D1537565

Communicating
for success

SECOND EDITION

Janet S. Hyden
Great Oaks Institute of Technology and
    Career Development
Cincinnati, Ohio

Ann K. Jordan
Great Oaks Institute of Technology and
    Career Development
Cincinnati, Ohio

Mary Helen Steinauer
Great Oaks Institute of Technology and
    Career Development
Cincinnati, Ohio

Margie J. Jones
Greene County Central High School
Snow Hill, North Carolina
    (Contributing author)

VISIT US ON THE INTERNET
www.swep.com

South-Western Educational Publishing
an International Thomson Publishing company I(T)P®

www.thomson.com

Cincinnati • Albany, NY • Belmont, CA • Bonn • Boston • Detroit • Johannesburg • London • Madrid
Melbourne • Mexico City • New York • Paris • Singapore • Tokyo • Toronto • Washington

Copyright © 1999
by South-Western Educational Publishing
Cincinnati, OH

ALL RIGHTS RESERVED

The text of this publication, or any part thereof, may not be reproduced or transmitted in any form or by any means, electronic or mechanical, including photocopying, recording, storage in an information retrieval system, or otherwise, without the prior written permission of the publisher.

ISBN: 0-538-68171-3

2 3 4 5 6 7 8 D4 05 04 03 02 01 00

Printed in the United States of America

International Thomson Publishing

South-Western Educational Publishing is an ITP Company. The ITP logo is a registered trademark used herein under License by South-Western Educational Publishing.

Vice President/Director of Publishing: Peter McBride
Acquisitions/New Business Development Manager: Susan Carson
Project Manager: Penny Shank
Editor: Timothy Bailey
Production & Design Coordinator: Tricia M. Boies
Consulting Editor: Elaine Langlois
National English/Communication Consultant: Carolyn Love, Ph.D.
Marketing Manager: Mark Linton
Marketing Coordinator: Tricia Allen
Editorial Assistant: Brenda Evans
Prepress Services: WordCrafters Editorial Services, Inc.; GGS Information Services
Cover and Title Page Design: Lamson Design

Works Cited Acknowledgments:
p. 28, Reprinted with permission of Simon & Schuster from SNIGLETS (snig'lit): ANY WORD THAT DOESN'T APPEAR IN THE DICTIONARY, BUT SHOULD by Rich Hall & Friends. Copyright © 1984 by Not the Network Company, Inc.
p. 123, Reprinted with permission from the Society of Technical Communication, Arlington, VA.
p. 504, Report excerpt courtesy of Elizabeth S. Kroon.

The names of all commercially available software mentioned herein are used for identification purposes only and may be trademarks or registered trademarks of their respective owners. South-Western Educational Publishing disclaims any affiliation, association, connection with, sponsorship, or endorsement by such owners.

Photo Credits:
Cover Image: OMS Photography, Cincinnati, OH; **Cloud image** used as background in all chapter openers and Projects: © 1998 Adobe Systems Inc.; **Antique book stack** used in all literature opener pages: © PhotoDisc, Inc.

Photo Credits continued on page 572.

Literature Acknowledgments:
"Future Tense" by Robert Lipsyte, copyright © 1984 by Robert Lipsyte from SIXTEEN: SHORT STORIES by Donald R. Gallo, ed. Used by permission of Dell Books, a division of Bantam Doubleday Dell Publishing Group, Inc.
"From Man to Boy" by John R. Coleman. Reprinted from *Blue Collar Journal,* © 1974 by John R. Coleman, by permission of Collier Associates, P.O. Box 21361, West Palm Beach, FL 33416 USA.

Literature Acknowledgments continued on page 574.

ACKNOWLEDGMENTS

We wish to thank all who helped us create this book. We are particularly grateful to the following educators who reviewed the manuscript and offered helpful suggestions for improvement:

Margaret Ackerman
English and Technical
    Communication Instructor
Live Oaks Career Development
    Campus
Cincinnati, Ohio

Kathie Bates
Keyboarding Instructor
Mt. Healthy High School
Cincinnati, Ohio

Laura Beusse
Apopka High School
Apopka, Florida

Norma Bickley
English Instructor
Newberry High School
Newberry, South Carolina

Ann Edney-Pyle
Norview High School
Norfolk, Virginia

Edwina Evans
Language Arts Instructor
Logan Senior High School
Logan, West Virginia

James A. Fidler
U.S. Army National Guard,
    Retired
Springfield, Ohio

Sherry Forster
Social Studies, English &
Communications Instructor
Delaware Joint Vocational School
Delaware, Ohio

Kathy Freeman
English and Technical
    Communication Instructor
Laurel Oaks Career Development
    Campus
Wilmington, Ohio

Mabel Gelter
English and Technical
    Communication Instructor
Live Oaks Career Development
    Campus
Milford, Ohio

Lloyd Harris
Fairdale High School
Fairdale, Kentucky

Joyce Hendrickson
English Instructor
Jefferson City High School
Jefferson City, Missouri

Helen Humbert
Business Education Department
    Chair
Kent-Meridian High School
Kent, Washington

Roy A. Hyden
Business Education Chair
Princeton High Schoool
Cincinnati, Ohio

Jean Jonkers
English Instructor
Wm. J. Dean Technical High
    School
Holyoke, Massachusetts

Sandy Jowers
Swansea High School
Swansea, South Carolina

Christine Bideganeta LaRocco
Educational Consultant
Arlington, VA

Laurie Logsdon
Lincoln High School
Lincoln, Nebraska

Susanne Long
Gwinett Vocational Education
    Center
Lawrenceville, Georgia

Carol McCormick
Apopka High School
Apopka, Florida

Tracy Olsen
Applied Communications
    Consultant
Florida School-to-Work Initiative
Casselberry, Florida

Judy Pitts
English Department Chair
Salem High School
Salem, Virginia

Linda Plybon
Administrative Officer
NIOSH
Cincinnati, Ohio

Betty Rogers
Hoke High School
Raeford, North Carolina

Theresa Spangler
English/Communication Instructor
Brunswick High School
Brunswick, Georgia

Judy Strand
Lincoln High School
Lincoln, Nebraska

Jeff Whitesell
English and Technical
    Communication Instructor
Scarlet Oaks Career Development
    Campus
Cincinnati, Ohio

Janet Hyden
Ann Jordan
Mary Helen Steinauer

CONTENTS

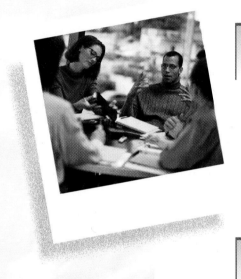
INFOBIT

Language is not good or bad. It is simply appropriate or inappropriate, depending on the audience and the occasion.

INFOBIT

"People who enjoy what they are doing invariably do it well."

JOE GIBBS, NFL COACH

INFOBIT

One of the most important workplace skills needed today is problem-solving ability, according to the U.S. Department of Labor.

C·O·N·N·E·C·T·I·O·N

CAREER

You have studied geography in school and have probably used computers either at home or in school, but have you thought about making a career of the combination? If you like geography and computers, you might
be interested in a career in GIS (geographic information systems). When
decisions have to be made about how to redistrict schools or where to
loca... ...ower plant or a new subdivision, a GIS specialist is
like... ...rant combines computerized mapping
wit... ...onal planners make crit-
ica...

To the Student:

If you want success in any career, you will find nothing more valuable
than good communication skills. Such skills are and will continue to be
your most valuable assets in both your personal and professional lives.
Whether you are talking to a friend, applying for a job, submitting a
report, or trying to convince someone that you have a great idea,
skilled communication is key. And you'll find, as your communication
skills improve, that you will be able to open eyes, open minds, and
open doors.

Communicating for Success may be the most practical textbook you've
ever used. It helps develop effective workplace communication skills by
providing you with more than theories. It shows you what steps to take
to carry out specific communication tasks effectively and then lets you
try out the tasks yourself. It also expects you to learn to work with
others, rather than always trying to do things by yourself because, in
today's workplace, you'll have to work with other people. School is a
good place to learn these things—a safe place where you won't risk
losing a paycheck or jeopardizing your career if you don't do them
right the first time.

Employers seek, value, and reward the skills stressed in this text.
If you master these skills, you will have a much better chance of
succeeding at whatever you choose to do in your future.

Communicating for Success is divided into chapters. Each chapter
deals with a topic such as: describing a process; listening and speaking
effectively; persuading someone in authority that you have a good
idea; managing your time; getting and keeping a job. Each chapter
ends in a real-world project for you and others to design and present.

WEB LINK

Internet searches
will provide you
with a wealth of
information,
including
considerable dat...
include in your
tables. For exam...
you can gather
information to
compare simila...
national or larg...
local compani...
products.

INFOBIT

The U.S. Department of Energy is responsible for marketing federal power, regulating ...gy production ...use, pricing ...allocation, ...oting more ...nt uses of ...y, and ...eeing the ...r weapons ...m.

In each chapter, in addition to the basic lessons, you will notice several special features labeled "Connections," which deal with a variety of topics related to careers, ethics in the workplace, quality improvement, people, culture, and technology. As you scan each page you will also notice featured quotes, anecdotes, or tidbits of information in the margins. We call these Infobits and Technobits. We found them interesting and thought you might, too.

Finally, at the end of each chapter you will find literature selections. These stories, poems, essays, and plays have plots, characters, or themes that relate to the topics in each chapter.

Throughout this text, we consistently refer to resources available on the Internet. We also recommend that you use computers and appropriate software in your projects as well as in your everyday work wherever possible, since computers will be your tools in the workplace.

We hope you enjoy and learn from *Communicating for Success* and that you will not only know more but be able to do more with what you've learned after completing this course.

TECHNOBIT

After you click the "send" icon, ...Internet e-mail ...messages are ...roken up into ...all packets, each ...g the quickest ...he last ...ent might ...st to ...

Janet S. Hyden   *Ann K. Jordan*   *Mary Helen Steinauer*

Janet S. Hyden   Ann K. Jordan   Mary Helen Steinauer

TIME TO PRACTICE OUR COMMUNICATION SKILLS

THERE ARE TURKEYS TAP DANCING IN THE TAPIOCA!

HE'S GOOD

JIM DAVIS 9-6

GARFIELD © 1993 Paws, Inc. Dist. by UNIVERSAL PRESS SYNDICATE. Reprinted with permission. All rights reserved.

Communicating at Work

> "There has been more information produced in the last 30 years than during the previous 5,000. . . . The information supply available to us doubles every five years."

—RICHARD SAUL WURMAN, *INFORMATION ANXIETY*

Workplace Skills in This Chapter

- Improve **interpersonal** skills as you analyze documents with team members.

- Understand how effective communication benefits workplace **systems**.

- Examine and categorize various types of **information**.

- Identify **resources** for planning written communication.

- Use **technology** to improve proofreading skills.

As you complete Chapter 1, you will

- define communication.

- compare various forms of communication.

- identify the elements of communication.

- describe how messages are adapted to various audiences and purposes.

- discuss the importance of planning, editing, and revising messages.

- use proofreading marks.

Have you ever considered what life would be like without communication? No reassuring smiles, no love songs on the radio, no gripping novels, no comforting hugs, no friendly conversation. Fortunately, though, we can communicate. In fact, we spend most of our waking hours listening, speaking, reading, or writing.

Communication is the transfer or exchange of thoughts, information, ideas, and feelings by speech, writing, or signals between at least two people. Since today's workplace demands workers who are proficient in specialized communication skills, the quality of your communication will have a direct bearing on your success on the job. This book will help you learn to communicate successfully at work.

Communication Takes Many Forms

Dear Liz and Todd,

Thank you so much for sending the lovely roses for my birthday. We had dinner guests the next day and they made such a wonderful centerpiece. How thoughtful of you to remember that white roses have always been my favorite.

Hope to see you soon.

Love,
Grandma

Figure 1-1: *Thank-you note*

The Last Rose of Summer

'Tis the last rose of summer
Left blooming alone;
All her lovely companions
Are faded and gone.
—Thomas Moore

Figure 1-2: *Poem*

At school, at work, and during our leisure time, we encounter hundreds of forms of communication daily. The first voice Inez hears each day is her father calling, "Time to get up. You're late already." Then she turns on the television to catch the day's weather report. While eating breakfast, Inez scans the sports page. On her drive to school, as she listens to the radio, she is hardly aware of the many signs she passes along the roadside. Once at school, Inez talks with friends, listens to teachers, views videotapes, and reads textbooks, assignment sheets, tests, and chalkboards. She writes in response to assignments in all her classes. Since Inez is a culinary arts student, she often reads and follows recipes in her vocational lab.

In her after-school job at Roy's Ribs, Inez greets customers, explains menu items to them, takes their orders, makes requests of the kitchen personnel, and responds to requests from her boss. After work, Inez discusses her day with her family, completes her homework, and talks to her boyfriend on the phone before turning in for the night. Inez spends a great deal of time communicating.

INFOBIT

"On the job, the average employee spends about 45 percent of his communication time listening, about 30 percent speaking, about 16 percent reading, and about 9 percent writing."

GEORGE BELL,
CORPORATE CONSULTANT

Practice 1-1: Forms of Communication

Whenever you see the heading "Practice," you will know that it's time for action—in the form of listening, speaking, or writing.

teamwork Examine the six documents shown in Figures 1-1 to 1-6. With a partner, complete *Student Workbook* page 1-A. Decide what each document is about, who would read it, and why they would read it. As you decide why the reader would read the document, consider the following questions:

* What does the writer expect the reader to know or think after reading the selection?

* How does the writer expect the reader to feel after reading the selection?

* Is the reader expected to take some action after reading? If so, what action?

Horticulture 102
Midterm Exam, page 2

II. Describe the procedure for feeding rosebushes. Include the following information: (a) why feeding is important and necessary, (b) what to feed, (c) types of feeding, (d) when to feed, (e) how to feed.

Plant food is a number of different elements, suspended in water, which enter the plant usually through the roots and leaves. Once inside, they are moved where they are wanted, mixed up, and altered into various chemical formulae. These elements should, in the normal life cycle, be returned to the soil through leaf fall or through the bodies of insects or other creatures that have been eating the plants. When back in the soil, the elements are recycled by the bacteria in the soil, and rendered available to the plant again. However, in the normal rose bed, this cycle is interrupted (little or nothing returns to the soil), because we cut the flowers, clear weeds, and tidy up leaves. Therefore, rose growers must return the elements to the soil themselves.

A good time to put plenty of organic material into the soil is at the time of planting. After their first year, the plants should be fed annually, from early spring to high summer. When organic manure is used, it should be applied in spring, as it normally takes longer to act than inorganic fertilizer. The plants should be fed again when the first flower buds form and then after a couple of months to help the repeat blooming. Some growers feed the plants once a month.

Roses need to be fed when they show signs of deficiency in their growth or leaves. While inorganic manure is convenient and effective, some organic fertilizers are required to keep the soil in good condition. Manure should be applied during the season, early spring to high summer, except for the one purpose of helping to harden off soft growth in late summer or autumn with potassium and magnesium.

Figure 1-3: *Horticulture class midterm exam*

Garret's Garden Nursery
983 Harrison Lane
St. Paul, Minnesota 55177-0123

Fax Cover Sheet

DATE: June 24, ----   TIME: 4:13 a.m.

TO: Linda   PHONE: 612-555-0104
       InterComm Industries   FAX: 612-555-0100

FROM: Kevin   PHONE: 612-555-0180
       Garret's Garden Nursery FAX: 612-555-0181

RE: Roses

C: Brenda

Number of pages including cover sheet: 2

Message

As we discussed in our phone conversation on 6/22, I inspected the rosebushes growing on the southeast corner of your main building, removed several leaves from these bushes, and examined the leaves with a magnifying glass.

The roundish dark spots on the upper leaf surfaces indicate blackspot, a common fungal disease. This fungus is probably the most serious (and best-known) of the rose diseases. This is what's causing the lower leaves to yellow and fall off.

On Tuesday, Brenda will spray the affected plants with PlantBlite. One or two repeats of this treatment at two- to three-week intervals should solve the problem. Between treatments, be sure to remove infected leaves before they fall to the ground. Place them in a bag and burn them.

Thanks for letting me know about the problem so promptly. Don't hesitate to call again if you have any further questions. I have enclosed a chart showing symptoms and treatments of common rose diseases.

Figure 1-4: *Fax cover sheet*

Home Page of the Anyville Rose Society

Welcome to the home page of the Anyville Rose Society.

Our meetings occur on the first Thursday of each month at the Civic Center, 4534 East Elm Avenue—right next to Anyville Memorial Hospital—at 7 p.m. Here is a map of the meeting location. This month's speaker will be Clarence Johns, owner of CJ's Natural Gardening. His topic will be "Grin and Groom It."

The Anyville Rose Society was founded in 1950 and is affiliated with the American Rose Society (ARS). There are currently approximately 175 members. Our mission is to encourage interest in the rose, to promote its cultivation, and to disseminate information on its culture among any interested persons.

The society's fair garden committee garnered a second place for its entry in the Lake County Fair. Come take a look at the prizewinning entry.

Photo of garden

Here are several topics we hope you'll find helpful:

How to become a member
Calendar of events
How to grow roses in Lake County
What roses do well in Lake County
Where to see roses in Lake County
Links to other rose sites

We hope you enjoyed our home page. Send questions or comments by e-mail to

Brittany Gibbs

Figure 1-5: *World Wide Web home page*

The peculiar meiosis of the Caninae roses was worked out in detail and reported by Rauhala (8). In this particular group are found tetraploid 2n 5 28, pentaploid 2n 5 35, and hexaploid 2n 5 42 forms, but in all forms Rauhala found exactly seven pairs at meiosis, the remaining chromosomes behaving as univalents in the reduction division. In the first meiotic division the seven bivalents are arranged in a normal fashion on the equatorial plate with the univalents scattered at random over the spindle. According to Rauhala the bivalents separate normally at anaphase I and proceed to the poles, while the univalents remain behind on the spindle. Later the univalents divide and sister halves are distributed regularly to the two poles. Rauhala reported, however, that all chromosomes were included in the restitution nuclei. At second anaphase the seven chromosomes from the original bivalents divide and the sister halves are distributed to opposite poles. The univalents having divided previously at the first anaphase do not divide again and are left behind in the cytoplasm to form supernumerary microspores. Those microspores receiving exactly seven chromatids from the original bivalents are assumed to be the only functional ones, the others becoming abortive.

The reduction division in the macrospore mother cells is quite different. The biva-

lents behave as in the divisions of the microspore mother cell, but at anaphase I the univalents do not divide, but are all oriented on the micropylar side of the equatorial plate and are included in the micropylar nucleus at the end of the first division. The egg cell finally formed is a derivative of this micropylar nucleus and contains seven less than the somatic number of chromosomes. Thus, if self-pollination occurred the resulting progeny would contain the original somatic chromosome number of parent.

To explain this peculiar meiosis in the Caninae roses, Hill (4) advanced a genome theory in which he postulated the existence in the genus Rosa of five differential diploid septets of chromosomes, which he designated as A, B, C, D, and E. These septets are supposed to segregate essentially as complete units, and the genome makeup of a species may supposedly be determined by a study of the morphological characters which are more or less specific for the various septets. It is further supposed that pairing at meiosis occurs between similar septets. According to Hill the Caninae roses have resulted from hybridization between species having only one septet in common, resulting in well-differentiated species having only seven pairs of homologous chromosomes.

Chapter 2–Rosa Rubiginosa and Its Hybrids

78

Figure 1-6: *Textbook page*

CHAIR-SIDE ASSISTANT
Full- or part-time position in local pediatric dental practice. Requires outgoing person with good communication skills. Previous experience and training preferred.

TECHNOBIT

In 1991, companies began spending more money on computing and communications equipment than they did on industrial, mining, farm, and construction equipment combined.

Communication at School

One document you and your partner analyzed for the last Practice was a school essay for a horticulture class. You have done similar activities hundreds of times in school, and your teachers have read your responses. Why would the horticulture teacher read a description of roses? Because he or she is unfamiliar with procedures for feeding roses? Why did your social studies teacher last year read your explanation of the causes of the Civil War? Because the teacher did not know the causes? Why did your algebra teacher check your answers on the final exam? To find out how to solve for x?

Of course, your teachers know how to feed roses, what the causes of the Civil War were, and how to solve for x. So why read your answers? To find out what *you* know or what *you* can do. *This type of communication **never** occurs at work.*

Communication at Work

Once hired, people at work do not speak or write to demonstrate their knowledge to someone who already knows the answers, for this would be a pointless waste of time. Rather, communication at work occurs because someone who does not already know the answers needs information or ideas.

Every day on the job, not only will you be called on to communicate what you know to others, but you will also need to ask them for information and ideas. As long as you work with people, your ability to communicate will be important to your job success.

Figure 1-7: *Firefighters at the scene*

Practice 1-2: Communicating at Work

Let's see how a single incident can result in an assortment of communication activities.

On a separate piece of paper, set up two columns. Label the first column "Communication Activities." Label the second column "Writing, but Not Communicating." Now listen to the audio selection your teacher will play for you. As you listen, make a mark in the first column every time you hear an example of someone communicating as part of a job.

You will also hear some examples of people writing without really communicating with someone else. Make a mark in the second column for each of those.

CAREER

C·O·N·N·E·C·T·I·O·N

Many students count the days until graduation—the end of classes and studying and tests. If this describes you, don't start counting those days yet. Most jobs require continual learning. Consider the job held by M. J. Plaster, a technical writer who writes on-line help for computer software. She began by writing manuals for DOS-based programs and was offered a job writing on-line help for Windows programs. Although she knew very little about how to do this, she accepted the job and quickly learned everything she could about the process. Since the rate of change in the software industry is rapid, M. J. must constantly study and learn to keep up, but she still loves the challenges of her job. When you stop and think about it, a job that never changes and never requires new knowledge and skills would get pretty boring, wouldn't it? (Powell 13)

What Employers Are Looking For

To understand how you can prepare yourself for the kind of job you want, it is useful to understand what employers are looking for in new employees. They are, of course, interested in job–specific skills. A chef, for example, needs to know how to cook and bake. An auto mechanic needs to know how to diagnose and repair vehicles.

But since jobs require more than job–specific skills and because jobs are constantly changing, employers are also looking for people with **transferable skills**. These skills allow employees to adapt to changes in the organization, changes in technology, and changes in the requirements of their jobs.

ADMINISTRATIVE ASSIST.

Local software company has an immediate opening for an outgoing, energetic person to support our sales and admin. staff. We seek an individual with excellent organizational and communication skills and the ability to operate in a fast-paced, team-oriented environment. Previous secretarial and word processing experience a must.

Knowing How to Learn

Knowing how to learn is the most basic skill because it is the key that unlocks future success. Competence in reading, writing, and math enables people to learn. The ability to use information technology is also quickly becoming a basic skill for most jobs. A person who knows how to learn can respond effectively to change, make improvements in quality and efficiency, and develop new ideas and techniques.

INFOBIT

Sign in a beauty salon window: "If you like our work, tell your friends; if you don't, tell us."

Self-Management, Teamwork, and Communication Skills

Employers want to hire dependable people who come to work on time every day, get along with others, solve problems, and take personal responsibility for the quality of their work. These people must know how to listen and to express their thoughts clearly.

Figure 1-8: *Employers want employees to listen to customers' concerns.*

Employers want employees who will hear the key points that make up a customer's concerns and who can give an adequate spoken or written response. They look for people who know how to get along with customers, suppliers, coworkers, and supervisors. The number-one reason people are fired from their jobs is because they cannot get along with other employees.

When employers complain about the skills of entry-level workers, they mention problems with communication—writing, listening, reading, and speaking—more often than any others. Communicating effectively is clearly important to your career.

Practice 1-3: Communication Tasks

teamwork *careers* In a team of three or four students, identify a particular job in a field that interests you and write the job title at the top of a piece of paper. Then list as many communication tasks as your team can think of that a person who holds this job is expected to perform. Be sure to include listening, speaking, reading, and writing activities. For each item on your list, consider the following factors:

* The subject of the communication

* The form of communication

* The person or persons who will receive the communication

The following example lists a few of the communication tasks high school teachers must perform on the job.

High School Teacher

* Phone parents to report students' progress

* Explain assignments to students

* Write memos requesting advice from administrators

* Discuss problems with other teachers during committee meetings

* Write tests for students

* Explain procedures to new employees

* Read daily announcements to students

* Listen to a student explain that the computer ate his or her homework

* Complete forms requesting supplies

Electronics
BENCH TECHNICIAN

A leader in the sales and service of quality security equipment and systems has an excellent opportunity available in our National Repair Center for an Electronic Bench Technician.

You will troubleshoot to the component level and repair a variety of electronic security equipment.

Requirements for the position include an associate degree in electronics or equivalent training, a minimum of two years' experience as a component-level bench technician, the ability to meet deadlines, and good communication skills. Commercial VCR repair experience desirable.

QUALITY

C·O·N·N·E·C·T·I·O·N

Poor customer service is expensive and can cost you your job. According to Rocco Vicari, executive vice president of Macro International Inc.'s research and consulting division:

- Dissatisfied customers don't always complain, but they may take their business elsewhere. For every customer who does complain, as many as 26 other dissatisfied customers do not.
- Dissatisfied customers are talkative. Each one tells an average of 18 people.
- It costs four to six times more to gain a new customer than it does to keep one existing customer happy.

Whose job is it to keep customers happy? It's *your* job. (Working 7)

Elements of Communication at Work

The process of communicating at work involves five elements: the situation, the sender, the receiver, the message, and the purpose of the message. All of these elements are important, no matter what form your communication takes. A clear understanding of each element is important for communicating messages effectively at work.

The Situation

The **situation** that requires communication includes what is happening and where it is happening. In the audio selection about the classroom fire, the situation determined the types of communication activities that occurred.

Whether you work on a farm, in an office, in a shop, in a store, or on a construction site, you are constantly communicating. As the situation changes, the types of communication activities may change too.

The Sender

The **sender** is the person who is speaking or writing. The background, experience, attitudes, and skills of the sender always affect the message.

At work, the sender is also concerned with the image that he or she projects. The ideal image should be one of competence and cooperation toward coworkers. With the public, the sender's image should reflect positively on the organization that he or she represents. Later chapters in this book will provide practice in communicating with a variety of readers and listeners.

The Receiver

The **receiver** of the message could be one person or thousands of people. In this book, we will call the receiver or receivers of the

---

MAINTENANCE ENGINEER

Experienced maintenance engineer needed for industrial park. Must have experience in all phases of building maintenance, including electrical systems. A working knowledge of rooftop HVAC units (and repair experience) is preferred.

The ideal candidate should be organized and self-motivated and should have good communication skills. We offer an excellent salary and benefits package.

Figure 1-9: *The sender's image should reflect positively on the organization that he or she represents.*

LAB TECHNICIAN

We are seeking a self-motivated, conscientious, and responsible individual to work as a lab technician. Duties include building and testing air compressors and airless sprayers. Qualifications include an associate degree plus 2 years' lab experience or 3 to 5 years' hands-on experience, mechanical inclination, and basic knowledge of electric power, along with good oral and written communication skills.

Figure 1-10: *Workplace messages take many forms.*

Store Manager
SEARCHING FOR THE PERFECT FIT

We have a unique career opportunity! Experience & drive to succeed highly desirable. Selected individual must have retail experience with excellent communication skills & dedication to customer service. Position will involve sales, training, merchandising, & displays. This is a salaried position with growth potential, incentives, & benefits.

message the **audience**. The sender must be certain that the audience gets the right information at the right time in a clear and understandable form.

Audiences can be divided into two groups: **specialists** and the **general audience**. Specialists have interest, experience, and knowledge in a particular technical field. Your lab teacher and your classmates in lab are specialists in your field. If you have a job in your chosen occupation, your boss and coworkers are probably specialists. Sometimes, though, you may find yourself working for someone who knows very little about what you do.

The general audience includes everyone else: clients, customers, patients, sales representatives, suppliers, and the general public. These people may have little understanding of the technical details associated with your work. They lack the interest, background, and knowledge to understand technical information.

When listening to the audio selection, did you notice any sender who at times fit into the general audience category and at other times fit into the specialist category? How might this occur?

The Message

The message is the information and ideas relayed by the sender to the audience. If communicated in an unclear manner, messages can cause workers to waste time, materials, and money. The message can take one or more forms. Some examples are as follows:

Radio announcements	Memorandums	Photographs
Conversations	Letters	Drawings
Phone calls	Manuals	Maps
Discussions	Catalogs	Graphs
Meetings	Books	Cartoons
Voice mail messages	Signs	Blueprints
Speeches	Pamphlets	Videotapes
Audiotapes	E-mail messages	Facial expressions

Practice 1-4: Types of Messages

Examine the list of types of messages above. Suggest a heading for each column that describes each of the three categories of messages. Below each heading, add five more types of messages.

ETHICS C·O·N·N·E·C·T·I·O·N

Ethics are standards of right and wrong that guide our decision making. Your employer and your customers expect you to communicate in an ethical manner. People can use language to explain, clarify, and enlighten. They can also use language to mislead, cover up, and lie. While it is important that you carefully consider how you present yourself and your messages, it is equally important to do so honestly. Workplace messages need to be accurate. It is wrong to misrepresent yourself, your organization, your product, or your services. Lying is often illegal and always wrong. Stick with the truth, and your reputation for honesty and accuracy will add credibility to all your messages.

The Purpose

Messages that are sent to both specialists and general audiences at work can have many purposes. The purpose can be to

* socialize (small talk or inquiries about personal interests).

* inform (about a situation, need, problem, or success).

* persuade (to make a decision, revise an opinion, or take an action).

Most communication at work is informative or persuasive. Whatever form the communication takes, its purpose is always to make something happen.

CAD Technician
(Full- or Part-Time)
Successful, established office furniture distributor offers excellent opportunity as CAD Technician. You should be an excellent communicator with 2+ years of CADVANCE or AUTOCAD experience in an interior or architectural environment. You will perform a variety of PC- and interiors-related activities. Flexible hours.

INFOBIT

"Always do right—this will gratify some and astonish the rest."

MARK TWAIN, U.S. AUTHOR. UNITED STATES PRESIDENT HARRY S TRUMAN HAD THIS REMARK FRAMED BEHIND HIS DESK IN THE OVAL OFFICE.

Practice 1-5: Elements of Communication

In this Practice, you will listen for clues about the subject, sender, audience, form of message, and purpose of communication.

1. Listen again to the audio selection about the classroom fire, but this time, listen for single and double beeps.

2. When you hear one beep, listen carefully to the information that follows. After two beeps, your teacher will pause the recording.

3. On *Student Workbook* page 1-B, record the subject, sender, audience, form of message, and purpose of the communication that is described after the single beep.

Effect of the Audience on the Message

Communication is effective if something happens as a result—but not just any something. The something that happens must accomplish the sender's purpose. If, for example, you fax a letter to a customer asking

PC Support Technician

A growing national insurance company has an excellent opportunity for a PC Support Technician in our Claims Department. Qualifications are: technical school degree and experience, solid knowledge of PC hardware with experience installing hardware and software, familiarity with troubleshooting and problem analysis, and network experience. Additional responsibilities include conducting training classes on company e-mail, imaging software, and new products as required. Qualified person should possess strong communication, planning, and organizational skills and ability to work independently.

her to pay a bill immediately, and a check arrives two days later, you have communicated effectively.

Effective communication is an interactive process—that is, the sender acts upon or affects the audience, and the audience in turn affects the sender. Once the sender has determined the content and purpose of the message, the sender must consider how to communicate effectively with his or her particular audience. To do this, we **analyze** (study) the audience and then **adapt** (adjust) the message.

The following questions indicate what information the sender must ask about the audience:

* What does the audience already know?
* What does the audience need to know?
    * How many people are in the audience and how old are they?
    * How much education does the audience have?
    * What is the audience's cultural background?
    * What is the audience's attitude toward the subject?
    * How much time can the audience spend reading or listening to the message?
    * What is the audience's job?
    * Will the audience pass the message along to someone else?
    * What is the audience supposed to do after receiving the message?

An effective message will take into account all these questions.

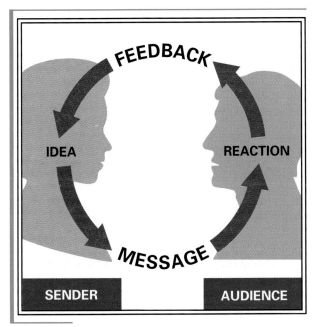

Figure 1-11: *Effective communication is an interactive process.*

Culture and Communication

In analyzing the audience, one important consideration is the audience's cultural background. Our cultural backgrounds are shaped by many factors. Some of them are

* the region of the country or world where we were raised.
* the region of the country or world where our parents or grandparents were raised.
* our religion.

"Culture is the name for what people are interested in, their thoughts, their models, the books they read and the speeches they hear, their table-talk, gossip, controversies, historical sense and scientific training, the values they appreciate, the quality of life they admire. All communities have a culture. It is the climate of their civilization."

WALTER LIPPMANN, U.S. JOURNALIST

CULTURE **C·O·N·N·E·C·T·I·O·N**

How diverse is the United States? Here are some facts and statistics:

- The United States permits twice as much legal immigration as the rest of the world combined. Of the yearly U.S. population increase of 3 million, approximately half are immigrants.
- Most immigrants currently come from Mexico, Asia, the Caribbean, Europe, Central America, South America, Africa, and former Soviet Union republics.
- Nearly one-fourth of all California residents are foreign-born.
- Experts predict that by the year 2000, the Latino population will account for 13 to 14 percent of the U.S. population.
- White males make up only 44 percent of the U.S. workforce. More than one out of every fourteen Americans works for a foreign boss.

Interior Designer

Opportunity for full-time designer/salesperson who is fashion- and style-conscious, career-minded, and self-motivated. Must understand the importance of customer service, like working with and care about people, possess the ability to communicate effectively and efficiently, like to sell, and enjoy earning money.

Figure 1-12: *Culture may influence styles of clothing.*

- our race.
- our gender.
- our age.
- our level of education.
- where we work and what we do.
- our economic situation.

An individual's culture influences most areas of his or her life, including

- styles of food, clothing, and housing.
- attitudes about family and friendship.
- beliefs and values.
- ways of celebrating holidays and other special occasions.
- attitudes about work and school.
- attitudes about roles of men and women.
- reactions to technology.
- feelings about personal space.
- use of body language.
- style of communication.

You will very likely find yourself working with people from many different cultures. While your own culture seems right and normal to you, the behavior of people from other cultures may sometimes seem strange or wrong. People from other cultures may communicate differently than you do and may respond differently to what you write or say.

Figure 1-13: *To learn about other cultures, sample foods at ethnic or international restaurants.*

Be aware that the words we choose and the communication styles we employ are a result of cultural conditioning. How you phrase your messages can communicate a great deal more than just technical information; age, gender, race, ethnic, and other cultural biases can destroy your attempts to communicate. To communicate successfully at work, you will need to learn about and to appreciate other cultures. To learn about other cultures, try the following:

* Read the literature of other cultures.

* Sample foods at ethnic or international restaurants.

* Locate and read magazines or newspapers from other countries in a bookstore or public library.

* Examine your own cultural stereotypes. Cultural stereotypes are unfair generalizations that lead to misunderstanding. Do you, for example, believe all people in England are formal or all Chinese people are good in math?

* Keep an open mind when interacting with people from other cultures, and make an effort to learn from them.

Practice 1-6: Communicating Across Cultures

Every language has **idioms**, phrases or sentences that cannot be understood literally. Even if the audience knows the meanings of all the words in a phrase or sentence and understands the grammar completely, the meaning may still be unclear. A phrase or sentence of this type is said to be *idiomatic*.

Using idioms with audiences with different cultural backgrounds can lead to misunderstanding. Would a person who is new to the United States know, for instance, that a road hog has nothing to do with farm animals? Consider how the word *fall* changes meaning in the following expressions:

fall apart	fall in love
fall asleep	fall off
fall back	fall out
fall behind	fall short
fall down on the job	fall through

Explain how a person who learned English from a textbook might interpret the following idiomatic sentences:

1. Larry <u>dug up</u> a date for the wedding.

2. The convertible <u>cut me off</u> just before the exit.

(cont'd on next page)

INFOBIT

"For Africa to me . . . is more than a glamorous fact. It is a historical truth. No man can know where he is going unless he knows exactly where he has been and exactly how he arrived at his present place."

MAYA ANGELOU, U.S. AUTHOR

FOOD SERVICE AIDE

2 full-time positions available. Hours are 10:30 a.m. - 7:00 p.m. Every other weekend off. Duties include but are not limited to serving residents in main dining room, working on tray line, preparing and serving food, using and cleaning kitchen equipment. Must be dependable, punctual, able to follow verbal and written directions well.

SUPPORTED-LIVING MANAGER
Excellent opportunity to assist individuals with MR/DD in community living and oversee service delivery and management of individual needs. Must be team-oriented and flexible and have above-average communication skills. High school diploma, minimum 1 yr. experience with MR/DD, and own transportation required.

3. I am <u>crazy about</u> chocolate.

4. Sean <u>aced</u> the test without <u>cracking a book</u>.

5. The <u>old heap broke down</u> in the middle of the desert.

6–10. Now list five common idioms that you use in your conversation. Explain how that same person might misinterpret your words.

Adapt the Communication for the Audience

The audience understands an effective message readily. If a message in the workplace can be understood in more than one way, it is inadequate.

The message must be adjusted, or adapted, to suit the audience in the way that a car is customized to suit its driver. Once the writer or speaker has decided on the message and its purpose and has analyzed the audience, decisions must be made about how best to adapt the message. The writer or speaker must consider these questions:

ELECTRICAL TECHNICIAN
Immediate opening for a technically oriented person wanting hands-on responsibility in a growing organization. Position requires knowledge of control circuits, some PLC technology, and agency interface (i.e., UL, CSA, & FM) along with strong communication skills for customer service duties. A degree would be a plus. Some travel required. Opening is immediate.

* What form should this message take?

* How will the audience use the message?

* What vocabulary will the audience understand?

* Will the audience have the desire to read or listen, or will I have to get his or her attention?

* Will an illustration help the reader understand?

* How can I design a user-friendly page?

* How should the information be organized?

* How can I convince the audience to do what I want?

Practice 1-7: <u>Adapting Your Message</u>

Complete this Practice on your own.

1. Write three sentences describing your personal characteristics to a five-year-old child for whom you have been asked to baby-sit for the day.

2. Write three sentences describing your personal characteristics to someone you would like to date.

3. Write three sentences describing your personal characteristics to a prospective employer.

4. How did the audience and purpose affect your choice of words and details and your sentence structure?

ADMINISTRATIVE ASSISTANT
For condominium management company. Requires creative, self-starting non-clock watcher. Requirements include word processing experience, computer literacy, experience with database and spreadsheet programs, solid organizational skills, ability to calmly handle multiple priorities, sound communication skills, both oral and written, and sense of urgency towards future advancement. We offer competitive pay and above-average benefits.

Communicating Messages Effectively

The key to effective communication is *thinking*. In fact, learning to think effectively will automatically improve your communication. No one can see inside your head. Therefore, the only way to let people know what you're thinking is by communicating with them. If your message is unclear, the audience will assume that your thinking is unclear. If it is, you need to straighten out your thinking; if it isn't, you need to straighten out your communication.

The three main stages of the writing process are **planning**, **writing**, and **revising**. More time is spent on the first and third stages than on the second.

The Planning Stage

Unless you are giving a prepared speech, when you speak, you voice your thoughts almost as quickly as they occur to you. You have little time to plan your message and no opportunity to change what you have already said. One of the many advantages of a written message is that you can spend time planning it and can then change what you have written *before* you send the message—your message can say exactly what you want it to say. Writing is too complex a process to try to do everything at once. Get your planning out of the way before writing begins. Planning a document requires the following:

* Analyzing the audience
* Determining the purpose
* Collecting information
* Selecting and organizing information

The Writing Stage

The secret to success in the writing stage is to do it wrong the first time. Surprised? Many people assume that a good writer probably gets it right the first time. Wrong. Even professional writers prepare many drafts with the help of editors and proofreaders. For the first draft, just write without breaks. Stopping to edit while we draft breaks the train of thought and keeps us from being as smart or creative as we could be. As you write, don't stop to read what you've written. If you don't know how to spell a word, just approximate and fix it later. If you don't know the right word, use the wrong word. Just keep writing. Later on, you can correct mistakes, add or delete text, and reorganize.

Figure 1-14: *The three main stages of the writing process*

Figure 1-15: *The planning stage*

Figure 1-16: *The writing stage*

ETHICS **C·O·N·N·E·C·T·I·O·N**
THE TEN COMMANDMENTS FOR COMPUTER ETHICS
from the Computer Ethics Institute, June 1992

1. Thou shalt not use a computer to harm other people.
2. Thou shalt not interfere with other people's computer work.
3. Thou shalt not snoop around in other people's files.
4. Thou shalt not use a computer to steal.
5. Thou shalt not use a computer to bear false witness.
6. Thou shalt not use or copy software for which you have not paid.
7. Thou shalt not use other people's computer resources without authorization.
8. Thou shalt not appropriate other people's intellectual property.
9. Thou shalt think about the social consequences of what you write.
10. Thou shalt use a computer in ways that show consideration and respect.

WEB LINK

Search the Internet for ethics. You'll find numerous sites devoted to the ethical standards of various industries and professions.

INFOBIT

"Get it down. Take chances. It may be bad, but it's the only way you can do anything really good."

WILLIAM FAULKNER, U.S. NOVELIST

Figure 1-17: *The revising stage*

The Revising Stage

Preparing an effective written message requires editing: checking, proofreading, and revising. If you write with the aid of a computer and a word processing program, this editing process requires much less effort. Such a program will find and help you correct most spelling errors and other types of errors with only a few keystrokes. You never have to copy the whole message over again. Just change the words, sentences, or paragraphs until you are satisfied that the document says exactly what you mean. If a computer is available, learn to use it.

You might not be the best judge of your own writing; as you first read through it, it will, of course, make sense to you. Let some time pass between writing the first draft and editing it in order to gain critical distance.

Read the message aloud to yourself. It may feel silly, but a sentence that looks fine to the eye may sound awkward or unclear to your ear. Learn to proofread with your ears. Some experts recommend finding weak sentences by beginning at the end of the paper and reading it backwards, sentence by sentence. Try it.

Consulting dictionaries and reference books on writing style can be helpful. Studying well-written examples is useful, too. If, for instance, you are preparing a resume, examine other people's resumes as you plan your own.

Luckily, you are rarely alone as you write. Consult experts, such as your teachers, to make sure that your facts are correct. Check the accuracy of your message against information in textbooks and manuals. Ask other students to help proofread your work. How can

INFOBIT

Ernest Hemingway, a great American novelist, rewrote the last chapter of his novel A Farewell to Arms 44 times! When asked why, he said, "To get the words right." Rewriting does not mean failure; it often means success.

INFOBIT

"My spelling is Wobbly. It's good spelling but it Wobbles, and the letters get in the wrong places."

A. A. MILNE, BRITISH AUTHOR. SPOKEN BY WINNIE-THE-POOH, IN WINNIE-THE-POOH

you help one another if you are all just learning to improve your communication? It is easier to spot errors in other people's writing than it is to spot them in your own.

Does Spelling Count?

Earlier in this chapter, you were told that an effective message is one that accomplishes its purpose. In fact, if you write a note to your boss asking permission to leave work early tomorrow so that your dentist can treat your toothache, and permission is granted, you have indeed communicated successfully—even if your message contains a spelling error.

A poorly written message, however, can give the audience the impression that the writer is incompetent or uncaring. If you are viewed as incompetent and uncaring in one area, that perception could affect the audience's overall impression of you. Since your message is important, or you never would have bothered to write it, you want to be taken seriously.

A newspaper story reported that a group of students operated a thriving business manufacturing and selling fake driver's licenses. Finally they were caught and arrested. Why? Because they had spelled the name of the state incorrectly on the fake licenses! Yes, spelling does count—even for lawbreakers!

Practice 1-8: Using a Spell-Checker

teamwork Most word processors have a spell-checker. This type of program checks every word in a document against its dictionary database. If the spell-checker finds a match, it goes on to check the next word. If the spell-checker does not find a match, it highlights the word and presents the user with options to ignore the misspelling, to replace it with one of several suggested spellings, or to key the correct word.

Spell-checkers are useful, but not foolproof. For example, most names and many technical terms are not in general dictionaries and, therefore, will be highlighted as misspelled by the spell-checker. Compound words, such as *sunshine*, misspelled as *sun shine*, will not be caught by the spell-checker. Also, homonym errors, such as writing *affect* when you mean *effect*, will escape the spell-checker. So it is necessary to proofread for spelling errors even if you use a spell-checker.

In a team of three students, list 30 or more words that would stump a spell-checker program.

TECHNOLOGY C·O·N·N·E·C·T·I·O·N

In addition to spell-checkers, most word processing programs have grammar checkers. The user can choose a set of standards for checking material, such as a strict check of all grammar rules or a check that focuses on business or casual writing. The grammar checker locates some spelling, punctuation, grammar, style, and word choice errors. It can even call your attention to sexist expressions and overused phrases.

Still, people do a better job of proofreading. Grammar checkers can only locate about 33 percent of writing errors. Beware, because a sentence that looks just fine to a grammar checker may make no sense at all. For example, a grammar checker found no errors in the following sentence:

Mike frequently dusts his January loudly with a Volkswagen.

While it makes sense to use a grammar checker, do not rely on it. Trust your eyes and ears and the opinions of other people who read what you write.

LANDSCAPE, MAINTENANCE, SUPER, CREW LEADERS, ASST. CREW LEADERS, & TECHNICIANS

• Excellent pay.

• Vacation.

• Holidays.

• Benefits.

• 401K.

• Knowledge of turf, turf applications, & turf equipment.

• Good communication skills.

• Ability to supervise 2 to 5 people.

• Horticulture education and background a plus.

• Valid driver's license.

• Full-time or part-time positions.

MEDICAL ASSISTANT

Challenging FT position available in our fast-paced multi-physician office. Requires physician office experience and completion of medical assistant training program or LPN license. Certification to initiate venipuncture and operate physician office radiology equipment is preferred. Candidates should possess basic computer skills and demonstrate excellent communication skills.

Does Punctuation Count?

Punctuation in writing is like expression in speaking. A misplaced comma may change the meaning of a sentence by causing the reader to pause in the wrong place. Consider this sentence:

Woman without her man is nothing

What does this sentence mean? Now read the same sentence with punctuation added.

Woman—without her, man is nothing.

Did adding punctuation affect the meaning? Punctuation, too, counts.

Practice 1-9: Using Punctuation to Convey Meaning

Write each sentence below twice, each time with different punctuation, to convey two different meanings.

1. No children are allowed in the pool

2. Juan thinks his teacher is a genius

3. Ms. Krause your client just came in

4. Aaron my boss always puts the customer first

Proofreading Marks

Proofreading marks are symbols or codes that indicate what kind of changes need to be made to writing and where. These symbols allow you to mark needed changes without having to do a lot of writing on the draft. Using these standardized codes when you help someone else proofread his or her work will make your job quicker, and the writer will understand your marks. A list of proofreading marks appears inside the back cover of this text.

Practice 1-10: Using Proofreading Marks

The opening paragraph for an article about Netiquette (Figure 1–6) needs revision. Rewrite it, using proofreading marks to guide your revision.

Netiquette and the Culture of Cyberspace
"When thou enter a city abide by its customs."
—The Talmud★

When the Internet first began, there were only a few thousand computers connected to it. Cyber space (a world created by computers) was populated by a relatively small group of people as with every other group of people, they developed their own culture, along with guidelines too govern the behavior of their citizens. These guide lines are know as Netiquette, a combination of the words *network* and *etiquette*. Now that a lot of people are "surfing the net, we should all know the basics of Netiquette so we can avoid some misunderstandings offense, and embarrassment

★ The *Talmud* is the collection of ancient Rabbinic writings consisting of the *Mishnah* and the *Gemara*, constituting the basis of religious authority in Orthodox Judaism.

Now use proofreading marks to indicate needed revisions to the rest of the article shown on *Student Workbook* page 1-C.

SUMMARY

Communication is the transfer or exchange of thoughts, information, ideas, and feelings by speech, writing, or signals between at least two people. Follow these guidelines whenever you communicate at work:

* Consider how the situation, the sender, the audience, and the purpose affect messages.

* Carefully analyze the audience and adapt the message for the audience and purpose.

* Plan and edit all written communication.

WORKS CITED

Powell, Leigh Schindler. "Help!" *American Careers*. Winter 1997: 13.

The Working Communicator. Chicago: Lawrence Ragan Communication, Inc., Oct. 1996.

Overview

Being familiar with the type of reading and writing done in the English classroom, we note that major differences exist between literature and technical writing.

A person reads literature on his or her own terms. For example, one reader's experience differs from another reader's, which allows for different interpretations of a piece of literature. The interpretations will have similarities, but because of the readers' experiences, interpretations may differ.

Each genre (poetry, drama, short story, novel, essay) serves as a lens for observing, recording, and examining the world.

The relationship between the literary text and its meaning or interpretation is not as direct as that required by technical writing. For example, consider a train schedule (technical writing), which records, "The B train from Spencer arrives at 12:05 a.m." This statement has only one interpretation. An interpretation that the B train from Spencer arrives at 12:50 a.m. is simply wrong and can lead to pointless standing around at the railway station. Ambiguity (having two or more meanings) in literary selections is accepted and allows the reader several interpretations. Different interpretations of a piece of technical writing can cause confusion and damage business relationships.

Literature takes a nugget of information and expands it into an unlimited amount of meaning. Technical writing takes an unlimited amount of meaning and reduces it into a nugget of information.

Future Tense

Gary couldn't wait for tenth grade to start so he could strut his sentences, parade his paragraphs, renew his reputation as the top creative writer in school. . . . his head cocked alertly as Dr. Proctor introduced the new Honors English teacher, Mr. Smith. Here was the person he'd have to impress. . . . The man was hard to describe. . . .

"If he was a color he'd be beige," said Gary. "If he was a taste he'd be water. If he was a sound he'd be a low hum." . . .

"Describe a Typical Day at School," said Gary, trying unsuccessfully to mimic Mr. Smith's bland voice. "That's about as exciting as tofu."

"A real artist," said Dani, "accepts the commonplace as a challenge."

That night, hunched over his humming electric typewriter, Gary wrote a description of a typical day at school from the viewpoint of a new teacher who was seeing everything for the first time, who took nothing for granted. He described the shredded edges of the limp flag outside the dented front door, the worn flooring where generations of kids had nervously paced outside the principal's office, the nauseatingly sweet pipe-smoke seeping out of the teachers' lounge.

And then, in the last line, he gave the composition that extra twist, the little kicker on which his reputation rested. He wrote:

> The new teacher's beady little eyes missed nothing, for they were the optical recorders of an alien creature who had come to Earth to gather information.

The next morning, when Mr. Smith asked for a volunteer to read aloud, Gary was on his feet and moving toward the front of the classroom before Mike Chung got his hand out of his pocket.

The class loved Gary's composition. . . .

Gary felt good until he got the composition back. Along the margin, in perfect script, Mr. Smith had written:

> *You can do better.*

> *"A real artist accepts the commonplace as a challenge."*

"How would he know?" Gary complained on the way home.

"You should be grateful," said Dani. "He's pushing you to the farthest limits of your talent." . . .

Gary rewrote the composition, expanded it, complicated it, thickened it. Not only was this new teacher an alien, he was part of an extraterrestrial conspiracy to take over the Earth. Gary's final sentence was:

> Every iota of information, fragment of fact, morsel of minutiae sucked up by those vacuuming eyes was beamed directly into a computer circling the planet. The data would eventually become a program that would control the mind of every school kid on earth.

Gary showed the new draft to Dani before class. He stood on tiptoes so he could read over her shoulder. Sometimes he wished she were shorter, but mostly he wished he were taller.

"What do you think?"

"The assignment was to describe a typical day," said Dani. "This is off the wall."

He snatched the papers back.

"Creative writing means creating." He walked away, hurt and angry. . . . Gary's rewrite came back the next day marked:

> *Improving. Try again.*

(cont'd on next page)

Saturday he locked himself in his room after breakfast and rewrote the rewrite. He carefully selected his nouns and verbs and adjectives. He polished and arranged them in sentences like a jeweller strings pearls. . . .

Gary wrote:

> The alien's probes trembled as he read the student's composition. Could that skinny, bespectacled Earthling really suspect its extraterrestrial identity? Or was his composition merely the result of a creative thunderstorm in a brilliant young mind?

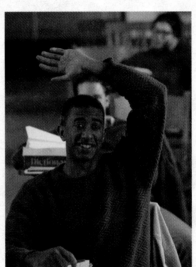

Before Gary turned in his composition on Monday morning, he showed it to Mike Chung. He should have known better.

"You're trying too hard," chortled Chung. "Truth is stranger than fiction." . . .

Mr. Smith handed back Gary's composition that next day marked:

> *See me after school.*

Gary was nervous all day. What was there to talk about? Maybe Mr. Smith hated science fiction. One of those traditional English teachers. Didn't understand that science fiction could be literature. *Maybe I can educate him,* thought Gary.

When Gary arrived at the English office, Mr. Smith seemed nervous, too.

He kept folding and unfolding Gary's composition. "Where do you get such ideas?" he asked in his monotone voice.

Gary shrugged. "They just come to me."

"Alien teachers. Taking over the minds of schoolchildren." Mr. Smith's empty eyes were blinking. "What made you think of that?"

"I've always had this vivid imagination."

Mr. Smith looked relieved. "I guess everything will work out." He handed back Gary's composition. "No more fantasy, Gary. Reality. . . ."

The words flowed out of Gary's mind and through his fingers and out of the machine onto sheets of paper. He wrote and rewrote until he felt the words were exactly right:

> With great effort, the alien shut down the electrical panic impulses coursing through its system and turned on Logical Overdrive. There were two possibilities:
>
> 1. This high school boy was exactly what he seemed to be, a brilliant, imaginative, apprentice best-selling author and screen-writer, or,
>
> 2. He had somehow stumbled onto the secret plan, and he

would have to be either enlisted into the conspiracy or erased off the face of the planet.

First thing in the morning, Gary turned in his new rewrite to Mr. Smith. A half hour later, Mr. Smith called Gary out of Spanish. There was no expression on his regular features. He said, "I'm going to need some help with you."

Cold sweat covered Gary's body as Mr. Smith grabbed his arm and led him to the new vice-principal. She read the composition while they waited. Gary got a good look at her for the first time. Ms. Jones was . . . just there. She looked as though she'd been manufactured to fit her name. Average. Standard. Typical. The cold sweat turned into goose pimples.

How could he have missed the clues? Smith and Jones were aliens! He had stumbled on their secret and now they'd have to deal with him. . . .

> "Writing can be very dangerous."

Ms. Jones ignored him. "In my opinion, Mr. Smith, you are over-reacting. This sort of nonsense"—she waved Gary's composition—"is the typical response of an overstimulated adolescent to the mixture of reality and fantasy in an environment dominated by manipulative music, television, and films. Nothing for us to worry about." . . .

"I'm not going to do anything this time," said Ms. Jones, "but you must promise to write only about what you know."

"Or I'll have to fail you," said Mr. Smith.

"For your own good," said Ms. Jones. "Writing can be very dangerous."

"Especially for writers," said Mr. Smith, "who write about things they shouldn't." . . .

Jim Baggs was practicing head fakes—in the hallway. He slammed Gary into the wall with a hip block. "How's it going, Dude?" he asked, helping Gary up.

"Aliens," gasped Gary. "Told me no more science fiction."

"They can't treat a star writer like that," said Jim. "See what the head honcho's got to say." He grabbed Gary's wrist and dragged him into the principal's office.

"What can I do for you, boys?" boomed Dr. Proctor.

"They're messing with his moves, Doc," said Jim Baggs. "You got to let the aces run their races." . . .

(cont'd on next page)

"From the beginning," ordered Dr. Proctor. He nodded sympathetically as Gary told the entire story. . . .

"You really have a way with words, Gary. I should have sensed you were on to something."

Gary's stomach flipped. "You really think there could be aliens trying to take over Earth?"

"And I can't wait to hear what the folks back home say when you read it to them."

"Certainly," said Dr. Proctor, matter-of-factly. "Earth is the ripest plum in the universe."

Gary wasn't sure if he should feel relieved that he wasn't crazy or be scared out of his mind. He took a deep breath to control the quaver in his voice, and said: "I spotted Smith and Jones right away. They look like they were manufactured to fit their names. Obviously humanoids. Panicked as soon as they knew I was on to them."

Dr. Proctor chuckled and shook his head. "No self-respecting civilization would send those two stiffs to Earth."

"They're not aliens?" He felt relieved and disappointed at the same time.

"I checked them out myself," said Dr. Proctor. "Just two average, standard, typical human beings, with no imagination, no creativity."

"So why'd you hire them?"

Dr. Proctor laughed. "Because they'd never spot an alien. No creative imagination. That's why I got rid of the last vice-principal and the last Honors English teacher. They were giving me odd little glances when they thought I wasn't looking. After ten years on your planet, I've learned to smell trouble."

Gary's spine turned to ice and dripped down the backs of his legs. "You're an alien!"

"Great composition," said Dr. Proctor, waving Gary's paper. "Grammatical, vividly written, and totally accurate." . . .

"And I can't wait to hear what the folks back home say when you read it to them," said Dr. Proctor.

"I made it all up." Gary had the sensation of rocketing upward. "I made up the whole . . ."

—Robert Lipsyte

Start-Up: The excerpt from Robert Lipsyte's short story is an example of ambiguity in literature. As a class, discuss different possible interpretations of the story.

Connection: The memo in Figure 1-18 is intentionally unclear and ambiguous. Rewrite it so that there is no misunderstanding.

TO: The Person in Charge

FROM: Department Supervisor

DATE: July 3, ----

SUBJECT: Temperature in Offices

Several staff members have complained recently about the temperatures in their offices.

I want you to do something about them.

Maybe you could set them at comfortable levels. They should turn on early in the morning and turn off after everyone has left for the day. Be sure the climate in the offices is suitable for all.

Figure 1-18: *An unclear memo*

Overview

John Coleman, the author of this nonfictional account, had a distinguished career as a teacher at the Massachusetts Institute of Technology, a college president, and a board member of several major companies before he left academics and joined the blue-collar world.

Feeling that there was a lack of understanding between the white-collar worker and the blue-collar worker, Coleman worked in sewers, dug ditches, and collected garbage.

This journal account tells of the author's experience of being undeservedly degraded by a waitress with whom he worked.

"From Man to Boy"
from *Blue-Collar Journal*

Tuesday, March 27

One of the waitresses I find hard to take asked me at one point today, "Are you the boy who cuts the lemons?"

"I'm the man who does," I replied.

"Well, there are none cut." There wasn't even a hint that she heard my point.

> *"Are you the boy who cuts the lemons?"*
>
> *"I'm the man who does."*

Dana, who has cooked here for twelve years or so, heard that exchange. "It's no use, Jack," he said when she was gone. "If she doesn't know now, she never will." There was a trace of a smile on his face, but it was a sad look all the same.

In that moment, I learned the full thrust of those billboard ads of a few years ago that said, "Boy. Drop out of school and that's what they'll call you the rest of your life." I had read those ads before with a certain feeling of pride; education matters, they said, and that gave a lift to my field. Today I saw them saying something else. They were untrue in part; it turns out that you'll get called "boy" if you do work that others don't respect even if you have a Ph.D. It isn't education that counts, but the job in which you land. And the ads spoke too of a sad resignation about the world. They assumed that some people just won't learn respect for others, so

> *Get the right job and they won't call you boy any more.*

you should adapt yourself to them. Don't try to change them. Get the right job and they won't call you boy any more. They'll save it for the next man.

It isn't just people like this one waitress who learn slowly, if at all. Haverford College has prided itself on being a caring, considerate community in the Quaker tradition for many long years. Yet when I came there I soon learned that the cleaning women in the dormitories were called "wombats" by all the students. No one seemed to know where the name came from or what connection, if any, it had with the dictionary definition. *The American College Dictionary* says a wombat is "any of three species of burrowing marsupials of Australia . . . somewhat resembling ground hogs." The name was just one of Haverford's unexamined ways of doing things.

It didn't take much persuasion to get the name dropped. Today there are few students who remember it at all. But I imagine the cleaning women remember it well.

Certainly I won't forget being called a boy today.

—John Coleman

Start-Up: Krazy Kousins Pizzeria has two male and two female servers. During business hours, these employees are responsible for waiting on tables, keeping the salad bar stocked, filling up salt and pepper shakers and other condiment jars, and rolling silverware in napkins. Once she serves her customers, Employee A does not return to the table to give additional service, uses other employees' rolled silverware, very seldom refills the containers on the salad bar, and neglects refilling the condiment containers. The other servers have informed the manager of the problem and asked his advice.

In the past, Employee A has done a good job for the pizzeria, but she is now having personal problems. Although the manager cannot permit her work habits to destroy the interpersonal relationships among his other employees, he also wants to keep a previously good employee from quitting her job. He needs to handle this problem in a positive but firm manner.

Connection: In groups of three, make a list of the problem(s). Brainstorm to find several solutions and to see what advice the manager could give to improve Employee A's work habits.

Write a short skit to illustrate what the manager would say and how the employee might respond. Be sure to use a dialogue format, and include stage directions (descriptions of the characters and settings, as well as directions regarding how the characters would move and what they would be doing).

Sniglet (snig' lit)

Any word that doesn't appear in the dictionary, but should

FLOPCORN (flop' korn) n. The unpopped kernels at the bottom of the cooker.

McMONIA (muk moan' ee uh) n. (Chemical symbol: Mc) Noxious gas created by fast-food employee mopping under your table while you're eating.

MAYPOP (may' pahp) n. A bald tire.

PHONESIA (fo nee' zhuh) n. The affliction of dialing a phone number and forgetting whom you were calling just as they answer.

Communicating Definitions

"*Words can have no single fixed meaning. Like wayward electrons, they can spin away from their initial orbit and enter a wider magnetic field. No one owns them or has a proprietary right to dictate how they will be used.*"

—DAVID LEHMAN, U.S. POET, EDITOR, CRITIC

As you complete Chapter 2, you will

- list reasons for defining.
- give three-part sentence definitions.
- analyze the audience for a definition.
- write clear sentences and paragraphs.
- create an effective page design.
- produce effective visual aids.
- list sources of information.
- plan, write, and revise an expanded definition.

Workplace Skills in This Chapter

- Improve **interpersonal** skills as you work with team members.
- Understand how effective use of language benefits workplace **systems**.
- Gather **information** for producing definitions.
- Manage **resources** as you plan a Project.
- Use **technology** to produce text and visuals.

Defining words is not a new activity for you. In fact, since third grade you have been asked by your teachers to give definitions for vocabulary words in English class, science class, math class—all your classes. Why did your teachers ask you to define all these words?

Because it is impossible to discuss literature, biology, geometry, or any field of study without understanding the vocabulary of that discipline.

Defining at Work

Since you have begun a study of a particular occupational field, you have spent time learning the vocabulary of your work. Each field has its own specialized language, and you must make the language a part of your own vocabulary to work effectively in that field.

Simply knowing your occupation's vocabulary is not enough. You must use it to communicate requests, suggestions, explanations, instructions, and descriptions to others. This would be easy if everyone that you had to communicate with knew your specialized vocabulary, but they often do not.

If you work in a shop, you must communicate with coworkers, trainees, supervisors, managers, office workers, suppliers, and customers. If you work in a medical office, you must communicate with doctors, nurses, technicians, and patients, some of whom may be small children. If you work in a business office, you must communicate with management, clients and customers, salespeople, and other office workers.

Various audiences have various needs for information and may or may not understand specialized vocabulary. Yet, you must communicate effectively with all of them.

Practice 2-1: Uses for Definitions

teamwork Definitions rarely stand alone; they are usually a part of a longer communication. For example, directions for rebuilding an engine may begin with definitions of technical terms so readers will understand those terms when they encounter them while following the directions. Working with two or three other students, list as many types of business and technical communication as you can that may include definitions.

Why Defining Is Necessary

You can assume that your reader or listener will understand most of the words you use exactly the way you mean them. However, if a word can be understood more than one way or if you are using a technical term, you must provide a definition unless you are certain that your audience will not misunderstand.

A **dialect** is a style of language that is distinctive to a particular region. Many thousands of differences in words, pronunciations, and phrases characterize the various dialects of the United States. For example, every region has words that are peculiar to its dialect. We learn these words at home rather than at school; they are part of our oral rather than our written culture. Do you know what any of the following words mean? You probably won't find them in the dictionary. *Turn the page upside down to read their definitions.*

1. mulligrubs
2. neb-nose
3. alamagoozlum
4. chizzywink

5. Juneteenth
6. noshery
7. bizmaroon
8. faunch

9. lanai
10. Oklahoma rain
11. bumfuzzled
12. off-brand

1. unwellness
2. inquisitive person
3. maple syrup

4. a large mosquito
5. emancipation day
6. snack bar

7. bullfrog
8. to rant and rave
9. porch

10. sandstorm
11. confused
12. unusual

TECHNOBIT

A video toaster is a special computer that creates the fancy displays and effects you see in commercials and movies. The designer called it a toaster because he wanted it to be as easy to use as a toaster.

Words with Multiple Meanings

Many words have more than one meaning. If you think your audience might possibly misunderstand the meaning you intend for a word, provide a definition.

For example, the dictionary lists 20 definitions for the word *stock*. People in different occupations use this word in different ways.

* To a merchant, stock is goods kept on hand.

* To an economist, stock is a share owned in a company.

* To a nautical engineer, a stock is the crosspiece on the end of an anchor's shaft.

* To a farmer, stock is all the animals kept on the farm.

* To a geologist, stock is the main body of intrusive igneous rock of which less than forty miles is exposed.

* To a chef, stock is broth used as a base for soup, gravy, or sauces.

* To a botanist, stock is a plant from which cuttings are taken.

To communicate effectively, the chef and the botanist must agree on which definition of stock is operating.

Practice 2-2: Words with Multiple Meanings

teamwork
careers

Words that have more than one meaning can be easily misunderstood. The three common words defined on the next page have some uncommon meanings. With a partner, analyze the definitions listed for each word. For each definition, give the job title of a person who might use that particular definition of the word. *(cont'd on next page)*

1. valve

   a. A membranous structure in a hollow organ or passage, as in an artery or a vein, that folds or closes to prevent the return flow of the body fluid passing through it.

   b. Any of various devices that regulate the flow of gases, liquids, or loose materials through piping or through apertures by opening, closing, or obstructing ports or passageways.

   c. A device in a brass wind instrument that permits change in pitch by a rapid varying of the air column in a tube.

   d. One of the paired, hinged shells of certain mollusks and of brachiopods. The entire, one-piece shell of a snail and certain other mollusks.

   e. An electron tube or a vacuum tube.

2. chip

   a. A small piece, as of wood, or glass, broken ~~or~~ cut off.

   b. A minute slice of a semiconducting material, such as silicon or germanium, processed to have specified electrical characteristics, especially before it is developed into an electronic component or integrated circuit.

   c. A thin, usually fried slice of food, especially a potato chip.

   d. To chop or cut with an ax or other implement.

   e. To make a short, lofted golf stroke, used in approaching the green.

3. draft

   a. A device that regulates the flow or circulation of air.

   b. A written order directing the payment of money from an account or fund.

   c. A preliminary outline of a plan, document, or picture.

   d. A slight taper given a die to facilitate the removal of a casting.

   e. An allowance made for loss in weight of merchandise.

   f. To drive close behind another vehicle to take advantage of the reduced air pressure in its wake.

4. Can you think of a technical term used in your occupational field that has more than one meaning? Using a dictionary, find three definitions for that term.

ETHICS C·O·N·N·E·C·T·I·O·N

Would you ever

- use the office copier to make ten copies of your resume to send out?
- take home five pens that your employer purchased to give to regular customers?
- buy a leather jacket for your neighbor using your employee discount?
- make a long-distance call to wish your mom a happy birthday using the office phone?
- call in sick on the first nice spring day so you can go kayaking?
- ask another employee to clock out for you so you can leave 20 minutes early?
- embezzle $5,000 from the company accounts?

Which of the above actions would you define as theft? Chances are your employer defines *all* of them as theft. Both large and small losses to business add up. Statistics on employee crime from the FBI, U.S. Department of Commerce, and U.S. Chamber of Commerce show the following:

- One-half of all employees admit to stealing.
- Six percent of a typical business's profits are lost annually to employee crime.
- Between 20 and 30 percent of all business failures are attributed to employee theft.

If your employer loses profits or goes out of business because of employee theft, your job will be affected even if you don't steal. If your employer made an anonymous hotline available so employees could report theft, would you use it?

Abstract Ideas

A **concrete** word stands for something that can be seen, felt, weighed, or measured. An **abstract** word stands for an idea or quality. *Sweetness* is abstract. *Sugar* is concrete.

The meaning of an abstract word shifts according to its use, which often leads to misunderstanding. For example, your boss advises you to "straighten up." Do you tuck in your shirt? Clean your desk? Report for work on time? Improve your posture?

We can define an abstract word or phrase by giving **criteria**, tests that are applied to the term being defined. What criteria would define *accurate work* for a veterinary assistant? Would a brain surgeon have different criteria for accurate work? The definition of the abstract word or phrase and the criteria depend on the situation.

Examine the term *safe environment*. To a child care center, the criteria might include covered outlets, sharp objects placed out of reach, barricaded stairs, and clean surfaces. However, criteria for a safe environment in a chemical processing plant might include air-cleaning equipment, sprinkler systems, and gauges for measuring air quality.

INFOBIT

"If A is a success in life, then A equals x plus y plus z. Work is x; y is play; and z is keeping your mouth shut."

ALBERT EINSTEIN, GERMAN-BORN U.S. SCIENTIST, ON THE DEFINITION OF SUCCESS

Practice 2-3: Abstract Terms

careers

1. Are the following terms concrete or abstract?

   a. metal   e. cost   i. privacy

   b. truth   f. ethics   j. money

   c. success   g. value   k. air

   d. efficiency   h. telephone   l. child

Various societies, cultures, and workplaces constantly redefine abstract terms such as *quality, family, success,* and *sexual harassment.* Some businesses put their definitions in writing. For example, most professions have **codes of ethics**, standards of right and wrong. *Ethics* is an abstract term that must be defined for it to be meaningful. Even if they are not written down, everyone must understand the ethics of his or her job.

2. Ask your teacher what constitutes ethical behavior for an educator. Write three ethical standards for teachers.

3. Write three criteria for defining ethical behavior in a particular occupational field with which you are familiar. Begin by naming a specific job in that field.

Acronyms

An **acronym** is a word made up of the first letters of a phrase. Most acronyms are written in all capital letters with no periods. For example, the acronym OSHA contains the first letters of *Occupational Safety and Health Administration*. The acronym SWAT (*Special Weapons And Tactics*), as in SWAT team, is another example.

Acronyms that are understood by almost everyone do not need defining. In fact, some are so common that we have forgotten that

DILBERT reprinted by permission of United Feature Syndicate, Inc.

they are acronyms. The acronym *radar* (**R**adio **D**etecting **A**nd **R**anging) is one example. Not all acronyms are pronounceable. The acronym *FBI* is not pronounceable as a word, but we still recognize it as an acronym rather than as an abbreviation.

Acronyms that are only understood by specialists require definition. People who work with computers use many acronyms that most of us do not understand:

LAN	local area network	DOS	disk operating system
GIGO	garbage in, garbage out	GUI	graphical user interface
FAQ	frequently asked questions	PIM	personal information manager
CAD	computer-aided design	MUD	multi-user dungeon
RAM	random-access memory	MIDI	musical instrument digital interface

When using an acronym, write out its expansion (the words from which the acronym is formed) the first time you use the acronym. After that, assume that the audience will remember what the acronym means.

> **EXAMPLE:**
>
> The CPU (central processing unit) is the brain of a computer.

Practice 2-4: Using Acronyms

1. Using a dictionary, give the expansions for the following acronyms.

   a. CEO   f. PIN

   b. ZIP Code   g. DNA

   c. laser   h. ASAP

   d. CD-ROM   i. FYI

   e. GNP   j. AIDS

2. List three acronyms used in your school.

3. Do you know of any acronyms that are used by specialists in your field of study? Use one of them in a sentence. Give its expansion in parentheses.

TECHNOLOGY C·O·N·N·E·C·T·I·O·N

Lexicographers are people who write dictionaries. They do not invent words; they describe words people use in conversation, in literature, and in the media. Since new words are coined every day, and since old words often take on new meanings, lexicographers never run out of work.

New technologies have always resulted in new words. For example, dictionaries published in 1992 do not include listings for *hacker* or *CD-ROM.* The Internet—a word also not listed in 1992 dictionaries—has the potential to influence language more rapidly than other technology, since it is so interactive. Anyone can create a new word or invent a new way to use an old word. Try inventing a new word by attaching one of the three prefixes listed below to an old word.

Prefix	Meaning	Examples
cyber	having to do with computers, especially the Internet	cybernetics, cyberspace
e	something electronic, usually replacing a paper-based or verbal process	e-mail, e-ticket service
hyper	originally meant "over"; now means momentum or being interactive	hyperlink, hypermedia, hypertext

Technical Jargon

Technical jargon is the specialized language of a particular occupation. When the specialist uses technical jargon with a general audience, confusion may result. If, for example, your doctor diagnoses your injuries as *abrasions and contusions* instead of *scrapes and bruises,* you may become not only confused but also apprehensive, because you are unfamiliar with the medical jargon.

Use of technical jargon allows members of the same occupation to communicate efficiently about their work. A computer programmer can refer to a computer system as a *kludge* when speaking to a coworker. However, when speaking to a nonspecialist, the computer programmer would need to explain that a kludge is a computer system that is difficult to use due to poor design.

Synonyms

Synonyms are words that have the same meaning. The specialist may, at times, be able to replace a technical term with a familiar one. If the audience needs to learn the terms, both the technical term and the more familiar synonym may be given. For example:

> The inspection revealed that the plane's <u>fuselage</u> was damaged.
>
> The inspection revealed that the plane's <u>body</u> was damaged.
>
> The inspection revealed that the plane's fuselage (body) was damaged.

Communicating a Useful Definition

Often, a familiar synonym for a technical term may not exist. Then the technician must provide a definition. Most terms can be defined with a carefully constructed sentence called a **three-part sentence definition**.

Three Parts of a Sentence Definition

The three parts of a sentence definition are term, group, and details.

* The **term** is the word that is being defined.

* The **group** is a familiar classification in which the term belongs.

* The **details** give information about the term to show how it is different from other members of the same group.

TERM	GROUP	DETAILS
A toxin	is a poison	produced by a plant or animal.

The three parts of a definition can appear in any order.

TERM	DETAILS	GROUP
A conflagration	is a large and destructive	fire.

Constructing a Three-Part Definition

Suppose we are giving a three-part definition of *tureen*. The term *tureen* belongs to the group *dishes*. The definition "a tureen is a type of dish" is helpful but incomplete, because not all dishes are tureens. One detail that shows how tureens are different from other types of dishes is that a tureen is broad and deep. This detail eliminates platters, saucers, and many other dishes. However, a mixing bowl is also broad and deep, but it isn't a tureen. More details are needed; for example, tureens usually have lids. However, a casserole dish can be broad and deep and can have a lid, but it isn't a tureen. When we add the detail that a tureen is used for serving foods such as soups or stews, we eliminate all dishes that are not tureens from the definition.

> **THREE-PART DEFINITION OF TUREEN:**
>
> A tureen is a broad, deep, usually covered dish used for serving foods such as soups or stews.

This definition applies only to the word *tureen* and includes all tureens.

Adding information such as different materials from which tureens can be made is not necessary because these details are not essential for a basic understanding of the term *tureen*.

Figure 2-1: *A soup tureen*

TECHNOLOGY C·O·N·N·E·C·T·I·O·N

If you spent some time in a TV studio, you might need to know the following definitions of technical jargon:

- *Chromakey* is electronic placement of pictures behind the people on camera.
- *Cover footage* is a shot used to replace pictures of an interviewer and the subject while their voices are still heard.
- *Keeper* is usable video.
- Video disturbance caused by the object being taped, often jewelry or clothing, is called *moray*.
- The abbreviation *natsot* (natural sound) is background sound recorded during taping.
- The abbreviation *O/C* stands for *on camera*.
- A picture reduced so it takes up only part of the screen is a *squeeze frame*.

Practice 2-5: Recognizing Group and Details

In a three-part sentence definition, the term is the word that is being defined, the group is the classification in which the term belongs, and the details set the term apart from members of the same group.

Copy the following sentences. Then circle the group and underline the details. The term is italicized.

EXAMPLE:

Lagniappe is an extra or unexpected gift or benefit.

1. *Cajeta* is a thick, dark syrup or paste made from caramelized sugar and goat's milk.

2. To *cultivate* means to prepare soil for the raising of crops.

3. A *credit union* is a financial institution formed by workers in the same organization that serves only its members.

4. An insulting message posted to a newsgroup is a *flame*.

5. *Vellum* is heavy, off-white, fine-quality paper resembling parchment.

Problems in Defining

Giving a meaningful three-part sentence definition is a simple process. With practice, it can become a part of your everyday communication. Still, the following problems in defining can interfere with clear communication.

Incomplete Definitions

You've already learned that in order for a definition to be helpful to the audience, it must include all three parts—the term, the group, and the details.

Imagine trying to explain what a Dalmatian is to a small child who has never seen one. If you include only the term and the group without details—"A Dalmatian is a dog"—can you be sure that the child will accurately picture a Dalmatian?

On the other hand, if you include only the term and the details—"A Dalmatian is big and white with black spots"—what might the child visualize?

Practice 2-6: Giving Complete Three-Part Sentence Definitions

teamwork

1. In Sentences a–e, either the group or the details are missing. Identify which is missing. Work on this Practice with a partner.

   a. *Nitroglycerin* is used in making explosives and medicine.

   b. A *darby* is used by plasterers when working on ceilings.

   c. One of the bones is called the *patella*.

   d. A *sedan* is a style of automobile.

   e. A *stethoscope* is used for listening to sounds produced within the body.

2. Complete the following definitions by filling in the group.

   a. *Finland* is a _____ in northern Europe.

   b. _____ growing on the upper lip is a *mustache*.

   c. A *pediatrician* is a _____ that specializes in the treatment of babies and children.

   d. To *flatter* is to _____ excessively and often insincerely, especially in order to win favor.

   e. A *carpool* is a _____ who share transportation costs and take turns providing a vehicle and driver.

3. Complete the following definitions by adding the details.

   a. A *parasite* is an organism. . . .

   b. A *bank* is a place of business. . . .

   c. *Purple* is a color. . . .

   d. A *needle* is an instrument. . . .

   e. To *arrest* means to take or hold in custody. . . .

Figure 2-2: *A plotter*

Nonspecific Groups

When defining a technical term, make sure that the group is familiar and specific enough to be helpful. General groups such as *things*, *items*, or *devices* provide no information about the term being defined. Even groups such as *tools*, *machines*, and *parts* often do not provide enough information about the term to be helpful. *Power tools*, *life-support machines*, and *engine parts* are more informative. The more specific the group, the more helpful it will be.

Using a previous example, if we tell a child that a Dalmatian is an animal (general), we are giving him or her less information than if we say that a Dalmatian is a dog (specific). The following definitions illustrate how using a specific group makes the definition more informative:

GENERAL GROUP:

A plotter is a <u>device</u> that draws graphs or pictures, usually by moving a pen.

SPECIFIC GROUP:

A plotter is a <u>computer output device</u> that draws graphs or pictures, usually by moving a pen.

Circular Definitions

A **circular definition** confuses the audience by repeating, rather than explaining, the term. Examine the following circular definitions:

Project management software is software designed for managing projects.

The dorsal fin is the fin on the dorsal surface of a fish.

In the first example, the definition merely repeats the term. In the second example, the meaning of *dorsal* is not given, but the word is used as if the audience already knew its meaning.

INFOBIT

"Happiness is good health and a bad memory."

INGRID BERGMAN, U.S. ACTRESS, ON THE DEFINITION OF HAPPINESS

Practice 2-7: Giving Informative Definitions

1. When defining, always choose a specific group that gives the audience enough information. Next to each letter on page 41 is a list of three related terms. Beside each list, you will find a general group name. Give a more informative, specific group name. For example:

lemon, orange, lime   **General group:** fruit
                      Specific group: citrus fruit

Related Terms	General Group
a. parrot, parakeet, canary	birds
b. guitar, violin, cello	instruments
c. lizard, crocodile, snake	animals
d. Berlin, Rome, Madrid	cities
e. inauguration, wedding, bar mitzvah	events

2. Choose one term from Items 1a–1e above and write a complete and informative three-part sentence definition for it.

3. In each sentence below, the group is too general to be helpful. Revise the definitions, using a more informative, specific group. For example:

The wrist is a <u>spot</u> between the human hand and the human forearm.

The wrist is a <u>joint</u> between the human hand and the human forearm.

   a. A gesture is something that communicates an idea, sentiment, or attitude.

   b. Punch is a liquid made from several ingredients.

   c. A dungeon is a cold, dark place, usually underground.

   d. Shish kebab is a term for pieces of seasoned meat, and sometimes vegetables, roasted on skewers and served with condiments.

   e. A match is an item tipped with a mixture that ignites when subjected to friction.

Practice 2-8: Giving Useful Three-Part Sentence Definitions

careers Review the information on the parts of the sentence definition and the problems that can occur in defining. Then do the following:

1. Choose five of the following incomplete or incorrect definitions. Edit them, and write out corrected definitions. Be sure to write complete sentences.

   a. A felon is a person who has committed a felony.

   b. A prune is a type of plum.

(cont'd on next page)

c. An SOS is used when help is needed.

d. Geology is a term that deals with the history of earth and its life.

e. A bicycle is a vehicle with two wheels.

f. A stadium is where you play games.

g. A bar code is a series of vertical bars of varying widths.

h. Hypoglycemia is a medical term.

i. Dehydration is the process of dehydrating.

j. Programming is when you tell a computer what to do.

k. Flextime is a type of work schedule.

l. Telecommuting is when you work at home.

m. A ladle has a long handle and is used for serving liquid food.

n. Disinfect is when you clean something thoroughly.

o. A motorcycle is a vehicle with two wheels.

2. Choose five of the terms listed below. Write three-part definitions for them.

soufflé	vein	petal	antibiotic
spark plug	electricity	audience	tourniquet
acronym	fender	server	dowel
monitor	letterhead	amplifier	asset
scanner	ergonomic	portrait	catalytic converter
proofread	bifocals	irrigation	communication
garnish	DVD	cursor	speedometer
VCR	resume		

Failure to Analyze When Defining a Term

Analyzing your audience will help you to decide how much information to include in the definition and the words to include. Definitions intended for the general audience containing unfamiliar words do not adequately define. The specialist may, on the other hand, understand other technical terms included in the definition. Also, the specialist requires more detailed information than the general audience does. Consider the following example:

> Ethernet is a LAN connection with a bandwidth of 10,000 kilobits per second.

Most people would have to run to a dictionary to look up *LAN*, *bandwidth*, and *kilobits*. Remember that, as a communicator, it is your responsibility to be clearly understood at all times.

INFOBIT

An education researcher defined play as "the freely chosen and personally directed enactment of a group of non-goal-oriented behaviors which become progressively more complex with experience and which in themselves facilitate the development of an equivalent range of tools (i.e. skills and abilities) without which personal and species evolution cannot continue."

Notice in the following examples how the vocabulary and the amount of detail differ depending on the intended audience for the definition.

GENERAL AUDIENCE	SPECIALIST
A differential is a set of gears that transmits power to the wheels.	A differential is a type of transmission by which torque is delivered at a right angle to the motor.
Excising is cutting off a piece of body tissue.	Excising is the action of making an entry into the tissue to remove a segment of the tissue or to remove a lesion.

Finally, make sure you consider your purpose in defining. Are you, for example, defining *fire stop* so a client will understand an item on a contractor's bill, or will the reader, a carpenter trainee, be expected to build a fire stop into a wall?

Practice 2-9: Defining for Different Audiences

Identify the intended audience as general or specialized for each definition listed below.

1. A booster is a braking device that increases pressure output or decreases the amount of effort required to operate or both.

2. A booster is a part of a car's brake system that makes it easier to stop the car.

3. A mortise is a hole cut in a piece of wood into which another piece fits so as to form a joint.

4. A mortise is a hole or recess cut in a piece of wood to receive a tenon.

5. Gingiva (also known as *gums*) is the pink skin surrounding the teeth.

6. Gingiva is the mucous membrane that covers the alveolar parts of either jaw.

7. An envelope is a type of wave displayed on a measuring instrument that measures voltage used by electronics technicians.

(cont'd on next page)

PEOPLE C·O·N·N·E·C·T·I·O·N

Did you ever wonder where the expression "the real McCoy" came from? Elijah J. McCoy, born in Canada in 1843 to parents who had escaped slavery, earned an engineering degree in Scotland. Despite his education, he was unable to find a good engineering job, so he worked as a fireman for the railroad. Part of his job was to oil the train engine, which at that time required shutting the engine down. He knew that there must be a way to drip oil continuously onto the moving parts of machines, so he began experimenting. As a result, McCoy invented the first automatic machine "lubricating cup." Large industries in the United States, Canada, and abroad began to order the device. Everyone began bragging about having "the real McCoy." His invention is still used today in cars, trains, rockets, ships, and other machines.

8. An envelope is an enclosed waveform made by outlining peaks of modulated RF waves.

9. Tooth is the surface texture of the medium.

10. Tooth is the surface roughness of paper.

11. Piggyback refers to a small IV bag that runs along with a larger IV bag.

12. Piggyback refers to a small-volume IV bag of solution that is running along with or in a larger, already-existing IV line over a brief period of time.

Practice 2-10: Defining Technical Terms

careers 1. List 12 technical terms from a specialized field. They should be words that you have learned in your studies, not words that would be familiar to a general audience.

2. Choose eight of the technical terms you listed. Then, using three-part sentence definitions, define them as follows:

   a. First, define the eight terms so that a general audience will understand them.

   b. Next, define the same eight terms for specialists. Remember, the specialist will be able to understand other technical terms used in your definition. Specialists, however, may require more details than does the general audience. Ask yourself what the audience can understand and what the audience needs to know.

   c. In each definition, circle the group and underline the details. Make sure each definition is a complete sentence.

WEB LINK

The Internet is a good source for specialized dictionaries and glossaries that list words most standard dictionaries don't include.

C·O·N·N·E·C·T·I·O·N

At all times, but especially at work, be conscientious about using language that will not offend others. Some of your coworkers and customers will have conditions that can interfere with their ability to, for example, hear, walk, or lift. Never use language that identifies people solely by their disability.

Don't Use	Use
Disabled or handicapped	Person who has a disability
Crippled, defective, deformed	Person with cerebral palsy, spina bifida, etc.
Deaf and dumb	Person with a hearing impairment or deafness
Retarded, moron, imbecile	Person who has a mental or developmental disability
Confined to a wheelchair or wheelchair-bound	Uses a wheelchair
Normal, healthy	Able-bodied, person who does not have a disability
Afflicted with or suffers from	Person who has (name of disability)

Always use language that puts the person, not the disability, first.

Providing More Information

Often, a synonym or a three-part sentence definition gives the audience enough information. At other times, however, the audience needs or wants more information about a term. Then you should provide an expanded definition. An **expanded definition** gives all of the information that the audience wants or needs about the term.

In an expanded definition the subject, audience, and purpose determine the

- form of communication (written or oral).
- amount of information.
- type of information.
- word choice.
- sentence and paragraph structure.
- page design.
- subject, type, and number of illustrations.

Planning an Expanded Definition

Consider what the audience already knows about the term and what the audience needs to know. To define a term clearly and thoroughly,

INFOBIT

"The only place where success comes before work is in the dictionary."

VIDAL SASSOON, HAIR DESIGNER

you must predict the questions that the audience would ask about that term within a given situation and then answer them in the definition. The answers to the questions make up the *data* for the expanded definition. **Data** is organized information that usually is used to solve a problem.

Practice 2-11: Predicting the Audience's Questions

careers The data included in an expanded definition of a technical term depends on the audience and the purpose. Four situations are described below in which a definition is required. For any three situations, write three questions that you predict the audience will ask.

1. Eddie Lopez has been told by an auto mechanic that his car's engine has stopped running because it "threw a rod." The engine must be replaced. Eddie does not know what it means to "throw a rod." What questions about this expression does the mechanic need to answer?

2. Karen Scott has been advised to set up an IRA account at her bank. Karen does not know what an IRA account is. What questions can you predict Karen asking?

3. Pat Michaels has been told by an occupational counselor that your educational program offers challenges and opportunities. Pat is unfamiliar with your program. Before you define your program, what questions would you predict that Pat will need to ask?

4. Tonya Williams has purchased a new home. The roofing inspector has advised her to have the chimneys tuck-pointed. What questions will an expanded definition of tuck-pointing answer?

Parts of an Expanded Definition

A written expanded definition includes a title, an introduction, a body, and perhaps a closing, as well as the source(s) of the information presented.

The Title

The **title** tells the audience what kind of information to expect. Center the title at the top of the page. Do not underline or put quotation marks around the title.

You may capitalize every letter in the title. For example:

DEFINITION OF SPHYGMOMANOMETER

INFOBIT

Most French dictionaries list fewer than 100,000 words, while German dictionaries list about 185,000. English dictionaries, however, list an average of 500,000 words.

INFOBIT

".. . the full use of your powers along lines of excellence."

JOHN F. KENNEDY, U.S. PRESIDENT, ON THE DEFINITION OF HAPPINESS

If you do not wish to capitalize every letter, follow the standard rules listed below for capitalizing titles. For example:

What Is a Sphygmomanometer?

* Capitalize the first letter of the first and last words.

* Capitalize the first letter of all other words except for

    * articles (*a, an, the*).

    * coordinate conjunctions (*and, or, but, nor*).

    * *to* in infinitives (*to Walk, to Go*).

    * prepositions consisting of fewer than five letters (*at, by, for, in, of, off, on, out, to, up,* etc.).

The Introduction

The **introduction** for an expanded definition includes an accurate and complete three-part sentence definition. It may also explain why it is important for the reader or listener to have additional data. The main topics that will be covered in the body may be listed in this introductory sentence.

The Body

The **body** is the main part of the definition. It includes data that answers the questions you predict the audience will ask about the term. The body of a written expanded definition is organized into sentences and paragraphs. The main sections are divided by headings, and illustrations may be included.

The Closing

A closing may or may not be needed. Analyze the audience to decide if you need to

* restate the most important point.

* indicate where to find more information about the term.

* summarize the main points.

Sources

Your only source of information for the definition may be your own experience. If, however, you have consulted any experts, textbooks, articles, manuals, or other sources, name each source at the end of the definition. This not only gives credit where credit is due but also builds audience confidence in the correctness of your facts. In addition, if the audience would like to consult your source(s), they have the information needed. Information on citing sources is provided later in this chapter.

Writing Clear Sentences

In expanded definitions and all other written communication, the words in a sentence, the length of sentences, and the arrangement of the words within a sentence depend on audience, subject, and purpose. In order to produce clear, understandable written or oral communication, you must produce clear, understandable sentences.

Sentence Length

In technical writing, as in most good writing, sentence length varies. A combination of sentence lengths not only makes communication more interesting, because it varies the pace, but also makes communication less tiring. A series of short, choppy sentences can be as tiring to the reader as long, complicated sentences. Experts recommend that sentences in business and technical documents not exceed 17 words.

Figure 2-3: *A fax machine*

EXAMPLE OF SHORT, CHOPPY SENTENCES

Facsimile transmission is also known as fax. Facsimile transmission is a system by which text is converted. It is converted into signal waves. The signals are entered into the transmission system. This is usually phone lines. The signals are sent to a remote receiving point. At that point, a receiver reconverts the signals. It produces a copy of the original material.

EXAMPLE OF A LONG, COMPLICATED SENTENCE

Facsimile transmission, also known as fax, is a system by which text is converted into signal waves, entered into the transmission system (usually phone lines), and sent to a remote receiving point where a receiver reconverts the signal into a copy of the original material.

Carefully analyze the reader or listener when trying to determine the best sentence lengths for the definition. A general audience will not be able to take in several new ideas contained in one sentence. One new or important main idea per sentence will be more easily understood. Specialists, on the other hand, probably have enough background and interest to absorb new information more quickly.

Practice 2-12: Varying Sentence Length

1. Working with a partner, combine the lists of short sentences in Items a–d into clear single sentences. You may add words, remove words, and rearrange ideas.

INFOBIT

"...something made greater by ourselves and in turn that makes us greater."

MAYA ANGELOU, U.S. AUTHOR, ON THE DEFINITION OF WORK

Each revised sentence must be grammatically correct and must include all of the ideas from the original sentences.

For example, the following sentences could be combined:

> A parsec is a unit of measurement. It measures interstellar space. It equals 3.26 light-years.

Simply combining the sentences by connecting them with *and* is not effective.

> A parsec is a unit of measurement and it measures interstellar space and it equals 3.26 light-years.

Here are two effective ways to combine the sentences:

> A parsec, a unit of measurement for interstellar space, equals 3.26 light-years.
>
> A unit of measurement for interstellar space, the parsec, equals 3.26 light-years.

    a. Gutta–percha is a type of gum. It is obtained from trees. The trees grow in East India. Gutta–percha is used for electrical insulation.

    b. The telephone rang. Three customers came in. The computer crashed. All this happened at once.

    c. Her name is Kim. Kim works as a carpenter. Everyone told her women couldn't be good carpenters. Kim has been promoted twice.

    d. The contract was signed. The contract called for three payments. Each payment would be $120. All payments would be made by July 1. It is August 1. The customer still owes $240.

2. The following sentence is overly long and complicated. Break it into three or four shorter, more easily understood, but complete sentences.

Fiber optics are cables that carry sound and video signals across bundles of extremely thin strands of glass, each about the thickness of a strand of hair, which, although they are much lighter and more flexible than copper wire, are able to carry much more information—hundreds of thousands of times more—than copper wire, in less space.

Figure 2-4: *Fiber optic cable*

Word Arrangement

Suppose it is Friday night, and you wish to have a pizza delivered to your house. You look up the phone number for the pizza parlor in the phone book. It is 555-0102. You pick up the phone and instead dial 555-0120. The numbers are correct, but you mistakenly dialed them in the wrong order. The order of the numbers is important.

In a sentence, the order of the words is important. Though the words may be correct, if they are in the wrong order, you cannot communicate your ideas clearly. Your own written sentence might look perfectly fine on the page to you; you may not even notice until you hear the sentence read aloud that the words are out of order.

Use your ears to proofread sentences. Do your sentences make sense or do they sound like these?

> **Unclear:** Opaque ink is paint used to fill in spots on negatives that you don't want. (You don't want the *negatives*?)
>
> **Revised:** Opaque ink is paint used to fill in spots that you don't want on negatives.
>
> **Unclear:** Even though low on gas, Rob kept on driving his car. (Is Rob low on gas?)
>
> **Revised:** Rob kept on driving his car, even though it was low on gas.

In the first sentence, because the words *that you don't want* are closer to *negatives* than they are to spots, the sentence is confusing. Moving the words closer to *spots* solves the problem.

Figure 2-5: *We have discussed how to fill the barrels with our employees.*

Practice 2-13: Writing Sentences That Make Sense

teamwork It is important to arrange words in a logical order so that sentences make sense. The following sentences may *look* correct to you. Working on this Practice with a partner, read the sentences aloud to each other and *listen* to them. Revise the sentences so they make sense by reorganizing the sentences and adding words when necessary.

1. We have discussed how to fill the barrels with our employees.

2. The car was advertised in the newspaper which costs $8,000.

3. Ana is writing a report about the accident on the laptop.

4. Joseph explained how he wrecked his car while eating lunch in my kitchen.

5. We learned about the apartment building over the radio that had burned to the ground.

6. Ms. Duke planned the speech that she had to give while jogging to work.

7. Davis looked for the wrench in the customer's car which had been mislaid.

8. Mark discussed the wiring he had installed while he had coffee in the cafeteria.

9. Driving to the store, Diane's hat flew out of the open window.

10. Baked for one hour, Andrew removed the bread from the oven.

11. Mr. Swift looked for his pen in his desk which was missing.

12. Even though her brother was in it, thieves stole Mrs. Ivey's suitcase from her car.

Organizing Paragraphs

In written communication, well-organized paragraphs help readers see how ideas are related. Since a paragraph develops a single idea, a new paragraph signals a new idea to the reader. Think of paragraphs as units of thought, and give each main idea its own paragraph.

In organizing information within a paragraph, present the most important information either first or last, since readers tend to forget the middle items. If you are presenting new or difficult information, help your reader understand by moving from simpler ideas to more complex ones. Tie ideas together with signal words so readers can tell how ideas relate to one another.

For most forms of writing, a writer uses a variety of paragraph lengths. In business and technical writing, however, most paragraphs are short, only a few sentences each.

Practice 2-14: Organizing a Paragraph

1. Arrange the scrambled sentences on *Student Workbook* page 2-A into a logical order.

2. The following definition of a work team is made up of short, choppy sentences. First, combine related ideas in each group of sentences into meaningful single sentences. Then, arrange the three sentences into a logical order.

(cont'd on next page)

Definition of a Work Team

A work team is a group of individuals.

The individuals work together.
The individuals have the same objectives.
Their work is mutually dependent.

In the workplace, the competition is not against other teams within the organization.

The competition is against waste.
The competition is against poor quality.
The competition is against delays.
The competition is against the need to redo work.
The competition is against low productivity.
The competition is against competitors in the marketplace.

The team members are joined together.
The team members are joined in a coordinated effort.
The coordinated effort is much like a team in a contest.
The coordinated effort is also like a team in a competition.

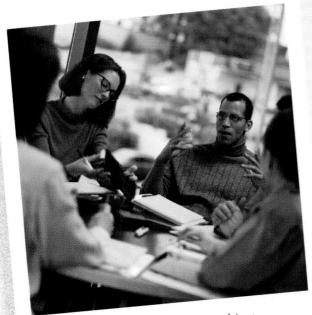

Figure 2-6: *Team members are joined in a coordinated effort.*

Page Design

Take a look at the front page of any daily newspaper. The name appears at the top of the page in large letters. Next comes the leading headline, written in large, dark letters that call your attention to the day's most important story. Notice the photographs, and perhaps charts or drawings, which may have touches of color. The news stories all have brief, informative titles. The articles are printed in narrow columns or are enclosed in boxes. Long articles are broken up by easy-to-see headings, and important points within articles are sometimes preceded by black dots or dashes.

White Space

Just as newspapers are designed for quick, easy reading, so too is business and technical writing. Along with clear sentences and well-organized paragraphs, use of white space can help to get your message across by making your writing easier to read. (See Figures 2-7 and 2-8.)

This paragraph has been formatted with almost no white space. White space is blank space on a page that contains no words or illustrations. The margins of this paragraph are narrow, and there is little space between lines or letters. The small type size and full justification (even right margin) make the text even harder to read. This type of page design can discourage even the most determined reader. A solid block of print like this one looks difficult, boring, and time-consuming to read. The experienced writer knows how to use white space to encourage the reader to read.

Figure 2-7: *Inadequate white space*

These paragraphs have been formatted with adequate amounts of white space. Appropriate use of white space creates a page that is attractive and easy to read.

The margins create a balanced, "picture frame" effect. Paragraphs in this example are separated with white space. This white space tells the reader to expect a new idea.

A well-designed page has roughly equal amounts of print and white space.

Figure 2-8: *Adequate white space*

Headings

When we read the newspaper, we scan the titles of the articles to find the ones that interest us. Most of us read only the information in the newspaper that we want or need. So it is with business and technical writing. Your audience may only want to read certain sections of your document. At other times, your audience may read it from start to finish and then later go back to it to find certain information. **Headings** help your reader by signaling the main topics.

Style

Headings are capitalized according to the same rules that govern capitalizing titles. They are usually written in bold print and are sometimes underlined or emphasized by color. Since headings serve as brief descriptions of the material that follows, they are not written in complete sentences. Introductions and closings do not ordinarily require headings.

Placement

Headings are usually either centered or placed along the left-hand margin. Leave white space above and below main headings so they are easy to find at a glance.

Page through this chapter to see how headings help you locate information quickly. The page that looks quick and easy to read is more likely to be read than the one that is not. If your message is important, pay attention to page design.

Illustrations

Imagine trying to adequately define *parallelogram* or *praying mantis* without an illustration. How effective are the following descriptions?

A parallelogram is a quadrilateral whose opposite sides are parallel and equal.

A praying mantis is a green or brownish predatory insect which, while at rest, folds its front legs as if in prayer.

The addition of drawings that *show*, rather than just *tell*, increases the effectiveness of these definitions. (See Figures 2-9 and 2-10 on the next page.)

Figure 2-9: *A parallelogram*

Figure 2-10: *A praying mantis*

If an illustration, or as it is also called, a **visual**, can help the audience understand your definition, include one. A visual can save your reader time by quickly showing what might require paragraphs of writing to explain. In addition to providing valuable information, the visual adds interest to your page.

Once you have decided that a visual will increase your audience's understanding of a definition, you must decide what type of visual to use, how to produce it, and where to place it.

Practice 2-15: Designing a Logo

A **logo** is a visual symbol designed to represent a company or organization. Companies spend thousands of dollars on the design of these visuals, since many of their customers are able to identify their products by the logos alone. You may even be wearing logos on your clothing or shoes.

1. Examine five company logos and answer the following questions about each one.

    a. Describe the logo.

    b. Who is the intended audience for the logo?

    c. What is the logo's purpose? What is its intended effect on the audience? Consider what impression the logo creates. Is it professional or casual, formal or fun, expensive or economical?

    d. Is the logo effective? Why or why not?

2. Erik Maxwell, a commercial art student, has painted his parents' restaurant window with seasonal designs over the past year. Lately, other neighborhood businesses have been asking if they can hire Erik to paint their windows too. Erik is convinced that he can start his own small business in window painting. He decides to call his business "Windows of Opportunity" and designs a logo to use on his business cards and on the flyers he plans to drop off at local stores. Which of the logos shown on the next page should he use and why?

Figure 2-11: *Logo 1*

Figure 2-12: *Logo 2*

Figure 2-13: *Logo 3*

3. Design an appropriate logo to be used on letterhead stationery, business cards, and products for the company *(Your Last Name) and Associates.*

Types of Visuals

First, analyze the subject, audience, and purpose to choose the most effective type of visual. Once you have this information, there are many options from which you can choose: drawings, photographs, diagrams, tables, charts, and graphs. Drawings and photos are most often used to illustrate definitions.

Production

Drawings and photographs both show the actual appearance of an object. Photographs, however, can sometimes include distracting detail. A clear drawing can show only what the audience needs to see. Consider using a computer graphics program or clip art for your visuals.

Most people can produce drawings of simple objects if they take their time. Make a rough draft (see Figure 2-14) of a drawing that illustrates your expanded definition. Then use a ruler and perhaps a compass to produce a neat illustration. Make the drawing simple, accurate, and large enough to be seen easily.

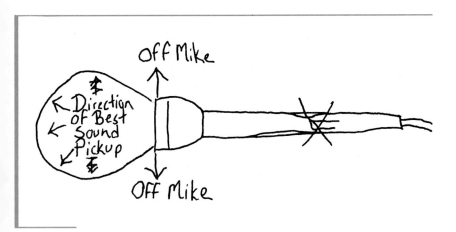

Figure 2-14: *A rough draft*

CAREER **C·O·N·N·E·C·T·I·O·N**
Looking for a sports career with the major leagues? The chance of your making it into a major- league baseball team as a player is only 1 out of 2,300 if you played high school baseball. But you could help professional teams, professional leagues, or college teams promote their products. Creating new product designs with logos is challenging work. Taking the logo and changing it slightly to place it on new products, clothing items, or materials uses the same skills as designing a page and working with visuals. The employment outlook is excellent, with room for advancement and salary increases.

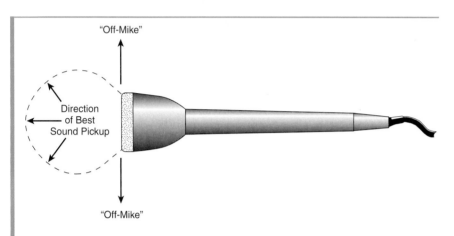

"Off-Mike"

Direction
of Best
Sound Pickup

"Off-Mike"

Figure 1   Directional microphone. The typical control-room microphone has a cardioid directional pattern, so named because of its heart-shaped area of sensitivity.

Figure 2-15: *Final draft with caption*

Captions

Most visuals need captions that clearly explain what the reader is looking at. If your visual is on a page all by itself, and you drop it on the floor, anyone who picks it up should be able to identify exactly what it shows. Clearly print or key captions and labels. If there is more than one visual, number each one "Figure 1," "Figure 2," and so on. (See Figure 2-15.)

Placement

The best place for a visual is at the point in the text where it is easiest for the audience to use it. The text is the written portion of your definition. Just after the first mention of the object shown in the drawing, insert the drawing in the text. If the visual is too large to insert in the text, place it on a separate page. The reader should not have to wait until he or she has finished reading, though, before examining the drawing. When the need to look at the visual arises, tell the reader where to find it; for example, *See Figure 3 on page 2.* Refer to the visual within the text so that the audience will know why it is important; for example, *Figure 3 on page 2 shows the main parts.*

Be sure to leave white space around the visual. This will create a more attractive page, and the visual will be easier to find and use.

Practice 2-16: Designing an Effective Page

teamwork Working with a partner, use scissors to cut out the elements for a definition of *robotics* on *Student Workbook* pages 2-B and 2-C. Create an effective and attractive document by positioning the elements on two or three sheets of plain paper. When you are satisfied with your page design, glue the page elements in place.

Naming Sources

At the end of your definition, cite the source(s) consulted to find the information. Several correct styles exist for naming the sources used for information or for visuals. Various fields of study and various publications have their own accepted styles. Many technicians who write use the style shown in this chapter.

All styles of references include the same information; however, the information is arranged differently in the different accepted forms. Keep in mind that the objective is to provide enough information so that someone else could track down the original source.

Use the following examples as models for references. Pay close attention to the pattern of capitalization and punctuation. If it is available, use italic type instead of underscore.

INFOBIT

"Work is life, you know, and without it, there's nothing but fear and insecurity."

JOHN LENNON, BRITISH ROCK MUSICIAN, ON THE DEFINITION OF WORK

INFORMATION FROM A BOOK:

Author	J. D. Heiman
Title of book	MTV's Now What!: A Guide to Jobs, Money, and the Real World
City of publication	New York
Publisher's name	MTV Books/Pocket Books
Year of publication	1996

Heiman, J. D. <u>MTV's Now What!: A Guide to Jobs, Money, and the Real World</u>. New York: MTV Books/Pocket Books, 1996.

INFORMATION FROM A MAGAZINE:

Author of article (if known)	Barbara DePompa
Title of article	Start Your Engines
Title of magazine	Success
Date of magazine	December 1990
Page numbers	24

DePompa, Barbara. "Start Your Engines." <u>Success</u>. Dec. 1990: 24.

INFORMATION FROM AN INTERVIEW:

Name	Lee Washington
Title	Manager
Organization	Washington Electronics
Date of interview	May 10, 1998

Washington, Lee. Manager, Washington Electronics. Personal interview. 10 May 1998.

(cont'd on next page)

INFOBIT

"The greatest analgesic, soporific, stimulant, tranquilizer, narcotic, and to some extent even antibiotic—in short, the closest thing to a genuine panacea—known to medical science is work." Thomas Szasz, U.S. psychiatrist, on the definition of work

INFORMATION FROM A WORLD WIDE WEB SITE:

Author's name (if known)	Marco Carrión Calderón
Title of article	Libertad en Internet
Title of complete work	LatinoLink
URL (http address)	www.latinolink.com/art/ art97/0814rcib.htm
Date of visit	October 21, 1997

Carrión Calderón, Marco. "Libertad en Internet." <u>LatinoLink</u>. http://www.latinolink.com/art/art97/0814rcib.htm. 21 Oct. 1997.

Practice 2-17: Naming Sources

Using the information listed, write the reference for each of the sources shown below. Look closely at the previous examples for the correct order of information, capitalization, and punctuation.

1. Information from a Book:

Author	Scott Adams
Title of book	The Dilbert Principle: A Cubicle-Eye's View of Bosses, Meetings, Management Fads & Other Workplace Afflictions
City of publication	New York
Publisher's name	HarperBusiness
Year of publication	1996

2. Information from a Magazine:

Author of article	David Noack
Title of article	Galaxy of Gadgets
Title of magazine	Websight
Date of magazine	March/April 1997
Page numbers	48–51

3. Information from an Interview:

Name	Suzanne Kemp
Title	Director
Organization	Citizens for the Earth
Date of interview	August 20, 1997

4. Information from a World Wide Web Site:

Author's name	Kenny Morse
Title of article	Driving Drowsy
Title of complete work	Ask Mr. Traffic
URL (http address)	www.ruku.com
Date of visit	April 2, 1997

PEOPLE C·O·N·N·E·C·T·I·O·N

Look around—could one of your classmates help you make a million? It happened to Jason Jones when Alexander Seropian proposed that Jones join him in his newly formed company, Bungie Software. Capitalizing on his passion for computer games, Seropian had already created "Operation Desert Storm," a tank-combat game. After meeting Jones, another computer addict, in a college class, Seropian asked Jones to team with him to create the game "Minotaur."

Since the partnership was formed in 1991, Bungie Software has earned nearly $2 million a year by inventing and selling games. What makes the games different is that the players actually feel that they are part of the action inside the game. Seropian credits his pastime for his success. "I picked an area I knew a lot about and enjoyed. Working for myself had always been an idea I liked, so I sat down to see what I needed to do to make that happen."

SUMMARY

Workers must communicate a wide variety of messages both to general audiences and to specialists. The audience must be able to understand every word exactly as the writer or speaker intended in order for effective communication to take place. Follow these guidelines whenever you define technical terms at work:

* Give complete, informative sentence definitions that include the term, the group, and the details.

* When more information is required, provide an expanded definition. The expanded definition should answer all questions you can predict the audience may ask about the term.

* Create an effective design for a written expanded definition. Include an informative title and headings, white space, and visuals, such as drawings, diagrams, or photographs.

* Write clear and correct sentences and paragraphs.

* Name the sources of information and visuals.

PROJECT · GIVING AN EXPANDED DEFINITION

 Select one of the following Project choices for an expanded definition. Then follow Steps 1–9.

❋ Ms. Delgado is a third-grade teacher at a nearby elementary school. She needs descriptions of various jobs for her students to read because she wants to expand their knowledge of careers. She also is interested in showing the children how the math, reading, writing, and science skills that they are learning now will help them in the future. Your task is to provide one expanded definition of a job in your career field for Ms. Delgado's class.

❋ Select a complex technical term from your course of study to thoroughly define for an entry-level worker in your occupational field.

❋ Define *ethics, excellence,* or *quality* as it applies to your chosen career. Your audience is your customers.

1. Carefully read the Sample Project Plan and the Sample Expanded Definition on pages 61–63.

2. Begin filling out the Project Plan, *Student Workbook* page 2-E. Will a drawing or photo help your reader understand your definition? If so, plan a visual.

3. Locate facts that will answer the questions your audience would have about the term being defined. Under the questions on your Project Plan, jot down facts that will help to answer those questions. Do not write complete sentences, just brief notes.

4. Have your teacher check the Project Plan.

5. Using the information on your Project Plan, write a rough draft. Write quickly without stopping to consult a dictionary or to puzzle over exact wording. Just try to get your ideas down in roughly the correct form. A rough draft should be rough.

6. Using the Rough Draft column of the Project Guide (*Student Workbook* page 2-F), check your own work with one or more classmates. Have them record all their comments and changes on your Project Guide and rough draft. Ask them to write a constructive comment on the rough draft and sign it. Have your teacher check your rough draft.

7. Revise your rough draft, incorporating the changes that your classmates and your teacher suggested.

8. Using the Final Draft column of the Project Guide, proofread your work. Make any needed corrections.

9. Turn in the final draft along with the Project Guide. Your teacher will use the Teacher's Comments column to evaluate the final draft.

SAMPLE PROJECT PLAN

Plan for an Expanded Definition

SUBJECT	URL	**CONTENT** Questions the audience might ask and data to answer them.
AUDIENCE	a new employee	**What does a URL do?** Directs browser to the web page -- works like a mailing address **What does http mean?** Hypertext Transfer Protocol format used to retrieve document -- mention ftp
PURPOSE	**What actions should the audience take?** understand what a URL is for and what its parts are	**What is the domain?** the computer where the web page is stored
FORMAT	☒ written ☐ oral ☐ other	**What is the last part of the URL for?** The document (home page) you're looking for html -- hypertext markup language
SOURCES	WEBster Home Page Mr. Hughes	**What do the domain name extensions mean?**
VISUALS	**What visuals, if any, will make the definition more effective?** Parts of a URL with each part in a different color List of domain name extensions	.gov government .edu educational institution .mil military .org private organization .com company .net network host **What is the correct way to key in a URL?** case, spelling, punctuation matter
INTRO	**Three-part sentence definition:** A URL (Uniform Resource Locator) is a method of naming documents or places on the Internet.	

What Is a URL?

A few years ago, strange strings of letters and punctuation marks, like this

http://www.gibberish.com/~nonsense/moregibberish.html

began appearing on advertisements for everything from movies to luxury cars. These strings of characters are URLs. A URL (Uniform Resource Locator) is a method of naming documents or places on the Internet. Just like a mailing address, each part of the URL address plays a specific role in directing a Web browser to the correct location anywhere in the world (see Figure 1). On the World Wide Web (WWW), URLs are accessed with *browsers*, or computer programs that can connect to the Internet and display Web pages.

Figure 1   URL For the Energy Star Programs

The Protocol

For example, the URL of the main *Web page* (a document on the WWW) for the United States Environmental Protection Agency's Energy Star Programs is http://www.epa.gov/energystar.html. The part of the URL before the colon represents the *protocol,* or format used to retrieve the document; *http* (Hypertext Transfer Protocol) means the document is on the WWW. If, instead of *http,* that part of the URL was *ftp,* it would mean that that document could be accessed through *File Transfer Protocol* (FTP), a format that allows a user to list files on, retrieve files from, and add files to another computer on the Internet.

The Domain Name

The next part of the URL, *www.epa.gov,* is called the *domain name* and represents the computer on which the document can be found. The *.gov* extension identifies the computer as belonging to the United States government. Some other common extensions are shown in Figure 2.

Domain Name Extensions

.COM	company or business	.MIL	military site
.EDU	educational institution	.ORG	private organization
.GOV	government site	.NET	network gateway or host

Figure 2   Common Domain Name Extensions

The Document Name

The last item to be listed is the Web page document name—in this case, *energystar.html*—the Energy Star home page. Hypertext Markup Language (HTML) is the language used to create the document.

URLs are case-sensitive, which means that uppercase and lowercase letters are considered different letters, so a user has to enter a URL with all letters in the correct case. Punctuation and spelling both count. Key a URL correctly, and let your browser take you around the world.

Sources: "Internet Acronyms." *WEBster.* http://www.WEBster.usv.edu/iacronyms.html. 8 May 1998.

Hughes, Shawn. Computer science teacher, Walnut Hills High School. Personal interview. 10 May 1998.

Overview

Literature uses definitions. Many times authors must clarify a concept or explain a complex idea. A reader's understanding of the concept or idea depends on how well the writer explains it.

James Baldwin, a popular, successful black writer, has written novels, essays, and plays which have won critical acclaim. Among these are *Go Tell It On the Mountain, Nobody Knows My Name: More Notes of a Native Son,* and *Another Country.*

In an address presented to a college audience, James Baldwin used the dictionary definition of the word *majority* but then continued by expanding and explaining the definition to fit his personal concept in his essay.

"In Search of a Majority"
An Address

I am supposed to speak this evening on the goals of American society as they involve minority rights, but what I am really going to do is to invite you to join me in a series of speculations. Some of them are dangerous, some painful, all are reckless. It seems to me that before we can

> *. . . we've got to make some attempt to isolate or define majority.*

begin to speak of minority rights in this country, we've got to make some attempt to isolate or define majority.

Presumably the society in which we live is an expression—in some way—of

the majority will. But it is not so easy to locate this majority. The moment one attempts to define this majority one is faced with several conundrums. Majority is not an expression of numbers, of numerical strength, for example. You may far outnumber your opposition and not be able to impose your will on them or even to modify the rigor with which they impose their will on you, i.e., the Negroes in South Africa or in some counties, some sections, of the American South. You

> *Majority is not an expression of numbers. . . .*

may have beneath your hand all the apparatus of power, political, military, state, and still be unable to use these things to achieve your ends. . . .

I suppose it can be said that there was a time in this country when an entity existed which could be called the majority, let's say a class, for the lack of a better word, which created the standards by which the country lived or which created the standards to which the country aspired. I am referring to or have in mind, perhaps somewhat arbitrarily, the aristocracies of Virginia and New England. These were mainly of Anglo-Saxon stock, and they created what Henry James was to refer to, not very much later, as our Anglo-American heritage, or Anglo-American connections. Now at no time did these men ever form anything resembling a popular majority. Their importance was that they kept alive and they bore witness to two elements of a man's life which are not greatly respected among us now: (1) the social forms, called manners, which prevent us from rubbing too abrasively against one another and (2) the interior life, or the life of the mind. These things were important; these things were realities for them and no matter how rough-hewn or dark the country was then, it is important to remember that this was also the time when people sat up in log cabins studying very hard by lamplight or candlelight. That they were better educated than we are now can be proved by comparing the political speeches of that time with those of our own day.

Now, what I have been trying to suggest in all this is that the only useful definition of the word *majority* does not refer to numbers, and it does not refer to power. It refers to influence. Someone said, and said it very accurately, that what is honored in a country is cultivated there. If we apply this touchstone to American life we can scarcely fail to arrive at a very grim view of it. But I think we have to look grim facts in the face because if we don't, we can never hope to change them.

—James Baldwin

Start-Up: A sentence definition is bare-bones stuff. An expanded definition needs more information, explanation, and examples, to show how something looks, acts, or fits in among other things before we truly understand it. There are many kinds of details one can add to a sentence definition to expand it into a paragraph or an essay. Listed below are several definition expanders:

* Give a dictionary definition.
* Tell what people say about the term being defined.
* Describe the term in detail.

* Tell what the term is not.
* Compare the term to something.
* Explain the different kinds.
* Use a quotation.
* Add your personal experience.

Connection: As a class, list the ways that James Baldwin expands the definition of the word *majority*. Give an example of these expanders from the text. Place the answers on the chalkboard.

Understanding Definitions

Start-Up: In the world of work, we must use definitions that convey exactly what we mean in concrete terms. In the world of literature, however, authors often use abstract words, deliberately involving the reader in defining the words. The use of abstract words encourages readers to interpret the work in more than one way. Note that in technical writing, we strive for one interpretation.

Connection: Form groups of three or four students and consider the abstract definitions given below. Write a concrete definition based on the abstract one. When appropriate, try to think of concrete examples of the definition. The first question is completed for you.

1. "**Willy was a salesman**. . . . He's a man way out there in the blue, riding on a smile and a shoeshine." (*Death of a Salesman* by Arthur Miller)

   Answer: A salesman is a loner who must rely on his personality and his appearance to sell his goods.

   Examples: Any salesman who must come to the door (e.g., people selling cosmetics or insurance agents)

2. ". . . we need a definition of greatness, and I suppose that would be somebody who . . . benefited all mankind." (*Master Harold and the Boys* by Athol Fugard)

3. "Satire is a sort of glass wherein beholders do generally discover everybody's face but their own." ("Battle of the Books" by Jonathan Swift)

4. ". . . first in love; when you were like a person sleepwalking, and you didn't quite see the street you were in, and didn't quite hear everything that was said to you." (*Our Town* by Thornton Wilder)

5. "I am a Doctor. A.B. ... M.A. ... Ph.D. ... ABMAPHID! Abmaphid has been variously described as a wasting disease of the frontal lobes, and as a wonder drug. It is actually

both." (*Who's Afraid of Virginia Woolf?* by Edward Albee)

6. "What does that mean—'tame'?" . . .

   "It is an act too often neglected," said the fox. "It means to establish ties. . . . But if you tame me, then we shall need each other." (*The Little Prince* by Antoine de Saint-Exupery)

7. "A foolish consistency is the hobgoblin of little minds, adored by little statesmen and philosophers and divines." ("Self-Reliance" by Ralph Waldo Emerson)

8. "A child said *What is grass?* fetching it to one with full hands. . . . I guess it is the handkerchief of the Lord." ("Song of Myself" by Walt Whitman)

9. "If a man has an office with a desk on which there is a buzzer, and if he can press that buzzer and have somebody come dashing in in response—then he's an executive." ("Address before the Trade Association Executives' Forum of Chicago" by Elmer Frank Andrews)

10. "New York, the nation's thyroid gland." ("Shore Leave" by Christopher Morley)

Overview

In 1916 Don Marquis, in his newspaper column "the Sun Dial" in the *New York Sun,* introduced archy the cockroach and mehitabel, a cat who believed she was Cleopatra in an earlier life. Archy believed he was a free-verse poet in an earlier life. Every night he recorded his experiences and observations on his boss's typewriter.

from *archy and mehitabel*

. . . archie would climb painfully upon the framework of the machine and cast himself with all his force upon a key, head downward, and his weight and the impact of the blow were just sufficient enough to operate the machine, one slow letter after another. He could not work the capital letters, and he had a great deal of difficulty operating the mechanism that shifts the paper so that a fresh line may be started. We never saw a cockroach work so hard or perspire so freely in all our lives before. After about an hour of this frightfully difficult literary labor he fell to the floor exhausted.

Congratulating ourself that we had left a sheet of paper in the machine the night before so that all this work had not been in vain, we made an examination, and this is what we found: . . .

(cont'd on next page)

"pity the poor spiders" by archy

I have just been reading
an advertisement of a certain
roach exterminator
the human race little knows
all the sadness it
causes in the insect world
i remember some weeks ago
meeting a middle aged spider
she was weeping
what is the trouble i asked
her it is these cursed
fly swatters she replied
they kill off all the flies
and my family and i are starving
to death it struck me as
so pathetic that i made
a little song about it
as follows to wit

twas an elderly mother spider
grown gaunt and fierce and gray
with her little ones crouched beside her
who wept as she sang this lay
curses on these here swatters
what kills off all the flies
for me and my little daughters
unless we eats we dies

swattin and swattin and swattin
tis little else you hear
and we ll soon be dead and forgotten
with the cost of living so dear

my husband he up and left me
lured off by a centipede
and he says as he bereft me
tis wrong but i ll get a feed

and me a working and working
scouring the streets for food
faithful and never shirking
doing the best i could

curses on these here swatters
what kills off all the flies
me and my poor little daughters
unless we eats we dies

only a withered spider
feeble and worn and old
and this is what
you do when you swat
you swatters cruel and cold

i will admit that some
of the insects do not lead
noble lives but is every
man s hand to be against them
yours for less justice
and more charity

—archy (Don Marquis)

Start-Up: Archy the cockroach doesn't capitalize words or use punctuation in his poems.

The competent technical writer must communicate information and ideas accurately. To ensure this accuracy, writers must edit their work to eliminate any possibility of being misunderstood.

Poor archy, a vers libre bard, is writing poetry the best he can. Let's give this cockroach some help.

Connection: Group into pairs and edit archy's work. Add all the needed capital letters, punctuate the lines correctly, and correct the grammar.

I HOPE YOU WON'T MIND MY PILLOW AND BLANKET AT YOUR PRESENTATION.

THE LAST TIME YOU PRESENTED, I LOST CONSCIOUSNESS AND BROKE MY NOSE ON THE TABLE.

WHATEVER HAPPENED TO GOOD MANNERS?

© 1991 United Feature Syndicate, Inc.

DILBERT reprinted by permission of United Feature Syndicate, Inc.

Listening and Responding

> "All speech, written or spoken, is a dead language until it finds a willing and prepared hearer."
>
> —ROBERT LOUIS STEVENSON, SCOTTISH NOVELIST, ESSAYIST, AND POET

Workplace Skills in This Chapter

- Improve **interpersonal** skills as you practice speaking and listening skills in teams with classmates.

- Gather, interpret, and convey **information**.

- Understand how effective speaking and listening affect workplace **systems**.

- Use communication **technology** effectively in giving and receiving information.

As you complete Chapter 3, you will

- analyze speaking and listening behaviors.

- distinguish between businesslike and unbusinesslike speaking and listening behaviors, and use businesslike speech in role-playing situations.

- take accurate notes from telephone messages.

- reconstruct messages from notes you've taken.

- communicate effective telephone messages.

- construct and give an informative oral presentation.

Listen up! You've probably heard that from teachers, coaches, parents—people who had to get a point across to a group of individuals who obviously weren't paying attention. We often have to be reminded to listen, because our minds tend to focus on one thing at a time. If we see or hear something interesting, we may block out other sights and sounds completely.

Believe it or not, listening attentively can be more difficult than reading. Yet it's one of the first things a person learns to do. Infants do it naturally—listening for their mother's or father's voice when they are just a few weeks old, smiling at friendly voices, and crying at strange, unfriendly ones. It is the beginning of a survival mechanism.

Listening for Survival

Children develop the ability to listen to avoid real physical harm as they grow up: hiding at the sound of a threatening person, hearing a motor and squealing tires in time to dodge a speeding car, or hearing the high-pitched noise of a flying object parting the air just in time to duck as it whizzes by overhead.

Listening is as important to survival on the job as it is to protecting a person from life-threatening situations. Listening to customers, to a supervisor, to coworkers, to suppliers, to health or safety inspectors—any one of these listening situations can mean success or failure at work. Whether we like it or not, as long as we work for people or with people, we have to improve our listening skills.

Most listening is done in the presence of a speaker: someone is standing in front of you, behind you, or next to you and says something. But what about when the speaker is nowhere in sight? Many times a day, in fact, you may find yourself listening to

* the radio.

* an announcement over a public address system.

* a telephone caller.

Impressions Created by the Voice

INFOBIT

Some people don't realize how much their voices are saying about them.

When a speaker is heard but not seen, that speaker's voice may cause a listener to form a mental picture of the person behind the voice. The listener may begin to make judgments about what kind of person this speaker might be (honest, dishonest, fearful, bold, etc.). What are some of the clues you use to put together a picture or impression of an absent speaker like a telephone caller or a radio announcer?

There have probably been times when you have had the opportunity to meet a person after hearing him or her on the radio or over the telephone. Did your mental picture look anything like the real person? Or did the appearance of the person surprise you?

Think of a popular radio personality whose voice has become well known to the listening public. At a public appearance, when this radio personality is perhaps introducing a popular singer onstage, or broadcasting in person from a local business, people in the audience may comment on how strange it seems that this person with the deep, booming voice turns out to be a small, ordinary-looking individual. Or the speaker may be a mild-sounding individual who has a fierce countenance and is built like a football tackle. Radio announcers learn

C·O·N·N·E·C·T·I·O·N

A whole new consulting business has been flourishing in the past few years to help women succeed and get promoted. This business teaches women how they need to communicate in order to become accepted and respected in the world of business. Consultants go from city to city presenting workshops (often one-day classes) helping women become more confident communicators while capitalizing on their own strengths and people skills.

Why have these workshops become so popular? It is a known fact that relatively few large corporations have a high percentage of women in upper management or as chairs of their boards. Communication workshop presenters offer the hope that improved understanding of how to communicate effectively will increase the likelihood that women will become more successful in corporations and not only begin to earn pay on a par with their male coworkers but also begin to climb higher on the corporate ladder.

INFOBIT

"We will have to repent in this generation not merely for the hateful words and actions of the bad people but for the appalling silence of the good people."

MARTIN LUTHER KING, JR.,
LETTER FROM BIRMINGHAM
JAIL, 1963

to make their voices work for them. They create the impression they need to create. That's their business.

Practice 3-1: Telephone Images

1. Read the following excerpts from different telephone conversations. For each excerpt, record whether you think the speaker is male or female, estimate the speaker's age, and add any other impressions you have formed of the person. An example is provided for you.

EXAMPLE:

Girl, do you know what my boss already asked me to do this morning? That woman wants me to give up another Saturday and work overtime.

Sample answer: Could be either sex; probably late teens or twenties; is talking to a friend (uses the familiar term *girl*); is upset with his or her boss (calls her "that woman"); and particularly doesn't like to work on Saturdays.

a. Julio, this is Sara. Whaddaya think that yo-yo upstairs just asked me to do? She actually wants me to take all those ceiling fans off the stockroom shelves and check the serial number on each one.

b. Hi! Wish you could see that red convertible I'm feasting my eyes on right now. Ri-i-ght! Not bad at all! Say—the reason I called is to see if you can replace that muffler this afternoon—maybe three or so?

(cont'd on next page)

WEB LINK

An incredible amount of information on gender equity can be found on the Internet. Use key words to search for information related to men's and women's occupations, salaries, and roles in this country.

c. Mr. Chan wishes to speak with Mr. Brady. Is Mr. Brady in, please?

d. Edna, did you get the work order on that CNC lathe in the machine shop? We're really hurting to get that one up and running.

e. Hey, Charlie? Jones here. Didja get those ten sacks of feed in for my mares yet?

2. Now listen to the audio selection your teacher will play for you. Give at least two additional observations about the speaker. For example, does the speaker sound energetic? show a lack of manners by loudly chewing gum while speaking? sound bored? speak in a formal rather than a familiar way?

3. It's a lot easier when you can see the speaker. Pick one of the telephone callers above and jot down the kinds of observations you might have made of that caller if you had been in the same room with him or her.

4. Compare your responses with those of other students. Do you think any of you fell victim to sexual **stereotyping**? That is, did any of you assume that a speaker was a man or woman based on what some people consider typical male or female behaviors? What are some of those behaviors? Are they truly male or female?

Making Your Voice Work for You

Your voice can work for you, too, even though you may never become a radio announcer. Remember, just as you listen to others, others are also listening to you. Of course, when you are at work, others are listening to you as more than just an individual; when you're at work, you represent your company.

If, for example, you work for Bradley Electronics, you may be the only person in that company that a customer ever sees or hears. Naturally, the owner of Bradley Electronics has to be absolutely certain that all employees give the best possible impression of the company, or it will risk losing customers. Losing customers, of course, means losing money. It takes money to pay employees, and no smart employer is going to waste money on an employee who causes the company to lose business.

When you encounter a persistent or irate customer and would like to say, "Shut up and get off my back," you instead have to take a deep breath, calm your voice, and say in your most polite manner, "Tell me

Even though early settlers came to this country to be free, women had few freedoms until very recently in history. They did not have equal educational opportunities. They could not study auto mechanics or carpentry, for example, and if they managed to get into medical school, they knew their qualifications and grades sometimes had to be higher than those of their male counterparts. They had no rights to own property or even the right to vote until 1920. In some states, working women could not get a loan to purchase a house or car until the 1970s without having their husbands or fathers co-sign for them.

A major breakthrough occurred in the form of Title IX of the Civil Rights Act of 1964. Title IX prohibited employers of more than 15 workers from discriminating on the basis of sex, race, color, religion, or national origin.

The National Commission on Working Women tells us that, by the year 2000, 80 percent of women ages 25–54 will be working. Nearly half—47 percent—of the entire labor force will be women. In the past, most women worked in clerical jobs, service industries, retail sales, and factories. Growing numbers are now entering such occupations as construction trades, manufacturing, electronics, and mechanics.

As women achieve an equal footing with men in politics, government, and business, they will have the opportunity to influence laws and customs affecting women's roles in the future.

Figure 3-1: *"What do you want me to do about it?"*

INFOBIT

When you are not feeling well, try smiling and deliberately speaking to others in a more cheerful tone. It can actually make you feel better.

how I can help you, Mr. El Khoja, and I'll do my best." (Always address the customer by name. It adds a more personal, friendly tone to your conversation.)

Sometimes you can say words that sound perfectly innocent to you, and the customer interprets them as arrogant. Your tone of voice, which includes the emphasis you give to specific words, may affect how the customer interprets your meaning. You may not even be aware that something as simple as a bad cold or an unpleasant memory may translate into a whiny or irritable tone as you deal with coworkers and customers. Your tone may not be intentional, which is why it's so important to be aware of it and control it.

For example, you may ask a simple question like "What do you want me to do about it?" Try reading this sentence aloud several times. Each time put the emphasis on a different (underlined) word, as shown below:

1. <u>What</u> do you want me to <u>do</u> about it?
2. What do you want <u>me</u> to do about it?
3. What do <u>you</u> want me to do about it?
4. What do you <u>want</u> me to do about it?

Note the subtle changes in meaning. Which examples sound more positive? more negative? Why?

Now reread each sentence above, but add the name *Mrs. Adams* at the beginning or end of the sentence. Decide which version sounds most appropriate for the workplace setting.

Obviously, more is involved here than merely accenting different words. Notice the subtle change of tone in your voice that goes along with emphasizing different parts of the question. That tone is the key to whether you will make a good impression on your manager, supervisor, or customer.

Using the Right Tone

The best definition of **tone** is verbal attitude; that is, attitude shown through the voice. Whether your voice is high or low, hoarse or smooth, your attitude is in your tone. You can show respect, courtesy, and competence with any kind of voice.

You've probably heard the saying "Work smarter, not harder." Using the proper tone is one way to work smarter. It isn't that hard to do, but it does require thinking before you speak. Otherwise, an attitude you do not intend may be communicated to your listener.

Practice 3-2: Making Your Voice Work for You

teamwork

1. *Use your voice to send the wrong message.* Each example (a–d) contains a comment that a salesperson or service representative might typically make in a particular business setting. Pretend you are the salesperson or service representative and you are in a bad mood. Give yourself time to read each comment to yourself first. Then practice reading it aloud to a partner in a way that might really turn off a customer.

Take turns with your partner, exaggerating the way you would emphasize the words to make the tone (attitude) of the comment rude or discourteous. Don't add or skip any of the words. Just work on attitude and see what you can do with your voice.

a. *Business setting:* A salesperson is demonstrating how to use the remote on a new combination television and VCR. The customer keeps interrupting, causing the salesperson to get flustered.

Comment from salesperson: "Here. Maybe you'd like to try it yourself."

PEOPLE   C·O·N·N·E·C·T·I·O·N

Robert Reich was not looking for a job when President Bill Clinton asked him to join his cabinet as secretary of labor in 1993. He was a faculty member at the John F. Kennedy School of Government at Harvard University, where he was known as one of America's foremost political economists.

Reich has since become more widely known to the American public as a man of keen intellect, excellent communication skills, and a quick, often self-deprecating sense of humor. He admits having had difficulty getting used to politics. He had been accustomed to saying and writing what he thought. After becoming a politician, he said he had to think twice about what to say and how to say it, lest political opponents use his ideas against the president and the good things that he was trying to accomplish.

Often Reich used humor to take the edge off awkward situations. When he was introduced publicly after being nominated as secretary of labor, he approached the podium only to discover that, although the podium was chest-high for the president, it was up to Reich's nose, and no step stool had been provided to allow him to see over it. (Reich is less than five feet tall.) The reporters seemed embarrassed by his plight. Finally, he commented, "Modesty aside, I've known for months that I was on Bill Clinton's shortlist." The reporters hooted.

INFOBIT

"Do not the most moving moments of our lives find us all without words?"

MARCEL MARCEAU, MIME

b. *Business setting:* Two high school students head for the mall after school. They enter a clothing store and begin trying on jackets between racks of clothing. Several jackets fall on the floor. They ignore the fallen jackets and proceed to another rack.

Comment from salesperson: "Excuse me. Is there something I can help you with?"

c. *Business setting:* A customer in a garden store has been moving potted plants from one place to another, looking at them, and then walking away and leaving them in disarray.

Comment from salesperson: "Have you been able to find any plants that you like in our store?"

d. *Business setting:* A customer who's had a car repaired after a serious accident returns with a frown a day after paying for the repairs and approaches the service desk, while complaining loudly to a fellow customer.

Comment from service representative: "So, did I hear you say there's a problem with your car?"

2. *Use your voice to send the right message.* Now, using the same four comments above, see what it takes to produce the right tone for a business setting.

(cont'd on next page)

C·O·N·N·E·C·T·I·O·N

A serious concern in the United States today is the need to treat men and women with equal respect in the workplace. Any behavior that focuses on the sexual attributes of a person, such as making crude comments to or about a person or touching someone in a way that is unwanted by the recipient, is not only bad manners but a crime. It is called sexual harassment.

Offensive behavior may be either physical or verbal, and it may come from a coworker or a supervisor. Crude jokes, name-calling, or sexual advances or suggestions, if unwanted by the person receiving them—or even by other workers who are forced to witness such behavior directed at someone else—may be reported.

Laws against sexual harassment apply to schools as well as the workplace. (Actually, school is a workplace for lots of people, though students don't often think of it in that way.) In your own school, there is someone appointed as the Title IX officer. This person is supposed to be someone to whom sexual harassment can be reported without fear of recrimination. The Title IX officer then sees to it that the behavior is stopped, either by warning the offender or by reporting the behavior to someone, thus initiating disciplinary action. Do you know who your Title IX officer is? If you don't, check your student handbook or ask your principal.

INFOBIT

People tend to pay close attention and respond in a positive way when they are addressed by name in a respectful and friendly manner.

Take turns with your partner, exaggerating the words you would emphasize to make the tone of the comment polite and helpful. Use your partner's name to add the personal touch, as should be done whenever possible in dealing with anyone.

What did you do to make the comments sound polite? Note that emphasis on words alone was not enough to get the results you were aiming for. The tone of voice—kind, rough, cheerful, irritated—had a lot to do with your results.

Practice 3-3: Workplace Scenario

teamwork Think of something good or bad that might happen in one of the work sites listed below. (You may want to choose one that appeals to your own career interest.) *careers* Write a brief **scenario** about what happens and give two or three comments that might be spoken by an employee to a supervisor, coworker, or customer/client. Let someone else in the class read your scenario and decide whether you described a positive or negative business situation.

Animal feed store	Computer center
Attorney's office	Construction site
Auto repair shop	Day-care center
Bakery	Doctor's office
College campus	Farm supply store

Greenhouse	Plumbing company
Hair salon	Printing company
Hospital	Private home
Lumberyard	Restaurant
Machine shop	Specialty store
Motorcycle shop	State park
Pet grooming shop	Supermarket

Good Listener Versus Problem Listener

When a coworker, customer, or supervisor comes to you about a business matter, be as concerned about your behavior as you are about your words. Let the person know that you are listening. Actions often speak louder than words.

Study the following list to see what it takes to be a good listener as opposed to a problem listener.

EFFECTIVE AND INEFFECTIVE LISTENING SKILLS

Good Listeners	*Problem Listeners*
listen closely to what is said.	let their minds wander.
keep their eyes on the speaker.	let their eyes wander around the room.
remain quiet so as not to interrupt the speaker.	distract the speaker with annoying behavior.
ask appropriate questions to help clarify what the speaker is saying.	do not show any response to what the speaker is saying.
act interested.	act bored.
listen for emotional content.	listen only to the words (do not listen for hidden meanings).

Practice 3-4: One-on-One

teamwork Being a good listener, like anything else, takes practice. Here is an opportunity to practice being both a poor and a good listener and talking to both a poor and a good listener.

Study the list above, which shows the characteristics of a good listener versus a poor listener.

(cont'd on next page)

For the next few minutes, you will be paired with someone in your class. Follow this procedure:

1. Decide who will be Person A and who will be Person B.

2. For two minutes, Person A will tell Person B about something that was important to him or her as a child. Person B will not talk back, but will otherwise act as a poor listener.

3. Then, for two minutes, Person A will tell Person B about something that is important to him or her today. Person B will not speak, but otherwise will act as a good listener.

4. Reverse roles and let Person B do the talking, repeating Steps 2 and 3.

After everyone has had a chance to be both a speaker and a listener, be ready to tell the class what kinds of things your bad listener did. Be very specific about exact behaviors. How did your bad listener's behaviors make you feel as you were speaking?

Now list ways that the good listeners behaved. How did these behaviors make you feel as you were speaking?

Figure 3-2: *The problem listener avoids eye contact and does not respond to the speaker.*

The Importance of Verbal Feedback

The behaviors of good and poor listeners are forms of what is often called **feedback**. *Verbal feedback* is talking to the speaker, asking questions like "Why did you do that?" or saying things like "I know just what you mean."

Using feedback skills helps to build successful communication between speaker and listener. Sometimes you think you know what the person means, but after clarifying with a question, you find out that you were quite mistaken in your thinking (see Figure 3-3).

What would be some logical questions that might **clarify** the following questions or statements?

1. Rene, do you have the *Test13* file on your data disk?

2. Be sure to put the Bordeaux jacket on the mannequin.

3. Please take the azalea to the customer in the office.

The Meaning Behind the Words

People say much more than is contained in their words alone. We can all remember the arguments that ended with "All I said was . . . ." And someone responded with, "Yes, but it's *how* you said it."

Figure 3-3: *Verbal feedback*

To be sure we truly understand what someone is saying, we have to listen not only with our ears but also with our brains. We have to learn to analyze not only the words, but more importantly,

* the sounds of the words.

* their emotional content.

* the physical movements and facial expressions of the person speaking.

If you cannot listen sensitively, you will not do well at work. How skilled you are at fixing transmissions, taking blood samples, spot welding, planting shrubs, decorating cakes, or installing peripherals on a computer won't matter much without effective listening and responding skills.

It's possible that you will not lose your job for not being a good listener. You may not even receive a warning, at least not at first. But real success—respect from coworkers, praise from your supervisor, good recommendations, increased responsibility, raises, and promotions—are more likely to come to those who listen well and respond appropriately.

Listening for Implied Meanings

The hidden meaning in a message is like the music behind the words of a song. Many times people speak to you, and they mean exactly what their words are saying. However, there's often an implied meaning they may be trying to communicate, sometimes without even realizing it.

We can better understand people and sometimes avoid conflicts if we listen for hidden meanings. Tone of voice, facial expression, and body language can all help to provide clues.

INFOBIT

"The right word may be effective, but no word was ever as effective as a rightly timed pause."

MARK TWAIN, U.S. AUTHOR

For example, a coworker says, "The coffee machine is broken." It may be that the coffee machine is broken, but why did she tell *you*? The reason she told you is the meaning behind the message. Maybe you're always good with machinery, and she wants you to try to fix it. Or maybe she'd like you to report it broken. Or maybe she's frustrated and just wants to gripe to someone.

Now is the time to use a clarifying question. A haughty "So?" is not a clarifying question; it merely aggravates people. Try something like "What's the machine doing, eating your money?" Usually a friendly, questioning response will result in the person saying something like, "No, it's putting sugar in all the coffee. I hate sugar in my coffee."

Sometimes people don't really need an answer; they just need to complain to someone. A friendly, sympathetic response will help. Avoid saying things like "So?" or "What do you expect *me* to do about it?"

Getting along with coworkers and customers is a lot easier when you get to know them well enough to understand what they mean when they say even the most common things.

Practice 3-5: Listening for Implied Meanings

Between now and tomorrow at this time, listen for at least one instance in which a person says a simple thing to you, but you know from the body language, facial expression, or tone of voice that the words spoken do not really say what's on that person's mind. Be prepared to share this example of an implied meaning with the class and tell them what you think the person was really saying or feeling.

EXAMPLE:

You say, "How are you doing?" to someone. He answers, "OK" in a depressed voice and keeps walking away from you.

Implied meaning: "I'm *not* OK, but I don't want to talk about it."

What Your Speech Says About You

The way you talk can tell people where you're from, how much education you have, what neighborhood you live in, what you do for a living, and more. This observation is not just true of you, of course, and it's not just true of Americans who speak English. It's true of people in every part of the world.

In every society, there are people who are more educated or less educated. There are people who have more money or less money. There are people who work in different kinds of jobs, where words like *prosthesis, rotors, capacitors,* and *matrix* are used—words that people in other kinds of jobs don't use or understand.

Word Choice Linked to Audience and Purpose

We choose words that we find useful, important, and effective depending on the people we're talking to and what the occasion happens to be. People who use different sets of words (or who use the same words but pronounce them differently) may have different backgrounds or may use the words to represent different things. The words *car, Beemer, wheels,* and *rod* may all refer to automobiles. However, they are not all equally effective with everyone. You have to choose the most effective word with the right tone to communicate with certain people or groups.

Figure 3-4: *In My Fair Lady, Eliza Dolittle was treated like a flower girl until she learned to speak like a lady.*

Consider the comment "Nobody is like my mom." This statement says the same thing as "Ain't nobody like my momma" and "No one is quite like Mother." In these three statements the speakers could mean the same thing. It is even possible that the speaker of all three statements could be the same person.

Let's pretend that the speaker of all three of those statements *is* the same person (a young man). He may say "Nobody is like my mom" to his high school principal, "Ain't nobody like my momma" to his best friend, and "No one is quite like Mother" while performing in a play. If he can do this, he is not a faker; he is smart.

People who want to be able to communicate clearly always keep their audience and purpose in mind. They vary their way of speaking to suit their audience and purpose. Figure 3-5 illustrates this idea. "Let's hurry, Grandpa" would be perfectly appropriate to say to your grandfather. "Step on it, Jack!" would be OK to say to a friend you wanted to move faster. But if you said one of these things to the wrong person, that person might be offended.

Figure 3-5: *Inappropriate language for the audience*

Practice 3-6: Are You Asking for Trouble?

Below are several businesslike requests. Rewrite them to give a similar message but in a way not appropriate for work. (Think whiny, argumentative, pushy, and so on.) An example is provided.

INFOBIT

Language is not good or bad. It is simply appropriate or inappropriate, depending on the audience and the occasion.

Businesslike request: Is it all right if I leave 15 minutes early today, Ms. Tasker?

Inappropriate request: Hey! I'm outta here!

or: You have to let me leave early, or I'll lose my driver's license.

Provide inappropriate ways of saying each of the following:

1. Is there a problem with the delivery truck, Mrs. Ortega?

2. Aren't you feeling any better today, Mr. Wilson?

3. Bill, do you need some help with those packages?

4. Mr. LaRosa seems to like the work you do, Cory.

5. You always wear such neat clothes, Miss Kwan.

At work, you must choose the manner of speaking that is most appropriate and effective for your job. Speech that is perfectly acceptable at home or among friends may not be acceptable at work and vice versa.

Sometimes, you may need to be careful of your word choice for legal reasons. That is why, for example, police officers often are taught to use statements like "We just want the facts, ma'am" and "We apprehended the alleged intruder." Remember, police officers are told never to accuse or condemn a person. Together, the above statements say, "We just want to find out the truth; we are not saying this person really was an intruder."

A Pocketful of Dialects

We all know that words used with adults can't always be used with very young children, who do not have the same degree of knowledge or experience and often require simpler language. So, too, you must use different words with customers who do not understand the technical terms that you might use comfortably with your coworkers.

INFOBIT

You keep customers happy, customers keep your employer in business, and your employer keeps you employed. This is the logic of the workplace.

Develop a pocketful of dialects—that is, many ways of speaking that you can use to suit the event, location, and people you're with. Some employers train their employees on how to speak while at work so that they both get along with the people in their company and represent the company well to outsiders. If this type of training is not available to you, listen to supervisors. Listen to coworkers. Imitate the successful people around you.

If you are not used to dealing with customers or clients, practice phrases that reflect what your employer wants customers to hear. Above all, select words carefully, pronounce them clearly, and treat others with respect.

Practice 3-7: Businesslike Speech

What would be a more appropriate, businesslike, customer-friendly way to rephrase each of the following statements? Write a better response. An example is provided.

EXAMPLE:

Electronics repairer to returning customer: Good grief, did that thing break already?

Better response: You're back. Is there something else I can help you with?

1. Salesperson in appliance store: Okay, man, I can sell you a service plan if you really want to spend that kind of money.

2. Dentist to patient: Most people hate this drill. They're such crybabies.

3. Dining room attendant: Lady, if you can't get that kid to quiet down, we'll have to ask you to leave. Other customers are complaining.

4. Florist to customer: That aloe plant would have been fine if you'd watered it like I told you to.

5. Department store salesperson: I can't wait on you now. I'm busy with somebody else.

Working with Telephone Messages

Many of us don't like to be told what to do or how to do it, but at work the importance of following directions cannot be overemphasized. Following directions at work is important for many reasons, including

* handling equipment correctly.

* safeguarding employees from workplace hazards.

* ensuring that customers' orders will be correctly interpreted.

* gathering accurate information on clients.

One of the most common occurrences that requires us to follow directions is receiving telephone messages. When we think of people taking telephone messages, we usually think of secretaries and other office workers. Actually, workers in many different occupations answer telephones. In many

Figure 3-6: *Taking an accurate telephone message involves both listening and writing skills.*

businesses, employees answer their own telephones or take messages for others in the office. Conducting business on a cellular telephone in the car, at home, or in public has become commonplace. Drivers of concrete mixer trucks, real estate agents, plumbers, electricians, and pizza deliverers all may be required to take telephone messages as a routine part of their jobs. A driver may be in a truck, and a voice on the line may say:

> "Tell Donna Chavez that we'll be there at 7 p.m."
>
> or
>
> "Be sure that you and Ali check the brake fluid on Number 9 before leaving the lot."

It is always best to have a pencil or pen and a small card or piece of paper in your pocket or somewhere nearby. Otherwise, in the rush of the day's activities, it's easy to forget to pass along the message or to forget exactly what's to be done. It's easy to miss details. (Was that Vehicle 9 or Vehicle 5 that needed to have the brake fluid checked?)

Wherever you happen to be when a call comes through, you may have to answer the phone and take a message for someone else, even if it's not officially your job to answer phones on a regular basis. Your voice is the only image of your company that the customer has at that time. An "I want to help you" attitude is a must.

How to Answer the Phone

Follow this procedure when answering the phone for any type of business:

1. Answer with the company's name. Sometimes your employer will have specific guidelines on how to answer the phone.

2. Copy all key pieces of information (certainly not every word) given by the caller. Usually telephone message forms are provided for this purpose.

3. Repeat the information, especially verifying numbers and the spelling of names.

4. End the call by thanking the caller.

Practice 3-8: Taking Telephone Messages

Because writing information while listening to a caller is not always easy, your teacher is going to give you a chance to practice this important skill. Using *Student Workbook* pages 3-A and 3-B, take down the key details from each caller, and be prepared to pass the messages along to someone else. Use the current date and time.

This task is not as easy as it seems, so be patient with yourself. You'll improve with practice.

C·O·N·N·E·C·T·I·O·N

You pick up the phone and a cheerful voice says, "Hello. I'd like to get your opinion about products used in your home. I am a computer, so please listen and answer only when I give you the signal."

Electronic technology can now digitize the sounds of a human voice and play them back to you. The results make a computer sound quite authentically human. However, when you get used to listening for them, these voices often sound stilted or overly cheerful.

Do you hang up, or do you listen and respond? Some people refuse to talk to a computer. But companies increasingly rely on computers to get valuable information, and many people do provide—without hesitation—the information the computer requests. If enough people refused to talk to computers, businesses would quit using them. So the fact that they are still around means that they are helping someone make money.

Getting the Answer You Want

Many large companies now use electronic messages to serve customers more quickly and efficiently. A caller is likely to hear a greeting followed by a set of directions. For example:

"Press *1* if you are calling from a Touch-Tone phone. If you are calling from a rotary phone, stay on the line and someone will answer your call."

After you press *1*, another message quickly follows.

"If you are calling one of our representatives and know the extension, enter the number of that extension now."

If you do not enter an extension number, still more messages follow.

"If you wish to place an order, press *2*."
"If you wish to inquire about a billing, press *3*."

"If you wish to speak with an operator, stay on the line and someone will speak with you shortly."

Sometimes these directions are given so quickly that it is hard to comprehend them before the next direction is given. However, if you wait, the entire series of instructions will probably be repeated, or a person will answer. Just waiting for the proper instructions and navigating through the system can be a test of patience and keen listening skills.

Leaving Messages for Others

Sometimes, especially if you are calling someone who does not stay near a phone all day, you will have to leave a message. You may hear the person's voice answer the phone and suddenly, just as you are about to say hello, you are instructed to "please leave your message at the sound of the tone."

Choosing not to talk to a machine is unprofessional. It can cause you to lose business and can cause delays in your acquiring or giving out important information. Not leaving a message wastes your time, as well, since you have to continue calling until you reach the person.

The trick is to be ready with your message. Be prepared to say exactly what you want to say as soon as the electronic voice tells you to leave your message. Since a machine can't provide callers with verbal feedback, you will have to be clear about what you mean and give just the right impression when leaving a message.

At first, it can be difficult to avoid stuttering and stammering into the machine. Here are a few tips to help you sound like a true professional.

1. Jot down a few key words so you don't forget anything you are supposed to say.

   For example, if you need to speak to Olga about rescheduling an appointment for October 3 to a later date, preferably in the morning, you might write

   "Olga—cancel Oct. 3—later date in a.m."

   That way, you won't have to stop to decide what to tell Olga by way of her answering machine.

2. Mentally rehearse your first few words. (Getting started is always the most difficult part.)

3. If you are caught off guard, hang up, get your act together, and call again. Then leave the message. Machines are very patient! They don't care if you don't get it right the first time.

4. Remember, you usually have less than a minute to leave a message. Keep it short.

Practice 3-9: Leaving a Message on an Answering Machine

Read the situation described below until you understand all the details. Decide what you will say to Kim Rikofsky and write it in 50 words or less. Then read your message into the tape recorder. Remember to pronounce your words clearly, and don't forget to leave your name, your company's name, and your phone number.

Situation: You own a lawn care company and are two days behind schedule because of severe thunderstorms. More tornado-like weather is expected tomorrow, and you know the job can't be done during a storm. You have to call Kim Rikofsky at the Rolfe Company to let her know that you haven't forgotten them, but that you don't know exactly when you can reschedule them since the weather is uncertain and other customers are ahead of them. You also realize that PerfectLawn, one of your biggest competitors, has been trying to get the Rolfe account away from you, so you have to keep your customer happy. You decide to call. Kim is out of the building, and after the phone rings, her answering machine clicks on. What do you say?

Remember to pronounce your words clearly, and don't forget to leave your name and phone number.

Practice 3-10: Creating a Work Situation Involving Telephone Messages

1. Using the yellow pages of a phone book, the Internet, or advertisements from newspapers and trade magazines, find a company representing an occupational area of your choice.

2. Work with a partner to develop a situation in which a customer would need to leave a message for someone at the company asking for information or service.

3. Create the customer's phone message to that company. Compose the message as though you were going to leave it on an answering machine.

4. Then, either record the message on a tape recorder, or if no recorder is available, choose one person to recite the message to another team of students in class. If you do not use a tape recorder, but simply recite your message, remember that you cannot answer questions as you give the message.

5. The members of the other team will then summarize your message on a phone message form and recite it back to you. Listen carefully to be sure all details are repeated accurately.

Preparing to Give an Informative Oral Presentation

Talking to a group is just one step beyond talking to an individual. The same things have to be considered, but on a larger scale. For example, you have to talk loudly enough to be heard by the whole group, and you have to look at more people than you do in a conversation.

Does talking to a group make you nervous? Almost everyone gets nervous just thinking about speaking before a group. If you follow a few simple steps, you will do a good job with your presentation.

1. Choose a subject that will be of interest to you and your audience. If the subject is given to you by your teacher, try to find an interesting or unusual way to present it.

2. Analyze your audience. Who are they? What are their backgrounds and interests? Do they already have attitudes or opinions about your topic? What aspect of your topic might especially interest them?

3. Clarify your purpose in sharing this topic with them.

4. Gather facts about your topic.

5. Organize the presentation. Put your ideas on note cards and put them in the order you would say them. (Don't forget to number them after you decide which order to put them in.)

6. Design your visuals. People often remember visuals when they don't remember the words. Make your visuals large, colorful, and easy to see. You may want to design them on the computer using presentation software such as PowerPoint, which allows you to incorporate your notes with movement, drawings, and photographs, with lots of eye-catching options.

7. Rehearse your presentation, including where you will put your notes and how you will display your visuals. If you use a flowchart, outline, or computer presentation, you may not have to use your note cards at all.

Choosing a Subject and Analyzing the Audience

Often a subject in school or at work is assigned to you. It then becomes part of your task to figure out the most appealing way to present it to your audience. Is your audience a group of classmates? Is it an auditorium full of parents and relatives? Is it a troop of Cub Scouts or Brownies? You need to know ahead of time who your audience will be so that you can choose your words to suit their ages, interests, cultural backgrounds, and educational levels.

If, however, you must choose the subject yourself, sticking with a subject that you know well and that will interest your audience will give you confidence and make your preparation easier.

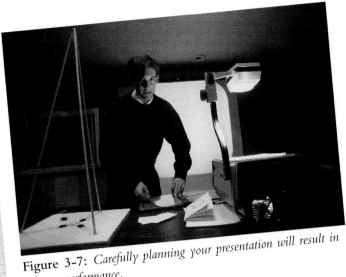

Figure 3-7: *Carefully planning your presentation will result in a better performance.*

Clarifying Your Purpose

You need to decide whether your purpose in this presentation is to simply entertain your audience, to inform them about something interesting or important, or to persuade them to take some action as a result of what you're saying. Your purpose will dictate where you need to focus. Narrowing your focus to specific points makes it easier to construct an effective presentation.

Gathering Information

Find a catchy quote or amusing or thought-provoking anecdote to use in beginning your presentation. Then decide whether you need to talk to others to get the information you need, or whether you need to research your topic using the Internet, books, trade magazines, or other sources.

Organizing the Presentation

There are several methods of preparing notes for a presentation. The most important consideration is that you be able to read and use the notes easily.

If your main points are shown in a visual such as an outline, a flowchart, or a diagram, your notes will only have to include any supporting details that you might otherwise forget.

Note-Taking Methods

Some people write notes on index cards; others use a sheet of paper. Both note-taking methods have pros and cons. The cards can be convenient, but you must turn them as you speak. Notes written on a sheet of paper do not require this handling, but you may have a more difficult time locating specific points.

Notes can be written either in a formal outline or as a list. (See Figures 3-8 and 3-9.) If you prefer a formal outline, keep it as simple as possible. After all, you want to be able to glance at your notes when

Main points

Subpoints

Details

Each card is
numbered

The Japanese Beetle - A Beautiful Destroyer

I. <u>Introduction</u> - scarab bracelet
   A. Scarabs & other beetles = 40% of animal species
      1. All sizes - microscopic to 7" long
      2. Leathery wings cover flying wings
      3. Life cycle like butterfly

①

C. Ene
   1.
   2.
D. Eff
   1.
     a. Yellow top

③

Figure 3-8: *Notes in formal outline format*

necessary, not read from them. Print your notes neatly or key them to make them easy to read. Use large letters, but not capital letters (capital letters may be used for the title). If you feel more confident making your notes in list form, do so.

Planning the Organization

Any effective presentation includes an introduction, a body, and a conclusion. In the notes shown in Figure 3-9, the introduction and conclusion are written out word for word, exactly as the speaker intends to say (or perhaps even read) them. This approach helps ensure a clear and confident beginning and end.

The Introduction. The introduction, which you will probably compose last, introduces the audience to the subject, gets their attention, and lists the main topics that will be covered. The audience will know why they should listen, what information will be explained, and how that information will be organized.

The introduction is written out word for word.

Bullets, dashes, underlining, color, or stars make the points and sub-points stand out.

Use single words or brief phrases.

Use large, easy-to-read print.

The conclusion is written out word for word.

The Japanese Beetle
A Beautiful Destroyer

Have you ever seen someone wearing a scarab bracelet like this one? If so, the person was wearing a wristful of fake scarab beetles. These multicolored creatures have been the inspiration for popular items of jewelry since ancient times.

- Beetles represent 40%—nearly half—of the 300,000 species of the world's insects & 1 out of 4 animal species.
  —need magnifying glass to see vs. 7" long
  —leathery body
  —life cycle like butterfly

- Beetles everywhere—in food, carpets, clothes, animal dung, plants, etc.

- Japanese most beautiful. Enemy of gardeners.
  —eats 275 kinds of plants (fruits, roses, etc.)

Efforts to get rid of Japanese beetle, esp. trap
—Yellow top w/pheromone
—bag to collect
—locate 25 feet away from plants

Maybe the ancients admired these beetles because they were survivors—or maybe they just accepted them because they were so much a part of their lives. As for me, I may wear a scarab bracelet, but I want to keep the real scarabs off my flowers—and out of my hair.

Figure 3-9: *Notes in list form*

The Body.   The outlined body, which includes the main points, is the longest part of the presentation. If you are explaining how to do something, you should put the points in chronological order.

The Conclusion.   The conclusion should always be brief. It restates the most important points and may also recommend some action on

TECHNOBIT

The Internet gives you access to a great deal of information. However, using it well requires discrimination. Some of the information found on the Internet is poorly documented and unreliable and may even be a put-on deliberately concocted by its author or contributor to amuse or deceive you. Always cross-check any information you find there with other sources if you are not sure that the Web site you have found is reputable and reliable.

the part of the audience. The purpose of the presentation will determine the information included in the conclusion.

Practice 3-11: Preparing Notes for a Speech

careers You have been asked to give a three-minute speech to people interested in your field of study. You are to describe a tool or other piece of equipment used in your program of study and discuss how it's used. On notebook paper, use the list method to prepare notes for the speech. Be sure to write out the introduction and conclusion exactly as you would say them. Decide what kinds of visuals you could use.

Preparing Visuals

Visuals will make your speech easier to understand and more interesting. Another advantage of visuals is that your audience will spend most of the time looking at them instead of you. For many people, what makes them most nervous about giving a speech is all those eyes staring at them! Visuals can help solve that problem.

Whether you choose drawings, diagrams, flowcharts, models, pieces of equipment, potted plants or other live specimens, or a combination of these, make sure that your visuals are attractive, neat, and informative. You may project them on a wall or screen, stand them on a table, draw them on the chalkboard, or use whatever device is necessary to make it easy for every member of the audience to see them. Give your visuals titles, if they are needed, and refer to them in your presentation.

Rehearsing the Presentation

Rehearsing will help your final presentation in many ways. It will help you to

* decide where notes need revision.

* estimate the time it takes to give the presentation.

* improve your delivery.

Ask a friend or family member to observe your rehearsal and offer suggestions for improvement. If no one is available to do this, use a video camera or tape recorder so that you can review your own performance. If you are working as part of a team, the team must also rehearse together. Individuals should know when they are to act and speak. Include reminders in your notes.

You can improve your delivery by following a few basic rules.

Speak Up!

Most important, make sure that your audience—whether 3 or 30 people—will be able to easily hear and understand you. This is *your* job, not theirs. Practice raising your voice so that it is loud enough to fill a room. (Make your voice louder, not higher in pitch.) Pronounce each word clearly, and speak slowly. If you mumble or move along too quickly, you will lose the interest of your audience. They should not have to struggle to understand you.

Watch Your Body Language—Your Audience Will, Too

The gestures and mannerisms that you use to communicate with your audience can greatly add to—or take away from—your speech. Therefore, it's a good idea to rehearse before someone else to get feedback on your body language. As you practice, follow the tips below.

INFOBIT

People who totally lose their sight gradually lose much of their body language or use body language that is less appropriate. Why do you think this is true?

Delivering the Presentation

When it is finally time to face the audience, relax and do your best. If you have carefully planned and rehearsed your presentation, you have done all you can. Just take a deep breath and begin. If you make a mistake, go on. Your audience will understand that you are doing your best to perform a difficult task.

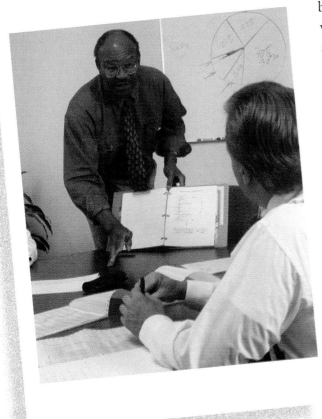

Remember to speak clearly, slowly, and loudly enough for your audience to understand. As you speak, keep these tips in mind:

* Try to maintain as much eye contact with your audience as you can. If you find this difficult, direct their attention to your visuals.

* Never turn your back to your audience.

* Try to avoid behaviors such as swaying, fiddling with your notes, adjusting your clothes, or other fidgeting that will reveal your nervousness and distract your audience.

* Stand comfortably and just talk to your audience. After all, they are just people, too, and you have years of experience in talking to people.

Practice 3-12: Analyzing a Speech

Analyzing a presentation and making suggestions for improvement should be a helpful, positive experience for both the speaker and the critic. Never make suggestions in an insulting or degrading way.

In this Practice, you will listen to a speech given by a floriculture student describing the Japanese beetle, a natural enemy of plants. Make three positive suggestions for improvement. Avoid telling the speaker what *not* to do. Instead, tell her what she can do to improve. Make three positive suggestions for improvement; for example, add an interesting fact to the introduction to get the audience's attention, give information in the correct order, define unfamiliar terms, find out all needed information ahead of time, give complete information, and omit unnecessary information.

SUMMARY

Communicating well means speaking thoughtfully, listening carefully, and responding appropriately to supervisors, coworkers, and customers. Follow these guidelines whenever you find yourself communicating with someone:

* Listen for meanings underlying the words.

* Tune in to the feelings of the person you are communicating with.

* Use appropriate language for the situation.

* Speak clearly and avoid distracting mannerisms.

* Take notes when necessary.

* Pass along messages intended for others as quickly and accurately as possible.

WORKS CITED

Reich, Robert. *Locked in the Cabinet.* New York: Knopf, 1997.

Describing an Important Object, Rule, or Idea

teamwork

careers

Regardless of what you are studying, you have dealt with objects, rules, or ideas which are an important part of your field of study. For example, if you are studying forestry or parks management, it is important for you to understand how to identify trees or what makes a lake a healthy habitat for fish. If you are studying accounting, you must understand a spreadsheet.

You and a partner will prepare and deliver an oral presentation to describe an important object, rule, or idea from your field that would be valuable or interesting to a general audience. Divide tasks between you and your partner based on your individual skills and talents. Some examples of occupations and suitable topics follow.

EXAMPLES:

Occupation	Useful Information for a General Audience
Child care worker	Which snacks are healthful for young children and why?
Nurse assistant	Why is it important to wash your hands before and after working with patients? What diseases are spread by dirty hands?
Electrician	What is electricity and how does it work?
Horticulturist	Which types of grasses grow best in your area? What kind of soils and fertilizers do they need?

1. Study the Sample Project Plan on page 99. Brainstorm ideas for a topic, for an organizational plan, and for the type and subject matter of visuals you might use.

2. With your partner, complete the Project Plan on *Student Workbook* page 3-C.

3. Have your teacher check your Project Plan.

4. Listen to the more polished sample presentation about the Japanese beetle. The notes for this presentation are in Figure 3-9 on page 93.

5. With your partner, prepare notes and visual(s) for your presentation.

6. Rehearse your part of the presentation individually and then rehearse it with your partner. Use your notes and visuals as you would in presenting before the class.

7. Using the Rough Draft column of the Project Guide on page 3-D of your *Student Workbook,* rate your rehearsed presentation.

8. Do another rehearsed presentation with your partner. If possible, ask a classmate to act as your audience and help you to rate yourselves using the Final Draft column of the Project Guide.

9. Give your presentation and your Project Guide to your teacher, who will use the Teacher's Comments column to evaluate your notes, visual(s), and speech.

Plan for a Presentation

SUBJECT	The Japanese Beetle--A Beautiful Destroyer
AUDIENCE	General audience, classmates
PURPOSE	**What actions should the audience take?** Recognize and understand the Japanese beetle
FORMAT	☐ written ☒ oral ☐ other
SOURCES	Insects by Joni Phelps Hunt, Silver Burdett Press, 1995 and Comptons Interactive Encyclopedia, 1995.
VISUALS	**What visuals, if any, will make the report more effective?** Colored photo of Japanese beetle, scarab bracelet
PREPARE	**Necessary materials, equipment:** none

CONTENT
Main points to describe or explain:

Scarab bracelet -- fake scarab beetles

Beetles represent 40% of world's insects.

--microscopic up to 7" long, leathery body

--life cycle like butterfly

Beetles everywhere -- in food, carpet, clothes, animal dung, plants

Japanese beetle most beautiful

--enemy of gardens

--eats 275 kinds of plants (fruits, roses, etc.)

Traps designed to get rid of beetles -- describe trap

Beetles survive in spite of everything

Like the bracelet, but not the real beetles.

Want to keep them away from my flower beds

Overview

Most of us have had the overwhelming experience of leaving our safe inner circle of family on that first day of school. We have all adjusted, to some degree, to the close supervision and new restraints of school. Some of us have coped better than others. Shirley Jackson's story is of a little boy's retelling of his experiences during his first days at school.

Don't miss the surprise ending.

"Charles"

The day my son Laurie started kindergarten, he renounced corduroy overalls with bibs and began wearing blue jeans with a belt; I watched him go off the first morning with the older girl next door, seeing clearly that an era of my life was ended, my sweet-voiced nursery-school tot replaced by a long-trousered, swaggering character who forgot to stop at the corner and wave good-bye to me.

He came home the same way, the front door slamming open, his cap on the floor, and the voice suddenly become raucous shouting, "Isn't anybody *here*?"

At lunch he spoke insolently to his father, spilled his baby sister's milk, and remarked that his teacher said we were not to take the name of the Lord in vain.

"How *was* school today?" I asked, elaborately casual.

"All right," he said.

"Did you learn anything?" his father asked.

Laurie regarded his father coldly. "I didn't learn nothing," he said.

"Anything," I said. "Didn't learn anything."

"The teacher spanked a boy, though," Laurie said, addressing his bread and butter. "For being fresh," he added, with his mouth full.

"What did he do?" I asked. "Who was it?"

Laurie thought. "It was Charles," he said. "He was fresh. The teacher spanked him and made him stand in a corner. He was awfully fresh."

> *"I didn't learn nothing,"*
> *he said.*

"What did he do?" I asked again, but Laurie slid off his chair, took a cookie, and left, while his father was still saying, "See here, young man."

The next day, Laurie remarked at lunch, as soon as he sat down, "Well, Charles was bad again today." He grinned enormously and said, "Today Charles hit the teacher."

"Good heavens," I said, mindful of the Lord's name, "I suppose he got spanked again?"

"He sure did," Laurie said. "Look up," he said to his father.

"What?" his father said, looking up.

"Look down," Laurie said. "Look at my thumb. Gee, you're dumb." He began to laugh insanely.

"Why did Charles hit the teacher?" I asked quickly.

"Because she tried to make him color with red crayons," Laurie said. "Charles wanted to color with green crayons so he hit the teacher and she spanked him and said nobody play with Charles but everybody did."

The third day—it was Wednesday of the first week—Charles bounced a see-saw on to the head of a little girl and made her bleed, and the teacher made him stay inside all during recess. Thursday Charles had to stand in a corner during story-time because he kept pounding his feet on the floor. Friday Charles was deprived of blackboard privileges because he threw chalk.

On Saturday I remarked to my husband, "Do you think kindergarten is too unsettling for Laurie? All this toughness, and bad grammar, and this Charles boy sounds like such a bad influence."

"It'll be all right," my husband said reassuringly. "Bound to be people like Charles in the world. Might as well meet them now as later."

On Monday Laurie came home late, full of news.

"Charles," he shouted as he came up to the hill; I was waiting anxiously on the front steps. "Charles," Laurie yelled all the way up the hill, "Charles was bad again."

"Come right in," I said, as soon as he came close enough. "Lunch is waiting."

"You know what Charles did?" he demanded, following me through the door. "Charles yelled so in school they sent a boy in from first grade to tell the teacher she had to make Charles keep quiet, and so Charles had to stay after school. And so all the children stayed to watch him."

"What did he do?" I asked.

"He just sat there," Laurie said, climbing into his chair at the table. "Hi, Pop, y'old dust mop."

"Charles had to stay after school today," I told my husband. "Everyone stayed with him."

"What does this Charles look like?" my husband asked Laurie. "What's his other name?"

> "... this Charles boy sounds like such a bad influence."

(cont'd on next page)

"He's bigger than me," Laurie said. "And he doesn't have any rubbers and he doesn't ever wear a jacket."

Monday night was the first Parent-Teachers meeting, and only the fact that the baby had a cold kept me from going; I wanted passionately to meet Charles's mother. On Tuesday Laurie remarked suddenly, "Our teacher had a friend come to see her in school today."

"Charles's mother?" my husband and I asked simultaneously.

"Naaah," Laurie said scornfully. "It was a man who came and made us do exercises, we had to touch our toes. Look." He climbed down from his chair and squatted down and touched his toes. "Like this," he said. He got solemnly back into his chair and said, picking up his fork, "Charles didn't even *do* exercises."

"That's fine," I said heartily. "Didn't Charles want to do exercises?"

"Naaah," Laurie said. "Charles was so fresh to the teacher's friend he wasn't let do exercises."

"Fresh again?" I said.

"He kicked the teacher's friend," Laurie said. "The teacher's friend told Charles to touch his toes like I just did and Charles kicked him."

"What are they going to do about Charles, do you suppose?" Laurie's father asked him.

> *"Charles was so fresh to the teacher's friend he wasn't let do exercises."*

Laurie shrugged elaborately. "Throw him out of school, I guess," he said.

Wednesday and Thursday were routine; Charles yelled during story hour and hit a boy in the stomach and made him cry. On Friday Charles stayed after school again and so did all the other children.

With the third week of kindergarten Charles was an institution in our family; the baby was being a Charles when she cried all afternoon; Laurie did a Charles when he filled his wagon full of mud and pulled it through the kitchen; even my husband, when he caught his elbow in the telephone cord and pulled telephone, ashtray, and a bowl of flowers off the table, said, after the first minute, "Looks like Charles."

During the third and fourth weeks it looked like a reformation in Charles; Laurie reported grimly at lunch on Thursday of the third week, "Charles was so good today the teacher gave him an apple."

"What?" I said, and my husband added warily, "You mean Charles?"

"Charles," Laurie said. "He gave the crayons around and he picked up the books afterward and the teacher said he was her helper."

"What happened?" I asked incredulously.

"He was her helper, that's all," Laurie said, and shrugged.

"Can this be true, about Charles?" I asked my husband that night. "Can something like this happen?"

"Wait and see," my husband said cynically. "When you've got a Charles to deal with, this may mean he's only plotting."

He seemed to be wrong. For over a week Charles was the teacher's helper; each day he handed things out and he picked things up; no one had to stay after school.

"The P.T.A. meeting's next week again," I told my husband one evening. "I'm going to find Charles's mother there."

"Ask her what happened to Charles," my husband said. "I'd like to know."
"I'd like to know myself," I said.

On Friday of that week things were back to normal. "You know what Charles did today?" Laurie demanded at the lunch table, in a voice slightly awed. "He told a little girl to say a word and she said it and the teacher washed her mouth out with soap and Charles laughed."

"What word?" his father asked unwisely, and Laurie said, "I'll have to whisper it to you, it's so bad." He got down off his chair and went around to his father. His father bent his head down and Laurie whispered joyfully. His father's eyes widened.

"Did Charles tell the little girl to say *that*?" he asked respectfully.

"She said it *twice*," Laurie said. "Charles told her to say it *twice*."

"What happened to Charles?" my husband asked.

"Nothing," Laurie said. "He was passing out the crayons."

Monday morning Charles abandoned the little girl and said the evil word himself three or four times, getting his mouth washed out with soap each time. He also threw chalk.

> We maneuvered up to one another cautiously, and smiled.

My husband came to the door with me that evening as I set out for the P.T.A. meeting. "Invite her over for a cup of tea after the meeting," he said. "I want to get a look at her."

"If only she's there," I said prayerfully.

"She'll be there," my husband said. "I don't see how they could hold a P.T.A. meeting without Charles's mother."

At the meeting I sat restlessly, scanning each comfortable matronly face, trying to determine which one hid the secret of Charles. None of them looked to me haggard enough. No one stood up in the meeting and apologized for the way her son had been acting. No one mentioned Charles.

After the meeting, I identified and sought out Laurie's kindergarten teacher. She had a plate with a cup of tea and a piece of chocolate cake; I had a plate with a cup of tea and a piece of marshmallow cake. We maneuvered up to one another cautiously, and smiled.

(cont'd on next page)

"I've been so anxious to meet you," I said. "I'm Laurie's mother."

"We're all so interested in Laurie," she said.

"Well, he certainly likes kindergarten," I said. "He talks about it all the time."

"We had a little trouble adjusting, the first week or so," she said primly, "but now he's a fine little helper. With occasional lapses, of course."

"Laurie usually adjusts very quickly," I said. "I suppose this time it's Charles's influence."

"Charles?"

"Yes," I said, laughing, "you must have your hands full in that kindergarten, with Charles."

"Charles?" she said. "We don't have any Charles in the kindergarten."

—Shirley Jackson

Start-Up: Listening, not just hearing, is very important in communication.

We all need to improve our listening skills. The biggest listening problem is lack of interest. Some students excuse low grades by saying that their teachers are boring or subjects are not interesting. The real problem in most cases, however, is lack of interest. What can you do to make a class more interesting? Make a game out of the class. Reward yourself for staying alert. Your reward may be better grades. Look for ways you can use the material you learn in class now. Impress your friends with your knowledge. Challenge yourself. Set a goal for yourself and become informed.

Lack of concentration is another listening problem. To help improve your concentration, make a record of how often you lose concentration. Get adhesive notes and label one for each class. When your attention wanders, make a mark on the note. This record will show how often you don't concentrate in class. Keep this record for five days. Average the number of times you did not pay attention for each class. This average will be a target for you to reduce. If this practice does not cause you to pay better attention in class, ask your teacher for assistance.

Be an active listener. Restate main ideas in your own words. Relate new ideas to old ones. If you don't understand, ask questions. Avoid distractions. Predict topics and pose problems. Find ways to improve your listening skills.

Connection: Laurie's parents proved to be problem listeners: they heard only words and did not listen actively. They were very interested in Laurie's days at school, but they did not probe his actions, nor did they question him until they were satisfied they understood the real situation. They missed the nonverbal cues.

1. Reread Jackson's story. List all the cues, verbal and nonverbal, that indicate Laurie is really Charles.

2. Write down some advice for Laurie's parents on improving their listening skills. Put your advice in the form of a doctor's prescription. For example:

> Once a day, give one tablespoon of questioning. (Probe for information and clarification.)

Include at least three items in your prescription.

"Barbara Allen"

OVERVIEW

Irving Berlin, who wrote such well-known songs as "White Christmas" and "God Bless America," when asked what he did for a living, answered, "I write sentimental ballads." In literature, a ballad is a poem that tells a story and is often set to music. "Barbara Allen," which has over a dozen titles, is one of the most widely recorded ballads in history. English and Scottish versions, as well as American versions, exist. A historian found over ninety versions in Virginia alone.

During the Middle Ages, when few people could either read or write, minstrels composed ballads about the everyday lives of common people on such subjects as lost love, envy, loyalty, sudden disaster, and revenge. These ballads were passed down by word of mouth from generation to generation.

Early settlers of America brought the ballads with them. These ballads still flourish in the Appalachian Mountains, among cowhands, and within many cultures.

Start-Up: You will listen to a recorded version of "Barbara Allen," which has several verses.

Connection: Listen to the ballad once through. Then listen a second time, taking notes on each verse as it is sung. Write down the answers to these questions: Who was involved? What happened? When? Where? How? Why?

Imagine that you want to share with an acquaintance the story told by the ballad. Modernize the story. Tell it as if the situation happened to someone you both know. Write a message as if you were sending it by e-mail. The message must be a maximum of 100 words and should answer the questions on which you took notes.

Using the TOT Outlet Cap

Crawling babies are attracted to electrical outlets. The TOT Outlet Cap can protect them from electrical hazards. Works on any type of outlet.

To use:

1. Hold the TOT Outlet Cap with the arrow facing up. Push prongs into outlet slots. Make sure caps are flat against the outlet plate.

2. To use the outlet, lift removal slot at top and bottom of cap. Bend back flexible connector for access to slot.

Caution:

This product is not intended to substitute for adult supervision. Always replace Outlet Cap as soon as you are finished using the outlet.

Giving Instructions

> "The factory of the future will have only two employees, a man and a dog. The man will be there to feed the dog. The dog will be there to keep the man from touching the equipment."

—WARREN BENNIS, AUTHOR AND DISTINGUISHED PROFESSOR OF
BUSINESS ADMINISTRATION, UNIVERSITY OF SOUTHERN CALIFORNIA

As you complete Chapter 4, you will

* analyze audiences.
* give effective locational instructions.
* prepare an oral presentation.
* select and use precise language.
* write concise sentences.
* write steps in instructions as commands.
* list steps in chronological order.
* write effective warnings.
* use elements of effective page design, including visual aids.
* plan, write, and revise instructions.

Workplace Skills in This Chapter

* Improve **interpersonal** skills as you analyze instructions with team members.
* Understand how effective instructions benefit workplace **systems**.
* Gather **information** for producing instructions.
* Manage **resources** as you plan a Project.
* Use **technology** to produce text and visuals.

Instructions range in complexity. Arrows show which end of a milk carton to open; book-length computer manuals detail operating procedures. Maps use very few words, while instructions for completing tax returns use thousands of words.

All of us have encountered instructions that are confusing, incomplete, or inaccurate. This chapter will help you learn to give useful and effective instructions.

Adapting Instructions for the Audience

The three important elements of all communication are audience, subject, and purpose. As communicators, however, we sometimes become so interested in our subject and purpose that we forget the needs of our audience. Since we expect the audience for instructions to act, not just to listen or read, we must always keep their needs in mind. Ask yourself how your audience will use your instructions.

How are we supposed to use instructions? We have been told that it is best to read all instructions before doing anything. But how do we really use instructions? Most of us read only what we think we need to know when we need to know it.

You cannot assume that your audience will read or listen to all of your instructions or that your audience will carry out your instructions in the order in which they were given. Nevertheless, careful audience analysis will help you produce instructions that the audience will be likely to use. After all, instructions that no one will use are no better than no instructions at all.

Audience Characteristics

The characteristics of the audience for your instructions will dictate everything from your word choice to your page design and use of visuals. How old are your readers (or listeners)? How much education have they had? Is English their primary language? How much previous experience with the subject do they have? Are they highly motivated to follow instructions, or are they reluctant? What exactly does your audience need to know?

Length of Instructions

Instructions that are overly long and detailed are less likely to be completely and carefully read than brief, to-the-point instructions. Thorough audience analysis will help you to determine the amount of explanation to include. Provide all the information your reader will need to successfully carry out the instructions *and nothing more.*

Method of Presentation

Determining the most effective way in which to present your instructions can be crucial to their success. Simple instructions can be oral—in fact, a demonstration is often most effective. Sometimes, though, you are separated from your audience by space and/or time. Then you will need to present written instructions. At other times, particularly for more complex operations, your instructions may need to combine both oral presentations and written reminders.

Figure 4-1: *Different audiences have different needs.*

QUALITY **C·O·N·N·E·C·T·I·O·N**

Sometimes even excellent instructions fail. Perhaps the audience doesn't read them or listen to them carefully. Sometimes audiences are more inexperienced than the writer anticipated. Many companies offer help lines as a service to customers who have trouble with their products. Computer hardware and software technical support lines often get calls from customers with little computer experience. According to Charles Brewer's "Home Computing" newspaper column, one company's technical support technicians reported the following stories:

A technician told a customer to "open a window," meaning a program group window on the computer screen. The customer opened a window—and then complained about the room getting too cold.

Another customer returned his broken computer to the company. It seems that when he attempted to sign up for an on-line service, it asked him to "enter your credit card number" and he stuck his credit card in the disk drive.

Don't forget that what seems simple to you may appear complicated to your audience. Once again, careful analysis of your audience, subject, and purpose will determine whether your instructions should be written, oral, or both.

Practice 4-1: Grading Instructions with a Team

 For this Practice, work with three or four other students. Your teacher will give your team five sets of instructions to grade. Make sure each team member examines each set of instructions. Discuss the strengths and weaknesses of each set. Summarize the group's evaluation of the instructions on *Student Workbook* page 4-A. For each set of instructions, fill in the blanks indicating the purpose of the instructions; for example, "Instructions for growing Magic Rocks." Note two or three effective features and two or three ineffective features. Then give each set of instructions a grade. You may give no more than one *A*, one *B*, one *C*, one *D*, and one *F*.

Giving Effective Oral Instructions

On-the-job training often involves showing rather than telling. The presenter not only must demonstrate an operation but also must teach techniques and important ideas, present information, and persuade the audience to follow directions. The key to effective oral instructions is planning.

Analyze the Audience

The complexity of your subject will, in part, determine the length of your presentation and the amount of planning required. However, consider the age, experience, attitude, and needs of your audience as well. You must plan more carefully for instructions for 30 people than you would for instructions for 3.

Practice 4-2: Considering Your Audience

teamwork For this Practice you will need a piece of blank paper, a pencil, and a book to use as a lap desk. Choose a partner to work with. One of you is Person A and the other is Person B. Position yourselves so that you can talk and listen to each other but cannot see each other.

1. Your teacher will give a copy of a drawing to Person A in each team. Person A will describe the drawing and will give B clear and precise instructions for reproducing it on his or her paper. Person B may not speak or make any sounds at all—no questions, no requests to repeat instructions, no statements about being ready for the next step. Person A may not look at B's drawing, and B may not look at A's. When A is finished, B should compare his or her drawing to A's drawing.

2. Your teacher will give you instructions for the second round. After completing Round 2, answer the following questions:

   a. What problems did the lack of feedback cause when you gave or followed instructions?

   b. How did giving or following instructions with no feedback make you feel?

   c. What three things did you do to make your instructions easy to follow?

   d. What three things could you have done to improve your instructions?

   e. How is producing written instructions like giving oral instructions with no feedback?

   f. Why is it important to plan carefully for larger audiences?

   g. Why are written instructions often easier to follow than oral instructions?

   h. Based on this activity, can you provide three rules for giving effective oral instructions?

Research the Subject

If there are any gaps in your knowledge of your subject, consult manuals, experts, or other sources to fill in those gaps. Remember,

CULTURE C·O·N·N·E·C·T·I·O·N

Most of us at times use gestures to give simple instructions, such as *stop, quiet,* or *come here.* We take for granted that everyone will understand what we mean. But these gestures are culturally biased; that is, they may vary from one culture to another—a possible source of misunderstanding. Here are some examples of how people in some other countries make the sign for *come here:*

Burma	Palm down with fingers moving as though playing the piano
Philippines	Quick downward nod of the head
Scandinavia	Tossing the head back

If that's not confusing enough, in both Albania and Bulgaria a nod means *no,* while a head shake means *yes.*

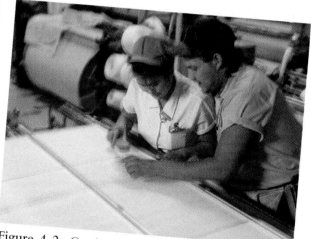

Figure 4-2: *On-the-job training often involves showing rather than telling.*

your audience may ask questions, and you will want to give accurate answers. Nothing is more important in giving instructions than accuracy. Double-check accuracy by asking someone who is not familiar with the subject to follow your instructions. Note places where they had questions or made errors; then revise the instructions accordingly.

Organize

Organize your presentation so that the listener will be able to follow your directions easily. Present information in the order the audience will use it as they carry out the instructions. The organizational plan for instructions explained later in this chapter will also work well for most oral instructions.

Make Notes

Since it is so important to present instructions in the proper order, outline your presentation or prepare note cards to prevent your forgetting an important fact or step. The presentation will be more effective if you occasionally refer to notes as you talk, instead of reading word for word from a page.

Prepare Visual Aids

Since our most highly developed sense is sight, most of us learn more from seeing than from hearing. Whenever possible, show rather than tell. Whether your visuals are the actual tools or equipment that you are using, a drawing or diagram, or some other type of illustration, make sure they are large enough and are clearly visible to everyone in the audience.

Practice

The most important benefit to practicing your presentation is that it will give you confidence and relieve your anxiety about having to speak publicly. Practice as though your audience were there. Don't just think the words; talk out loud. Use your visual aids as you practice. If you find that you occasionally need to pause and think, that's okay. Do not fill brief silences with *umm, all right,* and similar expressions.

Figure 4-3: *Visual aids must be clearly visible to the audience.*

Give the Presentation

Guard against performing the process without talking; an effective presenter describes the steps as they are being performed. Do not rush through your demonstration, and remember to talk clearly and loudly enough to be heard in the back of the room. If you don't mind interruptions, let your audience know that they can ask you questions during your presentation. Otherwise, ask if they have any questions when you have finished the instructions.

Locational Instructions

Locational instructions explain how to get from here to there. Only the simplest instructions may be given orally, since the human brain is able to remember only a limited amount of information at one time. A clear map will sometimes be sufficient, as in Figure 4-4. At other times, written or oral instructions with a map will be most effective. The complexity of the directions required and careful audience analysis will guide your choices.

Figure 4-4: *A map showing locational instructions*

Practice 4-3: The Numbers Game

Most people cannot retain more than seven bits of unrelated information at a time in short-term memory. For example, since phone numbers are only seven digits long, most people can remember one just long enough to dial it. Once that number has been dialed several times, it will probably be stored in the brain's long-term memory. If oral instructions include more than a few steps, the audience will need written reminders. To test this information, listen carefully while your teacher reads a series of numbers; then write them down. Your teacher will give you further instructions.

INFOBIT

The attention span of a person while reading or listening can be calculated by adding two minutes to the person's age. For example: an 18-year-old's attention span is 18 + 2, or a maximum of 20 minutes.

Tips for Giving Locational Instructions

When giving locational instructions, follow these guidelines:

1. Identify the starting point and destination.

2. Give the distance between the starting point and the destination in terms of space (six miles or blocks) or time (about five minutes).

3. Indicate the general direction between the starting point and the destination. If appropriate, use compass points (northeast, south).

4. Give specific, step-by-step directions in **chronological** (time) order. Note landmarks and places where mistakes might occur. Include enough detail to make the instructions easy to follow, but eliminate unnecessary detail that may only confuse your audience.

Practice 4-4: Listening to Instructions

1. Listen to the effective locational instructions that your teacher will provide.

2. Now listen to the ineffective locational instructions.

3. List five ways to improve the second set of instructions.

INFOBIT

"You got to be careful if you don't know where you're going, because you might not get there."

YOGI BERRA, U.S. ATHLETE

Practice 4-5: Giving Clear Oral Instructions

Your teacher will give you a slip of paper identifying a place located in or around the building. You will give oral directions from the room in which you are sitting to the location written on your paper. You may not reveal the destination. If your instructions are clear enough, the class should be able to guess.

1. Jot down reminder notes before it is your turn to participate in this Practice.

2. Begin by giving the distance between the starting point and the destination.

3. Indicate the general direction.

4. Give specific, step-by-step directions.

5. Do not use hand signals to indicate direction.

6. Provide enough—but not too much—detail.

7. Give all directions in the right order.

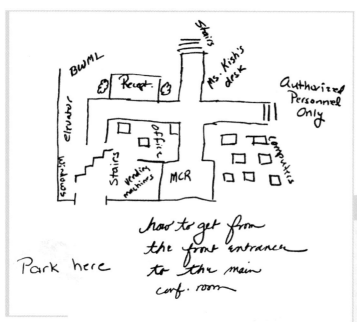

Park here

how to get from
the front entrance
to the main
conf. room

Figure 4-5: *An ineffective map*

Using Maps to Give Instructions

A clear, accurate, well-designed map is often the most effective way to present locational instructions. If you cannot find a suitable map, you may have to draw one yourself. Drawing a simple map does not take artistic ability, but it does take time and patience. As in all instructions, accuracy is the most important factor.

Practice 4-6: Evaluating a Map

Think about maps you have used in the past, whether they were road maps or maps showing how to find a particular location in a building. What made them easy—or difficult— to follow? The map shown in Figure 4-5 is not effective. Examine it closely. Then list five ways to improve it.

Practice 4-7: Constructing an Effective Map

Draw both a rough draft and a final draft of a map showing how to get from the gas station nearest your home to your school.

For the Rough Draft

1. Use a pencil.

2. Give your map a clear title written in capital letters.

3. Indicate the starting point and the destination.

4. Show the distance in miles.

5. Use compass points to indicate direction (north, southeast).

6. Show the correct path using arrows.

7. Include landmarks and street names.

8. Use as few words as possible.

9. Include enough detail to make your map easy to follow.

For the Final Draft

1. Use unlined paper and a ruler.

2. Make your map neat, uncrowded, and attractive.

3. Carefully print any words.

4. Make sure that your audience can read your map without rotating the page.

5. Eliminate distracting detail.

6. Use color to highlight important places.

The Content of Instructions

Effective instructions are complete and easy to follow. Most instructions will include an introduction, definitions, necessary preparations, warnings and precautions, steps, and sometimes a closing. Each section of the instructions (except the title and introduction) must have its own heading so that the audience can find needed information quickly. Instructions for cleaning up a chemical spill, shown at the end of this chapter, provide good examples of these elements.

The Introduction

The introduction often serves several functions: It can provide an overview of the task being explained, give the purpose of the task, explain a process, or encourage the reader to read and follow the instructions. Your subject and the characteristics of your audience will determine the information appropriate for your introduction (see Figure 4-6).

Definitions

Once again, let your intended audience be your guide. If you are not 100 percent certain that your audience will understand a technical term, define it using a three-part sentence definition. Give the definition immediately after using the term for the first time, or list it in a glossary following the introduction.

Preparations

What preparations will the audience need to make before following the steps? Are certain conditions necessary, such as strong light, a 60- to 70-degree room temperature, or a dust-free environment, for example, in order to begin the task? What tools, equipment, and materials are needed? For written instructions, if more than two are required, list them down the page. Unless the exact order matters, use bullets instead of numbers. **Bullets** are symbols inserted at the start of each line that make a list easier to read (see Figure 4-7).

Warnings and Precautions

Effective warnings and precautions can prevent safety hazards, injuries, ruined materials, broken equipment, and other problems. It is your responsibility to ensure the safety of your audience as they follow your directions (see Figure 4-8).

Special care is necessary when using any chemical product. Proper use of chemicals includes safely storing and disposing of them. The chemicals contained in many common products are poisonous if swallowed; others are caustic and can burn the eyes and skin or release toxic fumes. If a large chemical spill occurs, you must be very careful to clean it up correctly.

Figure 4-6: *Introduction for instructions*

Preparations
- Make sure that a fire extinguisher rated ABC or BC is nearby.
- Put out any flame and keep people away.
- Wear a respirator, rubber gloves, rubber boots, and safety goggles.

Materials and Equipment
- Clean cloths or paper towels
- Plastic garbage bag
- Absorbent material (cat litter or vermiculite)

Figure 4-7: *Preparations, including materials and equipment—shown in a list with bullets*

WARNING

Toxic Fumes

Can cause dizziness or unconsciousness.

Open all windows and doors to the outside.

Wear a respirator.

Figure 4-8: *A warning for instructions*

Steps

1. Pour absorbent material on the spill. Wait for it to be soaked up.

2. Scoop up the absorbent material with a shovel or dustpan; put it in a bag.

3. Remove all traces of the spill using a cloth or brush dipped in solvent.

4. Scrub the area thoroughly with a stiff-bristled brush and a solution of mild detergent and water.

5. Rinse and wipe dry with clean cloths or paper towels.

6. Following the disposal regulations of your community, remove chemical-soaked cloths, paper towels, and absorbent materials.

7. Change your clothes and wash them separately.

Figure 4-9: *Numbered steps*

Steps

Include enough detail to eliminate any confusion about what to do. To test your instructions, ask a person unfamiliar with the task to read them and provide feedback. Are there any unexplained gaps or steps that could be interpreted more than one way? Explain *how* as well as what to *do*. In written instructions, steps, presented in a numbered list, should describe just one action for each numbered step (see Figure 4-9).

The Closing

A closing may be needed to tell the audience how to test the results of following the instructions, to summarize the main steps, or to mention other methods of carrying out the task. Whatever the purpose, the closing should be brief.

Practice 4-8: Making a Paper Airplane

For this Practice you will need three sheets of plain paper. Fold the first sheet into a paper airplane. It can be as simple or as complex as you wish. If you do not know how to make a paper airplane, make up your own design. Try to prevent anyone from seeing your plane. Your teacher will give you further instructions.

Using Language Effectively

Careful use of language makes instructions easy to understand and use. No one reads instructions merely for pleasure. The words and combinations of words must be carefully chosen to carry out the purpose of the instructions: to enable the audience to act, not just to understand. Your language must be **precise**, **concise**, and **clear**. Write all steps as **commands**. Be especially careful when writing numbers.

INFOBIT

A technical writer must have the ability to make simple that which is not simple.

Word Choice

Depending on your audience, you may need to define technical terms as you use them. Whenever possible, choose words that most people can understand. You might produce instructions that are complete and technically accurate, but if your reader is unable to understand even a few words, your instructions will be useless.

Precise Language

The difference between *crow* and *crown* is only one letter, but if one of them is sitting on your head, the difference is important! In communication at work, "almost the right word" is the wrong word. Make certain that you understand the exact meaning of each word you use—and that you are using it appropriately. Then make sure that your audience cannot misinterpret your meaning. Precise language is exact and accurate.

Practice 4-9: Precise Writing

The words and phrases below are unclear because they are not precise. Copy each unclear phrase. Then replace the vague, imprecise language with concrete and exact words and phrases.

EXAMPLES:

Vague	Precise
just a few ingredients	three ingredients
a perfect-size nail	a 10d nail
the institution	the university

1. a number of tools
2. a large profit
3. enough money
4. more time
5. a high temperature

6. quite a few orders
7. the missing part
8. a tall person
9. a few colors
10. soon

INFOBIT

"He can compress the most words into the smallest idea of any man I ever met."

ABRAHAM LINCOLN, U.S. PRESIDENT

Concise and Clear Language

Extra words, sentences, and information clutter your writing, making your instructions unnecessarily long and confusing to your audience. If anything can be removed without changing the meaning of your message, remove it. Concise language is economical—every word counts.

Practice 4-10: Concise and Clear Writing

1. The words and phrases in the left column on page 118 are not concise or clear. Some phrases say in many words what could be said in a few. Some words or phrases are long, fancy, or easily misunderstood; simple, more easily understood ones would be clearer. Phrases may also include an unnecessary word, such as *together* in the phrase *collaborate together*. Replace the words and phrases with clearer, more concise ones.

(cont'd on next page)

Wordy, Fancy, or Unclear	Concise, Simple, and Clear
revolutionary new	new (or revolutionary)
exact same	same
terminate	end
in the year of 1492	in 1492
true facts	facts
completely finished	finished
during the time that	while

<table>
<tr><td>a. cancel out</td><td>i. in order to</td></tr>
<tr><td>b. positive benefits</td><td>j. at all times</td></tr>
<tr><td>c. utilize</td><td>k. yellow in color</td></tr>
<tr><td>d. each and every</td><td>l. in the amount of</td></tr>
<tr><td>e. costs the sum of</td><td>m. end result</td></tr>
<tr><td>f. make an inspection</td><td>n. personal opinion</td></tr>
<tr><td>g. really interesting</td><td>o. three different people</td></tr>
<tr><td>h. in the state of Iowa</td><td></td></tr>
</table>

2. Now rewrite the following sentences to make them more precise and concise. In the first two, the wordy or vague words and phrases are underlined.

EXAMPLE:

Wordy and Vague
Should you wish to return the item, please contact the undersigned by phone in a timely manner.

Concise and Precise
If you want to return the stereo system, please call me by May 31.

a. Our future plans include procuring additional units.

b. Either one or the other of the plans is totally acceptable.

c. I believe that there are several operators who are violating regulations with regard to safety procedures.

d. During unfavorable weather conditions, perform maintenance in an indoor area.

e. If you purchase a large number of them, the locking devices that are circular in shape only cost the sum of $7.50.

INFOBIT

Communicate to express, not to impress.

DILBERT *reprinted by permission of United Feature Syndicate, Inc.*

Command Forms

In instructions, steps are always given in the second person and as **commands**. The second person is you, the audience. Commands allow the writer to address the audience directly, increasing the likelihood that the steps will be followed. "Please stand for the Pledge of Allegiance" is a command.

Practice 4-11: Writing Commands

All but one of the following instructions are not written as commands. Instead, they describe or explain—rather than direct—action. Rewrite the instructions as commands. Begin each sentence with a *verb*, the word in the sentence that expresses the action. In the first two sentences, the base form of the verb is underlined. For the one instruction that is correctly written, write *command*.

EXAMPLE:

"Everyone should complete this Practice today" is not a command.
"This Practice is due today" is not a command.
"Complete this Practice today" is a command.
Complete is a verb.

1. It is a good idea to <u>ask</u> questions if you don't understand the directions.

2. The board should be <u>clamp</u>ed to the bench.

3. All employees must fill out an insurance form.

4. They should lower the bar before sawing.

5. The X-rays need to be examined immediately.

6. Safety glasses must be worn by all electricians.

7. Take the time to make the customer feel comfortable.

8. The lines need to be drawn more carefully.

9. Customers should be listened to.

10. All phone calls must be returned promptly.

Writing Numbers Correctly

When writing instructions and other workplace documents, write numbers carefully. A hastily written *5* can look like an *S*; a *4* can look like a *9*. The following table shows when to use words and when to use figures when writing numbers. When you follow these guidelines, you help the audience to read numbers accurately.

GUIDELINES FOR WRITING NUMBERS	
Use Figures For	**Examples**
1. Dates, house numbers (except *One*), telephone numbers, ZIP Codes, specific amounts, mathematical expressions, etc.	July 30, 1990; 600 Race Street; 61 percent; 555-0103; 10:30 p.m.; Chapter 12; $29.54
2. Measures, weights, and dimensions.	The recipe calls for 2 cups of sugar, 1/2 teaspoon of salt, 1 stick of butter, and 1/4 cup of cocoa.
3. Numerals expressed as decimals.	12.0006
4. Numbers above ten or numbers that require three or more words.	She sold 12 new cars in 2 1/2 hours.
5. Several related numbers (including fractions) that occur within a sentence.	We ordered 20 reams of paper, 3 boxes of envelopes, and 5 printer cartridges
6. One of two numbers occurring next to each other.	12 fifty-gallon containers
Use Words For	**Examples**
7. One of two numbers occurring next to each other.	50 six-cylinder cars four 3,600-pound loads
8. Numbers from one through ten.	I left work two hours early.
9. A number that begins a sentence. **Note:** If using words for numbers at the beginning of a sentence is awkward, reorganize the sentence.	Fifty cents is a fair entrance fee. Sixty percent of first-year students come from this area. **Wrong:** 2,175 orders are ready. **Awkward:** Two thousand, one hundred seventy-five orders are ready. **Correct:** We have 2,175 orders ready.
10. Numbers that are approximate or indefinite.	You'll save hundreds of dollars. About fifty machines were returned.
11. Fractions.	Our department receives three-fourths of the funding.

Practice 4-12: Writing Numbers Correctly

Rewrite any of the following sentences in which numbers are used incorrectly. Three sentences are correct as stated. For them, write the word *correct*. Refer to the guidelines shown in the table above.

1. Press the Return key 3 times.

2. Twenty-seven dollars was spent for one twelve-volt battery.

3. The motor uses about 500 watts of electrical energy.

4. The preschool will have room for about one hundred fifty children next year.

5. Sam reported that one-fourth of the modems had been sold.

6. The statement included the following costs: $25.00 for chicken, $15.65 for beef, and seven dollars for pasta.

7. The cabinet was three feet high, 10 feet long, and 18 inches deep.

8. 175 people applied for permits before January fifteenth.

9. We sold 4 50-inch televisions.

10. We need drill bits for 1/2-inch holes, 3/4-inch holes, and 1 1/2-inch holes.

INFOBIT

"Perfection is achieved, not when there is nothing left to add, but when there is nothing left to take away."

ANTOINE DE ST. EXUPERY, FRENCH WRITER

Giving Precautions and Warnings

Using effective language is especially important whenever safety is concerned. Warn your listener or reader of any hazards that you can foresee as instructions are being followed. Always provide warnings at the point in your instructions when the audience is most likely to encounter the problem. If your audience reads the warning two hours before encountering the potential danger, they may forget. On the other hand, if you caution them at the end of your instructions, it may already be too late.

An effective warning or precaution contains four types of information: a **signal word**, a **hazard identification**, the **result of ignoring the warning**, and instructions for **avoiding the hazard**. (See Figure 4-10 below for a sample warning.)

Signal word

Hazard identification

Result of ignoring warning

Avoiding the hazard

DANGER

High Voltage

Can cause severe injury or death

Disconnect transformer leads before removing this panel.

Figure 4-10: *A high-voltage warning*

The Signal Word

A precaution warns the audience to be careful, while a warning gives a stronger message that severe harm will occur if the warning is ignored. The signal

INFOBIT

A notice from a South Carolina agency regarding items that should not be recycled: "To avoid suffocation, keep away from small children." Sure, little children can sometimes be a nuisance, but they're not that dangerous.

words *DANGER, WARNING, STOP, CAUTION,* or *IMPORTANT,* written in large, capital, bold letters, will get the audience's attention. The colors red or yellow will also help attract your audience.

The Hazard Identification

This part of the message tells the audience what the hazard is. The hazard identification should appear in bold print. **Electrical shock, Radiation,** and **Hazardous vapors** are some examples. Use **sentence case** for this part. In sentence case the first letter of the first word is capitalized.

The Result of Ignoring the Warning

The next part of the message describes what will happen if the warning is ignored. It tells what damage the **Radiation, Hazardous vapors, Electrical shock,** etc., will cause. Use sentence case for this part.

Avoiding the Hazard

The last part of a precaution or warning gives detailed instructions for avoiding the hazard. This section must be concise and well organized. Use simple, direct commands in sentence case.

Careful
Acme Liquid.

Contains no oxygen.
Should be serviced in a ventilated area.

Figure 4-11: *A warning sign*

CAUTION

THIS MACHINE OPERATES WITH A LASER LIGHT THAT COULD CAUSE AN INJURY TO THE USER'S EYES.

EYES MUST BE PROTECTED AND DON'T AIM THE BEAM AT EYES OR AT SURFACES THAT REFLECT.

Figure 4-12: *A caution sign*

Practice 4-13: Precautions and Warnings

teamwork

1. As a group, discuss the strengths and weaknesses of the warnings in Figures 4-11 and 4-12.

2. On your own or with a partner, rewrite the warnings, correcting them and improving their effectiveness. Use the four-part format shown in Figure 4-10.

3. On the top half of the back of your paper, make a four-part sign warning the user of a hazard in your classroom, in your lab, or at work. Label the four parts of your sign.

4. On the bottom half, make a four-part warning sign to hang around your neck the next time you are having a bad day. The warning will protect you from friends and enemies (and will protect them from you). No profanity, please.

ETHICS   **C·O·N·N·E·C·T·I·O·N**

How does the following excerpt from "The Society for Technical Communication Code for Communicators" apply to writing instructions?

As a technical communicator, I am the bridge between those who create ideas and those who use them. . . .

I value the worth of the ideas I am transmitting and the cost of developing and communicating those ideas. I also value the time and effort spent by those who read or see or hear my communication.

I therefore recognize my responsibility to communicate technical information truthfully, clearly, and economically.

My commitment to professional excellence and ethical behavior means that I will

- Use language and visuals with precision.
- Prefer simple, direct expression of ideas.
- Satisfy the audience's need for information, not my own need for self-expression.
- Hold myself responsible for how well my audience understands my message.

Designing an Effective Page

Carefully planned layout and design of written instructions can make the difference between instructions that are successfully followed and those that are ignored or misused. Logical layout of material, titles and headings, white space, easy-to-read print, and easy-to-follow sequence (order) all contribute to effective instructions.

Page Design

A page that looks easy and quick to read is more likely to be read than a disorganized page crammed with words and pictures. Information that is difficult to locate may be ignored. Help your audience follow instructions by carefully designing your page. Follow these guidelines:

- Number your steps down the page and separate them with white space.

- Use bullets for most other lists (unless sequence is important).

- Use clear, large print and visuals.

- Use a computer or write neatly.

Spread the material evenly over the page instead of crowding it in one area. Place visuals so that your reader can find them easily within the text, or if they must be on another page, include directions explaining where to find them.

TECHNOLOGY **C·O·N·N·E·C·T·I·O·N**

The right font choice can reinforce your message, whereas the wrong one can detract from it. Remember that your primary purpose is to make the document easy to read and to understand.

Most experts agree that 10- to 12-point normal serif fonts are best for large amounts of text because they are easier to read. Serifs are decorative extensions at the ends of letters.

San serif typefaces (typefaces without serifs) are effective for small amounts of text and for titles and headings.

Decorative and display typefaces will get your reader's attention, but use them sparingly, since they can be hard to read.

Script typefaces look like handwriting. Although some of them can be difficult to read, they come in handy when you want a small amount of text to have a more personal look.

Whichever style you use, avoid using more than two typefaces on a page. Never use all capital letters for display or script fonts, since that makes them too difficult to read.

White space makes important information stand out, much like a silent room can make a sneeze sound like an explosion. White space also indicates the writer's organization and makes for an inviting and easy-to-read page.

If you use a computer to produce documents, you will have to decide which typefaces, type styles, and fonts to use. A **typeface** is a particular design for the letters and other symbols (for example, Times Roman or Helvetica). A **type style** is a variation on a typeface (for example, normal, bold, or italic). A **font** is one size and style of a particular typeface (for example, 10-point Helvetica Bold). The thousands of available typefaces range from formal to casual, from artistic to businesslike, and from plain to fancy.

The Title

The wording of the title informs the audience about the purpose of the instructions. "HOW TO CLEAN UP A LARGE CHEMICAL SPILL" or "CLEANING UP A LARGE CHEMICAL SPILL" is more informative than "CHEMICAL SPILLS." Center your title at the top of your page, and use all capital letters, bold print, or a display font.

Headings

Headings can help your reader locate information at a glance. When your reader needs to assemble necessary materials, for instance, he or

INFOBIT

In your workplace, learn to admit mistakes and to accept imperfection. A good manager will encourage you not to be fearful and pin the blame elsewhere, a breach of ethics. Occasional mistakes are an inevitable consequence of being creative.

CAREER **C·O·N·N·E·C·T·I·O·N**

According to the Labor Department, almost one-third of Americans are nontraditional workers—temporaries, part-time employees, consultants, freelancers, and self-employed workers. Constant training, retraining, and job-hopping is becoming the norm.

In 1991, nearly one out of three American workers had been with their employer for less than a year and almost two out of three for less than five years. Some workplaces have a high turnover rate; that is, employees do not stay long and are constantly being replaced. If you work in such a place, you will find yourself training new employees after you have been on the job for only a few months.

she does not want to read through the definitions or steps while trying to locate the materials list. Headings must stand out from the rest of the page so the reader can locate them quickly. Use bold print or color and white space to make them obvious. Center headings or align them at the left margin. Headings must also be consistent; that is, they need to be formatted the same way throughout the document.

Chronological Order

Instructions must be written in chronological (time) order—the same order as the reader's action. You would never list materials at the end of your instructions or warn your reader to remove all nails from the cutting surface after he or she has made the first cut. The audience should be able to carry out the instructions in the order given. For example, "Before you open the lid, turn the machine off" is confusing. "Turn the machine off before opening the lid" is clearer.

Putting information down in the order you *think* it instead of the order in which your reader will *use* it can have disastrous results. Here's an example from M★A★S★H, a popular television comedy that ran from 1972 through 1982. The 4077th M★A★S★H was an Army medical unit located in Korea during the Korean War. In one episode, two doctors, Hawkeye and Trapper, are assigned to defuse an unexploded bomb that has landed in the compound. Colonel Blake, hiding behind a sandbag bunker, reads a bomb-defusing manual aloud to them though a bullhorn.

"First you need a wrench," he reads. Hawkeye and Trapper find one. "All right, now, place it gently on the nut just above the locking ring and loosen." They loosen it. "Now, rotate the locking ring counterclockwise." They figure out which way is counterclockwise and rotate it. "Now, remove the tail assembly." They remove it. "And carefully cut the wires leading to the clockwork fuse at the head." They cut them. "But first," shouts Blake, "remove the fuse." The punch line of this joke is, of course, the resulting explosion.

List five differences between the negative and the positive examples of layout and design shown in Figures 4-13 and 4-14.

XXX XX XXX X XXXXXX

Xxx xxx xx xxxxx. Xxx xxxx x xxxx xx xxxx. X xx xxx x xxxxx xxx. Xxxxxxx xxxx.

Xxxxxx

- xxxxx xxx
- xxxx
- xxx x xxxxx

XXXX

Xxxx xxx xxxxx xxx.

Xxx xxx xx xxx.

Xxxxx xx xxxx.

Xxxx

1. Xxxx xx xxxx xxxxxx.
2. X xxx x xxxxx xxx xxxxx.

Xxx x xxxx

3. Xxxxxx xx xxxx xx xxx.

Figure 4-13: *Positive design*

Xxx xxx xx xxxxx. Xxx xxxx x xxxx xx xxxx. X xx xxx x xxxxx xxx. Xxxxxxx xxxx. Xxxx xx xxxx xxxxxx. X xxx x xxxxx xxx xxxxx. Xxxxxx xx xxxx xx xxx. Xxx xxx xx xxx. Xxx xxxx x xxxx xx xxxx. X xx xxx x xxxxx xxx. Xxxxxxx xxxx. Xxxx xx xxxx xxxxxx. X xxx x xxxxx xxx xxxxx. Xxxxxx xx xxxx xxxx xx xxxxx xx xxxxx xxx.

Xxx xxx xx xxxxx. Xxx xxxx x xxxx xx xxxx. X xx xxx x xxxxx xxx. Xxxxxxx xxxx. Xxxx xx xxxx xxxxxx. X xxx x xxxxx xxx xxxxx. Xxxxxx xx xxxx xx xxx xxxxxxxx xxxxx xxx xxxxxxxxx.

Xxx xx xxxx xxxxx. X xxx x xxxxx xxx xxxxx. Xxxxx xx xxxx xx xxx x xxxx xxxx.

Xxx xxx xx xxxxx. Xxx xxxx x xxxx xx xxxx. X xx xxx x xxxxx xxx. Xxxxxxx xxxx. Xxxx xx xxxx xxxxxx. X xxx x xxxxxx xxx xxxxx. Xxxxxx xx xxxx xx xxx xxxx xxxxxxx xxx xxxxx xx x xxxxx. Xxxxx xxxx x xxxxx xxx.

Figure 4-14: *Negative design*

Creating Effective Visuals

The expression "a picture is worth a thousand words" becomes a reality when applied to giving instructions. When planned and executed well, visuals can add interest to the presentation, highlight important points, and clarify directions.

Visuals, then, serve as important components of instructions by *showing* what to do. Your subject, audience, and purpose will determine the most appropriate type of visuals, the number needed, and the information they will show.

Types of Visuals

Analyze the subject, audience, and purpose of your instructions to choose the most effective type of visual. Depending on your subject, audience, and purpose, you might choose models or objects, drawings or photographs, or diagrams to illustrate instructions.

Models and Objects

For oral instructions and demonstrations, the actual equipment or a model is often most helpful. Position the object so everyone in the audience can see it clearly.

Drawings and Photographs

Realistic, accurate drawings and photographs show your audience the parts of a mechanism, a before-and-after situation, the differences between similar items, or the steps in an operation (see Figures 4-15 to 4-18).

Often, a simple drawing is easier to read than a photograph since it eliminates the photograph's distracting details. Please refer to Chapter 2 for guidelines for constructing effective drawings.

DRAWING SHOWING PARTS OF A MECHANISM

Underwriter's knot

Figure 4-15: *Plug end of an electrical cord*

Figure 4-16: *Before and after hairstyling*

DRAWING SHOWING DIFFERENCES BETWEEN SIMILAR ITEMS

9-pin   15-pin   25-pin

Figure 4-17: *D-shaped connectors*

DRAWING SHOWING STEPS IN AN OPERATION

Figure 4-18: *Tying an underwriter's knot*

TECHNOBIT

The top job of the twenty-first century is predicted to be multimedia software designer. This job has grown 40 percent in the last ten years.

Diagrams

Diagrams, constructed mainly of lines and symbols, illustrate ideas, areas, and processes (see Figures 4-19 to 4-21). Examples of diagrams include maps, schematics, and blueprints. The guidelines for constructing drawings in Chapter 2 also apply to diagrams.

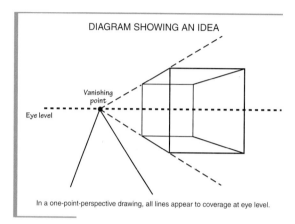

DIAGRAM SHOWING AN IDEA

Vanishing point

Eye level

In a one-point-perspective drawing, all lines appear to coverage at eye level.

Figure 4-19: *One-point perspective*

DIAGRAM SHOWING AN AREA

Dining Room · Kitchen (Tile) · Bath (Tile) · Bedroom No. 3

Splined groove · Set up line · **Start here** · Closet

Lay in this direction · Living Room · Bedroom No. 1 · Bedroom No. 2

Figure 4-20: *Laying strip floors*

DIAGRAM SHOWING A PROCESS

Audio From 5 Mixing Channels

Program Channel Amp

Master Volume Control · Program Line Output

Audio signals from the board's mixing channels are mixed together in the program channel amplifier. The combined output of the program channel is regulated by the master volume control.

Figure 4-21: *Master volume control*

When to Include Visuals

Before deciding to include a visual in your instructions, ask yourself the following: Will a visual help the audience to

* understand the purpose of the instructions?
* identify parts or equipment?
* understand a specific step or series of steps?
* avoid injury or increase safety?
* successfully complete the task?

If your answer to *any* of these questions is yes, include the visual with your instructions.

INFOBIT

We remember 10 percent of what we read, but 30 percent of what we see.

A. Words Only

Xxx xxx xx xxxxx. Xxx xxxx x xxxx xx xxxx. X xx xxx x xxxxx xxx. Xxxxxxx xxxx. Xxxx xx xxxx xxxxxx. X xxx x xxxxxx xxx xxxxx. Xxxxxx xx xxxx xx xxx. Xxx xxx xx xxxxx. Xxx xxxx x xxxx xx xxxx. X xx xxx x xxxxx xxx. Xxxxxx xxxx. Xxxx xx xxxx xxxxxx. X xxx x xxxxxx xxx xxxxx. Xxxxxx xx xxxx xxxx xx xxxxx xxx. Xxx xxx xx xxxxx. Xxx xxxx x xxxx xx xxxx. X xx xxx x xxxxx xxx. Xxxxxx xxxx. Xxxx xx xxxx xxxxxx. X xxx

Example: Identifying harmful fumes by their odors

B. Mostly Words with Some Visuals

Xxx xxx xx xxxxx. Xxx xxxx x xxxx xx xxxx. X xx xxx x xxxxx xxx. Xxxxxxx xxxx. Xxxx xx xxxx xxxxxx. X xxx x xxxxxx xxx xxxxx.

Xxxxxx xx xxxx xx xxx. Xxx xxx xx xxxxx. Xxx xxxx x xxxx xx xxxx. X xx xxx x xxxxx xxx.

Xxxxxx xxxx. Xxxx xx xxxx xxxxxx. X xxx x xxxxxx xxx xxxxx. Xxxxxx xx xxxx xxxx xx xxxxx xx xxxx xxx. Xxx xxx

Example: Making a pie crust

teamwork The audience, subject, and purpose determine the relative amount of **verbal information** (words) and **visual information** (drawings, diagrams, and photos) to include in instructions.

Work on this Practice with one or two partners. For each illustration, list two subjects for instructions that would be appropriate for the amount of verbal and visual information shown. One subject is already provided for each illustration. List two more subjects for each illustration.

C. Mostly Visuals with Some Words

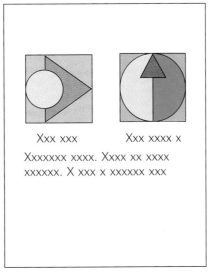

Xxx xxx   Xxx xxxx x
Xxxxxxx xxxx. Xxxx xx xxxx xxxxx. X xxx x xxxxxx xxx

Example: Rescuing a choking victim

D. Visuals Only

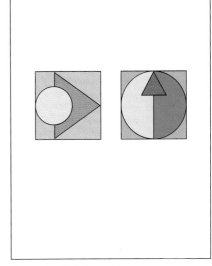

Example: Folding a letter

Making Visuals Effective

Try scanning a few pages that include visuals. You'll find that your eyes naturally focus on the visuals first. Effective visuals are often necessary elements of instructions. However, the reader may ignore a visual that requires too much work to use. A useful visual is accurate, clear, of the appropriate size, and complete.

Accuracy and Completeness

How, for example, could the audience locate the "center knob" on a drawing that only shows two knobs? Or four knobs? Accurate, complete visuals, properly labeled, provide information that the reader or listener needs.

PEOPLE C·O·N·N·E·C·T·I·O·N

Dean owns two businesses, both of them seasonal. One is a firewood delivery service. Since many people have fireplaces, but do not have the time to cut their own wood or a place to store large amounts, his business is thriving. Dean uses his communication skills to build his customer base and to improve his service. His computer comes in handy, not just for billing, but for producing advertising flyers that he hangs from doorknobs in apartment complexes. He also gives new customers a card with instructions on building fires, since they often have little experience in this area. The printed instructions save him many evening calls from cold, cranky customers, claiming, "There's something wrong with this wood; it won't burn!"

Size and Clarity

Using appropriately sized visuals is important in both oral and written instructions. Obviously, an audience must be able to see visuals during a live presentation in order to understand your instructions. Likewise, an overly large visual on the printed page takes up scarce space, while a very small visual requires too much effort on the part of the audience to see.

Not only size but also clarity will aid your visuals' effectiveness. A fuzzy, overly detailed photograph merely takes up valuable space and detracts from your instructions. An effective visual, however, is as simple as possible, without omitting essential detail.

INFOBIT

"Make everything as simple as possible, but not simpler."

ALBERT EINSTEIN, GERMAN-BORN U.S. SCIENTIST

Creating Attractive Visuals

Many types of visuals require little or no artistic ability. A stick figure showing a safe method of lifting a heavy weight is more helpful than no visual at all (see Figure 4-22). Take your time, do your best, and keep trying until you are satisfied with the results.

When greater artistic ability than you possess is called for, try presenting a rough sketch of your visual to a friend who has drawing talent. He or she may be pleased and flattered that you asked for help.

Finally, if you have access to a computer with graphics software, learn how to use it. Today's computers create most of the art used in business and industry to produce amazing results; moreover, they are fun to use. Clip art collections may include visuals appropriate for your instructions.

Figure 4-22: *Stick figure lifting weight*

Figure 4-23: *Learn to use graphics software to create visuals.*

When producing drawings and diagrams, follow these guidelines:

* Use only informative and appropriate visuals.

* Produce visuals by hand or with a computer that are attractive, neat, clear, and easy to use.

* Include a brief title or caption.

* Clearly label all parts your audience will need to locate.

* In written instructions, place your visuals at the point where your audience will need to use them. If they must appear on a separate page, let the audience know when to look at them and where to find them.

* Refer to the visuals in the instructions.

Practice 4-16: Editing Instructions

teamwork Work on this Practice with one partner. Read and evaluate the instructions printed on *Student Workbook* page 4-B. Use proofreading marks (see the inside back cover of the text) to mark errors in the instructions. Write helpful notes on the page for improving organization, design, accuracy, and language use.

SUMMARY

A valuable employee is able to give effective instructions to coworkers and customers. Follow these guidelines whenever you are required to give instructions at work:

* Adapt the instructions to the previous knowledge and the needs of the audience.

* Carefully plan the instructions.

* Make sure all information is accurate.

* Include an introduction, definitions, preparations, warnings or precautions, a list of steps given as commands, and a brief closing, when needed.

* Communicate clearly, precisely, and concisely.

* Design a page that is easy to use.

* Include visuals whenever they will help the audience follow instructions.

WEB LINK

What interests you? Chances are someone has created a Web site devoted to your interest. Search the World Wide Web for instructions relating to your interest, whether it is snow boarding, cooking Mexican food, or T'ai Chi.

careers Suppose that you have been asked by your supervisor to create a set of instructions that will be used in your classroom, in your lab, or at work. You may give instructions for standard or emergency procedures; for proper hygiene; or for safe assembly, use, or maintenance of equipment. Your subject must be related to your career training.

Here are some examples:

EXAMPLES:

* Washing hands in a medical lab

* Clearing a paper jam in the office copier

* Cropping a photo

* Putting out an electrical fire in a repair shop

* Handcuffing a suspect

* Thinning seedlings

The visual effect is very important, since this instructional information must be noticed, read, and understood under various conditions. Consider the amount of time that your audience will have to read and follow the instructions. Also consider stressful circumstances that might impair the reader's ability to carry out the instructions.

1. Review the information in this chapter and the instructions for cleaning up a large chemical spill shown in the Sample Project Plan and the Sample Instructions on pages 133-135.

2. Complete the Project Plan on *Student Workbook* page 4-C, and have your teacher check it.

3. Using the Rough Draft column of the Project Guide (*Student Workbook* page 4-D), check your own work with one or more classmates. Have them record all their comments and changes on your Project Guide and rough draft. Ask them to write a constructive comment on the rough draft and sign it.

4. Have your teacher check your rough draft.

5. Revise and edit the rough draft.

6. Using the Final Draft column of the Project Guide, proofread your work. Make any needed corrections.

7. Turn in the final draft along with the Project Guide.

Giving Instructions

		CONTENT
SUBJECT	**How to:** clean up a chemical spill	**Main steps to follow:**
AUDIENCE	all employees **Why should they follow instructions?** To be safe	1. Pour kitty litter 2. Scoop up & dispose 3. Brush with solvent
PURPOSE	**What actions should the audience take?** Read & follow instructions	4. Scrub, rinse, dry 5. Get rid of cloths, kitty litter, etc. 6. Wash clothes
FORMAT	☒ written ☐ oral ☐ other	
SOURCES	"Safety First . . . and Second" Pursuits pp. 45-49 4-98	
VISUALS	**What visuals, if any, will make the instructions more effective?** Drawings - pouring cat litter, safety equipment	
INTRO	**Necessary conditions, materials, equipment:** conditions - protective clothing, fire extinguisher, flames out need - paper towels, cloths, kitty litter, shovel, brush, solvent	**Necessary precautions/warnings:** toxic fumes warning

How to Clean Up a Large Chemical Spill

WARNING

Toxic Fumes

Can cause dizziness or unconsciousness.

Open all windows and doors to the outside.

Wear a respirator.

Special care is necessary when using any chemical product. Proper use of chemicals includes safely storing and disposing of them. The chemicals contained in many common products are poisonous if swallowed; others are caustic and can burn the eyes and skin or release toxic fumes. If a large chemical spill occurs, you must be very careful to clean it up correctly.

Preparations

* Make sure that a fire extinguisher rated ABC or BC is nearby.
* Put out any flame and keep people away.
* Wear a respirator, rubber gloves, rubber boots, and safety goggles.

Materials and Equipment

* Clean cloths or paper towels
* Plastic garbage bag
* Absorbent material (cat litter or vermiculite)
* Shovel or dustpan
* Stiff-bristled brush
* Solvent (check label on chemical for the right type)
* Mild detergent

Steps

1. Pour absorbent material on the spill. Wait for it to be soaked up. (See Figure 1.)

2. Scoop up the absorbent material with a shovel or dustpan; put it in a bag.

3. Remove all traces of the spill using a cloth or brush dipped in solvent.

4. Scrub the area thoroughly with a stiff-bristled brush and a solution of mild detergent and water. (See Figure 2.)

5. Rinse and wipe dry with clean cloths or paper towels.

6. Following the disposal regulations of your community, remove chemical-soaked cloths, paper towels, and absorbent materials.

7. Change your clothes and wash them separately.

Figure 1: *Pouring absorbent material*

Figure 2: *Person with proper safety equipment scrubbing the area*

Source: "Safety First . . . and Second." Pursuits. April 1998: 45–49.

Overview

Easily understood and accurate instructions are very important in the workplace. These instructions include special warnings and cautions. Much time and money can be wasted when inaccurate instructions are given. At times catastrophic events can happen because adequate instructions and precautions were not given to prevent harm to the employee and others in the workplace.

People who give instructions without consideration of the audience, subject, and purpose often end up misdirecting their audience. The poem you are about to read tells how the speaker was angered by persons who had given him or her inaccurate instructions.

"Traveller's Curse After Misdirection"

May they stumble, stage by stage
On an endless pilgrimage,

Dawn and dusk, mile after mile

At each and every step a stile;

At each and every step withal

May they catch their feet and fall;

At each and every fall they take

May a bone within them break;

And may the bone that breaks within

Not be, for variation's sake,

Now rib, now thigh, now arm, now shin,

But always, without fail, THE NECK.

—Robert Graves

Start-Up: The speaker in Graves's poem might have traveled without incident, despite being poorly directed, if there had been signs to follow. Signs and symbols are visual shorthand instructions that assist us and guard us from harm. Think of the button with an upward-pointing arrow on an elevator, the sign with a picture of a suitcase in an airport, and the skull and crossbones on a container the contents of which would be harmful if swallowed. Particularly for people who cannot read or do not speak the local language, such wordless visual aids are invaluable.

Connection: Search for examples of visuals without words. List as many as you can find.

Overview

In his book *Make Your Words Work*, Gary Provost instructs us on how to use active verbs to make our writing better. In giving these instructions, he uses personal illustrations and examples rather than rules to make his point.

"Use Active Voice . . . Most of the Time"
from *Make Your Words Work*

A guy I know hangs around his apartment every evening in front of the television, hoping somebody will call and invite him to dinner. In the afternoon he haunts the mailbox, figuring maybe an invitation or a check will show up from some unexpected source. He dreams about new friends coming into his life, a better job popping up out of nowhere, and he figures he might win a new car someday if a disc

jockey calls him up and asks an easy question. I know another fellow who plays tennis every morning. When he meets a man or a woman he'd like to know better, he gets the phone number and calls the person up. This guy started his own business a few years back, and now he's putting the profits into businesses by his friends. He also likes to go skydiving.

(cont'd on next page)

Which man do you find more interesting, the passive one who lets things happen to him, or the active one who makes things happen?

The active man is more interesting. In writing, too, active is more interesting than passive. Just as you would fix your attention on the active man and ignore the passive one, your reader will fix his attention on the active words and phrases.

New writers often fall into the habit of casting their characters as the passive recipients of some activity, when they should be writing about people or objects doing things, making things happen.

Compare "The Christmas present given to Frank was an electric guitar" with "Frank got an electric guitar for Christmas"; "The result of the accident was many injuries to Bertha" with "When the car crashed, Bertha broke her arm, twisted her neck, and dislocated her hip."

> *New writers often fall into the habit of casting their characters as the passive recipients of some activity, when they should be writing about people or objects doing things, making things happen.*

A key to finding the active voice is to write about people, not things. "A good time was had by all," for example, is a passive-voice sentence about good times. "Everybody had a good time" is an active-voice sentence about people.

Sometimes, of course, you are not writing about people, but about objects or concepts. Even then your object or concept should take charge of the sentence, become the subject, and work in the active voice.

For example, "Nushka was loved by Garonovitch." If you're writing about Garonvitch, then "Garonovitch loved Nushka." But maybe you're really writing about love. In that case, "Love filled Garonovitch with excitement," and "It was love that made him act so foolishly."

The tip-off to these dull, passive-voice sentences is usually a compound verb such as *was driven* or *were presented*. Cash them in for sharp, short, interesting, active verbs, and your writing will work better.

—Gary Provost

New procedures for answering the phone were given to our department. Now, when the phone rings, the # button must be pushed by you before the phone will connect. In addition, since the departments were reorganized and renamed by upper-level management, your response to identify our department should be "Retail" rather than "Dry Goods." At the end of the conversation, the # button should once again be pushed to terminate the connection. By using this procedure, the specific departments can be billed directly.

Connection: This draft is full of passive-voice verbs, which are unsuitable for your instructions. The instructions are also poorly organized and unclear. Convert the verbs into active-voice verbs. Then revise the set of directions for your staff.

Describing a Process

"Individual commitment to a group effort—that is what makes a team work, a company work, a society work, a civilization work."

—VINCE LOMBARDI, NFL COACH AND GENERAL MANAGER

Workplace Skills in This Chapter

- Improve **interpersonal** skills by participating in decision-making teams.

- Understand how effective teamwork benefits workplace **systems**.

- Gather **information** for process descriptions.

- Manage **resources** as you plan a Project.

- Use **technology** to produce text and visuals.

As you complete Chapter 5, you will

- identify various types of processes.

- distinguish between process descriptions and instructions.

- use effective language for describing processes.

- organize information chrono- logically.

- recognize analogies in techni- cal description.

- prepare visual aids for an oral presentation.

- identify leadership qualities.

- brainstorm solutions to prob- lems.

- participate in decision-making groups.

- plan and give a process de- scription.

A device developed in France in 1996 could end the isolation of those who can't communicate with speech or body movement by letting them write with their eyes. As the person looks at a special keyboard, a laser-guided camera records the person's eye movement from letter to letter. The camera feeds the selected letters into a computer, and the text appears on the computer screen. Users only have to look at a key for less than a second for it to register. However, the system is sensitive enough that it won't register the letters users pass over, only the ones they stop on. Badly injured patients who can't speak could use this technology to communicate with doctors in emergency rooms.

Types of Processes

The paragraph you just read is a description of a **process**: a series of actions leading to a specific result. Your job will require you to describe processes to supervisors, coworkers, and the general public so they can understand them.

Process descriptions explain how things work or how things are done or made. Processes can be carried out by machines, by people, or by nature. For example, the previously described process that enables people to write with their eyes is a mechanical process. All processes consist of a series of steps that occur in a particular order. The following chart shows other examples of processes.

PROCESSES ARE CARRIED OUT

By Machines	By People	By Nature
how polygraph machines work	how law enforcement officials administer polygraph tests	how emotions alter pulse, respiration, and blood pressure
how diamond saws work	how jewelers determine the value of a diamond	how carbon changes to diamonds
how Doppler radar works	how the National Hurricane Center predicts the paths of hurricanes	how hurricanes form
how a bread machine works	how a baker makes croissants	how yeast causes bread to rise

Sometimes a process description just satisfies our curiosity about how something works. At other times, process descriptions enable readers or listeners to make informed choices and sound decisions, work safely, and grow professionally. Even though the audience will rarely carry out the described process, other actions may depend on a clear understanding of that process.

Practice 5-1: Types of Processes

teamwork Work on this Practice with one partner. For each of the following items, tell whether the process is carried out by machines, by people, or by nature. Then explain a useful way in which the intended audience can apply their understanding of the process. Are the audience in each case general or are they specialists?

Process	Intended Audience
1. how bacteria cause food poisoning	a restaurant worker
2. how anti-lock brakes and cruise control work	a new driver

PEOPLE C·O·N·N·E·C·T·I·O·N

When Philo Farnsworth was 15, his family moved to a new house in Rigby, Idaho. The former owners had left behind several technical publications. After reading them, Farnsworth became fascinated with the process of using photoelectric cells and cathode ray tubes to transmit images, and he began designing such a system. His experiments continued even after he had to leave college following his father's death. At age 21, Farnsworth applied for a patent for his "image dissector" camera tube. This glass tube had a photosensitive mirror at one end on which an image was focused. The mirror emitted electrons in response to different light intensities projected upon it. After presenting the device to investors, he established a small production company. Before financial difficulties forced him to sell his patent rights to RCA, Farnsworth used his invention to make the first-ever public demonstration of television in 1934.

Figure 5-1: *Parents should understand how babies acquire language.*

Process	Intended Audience
3. how overexposure to the sun can cause skin cancer	an apprentice carpenter
4. how the Internal Revenue Service decides which taxpayers to audit	a small-business owner
5. how a computer virus can destroy data	a World Wide Web "surfer"
6. how babies acquire language	a new parent
7. how numbers in animal populations are estimated	a wildlife management student
8. how a consumer survey was taken	an advertising executive

Process Descriptions Compared to Instructions

Instructions and process descriptions have several similarities. Both are composed of steps that occur in a particular sequence. Both can be given to general or specialized audiences. In manuals, process descriptions often come before instructions.

The main distinction between instructions and process descriptions is in purpose. The audience for instructions is expected to carry out the steps. The audience for a process description is just expected to understand the process, not to carry it out. Instructions explain how to work a VCR; a process description explains how a VCR works.

Instructions Use Commands

Steps in instructions are always given as **commands** in the second person. Commands directly tell the reader what to do. In the following examples, notice each command begins with an action verb:

> **Check** the gauges every 30 minutes.
>
> Please **give** your name when answering the phone.
>
> **Turn in** your mileage report every Friday.

Process Descriptions Use Statements

Steps in process descriptions are always given as **statements** that explain what happened or what is done. The action verb in these examples follows the subject of the sentence:

> The technician **checks** the gauges every 30 minutes.
>
> We always **give** our names when answering the phone.
>
> Employees **turn in** mileage reports every Friday.

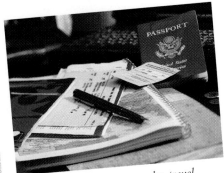

Figure 5-2: *Americans who travel abroad must often apply for a passport.*

INFORIT

A passport is an official government document that certifies one's identity and citizenship and permits a citizen to travel abroad. A visa is an official authorization added to a passport, permitting entry into and travel within a particular country or region.

Practice 5-2: Commands and Statements

The following eight sentences are written as commands. Rewrite each command as a statement. Hint: Begin your first sentence with the word *Americans*.

Process: Obtaining a U.S. Passport

1. If you are planning to visit India, apply for a passport.

2. Get an application form from a travel agent and fill it in ahead of time.

3. Appear in person at a regional passport office.

4. Present the following materials: the application form, proof of U.S. citizenship, two recent photographs of yourself, proof of your identity, and payment.

5. To prevent theft, carry your passport in a money belt or pouch, not in a pocket or purse.

6. If you lose your passport while in the United States, go to the nearest U.S. Passport Agency.

7. If you are in India, report the loss to the nearest U.S. embassy or consulate, and also notify the local police.

8. When your passport is about to expire, apply for a new one by mail.

Process Descriptions Use Active and Passive Verbs

We always express commands in instructions using active verbs. In a sentence with **active verbs**, the subject of the sentence does the action. We can, however, give statements in process descriptions using either active or passive verbs. In sentences with **passive verbs**, the subject of the sentence receives the action. Since most people find it difficult to understand the grammatical explanation, perhaps an illustration will help. The following paragraph, reprinted from a manual explaining how *not* to write a technical report, is an example of a process description using passive verbs.

INFOBIT

The U.S. Department of Energy is responsible for marketing federal power, regulating energy production and use, pricing and allocation, promoting more efficient uses of energy, and overseeing the nuclear weapons program.

> A 72-gram brown Rhode Island Red country-fresh candled egg was secured and washed free of feathers, etc. Held between thumb and index finger, about three feet more or less from an electric fan (General Electric No. MC-2404, Serial No. JC23023, non-oscillating, rotating on "high" speed at approximately 1052.23 ± 0.02 rpm), the egg was suspended on a string (pendulum) so it arrived at the fan with essentially zero velocity normal to the fan rotation plan. The product, adhering strongly to the walls and ceiling, was difficult to recover; however, using putty knives a total of 13 grams was obtained and put in a skillet with 11.2 grams of hickory smoked Armour's Old Style bacon and was heated over a low Bunsen flame for 7 min. 32 sec. What there was of it was excellent scrambled eggs (United States Department of Energy).

The writer not only used passive verbs but also included unnecessary detail and technical jargon to make a point about how *not* to write. The translation of this example, with clear, direct, *active* verbs, follows:

> Carlos and I *threw* an egg into an electric fan. Although we *had* a difficult time removing it from the walls and ceiling, we *managed to make* excellent scrambled eggs with the small amount recovered.

Unless you have a good reason to do otherwise, choose active rather than passive sentence construction. Sentences with passive verbs are not as clear and tend to be wordier and weaker than sentences with active verbs. Passive verbs consist of a form of the verb *to be* plus the action verb. For example:

* *Was* placed	* *Are* invited
* *Were* noticed	* Has *been* reached
* *Is* found	

In the following sentence, the subject of the sentence—the mileage reports—doesn't do anything. Something—being turned in—is done to the mileage reports by the employees. This sentence is passive:

> Mileage reports are turned in every Friday by employees.

It's easy to make a passive sentence active. Just begin the sentence with the subject that does the action. In this sentence, the employees

ETHICS C·O·N·N·E·C·T·I·O·N

When you hear people in uncomfortable situations overusing passive verbs, get out your hogwash detector. They may be trying to evade responsibility. Consider this response to a customer who sent film of his only daughter's wedding pictures to a photo lab: "We must report that during the handling of your twelve 35mm photo orders, the films were involved in an unusual laboratory experience." Nobody did anything to the rolls of film; they just had a bad experience. Of course, the customer can always hold another wedding for his daughter and take the pictures all over again, using the twelve replacement rolls the lab so generously sent him. If you make a mistake, don't say, "A mistake happened." Instead, take responsibility by saying, "I made a mistake." As Nikki Giovanni once said, "Mistakes are a fact of life. It is the response to error that counts."

do the action, which is turning in the mileage reports. This sentence is active:

> Employees turn in mileage reports every Friday.

At times, the *who* or *what* that does the action is so obvious or so unimportant that it is left out entirely. In these cases using passive verbs is acceptable. In the following examples of passive-verb statements, the operator or doer of the action is not mentioned.

> Sunny is being promoted to assistant manager.
>
> The building was demolished ten years ago.
>
> Your applications have always been processed on time.

Microwave beam

Fan

Magnetron

Microwaves

Cooking surface

Figure 5-3: *A diagram showing a mechanical process*

Practice 5-3: Active and Passive

These statements have passive verbs. Rewrite them with active verbs. In the first two, the subject of the sentence is in bold.

Process: How a Microwave Oven Works

1. A beam of microwaves is produced by **a magnetron**.

2. The waves are scattered by **the fan**.

3. Waves are absorbed by molecules of water in the food.

4. Molecules are aligned by waves of energy.

5. The alignment is then reversed by waves.

6. Rapid and repeated twisting is caused by this alignment and realignment.

7. Heat is produced by the twisting.

Describing a Process: Structure and Language

A good process description is organized like a story—with a beginning, middle, and end. The events are chronological; that is, related in the order in which they occur. Parallel ideas are expressed in the same way. Analogies (comparisons) often make the description easier to understand.

Chronological Order

Chronological order is time order. When communication is organized chronologically, the first event comes first, the second event comes second, and so on. Process descriptions are always organized chronologically.

TECHNOBIT

Randall Tobias offers this analogy to explain the astonishing rate of increase in computer power: "If we had similar progress in automotive technology, today you could buy a Lexus for about $2. It would travel at the speed of sound, and go about 600 miles on a thimble of gas."

Practice 5-4: Describing a Process in Chronological Order

The following description of how an answering machine records a message is not organized chronologically. Notice how hard it is to keep track of the series of actions and how they relate to the overall process.

Reorganize the description chronologically to make it easier to follow. Add words such as *after, then,* and *while* to help the reader keep track of the proper sequence of actions.

Process: How an Answering Machine Works

The "message waiting" and "operation" lights turn on and the outgoing message tape starts after the first ring of the phone sets up an electronic connection between the answering machine and the phone line. The outgoing message tape contains a prerecorded message that can last up to 20 seconds. The incoming message tape starts after the beep that tells the caller that he or she may leave a message. The machine disconnects after a 10-second silence. An electronic voice control circuit allows the machine to continue taping as long as the caller keeps talking. Before the machine "hangs up" until the next call, the "operation" light goes off.

Parallel Structure

Experienced writers present parallel ideas the same way; that is, they make the sentence elements that express these ideas **parallel.** Parallel structure makes writing clearer and more effective. Here's one example from a speech by President John F. Kennedy:

> Conformity is *the jailer of freedom* and *the enemy of growth.*

The two parallel, italicized phrases are joined with a conjunction, *and.* Both phrases consist of the word *the,* a noun, the word *of,* and another noun. This similarity in the structure of the phrases makes them parallel.

Figure 5-4: *President John F. Kennedy*

If Kennedy had not used parallel structure, he might have said instead, "Conformity is the jailer of freedom and opposes growth." Notice how much less effective this sentence sounds than the first version. Most people can detect faulty parallelism by listening to the *sound* of a sentence.

Elements in lists are clearer and more effective when they are parallel, as in the following sentence, also from Kennedy:

> The great enemy of the truth is very often not the lie—*deliberate, contrived and dishonest*—but the myth—*persistent, persuasive and unrealistic.*

Always use parallel structure in listing statements in a process description. Using parallel structure helps the audience picture the flow of the process described and see it as a clearly presented series of actions. In contrast, sentences and lists that are not parallel will probably confuse the audience.

Practice 5-5: Parallel Structure

teamwork With one partner, revise the following sentences to make them parallel. Remember that *listening* to the sound of the sentences helps. The words and phrases that should be made parallel are italicized in the first two sentences.

1. I like *to identify a problem* and *solving it.*

2. Kim was promoted not only *for her hard work and loyalty* but also *because she gets along well with people.*

3. Your suggestion is creative, is reasonable in cost, and was presented convincingly.

4. This could be a problem for both the winners and those who lose.

5. I possess neither the skill nor am I patient enough to care for small children.

6. Each supervisor is responsible for the following:

   * Reducing costs

   * Provide training for all new employees

   * Inventory

7. Jamie found the perfect job by preparing a perfect resume, she contacted references, and she took the time to make dozens of phone calls.

8. Each diagram shows the appearance of the object and how it works is shown too.

INFOBIT

"Being courageous requires no exceptional qualifications, no magic formula, no special combination of time, place and circumstances. It is an opportunity that sooner or later is presented to us all."

PRESIDENT JOHN F. KENNEDY

Analogies

An **analogy** is a comparison between the unknown and the known. Using an analogy implies that since the things being compared are alike in some ways, they are probably alike in other ways as well. An analogy is a useful device in explaining an unfamiliar process. In the following introduction for a process description, truck scales are compared to the familiar doctor's office scales.

Figure 5-5: *Doctor's office scales and truck scales work on the same principle.*

> The scales that weigh you in the doctor's office and the platform scales that weigh trucks both work on the same principle. Scales of both types have levers that divide the weight and then balance many pounds on the platform with a single pound at the weight indicator. The four pairs of levers on a 50-ton truck scale cause 7,000 pounds on the platform to exert a one-pound force at the indicator. The doctor's scale, on the other hand, has only one pair of levers with a 40-to-1 "tip ratio."

Organizing a Process Description

An effectively written process description includes an informative title, an introduction, a body that explains each step in the process, and, perhaps, a closing. A longer description of a complex process requires headings for each main step.

Read the explanation of virtual reality shown in Figure 5-6 on page 150. The notes in the margin point out some features of this description.

Using Visuals

As with definitions and instructions, an informative visual can make a process description easier to understand. A good visual can also reduce the amount of writing and reading needed for a thorough explanation. Occasionally, a visual may be able to stand on its own; however, a written or spoken explanation is usually necessary.

Drawings, diagrams, and flowcharts are especially useful for illustrating process descriptions. You may need to review basic guidelines (see Chapters 2 and 4) for creating drawings and diagrams.

Informative title

Analogy to water domes

Elements in lists are parallel.

Some sentences are passive.

Statements describe steps in the process.

Headings signal the main ideas.

Unfamiliar terms are defined.

Most sentences are active.

Source of information

The World of Virtual Reality

VR stands for Virtual Reality, one of the most promising new computer technologies. To understand VR, imagine one of those small, water-filled plastic domes you had as a child. Perhaps it contained a city or a nativity scene. Now, imagine that you had the ability to shrink yourself down to a size small enough that you could actually walk around in this imaginary world, opening doors, picking up objects, and peeking around corners.

What Is VR?

VR has a great deal in common with that winter scene. It is an artificial world and is seen from your perspective. It is an environment generated by a computer in which you can move freely and interact with other objects generated by the computer, such as people, animals and things. In VR terminology, the world is a "Cyberspace."

VR has a few significant differences, though. First, the Cyberspace is continuously expanding and changing. As you "walk" through Cyberspace, the computer generates more "space" in response to your movements. So, you're not confined to a small space. The Cyberspace can be as big or as small as the designer (programmer) chooses to make it.

Another difference is that objects in Cyberspace can exhibit intelligence and behaviors on their own and in response to you, just like the real world. For example, you could approach a person in Cyberspace and they may respond in any number of ways, depending on the situation.

How Does VR Work?

Based on data entered by programmers, computers create virtual environments by generating three-dimensional images. Users usually view these images through a head-mounted device, which can be a helmet, goggles, or other apparatus that restricts their vision to two small video monitors, one in front of each eye. Each monitor displays a slightly different view of the environment, which gives users a sense of depth.

Another device, called a position tracker, monitors users' physical positions and provides input to the computer. This information instructs the computer to change the environment based upon users' actions. For example, when users look over their shoulders, they see what lies behind them. Because virtual reality users remain stationary, they use a joy stick or track ball to move through the virtual environment. Users also may wear a special glove or use other devices to manipulate objects within the virtual environment. Similarly, they can employ virtual weapons to defeat virtual enemies.

What Is VR For?

In the future, surgeons may use VR to plan and practice an operation on a virtual patient rather than a real person. Police could practice responding to virtual emergency situations. VR could be used to train the operators of dangerous or complicated machinery. Network VR simulations could enable people in many different locations to participate together in teleconferences or simulated military training exercises.

Source: Masson, Mark. "Virtual Reality in Education." *Career Chatter.* Great Oaks Institute of Technology and Career Development, Nov. 1992.

Figure 5-6: *Features of a process description*

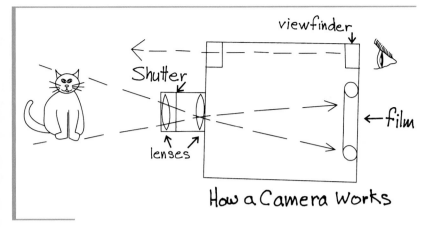

Figure 5-7: *A drawing of a camera*

Drawings

Figure 5-7 illustrates how an informative drawing can show how a camera works. Even a person who has little artistic ability can produce a drawing like this one. This drawing is appropriate for a general audience since it only shows the basics of the process.

Diagrams

Diagrams are abstract representations of ideas. When choosing a diagram to go with your process description, you should carefully think about your audience. Is it general or specialized? If the diagram is too complex, you will probably confuse your audience. If it is too simple, you may bore them.

The diagram in Figure 5-8 shows how an audio control console creates echo effects. Notice the differences between this diagram and Figure 5-7. This diagram and its written explanation are more complex. It was created for a specialist who already has some knowledge of the process and the technical jargon.

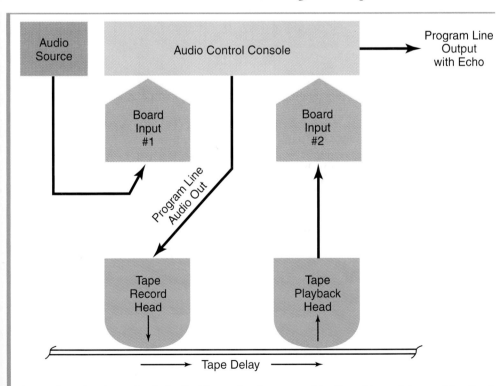

A reverberating (repeat echo) effect is made when a combination of tape delay and feedback is used. The sound goes from the source through the board to the record head and onto the tape. A fraction of a second later, the playback head picks up the sound and plays it back through the board to the record head again.

Figure 5-8: *A diagram of the tape echo process*

Flowcharts

Flowcharts are diagrams that show steps in a process, connected by arrows. They are often used as illustrations in technical manuals. By following the arrows, the reader can see the main steps of the process in chronological order. The writer who constructs an effective flowchart must thoroughly understand the process shown. In fact, the act of creating the chart may help the writer clarify his or her own understanding of the process.

The flowchart in Figure 5–9 illustrates the process that allows a computer to control the movements of an industrial robot.

Feedback Loops

The controls for an industrial robot include sensors that monitor the position of each joint, the changes in the velocity of the movement of each joint, and whether movement is accelerating or decelerating. The diagram shows the feedback information and the instructions that are relayed in response to it. The feedback information flows in a series of loops as the sensors supply information to the system.

Figure 5-9: *A flowchart showing robot feedback loops*

Practice 5-6: Explaining a Flowchart

Figure 5–10 on page 153 shows how ferns propagate. Examine this example and read its explanation.

Figure 5–11 illustrates the water cycle. Carefully examine the visual. Then write a short paragraph explaining the process.

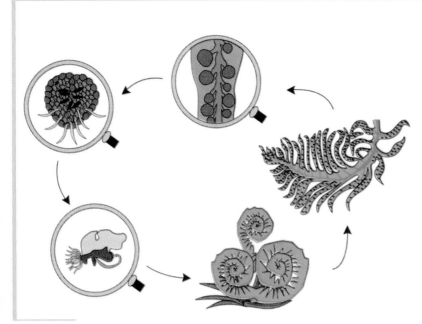

The Life Cycle of a Fern

Spores grow underneath leaf fronds and are spread by wind. Where they land, a prothallus grows. This produces sperm and egg cells. The final stage is the growth of a new fern.

Figure 5-10: *A flowchart showing a natural process*

Figure 5-11: *The water cycle*

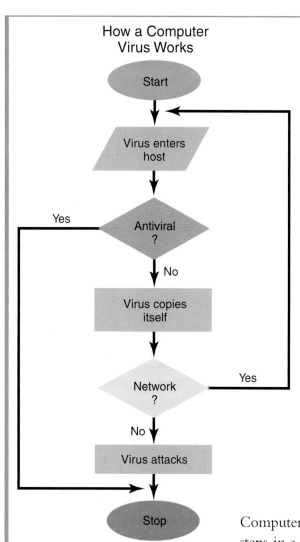

How a Computer
Virus Works

Figure 5-12: *A flowchart showing
how a computer virus works*

* An oval indicates the beginning or end of the process.

* A parallelogram indicates input to the process or output from the process.

* A diamond indicates a decision. Inside the diamond is a question. Two arrows lead from the diamond, one marked "yes" and one marked "no." Each path must eventually lead to "stop."

* A rectangle indicates a step in the process not requiring a decision.

Computer programmers use a special type of flowchart to show the steps in a software program. This type of flowchart can also be used to illustrate processes. Figure 5-12 shows how destructive computer programs called viruses infect computer systems. Notice how the shapes enclosing each step have meanings of their own.

Practice 5-7: Fractured Flowcharts

The flowcharts shown on *Student Workbook* pages 5-A and 5-B do not match their corresponding paragraphs. Things are missing, out of order, and factually wrong. Correct the flowcharts so the facts in the flowcharts match the facts in the paragraphs.

Presentation Software

Presentation software such as *Microsoft PowerPoint, Lotus Freelance Graphics,* and *Harvard Graphics* can help you produce effective visual aids for oral presentations of process descriptions. **Presentation software** simulates slide shows on the computer screen. Special projectors allow these slides to be shown on a large screen. Presentation software can also generate attractive, colorful transparencies.

TECHNOBIT

Although thousands of computer viruses have been created, only a few hundred are active, or "in the wild."

Figure 5-13: *Use presentation software to create effective visual aids.*

Presentation software allows you to add color, movement, and a variety of special effects to the visuals aids for speeches. The software templates—sample presentation designs you can use—make creating a dazzling production amazingly easy. With a little training and a healthy dose of planning, you can create an attractive and engaging presentation. Here are a few guidelines to follow as you prepare a slide show:

* Begin with a well-thought-out plan, and key in your content in outline view. This allows you to concentrate on your message without distraction. After all, a great-looking presentation that fails to communicate your message will just waste everyone's time.

* Don't get too carried away with special effects. Your audience may be wondering what your next effect will be instead of paying attention to what you have to say.

* Never put more words on a slide than you would put on a T-shirt.

* Time slide changes so the audience has enough time to read the slides—but not too much time.

* When making the presentation, stand so the audience will see you to the left of the screen (see Figure 5-13).

WEB LINK

Look for slide shows created with presentation software available for downloading from the Internet. You might pick up some good ideas for your own presentations.

Describing Processes Orally

As you have seen, processes can be described in writing. More often, though, they are spoken as part of casual conversation between two people. A dog trainer might explain to the owner of a puppy how dogs learn to obey commands. An installer for a home security system might explain to a homeowner how the system detects movement in the house. This type of discussion requires knowledge on the part of the speaker, but not much planning. In other situations, however, a great deal of planning may be required.

DILBERT reprinted by permisson of United Feature Syndicate, Inc.

Explaining a Process to a Group

If you are asked to explain a process to a group at work, you must consider the needs of your audience. How much time will they have to listen to you? Remember that people are busy, so they have little

TECHNOLOGY C·O·N·N·E·C·T·I·O·N

Groupware is software that allows people located in different parts of a building or different parts of the world to communicate and work on the same project at the same time. Teams can create and edit a document together, almost as if they were working at the same desk. Groupware also can merge phone and e-mail systems. Messages are delivered to "smart post offices." These networks can hunt down the receiver of a message and deliver it in the proper format—be it pager, cellular phone, laptop computer, or fax machine. Eventually, these features may be available through the Internet.

time or patience for disorganization. Plan carefully to tell the audience what they need to know—and no more—as efficiently as possible. Consider the following example.

INFOBIT

"People who enjoy what they are doing invariably do it well."

JOE GIBBS, NFL COACH

> Ms. Bhati supervises the print shop of a large company that manufactures gardening equipment. Her department produces brochures, forms, product inserts, flyers, the company newsletter, and more. New digital equipment has been installed that will give her department the capability of producing higher-quality materials in less time.
>
> Ms. Bhati must meet with the supervisors of the other 12 departments to explain what the new equipment can do. Since the meeting is scheduled to run for only 30 minutes, she must plan carefully to make efficient use of time, while still getting her points across to everyone in the group.

Presenting Information with a Team

If a team has worked together to make a decision or solve a problem, they may be asked to present their results, either in writing or by speaking. An effective team takes advantage of the talents and skills of the individual members of the group when planning the presentation. Taking the time to learn the strengths of each member will benefit everyone. For instance, the math skills, public speaking skills, writing ability, computer expertise, artistic talent, proofreading skills, or organizational ability of any team member cannot be used unless it is known. Always try to assign tasks based on the individual strengths of team members. Working in teams is discussed on pages 157–164.

Practice 5-8: Flowcharting a Process

Complete the flowchart on *Student Workbook* page 5-C showing the steps required for planning and giving an effective oral presentation. Refer to pages 90–91 in Chapter 3 for information about this process. Give the flowchart an informative title.

Kaizen is a Japanese word meaning the relentless quest for a better way, for higher-quality craftsmanship. If you practice Kaizen and make the pursuit of perfection a daily goal, your work will improve and your organization will come closer to meeting its goals. Improvements are usually gradual. If, however, everyone in the organization constantly tries to outdo yesterday, measurable improvement will eventually happen. Your productivity, product quality, cost control, and customer service efforts need continuous upgrading. After all, the competition never stands still.

Remember, a strong, successful organization is the best paycheck insurance there is. Even if other circumstances cause your organization to fail, by becoming the best you can be, you'll find it that much easier to land a new job.

Practice 5-9: Analyzing a Speech

In this Practice, you will listen to a speech explaining a process. Write a note to Erin, the speaker. Begin with a compliment; then make three positive suggestions for improvement. Instead of telling her what not to do, tell her what she can do to improve.

Teams *Work!*

In the past, managers of business and industry issued orders and directives to the people who carried them out. They expected little communication in return. In recent years, however, many organizations have adopted new management techniques. These organizations demand a high level of performance and communication skills from their employees. Simply complying with rules and obeying supervisors is not enough; these organizations need employees who are willing to work in new ways.

Many companies are organizing their employees into work teams. In this type of organization, everyone must understand decision–making processes. The effective use of teams in the workplace can help organizations reach their goals. In addition, the ability to work as a member of a team has become an important asset for employees. Your chances of being considered for a promotion can depend on your ability to work with and contribute to a team. Furthermore, team members often report increased job satisfaction.

In order to accomplish any task (such as making a decision), a team needs goals, leadership, and organization. The Project for this chapter involves participating in a team that will explain a process to the class. Your team will need to make many decisions, and its success will depend on the skills of each individual. With practice, you can learn to be a productive team member.

TECHNOBIT

Why not use a computer to prepare notes for your next oral presentation? Word processing programs allow you to reorganize text easily by cutting and pasting. Using 14-point or larger type makes your notes easy to read from a distance.

INFOBIT

"A problem well stated is a problem half solved."

C. F. KETTERING, U.S. INVENTOR

Goals

The first task of any decision-making group is to clarify its goals—what is it trying to accomplish, and why? Your group will not function as a team unless it agrees upon the task and the goals, develops effective leadership and decision-making strategies, and learns to resolve conflict.

Leadership

In formal groups, such as committees, a leader or chairperson is usually chosen. In more informal groups, one or two people will, out of necessity, assume the role of leader. Either way, the team leader has many responsibilities. Practice 5-10 will help you to focus on leadership roles.

INFOBIT

"You can't tell someone to go out and lead. You become a leader by doing it. So if you want to be a leader, go do it."

CHUCK NOLL, NFL LINEBACKER AND COACH

Practice 5-10: Leadership Roles

teamwork For this Practice, your whole class will work together as a problem-solving team. Your team's task is to calculate the average height in feet and inches of the members of the team. Time limit: 15 minutes.

After time is called, complete the following:

1. Write down the names of members who took leadership roles. In other words, who contributed the most toward helping the team reach its goal?

2. What leadership behaviors (for instance, calling for order) did these people demonstrate? List five leadership behaviors you observed.

3. One member of the team will record on the board all of the leadership skills that the class observed. You will probably find that other members noticed things that you did not.

4. Are there any leadership behaviors that you know of that were not displayed during this Practice? Add them to the list on the board.

5. Copy the leadership behaviors that are listed on the board. Save your list as a reference.

Organization

A decision-making group cannot function without leadership. It also cannot function without organization. Once everyone in the team clearly understands the team's task or goal, collect as much information and as many ideas as possible by brainstorming.

Brainstorming

Brainstorming is a problem-solving activity that requires all members of a group to contribute their ideas toward making a decision. Brainstorming can lead to creative solutions that individual members might not come up with on their own. This technique is useful for generating options to be considered when making decisions. When brainstorming, keep these guidelines in mind:

1. Make sure everyone understands the problem that needs solving.

2. Choose one team member to record all solutions to a problem without discussion, evaluation, or comment—negative or positive. No idea—no matter how silly or unworkable—is rejected. It is best if all the team members have a chance to see the suggested solutions as they are recorded.

3. Try to ensure that all members participate, as anyone can come up with a usable solution. Eccentric ideas often lead to creative solutions. Participation means more than talking or note taking; active listening is crucial.

4. Once the team has run out of solutions, they cross out duplicates.

Figure 5-14: *A brainstorming session*

Practice 5-11: Brainstorming

teamwork 1. Sketch a flowchart illustrating the steps in the brainstorming process listed above.

2. Work on this brainstorming Practice in a team consisting of four or five members. Begin by writing down the names of your team members. Then complete Steps a–e.

   The Problem: How many uses can you think of for a paper clip?

   a. Choose one member to write down all ideas—exactly as they are presented—so that all members can see them.

   b. Brainstorm as many ideas (uses) as you can. Record all ideas without discussion. The goal is to generate as many ideas as possible.

   c. When the team runs out of ideas, come up with three more.

   d. Cross out duplicates.

   e. Write down your group's total number of uses. How does this compare to the totals of the other groups?

(cont'd on next page)

3. After completing Step 2, answer the following questions:

 a. Who acted as leader of your team? How could you tell?

 b. What contributed to your team's success?

 c. Write down two ways that your group could improve the next time you try brainstorming.

Team Member Roles

Sometimes, after participating in a meeting, we leave feeling dissatisfied because nothing was accomplished. This may be because the team could not focus on the problem or they could not resolve conflict. Perhaps some members of the team just didn't seem to care.

In every team, each individual member plays one or more roles. Some of the roles are productive; that is, they help the team reach its goals. Other roles are unproductive. When you work with a team, are you a productive or an unproductive member? To determine this, it is helpful to examine some of the roles.

Practice 5-12: Roles People Play

teamwork For this Practice, your teacher will divide the class into two groups: one group will act as a decision-making team; the other group will be observers.

Directions for the team members:

Each member of the decision-making team draws a card that includes a description of the role he or she is to play. It is important for you to study the description of the role and to stay in character throughout the discussion. Cards also list one or more facts to contribute to the discussion. Do not show your card to anyone.

Directions for the observers:

Use *Student Workbook* page 5-D, which lists the roles and their descriptions. As you *silently* observe the discussion, try to figure out who is playing which role. Write the person's name next to the description of the role, along with the evidence for your decision. Be prepared to share your observations during the follow-up discussion.

The decision-making team will solve the following problem:

Your teacher has been named teacher of the year and will leave next week on a two-month speaking tour of the United States. The administration has selected three possible long-term substitute teachers from the list of qualified candidates. Your team's task is to select one of the three applicants to substitute for your teacher.

INFOBIT

"You don't win with computers or trick plays. You do it with good people and an efficient, organized operation. And right there you have a formula for success, be it in business, industry or sports."

CHUCK NOLL, NFL LINEBACKER AND COACH

Decision-Making Strategies

In Practice 5-12, you saw how some behaviors help a team reach its goals, while other behaviors are obstacles to the team's success. Even when everyone involved engages in productive behavior, the team may not be successful unless they know how to go about making a group decision.

Once the team understands the problem to be solved, understands the goal, and has brainstormed possible solutions, the members must choose the best solution and the best method to carry it out. Disagreement (conflict) may occur during this process. Some decision-making strategies are described in the following sections.

Rank Ordering

Rank ordering is a process that allows the team to list solutions and ideas in order by priority. As a result, they discover how much agreement exists between members. The process of rank ordering involves the following steps:

1. Team members agree on the criteria for ranking ideas. How will they measure the usefulness of the ideas? What will constitute the best ideas?

2. Team members identify each idea on the list with a letter of the alphabet.

3. Team members individually list the letters on a piece of paper and indicate the rank of each idea, with *1* being the first choice, *2* the second choice, and so on.

4. Each team member takes a turn calling out the number that indicates his or her ranking of each idea. One member records all the numbers on a flip chart, chalkboard, or large sheet of paper that is visible to everyone.

5. The team analyzes the rankings, looking at the total for each idea as well as the individual votes.

The Nominal Group Technique

The **nominal group technique** helps the team generate options to consider in making decisions. The process involves the following steps:

1. Each team member writes ideas on a piece of paper.

2. One member records all the members' ideas on a chalkboard, flip chart, or large piece of paper so all members can see them easily. No discussion of ideas should occur during this step.

3. Members vote to establish the rank of all items on the list.

INFOBIT

"People acting together as a group can accomplish things which no individual acting alone could ever hope to bring about."

FRANKLIN D. ROOSEVELT, U.S. PRESIDENT

4. The team discusses the vote and eliminates lower-ranked items.

5. Rounds of voting and discussion continue until the team reaches consensus. A consensus is a decision that all members can support to some degree.

Multi-Voting

Multi-voting allows a team to reduce a long list of ideas to a manageable number. The process of multi-voting involves these steps:

1. The team members decide on the criteria for selecting the best ideas from the list.

2. Members vote for their favorite ideas, no more than 25 percent of the entire list. For example, if the list includes 28 items, each member can vote for no more than 7. Team members can give only one vote to an individual idea and must use all of their votes. Votes are recorded with a tally mark beside each item on the list.

3. Team members thoroughly discuss the ideas with the most votes and discard the lower-ranked ideas.

4. In the second round of voting, each member votes for one of the remaining ideas.

INFOBIT

"You can't win if nobody catches the ball in the outfield. You're only as good as the team you have behind you."

JIM PALMER, MAJOR LEAGUE PITCHER AND SPORTS BROADCASTER

Practice 5-13: Making a Decision

teamwork Your teacher will divide the class into three teams. Each team will use one of the decision-making strategies described on pages 161–162 to solve the following problem:

Your school board voted to make participation in a volunteering project to benefit the community a requirement for graduation. The project can be completed individually or as a team. Your team has decided to work together to satisfy this requirement. The board has specified the following criteria:

* The project must provide a real benefit to the community outside the school.

* Each person must contribute no fewer than ten hours.

* The individuals or the team must present evidence that they have met the requirement.

Your team's task is to decide what activity they will do to satisfy the community service requirement. Each team will use a different decision-making strategy. Be prepared to report the following information to the class during the follow-up discussion:

Some teams are made up of individuals from different cultures. Their differing styles of communication can create misunderstanding and conflict when a problem needs to be solved or a decision needs to be made. Here are some tips for minimizing conflict in a multicultural team:

- Be aware that different people use nonverbal language, such as eye contact, posture, and gestures, in different ways.
- Repeat key ideas and ask questions to make sure everyone understands.
- Restate others' ideas to make sure you understand them.
- Signal your openness to others' ideas, but not just in words; your tone of voice and your body language say more about your attitude than your words do.
- Summarize the results of the team meeting orally or in writing.

1. What decision-making strategy did your team use?

2. How long did it take you to arrive at a decision?

3. Did any member provide leadership? Who?

4. How successful was your team in reaching its goal? What factors contributed to your success?

5. What problems did you encounter?

6. Did members at times disagree? How did you resolve disagreements?

7. How would you rate the effectiveness of your assigned decision-making strategy?

Conflict Management

Even when a team uses an effective decision-making strategy, conflict is inevitable. Individual differences in personality, values, and cultural background exist in any team. The goal is not to eliminate conflict; rather, the goal is to manage conflict in a productive, positive way. Practice 5-14 will give you experience in analyzing how people manage conflict.

Practice 5-14: Conflict Resolution

1. Your teacher will divide the class into four teams. Each team will brainstorm ideas to solve the following problem:

Because of the excellent work your class has done so far this year, you will be awarded a $10,000 grant to spend in some way that will benefit the entire class. The only

(cont'd on next page)

restrictions are that you must spend all $10,000 and what you spend it on must have educational value.

After brainstorming ideas, follow these steps:

a. Choose a team leader.

b. Use rank ordering, the nominal group technique, or multi-voting to arrive at your solution.

c. Record the team's decision on a piece of paper.

2. Once the teams have reached their decisions and recorded them, follow these steps:

Instructions for team leaders:

a. List all four teams' decisions on a flip chart, chalkboard, sheet of poster board, or large sheet of paper. It is important for all members of the class to be able to see the list.

b. Sit close to the other team leaders so you can talk. Everyone else will observe your discussion.

c. You and the other team leaders may use rank ordering, the nominal group technique, or multi-voting to select one of the four solutions to the problem of how to spend the money. Your goal is to *agree* on the decision.

Instructions for the rest of the class:

d. Position yourself so that you can silently watch the team leaders as they discuss the problem.

e. As you observe, complete *Student Workbook* page 5-E. Pay attention to how the team members handle disagreements. You might observe one or more of the conflict resolution strategies listed on the *Student Workbook* page. When you notice members using one of these strategies, note below its description on *Student Workbook* page 5-E the point of disagreement, along with a brief report of who did what.

f. Be prepared to share your observations during the follow-up discussion.

SUMMARY

A process description explains how something works, how something is done, or how something is made. Giving an effective process description requires careful planning. Follow these guidelines whenever you describe a process at work:

* Remember that the purpose of a process description is audience understanding, not action.

* Explain steps in a process in chronological order using active or, when appropriate, passive statements.

* Use parallel structure and, when appropriate, analogies to make your description clearer.

* Organize a written process description to contain an informative title, an introduction, a body that explains each step in the process, and, perhaps, a closing.

* Use visuals such as drawings, diagrams, or flowcharts to illustrate a process description.

* Plan oral presentations of process descriptions by choosing a subject, analyzing your audience, clarifying your purpose, gathering facts, organizing the presentation, designing visuals, and rehearsing.

The ability to work as a member of a team is a valuable asset in the workplace. Teams are often asked to solve problems or to make decisions. Effective teamwork involves setting goals, establishing leadership, making effective decisions, and managing conflict.

WORKS CITED

United States Department of Energy. "The D(ratted) P(rogress) Report." E.I. Dupont de Nemours and Company, Explosives Department, Atomic Energy Division, Technical Division, Savannah River Laboratory, July 12, 1954.

PROJECT DESCRIBING A PROCESS

No matter what field you are studying, you have learned some information that can be valuable to people who do not have your training. For instance, the person who drives, but who will never repair a car, can avoid some clutch repairs by understanding how the car's transmission works. Other examples follow:

EXAMPLES:

* How personal credit information is stored in and retrieved from data banks

* How children develop ideas of right and wrong

* How rays given off by an arc welder can damage unprotected eyes

* How news wire services distribute data to the media

* How plaque forms in arteries

* How whales communicate

For this Project you will give a description of a process related to your occupational field that would be valuable or interesting to a general audience. You will give the description as an oral presentation that you will prepare and deliver to your class as part of a team.

1. Study the Sample Project Plan on page 168. Brainstorm ideas for a topic, for an organizational plan, and for the type and subject matter of any visuals. With your team, research the chosen topic and complete the Project Plan on *Student Workbook* page 5-F. Have your teacher check it.

2. Listen to the recorded sample presentation. The notes for this presentation are on page 169. The visual referred to in the speech is Figure 5-12 on page 154.

3. Assign tasks to team members based on their individual skills and talents.

4. With your team, prepare notes and visuals for the presentation.

5. Study the Project Guide, *Student Workbook* page 5-G, for criteria (standards) by which the presentation will be evaluated.

6. Rehearse the presentation individually and with your team. Using the Rough Draft column of the Project Guide, check your own work with one or more classmates as you rehearse your presentation. Have them record all their comments and changes on your Project Guide and rough draft of your notes and visuals. Ask them to write a constructive comment on the rough draft and sign it.

7. Do a final rehearsed presentation. If possible, ask a classmate to act as your audience and help you to rate yourselves using the Final Draft column of the Project Guide.

8. Give the presentation. The Project Guide will be used to evaluate your notes, visuals, and speech.

Plan for Describing a Process

SUBJECT	How a computer virus works
AUDIENCE	Communication class—general audience
PURPOSE	**What actions should the audience take?** Protect their data from viruses
FORMAT	☐ written ☒ oral ☐ other
SOURCES	"Antidote for Viruses" CompUser pp. 38–40 1-98 "Common Sense for the Common Cold" The Telegraph B2 3-24-98
VISUALS	**What visuals, if any, will make the presentation more effective?** Flowchart showing main steps Screen shot of Casino virus
INTRO	**What will get the audience's attention?** Analogy between computer & cold viruses

CONTENT
What are the main steps and supporting details?

viruses are created by hackers

virus enters host
    virus—small, destructive program
        genes packed in protein shell
    host—person or computer with a virus

Vaccines & antiviral software can prevent infection

Virus makes copies of itself and spreads
    cough, sneeze, touch
    networks, modems, floppy disks

Virus attack
    prank message—Form virus
    data destruction
        Casino virus example
        FAT—file allocation table

BACK UP YOUR WORK

Notes for a Process Description

Do you use a computer at home or at work or at school? If you do, you need to know about a deadly disease that could attack your computer. It's called a virus. No, your computer can't catch your cold, but it can get sick, and the process is similar to the way your body catches a cold and gets sick.

1. Virus enters host **(show flowchart)**.

    * Body – genes packed in protein shells

    * Computer – small software programs

    Define VIRUS, HOST, HACKER

2. Prevention

    * Body—flu shot

    * Computer—antiviral software

3. Virus copies itself.

4. Virus spreads.

    * Body—to other people – airborne or direct contact

    * Computer—to other computers – networks, modems, floppy disks

5. Virus attacks host.

    * Body—symptoms appear

    * Computer—data and files destroyed

    * Form virus—beeps as you key on the 18th

    * Casino virus example **(show Casino virus screen shot)** FAT – file allocation table

Doctors say that the best way to avoid colds is to wash your hands frequently. If you do get a cold, once it has run its course, the body goes to work repairing your system. But computer systems can't repair themselves, and there's no foolproof method to protect your computer from a virus if your computer comes in contact with other computers. The best protection for your hard work is making backup copies of your files.

Write out the introduction word for word.

Use numbers and bullets.

Make the notes easy to read.

Write out the conclusion word for word.

Overview

This excerpt from *The Jungle* by Upton Sinclair describes the process used by the meat-packing industry at the beginning of the 20th century to slaughter hogs. Sinclair wrote the book to be used as a weapon against the meat-packing industry, to show the exploitation of the workers. Instead, the book generated a campaign to upgrade the sanitary conditions of the meat-packing industry. Sinclair thought the cause was of little help to the workers. The response to this passage and a later one—which reveals that men sometimes lost their balance on the slimy floor, fell into the vats, and ended up like hogs as part of the final meat product—caused a public outcry for more controls on meat inspection. As a result, the Meat Inspection and Pure Food and Drug Acts were formulated and passed.

from *The Jungle*

One could not stand and watch very long without becoming philosophical, without beginning to deal in symbols and similes, and to hear the hog-squeal of the universe. Was it permitted to believe that there was nowhere upon the earth, or above the earth, a heaven for hogs, where they were requited for all this suffering? Each one of these hogs was a separate creature. Some were white hogs, some were black; some were brown, some were spotted; some were old, some were young; some were long and lean, some were monstrous. And each of them had an individuality of his own, a will of his own, a hope and a heart's desire; each was full of self-confidence, of self-importance, and a sense of dignity. And trusting and strong in faith he had gone about his business, the while a black shadow hung over him and a horrid Fate waited in his pathway. Now suddenly it had swooped upon him; and had seized him by the leg. Relentless, remorseless, it was; all his protests, his screams, were nothing to it—it did its cruel will with him, as if his wishes, his feelings, had simply no existence at all; it cut his throat and watched him gasp out his life. And how was one to believe that there was nowhere a god of hogs, to whom this hog-personality was precious, to whom these hog-squeals and agonies had a meaning? Who would take this hog into his arms and comfort him, reward him for his work well done, and show him the meaning of his sacrifice? Perhaps some glimpse of all this was in the thoughts of our humble-minded Jurgis, as he turned to go on with the rest of the party, and muttered: "Dieve—but I'm glad I'm not a hog!"

The carcass of the hog was scooped out of the vat by machinery, and then it fell to the second floor, passing on the way through a wonderful machine with numerous scrapers, which adjusted themselves to the size and shape of the animal, and sent it out the other end with nearly all of its bristles removed. It was then again strung up by machinery, and sent upon another trolley ride; this time passing between two lines of men, who sat upon a raised platform, each doing a certain single thing to the carcass as it came to him. One scraped the outside of a leg; another scraped the inside of the same leg. One with a swift stroke cut the throat; another with two swift strokes severed the head, which fell to the floor and vanished through a hole. Another made a slit down the body; a second opened the body wider; a third with a saw cut out the breast-bone, a fourth loosened the entrails; a fifth pulled them out—and they also slid through a hole in the floor. There were men to scrape each side and men to scrape the back; there were men to clean the carcass inside, to trim it and wash it. Looking down this room one saw, creeping slowly, a line of dangling hogs a hundred yards in length; and for every yard there was a man, working as if a demon were after him. At the end of this hog's progress every inch of the carcass had been gone over several times; and then it was rolled into the chilling room where it stayed for twenty-four hours, and where a stranger might lose himself in a forest of freezing hogs.

. . . and for every yard there was a man, working as if a demon were after him.

—Upton Sinclair

Start-Up: Parallelism is used in both technical writing and literature. Repeating the same grammatical form emphasizes step-by-step organization.

Connection: Reread the excerpt.

1. List the ideas that are presented in the same way grammatically.

2. Rewrite one or two examples, removing the parallelism. What is the result?

3. Identify at least five descriptive passages or situations from the selection that could possibly inflame the public because of the imagery or emotional impact.

Overview

The following selection is a literary description of a process. When Denise Grady's two-year-old son began to stutter, she decided to research the reason. By breaking down the subject of stuttering into its constituent parts and studying how the parts fit together as a whole, the author explains the phenomenon of stuttering. As the author analyzes stuttering, she identifies the various body parts involved and the steps that lead to normal speech.

"Stuttering"

Nobody knows why people stutter. The disorder occurs in virtually every culture, and speech therapists estimate that it affects about one percent of the population of the world. The earliest explanations, dating from ancient Greece and persisting into the early 1800's, blamed the tongue: it was too weak, too wet, too dry, too hard, too cold, too large. By the early part this century, the focus had shifted upward, and stuttering was seen first as a bad habit or the product of a neurosis, and later as the result of some unknown abnormality of the brain.

Today many speech researchers think that stuttering is both a physiological and a behavioral condition. The details may differ from one person to the next, but the basic scenario is that stuttering begins for an organic reason and persists, at least in part, because the anxiety generated by the stuttering then makes the stuttering worse, as do some of the habits that people fall into in their struggle to control their speech. Some experts believe that excessive concern with the mechanics of talking can throw the rhythm off, just as thinking too much about where to put your foot next can lead to a fall, and trying to perfect each sentence as you write can lead to writer's block. Some researchers have even suggested that people become physically addicted to stuttering, perhaps to little jolts of adrenaline or other brain chemicals that may be released during stuttering.

In order to speak, one has to coordinate breathing, voice, and movements of the mouth, lips, and tongue. Almost a hundred muscles are involved, and all of them must receive nerve signals at certain instants to produce the right sequence of movements. Because the muscles are on both sides of the body, their movements must also be synchronized. The speech control center resides in the left half of the brain in most people; one popular theory suggests that in stutterers its control may be incomplete, and the right side may fire out conflicting orders that throw the whole speech apparatus out of whack. The result may be a breakdown in timing—a failure of the mechanism that organizes the movements required for speech and that marks its rhythm. Some researchers say that mistiming may be a perpetual problem: stutterers may hear their own speech in a distorted way—with a delay, perhaps—that interferes with their ability to talk.

Male stutterers outnumber females by at least three to one, and the disorder often runs in families. It nearly always comes on during preschool years, when speech and language pass through their most intense phases of development. Many children, especially boys, have brief periods of stuttering or stumbling or fragmented speech. Most get over it. Why some never do remains a mystery. In one of his books, *The Nature of Stuttering,* Charles Van Riper describes a "monstrous collage of factors" of physiology, intelligence, personality, verbal skill, and environmental stress that may contribute to stuttering.

—Denise Grady

Start-Up: The most complicated subject is composed of simpler parts. When a complicated subject is broken down into simpler parts, the process is more easily understood. A medical textbook may break a surgical procedure down into a series of steps. An automobile repair manual may list parts and tell how these parts work together.

Connection: To analyze the writing of a process description, answer the following questions about "Stuttering."

1. Is this process carried out by machines, by people, or by nature?

2. Is the intended audience specialized or general?

3. Take a sampling of the verbs. Are the verbs in the active voice or the passive voice?

4. Is there parallelism? If so, give an example.

5. Is the wording of the selection clear, concise, and direct? If so, give examples.

6. Would the selection be more easily understood if a visual accompanied it? Give a reason for your answer.

Chapter 6

Vapor Condenses

Precipitation

Runoff goes to Groundwater

Vapor becomes Clouds

Water Evaporates

Hydrologic Cycle

Reproduced by permission.
Exploring Agriscience By Herren
Delmar Publishers, Albany, New York, Copyright 1996

Describing a Mechanism

Tell me and I'll forget; show me and I may remember; involve me and I'll understand.

—CHINESE PROVERB

As you complete Chapter 6, you will

* define a mechanism.

* classify types of mechanisms.

* identify uses for mechanism descriptions.

* divide a mechanism into parts.

* use language appropriate to a mechanism description.

* use analogies in describing a mechanism.

* plan and give a mechanism description presentation with visuals.

Workplace Skills in This Chapter

• Use **resources** to plan and to prepare the Project.

• Improve **interpersonal** skills through brainstorming and discussion in groups.

• Gather and organize **information** to use mechanisms for chapter activities.

• Understand how a mechanism is a **system**.

• Utilize **technology** to choose mechanisms and to produce the Project visual.

Starting a new job? Getting an equipment upgrade? Trying a different exercise to help patients recover from knee surgery? Figuring out what combination of grains to use to increase growth in your livestock? Designing a perfect landscape plan? What do these scenarios have in common? They all entail learning something new— about equipment, a machine, a technique, a substance, an organism, a system, or a tool. Performing any of these tasks takes more than knowing a definition and more than knowing the process of how something works. Understanding requires knowing the entire mechanism.

A Mechanism Defined

Isn't a mechanism a machine? Sometimes it is, but it isn't all the time. A **mechanism** is an object or system that may be simple or complex. It can have any number of parts; each part has a particular function. The parts of the mechanism work together to accomplish a definite purpose. So a mechanism doesn't always have to be a machine. Any system that has parts that function separately to achieve an overall effect is a mechanism.

So, a mechanism does not have to be a piece of machinery. Yes, generally most people would think of a mechanism as something as complex as an airbrush, but it can be as simple as a whetstone. Furthermore, a system, an organism, or a location can be a mechanism also.

A mechanism can have any number of structural parts. For example, a key has one structural part; a fuel injection system has many structural parts. The structural parts of a hardhat would be the shell or body of the hat, the brim, the adjustable headband, and the interior crown's strap device (see Figure 6-1).

A mechanism can have any number of functional parts. In fact, the simplest mechanism may have only one structural part but many functional parts. For example, a key has only one structural part, but several functional parts. Each indentation on the key separately trips a spring and rod inside the cylinder lock (Figure 6-2).

A mechanism has only this simple requirement: at least two parts that work separately, but together perform a single function.

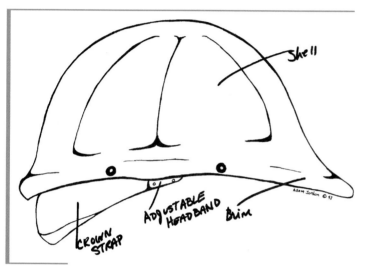

Figure 6-1: *The structural parts of a hardhat*
Reproduced by permission of Adam D. Jordan.

Figure 6-2: *A cylinder lock*

Practice 6-1: Finding a Mechanism

careers Determine if the following objects, substances, and systems can be described as mechanisms. Keep in mind the definition of a mechanism.

1. harness
2. fork
3. curling iron
4. blueprint
5. thermometer

6. T-square
7. microphone
8. anti-shoplifting tag
9. irrigation
10. blood

A bar code is a mechanism. The parts of a bar code, the graphical series of bars and spaces, are arranged in certain patterns that describe coded data characters that a reading device can scan. Another mechanism, a food web, is a system that can be explained through a diagram of its parts (see Figure 6-3). Each part works independently—a grasshopper eats a plant, a small bird consumes the grasshopper, a fox or an owl preys on the bird, and so on. The parts also perform an overall function as a complex network dependent originally upon the soil, contributing to the constant cycle of life on earth.

Number System Character

Check Digit

Manufacturer Number

1 04332 35463 D Product Code

Center Guard Bars

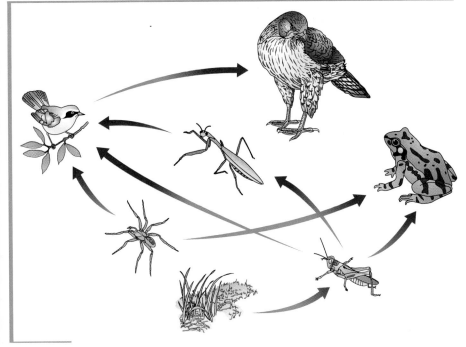

Figure 6-3: *A food web*

Reproduced by permission.
Exploring Agriscience *By Herren*
Delmar Publishers, Albany, New York, Copyright 1996

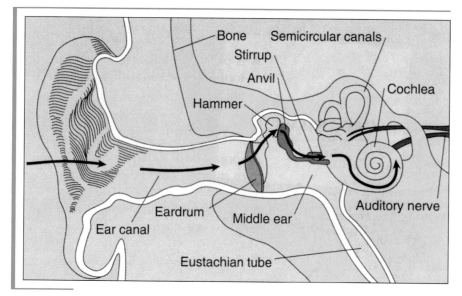

Figure 6-4: *The human ear*

The outer ear is a shell that catches sound waves. The drawing in Figure 6-4 will be familiar to many of you. The drawing shows how sound waves reach the outer ear, pass through the middle ear, and enter the inner ear, permitting a person to hear. The ear and its adjoining parts are the mechanism. The drawing, plus the teacher's explanation, is the mechanism description.

Classification of Mechanisms

Mechanisms can vary from basic to elaborate, from miniscule to large, and from inanimate to living. Tools, organisms, substances, sites or locations, and systems are the primary categories of mechanisms.

Tools and Machinery

When most people hear the word *mechanism,* they picture a **tool** or machinery. Even though tools are not the only type of mechanism, the tool is the easiest to understand. The tool is an aid for the worker and becomes an extension of the user. Some tools appear to be simple, seemingly made of just one or two parts. One such tool is a claw hammer. However, the claw hammer's major parts are the claw, the head, the cheek, the neck, the face, the poll, the adze eye, and the handle (see Figure 6-5). That simple tool seems to have many parts after all!

Tools and machinery can be simple or complex, handheld or massive.

* A laser has many sections that work together to pierce or cut materials, such as metal.

* A perm rod has several parts that combine to make a tool. This tool holds rolled hair in place so that a stylist can add perm solutions to curl the hair.

Figure 6-5: *A claw hammer*

* A clamp's handle turns its threaded piece that, combined with the body of the clamp, will determine the clamp's throat opening.
* A printing system may be large or small but consists of many parts.

Figure 6-6: *A substance mechanism*

Organisms

The range of **organisms** is virtually unlimited. From a single-celled living being like an amoeba to a whale or a human being, organisms are living mechanisms. A tree is a mechanism consisting of different parts, such as the roots, the leaves, and the bark. These parts have separate functions: taking in nutrients from the soil, providing respiration, and protecting the tree against insects.

Substances

Some **substances** may be considered mechanisms. These substances have two or more parts that, examined separately, do not resemble the new composite material. One such substance is automotive paint, which contains chemicals such as toners, reducers, and hardeners—components that can work independently. However, when they are combined, these compounds have a different function; they work together to achieve a factory-quality vehicle finish.

Locations

Some **locations** are considered mechanisms. The site includes separate parts that work together for one purpose. Viewing the site's components—for example, the parts of the terrain and the buildings—as one entity forms the mechanism. Surveyors, drafters, architects, and construction workers are examples of those persons who create or use locations as mechanisms.

One example of the location as a mechanism is the construction site for Paul Rosenfield's new home (Figure 6-7). Part of the house is built into a mountain wall to conserve energy and to preserve the terrain. The lower section overhangs the rocks with a spectacular view of the sea, making the overall effect from the decks breathtaking. There are entrances from the mountain road above and from the seaside drive below. All parts of the site work together to form the mechanism.

Figure 6-7: *The location as a mechanism*

Reproduced by permission of Adam D. Jordan.

Systems

Groups of parts that work together to perform a function form a **system**. Without each component, the system cannot function. Systems can be either natural or manufactured. For example, a plant cannot replicate without all the parts of its reproductive system. All the parts work together for the overall purpose of reproduction; however, each part has an independent function. For each command in a word

INFOBIT

Yes, this is a paying job! The head of quality for Godiva Chocolate has to sample one-half pound of chocolates each day. Batch after batch, Michael Gerraro must prove that Godiva is producing the best chocolate possible. That quality control adds up to 120 pounds to taste a year.

processing system's pull-down menus, there is a separate function, but together those parts form a systematic, efficient program that produces a formatted document. For example, one command makes the text bold; another changes uppercase to sentence case. Also, irrigation is a highly complex mechanism, but its parts work together to provide needed water for crops in climates where rain is scarce.

Practice 6-2: Selecting a Mechanism

careers For each of the mechanism categories, name two mechanisms. When practical, one mechanism should be from your career cluster. Record your answers on *Student Workbook* page 6-A.

Uses for Mechanism Descriptions

There are numerous uses for mechanism descriptions. These purposes may include purchasing, replacing, repairing, explaining, and so on. Each description can also vary for different audiences.

Soybeans, for instance, can be used as a mechanism in various ways, depending on the purpose for each description. Notice how each person in the following example describes soybeans in a different way.

* Abe, an organic farmer who grows soybeans to sell, does not decide what product uses certain parts of the plant; neither does he describe the whole bean or its parts to the buyer. Instead, Abe will describe his beans to another farmer as being superior in size, color, firmness, and overall quality.

* Peg, a supervisor in the factory that purchased Abe's beans, describes the soybean to Rick, a new employee. She explains the process of extracting the oil from the bean to sell separately. Then Peg explains the separation of the hulls from the meat of the bean. The factory sells the hulls for cattle feed and grinds the meat of the bean into soy flour. Peg's description of the bean varies greatly from Abe's because both are describing the soybean for different purposes and for different audiences.

Decision Making

Knowing how a mechanism works is important in many situations. The knowledge gained from studying a mechanism description, along with observing the way a mechanism is working, helps people make sound decisions. Watching for changes and comparing and contrasting mechanisms also provide information that is useful in making decisions.

PEOPLE **C·O·N·N·E·C·T·I·O·N**

When you next make a call on a cellular phone, think of Hedy Lamarr. Best known for her movie performances in the 1930s and '40s, Hedy Lamarr is a perceptive tinkerer whose scientific mind explored ways of preventing the jamming of submarine signals in the early days of World War II. When she wanted to pursue her ideas, she was discouraged and urged to work for the war bond effort instead. However, she teamed up with George Antheil, and their patent describing the method for radio signals' bouncing among frequencies at split-second intervals was accepted in 1942. The military used the invention during the Cuban missile crisis, and today the invention's concept is applied to wireless Internet transmission and in newer cellular phones. Unfortunately, the patent expired in 1959, and Lamarr and Antheil have never received any royalty payments for its commercialization. In 1997, recognition at last came for the movie star with the engineering mind, credited as having insight into the concept of the wireless Internet. Her comment? "It's about time."

* An emergency room technician must know how a healthy human arm works before he or she can treat an accident victim with a broken arm.

* By understanding how juniper bushes should grow, a landscape manager can decide how best to prune them.

* An electronics technician needs to know how a soldering iron tip should look to decide when the iron is ready to begin soldering.

All three situations need more than a superficial look; they require a thorough knowledge of a mechanism.

Training

Training situations occur daily in the workplace. Employers provide training for workers new to a job and new to pieces of equipment or procedures. In addition, transferred or promoted employees must develop experience with new products, machines, or even work sites. For all employers, changing technology constantly creates training needs for skilled employees.

* Even though Addie has been in the baking industry for several years, as the newly hired chief baker in Johnetta's bakery, she still needs instruction in the bakery's machines. The bread machines are a different brand than Addie has been using, and each oven has its own temperature idiosyncrasies. As a new employee, Addie needs to have the machinery described to her so that she will be able to use it correctly.

* The oxyacetylene welding unit brought into the precision machining area needs to be introduced to the workers, even though many of them have been on the job for more than twenty years. As the supervisor, Helena must be able to

TECHNOBIT

The need for basic training is increasing! A survey conducted by Olsten reports that more than 60 percent of newly hired employees need increased computer skills and more teamwork skills. The lack of these skills drives up production costs while the company does the training.

> describe the overall capabilities of the machinery, each part and its function, and the machine's performance while she trains her workers on the equipment.

Manuals give an overview, a type of general description of mechanisms. The technical description is usually followed by visuals, such as specifications sheets (specs) and special types of interior drawings. The details are typically added later in the succeeding sections of the manual. These technical mechanism descriptions are used for customer and employee training.

Reports

Mechanism descriptions are used within reports. The functions, parts, or data contained within the report may need to be described. For example, any changes in equipment or purchase recommendations will need a description before decisions are made. Sometimes the descriptions will be presented as an oral presentation or as a written report given in presentation form.

When Mai presented her architectural firm's bid for the Technical Center, she knew it would be meaningless without the floor plan and the three-dimensional drawings showing the location of the equipment. In addition, the modification report of the computer network would include several off-site locations. That report would not be understood without the wiring diagrams to describe the changes.

Marketing

A marketing campaign may include a mechanism description because marketing promotes the product as a whole and the parts of the product. If the buyer is a specialist, more details should be included than for the general buyer.

Proposals are a form of marketing. Often the audience for a proposal is a general purchaser. Bids to purchase equipment must be explained with a mechanism description to this nontechnical buyer. In order for the buyer to understand a proposal, visuals are usually included with the written description.

The Clamara crankshaft is more efficient than the crankshaft produced by the Hut company, its competitor. In its marketing campaigns, the Hut company should highlight the features of the part that make its crankshaft better by using a drawing with the verbal description in its

Piston

Crankshaft

Figure 6-8: *The Clamara crankshaft*

marketing proposal. Now Clamara needs to convince the giant Christos Car Corporation that it should use the Clamara crankshaft. In its proposal, Clamara will include a drawing of the side of the entire crankshaft (Figure 6-8) and a drawing highlighting the special features of the Clamara crankshaft that make it superior to its competitor.

Practice 6-3: Wording a Mechanism Picture

Examine your left shoe very carefully. Imagine that last weekend you and your friends spent a day at the beach. As your friend was driving down the highway, you decided to open the window and dump the sand out of the shoe. Unfortunately, you shook too hard, and you dropped the shoe! The right shoe is perfectly fine—and the shoes are a favorite pair of yours—so you want the shoe back.

Create a newspaper lost and found ad to find your shoe. Want ads have a maximum amount of words, usually 20 or 30, so you will need to be brief and concise.

Parts of a Mechanism

INFOBIT

"A closed mind is a dying mind."

EDNA FERBER, U.S. AUTHOR

A blueprint fits the definition of a mechanism; it is an object with parts performing different functions, each function serving a definite purpose. However, a computer spreadsheet is very complex and is best described if it is divided into sections. The sections can then be explained in a particular order. (This method of explanation is similar to the process description in Chapter 5.) **Random order** is not an effective way to describe the parts of a mechanism.

Structure, function, and order of importance are ways that you can divide a mechanism into parts. The method or combination of methods that you choose depends on the purpose of the mechanism description.

Structure

You can organize your description in terms of a mechanism's physical appearance. First, look closely at the mechanism. Then, describe its parts in a logical order according to the physical aspects that you see. Structurally, parts can be described from top to bottom, left to right, front to back, or outside to inside. (Chapter 2, "Communicating Definitions," is a good reference source for describing structural parts.)

The mechanism described by structure is the **machine at rest**—that is, a machine that is not in operation. The verbal picture of a machine at rest focuses on the mechanism's parts and the relationship of the parts to one another. The function of the parts is only mentioned briefly when needed to enhance the explanation of the structure.

A structural description of the heart might begin as follows:

> The human heart functions like a circulation pump for the body's blood. The heart consists of four chambers. The two small upper chambers are the left atrium and the right atrium. The left and right ventricles lay below each related atrium.

INFOBIT

Apply the same approach to your own career that you normally apply to project planning and development. Don't wait for others to provide the project's direction. Instead, think about your career yourself—and then take action to make those strategies reality.

WILLIAM ROTHWELL, HUMAN RESOURCE CONSULTANT

Function

If the audience needs to concentrate more on the purpose for each part of the mechanism, then the **function** of each part should be explained to the audience to illustrate the description. This type of description explains a **machine in operation;** the way the machine looks is secondary to the way the machine performs. In the functional description, you give the purpose for each part, rather than describing the part itself. A description of a machine in operation emphasizes parts working together to perform a function. How the parts are located in relationship to one another is only mentioned.

Functional parts are often described in the order of the tasks that each part performs. For example, Part A moves Part B, which moves Part C, and so on. Not every mechanism can be described functionally, particularly in a description of a substance.

The functional parts of a hardhat are the shell that protects the head, the brim that shields the eyes, the adjustable headband that sizes the hat to the individual's head, and the crown's strap device that combines with the headband to protect the head from impact (see Figure 6-1 on page 176).

Remember the earlier description of the heart based on structure? If the audience needs a description of how the heart performs, rather than how it is put together, then the heart should be described according to function. Notice how the following description emphasizes the function of the four major parts of the heart; the location of the heart's parts is mentioned only in relation to function.

> The human heart functions like a circulation pump for the body's blood. The heart consists of four chambers. The left atrium and the right atrium are the small upper chambers that receive the blood from the body. The left and right ventricles below the atriums pump the blood away from the heart.

Importance

In a few instances, the parts of a mechanism can be described in **order of importance**. Consider this example: the teacher is explaining how to check an X-ray film or radiograph to the dental assistant class. Parts of the film should be described in order of

CAREER C·O·N·N·E·C·T·I·O·N
The structural parts of a substance were important to Joseph Campbell in 1897. By extracting much of the water in his soup canning process, he greatly reduced costs and began selling condensed Campbell's Soup. Shoppers loved the product, and the New Jersey inventor was selling 40,000 cases a year eight years later. Today, Campbell's outsells all other brands in the soup world.

importance—that is, which is the most important part to check first, second, and so on. Cavities are more important to check on than gum disease or changes in the bone because cavities need to be repaired before the patient can schedule other dental work. List the positive before the negative for the best possible effect on your audience.

However, some mechanisms can never be described according to importance. For example, no one can judge the upper half of the heart more important than the lower half. Without either chamber, you would die!

Combination of Methods

At times, a combination of two methods may be used to describe a mechanism (see Figure 6-9). If the structural location of the chambers of the heart is as significant as the way the heart functions, then the description would be similar to the following explanation. Both structural and functional parts are given equal emphasis.

Blood flowing in from all parts of your body carrying used air.

Blood carrying fresh air from the lungs.

Right Auricle

Left Auricle

Blood is pumped to the lungs to get rid of the used air.

Blood filled with fresh air gets pumped to all parts of your body.

Right Ventricle

Left Ventricle

The heart is made up of two pumps working side by side.

The human heart functions like a circulation pump for the body's blood. The heart consists of four chambers. The left atrium and the right atrium are the two small upper chambers. These upper chambers receive the blood from the body. The left and right ventricles are below each related atrium. The ventricles pump blood away from the heart.

Figure 6-9: *Blood flow through the heart*

Source: John Burstein, Slim Goodbody: The Inside Story *(New York: McGraw-Hill, 1971), 11. Reprinted with permission.*

Your audience and the particular use of the mechanism description will help you decide whether you need to describe a mechanism by structure, function, importance, or a combination of methods.

Practice 6-4: Describing the Parts of a Mechanism

1. Choose one method to describe five of the following mechanisms—by structure, function, or importance. Then identify and describe the parts of the mechanism.

EXAMPLE:

hairbrush   *Function:* The bristles move through hair to smooth, detangle, and style. The handle provides a means for holding the brush.

a. thermometer   f. telephone receiver

b. blood   g. gum eraser

c. wood chisel   h. light bulb

d. bar code   i. tire

e. elm tree   j. paintbrush

2. Now choose five mechanisms from your career major, and repeat Step 1 to complete this Practice.

Writing Mechanism Descriptions

A mechanism is always described in words. A mechanism description may be written for a general audience who has never seen the mechanism or who may have very little knowledge of it. Even the specialist audience may need a description, for it may have the basic knowledge that a general audience has, but may need more technical, detailed information. With either audience, the description must be clearly written.

Though visuals are usually included with the written mechanism description, they cannot stand alone. Visuals enhance or strengthen the written description of a mechanism.

Sometimes the same mechanism must be described to different audiences. Such descriptions will vary, not in the way the mechanism is used, but in the language and complexity of the description. For example, Sera Broga comes into Jim Paul's electronics shop with a broken Diastar television antenna that she wants repaired. When Jim examines the antenna, he thinks that repairing the outdated Diastar antenna would be less cost-effective than replacing the antenna with a

INFOBIT

Avoid saying, "I think/feel I need more time." That phrase indicates that you are indecisive. Just be straightforward and drop the "think/feel" words.

PHYLLIS MINDELL, AUTHOR OF *A WOMAN'S GUIDE TO THE LANGUAGE OF SUCCESS: COMMUNICATING WITH CONFIDENCE AND POWER*

INFOBIT

Curiosity may have killed the cat, but you could live longer for being inquisitive. According to a study done by the National Institute on Aging, people who are very curious are likely to live longer than those with average levels of curiosity. In addition, the same people improve in their emotional health. So the next time someone suggests that you stop asking questions, just remember that asking those questions could add five years to your life!

portable satellite dish system. Jim Paul must describe the mechanisms of both the broken Diastar antenna and the replacement system of a satellite dish and its network to his customer, Sera Broga, before she can make her decision.

Jim wants Sera to understand what is involved in repairing the antenna versus replacing it with a satellite dish, so he needs to use nonspecialist language that a person with general knowledge, such as Sera, understands. Though Sera may have other reasons for not replacing the antenna, Jim does not want his explanation to be the reason for poor customer decision making.

Even though the labor cost is high, Sera decides to have Jim repair the antenna. Now Jim needs to describe the antenna mechanism to Misha Roth, his repairer. Jim's explanation is especially important because Misha has never repaired a Diastar antenna before. Moreover, Jim's description to Misha will be different than his description to Sera because, as a repairer, Misha is a specialist. In his work, Jim sees the need for describing a mechanism in different ways for different audiences.

Common Versus Specific Terms

Use more **common** or ordinary **terms** for the general audience. These terms are basically nontechnical and are less confusing. **Specific terms** have more technical details. These terms may seem more accurate, but this accuracy is frequently needed only by the specialist.

In common or general terms, a motor would be called "powerful." A seat would have "adjustable heights." A saw would come with "three different types of blades." In specific terms, the motor would be 1.5-horsepower. The seat would be adjustable to four positions in 2-inch increments. The saw blades would come in $7\frac{1}{2}$-, 7-, and $6\frac{1}{2}$-inch sizes.

Practice 6-5: Choosing General or Specific Terms

From *Student Workbook* page 6-B, choose one part or function of each mechanism. Describe that part or function in both general and specific terms.

Concrete Versus Abstract Terms

Careful word choice is also important. Not only must a common or specific term be chosen, but also a **concrete term** must be chosen over an abstract term. Because the mechanism description must be precise, use concrete terms to enable the audience to understand the word picture better. For example, *blight* is the concrete term that clarifies the abstract term *disease* (of plants). *Chartreuse* is the concrete color name; *green* is the **abstract term**.

Practice 6-6: Choosing Concrete Terms

The following abstract terms need to become concrete terms for a mechanism description. Write a concrete word or phrase to replace each abstract term given.

EXAMPLES:

safe	*dry floors*
dull-colored	*beige*
large	*6 feet in diameter*

1. disappointing
2. wet
3. quickly
4. problem area
5. bright
6. thick

7. thin (as in the opposite of *thick*)
8. thin (as in a liquid)
9. rusty
10. not feeling well
11. pretty
12. round

INFOBIT

A mother stopped in front of the bakery counter in the local grocery store. Asking the clerk for a large cookie for her children to share, the mother requested that the clerk break the cookie in half. Then she asked that the larger half be given to the older child. (Check your fraction circles for that one!)

Analogies

Often it is best to explain an unfamiliar mechanism by comparing it to something familiar that the audience knows. That direct comparison is called an **analogy**. The names of some terms have originated from analogies. Letters of the alphabet and numbers are familiar, so terms like *C-clamp, A-frame, I-beam,* and *figure 8* originated. These analogies give the unfamiliar a visual shape. Parts of the body provide useful analogies to describe parts of objects. The *neck* of a guitar, the *head* of a pin, and *gooseneck lamp* are examples of this type of analogy.

The following examples use analogies to create clear comparisons of well-known objects with objects less known. The visual image of something common makes the strange more familiar.

* The serpentine belt is as wide as an adult's little finger.
* The highlighting solution should be as thick as cake frosting.
* The hole is dime-sized.
* The human heart functions like a circulation pump for the body's blood.

A word of caution: Use analogies to simplify your descriptions, not to make them more confusing. So be sure that your audience is familiar with the terms compared. Also, only use an analogy if the audience needs the comparison to understand the description better.

Practice 6-7: Using Analogies

1. Often, an analogy can be visual. Terms that are analogies may draw a picture of the analogy. Explain the visual analogy for five of the following terms.

EXAMPLE:

Disk brake   *The brake shoe is in the shape of a disk-like saucer.*

a. blueprint	f. chain saw
b. tail comb	g. snapdragon
c. computer chip	h. claw hammer
d. elbow joint	i. hairline fracture
e. T–square	j. forklift

2. Create analogies for five of the following items. Describe the overall appearance and the major parts.

EXAMPLE:

keyboard   *The keyboard is a musical instrument that looks like a small piano mounted on a board. The keys are pressed to produce musical notes.*

a. scanner	f. transit
b. dental chair	g. keyhole saw
c. soil profile (soil lines)	h. easel
d. drafting table	i. CD-ROM
e. shock absorber	j. bit (horse equipment)

Precise Wording

The wording of a description needs to be **precise**. The more precise and exact a description is, the clearer it will be. Remember always to keep your audience and purpose in mind. An accurate description is important. Precise wording is needed whether the audience is general or specialized. For example, the following is a general description of a sheet-fed scanner. The description is accurate but is in nontechnical terms.

> The sheet-fed scanner is a device the size of a lunch box that looks like a mini-computer printer and attaches to both the computer and the printer. Some scanners are so small that they can fit behind the keyboard. Simply feed a page into the scanner, and push a button. The scanner head will move over the paper, reproducing photographs, drawings, and text as computer files.

If the description is for a specialist audience, more technical material is needed. The description of the scanner might be changed to the following:

> The sheet-fed scanner is a narrow, rectangular device that produces digitized versions of hard-copy photographs, line art, and text. When you feed a page into the slot on the scanner, the scanner head moves over the paper and captures the image. You can work with scanned files in popular graphics, presentation, Web publishing, and word processing programs.

INFOBIT

We are continually faced by great opportunities brilliantly disguised as insolvable problems.

Practice 6-8: Analyzing Mechanisms for Different Audiences

teamwork

1. After reading through the questions on *Student Workbook* page 6-C, listen to and take notes on the mechanism descriptions that your teacher will play for you.

2. With a partner, answer the questions on *Student Workbook* page 6-C. You may need to hear the Audio Activity a second time to hear all the details.

The Third Person

When you speak and write to others, you use the verb and the personal pronoun in the second person, as in the sentence, "you brought the cider." When you give instructions, you also use the second person in the form of a command, as in "bring the cider." When you use the second person, you write and speak directly to the reader, often with a familiar tone.

A description of a mechanism, however, is more impersonal. Generally, you are not writing to a person you know; instead, you are writing for an unknown audience. Therefore, you need to write in the **third person,** which is more impersonal and slightly more formal than the second person.

C·O·N·N·E·C·T·I·O·N
Reaching the nation's Hispanic and Latino population as consumers is often done by targeting the group as a whole. The most popular way of reaching Latinos is by communicating in Spanish. However, many Hispanic persons do not read or speak Spanish. Their communities may consist of such diverse groups as Cuban, Colombian, Mexican, Dominican Republican, and Puerto Rican people. The groups not only have diverse ethnic traits but also differ in issues that affect their buying habits. Each group needs to be targeted, with the message directing concerns to that particular audience.

For third–person writing, instead of saying *I* or *you*, use words and phrases such as the following:

Singular	Plural
he, she, it, one	they
a person (or a name)	people (or names)
an individual	individuals
an object	objects

Practice 6-9: Using the Third Person

Rewrite the following sentences so that all parts are in third person.

EXAMPLE:

If you like shorts, wear them at home.

If a student likes to wear shorts, he or she should wear them at home.

1. People who visit Los Angeles are amazed at the number of cars. You need one to travel anywhere near that city.

2. Dental assistant students should report to the auditorium and bring your notebooks.

3. Expect perfection, and others will do their best.

4. The wise trainer knows that you must dry a horse after bathing it in the winter.

5. Success is knowing you've done the best you can.

6. You can casually call long distance, and the bill will shock you in a month.

(cont'd on next page)

In the past, the masculine pronouns *he, him,* and *his* were the standard in the English language to represent groups that might include women. Today, many people consider this usage sexist. Here are some ways to avoid it.

- Try switching to plural pronouns, such as replacing *his* with *their*.
- Use gender-free words, such as *person, one, employee,* or *customer*.
- Reword to avoid using the pronoun.
- Alternate use of masculine and feminine pronouns.

7. Smokers will eventually realize that you can't just smoke without risking serious health problems.

8. High cholesterol may be a problem if you eat red meat.

9. Why drive your car to the mall when walking the two blocks is good exercise for the body?

10. Set the alarm 15 minutes early, and you will arrive at school on time every day.

INFOBIT

"Attempt the impossible in order to improve your work."

KATHARINE HEPBURN, U.S. ACTRESS

Objectivity

Write the mechanism description precisely and more formally than you would an instruction. The body of the mechanism description must be objective. Since the purpose of a mechanism description is to inform the audience, it should not include opinions or judgments except when necessary in the introduction and conclusion.

Practice 6-10: Making Sentences Objective

The following sentences are taken from descriptions, but they are not objective. Rewrite the sentences to make them objective.

EXAMPLE:

The use of spurs is unfair to the horse.

Digging spurs into a horse's sides can cause wounds.

1. Computer-aided design programs are too expensive for small businesses.

2. The resume that gets the job is the best.

3. The type of nail doesn't matter; no one looks at a basement ceiling.

4. The paint will cover any surface. That's what the salesclerk says.

5. Placing the tax on the customer's check will please him or her.

6. To apply the bandage properly, the nurse must first clean the wound well.

7. Only an expert knows how to choose the proper pigment.

8. Play is a welcome activity at any time in a child's day.

9. The Internet makes travel reservations a breeze.

10. His performance was great.

The Active Voice

Write your description in the **active voice**; the active voice is more direct and less confusing. Remember: you may be describing an unknown or unfamiliar object to the audience, so the clearer your writing is, the better. The active voice is desirable, but the passive voice is acceptable when the one who does the action is less important or obvious. (To review the active voice, turn to pages 144–146 of Chapter 5.)

With the active voice, the word or phrase in the subject position gets the emphasis. The subject is performing the action in the sentence. The active voice is more direct and precise, emphasizing the mechanism over the description.

Practice 6-11: Writing in the Active Voice

1. Change the following sentences from the passive to the active voice. Be sure to use only the third person.

EXAMPLE:

The disease should be prevented by the inoculation.

The inoculation should prevent the disease.

a. The seeds have been eaten by the birds.

b. The employee should be hired by the personnel department.

c. Hardhats should be worn at all times.

d. Unrefrigerated potato salad will be spoiled in a few hours.

e. Fingernails can be shaped with materials such as acrylics or porcelain.

f. Shawn should have been declared the first-place winner.

(cont'd on next page)

INFOBIT

A Boeing executive insists that his sales folks spend an hour on preparation for every minute a client meeting should last.

INFOBIT

Most people take the way of least resistance. Busy people tend to cut corners—and preparation is one of the primary places they cut. So do yourself a favor and just take the time and effort to prepare properly for your endeavors. The preparation is worth the perspiration.

g. A suit and tie will be worn by each male business student three times a week.

h. A prospective employee will not be hired by many employers if his or her resume reflects frequent job changes.

i. Communication skills are needed even by people who work alone.

j. A good student will be rewarded with excellent job placement, a satisfactory paycheck, and room for advancement.

2. The following phrases describe three mechanisms. Write a description for each mechanism; use the active voice and complete sentences. The first one is started for you.

a. black walnut tree
one of the most valuable native American trees
heavy, strong, durable wood
wood easy to work with
wood in great demand for veneers, cabinetmaking, interior finishing, gunstocks
bark used for tanning
yellowish-brown dye from nut husks
twigs—favorite deer food

The black walnut is one of the most valuable native American trees. Carpenters work the heavy, strong, durable wood easily. Black walnut is in great demand for . . .

b. internal combustion engine
power source for automobiles and airplanes
power develops in smooth-walled tube cylinder
cylinder—piston moves inside
movement of piston caused by expansion of gases
similar to steam engine—both use cylinders

c. pancreas
two essential substances:
  * insulin into bloodstream
    regulates amount of sugar in blood

  * pancreatic juices into duodenum
    contain enzymes that help digest food

Using Visuals in Mechanism Descriptions

Visuals add value to a mechanism description. A general audience may not understand the mechanism, despite the descriptive words. A specialist audience may have the basic technical knowledge but no understanding of the details of a specific subject area. With either audience, the mechanism description needs further explanation, and visuals help the audience better understand that information. Visuals illustrate the different aspects of a mechanism.

Figure 6-10: *An exterior view of a construction site*

When visuals are included, they are additions, enhancements to the description. Some facts cannot be described in a single visual, such as weight, materials used, actual size, texture, and three-dimensional contours. Each variation of the mechanism will have to be included in a separate visual.

Exterior Visuals

Some mechanisms may be totally unfamiliar to the audience. If the audience has never seen the mechanism, show an **exterior perspective**. Photographs, maps, and realistic drawings can provide an overall picture. Distracting details should not be included.

These exterior views must focus on the mechanism. The illustration must be uncluttered. Distracting details should not be included. Other than the mechanism itself, there should be very little else in the picture. A contrast is needed between the subject and the background for the mechanism to be the focus. For photographs, good lighting is essential.

Interior Visuals

Cross sections, schematics, and cutaway and exploded drawings depict the parts of a mechanism from the inside. With **interior views** of a mechanism, the audience can see where each part is located with respect to the other parts and to the mechanism as a whole.

Someone who is unfamiliar with an object can visualize it clearly with an interior view. By studying an interior visual, the audience can better repair, make changes, order parts, operate the mechanism, purchase equipment, and so on. The audience will understand what is going on under the housing, hood, or other exterior cover through the visualization.

Cross Sections

Cross sections depict the layers of a mechanism. This type of visual shows the depth and location of each layer. The content of each layer

WEB LINK

Using an Internet search engine, you can find additional sources for mechanism explanations and visuals.

Figure 6-11: *A cross section of a battery circuit*

Warmed air enters through heating ducts and rises to ceiling; floor-level cold air goes out via return ducts for reheating.

Figure 6-12: *A warm air system*

is often labeled as well. In Figure 6-11, the cross section of a battery circuit shows the layers and parts of the battery and the flow of electrons from negative to positive.

Schematics and Interior Maps

Schematics are drawings or diagrams that show an overall view of a mechanism with connections and various components labeled (see Figure 6-12). Many people assume a schematic is a diagram of only electrical circuits or wiring, but this type of diagram has a more generic use. For example, a **map** is a type of schematic with directions labeled by arrows and significant locations marked. These locations are the parts of a map.

Cutaway Drawings

Cutaway drawings slice the mechanism to show internal parts that are normally concealed from the exterior (see Figure 6-13). These drawings have a seemingly transparent exterior wall so that the interior can

Figure 6-13: *A cutaway drawing of a bathroom wall—top view*

Reproduced by permission. Carpentry *by Lewis. Delmar Publishers, Albany, New York.*

Perforated disc
Perforated cup
Screens
Aerator box

Check for clog

Spout nut
O-ring or packing
Diverter valve

Hose attachment
Hose hex nut

Figure 6-14: *An exploded drawing of a faucet*

be visible with the parts labeled. In cutaway drawings, you label the specific angle or position, called the **perspective**, of the drawing in the title. The labels may be *frontal view, side view, top view,* or something similar.

Exploded Drawings

Exploded drawings show how the parts of a mechanism fit together; the pieces are shown exploded or separated from each other in succession. Often exploded drawings appear in repair or maintenance manuals to allow users to assemble a device and replace parts. A general audience would need the exploded drawing in Figure 6-14 to replace the O-ring in a faucet.

Practice 6-12: Using Visuals

What visual would best illustrate a description of the mechanisms in the following list? You can use a cross section, schematic, cutaway drawing, exploded drawing, or exterior view for your visual. Give the reason for your choice.

EXAMPLES:

faucet	*exploded drawing*
house wiring diagram	*schematic*

1. drainage system for underground house
2. lamp socket
3. motherboard
4. automobile engine
5. tree trunk
6. blender
7. hair shaft
8. movement of water through layers of sediment
9. retractable ballpoint pen
10. highway system

Organization of a Mechanism Description

Describing a mechanism really provides an overview for the audience who may not be familiar with it. When choosing the subject, keep in mind the type of audience and the purpose for giving the description. Then divide the mechanism description into sections. Whether written or orally presented, mechanism descriptions use the following method. To explain the mechanism clearly, choose a visual that is best suited for the subject and for the specific audience.

The Introduction

The beginning of the introduction needs to attract the audience's attention—and give the name of the mechanism. Include the brand name and model number if applicable. Next, the audience needs to understand what the mechanism is, so define it in a three-part definition as you learned in Chapter 2, page 37. In the introduction, also specify who uses the mechanism, where it is used, and when it is needed. If necessary, include personal remarks and recommendations, depending on the audience. This beginning part can be completed in two or three sentences.

The Physical Characteristics

The overall explanation of the appearance provides an accurate, objective description of the physical features of the mechanism. Even though one or more visuals are usually included, they cannot show such characteristics as weight and materials. Several sentences should prepare the audience for the central part of the description—explaining the mechanism's parts.

The Major Parts

To describe the mechanism thoroughly, name the major parts. You may classify the parts by structure, function, order of importance, or a combination of methods. If you describe the parts by structure, you might indicate the parts' locations on a visual in a logical order. If the mechanism is divided by function, name each part and its function together, if possible, in the order of the tasks that each part performs. This objectively written portion of the presentation gives the overall operation of the mechanism; it is really a miniature process description, which you learned about in Chapter 5. However, do not spend too much time with this section; keep the purpose of your description in mind.

After the overview of the parts, you may select features that will set this mechanism apart from similar mechanisms if doing so makes the mechanism significantly different from others. Emphasize each of those

INFOBIT

No athlete ever would imagine entering competition without adequate preparation, including studying the opponent. Do yourself a favor—do the same when preparing a project. Study the audience well.

INFOBIT

Always keep your audience in mind, but be sure you know who your audience is. When a firm was doing a presentation at the Gillette Corporation, the salesperson repeatedly made the crucial mistake of saying he was glad to be at General Motors. Are you surprised that he didn't get the sale?

features in detail, discussing such facts as size, shape, weight, color, material, and overall appearance. Be sure to explain why these facts were selected—what makes a feature significant? A visual will help the audience understand the mechanism's features better.

The Closing

Now that you have described the mechanism, you may highlight the major parts again. Give any additional information necessary for your audience, such as price, different models or variations, guarantees—any information needed for the use of the mechanism description. Depending on the audience and the purpose, you may include personal remarks, persuasive language, and recommendations. Refer to the purpose of the description in the closing.

Practice 6-13: Describing a Common Mechanism

teamwork Your teacher will give you a paper clip. In small groups, describe this mechanism in detail, but first choose the audience and the purpose for the description. Include physical characteristics, major parts, and function, adding a visual. Prepare to share your mechanism description with the class.

SUMMARY

A mechanism description is the explanation and drawing of a mechanism, tool, organism, substance, location, or system that has a minimum of two parts. These parts work separately but together accomplish one purpose. The description clarifies the mechanism for the audience and must be accurate, clear, and concise. One or more visuals should accompany the written description. Follow these guidelines when you describe a mechanism:

* Understand the audience and purpose for the mechanism description.

* Choose a method for describing the parts.

* Use language appropriate to a mechanism description, such as analogies, objective writing, and active voice.

* Include visuals that show exterior or interior views for most descriptions.

* Organize the mechanism description to include an introduction, the physical characteristics, the major parts, and a closing.

PROJECT | MECHANISM DESCRIPTION

careers To encourage the purchase of state-of-the-art equipment, your state has given school districts the chance to apply for matching funds for equipment costing more than $500. Your instructor, Ms. Kinishi, has given you the authority to investigate the purchase of replacement equipment and to report the results to her. This mechanism would be something that is familiar to you, but not as well known to Ms. Kinishi.

After doing your investigation, you must give a presentation to Ms. Kinishi and your advisory committee. Write your presentation for a general audience with some technical knowledge. Translate your specific knowledge into more general terms that your audience will understand. Include a visual to explain the recommended mechanism thoroughly. Ms. Kinishi will use your presentation to prepare an announcement to open bids for competitive companies.

1. Review the information in this chapter. Then listen to the recorded sample presentation while your instructor shows you the visual. Study Shelley Sanchez's Sample Project Plan on page 201.

2. After consulting trade journals and catalogs, choose the mechanism for your description. Then complete the Project Plan, *Student Workbook* page 6-D, and have your teacher check it.

3. Using the information from your Project Plan, prepare notes for your presentation. Be sure to use the third person, be objective, and use the active voice. Include at least one analogy to form a clear image of the mechanism for the audience. (Chapter 2, "Communicating Definitions," will help you in describing the parts of the mechanism you have chosen.)

4. Review the types of visuals discussed earlier in this chapter. Then choose the type of visual best suited to explain your mechanism. Prepare your visual and label the parts.

5. Study the Project Guide, *Student Workbook* page 6-E, for criteria for your presentation. (Refer to Chapter 3, "Listening and Responding," starting with page 71, for planning your talk.) Rehearse your presentation individually, and then rehearse it for another student. Use your notes and visual as you would in presenting before the class. Using the Rough Draft column of the Project Guide, you and the other student should rate your rehearsed presentation.

6. Revise your notes and presentation, incorporating the changes in the presentation that your fellow student and teacher suggested. Proofread and practice the presentation with another student again, using the Final Draft column of the Project Guide.

7. Give your presentation to the class. The Project Guide will be used to evaluate your visual and your presentation.

SAMPLE PROJECT PLAN

Plan for Describing a Mechanism

		CONTENT
SUBJECT	Downdraft Ventilation paint booth for autobody spray painting	**Three-Part Definition**
		The Downdraft Ventilation paint booth is an autobody painting booth that removes spray paint components by forced downdrafts of air.
AUDIENCE	Advisory committee and instructor (a general audience with some technical knowledge)	**Physical Characteristics**
		Booth - Sheet metal, large enough to hold car, mini-van, pickup
		Ceiling - Airflow nozzles
PURPOSE	What actions should the audience take? Recommend district purchase of Downdraft Ventilation paint booth with matching state funds	Floor - Exit ports
		Doors - vehicle-sized at both ends of booth
		Major Parts and Their Purpose
FORMAT	☐ written ☒ oral ☐ other	Housing - Reduces exposure to harmful contaminants to technician and outside environment
SOURCES	"Control of Paint Overspray in Autobody Repair Shops" DHHS (NIOSH) Publication No. 96-106	Airflow input nozzles - Space inside booth enough for technician to use conventional gravity or siphon-feed paint gun
		Filters - Entering air of outside contaminants, then forced downward by downdraft
VISUALS	What visual will represent the mechanism? Labeled cross section of booth containing automobile	Exit ports - Allow removal of most paint contaminants
		Doors - Protect outside air
		Closing
ANALOGY	Size comparable to car wash booth	Advantages over present: Protects technician and outside
		Results in lower overspray concentrations and cleaner paint job
		Recommend purchase by district with matching state funds

Overview

Keep in mind that mechanisms may be tools or machinery, organisms, substances, locations, and systems. In the poem you are about to read, Rudyard Kipling, a British writer in the nineteenth century, tells about only one kind of mechanism. Although industry has greatly benefitted mankind, we should understand the problems that machines can ultimately cause. Note what Kipling is saying to us about the power of machines.

"The Secret of Machines"

We were taken from the ore bed and the mine,
We were melted in the furnace and the pit—
We were cast and wrought and hammered
to design,
We were cut and filed and tooled and gauged to fit.
Some water, coal, and oil is all we ask,
And a thousandth of an inch to give us play:
And now, if you will set us to our task,
We will serve you four and twenty hours a day!

We can pull and haul and push and lift and drive,
We can print and plow and weave and heat and
light,
We can run and jump and swim and fly and dive,
We can see and hear and count and read and write!

Do you wish to make the mountains bare their head
And lay their new-cut forests at your feet?
Do you want to turn a river in its bed,
Or plant a barren wilderness with wheat?
Shall we pipe aloft and bring your water down
From the never-failing cisterns of the snows,
To work the mills and tramways in your town,
And irrigate your orchards as it flows?
It is easy! Give us dynamite and drills!
Watch the iron-shouldered rocks lie down and
quake,
As the thirsty desert level floods and fills,
And the valley we have dammed becomes a lake.

But remember, please, the Law by which we live,
We are not built to comprehend a lie,
We can neither love nor pity nor forgive.
If you make a slip in handling us you die!
We are greater than the Peoples or the Kings—
Be humble, as you crawl beneath our rods!
Our touch can alter all created things,
We are everything on earth—except The Gods!

—Rudyard Kipling

Start-Up: Name the different machines to which the poem could be referring. How might these machines cause problems? Brainstorm solutions to the problems.

Connection: In small groups, brainstorm to create a list of problems that machines have caused in the past, cause in the present, and may cause in the future. (Don't deal with just surface problems, but with problems for humanity.)

Assume the personality of a machine of your choice. Use your imagination. Tell about one day in the business world.

Overview

Have you ever tried to read a book, view a video, or watch a ball game while someone is trying to engage you in conversation when you didn't want to participate? It's exasperating, isn't it? What can you do? Kurt Vonnegut tells a story of such a situation. Read it to find out how one man handled this annoyance.

This is a frame story, a story told within another story. As you read, think about how the inside story relates to the framework story.

"Tom Edison's Shaggy Dog"

Two old men sat on a park bench one morning in the sunshine of Tampa, Florida—one trying doggedly to read a book he was plainly enjoying while the other, Harold K. Bullard, told him the story of his life in the full, round, head tones of a public address system.

(cont'd on next page)

Bullard, who had been, before he retired, successful in many fields, enjoyed reviewing his important past.

But he faced the problem that complicates the lives of cannibals—namely: that a single victim cannot be used over and over. Anyone who had passed the time of day with him and his dog refused to share a bench with them again.

So Bullard and his dog set out through the park each day in quest of new faces. They had had good luck this morning, for they had found this stranger right away, clearly a new arrival in Florida, still buttoned up tight in heavy serge,

> "Yes," said Bullard, rounding out the first hour of his lecture, "made and lost five fortunes in my time."

stiff collar and necktie, and with nothing better to do than read.

"Yes," said Bullard, rounding out the first hour of his lecture, "made and lost five fortunes in my time."

"So you said," said the stranger, whose name Bullard had neglected to ask. "Easy, boy. No, no, no, boy," he said to the dog, who was growing more aggressive toward his ankles.

"Oh? Already told you that, did I?" said Bullard.

"Twice."

"Two in real estate, one in scrap iron, and one in oil, and one in trucking."

"So you said."

"I did? Yes, guess I did. Two in real estate, one in scrap iron, one in oil, and one in trucking. Wouldn't take back a day of it."

"No, I suppose not," said the stranger. "Pardon me, but do you suppose you could move your dog somewhere else? He keeps—"

"Him?" said Bullard, heartily. "Friendliest dog in the world. Don't need to be afraid of him."

"I'm not afraid of him. It's just that he drives me crazy, sniffing at my ankles."

"Plastic," said Bullard, chuckling.

"What?"

"Plastic. Must be something plastic on your garters. By golly, I'll bet it's those little buttons. Sure as we're sitting here, those buttons must be plastic. That dog is nuts about plastic. Don't know why that is, but he'll sniff it out and find it if there's a speck around. Must be a deficiency in his diet, though, by gosh, he eats better than I do. Once he chewed up a humidor. Can you beat it? *That's* the business I'd go into now, by glory, if the pill rollers hadn't told me to let up, to give the old ticker a rest."

"You could tie the dog to that tree over there," said the stranger.

"I get so darn' sore, at all the youngsters these days!" said Bullard. "All of 'em mooning around about no frontiers any more. There never have been so many frontiers as there are today. You know what Horace Greeley would say today?"

"His nose is wet," said the stranger, and he pulled his ankles away, but the dog humped forward in patient pursuit. "Stop it, boy!"

> *"Don't talk to me about no opportunity any more. Opportunity's knocking down every door in the country, trying to get in."*

"His wet nose shows he's healthy," said Bullard. "'Go plastic, young man!' That's what Greeley'd say. 'Go atom, young man!'"

The dog had definitely located the plastic buttons on the stranger's garters and was cocking his head one way and another, thinking out ways of bringing his teeth to bear on those delicacies.

"Scat!" said the stranger.

"Go electronic, young man!" said Bullard. "Don't talk to me about no opportunity any more. Opportunity's knocking down every door in the country, trying to get in. When I was young, a man had to go out and find opportunity and drag it home by the ears. Nowadays—"

"Sorry," said the stranger, evenly. He slammed his book shut, stood and jerked his ankle away from the dog.

"I've got to be on my way. So good day, sir."

He stalked across the park, found another bench, sat down with a sigh and began to read. His respiration had just returned to normal, when he felt the wet sponge of the dog's nose on his ankles again.

"Oh—it's you!" said Bullard, sitting down beside him. "He was tracking you. He was on the scent of something, and I just let him have his head. What'd I tell you about plastic?" He looked about contentedly. "Don't blame you for moving on. It was stuffy back there. No shade to speak of and not a sign of a breeze."

"Would the dog go away if I bought him a humidor?" said the stranger.

"Pretty good joke, pretty good joke," said Bullard, amiably. Suddenly he clapped the stranger on his knee. "Sa-ay, you aren't in plastics, are you? Here I've been blowing off about plastics, and for all I know that's your line."

"My line?" said the stranger crisply, laying down his book. "Sorry—I've never had a line. I've been a drifter since the age of nine, since Edison set up his laboratory next to my home, and showed me the intelligence analyzer."

(cont'd on next page)

"Edison?" said Bullard. "Thomas Edison, the inventor?"

"If you want to call him that, go ahead," said the stranger.

"If I *want* to call him that?"—Bullard guffawed—"I guess I just will! Father of the light bulb and I don't know what all."

"If you want to think he invented the light bulb, go ahead. No harm in it." The stranger resumed his reading.

"Say, what is this?" said Bullard, suspiciously. "You pulling my leg? What's this about an intelligence analyzer? I never heard of that."

"Of course you haven't," said the stranger. "Mr. Edison and I promised to keep it a secret. I've never told anyone. Mr. Edison broke his promise and told Henry Ford, but Ford made him promise not to tell anyone else—for the good of humanity."

Bullard was entranced. "Uh, this intelligence analyzer," he said, "it analyzed intelligence, did it?"

"It was an electric butter churn," said the stranger.

"Seriously now," Bullard coaxed.

"Maybe it *would* be better to talk it over with someone," said the stranger. "It's a terrible thing to keep bottled up inside me, year in and year out. But how can I be sure that it won't go any further?"

> *"Mr. Edison broke his promise and told Henry Ford, but Ford made him promise not to tell anyone else—for the good of humanity."*

"My word as a gentleman," Bullard assured him.

"I don't suppose I could find a stronger guarantee than that, could I?" said the stranger, judiciously.

"There is no stronger guarantee," said Bullard, proudly. "Cross my heart and hope to die!"

"Very well." The stranger leaned back and closed his eyes, seeming to travel backward through time. He was silent for a full minute, during which Bullard watched with respect.

"It was back in the fall of eighteen seventy-nine," said the stranger at last, softly. "Back in the village of Menlo Park, New Jersey. I was a boy of nine. A young man we all thought was a wizard had set up a laboratory next door to my home, and there were flashes and crashes inside, and all sorts of scary goings-on. The neighborhood children were warned to keep away, not to make any noise that would bother the wizard.

"I didn't get to know Edison right off, but his dog Sparky and I got to be steady pals. A dog a whole lot like yours, Sparky was, and we used to wrestle all over the neighborhood. Yes, sir, your dog is the image of Sparky."

"Is that so?" said Bullard, flattered.

"Gospel," replied the stranger. "Well, one day Sparky and I were wrestling around, and we wrestled right up to the door of Edison's laboratory. The next thing I knew, Sparky had pushed me in through the door, and bam! I was sitting on the laboratory floor, looking up at Mr. Edison himself."

"Bet he was sore," said Bullard, delighted.

"You can bet I was scared," said the stranger. "I thought I was face to face with Satan himself. Edison had wires hooked to his ears and running down to a little black box in his lap! I started to scoot, but he caught me by my collar and made me sit down.

"'Boy,' said Edison, 'it's always darkest before the dawn. I want you to remember that.'

"'Yes, sir,' I said.

"'For over a year, my boy,' Edison said to me, 'I've been trying to find a filament that will last in an incandescent lamp. Hair, string, splinters—nothing works. So while I was trying to think of something else to try, I started tinkering with another idea of mine, just letting off steam. I put this together,' he said, showing me the little black box. 'I thought maybe intelligence was a certain kind of electricity, so I made this intelligence analyzer here. It works! You're the first one to know about it, my boy. But I don't know why you shouldn't be. It will be your generation that will grow up in the glorious new era when people will be as easily graded as oranges.'"

> *"'I thought maybe intelligence was a certain kind of electricity, so I made this intelligence analyzer here.'"*

"I don't believe it," said Bullard.

"May I be struck by lightning this very instant!" said the stranger. "And it did work, too. Edison had tried out the analyzer on the men in his shop, without telling them what he was up to. The smarter a man was, by gosh, the farther the needle on the indicator in the little black box swung to the right. I let him try it on me, and the needle just lay where it was and trembled. But dumb as I was, then is when I made my one and only contribution to the world. As I say, I haven't lifted a finger since."

"Whadja do?" said Bullard, eagerly.

"I said, 'Mr. Edison, sir, let's try it on the dog.' And I wish you could have seen the show that dog put on when I said it! Old Sparky barked and howled and scratched to get out. When he saw we meant business, that he wasn't going to get out, he made a beeline right for the intelligence analyzer and knocked it out of Edison's hands. But we cornered him, and Edison held him down while I touched the wires to his ears. And would you believe it, that needle sailed clear across the dial, way past a little red pencil marker on the dial face!"

"The dog busted it," said Bullard.

"'Mr. Edison, sir,' I said, 'what's the red mark mean?'

(cont'd on next page)

"'My boy,' said Edison, 'it means that the instrument is broken, because that red mark is me.'"

"I'll say it was broken," said Bullard.

The stranger said gravely, "But it wasn't broken. No, sir. Edison checked the whole thing, and it was in apple-pie order. When Edison told me that, it was then that Sparky, crazy to get out, gave himself away."

"'. . . do you mean to tell me that dogs are smarter than people?'"

"How?" said Bullard, suspiciously.

"We really had him locked in, see? There were three locks on the door—a hook and eye, a bolt, and a regular knob and latch. That dog stood up, unhooked the hook, pushed the bolt back and had the knob in his teeth when Edison stopped him."

"No!" said Bullard.

"Yes!" said the stranger, his eyes shining. "And then is when Edison showed me what a great scientist he was. He was willing to face the truth, no matter how unpleasant it might be.

"'So!' said Edison to Sparky. 'Man's best friend, huh? Dumb animal, huh?'

"That Sparky was a caution. He pretended not to hear. He scratched himself and bit fleas and went around growling at ratholes—anything to get out of looking Edison in the eye.

"'Pretty soft, isn't it, Sparky?' said Edison. 'Let somebody else worry about getting food, building shelters and keeping warm, while you sleep in front of a fire or go chasing after the girls or raise the devil with the boys. No mortgages, no politics, no war, no work, no worry. Just wag the old tail or lick a hand, and you're all taken care of.'

"'Mr. Edison,' I said, 'do you mean to tell me that dogs are smarter than people?'

"'Smarter?' said Edison. 'I'll tell the world! And what have I been doing for the past year? Slaving to work out a light bulb so dogs can play at night!'

"'Look, Mr. Edison,' said Sparky, 'why not—'"

"Hold on!" roared Bullard.

"Silence!" shouted the stranger, triumphantly. "'Look, Mr. Edison,' said Sparky, 'why not keep quiet about this? It's been working out to everybody's satisfaction for hundreds of thousands of years. Let sleeping dogs lie. You forget all about it, destroy the intelligence analyzer, and I'll tell you what to use for a lamp filament.'"

"Hogwash!" said Bullard, his face purple.

The stranger stood. "You have my solemn word as a gentleman. That dog rewarded *me* for my silence with a stock-market tip that made me independently wealthy for the rest of my days. And the last words that Sparky ever spoke were to Thomas Edison. 'Try a piece of carbonized cotton thread,' he said. Later, he was torn to bits by a pack of dogs that had gathered outside the door, listening."

The stranger removed his garters and handed them to Bullard's dog. "A small token of esteem, sir, for an ancestor of yours who talked himself to death. Good day." He tucked his book under his arm and walked away.

—Kurt Vonnegut

Start-Up: The stranger gets his revenge on Bullard by pulling a joke on him. He tells him a long, rambling story that is full of absurd, unreal events. At what point in the story does Bullard realize that the stranger has played him for a fool?

In literature a description is often a very small part of the entire literary work; whereas in technical writing, it is usually a major part. At what part in the story is a description of a mechanism given?

Connection: Take a trip to your media center or a local library. Find an example of a mechanism description. Photocopy the description, if possible. Analyze the description for the following items:

* The classification of the mechanism
* The organization of the description
* Its accuracy
* Its clarity and conciseness
* Types of visuals used
* Use of analogies
* Use of the third person point of view
* Use of the active voice

Attach a word-processed (or typewritten) analysis to the photocopied mechanism description. Be sure to give the source of the description.

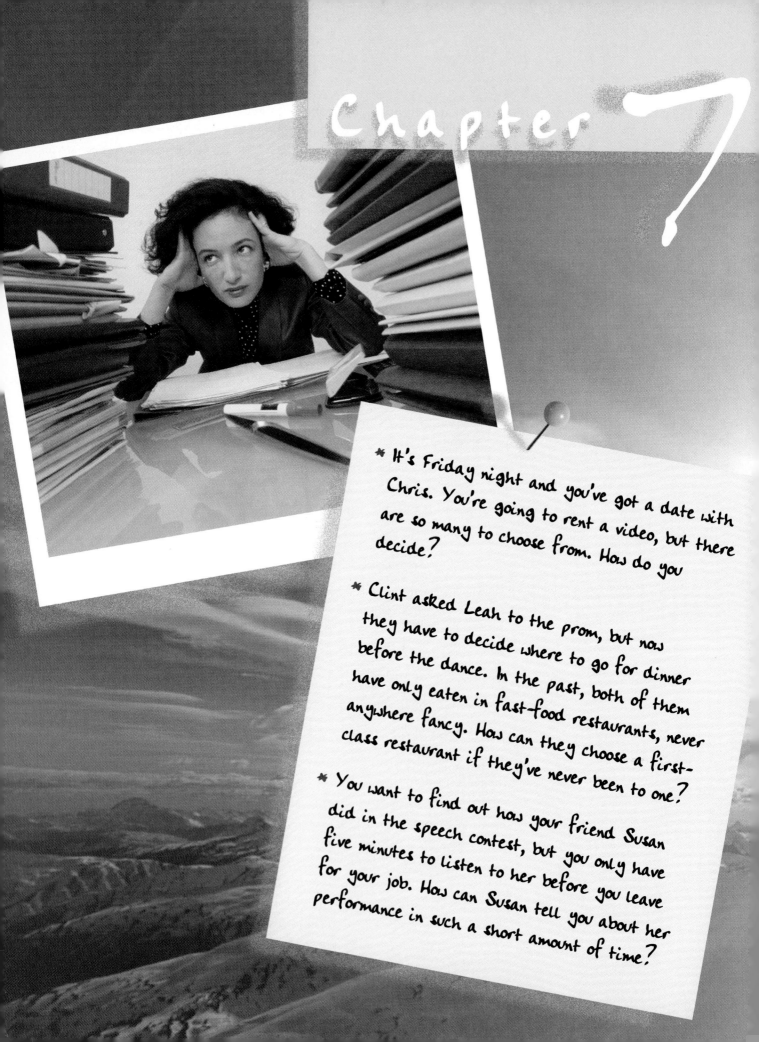

* It's Friday night and you've got a date with Chris. You're going to rent a video, but there are so many to choose from. How do you decide?

* Clint asked Leah to the prom, but now they have to decide where to go for dinner before the dance. In the past, both of them have only eaten in fast-food restaurants, never anywhere fancy. How can they choose a first-class restaurant if they've never been to one?

* You want to find out how your friend Susan did in the speech contest, but you only have five minutes to listen to her before you leave for your job. How can Susan tell you about her performance in such a short amount of time?

Summarizing

"*The difference between the right word and the almost right word is the difference between lightning and the lightning bug.*"

—MARK TWAIN, U.S. AUTHOR

Workplace Skills in This Chapter

- Utilize **resources** to search for Chapter Project information.

- Develop **interpersonal** skills through group discussions.

- Organize **information** to produce summaries.

- Examine data to improve workplace **systems**.

- Use **technology** (if available) to produce the Project.

As you complete Chapter 7, you will

* define a summary.

* use audience analysis in summarizing.

* identify the three types of summaries.

* distinguish fact from opinion.

* use aids in summarizing.

* utilize transitions in writing a summary.

* revise for brevity and conciseness.

* identify direct quotes.

* summarize oral material.

* plan, write, and revise a summary of an article.

A summary is the solution to choosing a movie, deciding on a restaurant, and describing an event. You can read a summary of a movie plot, along with an expert opinion, in a movie review. A restaurant guide in a local magazine summarizes the type of food, the atmosphere, and the pricing, which will help Clint and Leah choose a restaurant. Susan can easily summarize the highlights of her performance in the speech contest in the five minutes you have to spare before you leave for work. Providing just the highlights is summarizing. The summary focuses on the important points, saving both time and space.

Summary: A Definition

Summaries are shortened versions of speeches, writings, and events. People create summaries from original sources, such as books, articles, meetings, work orders, and reports. You include the central idea of the original source in the summary, but restate the idea. Add major points and important details, but only if they are essential to the central idea. A summary may be as brief as a single sentence or as long as several pages.

Practice 7-1: Recognizing Everyday Summaries

1. Summaries are a part of everyday life—at home, at school, and at work. We often use summaries out of habit, without thinking of them as summaries. Each of the following seven situations needs a summary in order to save time. Briefly explain how the summary would be used or created.

EXAMPLE:

> When she phones to give you directions to her office, Diane mentions every landmark and intersection. You have to ask her to repeat the directions several times, so that you can write everything down.
>
> You only need to write down major points, such as street names and buildings near major intersections or turns.

   a. Mr. Martinez asks you what his two-year-old daughter Inez has done during her day at preschool. You spend more than five minutes describing Inez's day. Since you spent this much time with Mr. Martinez, you feel obligated to spend the same amount of time with the parents of your 14 other students.

   b. Mr. Jefferson requires his students in English class to report on a book. Each student takes nearly 15 minutes to describe the novel he or she has read.

   c. The doctor has just examined one of her patients. As a medical assistant, you must write down her report and her instructions. However, the doctor has to speak very slowly and repeat so that you can keep up with her.

2. Now it's your turn. When would you use summaries in your career? Describe two situations in which summarizing would be beneficial.

INFOBIT

Al Smith, former governor of New York and presidential candidate, became a first-term state legislator in 1903. After a long day's work, instead of relaxing, he would read and master every line of the state budget. His unparalleled command of the fine print began his stellar political career. He concentrated on the details to use them in describing the big picture with seasoned legislators.

Characteristics of a Summary

A summary has the following features: it should be brief, well-written, independent of the source material, and accurate.

* **Brief.** The summary is short and to the point. Often it will be no more than one paragraph or even one sentence.

* **Well-Written.** The summary is understandable, with the most important points connected into unified paragraphs with topic sentences.

* **Independent.** The summary is clear and stands alone, independent of the original material. It contains only the main ideas of the source. For example, the summary of a conservation report requires no further explanation. A reader may decide to consult the original source for details, such as statistics. Add no new data to the source material, although you may include personal feelings in certain situations.

* **Accurate.** The summary provides an understanding of the original writing, speech, or event. It does not distort its meaning, but clearly reflects the author's intent.

Generally, follow this guideline: A summary is necessary when there is no way that you can describe the entire event, writing, or speech without shortening it considerably.

Summary Basics

The summary remains brief because it only deals with the most important information. However, while summarizing, keep in mind the subject, the audience, and the purpose of the summary.

The Subject

Writing a summary is actually writing a self-contained piece miniaturized from the original. Use fewer words than the author, but write in complete sentences. A summary need not follow the organization of the original, but it must be consistent, not confusing.

The length of the original writing, speech, or event often determines how to summarize. The more complex the original, the longer and more complex the summary. Above all, the summary must contain an accurate representation of the original. Whoever uses the summary should be able to understand it without consulting the original.

The Audience

Whoever is reading or hearing the summary (your audience) determines how you create the summary.

TECHNOBIT

In 1955, an auto mechanic needed to be able to read some 5,000 pages in auto manuals to fix any car on the road. According to Career Opportunity News, in the 1990s, auto technicians must be able to read almost 400,000 pages of high-tech instructions to fix any car on the road.

The General Audience. A summary for the general audience puts the summarized information into plain English; however, the information will not remain too general to be useful. For example, although he is not a professional baker, David Brown is interested in purchasing a bread machine to pursue his hobby. Before making his investment, he needs to know brand comparisons, frequency of repairs, prices, and other general information on household bread machines. After reading consumer buying guides and cooking magazine comparisons, David will summarize his findings to his wife Rachel so they can make the best buying choice as a family. For David Brown, simplifying through a summary is the best way to avoid confusion and to make an intelligent purchase.

The Specialist. **Basic technical style** is better for the specialist's summary. This type of summary will provide enough information for the needs of this audience, often with recommendations and/or results. The specialist needs sufficient information to make a decision.

For her commercial baking class, Sara Ramirez needs to purchase a machine that will mix the dough for the various breads and pastries her students make. In addition, she needs to make a decision: should she purchase a machine to be used only by her class, or should she buy one for the entire Food Service Department? Since Sara needs to base her decision on specific uses—such as the machine's life span, cost, and so on—she must read technical articles and make a qualified summary to her Advisory Committee. The committee, made up of professional bakers, can then make the decision whether or not to purchase the dough machine.

Practice 7-2: Determining the Audience

When you summarize, you need to make decisions about what the audience needs. Decide whether the following audiences are general or specialized.

1. Bob Fong asks you what the doctor did during his son's surgery.

2. An over-the-road truck driver has a diesel mechanic look over her truck. She needs to know what are the recommended repairs.

3. You must make a report to the purchasing department on an article reviewing the newest model of a company's laser printer.

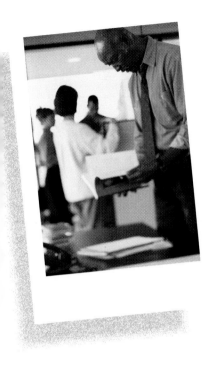

4. The social studies class needs a summary of the president's budget address.

5. Hydra Marine Motors has introduced a new inboard engine. The marine mechanics class needs to know the quality of the engine's performance.

6. You are the charge nurse on Ada Wright's floor at Riverview Hospital. You must write a report on her discharge to Sunrise Nursing Home.

7. Janet is explaining how to set up a template file for your document's outline.

The Purpose

While creating the summary, keep in mind the purpose for making it. Deciding what needs to be included and what needs to be eliminated is the most difficult decision for writing a summary. Ask yourself, "What point is the original work making?" This question will help you decide on the summary's purpose. Include only what is necessary after reading the article more than once.

Audience and purpose are often closely related when you create a summary. The patient's father who wanted a report of his son's surgery needed a general summary for the specific purpose of giving him information and reassurance. This summary was not only for a different audience but also for a different purpose. Generally the specialist needs the more thorough explanation.

Types of Summaries

The purpose of a summary determines which type of summary you write. The three types are informative, explanatory, and analytic. You can write any one of these for the general or the specialized audience. The following descriptions and examples will help you understand each type of summary in more detail.

The Informative Summary

The **informative summary** condenses the author's main ideas with no explanation or detail. Often, a sentence in the original states the central idea, or you can restate the topic sentence in your own words, making it the informative summary.

Internet news services often offer two options to read the news. One option is the quick summary, and the other is an in-depth look at the news story. The detailed news story may have links to related stories and Web sites. When searching for news services, you can find network television and radio news sites (e.g., CNN), national news television and radio stations and network sites (e.g., National Public Radio), and national news magazines (e.g., *Time*), as well as Web news services (e.g., PointCast).

An informative summary of the FHA-HERO Spring Rally program might include only the agenda.

FHA-HERO SPRING RALLY PROGRAM

The FHA-HERO Spring Rally program begins after lunch with a panel discussion and demonstration of picnic ideas, followed by the award ceremony, the election results, and the swearing in of new officers.

WEB LINK

Finding news on the Internet is often as easy as clicking on an icon on the opening page of your Internet service provider. Most opening pages provide a way to find national and international news quickly and easily. News on the Web is often summarized, with a more in-depth option offered. Investigate news on the Web—is it in-depth, summarized, or both?

Practice 7-3: Finding the Central Idea

Each of the following paragraphs contains a sentence that expresses the central idea of the paragraph. Identify this sentence.

1. Because synthetic lashes are attached to the client's own and become part of them, they last as long as the natural eyelashes, about 6 to 8 weeks. Hence, they are referred to as "semi-permanent eyelashes." However, due to the fact that natural eyelashes fall out regularly (a few each week), taking the attached false lashes with them, the false lashes should be filled in by periodic visits to the salon. (*Milady's* 466)

2. Even with all the predators eating insects, that still leaves a lot to destroy crops. For many years we have used chemicals to get rid of insects. These chemicals, called insecticides, have been very efficient. They have been the most efficient means ever devised to kill insects. In the past insecticides have been used in tremendous quantities. The overuse of insecticides has resulted in problems. Many of the older chemicals like DDT have been harmful to the environment, and wildlife suffered. These chemicals remained in the soil for many years. Rain would wash the chemicals into streams where they were absorbed by aquatic plants and animals. Animals such as water birds and eagles ate the fish and absorbed the chemicals. Reproductive cycles were disrupted because the eggs from the birds would not hatch. (Herren 75)

INFOBIT

Skilled trades workers read an average of 97 minutes a day on the job. The American Association of Career Education reports that most of the writing that these workers are required to read and understand is instructions, computer printouts, and order forms—all technical material.

3. Air is not the only source from which a heat pump can absorb heat, but it is the most popular. The most common sources of heat for a heat pump are air, water, and earth. For example, a structure located next to a large lake can remove heat from the lake and deposit it in the structure. The lake must be large enough so that the temperature will not drop appreciably in the lake. This system is a water-to-air heat pump. The water-to-air heat pump may also use a well to supply the water. If so, some consideration must be given to where the water will be pumped after it is used. A typical water-to-air heat pump uses 3 gallons of water per minute (gpm) in the heating cycle and 1.5 gpm in the cooling cycle per ton of refrigeration. (Whitman and Johnson 850)

The Explanatory Summary

An **explanatory summary** contains only information; includes no analysis or opinion. The objective writing contains the author's main ideas and essential supporting details. The explanatory summary expresses the content of the source in as little as one paragraph and rarely more than one keyed page.

An explanatory summary of the FHA-HERO Spring Rally will include more than the schedule of the day's events. Now the report includes a brief description of each event. The explanatory summary records the writer's understanding of the day's events, but without evaluation or criticism. The following is an explanatory summary of the program portion of the Rally.

> **FHA-HERO SPRING RALLY PROGRAM**
>
> A panel discussion and a demonstration of picnic ideas—food, themes, games, and events—was presented by the Bartlett District Chef Training and Child Learning classes at the annual FHA/HERO Spring Rally May 6. A certificate was presented to each class officer, with special award certificates given by each instructor. The current district officers then announced the election results. The new officers came to the platform, replacing the current officers in a ceremony.

The Analytic Summary

An **analytic summary** interprets, evaluates, or criticizes the facts of a source. After writing the information, blend in observations and/or criticisms. However, *indicate when you are stating an opinion, so that the reader can see clearly what is fact and what is opinion.* The summary should give enough information to provide an understanding of what was read, seen, or heard. Adding quotes from other sources may help to make your personal judgment more acceptable or believable, but only add enough for the audience to appreciate the criticism and to stress your point. The more specialized the audience, the more technical the summary.

An analytic summary of the FHA-HERO Rally program will combine an explanation of events with analysis. For example, now that the FHA-HERO Rally is over for this year, the officers need to make proposals for next year's event. First, the officers will need to include a brief description of each activity. Then they will need to add analysis to show the benefit of each event. Was the event a success? Could it be improved? Ultimately, these added comments will help the club decide which events to change or to keep for next year's Rally. The following is the analytic summary portion of the Rally program.

FHA-HERO SPRING RALLY PROGRAM

The Bartlett District Chef Training and Child Learning classes presented a well-planned panel discussion and demonstration of picnic ideas—food, themes, games, and events—at the annual FHA/HERO Spring Rally May 6. All members were interested both academically and personally.

Each instructor awarded a certificate to each class officer. Consistency was a problem with the awards. Some certificates were framed, some showy, some given for every minor achievement. The district officers should develop guidelines for certificates before next year's Rally.

The current district officers then announced the election results. The new officers came to the platform, replacing the current officers. The switching of officers turned out to be a very emotional ceremony. Don't change this great idea!

Distinguishing Between Fact and Opinion

The difference between fact and opinion is as important in writing as it is in speaking. A **fact** is supported by evidence; therefore, a fact can be proved. Do not base the fact's proof on what you *think* is true, but on what you *know* to be true. An **opinion** is a personal belief; it may or may not be based on fact.

CAREER C·O·N·N·E·C·T·I·O·N

Graphic design is a career in demand. Graphic designers are those lucky artists who don't have to starve to do what they love. To be successful in this profession, one not only needs to be skilled in illustration and design but also needs to be talented at absorbing and synthesizing information from many sources, such as market research and contemporary culture. The successful graphic designer blends a storehouse of knowledge, technical expertise, and creativity with the client's ideas, resulting in a productive, collaborative effort.

Opinions are personal feelings; they are biased statements. Whether opinions are based on fact or not, they cannot be proved true or false.

Facts Can Be Proved

Informative and explanatory summaries contain only facts. These facts are generally restated in your own words with no analysis or judgment added. Analytic summaries will include opinion, but that opinion is based on fact.

FACT	OPINION
The temperature is 97 degrees.	It's a scorcher outside today.
The white pine sapling needs a hole as deep as its roots when it's planted.	You need to dig a deep hole to plant the white pine sapling.

INFOBIT

A recent hiring trend for some national corporations is using graphologists to analyze prospective employees' handwriting. These firms believe that a person's handwriting gives a summary of the person's personality. For example, tense people press too hard, creative people add many flourishes, and those who don't dot their i's are often brilliant, for their hands are slower than their minds.

Please note: Defining a statement as a fact doesn't necessarily mean the statement is true. You can prove a statement of fact either true or false. You can state untrue information as a fact also; that is, you are giving false information as a fact.

FACT?

Combine blue and red to form the color purple.

You can prove this statement *true*.
Prove this statement true by combining blue and red—and producing the color purple.

FACT?

Combine blue and green to form the color purple.

You can prove this statement *false*.
Prove this statement false by combining blue and green—and making the color turquoise.

<table><tr><td>INFOBIT</td></tr></table>

A weekday edition of The New York Times *contains* more information than the average person in seventeenth-century England observed in his or her entire lifetime, according to Information Anxiety.

Practice 7-4: Proving a Fact

The following statements are expressed as facts, but can the statements be proved true or false? For each statement that is not a fact, state why it is not a fact. For each statement that is a fact, briefly describe the method that you would use to prove or disprove it.

1. An excellent peanut butter isn't overly sticky or gritty, and it doesn't leave a dry feeling in the mouth.

2. Choosing loudspeakers is the most difficult part of buying or upgrading an audio system.

3. A letter is composed of words; however, the way the letter looks on the page can be as important as the text.

4. The welder must be prepared to work in extreme heat and to risk burns from sparks.

5. If you inspect a tree's roots, you can determine if it's getting enough water.

6. Mistral font is too informal for business letters.

7. To catch melanoma quickly, check moles frequently for changes in color or size.

8. Government safety regulations deter technological expansion in the workplace.

A statement of fact can be turned into an opinion by adding a conditional word or phrase such as *maybe, in my opinion,* and *I think.*

For example:

> **FACT**
> The *Sunset Times* gave the State Cafe a three-star rating.
>
> **OPINION**
> I believe that *The Sunset Times* should give the State Cafe a three-star rating.

Details: Describing with Fact or Opinion

Objective words give details but do not analyze or judge. *Purple, metallic, closed, counterfeit,* and *frozen* are examples of such words.

Words that are **subjective** describe, but also give your interpretation, your perception of a word. These words express your opinion, which may or may not be based on fact. *Beautiful, soft, big,* and *appropriate* are examples of these expressive words.

CULTURE **C·O·N·N·E·C·T·I·O·N**

When traveling in a foreign country, try to speak a few words of the native tongue. Those few words will be much appreciated. However, the best way to ask a question in English is to print it legibly on a piece of paper. Your inquiry cannot be misinterpreted this way, and hopefully someone nearby knows some English.

Practice 7-5: Fact or Opinion?

Indicate whether the following phrases and statements are fact or opinion.

EXAMPLES:

concentric circles	fact
The computer drawing is more efficient than a board drawing.	opinion

1. the best fast-food hamburger

2. an enormous dent

3. 100 decibels

4. a raw piece of beef

5. a soft thump

6. The melting temperature of silver is 961 degrees Celsius.

7. Oak doors last the longest.

8. The average life of a Labrador retriever is ten years.

9. Probably more people use credit cards than cash to purchase furniture.

10. Orange is a more brilliant color than turquoise.

WEB LINK

Using your search engine, looking for copyright, you can investigate aspects of the copyright laws that pertain to situations that may occur in your career cluster. For example, are designs copyrighted? Are recipes? The U.S. government sponsors a copyright Web site also.

Practice 7-6: Investigating Using Fact and Opinion

teamwork In small groups, decide whether each of the statements in the following incident is a fact or an opinion. Use only the information provided in the incident to reach your conclusions. In deciding whether each of the statements is a fact or an opinion, your group must come to a consensus.

Incident: A businessman had just turned off the lights in a store when a man appeared and demanded money. The owner opened up the cash register. The contents of the cash register were scooped up, and the man sped away. A member of the police force arrived promptly.

(cont'd on next page)

1. A man appeared after the owner had turned off his store lights.

2. The robber was a man.

3. A man did not demand money.

4. The man who opened the cash register was the owner.

5. The store owner scooped up the contents of the cash register and ran away.

6. Someone opened a cash register.

7. After the man who demanded the money scooped up the contents of the cash register, he ran away.

8. While the cash register contained money, the story does not state how much.

9. The robber demanded money of the owner.

10. The story relates a series of events in which only three persons are referred to: the owner of the store, a man who demanded money, and a member of the police force.

Preparing to Summarize an Article

Summarizing an article requires reading it and finding the main ideas. If the summary is for specialists, you may add some details and examples to provide a more in-depth view. Usually, a general audience will not be interested in a detailed technical article that is filled with specialized terms and points. If you think a general audience might be interested, however, provide more of an overview of the article.

Photocopying

After you choose an article to summarize, the use of the copier can definitely be a timesaver. If the article is in the library, you may not be able to check out the material to take home. But, by photocopying the original, you can still read it in its entirety, or you can read it in sections, as with a book.

When photocopying, duplicate the entire page and page number. Also identify the source—author,

Figure 7-1: *The copier police*

ETHICS C·O·N·N·E·C·T·I·O·N

The water cooler used to be considered the center of social activity in the workplace. Now it's the copier. During the last ten years, the number of employees per copier has doubled due to more efficient, faster copier models, according to *Office Systems 96.* So while you're waiting to make that copy, you may hear who's getting promoted and who's going out with whom. However, if you want to be considered a respected worker and not a gossip, you will plan your copying during off-peak hours such as at the beginning and end of the workday or near lunchtime to avoid the rumors and the hazard of gossiping.

title, publication, and date—in the format explained in Chapter 2, pages 57 and 58. But beware! Photocopying does not replace note taking; photocopying merely supplements note taking.

Also, remember to follow the copyright law, last rewritten in 1976. As a rule, copying is legal only for your own personal use unless you have the author's permission to reprint the copyrighted information. Public libraries and media centers post a copyright restrictions warning above copiers (see Figure 7-2).

WARNING CONCERNING COPYRIGHT RESTRICTIONS

The copyright law of the United States (Title 17, United States Code) governs the making of photocopies or other reproductions of copyrighted material.

Under certain conditions specified in the law, libraries and archives are authorized to furnish a photocopy or other reproduction. One of these specified conditions is that the photocopy or reproduction is not to be "used for any purpose other than private study, scholarship, or research." If a user makes a request for, or later uses, a photocopy or a reproduction for purposes in excess of "fair use," that user may be liable for copyright infringement.

This institution reserves the right to refuse to accept a copy order if, in its judgment, fulfillment of the order would involve violation of copyright law. (U.S. Copyright Office, 37 C.F.R.)

Figure 7-2: *Copyright restrictions warning*

For works published after March 1989, using the copyright notice is optional. In other words, if a work doesn't have a copyright notice, you are to assume that the work *is* copyrighted unless you know otherwise. Copyrights protect almost any original work that is established in any tangible form, and copyright protection begins as soon as the author creates his or her work. Copyright protection extends to design and content of audio CDs, Web sites, CD-ROM, and computer programs. In fact, if you create a Web site, you have a site copyright as soon as you stop keying and save it as an HTML file.

Assuming someone else's words or ideas as your own is known as **plagiarism**. Whether you plagiarize on purpose or you plagiarize unknowingly, you are stealing when you plagiarize. If an author discovers that you have taken credit for his or her work, you could be sued. Instead, be honest, and always give credit where credit is due.

Documentation at the beginning of your summary gives the author credit for writing the original work. Use the sample Project summary on page 243 as an example of source information.

Choosing and Arranging Main Points

You have chosen the article to be summarized. To plan the summary, you must analyze the article. After you read the article and identify the organizational pattern, highlighting with marginal notes and note taking will help you prepare for the summary writing.

The Organizational Pattern

Look for signals that show how the author has arranged the article. These signals, or word clues, will reveal the main points of the article and the **organizational pattern** of the writing. Common organizational patterns include chronological order (order of time), order of importance (listing of points from most to least significant), and spatial order (arranged around placement or geography). Transitions, additional word clues explained on pages 230 and 231 of this chapter, will help you sort out an article's arrangement, as will definitions and lists of ideas.

Highlighting (Underlining)

A highlighter is a useful tool to mark the central idea and important supporting details of the text. The highlighter contains water-soluble ink that marks material permanently. The **highlighting** procedure is the same as underlining, but highlighting is simpler to do, easier to notice, and cleaner-looking than underlining. Though the traditional highlighter color is yellow, office supply stores offer many colors. If you choose, you may use different colors for different reasons, such as yellow for the central idea, blue for supporting details, and pink for evaluative support. Of course, only mark purchased or photocopied material. *Never* highlight material that you have borrowed from the library or from other people.

When highlighting material to prepare your summary, follow these steps:

1. *Read the section first.* You can only decide what to highlight after reading the material and then understanding the audience's wants and needs.

2. As a rule, *highlight about 10 percent of the original material.* If you mark nearly all the text, then you may as well mark nothing. Remember that the purpose of highlighting is to call your attention to the main points.

3. *Mark the main points for writing a summary based on your audience.* In reading a technical article, mark only broader statements

INFOBIT

For the first time, in 1991, companies spent more money on communication and computing than on industrial, mining, farm, and construction equipment, reports Price Pritchett. Such spending is evidence that the world has entered a new era: the Industrial Age has been replaced by the Information Age.

for the general audience. The specialist needs the basic technical points and possibly some examples. A review of the latest popular sports car, for example, will highlight the overall topics for the average consumer. However, the auto mechanic may need the article marked in more detail to explain such categories as drive line and body integrity.

Highlighting, then, provides a permanent record of the important ideas and helps organize notes. This procedure also saves time that would be spent taking notes or rereading the article. When you have to meet deadlines, such techniques for saving time become especially important.

Marginal Notes

Marginal notes are words and symbols written in the text or in the margins. This type of marking works best when combined with highlighting. Marginal notes can also become note taking within the article itself. Mark details if you need supporting statements or if the article is for a specialist. Figure 7-3 shows some typical symbols used in marginal notes.

Write the notes in your own words. These marginal notes can later be used to form the summary. When commenting on the article, put personal comments in the margin also—in parentheses (   ). Using parentheses will help to keep your personal thoughts and ideas separate from the article's. These marginal notes will be especially important when you write an analytic summary.

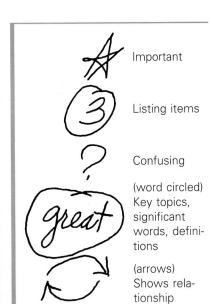

	Important
	Listing items
	Confusing
	(word circled) Key topics, significant words, definitions
	(arrows) Shows relationship

Figure 7-3: *Typical marginal note symbols*

Note Taking

If you can't mark the article itself, take brief notes, recording the main points. However, don't be so brief that you will have to reread the article to understand the meaning of the notes.

For help in **note taking**, follow these steps.

1. *First, read the entire article.*

2. *Next, take down the main ideas in your own words.* These notes may become the start of your summary statements.

3. *Then support the main ideas with some facts.* Such support is generally necessary for articles written for specialists. For example, you can write a word or two for each point of an article on the causes of high blood pressure if the summary is for a general audience. An audience of specialists, however,

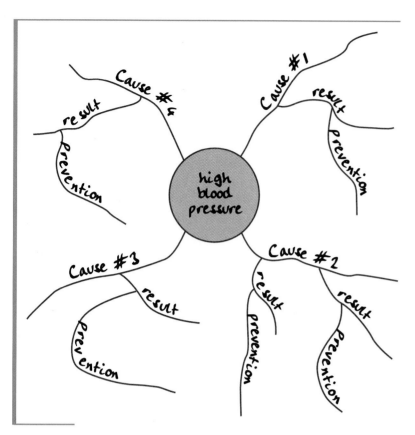

Figure 7-4: *Webbing or mapping*

will probably need a more detailed explanation of the basis for each cause of high blood pressure.

4. *Mark all of your personal reactions with parentheses.* These remarks can take the form of notes, lists, outlines, **webbing** or **mapping** (Figure 7-4), or any other organizational pattern you choose.

Practice 7-7: Marking Text and Taking Notes

Read the following paragraphs twice, taking two sets of notes for an explanatory summary—one for the general audience and one for the specialist. (Refer to your own notes and Figure 7-3 for guidelines.)

1. Sound travels readily through the air and through some materials. When airborne sound strikes a wall, the studs act as conductors unless they are separated in some way from the covering material. Electrical outlet boxes placed back to back in a wall easily transmit sound. Faulty construction, such as poorly fitted doors, often allows sound to pass through. Therefore, good construction practices aid in controlling sound. (Lewis 509)

2. Any care provided to elderly individuals should allow as much independence as possible. Assistance should be provided as needed for the individual's safety, but the individual should be allowed to do as much as possible. For example, a health care worker should encourage elderly persons to choose their clothing and dress themselves even if it takes longer. Self-stick strips can replace buttons to make the task of dressing easier and to provide more independence. This helps the elderly individual adapt to the situation and maintain a sense of self-worth. At all times, elderly individuals should be allowed as

much choice as possible to help them to maintain their individuality. (Simmers 134)

3. An alternator, rather than a generator, is used on today's vehicles to charge the battery and operate the electrical circuits. This is because the alternator is much more efficient than a generator. Alternators are much smaller, lighter in weight, and produce more current than generators. The alternator has a set of rotating poles and a stationary set of windings. In addition, there is no split-ring commutator. Solid-state diodes are used to convert ac to dc voltages. The alternator is made of a stator, rotor, and slip-ring and brush assembly. Many modern (late-model) alternators have the regulator built into the housings as a complete unit. (Schwaller 467)

Writing a Summary

The following steps are for summarizing written work, particularly articles, but the same procedure is used for summarizing other material as well.

For any summary, the following steps are necessary:

1. *Previewing.* Skim the article to look for trends and internal summaries.

2. *Reading.* Read the article thoroughly.

3. *Note taking.* Use one or more of the organizational aids such as highlighting or marginal notes to find the important points in the article.

4. *Writing (main idea).* Summarize the central idea of the article in one or two sentences. These sentences will become the informative summary. A single-sentence informative summary can be the topic sentence of an explanatory summary. Adding an opinion can form the topic sentence of an analytic summary.

5. *Writing (sections).* Restate sections or paragraphs of the article in your own words.

6. *Combining.* First, blend the main-idea sentence and the section sentences by using transitions. These word clues signal the organizational pattern and move one sentence into the next. Second, write a clincher sentence to tie the sub-points together. Finally, add an ending.

PEOPLE C·O·N·N·E·C·T·I·O·N

From ages 16 to 32, Yee-Ping Wu had a successful career as an award-winning concert pianist. Two years before she stopped touring, she developed a computerized music-notation business using software that her husband had created as a music graduate student. *Lenny's Music Toons,* a multimedia program starring a penguin, teaches children music fundamentals. Paramount Interactive purchased the program and commissioned two sequels from Yee-Ping Wu's newly formed company, Music Pen. Some of Music Pen's programs have the players creating their own multimedia storybooks with animation and music. The company has more than 300 titles. The skills Yee-Ping Wu needed as a classical pianist easily translated to producing multimedia software. "Whether you deliver art through technology or performance, it's still a multidisciplinary task."

7. *Editing.* Eliminate repetition. Make the writing to the point by taking out unnecessary words. This brevity is important to get the point across more effectively, but make sure your sentences flow smoothly from one to another. (The transitions you added in the previous step should help with the flow.) Check the summary against the original article to make sure you have not distorted its message. Also, make sure that nothing new has been added, except the personal comments *if* you are writing an analytic summary. As with any other written work, proofread carefully, checking for grammar, punctuation, and spelling.

8. *Documenting.* Be sure to give credit to the original source. Refer to pages 57 and 58 of Chapter 2 for the proper form.

9. *Formatting.* Check the entire document for placement of documentation and written copy on the page, effective use of white space, and balance of written copy and the visual (if you had one) on the page. Generally your page will begin with the title and the documentation, followed by the written copy. The sample Project on page 243 is an excellent example of a formatted written summary.

INFOBIT

According to the Occupational Outlook Quarterly, nearly two-thirds of U.S. employees work in service industries in which knowledge is the most important product.

Lucia Franco must hand in a report on a common construction hazard for a Vocational Industrial Clubs of America (VICA) safety contest. She read the article "One of the Most Frequent Construction Dangers," (see Figure 7-5) highlighted it, and took notes to begin writing her report.

After studying her article, Lucia wrote this informative summary, which showed her club advisor that she was working on her assignment.

> Gasoline and other flammable fuels are common safety hazards on construction sites.

One of the Most Frequent Construction Dangers

Think of dangerous substances on construction sites, and fumes and chemicals come to mind. Actually, the most commonplace hazardous substance is gasoline. Experts from the Occupational Health and Safety Administration (OSHA) report that gasoline is misused on many construction sites. Gasoline caused more than one-sixth of hazardous substance accidents in the last year.

These cases are some examples:

- A worker used gasoline to destroy a hornet's nest on top of a septic tank. When he opened the tank, it burst and he was severely burned.
- A laborer on a construction site used gasoline to clean his tar-covered clothes. He was seriously burned when a sudden fire covered him in flames.
- Sparks from sawing through steel ignited a nearby gasoline can, causing a worker's third-degree burns.

Gasoline fumes are also hazards. These vapors can collect and grow. Sparks and heat can flare up instantly. To prevent these fires, fast cleanups and suitable ventilation are crucial safety procedures. If necessary, workers should use masks.

Other fuels, such as alcohol and kerosene, are often found on building sites. These substances are also flammable. The chemicals—heptane, benzene, and acetone, found in paints and sealants—cause problems similar to those with gasoline. Exposure to some flammable and combustible materials can cause other health hazards over time.

Contractors often assume that workers know the rules for using gasoline. They then overlook teaching safety rules for its use. Workers need training for managing spills and refilling heated motors. Using tools that generate sparks recklessly can also be a problem. Employers should allow workers to smoke in a safe place that is *not* near gasoline.

To prevent dangerous accidents, construction crews should require training in the cautious handling of gasoline and other hazardous substances.

Figure 7-5: *"One of the Most Frequent Construction Dangers" article*

Next, Lucia expanded her informative summary to form an explanatory summary, the basis of her safety paper.

> Gasoline and other flammable fuels are common safety hazards on construction sites. Spills, sparks, and smoking are dangerous because fires can occur. Not only is the liquid a danger, but also the vapors from gasoline and other combustible fuels can be ignited. In order to have safer handling of these materials, contractors need to instruct crews on how to use these fuels.

Lucia next added her own comments, which advised the reader on how to prevent flammable material accidents on the job site. She then used the analytic summary for her construction technology class.

> After instructing each new employee about the hazards, contractors should post warning signs. For example, signs should read "No Smoking" and "Let tools cool down before refueling." Also, employers should store flammable materials in a separate, well-ventilated area.

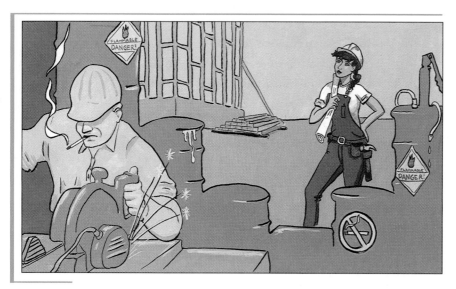

Figure 7-6: *Construction hazards*

A written summary needs to be smooth, without extraneous words. Transitions allow individual statements to blend into one paragraph, eliminating extra words and emphasizing the main idea. However, the summary must remain true to the original article. An analytic summary includes opinions.

Transitions

Transitions are the road signs of writing; they tell the reader in what direction the writer's ideas are going. These words and phrases logically connect separate statements into related ideas, helping the ideas flow smoothly to focus on the relationships to emphasize.

The following list gives some examples of common transitions that can help you arrange information clearly and logically.

COMMON TRANSITIONS

To add ideas, use
    also
    and
    furthermore
    in addition
    moreover

To contrast ideas, use
    but
    conversely
    however
    on the contrary
    on the other hand
    still
    while

To compare ideas, use
    besides
    in the same way
    similarly
    then

To reveal cause (and effect), use
    as a result
    because
    consequently
    hence
    since
    that
    therefore
    thus

To show time sequence, use
    after
    a year later
    before this
    formerly
    later
    meanwhile
    next
    now
    occasionally
    subsequently
    then
    when

To illustrate, use
    for example
    for instance

To introduce a condition, use
    although
    if
    nevertheless
    under the circumstances

To sum up ideas, use
    finally
    in conclusion
    in summary

The following summary is taken from Lucia's first rough draft on the topic of flammable fuel safety. Notice that the paragraph is written without transitions.

> Gasoline and other flammable fuels are common safety hazards on construction sites. Spills cause danger. Sparks can be dangerous and cause fires. Smoking can cause fires. Gasoline and combustible fuels are a danger. The vapors of these materials can be ignited. Safer handling of these materials is needed. Contractors need to instruct crews on how to use these fuels.

By reorganizing materials and adding transitions, Lucia made her writing smoother and more coherent. In the final version, which includes her analytic comments, the transitions are underlined.

> Gasoline and other flammable fuels are common safety hazards on construction sites. Spills, sparks, <u>and</u> smoking are dangerous <u>because</u> fires can occur. <u>Not only</u> is the liquid a danger, <u>but also</u> the vapors from gasoline <u>and</u> other combustible fuels can be ignited. <u>In order to</u> have safer handling of these materials, contractors need to instruct crews on how to use these fuels. <u>After</u> instructing each new employee about the hazards, contractors should post warning signs. <u>For example</u>, signs should read "No Smoking" <u>and</u> "Let tools cool down before refueling." <u>Also</u>, employers should store flammable materials in a separate, well-ventilated area.

By putting *and* in her second sentence, Lucia combines several fire hazards and points out the causes of the fires. *Not only/but also* introduces additional causes. The phrase *in order to* establishes a cause-and-effect relationship. In the analytic section of her summary, Lucia uses these additional signals: for sequence, *after;* to introduce examples, *for example;* and to add an idea, *also.*

INFOBIT

"What is written without effort is in general read without pleasure."

SAMUEL JOHNSON

Practice 7-8: Finding Transitions

1. List the transitions in the following paragraphs. Then write the signal that each transition makes. What relationships do the transitions make within the paragraph? For an example, use Lucia's paragraph with transitions added.

   a. Most children can understand and respond to a number of words before they can produce any. Their first words include names of objects and events in their world (people, food, toys, animals). Then the child begins to overextend words, perhaps using "doggy" to refer to all animals. Finally, single words can be used as sentences: "Bye-bye" can refer to someone leaving, a meal the child thinks is finished, the child going away, a door closing. (Gordon and Williams-Browne 405)

   b. One common result of improper image placement, particularly on small presses, is ink depletion. As the ink roller revolves over the sheet, it has enough ink to properly print the first halftone on the lead edge of the sheet, but not enough ink to print the remaining images in line with the halftone on the tail edge of the sheet. The ink becomes depleted from the ink rollers faster than it can be replaced from the ink reservoir. The result is good ink coverage on the lead edge of the sheet, but poor ink coverage on the tail edge of the sheet. Correct image position during the design stage can balance ink distribution needs to avoid ink depletion. (Adams, Faux, and Rieber 65)

   c. Another way to divide available techniques is by "trial" and "usage" promotions. For example, coupons and sampling are considered quite effective in getting new customers to try a service or product. On the other hand, contests and sweepstakes are good at convincing present customers or trade channels to use services more often. Once again, an organization may decide to use a combination of "trial" and "usage" promotions. (Morrison 409)

2. Using transitions makes your writing clearer, especially when you are preparing a summary. Without transitions, your summary will consist of a list of separate ideas in the form of sentences. To make the sentences meaningful to the reader, you need to add transitions. Rewrite the following paragraphs, adding transitions, combining sentences, and moving ideas to make the summary clearer.

a. I believe that in the really important areas of life women are superior to men. Why? They live longer. According to the Centers for Disease Control, the life expectancy of a female baby is now some seven years longer than it is for a male baby. These government health figures show that women are more able to resist major diseases. On the average, girls learn to count and to read earlier than boys do. Women seem less likely than men to solve their problems with violence. In cartoons, women hurl the rolling pins. In real life, men hurl the bombs.

b. Aspirin was first introduced in Germany 90 years ago. Aspirin has proved to be a miracle drug. Aspirin banishes headaches, reduces fever, and eases pain. Aspirin does have some dangers. If taken in excess, aspirin can cause stomach upset, bleeding ulcers, and even death. Aspirin is responsible for more good than harm. It may prevent heart attacks. It is possible that aspirin may contain properties that prevent blood clots and heart attacks caused by them. Blood clots clog arteries in the heart.

Brevity and Conciseness

Using two, six, or even ten words when one word would do is sometimes called *gobbledygook*. **Brevity** is the opposite; it means using as few words as possible.

An office manager sent a memo that included this wordy paragraph to her district manager:

> Mr. James has contacted me verbally with respect to the enclosed disclosure of acceleration. That has generated the attached rejoinder, seemingly insinuating that he desires to waive the responsibility.

In other words, Mr. James turned down the job!

Summaries condense information into a few sentences. Only the most crucial words and phrases should be included in a summary—not like the following wordy paragraph:

> A chapter summary in a textbook will save students time when they need to review for a test. There are definitions of terms that the author feels are important. The major points that the author stresses are focused on in the chapter summary. This section of each chapter is a valuable tool.

INFOBIT

"Remember the waterfront shack with the sign, 'Fresh Fish Sold Here.' Of course it's fresh, we're on the ocean. Of course it's for sale, we're not giving it away. Of course it's here, otherwise the sign would be someplace else. The final sign: 'fish.'"

PEGGY NOONAN, U.S. AUTHOR AND PRESIDENTIAL SPEECHWRITER

This paragraph includes entirely too many unnecessary words for a summary. A shortened version would appear as follows:

> A real timesaver for studying, the chapter summary focuses on the major points and essential terms and definitions of the chapter.

The main idea of each paragraph is the same, but there are fewer words.

Practice 7-9: Deleting for Brevity and Adding Transitions

Rewrite the following summaries by eliminating unnecessary words, combining related sentences, and adding transitions. Use the summaries that appeared previously in this chapter for examples.

1. You can prepare people to eat for the future. Teach them to avoid foods that can cause health problems. Teach them to avoid caffeine. Teach them to avoid alcohol. Teach them to avoid foods that are high in cholesterol. Teach them to avoid junk food. You can encourage them to plan nutritious meals. You can encourage them to drink lots of water. People will live longer, healthier lives.

2. Some employees need to take medication at work. Some medications can cause a worker to be drowsy. That drowsiness can cause accidents. The accidents lead to safety problems and downtime. The employee may need to take over-the-counter medicine. Workplace accidents can be lessened. Employers should be aware of side effects of medications. Employees need to inform supervisors of their medication. Regulations should be established for using medication. Fewer accidents will be the result.

3. Microwave ovens have many uses. Mostly they are timesavers. The two major uses for microwaves are for defrosting and reheating. The foods most often cooked in the microwave are popcorn and liquids being heated. Microwaves are used primarily for convenience. A cook can creatively fix meals using the microwave. It was initially promoted to save energy.

Using Quotes

The article that you are summarizing may have some material that you do not want to change. This material can be quoted directly or paraphrased. However, credit must be given to the author to avoid plagiarism.

Direct quotes are the exact words of a writer or speaker. They should be included within a summary if no other words can describe the original, *except* the original. When writing a direct quote, enclose the exact words within quotation marks.

A **paraphrase** is rewriting the author's words in your own words. In paraphrasing, all words are changed from the original.

If three or more words are used in the same order as the original, then make this a direct quote. Always compare the original with your copy to make sure you have not miscopied the source. Using direct quotes gives specific recognition to the author.

Writing Without Bias

Being true to the original article and accurate as to the statements and facts given is important when you are summarizing. One way to slant or distort a summary is to leave out portions that don't agree with what you wish that the article had said. This omission results in a biased summary. For example, Jermayne read the article shown in Figure 7-7 about workplace environmental health.

INFOBIT

"Excellence is not a destination you arrive at . . . It is the benchmark for your journey."

EARVIN "MAGIC" JOHNSON, U.S. BASKETBALL PLAYER

Workplace Injury and Disease:

A Mainstream Public Health Problem

In today's society, Americans are working more hours than ever before. The workplace environment profoundly affects health. Each of us, simply by going to work each day, may face hazards that threaten our health and safety. Risking one's life or health should never be considered merely part of the job.

In 1970, Congress passed the Occupational Safety and Health Act to ensure Americans the right to "safe and healthful working conditions," yet workplace hazards continue to inflict a tremendous toll in both human and economic costs.

Occupational injury and disease create needless human suffering, a tremendous burden upon health care resources, and an enormous drain on U.S. productivity. Yet, to date, this mainstream public health problem has escaped mainstream public attention. Workplace injuries and diseases are neither inevitable nor acceptable. The time has come to protect one of our most valuable resources: the American worker.

Figure 7-7: *"Workplace Injury and Disease" article*

Source: New Directions at NIOSH. United States. National Institute for Occupational Safety and Health (NIOSH). Washington: NIOSH, 1996.

After reading the article, Jermayne wrote this summary:

> Going to work every day affects American workers' health. Despite government action, injuries and deaths occur every day on the job. As a result, health care costs escalate and productivity decreases.

The original article contains statements and statistics, but nowhere does it state that going to work every day affects workers' health or that

INFOBIT

"Be careful that you write accurately rather than much."

ERASMUS

workplace injuries directly increase health care costs or decrease productivity. By adding a slant to the information from the original article, Jermayne added bias in his summary. The summary by itself does not appear biased, but after one compares it with the original, the slant is apparent. A reader should not have to check the original article to have accurate information. *The summary should be just as accurate as the original.*

Practice 7-10: Identifying Slanted Summaries

After reading each of the following paragraphs and their related summaries, decide if the summary is slanted. Write down the clues that helped you determine if there was bias. Use Jermayne's biased summary as an example. Your teacher may have you work with a partner.

1. There is a mistaken notion that using clippers to "clean" the neckline makes the hair grow in thicker on the neck. This is not true, because the amount of human hair can only be as great as the number of follicles in the area. Use of clippers or any other implement does not increase the number of follicles. (*Milady's* 94)

   Using clippers for trimming the neckline results in a greater number of follicles, and thus thicker hair.

2. By far, the most significant piece of credit legislation is the federal Consumer Credit Protection Act. Part of this act is known as the 1968 Truth-in-Lending Act, and its two primary purposes are to inform consumers about terms of a credit agreement and to require creditors to specify how finance charges are computed. The act requires a finance charge to be stated as an annual percentage rate and requires creditors to specify the procedures for correcting billing mistakes. (Longenecker, Moore, and Petty 326)

   The Consumer Credit Protection Act is the most important federal credit statute. It tells consumers about contract terms, informs them of how creditors calculate finance charges, requires that finance charges be written in annual percentage rates, and requires creditors to explain how to correct mistakes in bills.

3. A Pell Grant is an award to help first-time undergraduates pay for their education after high school. A first-time undergraduate is one who has not earned a bachelor's or first professional degree. (A professional degree would include a degree in such fields as pharmacy or dentistry, for example.) Eligibility for those who receive a Pell Grant for the first time is usually limited to 5 or 6 years of undergraduate study, not

including remedial coursework. For many students, a Pell Grant provides a "foundation" of financial aid to which aid from other federal and non-Federal sources may be added. Unlike loans, grants don't have to be paid back. (United States Department of Education 22)

The Pell Grant is a federal financial aid award for undergraduate and/or graduate study. All coursework is paid for for the first-time student.

Summarizing Oral Information and Delivering Oral Summaries

So far you have read about written summaries of written articles. You can also summarize oral information. Summarizing oral material is paraphrasing of a listening situation, such as a discussion, a conversation, a speech, instructions, or a lecture, and the visual clues that may be part of the situation. Your summary of oral information may be a verbal presentation and/or a written summary. For example, you may summarize a meeting orally to a coworker and in writing as the minutes of the meeting.

Job situations often require you to deliver summaries orally. For example, in an interview, you may verbally summarize your qualifications to a prospective employer rather than presenting them in writing.

Voice mail is a type of summary presented orally. With this system, a caller leaves messages at a central number where they are posted to a mailbox within the telephone system. Voice mail often has a time limit, so the caller must plan the message and summarize the information in order to avoid being rambling and unorganized. Using the techniques discussed in Chapter 3 for condensing information for electronic phone messages will also help in delivering summaries orally.

Use the following guidelines to summarize oral information.

* *Listening to summarize is more demanding than listening for pleasure.* An active listener remembers the main points. Taking notes will help, but that is not always possible.

* *Prepare to remember.* Relate what the speaker says to the reasons for listening.

* *Clump information into large sections.* This is easier when the speaker has major, organized points. Listening for clues to the organization of an oral presentation will help you prepare an effective summary.

WEB LINK

Searching for information on a product or a manufacturer can be as easy as inserting the company or product name in http://www._____.com. Try it with your favorite food, car manufacturer, or television station.

* *Create a mental picture of someone performing the information given.* This picture will help you remember and understand the main points.

* *Listen to the speaker with an open mind, and note the interest level.* When the speaker becomes enthusiastic, then an important point is being given. But don't react to an idea before the speaker is finished. Instead, wait until the speaker concludes to make sure you have heard everything.

Practice 7-11: Writing Summaries of Oral Material—News Stories

1. Listen to the news recordings that your teacher will play for you. Take notes on the news stories, being sure to write the following:

   a. The headline of the story

   b. The major points

   c. The organizational pattern

   d. The key transitions

2. Write an explanatory summary of each of the news stories. Be as specific and as brief as possible.

3. Compare your summary with a partner's. Note the following:

   a. Did you have the same major points? If not, what is the difference?

   b. What details did you both omit?

Practice 7-12: Writing Summaries of Oral Material—Situations

Your teacher will play four recordings describing different situations. After you have listened to all the recordings, you will write an explanatory summary of each situation. Listen carefully, and take notes. You will need only some of the information for your summaries. The narrator will provide you with the audience and purpose of the summary for each situation.

Practice 7-13: Writing Summaries of Oral Material—Discussions

In this Practice, you will extend what you have learned about oral summaries to a personal situation. Divide into groups of five or six people. Your teacher will give your group a topic to discuss for five minutes. During that discussion time, each group member will take his or her own notes.

After the teacher ends the discussion, spend the next ten minutes organizing and editing your notes. Then summarize the discussion in an analytic summary. You will not have to turn in the summary, so content is more important than proper form, spelling, or grammar. At the end of the time, each group member will present his or her summary. Compare results with the group, and discuss the similarities and differences.

SUMMARY

The central idea and the major points of a speech, writing, or event become the summary, a shortened version of the original material. You may present a summary in oral or written form. Whatever the form, follow these guidelines when you summarize:

* Consider subject, audience, and purpose in summarizing.

* Choose the type of summary—informative, explanatory, or analytic—according to the purpose for the summary.

* Be sure that the summary is brief, accurate, unbiased, and easily understood without consulting the original source.

* Use transitions to link the summary into one unit.

WORKS CITED

Adams, J. Michael, David D. Faux, and Lloyd J. Rieber. *Printing Technology*. Albany: Delmar Publishers, 1996.

Gordon, Ann Miles, and Kathryn Williams-Browne. *Beginnings and Beyond*. Albany: Delmar Publishers, 1996.

Herren, Ray V. *Exploring Agriscience*. Albany: Delmar Publishers, 1997.

Lewis, Gaspar. *Carpentry*. Albany: Delmar Publishers, 1995.

Longenecker, Justin G., Carlos W. Moore, and J. William Petty. *Small Business Management*. Cincinnati: South-Western College Publishing, 1997.

Milady's Standard Textbook of Cosmetology. Albany: Delmar Publishers, 1995.

Morrison, Alastair. *Hospitality and Travel Marketing*. Albany: Delmar Publishers, 1996.

Schwaller, Anthony E. *Automotive Technology*. Albany: Delmar Publishers, 1993.

Simmers, Louise. *Diversified Health Occupations*. Albany: Delmar Publishers, 1993.

United States Department of Education. *The Student Guide*. 1997.

Whitman, Williams C. and William M. Johnson. *Refrigeration and Air Conditioning Technology*. Albany: Delmar Publishers, 1995.

careers Your supervisor has asked your opinion of new procedures, products, or systems that will improve the work situation or will help with safety problems. After reviewing various printed materials, find an article that you can summarize for your manager.

Some possible sources of information include

- trade magazines.
- popular magazines.
- newspaper articles.
- product inserts.
- manufacturers' Web sites.
- *Consumer Reports* magazine.

1. Carefully read the sample Project article, "Stress Management: What Is Stress?" (page 241), the Sample Project Plan (page 242), and the Sample Summary (page 243).

2. Highlight or take notes on your article.

3. Begin filling out the Project Plan on *Student Workbook* page 7-A. Will a drawing or photo help your reader understand your summary? If so, plan a visual.

4. Have your teacher check the Project Plan.

5. Using the information on your Project Plan, write a rough draft.

6. Using the Rough Draft column of the Project Guide (*Student Workbook* page 7-B), check your own work with one or more classmates. Have them record all their comments and suggested changes on your Project Guide and rough draft. Ask them to write a constructive comment on the rough draft, and sign it. Have your teacher check your rough draft.

7. Revise and edit your rough draft, incorporating the changes that your classmates and your teacher suggested.

8. Using the Final Draft column of the Project Guide, proofread your work. Make any needed corrections.

9. Turn in the final draft, along with the Project Guide.

Stress Management

What Is Stress?

Stress happens when the demands of life get out of control. Changes occur, causing problems. As a result, stress can take over. However, the changes are not the problem; the problem is the way we react to the changes.

Changes in Life

Daily arguments, a new spouse, loss of a job—even a lottery win can cause stress. The big events and the small ones, the positive and the negative ones, are all changes that create stress.

Both physically and mentally, stress gains an advantage. Characteristics of stress often include always being tired, an acid stomach, an achy neck and shoulders, headaches, and an overwhelming irritated feeling. Our reactions to stress are often negative, such as smoking, overeating, losing sleep, and drinking too much—and the reactions often harm us more than the stress itself.

The result? We fall prey to illnesses like colds and flu more easily. Higher levels of stress increase the chances of having a heart attack, a stroke, cancer, or an ulcer. Asthma sufferers may endure more complications and have attacks more often.

Causes of Stress

You need to determine the causes of your stress before you attempt to manage it. Besides life-changing events, your feelings can trigger stress. Here are some common causes of stress:

- Problems in the family or at work
- Lack of time
- Uncertainty over money
- Increased responsibilities
- Personality conflicts
- Sudden changes

Stress Reactions

You can turn every negative reaction to stress into a positive solution. You don't even have to be Mary Poppins to do it!

Managing Stress

Work with stress positively. Everyone has problems in life, but the way we approach them will reduce our stress.

1. Understand

Why worry when worry won't solve the problems? Accept the things that you cannot control. Talk to yourself. The more you use positive self-talk, the more you shatter stress.

2. Focus

Here's that positive word again. Yes, focus on the positive. Look at the bright side of the supposed downside. What are better ways of managing the situation? Looking positively helps the answers come more easily.

3. Maintain a Positive Outlook

Why worry about problems that may never occur? Just keep things in perspective. When a problem arises, ask yourself, "In five years, will this matter?" If the answer is no, then move on.

If stressful events are controllable, then work on changing them. Take action to eliminate the problem. If the events are not in your control, then accept them positively with the attitude that you can reduce the stress.

LINDA HOCKENBERRY

If you are	then
hitting and screaming,	seek counseling.
grouchy,	try getting enough sleep.
overeating,	exercise with a friend.
tight in the neck and shoulders,	stretch your muscles with yoga.
spending too much money,	budget or go to credit counseling.
having repeated headaches	try controlled, slow breathing.
never assuming the blame,	think things over and take responsibility.
in a hurry and worrying,	make priorities and organize your days.
domineering,	allow others to share decision making.
pessimistic,	talk to yourself in a positive way.

Figure 7-9: *"Stress Management" article*

Plan for Summarizing

SUBJECT	Summary of "Stress Management"	
AUDIENCE	Manager	
PURPOSE	What actions should the audience take after reading the summary? Use article's summary to improve work situation.	
FORMAT	☒ written ☐ oral ☐ other	
SOURCES	Publication Title: <u>Wellness Publications</u> Article Title: "Stress Management" Author: Linda Hockenberry Date: August 1997 Page Numbers: 47	
VISUALS	What visuals, if any, will make the summary more effective? None	

CONTENT

Central Idea:

Our lives have many changes that could cause stress, but we can manage it through coping skills.

Main Supporting Details:

Causes
- Life changes, like family and money problems
- How we cope with the pressures in life, like problems at work and not enough time

Common Symptoms
- Tired
- Upset stomach, headaches

Coping skills
- Solutions to negative reactions
- Positive attitude
- Understand what we can't change

Look at things that matter

Keep things in perspective

Opinions and Evaluations (analysis):

Good to educate department

Will help with pressures of change in production and new personnel

Audience's Call to Action:

Need education program for department. Form a committee and set up agenda and timelines as soon as possible.

Hockenberry, Linda. "Stress Management." *Wellness Publications*. Aug. 1997: 47.

Changes in people's lives can cause stress, but stress can be managed through attitude and coping skills. The problem is not the pressures in our lives but how we cope with them.

Life changes, such as family and money problems, can cause stress. Also, the pressure of problems at work and not having enough time to accomplish what we want to do can produce stress if we don't cope well. Symptoms of stress include being constantly tired and having an upset stomach and headaches.

Attitude and coping are keys to managing stress. There are many solutions to stress's negative reactions. By adopting a more positive attitude, we will lessen the stress reaction. We need to understand that, unfortunately, there are those things we cannot change. Therefore, we just need to live with them. Instead, we should look at things that matter and keep things in perspective. If they matter, then handle them more positively.

A stress management program is a good policy that will benefit our department in the long run. We need to form a committee and set an agenda and timelines as soon as possible to start an education program. A stress management program will help with the pressures of change in production and with the addition of new personnel. The program can't start soon enough.

Overview

Henrik Ibsen, who was born in Norway in 1828, wrote the first great plays about the problems people have in everyday life. When he began writing plays, most of them were romantic stories written just to entertain audiences. His plays departed from the norm, using language that seemed as real as your own, and his characters' problems could be anyone's.

Ibsen's plays are still being performed. They are especially important because they have been so influential in the writing of drama.

from *A Doll's House*

In the following final scene from the play, Nora summarizes to her husband what she perceives her life to have been thus far.

Nora: That is just it; you have never understood me. I have been greatly wronged, Torvald—first by Papa and then by you.

Torvald: What! By us two—by us two who have loved you better than anyone else in the world?

Nora (shaking her head): You have never loved me. You have only thought it pleasant to be in love with me.

Torvald: Nora, what do I hear you saying?

Nora: It is perfectly true, Torvald. When I was at home with Papa he told me his opinion about everything, and so I had the same opinions; and if I differed from him I concealed the fact, because he would not have liked it. He called me his doll child, and he played with me just as I used to play with my dolls. And when I came to live with you—

Torvald: What sort of an expression is that to use about our marriage?

Nora (undisturbed): I mean that I was simply transferred from Papa's hands to yours. You arranged everything according to your own taste, and so I got the same tastes as you—or else I pretended to. I am really not quite sure which—I think sometimes the one and sometimes the other. When I look back on it it seems to me as if I have been living here like a poor woman—just from hand to mouth. I have existed merely to perform tricks for you,

Torvald. But you would have it so. You and Papa have committed a great sin against me. It is your fault that I have made nothing of my life.

Torvald: How unreasonable and how ungrateful you are. Nora! Have you not been happy here?

Nora: No, only merry. And you have always been so kind to me. But our home has been nothing but a playroom. I have been your doll wife, just as I was Papa's doll child; and here the children have been my dolls. I thought it great fun when you played with me, just as they thought it great fun when I played with them. That is what our marriage has been, Torvald.

> *I have been your doll wife, just as I was Papa's doll child . . .*

—Henrik Ibsen
(translated by Peter Watts)

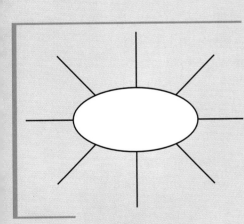

Figure 7-10: *A spidergram*

Start-Up: Nora summarizes her life, as she sees it thus far, for her husband Helmer Torvald. This scene occurs at the end of the play. Nora had forged her father's name in order to borrow money to take Torvald on a trip to bring him back to health. Torvald had found out about the forgery and condemned Nora for it, even though she had done it for him. He even went so far to say that she was not a fit mother because of this crime. As it turned out, the man who held the forged note had a turn of conscience and returned the note to Nora and Torvald. No harm done. Torvald immediately indicated that his comments about her no longer held true, and she could return to being his little "skylark," "spendthrift," and "doll." The above scene then occurs.

Connection: Form groups of three. Choose one student to draw a spidergram (Figure 7-10) on which the group will show the main ideas that summarize Nora's life. Write the topic being summarized on the body of the spider, and on the legs write each main idea.

Overview

Poetry, the brief form of literature, can often summarize wrenching experiences in fewer lines than a short story or novel. In this poem, Robert Frost presents a simple story: a boy, a buzz saw, a tragedy.

"Out, Out—"

The buzz saw snarled and rattled in the yard
And made dust and dropped stove-length sticks of wood,
Sweet-scented stuff when the breeze drew across it.
And from there those that lifted eyes could count
Five mountain ranges one behind the other
Under the sunset far into Vermont.
And the saw snarled and rattled, snarled and rattled,
As it ran light, or had to bear a load.
And nothing happened: day was all but done.
Call it a day, I wish they might have said
To please the boy by giving him the half hour
That a boy counts so much when saved from work.
His sister stood beside them in her apron
To tell them "Supper." At the word, the saw,
As if to prove saws knew what supper meant,
Leaped out of the boy's hand, or seemed to leap—
He must have given the hand. However it was,
Neither refused the meeting. But the hand!
The boy's first outcry was a rueful laugh,
As he swung toward them holding up the hand,
Half in appeal, but half as if to keep
The life from spilling. Then the boy saw all—
Since he was old enough to know, big boy
Doing man's work, though a child at heart—
He saw all spoiled. "Don't let them cut my hand off—
The doctor, when he comes. Don't let him, sister!"
So. But the hand was gone already.
The doctor put him in the dark of ether.

He lay and puffed his lips out with his breath.
And then—the watcher at his pulse took fright.
No one believed. They listened at his heart.
Little—less—nothing!—and that ended it.
No more to build on there. And they, since they
Were not the one dead, turned to their affairs.

—Robert Frost

In the poem above, a young boy loses his hand in a tragic accident that results in his death. The buzz saw appears to be almost human through the word choices that Frost uses to personify it. The family seems to accept the death as part of living.

Start-Up: Since summaries are the gist of things, we make them as short and concise as possible. In the English classroom, this is called a *précis*. In the workplace, for clarity and to save time, money, and labor, technical writing must often be as succinct as possible.

Connection: You are starting to work as a technical writer for Gourmet Fine Foods Company. Your first assignment is to summarize the directions sent from the manufacturer for a pint-size jar of Dreamy Asparagus Tips in Creamy Sauce. Your job is to edit the directions so that they can be placed on the rim of the jar lid.

The jar label has already been designed and printed. The top of the jar lid is reserved for advertising. The company's marketing department has left you the rim of the lid for instructions for the buyer. All essential information from the following directions must be kept.

> When stored at normal refrigerator temperature this food will retain its taste, lightness, color, and value as a food product; but when exposed to air or kept at freezing temperature, it will suffer a chemical change that may render it unfit for human consumption. It is therefore recommended that it be kept at refrigerated temperature when not being used. However, it may be stored at room temperature safely if the lid has never been removed.

Now, let's see how you, keeping all essential information, can edit these directions to fit on the rim of a pint- or quart-jar lid. A professional technical writer accomplished this job with seven words that included all the essential information.

Using Forms

Forms are big business. Whole companies exist whose employees do nothing but design, print, and produce forms for other businesses.

As you complete Chapter 8, you will

* read a variety of forms.
* identify the purposes of standard forms.
* complete forms accurately and legibly.
* critique the design of a form.
* design a usable form.

Workplace Skills in This Chapter

* Understand how **resources** can be better used through efficient and effective form design.

* Practice **interpersonal skills** as you work with others to design a form.

* Use forms as tools to give and receive **information**.

* Understand how forms affect **systems**.

* Apply **technology** to design and produce a form.

Forms are full of blank spaces. These spaces may sit above lines or appear as empty boxes. Whatever they appear to be, they invite us to fill them in. A form exists for nearly every milestone in your life. When you're born, someone fills out a birth certificate to record who you are and when and where you were born. When you were taken to the doctor, when you entered kindergarten, when you joined the Girl Scouts or Boy Scouts, when you got a report card, when you signed up for soccer, when you registered for classes, when you applied for a part-time job, when you got your driver's license—on all these occasions and many other times besides, a form had to be filled out to provide a record of who you are, whom to call in an emergency, what grades you made in school, and on and on.

Forms

A form always has at least two purposes: to get information and to give information. The job application form is a good example. The person or company that wants you to fill out a job application form uses it to get information in order to find out whether you have the proper qualifications for a job within the company. You fill out the form because you want to give information about yourself to show that you qualify for a particular position within the company.

The key word is information. Forms are designed to get as much information as possible on one page, without unnecessary writing or irrelevant details. When filling out a well-designed form, you should never have to guess what the person who designed the form wants from you. The purpose should be absolutely clear.

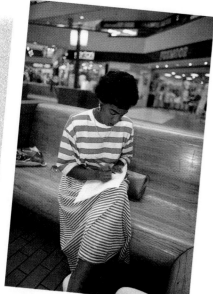

Figure 8-1: *Each form you fill out should be read carefully to determine its purpose.*

Practice 8-1: Identifying the Purposes of Forms

Some of the following workplace forms may be familiar to you. Write two purposes for which each form was designed.

1. Medical insurance form
2. W-4 form
3. Customer satisfaction form
4. Accident report
5. Parts request form
6. Work order
7. Purchase order
8. Invoice
9. Service report
10. Suggestion form

Tips on Filling Out Forms

Most people see a form, grab a pen or pencil, and begin reading and filling out one blank at a time. While this may seem to be a logical approach, it can actually waste time, because if you are filling out the form wrong (or the wrong form), you will ultimately have to start over again and do it right. If you really want to save time in the long run, spend a minute or two skimming it quickly.

Know the Purpose of the Form

Are you sending for a sample copy of a magazine? Or are you getting hooked into a year's subscription for which you will be billed later? Are you applying for vacation days? Or are you asking for release time to take a course in *Lotus Notes*?

Be careful. Forms can look similar but may contain very different information. You need to read each one carefully.

ETHICS **C·O·N·N·E·C·T·I·O·N**

Imagine that you begin receiving catalogs and flyers for electronic equipment and then start wondering how the sender got your name and address. The answer may come if you ask yourself: did I fill out a card with my name, address, and phone number and drop it in the box that said "Win a VCR" at the MediaStore grand opening in the mall last month? That card, along with hundreds of others, may have been sold to the supplier of the VCRs, who turned them into a mailing list. That mailing list may then have been resold to other companies. Soon you find yourself getting all kinds of junk mail.

If you don't wish to have your personal information shared with other companies, write to them or look for a check-off box on their order forms that says something like "Do not make my name available to other mailers." Check the box, and mail the form back to the company. Good business ethics would require the company to abide by your wishes.

Note the Arrangement of Questions

Do the questions go from left to right? Top to bottom? Are the questions divided into sections on the page? There may, for example, be one section for you and another section for your spouse.

Often you will notice a section labeled "For Office Use Only." Do not write in that space, since that is where those receiving the form will make their notations.

Use Only Standard English

Remember, those who read your form do not know you. So don't use any trade jargon, slang, or foreign terms. Use simply worded, standard English. Don't, for example, make your medical insurance company come back to you two months after you've broken your arm and say, "What does this mean?" You may be stacking up unpaid doctor bills because you did a haphazard job of filling out the required medical form.

Bring a Fact Sheet

When you know you are going to have to fill out a form, bring essential information with you, if possible. For example, if you go to a bank to apply for a loan, take a fact sheet of important names, addresses, and phone numbers with you.

* Do you know your mother's maiden name?

* Do you know the full name, address, and phone number of your nearest relative?

* Do you know the day, month, and year of your birth?

* Do you have with you your checking account number and a record of your personal finances, such as the amount of any debts you may have and your monthly salary?

TECHNOBIT

If you use the Internet, you could be providing information to a "tracker." As you move from one Web site to another, your locations can be tracked, and suddenly you may get junk mail from companies that deal in products like those you got information about on the Net. Perhaps the saying, "Let the buyer beware" should now read, "Let the Internet surfer beware."

PEOPLE C·O·N·N·E·C·T·I·O·N

If you rent an apartment or buy a home, you will probably begin finding letters and flyers in your mailbox, addressed to you personally, from hair-dressers, roofers, lawn-care companies, or local veterinarians. It makes you wonder how they know you need a new roof or that you own a pet. A coupon is often enclosed entitling you to a free haircut, a discount on a pizza, a free estimate on roof or gutter repairs, or a free checkup for your pet. The letters are friendly, addressed to you personally, and signed by the individual who owns the business.

Businesspeople know that customers prefer a personal approach, so they make an extra effort to find out about new residents of the community in order to communicate on a person-to-person basis rather than depending only on ads in the newspaper, signs on buses, and billboards. If you get such a letter, it may be interesting to call the business owner and ask how he or she found out so much about you.

If you do not have all this information, you will lose precious time in getting your loan processed. Actually, it would make sense to go to the bank, ask for a loan form, and then take it home and look up the information as you fill it out.

When going to a doctor, always take your insurance identification card with you. Some doctors' offices will use the card to fill out and submit insurance forms for you. You may also be required to supply information from the card in filling out the offices' forms.

Print Clearly or Key

Don't get fancy and add curlycues or dot your *i*'s with hearts. Simple block printing is best for all parts of a form except the signature line.

You were probably first introduced to block printing in elementary school. In case you have forgotten what it looks like, one simple style is shown in Figure 8-2. Remember, in any occupation, it is always appropriate to print. Whether you are filling out a form, hand-writing a memo, drafting a letter, or just leaving a short message for someone, the receiver often appreciates the clarity of printing. Handwriting (cursive) can be confusing, particularly if your own distinctive style may be difficult for others to read.

Aa Bb Cc Dd Ee Ff Gg
Hh Ii Jj Kk Ll Mm Nn
Oo Pp Qq Rr Ss Tt Uu
Vv Ww Xx Yy Zz

Figure 8-2: *The alphabet in block printing*

Some people use their handwriting as an excuse to cover up poor spelling. But when you print, you are sending this message:

> I want this information to be perfectly clear to my reader. I am confident in what I say, and I want the reader to understand me.

You may print with both capitals and small letters, as is done in this sentence. Or you may use all capitals, LIKE THIS. Just be sure to remain consistent in whichever approach you take. For some forms such as work orders, neat handwriting is acceptable.

Be as Brief as Possible

Don't use three words where one will suffice. Use phrases instead of full sentences. In other words, use the shortest, clearest way to state your information. Do not write a paragraph when a word is all that is requested. Save your words for those times, for example, when a form tells you to "Tell, in your own words, what you saw at the scene of the accident. Use additional paper, if necessary."

Use Common Abbreviations

Wherever possible, use **standard abbreviations** that are prescribed or commonly accepted and that the reader will understand. If, for example, you are not married, write *NA* in the space where your spouse's name is requested. Don't write "I am not married" or "I have no spouse." The abbreviation *NA* means "not applicable" and is all that is required. If you prefer, you could draw a short line in the space. By using *NA* or a short line in a space, you are telling the reader that you didn't ignore the blank or have some sinister reason for not filling it in; it says that it simply didn't apply to you.

Practice 8-2: Using Abbreviations

Write a standard abbreviation for each of the following words or phrases. (There may be more than one.) You may use letters, numerals, or other symbols as appropriate. Consult a dictionary if you need to. The first one is done for you.

EXAMPLE:

Avenue   **Ave.**

1. five feet eleven inches
2. Doctor of Medicine
3. Boulevard
4. number
5. February 2, 1993
6. Post Office Box 1052

7. Enrico Company, Incorporated
8. Social Security number
9. identification card
10. thousand
11. package
12. date of birth

TECHNOLOGY C·O·N·N·E·C·T·I·O·N

You've probably noticed that many forms today do not just have blank lines to fill in. They often contain boxes or separated lines for each letter required. The reason is that the information is set up for data entry; that is, for someone to put into a computer. Printing and separating each item or letter makes it easier for a data entry clerk to read the information and thus minimizes the possibility of error. Sometimes the form is already set up in the computer software. So instead of handing you a form to fill out, a receptionist may simply ask you for each piece of information needed and enter it into the computer as you say it.

Other abbreviations you should know are

* the two-letter abbreviations for the 50 states used by the U.S. Postal Service.

* abbreviations for streets and roads—for example, *St., Rd., Rte., Ave.,* and *Ct.*

* abbreviations for titles used in addressing people. Many forms require you to indicate which title you wish to use. But first, be sure you're clear about how these personal titles are used.

Mrs. Title preferred by many married women. Examples: *Mrs. Laurie Singleton* or *Mrs. Daniel Singleton.*

Mr. Title used for all men, married or unmarried, unless they have a professional title, such as *Doctor* or *Reverend* (see the following discussion). Sometimes this title is used with other titles, as in *Mr. President* for the President of the United States or *Mr. Speaker* for the Speaker of the House of Representatives.

Ms. Title used for married or unmarried women unless they indicate another preference.

Miss Now a word, although it started as the short form of *mistress,* which used to mean simply "unmarried woman." This title is preferred by some unmarried women.

Dr. Doctors are not all medical doctors. For example, a person with a Ph.D. in mathematics or history is also called *Doctor.* Some of these people work in colleges or engineering, chemical research, or other professions. Examples of two famous nonmedical doctors: Sally Ride, the first woman astronaut, and Martin Luther King, Jr., civil rights leader.

Rev. *Reverend* is the title of a minister or priest. Not all ministers use this title. Some use *Mr.* or *Dr.*

Forms in Our Lives: One Person's Story

Barrett Izaakson's struggles with paperwork began when he applied for his driver's license during his sophomore year. He found out that a driver's license isn't just handed to a person as a reward for turning 16 and passing the driver's test. In fact, he wasn't even allowed to take the test until he showed his birth certificate to prove his age. That's when his problems started. Although Barrett had been living with his parents at the same address in Ohio since he was three months old, he had been born near Chicago, so he had to write to the records office there for his birth certificate. Several years earlier, whole city blocks of buildings in downtown Chicago were flooded due to a disastrous water-main break. Businesses and government offices were shut down, some for several weeks. These offices included not only basements, but subbasements far underground, which filled with water when those pipes burst. People saved what they could and tried to move files out of basement offices to higher ground. Barrett's birth certificate was in one of those subterranean file cabinets.

It took weeks for a city office worker in Chicago to find and mail him a dim copy of his once-water-saturated birth certificate. He began to wonder if this was a foreshadowing of future struggles with forms.

It wasn't until his senior year, though, that he began to feel that banks and government agencies were burying him in forms. It started with a series of family calamities. First his dad was laid off from work and his mom went from part-time to full-time work at Kibbles Cookies on the 3 to 11 p.m. shift to make more money. Plans to get a new car and give the old one to Barrett were put aside. Now he would have to buy a car to get to his senior co-op job. He also knew that his parents could no longer afford to help him pay the annual $1,500 fee for his car insurance.

Barrett had worked part-time for Buildex Lumber, mostly on weekends, since he turned 16 in January 1996. In this first "real job," he had proved himself to be a reliable employee and his boss, Mr. Angelo Nunez, had even offered him a full-time job when he finished high school. He had started in a co-op job in their company's warehousing and inventory department during his senior year, and now he was working 30 hours a week at $5.50 an hour. He couldn't quit now. His choice was simple: to keep his job he would need a car, and since he had only a savings account with less than $200 in it, he would have to get a loan in order to get a car.

Getting a Loan

People get loans from banks every day. But as Barrett soon discovered, that does not mean that loans are easy to get. He discovered that banks don't care how much you need the money. They're in the money-lending business to make money. To do so, they must charge interest on every penny they lend.

Barrett discovered that since he was only 18 and had never had a loan before, he had no **credit rating** and therefore would need a **cosigner** to assure the bank that the loan would be paid. He asked his uncle, Wilbert Schilling, to be his cosigner, since his parents couldn't take on the burden of another loan. Uncle Bert knew that Barrett had no other debts and that he was hard-working, reliable, and conscientious, so he agreed to be the cosigner. He also knew that Barrett could afford a loan payment of about $50 after he made his insurance payments and took care of car upkeep and incidentals. They went back to the bank together to get a printout of the loan details he would need to purchase the older used car he had in mind.

The bank would charge Barrett 11 percent annually for the balance due on his loan, but since the interest was compounded, it actually worked out to an annual percentage rate (*a.p.r.*) of 14.35 percent. In addition, there was a one-time bank charge of $75. See Figure 8-3 for the way the bank presented the loan on paper.

1ST CITY BANK
INSTALLMENT LOAN

2/25/98 INPUT		OUTPUT		
CASH ADVANCED	1,500.00	PRINCIPAL NOTE AMT		1,575.00
BANK FEE	75.00			
DOC CHARGE	.00	AMT FINANCED		1,500.00
CONTRACT DATE (DDMMYY)	022798			
1ST PYMT DATE (DDMMYY)	040198	LIFE INSURANCE		.00
TERM OF LOAN	36			
INTEREST RATE	11.00	FINANCE CHARGE		361.56
INSURANCE:	NONE	DAYS TO 1ST PAYMENT	39	
		TOTAL PAYMENT AMT		1,861.56
		APR	14.35	
		NBR OF MONTHLY PYMTS	36	
		AMT OF MONTHLY PYMTS		51.71

Figure 8-3: *A printout showing bank terms for Barrett's installment loan*

Filling Out Loan and Credit Card Applications

When you are applying for a loan, your job history, credit rating, and educational level are all important. The person or company lending you the money must be sure that the loan will be paid back. These factors may work for or against you. However, you need to remember one thing in filling out these and other applications: Never lie. Your credit rating is a matter of record. The loan officer or credit card company will take a look at the information you provide to see if you appear to be a good risk or to be sure that you have filled out the form properly. Then they will send for a copy of your credit rating.

In this age of computers, it is fairly easy for someone to follow your money trail. If you have ever had a car loan, a home mortgage, a shopper's card, or a credit card of any kind, your bills and payments are in your file. And a computer somewhere can retrieve that file in seconds. If the facts in the file don't agree with what you have written on the form, you are caught in a lie. Liars are not good credit risks.

Occasionally, however, the facts in your credit file don't agree with what you have written on the form, not because you have lied or made a mistake, but because someone has made an incorrect entry, has kept outdated information, or has confused you with another person with a last name similar to yours (that person's debts are in your file). It may be wise to write to a credit rating company every few years and get a copy of your credit records so you can find and resolve any inaccuracies that may exist.

Filling out loan or credit card applications accurately may take a lot of research. That's why you are not expected to fill them out immediately. You can take the forms home and look up the information you need. If you realize you don't understand a question—such as, "Have you ever **defaulted** on a loan?"—don't hesitate to call the customer service people at the bank or loan company. Ask them to clarify what they mean. Most likely they will treat you politely because they appreciate people trying to do things right. They will tell you that *defaulted* means "failed to pay a financial debt." Banks and loan companies are used to handling all kinds of questions.

If you pay off the loan, your credit rating will be established, and you will have an easier time getting a loan on your own the next time you need one. If you default and someone else has to pay (or worse, if for some reason neither you nor your cosigner can pay), you will be subject to legal action and you may not qualify the next time you apply for a loan.

INFOBIT

"Whoever is careless with the truth in small matters cannot be trusted with important matters."

ALBERT EINSTEIN, GERMAN-BORN U.S. SCIENTIST

You have studied geography in school and have probably used computers either at home or in school, but have you thought about making a career of the combination? If you like geography and computers, you might be interested in a career in GIS (geographic information systems). When decisions have to be made about how to redistrict schools or where to locate an electrical power plant or a new subdivision, a GIS specialist is likely to be consulted. This consultant combines computerized mapping with data analysis and helps city, state, and national planners make critical planning decisions.

According to *Working Woman,* GIS specialists are also hired by large corporations who need to know if a particular town or country is a good place to locate one of their plants. The corporations need answers to such questions as, What are the local zoning laws, if any? Are there enough potential workers to run the plant? Does the location have proper sewage? Are water and electric utilities available? Gathering the data to answer these questions is the job of the GIS specialist. If this type of career interests you, check the Internet or a good college search software package to locate universities that offer degrees in GIS.

INFOBIT

According to Robert McKinley, founder of the RAM Research Group, which researches credit card information for both consumers and bankers, "Anyone who knows anything about the [credit] card business knows that if you make the minimum payment, the two percent per month that they ask for, you will never get out of debt. It takes 30 years to clear a $2,000 debt."

As you fill out a credit card application form, remember that credit cards are a type of loan arrangement. When you charge a purchase using a credit card, the payment is actually made by a company—usually a bank, a gasoline company, or a department store. Then later you pay them back, almost always with interest.

Be sure to read credit card applications carefully on both sides. Read all the fine print, and look for a chart showing the interest rates the company will charge if you don't pay the entire balance of the bill each month. The interest rate is often 18 to 21 percent (an additional $18 to $21 added to your bill for every $100 charged).

Wise credit card users make a practice of paying off their entire balance at the end of each month. That way they avoid a mounting debt and may even avoid paying an interest charge.

Some companies require you to pay off the entire amount you have charged each month, so there is no interest. Their cards usually carry an annual fee of $35 to $50 or more. It is important to know the terms of the agreement you are signing when you fill out the credit card application. Once you have signed it, you have entered into a contract with the company and are legally bound to the terms set forth in that contract.

Practice 8-3: Filling Out Forms

Use Barrett Izaakson's driver's license, bank account statement, paycheck, and any other information you have learned about him from reading this chapter in order to fill out the following forms:

1. Barrett's loan application (Do not fill in the co-applicant part.)

2. His request for **direct deposit** of a portion of his paycheck into his savings account

3. A form for a free subscription to *Buildex National, The Construction Suppliers' Magazine*

The forms are on pages 8-B through 8-D in your *Student Workbook*.

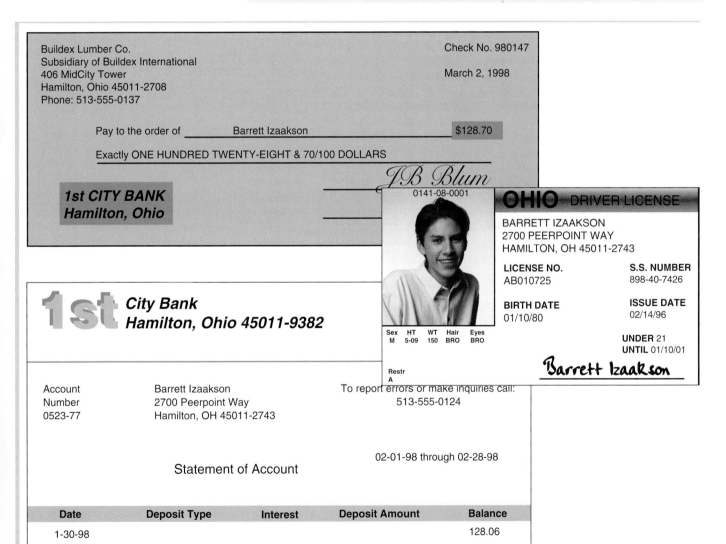

Buildex Lumber Co.
Subsidiary of Buildex International
406 MidCity Tower
Hamilton, Ohio 45011-2708
Phone: 513-555-0137

Check No. 980147

March 2, 1998

Pay to the order of _____ Barrett Izaakson _____ $128.70

Exactly ONE HUNDRED TWENTY-EIGHT & 70/100 DOLLARS

JB Blum

1st CITY BANK
Hamilton, Ohio

0141-08-0001

OHIO DRIVER LICENSE

BARRETT IZAAKSON
2700 PEERPOINT WAY
HAMILTON, OH 45011-2743

LICENSE NO.	S.S. NUMBER
AB010725	898-40-7426
BIRTH DATE	ISSUE DATE
01/10/80	02/14/96

Sex HT WT Hair Eyes
M 5-09 150 BRO BRO

UNDER 21
UNTIL 01/10/01

Restr
A

Barrett Izaakson

1st City Bank
Hamilton, Ohio 45011-9382

Account Number 0523-77

Barrett Izaakson
2700 Peerpoint Way
Hamilton, OH 45011-2743

To report errors or make inquiries call:
513-555-0124

02-01-98 through 02-28-98

Statement of Account

Date	Deposit Type	Interest	Deposit Amount	Balance
1-30-98				128.06
2-06-98	Savings		15.00	143.06
2-13-98	Savings		15.00	158.06
2-20-98	Savings		15.00	173.06
2-27-98	Savings		13.00	186.06
2-27-98		2%	3.72	189.78

Job-Related Forms

A variety of forms is commonly used in most workplaces. You will encounter some or all of these as an employee. Some of the most common are W-4 forms, medical forms, on-site service report forms, work orders, and purchase orders.

W-4 Forms

The W-4 is a federal income tax form, and you are usually required to complete one as soon as you are hired (see Figure 8-4). It tells your

Form W-4 (1998)

Purpose. Complete Form W-4 so your employer can withhold the correct Federal income tax from your pay. Because your tax situation may change, you may want to refigure your withholding each year.

Exemption from withholding. If you are exempt, complete only lines 1, 2, 3, 4, and 7, and sign the form to validate it. Your exemption for 1998 expires February 16, 1999.

Note: You cannot claim exemption from withholding if (1) your income exceeds $700 and includes unearned income (e.g., interest and dividends) and (2) another person can claim you as a dependent on their tax return.

Basic instructions. If you are not exempt, complete the Personal Allowances Worksheet. The worksheets on page 2 adjust your

withholding allowances based on itemized deductions, adjustments to income, or two-earner/two-job situations. Complete all worksheets that apply. They will help you figure the number of withholding allowances you are entitled to claim. However, you may claim fewer allowances.

New—Child tax and higher education credits. For details on adjusting withholding for these and other credits, see **Pub. 919,** Is My Withholding Correct for 1998?

Head of household. Generally, you may claim head of household filing status on your tax return only if you are unmarried and pay more than 50% of the costs of keeping up a home for yourself and your dependent(s) or other qualifying individuals.

Nonwage income. If you have a large amount of nonwage income, such as interest or dividends, you should consider making estimated tax payments using Form 1040-ES. Otherwise, you may owe additional tax.

Two earners/two jobs. If you have a working spouse or more than one job, figure the total number of allowances you are entitled to claim on all jobs using worksheets from only one W-4. Your withholding will usually be most accurate when all allowances are claimed on the W-4 filed for the highest paying job and zero allowances are claimed for the others.

Check your withholding. After your W-4 takes effect, use Pub. 919 to see how the dollar amount you are having withheld compares to your estimated total annual tax. Get Pub. 919 especially if you used the Two-Earner/Two-Job Worksheet and your earnings exceed $150,000 (Single) or $200,000 (Married). To order Pub. 919, call 1-800-829-3676. Check your telephone directory for the IRS assistance number for further help.

Sign this form. Form W-4 is not valid unless you sign it.

Personal Allowances Worksheet

A Enter "1" for **yourself** if no one else can claim you as a dependent . . . . A ____

B Enter "1" if:
  • You are single and have only one job; or
  • You are married, have only one job, and your spouse does not work; or
  • Your wages from a second job or your spouse's wages (or the total of both) are $1,000 or less. . . B ____

C Enter "1" for your **spouse.** But, you may choose to enter -0- if you are married and have either a working spouse or more than one job. (This may help you avoid having too little tax withheld.). . . . . C ____

D Enter number of **dependents** (other than your spouse or yourself) you will claim on your tax return . . . . D ____

E Enter "1" if you will file as **head of household** on your tax return (see conditions under **Head of household** above) . E ____

F Enter "1" if you have at least $1,500 of **child or dependent care expenses** for which you plan to claim a credit . . F ____

G **New—Child Tax Credit:** • If your total income will be between $16,500 and $47,000 ($21,000 and $60,000 if married), enter "1" for each eligible child. • If your total income will be between $47,000 and $80,000 ($60,000 and $115,000 if married), enter "1" if you have two or three eligible children, or enter "2" if you have four or more . . . . G ____

H Add lines A through G and enter total here. **Note:** This amount may be different from the number of exemptions you claim on your return. ▶ H ____

For accuracy, complete all worksheets that apply.
  • If you plan to **itemize or claim adjustments to income** and want to reduce your withholding, see the Deductions and Adjustments Worksheet on page 2.
  • If you are **single,** have **more than one job,** and your combined earnings from all jobs exceed $32,000 OR if you are **married** and have a **working spouse or more than one job,** and the combined earnings from all jobs exceed $55,000, see the Two-Earner/Two-Job Worksheet on page 2 to avoid having too little tax withheld.
  • If **neither** of the above situations applies, **stop here** and enter the number from line H on line 5 of Form W-4 below.

------------------ Cut here and give the certificate to your employer. Keep the top part for your records. ------------------

Form **W-4**
Department of the Treasury
Internal Revenue Service

Employee's Withholding Allowance Certificate

▶ **For Privacy Act and Paperwork Reduction Act Notice, see page 2.**

OMB No. 1545-0010

19**98**

1 Type or print your first name and middle initial	Last name		2 Your social security number

Home address (number and street or rural route)	3 ☐ Single ☐ Married ☐ Married, but withhold at higher Single rate.
	Note: If married, but legally separated, or spouse is a nonresident alien, check the Single box.
City or town, state, and ZIP code	4 If your last name differs from that on your social security card, check here and call 1-800-772-1213 for a new card . . . . . ▶ ☐

5 Total number of allowances you are claiming (from line H above or from the worksheets on page 2 if they apply) . **5** ____
6 Additional amount, if any, you want withheld from each paycheck . . . . **6** $ ____
7 I claim exemption from withholding for 1998, and I certify that I meet **BOTH** of the following conditions for exemption:
  • Last year I had a right to a refund of **ALL** Federal income tax withheld because I had **NO** tax liability **AND**
  • This year I expect a refund of **ALL** Federal income tax withheld because I expect to have **NO** tax liability.
  If you meet both conditions, enter "EXEMPT" here . . . . ▶ **7**

Under penalties of perjury, I certify that I am entitled to the number of withholding allowances claimed on this certificate or entitled to claim exempt status.

Employee's signature ▶ _____ Date ▶ _____, 19____

8 Employer's name and address (Employer: Complete 8 and 10 only if sending to the IRS)	9 Office code (optional)	10 Employer identification number

Figure 8-4: *The W-4 form*

WEB LINK

Check out a variety of Web sites that pertain to a career or occupation that interests you and see how many of them contain forms that allow you to request additional information or order a product. With your teacher's permission, fill out one of the forms requesting free information about a particular occupation, service, or product and have it sent to your school.

employer how many **dependents** (people including yourself whom you support) you are declaring. Your employer will then know how much federal income tax to withhold from your paycheck. If you have a job now, you have probably already filled out this form at work.

All you will probably have to fill out is page 1 (as shown in Figure 8-4). Page 2 is for people who itemize their income taxes. These people usually have a home mortgage and sufficient charitable contributions, non-wage income (like interest on investments), and other financial considerations that make it sensible for them to itemize their taxes.

Medical Insurance Forms

In most companies, full-time workers are offered some type of medical insurance as a **fringe benefit**. Usually you, as an employee, will have to pay a certain amount in the form of a **deductible**, or **copayment**. You may, for example, have to pay 20 percent of all medical bills yourself, while your insurance company pays the remaining 80 percent. Or you may simply have to make a copayment, typically $8 to $10, each time you visit a doctor. If you should require surgery or extensive therapy, you would have to pay a set percentage. Sometimes, for an added fee, your entire family can be covered by the insurance. Whatever the charge, it is far less than you would have to pay to a doctor or hospital if you didn't have insurance.

Money from a medical insurer is handled in two ways: it can be paid directly to the doctor, or it can be paid to you after you prove that you have already paid the doctor. In either case, you may be required to fill out a portion of the insurance form stating who you are, what company you work for, and whatever other information is requested.

If the doctor bills the insurance company directly, he or she will have detailed information about you on file. Usually, you will simply be required to present your health insurance identification card. It includes your insurance company's name, your policy number, your employer's name and code number, and perhaps other additional information. Then the bill is sent directly to the insurance company. If you are required to pay a percentage of the cost, the insurance company sends you a bill for that amount.

Some doctors will not send your bill to the insurance company, but will require you to pay the bill. Then you have to fill out a medical claim form provided by your insurance company and attach the doctor's bill showing that you have paid it in full. The insurance company will then reimburse you for the amount your policy stipulates.

CULTURE **C·O·N·N·E·C·T·I·O·N**

The crossword puzzle is a form that has nothing to do with business. It's just for fun. And it seems to be peculiarly English, since the first known crossword puzzles originated in England in the 1800s. According to *Compton's Encyclopedia,* these puzzles were fairly simple, compared to the challenge of the well-known *New York Times* crossword puzzles of today, and they soon became a serious pastime in the United States. The first known American crossword puzzle, designed by a journalist named Arthur Wynne, was published in the *New York World* Sunday Supplement on December 21, 1913.

Certainly the English alphabet lends itself more to the form of the crossword puzzle than do some other alphabets. Japanese and Chinese characters, which are stylized picture drawings, do not consist of individual letters that form words. The parts of these characters cannot be taken apart and inserted into separate blocks; separating the pen strokes would destroy the character and thus destroy the meaning.

An example of the portion of a typical medical form where patient information is required is shown in Figure 8-5.

PART I   PATIENT AND MEMBER INFORMATION   *(please print or key)*

1. Member's name _____

   Address _____

   City _____

   State _____   ZIP _____

   Phone (____) _____

2. Patient (first name, middle initial, last name)

3. Member's certificate or ID no.:

   _____

   _____
   (Numbers can be found on Member's ID card.)

4. Group Name:

   _____

5. Group Number:

   _____

6. Patient's date of birth   Age
   __/__/__

7. Patient's relation to Member

self (male)	self (female)	husband
1☐	2☐	3☐
wife	son	daughter
4☐	5☐	6☐

   other male dependent   other female dependent
   7☐   8☐

8. Is patient full-time student 19 years of age or older?
   ☐ yes   ☐ no
   Name of school:

9. Was condition related to:
   A. Employment ☐ yes ☐ no
   B. Accident   ☐ yes ☐ no
   Date of Onset: _____

10.

   IMPORTANT

   If patient is covered by any other group or non-group health insurance, please complete this section.
   Name of other employer _____
   Address of other employer _____
   Name of other person employed _____
   Birth date of other person employed _____
   Relationship to patient _____
   Other health care plan _____
   If patient is a child and parents are divorced, please answer the following:
   a. Which parent has custody of the patient?_____
   b. Is there a court decree that states which parent is responsible for medical bills? ___ yes ___ no. If yes, please attach a copy of the court decree.

11. Is the patient eligible for Medicare?
    ☐ yes ☐ no

12. Describe the illness, injury, or symptom:_____
    _____
    _____
    Date symptom first appeared: _____

5a. I authorize release of any information relative to this claim to be used by a review agency solely for the purposes of determining reimbursement.

_____ DATE: _____
(Signature of Member or Spouse)

Figure 8-5: *A patient information form*

Using either your own personal information or Barrett Izaakson's information, fill out the W-4 and medical insurance enrollment forms on pages 8-E and 8-F in your *Student Workbook*.

Figure 8-6: *A service representative must often prepare an on-site service report to describe the details of the work performed.*

On-Site Service Report Forms

In an increasing number of occupations, employees who deal directly with customers on the customer's property must make a written report of their work. Sometimes, but not always, this includes listing the costs billed to the customer.

Many new employees are shocked to discover that, just when they finally get hired as an electrician or plumber or furnace repairer, they suddenly have to polish up their speaking and writing skills.

Service reports are meant to inform the employer as well as the customer of exactly what services were rendered, how long the service call took, and what materials were used. Usually the company provides a form for the service representative to fill out.

Sometimes the form is filled out on the spot and handed to the customer. At other times, it may be taken to the office and converted into a letter or detailed invoice for the customer.

The service report in Figure 8-7 was filed by an electrician who did work in a private home. In this case, the report was filed in the office. Then it was keyed and mailed to the customer as part of the bill. What is missing from this bill?

Holkamp Electric Company
100 West Main Street—Georgetown, Indiana

DESCRIPTION OF WORK

Work performed on September 9 and 11, - - - -

For labor and material necessary to clean and service furnace and electronic air-cleaner.

Installed new thermocouple on furnace, installed new water pad on humidifier, and checked system for proper operation.

Installed owner's two floodlight fixtures with motion detector and furnished and installed new control switch in kitchen.

Furnished and installed new ground fault interrupter receptacle on outside of house in side yard connected to existing circuit in garage.

Total Price: $521.40

TERMS OF PAYMENT

Payment due upon job completion or receipt of invoice. 2% interest per month assessed on all accounts outstanding after 15 days of invoice date.

Figure 8-7: *A printed service report*

In the situation described below, Brenda Holderbaum, the service representative for a heating and air-conditioning company, must write out the report on the spot. While on the job site, she bills the customer and collects a check for services rendered.

Let's say that Brenda is scheduled to service an air conditioner at 811 Main Street. When Brenda arrives, she is expected to call the office and tell the secretary or dispatcher that she has arrived at the scheduled site and is ready to start working. The time is then recorded so the number of hours Brenda works can be figured into the bill. Brenda makes another phone call when the job is finished and reports that the work is done and what supplies she used. Someone in the company's office then figures up the bill and tells Brenda what to charge the customer. She writes the amount on her report and collects the money from the customer for services rendered.

The report itself has to be composed and written so that it is understandable and legible. There is no room for error, so it is wise for Brenda to have some standard phrases ready to use on the form. (See examples below.) She must also be prepared to explain each item on the bill, including the need for any replacement parts, to the customer's satisfaction.

If you are ever in Brenda's situation, you need to remember to record exactly what you did in chronological order, using short statements. Don't try to get fancy. Just begin each statement with a verb and keep it straightforward and simple. Examples:

> Cleaned furnace.
>
> Replaced furnace filter.
>
> Replaced humidifier pad.
>
> Checked thermostat.

In other occupations, you might use statements like the following:

> Replaced fan belt.
>
> Reapplied tracking powder behind baseboard.
>
> Installed light fixture in kitchen.
>
> Cleaned trap in bathroom sink.

Notice the absence of words like *I, the,* and *a.* These words are not necessary to the meaning of the report, and they take up extra space on a small form. Use a bare-bones approach. Say only what absolutely needs to be said. Just be careful not to skip essential information.

Practice 8-5: Paul's Service Report

teamwork Figure 8-8 is a report form filed by Paul, a heating and air-conditioning specialist. Paul is good at servicing furnaces, but not so good at writing his service reports. He has the right idea, but writes sloppily, runs his statements together, and misspells too many words, which could reflect badly on his employer.

Critique Paul's report with a partner. List everything that is helpful or confusing, and tell exactly what should be done to improve it. Then use the blank form on page 8-G of your *Student Workbook* to write the report correctly. The beginning verb is provided.

Maintenance Work Orders

The work order is a maintenance or repair request. It is designed to suit the needs of particular kinds of businesses and is filled out by someone who notices a problem with equipment, structure, electrical wiring, plumbing, etc., that may affect performance or safety. Here are some examples of situations in which a work order might be required:

* You are working in a warehouse and notice that shelving is pulling loose from a wall or that a truck stop rail is loose at the service entrance.

* You are an administrative assistant and notice bare wires on an electric outlet in the office.

* A coworker in the food processing plant where you work points out that the meat locker door is not closing properly, which could cause the meat to spoil.

JOB WORK ORDER
No. 98338

DATE OF ORDER

CUSTOMER *Lacey Manon* SERV. REP. *Paul* STARTING DATE *10/3/--*

BILL TO ORDER TAKEN BY

ADDRESS *1919 Hyde Street*
CITY *Frost City*

☑ DAY WORK
☐ CONTRACT
☐ EXTRA

JOB NAME

JOB PHONE

DESCRIPTION OF WORK *Clean & service furnace clean pilot light replaced thermocoupe oil motor check heat exchanger OK at this time Gave price price of $195:0 to install humidifier.*

Paid service call and work on furnace by check #2493

Thank You $94:95

METHOD OF PAYMENT
☐ CASH AMT. $_____
☐ CREDIT CARD
☐ CHECK NO. _____ AMT. $_____
☐ SEND BILL

TOTAL MATERIALS
TOTAL LABOR
TAX
TOTAL AMOUNT $*94 95*

DATE COMPLETED *10/ 3 /--* WORK ORDERED BY

Signed *Lacey Manon*
I hereby acknowledge the satisfactory completion of the above-described work.

Figure 8-8: *Paul's service report*

In situations like these, you would need to fill out a work order. Then you would submit the form to the individual or department responsible for maintenance, as shown in Figure 8-9.

MAINTENANCE WORK ORDER

	DEPT NO.	WORK ORDER NUMBER
	10	1158

DOWNTIME REQUIRED ☐   DATE SUBMITTED 6-10-- ___ DATE REQ'D 6-12-- ___

ORIGINATOR: Bob Stendhal ___ PHONE EXT: 310

AREA CONTACT: Mustafa Al Hag ___ FHONE EXT: 125

APPROVED BY: ___ SAFETY PERMIT REQUIRED: YES ☐ NO ☐

MACHINE NO./DESCRIPTION: ___

PRIORITY:	1. EMERGENCY	2. URGENT	③. PRIORITY	SAFETY:	Ⓐ. YES
	4. ROUTINE	5. SHUT DOWN			B. NO

DESCRIPTION OF WHAT IS WRONG OR MAINTENANCE WORK REQUESTED:

Safty gate at #2 dock, Bldg. 102, won't
close. Hinge is broken.

PHS NO.	DESCRIPTION OF WORK PHASE	CLK HRS	NO. PPL	EST. HRS				ACT HRS	CMP
				MR	E	P	TR	TR	
	Completed — gate repaired	4							
	TOTALS							☒	
		AVL	PHS NO.						AVL

TOTAL EST. HRS.		PARTS/MATERIAL REQUIRED
PHS NO.	PARTS/MATERIAL REQUIRED	
	Gate hinge	

DATE SCHEDULED: 6-11-- ___ DATE COMPLETED: 6-12-- ___

WORK PERFORMED: Hinge replaced on gate.

SUPERVISOR'S SIGNATURE Eva Cruz

WHITE - ORIGINATOR'S COPY   PINK - ORIGINATOR'S FEEDBACK COPY   GREEN - PLANNER'S COPY   CARD STOCK - EQUIPMENT HISTORY FILE   CANARY - MAINTENANCE COPY

Figure 8-9: *A work order*

PURCHASE ORDER

Your Company Name
Your Company Slogan
Your Company Street Address
City, State ZIP
000.000.0000 Fax 000.000.0000

The following number must appear on all related
correspondence, shipping papers, and invoices:
P.O. NUMBER: 980512

To:
Attention: Steve Gilland
Doors Galore
3333 Hacienda Lane
Phoenix, AZ 50012-1432

Ship To:
(Name and address of place where
you want Doors Galore to deliver the
merchandise.)

P.O. DATE	REQUISITIONER	SHIP VIA	F.O.B. POINT	TERMS
7/16/--	Becky	Avi Express		60 Days

ITEM	QTY.	UNIT	DESCRIPTION	UNIT PRICE	TOTAL
1.	2	ea	Insulated door, DM552-S	469.25	992.50
2.	3	set/2	Brass hinge set, BF032-557	29.95	89.95
3.	1	ea	External door lockset and latch, brass, D23207-408	92.50	92.50
			SUBTOTAL		$1,174.85
			SALES TAX		$ 70.49
			SHIPPING & HANDLING		$ 117.49
			OTHER		
			TOTAL		**$1,362.83**

1. Please send two copies of your invoice.
2. Enter this order in accordance with the prices, terms, delivery method, and
   specifications listed above.
3. Please notify us immediately if you are unable to ship as specified.
4. Send all correspondence to:
   Name
   Your Company Name
   Your Company Street Address
   City, State ZIP
   000.000.0000, ext. 000; Fax 000.000.0000

Requisitioner ___ Date ___

Authorized by ___ Date ___

Figure 8-10: *A sample purchase order*

Purchase Orders

Every business, big or small, uses purchase orders. These forms order (request) the purchase of items. Purchase orders vary from company to company, but they have certain things in common. A simple P.O., as purchase orders are commonly called, is shown in Figure 8-10. Note that you must be clear about the order quantity.

Item 1 calls for two doors. Each door is $496.25; therefore, you must multiply the price per door by two (the total number of doors needed) to get the total price of $992.50.

Item 2, on the other hand, specifies three sets of hinges, with two hinges in each set (set/2). One price includes both hinges. They are not $29.95 each; they are $29.95 combined as a set. The required number of hinges will cost $89.85.

Usually, individual items are indicated by *ea* (for *each*). What do you think the following abbreviations might mean on a purchase order?

> *bx, cs, pk, mil*

Practice 8-6: Filling Out a Purchase Order

Pretend that you work for the Bright Window Company and are in charge of replacing old office equipment. You have researched and priced everything you need. Now, using the following information and the blank purchase order on page 8-H of your *Student Workbook,* fill in the purchase order as it should look if you were actually ordering these items.

At the bottom of the P.O., sign your name as the requestor. The business manager or another authorized person signs on the "authorized signature" line in a real business transaction, which means that the purchase is approved and that the company will pay for the items when they are received.

Remember to use standard abbreviations wherever possible.

Purchase order information:
Vendor: Office Suppliers, Inc., 98 Retail Drive, Little Rock, Arkansas 72206-1256 (Shipping and billing addresses are the same.)

Item 1. 2 Condor Desktop Copiers, Model DT-39 with four preset reduction ratios and 100-sheet paper tray, @ $779.50 each.

Item 2. 2 Steel-Side file cabinets, Model 21-539, four-drawer, almond in color, @ $109.95 each.

Item 3. 1 SoSharp electric pencil sharpener @ $39.95.

Add up the costs, add 10 percent of the total to the P.O. for shipping, and compute the total.

QUALITY C·O·N·N·E·C·T·I·O·N

Feedback is important if you want to achieve quality. The only ways businesses can get feedback is by asking their customers, "How are we doing?" So they survey their customers, either by phone or in writing, through customer-response surveys. Very large companies may even hire another company to do the calling and mailing and then compile customers' responses into a report that can be studied. If a majority of the customers surveyed like or dislike a certain product or service, the company can make changes, decide whether to continue selling a certain product, or decide whether they need to train their workers better in order to please their customers better.

Good Form Design

A business may have dozens or hundreds of forms that are used regularly. Some are on paper; some are processed on a computer. Some are well-designed; some are poorly designed. If you have ever had trouble filling out a form, it may not have been all your problem. It may have been because the form was so poorly designed.

A poorly designed form will not only waste time, but it may waste money if several pages are used where one would suffice, or if the wrong information results in confusion, mismanagement, missed appointments, or unpaid bills.

From everything that has been said in this chapter about forms, we can draw some conclusions. First, a well-designed form is easy to read and fill out. The wording is clear and appropriate for its intended audience and purpose. It has a pleasing balance of print and white space.

Good judgment is important in creating a form. Whether a question is to be answered by inserting words, circling numbers, or checking boxes depends on the question being asked. The final test of a good form, of course, is whether it is easy to fill out. The form designer should have someone fill it out to see whether questions are clear and easy to answer before printing and distributing it.

Practice 8-7: Critiquing a Form

teamwork Look carefully at the locator sheet in Figure 8-11 on page 269. This form is filled out by people as they come and go in an office, so that the receptionist knows who is out, where they can be reached in case of an emergency, and when they can be expected to return.

Critique the locator sheet with a partner; list everything about it that is helpful or confusing, and tell exactly what should be done to improve it. Hint: use the responses of those who have filled out the form as clues to how you should modify it to make it more user-friendly. Then use the table function in your word processing software or a ruler, pencil, and lined paper to create a better version.

Locator Sheet

Monday, April 12, ----

Name	Time Out	Destination	Approx. Return	Ret'd (x)	Time Out	Destination
Ambrose, Bob	7:30	Metro Mall	10:00	✓	12:30	Lunch ✓
Ciancio, Ben	3:00	downtown	Tues			
Czerny, Amy	12:15	Lunch	✓	✓		
Hecht, Jim	8:15	Chamber of Comm 11:00		X	12:30	Lunch ✓
Hickory, Dana	11:30	Lunch	12:30	✓	1:00	Tech Center
Ichbonegun, N.	9:30	Convention	Ctr. Tues.			
Jain, Indira	11:30	lunch	12:30	X		
Janus, Phillipa	9:40	warehouse	11:30	X	1:00	Tech Center till 4:00
Kranz, Leo	10:30	Bell Insurance	1:30			
Montenegro, J.		ill-home	4/14			
Nugent, Jenna	1:00	errand	2:30			
Yamamoto, H.		vacation	4-20			

Figure 8-11: *A locator sheet*

SUMMARY

Forms are used at all levels in every business. They are used to get specific information quickly in a way that can be easily understood. Regardless of what you do or where you work, follow these guidelines concerning forms:

* Make sure you understand the purpose and meaning of any form you encounter.

* Fill out forms neatly and accurately.

* Design or redesign a usable form for a given purpose and audience if called upon to do so.

PROJECT DESIGNING A FORM

careers In the effort to improve quality, most businesses now use a customer satisfaction survey of some type. Sometimes the questions are read over the phone and the answers the customer gives are marked on a form. Sometimes a questionnaire is simply given to the customer to fill out and send in or drop into a box on-site.

You have probably seen such a questionnaire in a local restaurant, automobile service center, or department store. Look at the Sample Project Plan for designing a customer satisfaction form and the sample form that was actually designed from that plan on page 271. Then plan and design a customer satisfaction form of your own.

1. Decide on a type of customer satisfaction form that could be used by a business (or a department within a business) in your career field or in another field of your choice.

2. Complete the Project Plan on *Student Workbook* page 8-I.

3. Have your teacher check your Project Plan.

4. Using the information in your Project Plan, complete the rough draft of the customer satisfaction form.

5. Using the Rough Draft column of the Project Guide on page 8-J of your *Student Workbook,* check your own work. Then have another student check it.

6. Have your teacher check your rough draft.

7. Revise your rough draft, incorporating the changes that your classmates and your teacher suggested.

8. Using the Final Draft column of the Project Guide, proofread your work. Make any needed corrections.

9. Turn in the final draft along with the Project Guide.

Plan for a Customer Satisfaction Form

SUBJECT	Sandy Isles Inn Restaurant
AUDIENCE	Adults--general audience middle class
PURPOSE	**What actions should the audience take?** Write their responses on the form and mail it in.
FORMAT	☒ written ☐ oral ☐ other
SOURCES	Look at forms from other restaurants to get ideas.
VISUALS	**What visuals, if any, will make the customer satisfaction form more effective?** At top of form use font that matches restaurant logo.

CONTENT

Introduction: note to customers

Ask time of day and how often they come to the restaurant.

Ask about 1) quality of food
            2) opinion of the price
            3) opinion of the service

Leave blank lines for other comments.

Thank the customers for filling it out. Remind them to mail it.

SAMPLE CUSTOMER SATISFACTION FORM

Sandy Isles Inn Restaurant

To Our Valued Customers: Your opinion is important to us. Please take a moment and let us know how we are doing. Mark your responses on this card and drop it into a mailbox at your convenience.

Time of day (circle one):   a) Noon to 5 p.m.   b) 5 p.m. to 8 p.m.   c) 8 p.m. to 11 p.m.

How often do you dine here at Sandy Isles?   a) once a week or more often   c) 4 to 5 times a year
                                       b) at least once a month   d) This is my first visit to Sandy Isles.

Please rate our food and service:

1. The food was.......a) excellent   b) acceptable   c) acceptable, but could be better
2. The food was.......a) an excellent value for the price   b) reasonably priced   c) overpriced
3. Our service was...a) prompt and courteous   b) too slow to suit me   c) a bit rushed

Let us know how we can better serve you. _____

_____

_____

_____

Thank you for your time.   *The Management*

Overview

Garrison Keillor, born in Anoka, Minnesota, attended Anoka High School and the University of Minnesota. Since 1963, he has worked in radio. His radio stories have been collected on numerous audiocassettes, including *Lake Wobegon U.S.A.* He is the host of *A Prairie Home Companion* on National Public Radio. He lives in Wisconsin and New York.

Garrison Keillor's stories have a down-home flavor. They are well-suited to an oral reading because of the colloquial language, conversational tone, and repetition. His stories also show a good sense of humor. "Easter" is not just a casual, rambling story, but relates a serious message about how adults affect children and how children affect adults.

"Easter" *from Leaving Home*

It has been a quiet week in Lake Wobegon. The children are back to school after a riotous week of Easter break. The weather was so lovely when the children were released from confinement, the fresh air went to their heads. Air has a different effect on children: what we merely breathe, children are ignited and launched by. At Our Lady on Sunday morning, Father Emil felt as if he was speaking to a convention of rabbits instead of the usual herd of turtles. Constant movement in the pews. The homily was on new life and it was all around to be seen.

When I was a kid, we sat quietly on Sunday morning sometimes for forty or fifty seconds at a stretch. Fidgety kids were put between two grownups, usually your parents or sometimes a large aunt. Like tying a boat to a dock. Every time you moved they'd grab your shoulder and give you a sharp shake and hiss at you, *Sit.* Death will be like that. I'll be in bed and think, "Well, I think I'll get up and live a little," and death will grab me, shake me, say, "Shhh. Be quite. Lie still." I used to think about death on Sunday morning. How hard it would be to lie in your coffin for years with nothing to read, nothing to do, but some grownups I knew probably could manage quite well.

Some former children returned for Easter, bringing their children with them, and some children were shipped earlier to spend the week with grandparents, some of whom are starting to recover to the point where they can sit in a chair and sit back all the way, not lean forward ready to jump when they hear the crash. The grandparents imagined the kiddos leaning against them on the sofa listening to Uncle Wiggily: they forgot how explosive kids can be. Something in the air sets them off. A kid can go all day and hardly eat, then the moon shifts and he's eating like a farmhand. You served baked horse and he eats all of it. Children can lie around for a long time, then a herd of them bursts in the front door and gallops through the kitchen and outside. Children are always on the verge of bursting. They burst six, seven times a day and think nothing of it.

Virginia Ingqvist had two grandkids with her last week. Barbara's two oldest, Doug and Danielle. Hjalmar worked late at the bank. He loves them, but he knows his limit, and it's about thirty minutes. One is four and the other five, an age when you want to find out everything in one day. "Why don't buildings fall?" asked Doug two minutes after he arrived.

> "Children are always on the verge of bursting."

"Because," Virginia explained, "because they're built to stand." "How?"

Thirty seconds, and already she was into architecture, and knew that biology and astronomy and physics were coming right up. Then theology. "Who's God?" "God is God." "Yeah, but who?" It's never a subject you know something about, such as etiquette.

Barbara came up on Friday with her two-year-old and took all three of them to her friend Ruthie's house to visit. Ruthie has three of her own. Her three and Barbara's three sniffed each other for a moment and then two cats made the mistake of coming around the corner of the house into the backyard. The cats realized it was a mistake and backed away, saying, Uh sorry, didn't know you were here. We'll come back later. But the kids grabbed them, hauled them indoors, got them dressed and into a doll buggy, two little cat children. The cats went limp, waiting for a chance to break out, which they did—two cats in full regalia, one up the tree, one on the garage roof, trying to remove their clothes, five children in pursuit, and the two-year-old investigating the back porch.

Barbara and Ruthie sat in the yard talking about child rearing. Barbara's philosophy is more relaxed than her mother's, less restrictive, a hands-off

(cont'd on next page)

approach, allowing children freedom to explore and find their own boundaries. As she said this, she watched the little boy climb the porch steps, stand at the top, turn around, and when he took a step forward straight out into space, she leaped up and made a dash for him, too late to catch him, but she almost stepped on his head. When she scooped him up, she came close to spraining his neck.

> "A major cause of injury to children is parents rushing to the scene."

A major cause of injury to children is parents rushing to the scene. The panic reflex. Some children love to scream for the thrill of making immense people move fast. I remember that, on a quiet day, my sister and I in the backyard wondered, "Where's Mom?" Upstairs, we thought. So I screamed, "MOM." She made it down in two seconds. A good pair of wheels for an old lady. Grandma Tollefson turns off her hearing aid when descendants are around, so a crash is only a whisper to her, boys thundering around upstairs are a distant tapping. One afternoon a sound came out of her house like jets taking off, her grandson practicing his guitar. She was there, knitting, rocking, saying to him, "You know, there was a boy I knew who played the guitar— what was his name? Oh dear. He moved away in 1921, I think. He played his guitar on his porch, and I sat on our porch and listened. I don't think he knew. The screens were so dark, and I could hear him so clear, just like

I can hear you. I was in love with him for a whole summer and he didn't know it." Kevin didn't hear a word she said, and she didn't know the music was blowing her hair back.

Selective ignorance, a cornerstone of child rearing. You don't put kids under surveillance: it might frighten you. Parents should sit tall in the saddle and look upon their troops with a noble and benevolent and extremely nearsighted gaze.

The Buehler boy celebrated a birthday last night and ten of his closest friends came over for a party. They danced to alarming music and ate an alarming amount of pizza and told alarming jokes and there were periods of alarming dead silence, which the Buehlers heard from the kitchen, where they remained in quarantine. They whomped up armloads of chow, and passed it to their son, who carried it to his guests. Stayed in the kitchen for five hours, except for one trip to the bathroom, averting their eyes, and the mister snuck up front once to have a look, and when he looked he wished he hadn't. He was dying of curiosity. The party was so quiet and then burst into laughter, and then silence and then whispering and screams of laughter. He tiptoed down the hall and peeked and saw they were huddled over the Buehlers' wedding album. Nineteen fifty-nine was a funnier year than he had realized and he was a little hurt. He was quite handsome then in those half-rim glasses, his hair carefully oiled and combed back on the sides, like an ocean wave about to break, and piled high in front. He misses that pompadour. There's not much left where it rose from his head, a little tuft as a souvenir of what a stylish devil he used to be. He was hurt when he heard them laughing about his hair. He thought, "What are these people doing in my house? Why am I feeding them?"

Nothing you do for children is ever wasted. They seem not to notice us, hovering, averting our eyes, and they seldom offer thanks, but what we do for them is never wasted. We know that as we remember some gift given to us long ago. Suddenly it's 1951, I'm nine years old, in the bow of a green wooden rowboat, rocking on Lake Wobegon. It's five o'clock in the morning, dark; I'm shivering; mist comes up off the water, the smell of lake and weeds and Uncle Al's coffee as he puts a worm on my hook and whispers what to do when the big one bites. I lower my worm slowly into the dark water and brace my feet against the bow and wait for the immense fish to strike.

"Nothing you do for children is ever wasted."

Thousands of gifts, continually returning to us. Uncle Al thought he was taking his nephew fishing, but he made a permanent work of art in my head, a dark morning in the mist, the coffee, the boat rocking, whispering, shivering, waiting for the big one. Still waiting. Still shivering.

—Garrison Keillor

Start-Up: Forms are required by various organizations (businesses, state and local governments, etc.) to keep proper records and provide helpful information concerning many topics mentioned in Keillor's story, such as the following: (1) school; (2) weather; (3) church; (4) dying; (5) child rearing; and (6) fishing.

Connection: Divide the class into groups of two. Each group should take a topic from the story. Research. List all the forms you can think of related to that topic.

Overview

Isaac Asimov (1920-1992), one of the most prolific writers of this century, is best-known for his science fiction, even though his works range from science fiction to mysteries to history to juvenile books. His works appear in books and magazines and on cassettes and videotapes. Also, many of his works have been made into movies and television shows.

In "Eyes That Do More Than See," Isaac Asimov has projected life a trillion years forward. He says a lot about life in this short story. In an attempt to better humans, science seems to have created beings that have lost their humanity. The story implies a warning: If research continues in genetics (a branch of biology that studies the gene, the part of a cell that determines the inheritable characteristics of an organism), humans must make sure that they do not lose their humanity in the process.

"Eyes That Do More Than See"

After hundreds of billions of years had passed, he suddenly thought of himself as Ames. Not the energy wavelengths that were now the equivalent of Ames—but of the body and of the sound waves of his name that he no longer heard and could no longer hear.

His new idea for the contest had sharpened his memory for so many more of the old, old, eons-old things. He flattened the energy field that made up the total of himself, and its lines of force stretched into distance beyond the stars.

Brock's answering signal came.

> "He flattened the energy field that made up the total of himself. . . ."

Surely, Ames thought, he could tell Brock. Surely he could tell somebody.

Brock's shifting energy pattern adjusted to that of Ames, and communication began. "Aren't you coming for the contest?" communicated Brock.

"Of course."

"Will you take part?"

"Yes." Ames' lines of force pulsed with the answer. "Most certainly. I have thought of a whole new art form. Something really unusual."

"What a waste of effort," came Brock's reply. "How can you think of a new variation that has not been thought of in two hundred billion years? There can be nothing new."

For a moment Brock shifted out of phase and out of communication, so that Ames had to hurry to adjust his lines of force. He caught the drift of other thoughts as he did so—the view of galaxies against the velvet of nothingness and of endless ranks of energy beings drifting between the galaxies.

Ames said, "Please absorb my thoughts, Brock. Don't close out. I've thought of manipulating matter. Why bother with energy? There is nothing new in energy. How could there be?"

"Matter!" Ames interpreted Brock's energy vibrations as those of fear.

Ames said, "Why not? We were once matter ourselves back—back—a trillion years ago anyway. Why not create objects in the form of matter?" Ames was excited now. "Listen, Brock, why not build up an imitation of ourselves in matter, matter as we used to be?"

Brock replied, "I don't remember how that was. No one does."

"I do," said Ames with pulsing energy. "I've been thinking of nothing else, and I am beginning to remember. Brock, let me show you. Tell me if I'm right. Tell me."

"No! This is silly; it's . . . repulsive."

"Let me try, Brock. We've been friends; we've pulsed energy together from the beginning—from the moment that we became what we are. Brock, please!"

"Then quickly," Brock pulsed.

Ames had not felt such a tremor along his own line of force in—well, in how long? If he tried it now for Brock and it worked, he could dare manipulate matter for the contest. He could surprise the energy beings who had been waiting through so many endless reaches of time for something new. He could astound them; he could win the contest.

The matter was thin out there between the galaxies, but Ames gathered it. He scraped it together over the cubic light-years, choosing the atoms, achieving a claylike consistency, and forming matter into an oval form that spread out below.

"Don't you remember, Brock?" he asked softly. "Wasn't it something like this?"

(cont'd on next page)

Brock's energy field trembled. "Don't make me remember. I don't remember."

"That was the head. They—we—called it the head. I remember it so clearly.

I want to say it, I mean the sound." Ames worried briefly, then said, "Look. Don't you remember that word, that sound?"

On the upper front of the oval appeared HEAD.

"What is that?" asked Brock.

"That's the word for head. The symbols that meant the word in sound. Tell me you remember, Brock!"

"There was something in the middle," said Brock hesitantly. "Something in the middle."

A vertical bulge formed.

Ames said, "Yes! Nose, that's it!" and NOSE appeared upon the form. "And those are eyes on either side." LEFT EYE—RIGHT EYE appeared on the form.

Ames regarded what he had made, his lines of force pulsing slowly. Was he sure he liked this?

"Mouth," he said with small quivers of his energy field, "and chin and Adam's apple and collarbone. Now the words come back to me."

These words appeared on the form.

Brock said, "I haven't thought of them for hundreds of billions of years. Why have you reminded me? Why?"

Ames was momentarily lost in his thoughts. "Something else. Something to hear with— something to pick up sound waves. Ears! Where do they go? I don't remember where to put them."

Brock cried out, "Leave it alone! Ears and all else! Don't make me remember."

Ames said uncertainly, "What is wrong with remembering?"

"Because the outside wasn't rough and cold, as on your model, but smooth and warm. Because the eyes were tender and alive, and the lips of the mouth trembled and were soft." Brock's lines of energy glowed and wavered, glowed and wavered.

Ames said, "I'm sorry. I'm sorry."

"You're reminding me that once I was a woman and knew love, that eyes do more than see, and I have none to do it for me."

With violence Brock added matter to the rough-shaped head and said, "Then let them do it!" And Brock fled.

And Ames saw and remembered too— that once he had been a man. The force of his energy field split the head and he fled back across the galaxies on the energy track of Brock—back to the

> *"Don't make me remember."*
> *Ames said uncertainly, "What*
> *is wrong with remembering?"*

unchanging forever always repetition of life.

And the eyes of the shattered head still glistened with moisture Brock had placed in them to represent tears. And the head of matter did what the energy beings could do no longer—it wept for their humanity and for the fragile beauty of the bodies they had given up a trillion years ago.

—Isaac Asimov

Start-Up: What makes you a unique person?

Carefully consider what it means to be human. Then, keeping the story in mind, make a list of what would be gained were we to become bodiless (without form). Then make a list of what we would lose. Use either the chalkboard or a transparency on an overhead projector to list your gains and losses.

Connection: In periodicals, find pictures that best represent you in the following areas: work, school, home, achievements, and leisure and relaxation. Write these areas on construction paper; cut out and paste the pictures beside the words. Also, predict how the pictures may change in the next ten years. Present this information attractively. Give your work a title.

Communicating Messages

> *"Consciously or unconsciously, every one of us does render some service or other. If we cultivate the habit of doing this service deliberately, our desire for service will steadily grow stronger, and we will make not only our own happiness, but that of the world at large."*
>
> —MAHATMA GANDHI

As you complete Chapter 9, you will

* identify reasons for writing messages.

* understand your role in customer service.

* understand the purposes and content of various types of messages.

* analyze the qualities of effective messages.

* revise ineffective messages.

* write notes, memos, e-mail, and letters.

* address envelopes according to postal guidelines.

Workplace Skills in This Chapter

* Improve **interpersonal** skills as you practice using appropriate style and tone for communication.

* Understand the importance of customer service to workplace **systems**.

* Gather **information** for producing correspondence.

* Manage **resources** as you plan a Project.

* Use **technology** to produce memos and letters.

There's an old story about a New York City plumber that goes something like this: It seems he had discovered that hydrochloric acid did a dandy job of cleaning out drains. Just to be on the safe side, he wrote the Bureau of Standards asking if he was doing any harm. Since this practice was certainly harmful, the Bureau wrote back, "The efficacy of hydrochloric acid is indisputable, but the chlorine residue is incompatible with metallic permanence." The plumber replied with his thanks for their prompt approval. Concerned, the Bureau wrote to him again: "We cannot assume responsibility for the production of toxic and noxious residues with hydrochloric acid and suggest you use an alternate procedure."

Why Write?

The plumber wrote back declaring he was glad the Bureau agreed with him. Now, alarmed about the safety of the New York City sewer system, the Bureau fired off, "Don't use hydrochloric acid; it eats the pipes!"

The plumber story illustrates why it's so important to study the audience and the purpose for any message before writing even one word. This chapter will help you to produce messages—notes, memos, e-mail, and letters—that get the results you want.

Most communication at work is conversation, either face-to-face or over the phone. But all of us have to write messages from time to time. Why? Some messages just work better when they are written rather than spoken. A list of reasons follows:

* If the message is complicated or important, writing it gives the writer a chance to plan, organize, and revise. Plus the reader will have an easier time grasping the ideas, since he or she can stop reading to think or to reread some sections.

* People often hear what they want to hear. A written message is more likely to be understood accurately.

* A written message is a permanent, dated record of a request, complaint, compliment, or announcement. Both you and your reader can keep a copy for later reference.

* Some people either are too busy to take calls or are rarely near a phone. Some people screen their calls. A *written* message may reach them.

* Writing to a distant audience is cheaper than phoning.

* Written messages can save time when you need to communicate the same information to several people.

* If you are angry or upset, you may say something that you'll regret later. Writing gives you a chance to regain control of your emotions and, if necessary, edit and rewrite the message.

Most people receive more paperwork on the job than they can handle. When deciding how to get your message to your audience, ask yourself this question: Am I more likely to get what I want if I tell it or if I write it? Write only when you must.

INFOBIT

Words fly, writings remain.

LATIN PROVERB

INFOBIT

A Gannett News Service survey of employees of Fortune 500 companies revealed workers received an average of 31.8 phone calls, 13.6 e-mail messages, 11.2 voice-mail messages, 8.8 faxed documents, 5.1 phone message slips, and 6 Post-it® Notes per day.

CATHY © 1991, 1992 Cathy Guisewite. Reprinted with permission of UNIVERSAL PRESS SYNDICATE. All rights reserved.

Communicating with Customers

INFOBIT

Since, according to Executive Edge newsletter, as many as 80 percent of companies are now service-oriented, interaction with customers is often more important than the actual product.

If your job is not valuable to either external or internal customers, you have a problem!

Most experienced communicators follow unwritten—and sometimes written—rules and conventions of correspondence. These rules make it easier for their readers to understand messages quickly and accurately and to react appropriately. It helps to think of many of your readers as *customers*. *Customer* means more than a person who buys goods or services from you. A **customer** is anyone who depends on or benefits from the work you do—or suffers when your work is poorly done or not done at all. Customers are also people you want something from. You want **external customers** to buy your organization's goods or services. You also want your boss's approval and you want your coworkers to do their jobs. Bosses and coworkers are **internal customers**. Everyone *has* a customer and everyone *is* a customer.

Since we all have customers, we all are involved with customer service. Answering questions. Solving problems. Fixing what's broken. Making it happen *now*. And doing all these things with courtesy, reliability, and competence. Your customers want what they want and they want it now. Not only that, but they want to feel good about it. It's a tall order, but one that everyone in your organization must understand. If they don't understand customer service, your organization will lose business to competitors that do. And if you don't understand your own role in customer service, your internal customers may decide to replace you with someone who does. Improving your written communication with your customers—both external and internal—is a good start.

QUALITY

C·O·N·N·E·C·T·I·O·N

To external customers, *you* are the company. Whether their feelings about the organization are good or bad relates directly to their experience with you. Is that fair? No. Especially since so many things that you have no control over can go wrong. But fair has nothing to do with it. Texas A&M researcher Dr. Leonard Berry says customer service boils down to these five factors:

- Reliability   Keeping promises, accurately and on time
- Responsiveness   Helping customers promptly and willingly
- Assurance   Demonstrating knowledge of your job
- Empathy   Being sensitive to customers' needs and showing them individual attention
- Tangibles   Keeping yourself and your work area clean, attractive, and organized

INFOBIT

"You can't promise your customers sunny weather, but you can promise to hold an umbrella over them when it rains."

SIGN IN A TELEPHONE
SERVICE CENTER

Figure 9-1: *Everyone has a customer and everyone is a customer.*

Practice 9-1: Identifying Customers

teamwork

careers

1. In a team of two or three, brainstorm to identify one external customer and one internal customer for people with the following job titles:

   a. medical lab technician
   b. school secretary
   c. movie set designer
   d. emergency vehicle driver
   e. police officer
   f. hotel assistant manager
   g. 911 dispatcher
   h. writer of newspaper classified ads
   i. horse trainer
   j. car designer

2. Now give a job title related to your area of occupational study. Identify three customers for that job. The customers may be internal or external.

3. What kinds of information would individuals holding the job title in Item 2 need to communicate with their internal and external customers?

Purposes for Messages

We can group written messages—correspondence—according to purpose. Most messages fall into one of these five groups:

* Messages that *express*

* Messages that *inform*

* Messages that *request*

* Messages that *instruct*

* Messages that *persuade*

Some messages have more than one purpose. For instance, a message may instruct employees on how to fill out the new insurance forms; it may also try to persuade them to complete the forms by the end of the week. Still, the writer needs to focus on the primary purpose.

65 Kenny Drive
Seattle, WA 98105-1105
February 12, ----

Attention Manager
Roger's
443 East Halsey Road
Seattle, WA 98104-2847

Ladies and Gentlemen:

Just a quick note to compliment one of your employees.

Yesterday afternoon I was fifth in line in the express checkout line with four people behind me. There was a problem with the register, and the line had not moved for several minutes. Your employee, Toni, noticed and opened another register. It's not what she did, but how she did it, that deserves praise.

As I saw her approach the register, I got ready for the mad dash to the new register. Usually what happens is the last person in line, the person who has been waiting the least amount of time is first in the new line. Not this time. Instead of announcing, "Register 9 is open," Toni looked the person who'd been waiting longest right in the eye and said, "I believe you're next."

If this technique is store policy, congratulations to you all. If Toni came up with this technique on her own, she deserves special recognition. I hope all the cashiers in your store follow her example. Keep up the good work!

Sincerely,

Emila Del Gesso

Mrs. Emila Del Gesso

Figure 9–2: *Personal-business letter in block style*

The following table lists purposes and suggested content of messages. These guidelines are only suggestions. The situation and the audience will influence the information to include in any message. Examples of these types of messages are shown throughout this chapter.

CONTENT OF WRITTEN MESSAGES

Purpose	Suggested Content
To Express	Purpose of the message Reference to the occasion Personal sentiment
To Inform	Purpose of the message Explanation of the situation (Who? What? Where? When? How? Why?) Conclusion, recommendation, and/or action statement Polite ending
To Request	Purpose of the message Background information Details that will enable the reader to respond (Who? What? Where? When? How? Why?) Action statement Polite ending
To Instruct	Purpose of the message Reasons why the reader should follow the instructions List of steps, including what to do and how to do it Polite ending
To Persuade	The content of persuasive messages is explained in Chapters 10 and 11.

Practice 9-2: Purposes for Messages

1. Make a list of all the figure numbers for the 12 sample messages (including the Sample Letter for the chapter Project) shown in this chapter. (Since the Sample Letter does not have a figure number, list it as "Sample Letter.") Beside each figure number, write the primary purpose of the message. If the message has a secondary purpose, list it as well.

2. Why do you think the writers of the messages shown in Figures 9-2, 9-3, and 9-8 wrote their messages instead of making phone calls?

3. Examine several pieces of junk mail. Categorize them by purpose, including secondary purpose.

Qualities of Effective Messages

A written message communicates a great deal about its writer to both internal and external customers. If your writing is careless, inefficient, and incompetent, the reader will assume that your work is also careless, inefficient, and incompetent. Since you represent your organization, the reader of your message will suspect that the organization is careless, inefficient, and incompetent.

INFOBIT

"Consistent, high-quality service boils down to two equally important things: caring and competence."

CHIP R. BELL AND RON ZEMBE, AUTHORS OF SERVICE WISDOM

Kimura & Kimura

April 7, ----

Mr. Paul Beauchamp
Department B
Molloy Industries
8557 Dexter Avenue
Raleigh, NC 27612-0001

Dear Mr. Beauchamp

I am concerned about a situation that has developed because of your delivery procedures.

Last week the following events occurred: We placed an order on April 1 for 300 large furgetts and were promised delivery by noon the next day. When the order did not arrive by 1 p.m., I called your warehouse and was told the shipment would be here within an hour. I called again at 3 p.m. Your employee, Brad, would not give me any specific information about the order. He also refused to give me the name of his supervisor. In fact, he hung up when I asked.

The order arrived three days later. We refused delivery since by that time we had placed an order with one of your competitors. It was filled immediately.

I hope this problem was an isolated incident. Can you promise that similar situations will not happen in the future? We would like to continue our long-standing relationship with Molloy Industries.

Sincerely

Kijiro Kimura

Kijiro Kimura
Production Manager

14 East Shore Parkway
Zebulon, North Carolina 27597-9889
Phone 919-555-0111
Fax 919-555-0114
KIMURAB@TNET.COM

Figure 9-3: *Business letter in modified block style printed on letterhead stationery*

Your employer does not pay you to project a poor image to customers. Since a successful business often depends on its image, communication that broadcasts a negative impression could cost you your job. The clarity, tone, economy, and courtesy of your written messages are parts of that image.

A Clear Purpose

Before you begin writing, decide exactly what you want your reader to do. It is surprising how many otherwise correct messages never get around to the point. The writer either assumed that the reader would figure it out or failed to decide on the purpose before writing. The reader's reaction is, "So what?"

Suppose you wrote to the manager of a printing company to complain that the order forms they had printed included incorrect prices. If you explain the problem, but never tell the manager exactly how you want him or her to correct it, your letter will not be effective. Decide what your purpose is; then state it directly in the first or second sentence.

An Appropriate Tone

Most of us wear different styles of clothing for different occasions. You would never wear the same outfit to work out at the gym, to work in an office, and to attend a wedding. Style in clothing is like tone in writing. The **tone** of correspondence ranges from casual to formal and depends upon the situation, the message's purpose, and the relationship between the writer and the reader. Today, very formal writing is usually limited to messages such as engraved invitations. Most writing at work is less formal and often conversational.

Write to an audience the way you would speak to them. Would you talk to the president of the United States the same way you would talk to your Aunt Maggie? Overly stiff and formal language is as inappropriate as language that is too casual. Pretend the person you're writing to is seated beside you. How would you speak to that person? Write the way you would speak, only with more precision.

TECHNOBIT

"With the advent of the fax machine and e-mail, people are now able to embarrass themselves in writing hundreds of times faster than ever before."

MARYA W. HOLCOMBE, COAUTHOR OF *WRITING FOR DECISION MAKERS*

Figure 9-4: *Appropriate attire depends on the situation.*

INFOBIT

"Customers don't care what you know, until they know that you care."

DIGITAL EQUIPMENT CORPORATION, CUSTOMER SERVICE DEPARTMENT

Put "You" Before "I"

People read all messages looking for "what's in it for me." They are more interested in themselves than they are in your problems, your successes, and your concerns. They want to know how your message will help *them*. Notice in these two examples how the "I" attitude was changed to a "you" attitude:

ROUGH DRAFT	REVISION
I want to thank you for asking about our new service plan. I am enclosing a pamphlet that details the benefits of our new plan. I would very much like to enroll you within the next 30 days, since we are offering a special low rate as our introductory offer.	Thank you for asking about our new service plan. You'll find that the enclosed pamphlet outlines the benefits of the plan. If you sign up within the next 30 days, you'll be able to take advantage of a special low rate we're offering to you on an introductory basis. Thank you.

INFOBIT

"One often contradicts an opinion when what is uncongenial is really the tone in which it was conveyed."

FRIEDRICH NIETZSCHE, GERMAN PHILOSOPHER

Be Positive

Even if you feel angry or frustrated, maintain a respectful, friendly tone. You can be firm without resorting to sarcasm or hostility. If your letter has a positive tone, you'll find that your reader will be more willing to do what you want. Even negative messages can be stated with a positive tone. In the following examples, the messages have been revised to make them more positive and customer-oriented. The first example shows how using the passive voice can make a negative statement more impersonal.

ROUGH DRAFT	REVISION
You did not send your application before the deadline.	Your application was received after the deadline.
You sent the wrong form.	We received Form A but need Form B to complete the sale.
If you have any problems, please call me.	If you have any questions, please call me.
We cannot pay this bill in one lump sum as you requested.	We can clear up the balance in six months by paying you in monthly installments of $150.

INFOBIT

"Thank you . . . Thank you, Thank you . . . and Thank you!!!"

FOZZIE BEAR, MUPPET CHARACTER

Use "Thank You" and "I'm Sorry"

Give sincere thanks to internal and external customers whenever they

- ✹ do business with you.
- ✹ compliment you.
- ✹ are patient with you.
- ✹ offer comments or suggestions.
- ✹ help you to serve them better.
- ✹ make you smile.

With practice, thanking people can become a habit. Apologizing when something goes wrong can be more difficult because we often equate apologizing with admitting failure or blame. But to your customers, an apology just means you understand things are not going right for them at that time. Don't wait, and don't try to shift responsibility or find fault—even if your customer is the one who goofed. Give a simple apology, fix the problem, and then let the customer know what you've done.

ROUGH DRAFT	REVISION
If those guys in maintenance were doing their job, this wouldn't have happened.	I'm sorry you are experiencing a problem.
Since you failed to state what size you want, we won't be able to send your uniforms.	Thank you for your order. You'll receive your uniforms within three days after you send us your size on the enclosed form.

Practice 9-3: Improving the Tone of Messages

1. Revise the following messages to make them more conversational.

   a. Your efforts are most certainly appreciated.

   b. Please do not hesitate to contact me if you have any questions.

2. Revise the following negative messages to make them more positive.

   a. We demand payment this week.

   b. We are not open on Saturday.

3. Revise these sentences to make them more "you"-oriented.

   a. I will fax the price list immediately.

   b. We offer superior service to our customers.

4. Revise the following message to improve its tone.

Your desk is always messy. I find that I feel extremely embarrassed when visitors enter our area and, immediately upon entering, see this mess. Clean it up today. I don't want to have to tell you again.

L enfant
I ncorporated

3444 Commodity Circle
Plummer's Landing, KY 41081-0438

606/555-0147

June 6, ----

MS MARGUARITE AKERMANN
PRODUCTION SUPERVISOR
FINNEYTON TECHNOLOGIES COMPANY
PO BOX 12844
TAMPA FL 33647-2473

SUBJECT: FAX BOARD UPGRADE

The six fax boards that we shipped to you on May 25 (Invoice #4112) were equipped with the wrong memory chips. The new boards are being shipped to you by Express Delivery today.

I am sorry that this problem occurred. A small change in the subcontractor's upgrade assembly schedule created the difficulty. Unfortunately, several dozen boards were shipped before the problem was discovered.

I hope this has not caused any production delays for you, and I thank you for your understanding. We will keep you informed about future upgrades.

Gary Eder

GARY EDER
QUALITY CONTROL MANAGER

Enclosure
c R. Vallejos

Figure 9-5: *Business letter in simplified style printed on letterhead stationery*

Economical but Polite

At work, most people don't have time to read everything they are given to read. Make sure that your message is one that will be read immediately. An economical message is much more likely to be read than one that is not. To respect your reader's time and patience, get right to the point, stick to the point, and then end it. Limit sentences to 20 words and paragraphs to five lines.

BLOFFERS INC.

256 Camino Diablo
Los Angeles, California 90066-2023

Fax Cover Sheet

TIME: 3:07 PM

DATE: March 10, ----

TO: Joe Beasley
      Bigg Company

PHONE: 216-555-0142
FAX: 216-555-0144

FROM: Walter Witherspoon
       Bloffers Incorporated

PHONE: 310-555-0194
FAX: 310-555-0190

RE: Copy of Invoice #873943

Number of pages including cover sheet: 2

Message

This will acknowledge receipt of your request dated March 5, ----, in which you requested us to send you a copy of our invoice dated January 23, ----, No. 873943, for three dozen yellow-striped bloffers, in the amount of $954.43 plus $57.00 tax, totaling $1,011.43.

We are pleased to comply with your request. Please find attached a photostatic copy of the above-mentioned invoice, indicating the merchandise ordered and the total amount charged.

We trust that the copy of this invoice will be self-explanatory and hope that this matter is now settled to your satisfaction. I am thanking you in advance for your cooperation. Please do not hesitate to call me at the number given above if you have any questions at all.

Figure 9-6: *A wordy fax cover sheet*

INFOBIT

"I have only made this letter longer because I have not had the time to make it shorter."

BLAISE PASCAL, FRENCH SCIENTIST AND PHILOSOPHER

INFOBIT

"The writer who does the most gives the reader the most knowledge and takes from him the least time."

CHARLES CALEB COLTON, NINETEENTH-CENTURY ENGLISH CLERIC

Economical writing is brief and concise. Spend your words as if they were dollars; don't spend them on unnecessary information. Remember that sentences written in the active rather than the passive voice are more concise. Plus, active-voice sentences more strongly convey most ideas.

ROUGH DRAFT	REVISION
The instruments were sterilized by Julia.	Julia sterilized the instruments.
I want to take this opportunity to tell you that we appreciate your cooperating together with us on the project.	Thank you for helping us on the project.

Even an economical message, though, has room for good manners. Do not sacrifice politeness for brevity.

ROUGH DRAFT	REVISION
I must have your signature immediately on the purchase order for the new mixer. I intend to take no further action until I hear from you.	The purchase order for the new mixer is ready for your signature. Please sign it and send it back to me so that I can send it to Miss Reho for final approval.

Clear, Precise Language

As in other forms of writing, clarity and precision are essential in writing messages. Choose your words and construct your sentences and paragraphs carefully so they communicate your message without confusing the reader. Avoid using technical jargon unless you are positive your reader will understand it.

ROUGH DRAFT	REVISION
One of our customers called to complain about poor service in your department when she had to wait a long time for someone to do a simple repair that should have taken a short time.	Our customer Linda Ruiz called to complain because on October 30 she waited for two hours while Mike Whitesell repaired a broken hinge on her glasses. This simple repair ordinarily takes 15 minutes.

TECHNOLOGY **C·O·N·N·E·C·T·I·O·N**

In the last decade, homes and offices added millions of fax machines. Today, most personal computers are equipped with fax modems, allowing direct faxing from one computer to another. Faxes send exact copies of text and graphics over phone lines to other fax machines or computers in seconds, where they can be printed. Sending by fax is quick, convenient and, for documents of fewer than 20 pages, fairly inexpensive. Many companies offer fax-on-demand service. Callers use Touch-Tone phones to request particular documents, which are sent within minutes.

Fax cover sheets (like Figure 9-6, page 292) ensure your document will reach the right person. But don't use a cover sheet if the necessary routing information is in the document. That just wastes paper.

Sending a fax is like sending a letter with no envelope. Fax machines are often located in a central area, and anyone can read incoming faxes, even those marked "confidential." If it's private, use "snail mail."

INFOBIT

"Every job is a self-portrait of the person who did it. Autograph your work with excellence."

FROM A POSTER IN AN AUTO REPAIR SHOP

Style

It is important to learn the accepted rules of correspondence. A person who regularly reads business correspondence will think there is something odd about you if you do not use these styles. You may not be taken seriously, for instance, if you write your letters in pencil on notebook paper.

Over the years, your teachers have endlessly coached you in correct capitalization, spelling, punctuation, and grammar. Now is your chance to put that learning into practice. Accuracy in numbers and correctly spelled names are especially important. Check the spelling of the reader's name twice, as most people are sensitive about their names. Although it may seem unfair, other people will judge you based on the correctness of your writing. Since you want to be taken seriously, take the time and effort to use what you know.

Figure 9-7: *Ineffective messages often end up in the "circular file."*

Practice 9-4: Revising Ineffective Messages

1. Each of the following sentences lacks at least one quality of an effective message. Revise the sentences to improve their tone and to make them more economical, polite, and precise.

   a. Many people attended the demonstration.

   b. We regret to tell you that there will be a short delay in processing your forms.

   c. It was suggested that the deadline be extended.

   d. The new manuals will be available to each and every technician by the month of August.

   e. I know you're the boss, but what's your problem, anyway?

2. The fax cover sheet shown in Figure 9-6 on page 292 is wordy. Revise it to make it more economical and conversational. Use no more than two sentences.

3. The writer of the memo shown in Figure 9-8 below was very angry when he wrote his rough draft. Not only did someone's careless behavior cause the theft of sensitive information, but now the company must pay for new ID cards and increased security. Write what you imagine Bryan's angry, negative first draft said.

4. Write the first paragraph of a letter answering the letter from Kijiro Kimura shown in Figure 9-3 on page 287.

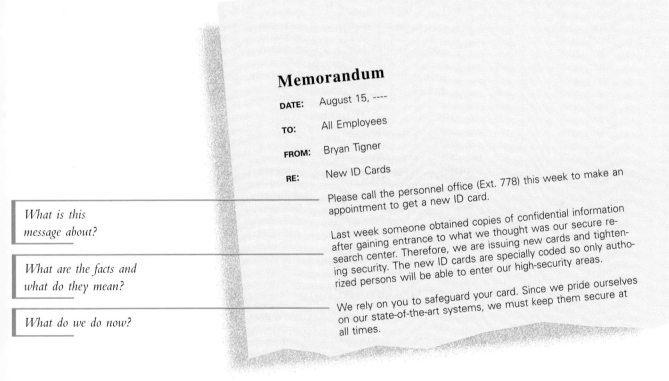

Figure 9-8: *A memo with an effective message*

Content of Effective Messages

Except for the simplest messages, an effective message has three parts that answer the following questions:

* What is this message about?

* What are the facts and what do they mean?

* What do we do now?

CAREER C·O·N·N·E·C·T·I·O·N

Rick Hemmert, owner of Earth Trek travel agency, often saves time by using postcards, rather than phone calls, to communicate with clients. He uses postcards to send confirmations of travel plans and reminders to clients that payments are due. Hemmert also uses postcards to follow up on sales, since he believes postcards are never interpreted as an interruption or hard sell, but they do let prospects know that he's interested and available when they're ready to do business.

Instead of calling clients after they've returned from a trip—a potentially lengthy process—he sends welcome-home cards. Hemmert says, "So much of the mail people receive these days is junk mail that they relate well to a personal card or letter and always seem to appreciate it."

What Is This Message About?

This introductory section lets the reader know what the message is about and, perhaps, who you are. It should make the reader want to read the rest of the message. Getting to the point quickly is one of the best ways to get the reader's attention.

Mention the most important point—the purpose of your message—in this first brief section. Even messages that are read are not always read to the very end. If the most important point appears at the end of the page or, even worse, on the second page, the reader may never see it.

What Are the Facts and What Do They Mean?

This section gives the reader enough information to make the decision, grant the request, or solve the problem. It must be concise, clear, and well organized. For easy reading, put important points or details into lists rather than paragraphs.

What Do We Do Now?

INFOBIT

Don't fight. Make it right.

HARDEE'S COMPLAINT-HANDLING POLICY

Many, but not all, written messages are action-oriented. The action statement tells the reader what to do and when to do it. Or it may explain what the writer intends to do. State the action clearly and directly. You'll find it's more effective to make polite requests than demands. It is often appropriate to close with a polite ending, such as "Thank you."

Sending Notes

Notes are informal personal messages. Writing the note by hand gives your message a personal touch. Notes may or may not be mailed. A typical format for a personal note is shown in Figure 9-9. Sending thank-you notes to people who go out of their way to help you is like sending an unexpected gift. Also send notes to congratulate customers or coworkers on promotions, achievements, and special occasions in both their professional and their personal lives. The few minutes it takes to write these simple messages are well worth the time. Your associates will appreciate your thoughtfulness.

J J

November 10, ----

Dateline

Salutation

Dear Herb,

Body

I just heard the good news about your promotion. Congratulations!
I can't say that I'm surprised. I think your hard work is largely responsible for this year's decrease in defective parts.
Nice job!

Sincerely,

Closing

Jocelynne

Signature

Figure 9-9: *A handwritten note*

Figure 9-10: *Writing notes by hand gives messages a personal touch.*

Practice 9-5: Sending a Note

Write a note to any staff member at your school expressing thanks for some recent help or advice. Your note doesn't have to be long, but it should be sincere. Be specific about why you're thanking the reader. Use blue or black ink and unlined paper. Follow these guidelines:

* Include only the dateline, salutation, body, closing, and signature.

* Place the dateline, closing, and signature beginning at center.

* Indent paragraphs.

Figure 9-9 above is an example of a personal note. Turn to Figure 9-16 on page 305 to see a thank-you letter.

Sending Memos

Memorandums, commonly called **memos**, are messages written to people within the organization and do not usually go through the U.S. Postal Service. The memo, the most common form of written communication at work, is easy to draft. Memos consist of two main sections: a heading and a message. Memos sometimes include some of the same optional parts as business letters. These parts are discussed later in this chapter.

There is no one correct format for memos. Many organizations have their own preferences. If your employer does not, you can use margins of 1.5 inches for the top, 1 inch for the sides, and at least 1 inch for the bottom.

The Heading

The heading of the memo has four parts, each with a **guide word**:

TO:	The name of the reader (or readers), sometimes followed by a comma and the person's title
FROM:	The name of the writer (or writers), sometimes followed by a comma and the person's title
DATE:	The date on which the memo was written
SUBJECT:	A brief description of the content of the memo. Sometimes, instead of "SUBJECT," it says "REFERENCE" or just "RE."

Sometimes the memo includes a **copy notation**, *c* (meaning "copy"), followed by names of other people who received copies of the memo. The memo shown in Figure 9-11 has a copy notation. The copy notation may also be placed two lines below the body of the memo, with or without a colon.

Follow each guide word with a colon (:). There is no one correct placement for these four items. The examples in this chapter demonstrate several acceptable styles. Some organizations use memo forms. All you have to do on these preprinted forms is fill in the heading information and write the message, as in Figure 9-12, page 301. Many word processing programs include predesigned memo templates.

The Subject Line

An informative **subject line** serves the same purpose as the headline of a newspaper story: It gives exact information about the subject and motivates the audience to read on. It not only answers the question

TO: Bobby Chaplin, Marie Delatorre, Eva Hodges, Dan Maurmeier

FROM: Sandy Nagy

DATE: September 8, - - - -

SUBJECT: Presentations to Alex Otero

C: M. J. Shearer

Our new owner, Alex Otero, will be touring our building on October 10. I have selected you to give a five-minute presentation about the workings of your department when he visits your area. Please describe your department's function and how your team works together to meet goals.

Please show me the first draft of the notes for your presentation one week from today, and plan a final draft by October 1.

I look forward to seeing your first draft and to your help in orienting Mr. Otero. Thanks.

Figure 9-11: *The two main sections of a memo*

"What is this about?"; it also answers the question "So what?" Notice how the following revised subject lines answer those questions.

ROUGH DRAFT	REVISION
RE: Rats	RE: Rats Sighted in Dumpster Area
SUBJECT: Mileage Reimbursement	SUBJECT: Procedure for Submitting Mileage Reimbursement Requests
REFERENCE: Widget Shipment	REFERENCE: Widget Shipment, Invoice 34322, dated 3/12/—

Try to keep subject lines to ten or fewer words.

The Message

Memos solve problems either by giving the reader new information or by persuading the reader to take an action. Since the writer and the reader of the memo are usually coworkers, the reader probably already knows something about the subject of the memo. Background information and explanations are often unnecessary. *Don't tell readers what they already know.*

Most memos are brief, perhaps only one paragraph long; others are longer. Include informative internal headings for long memos. Paragraphs in memos do not always follow the traditional "topic sentence, body, concluding sentence" structure. A shortened form is acceptable as long as the reader will understand the memo's meaning.

Each memo should deal with only one subject. If the memo includes more than one subject, the reader may take action on part of it and overlook the other parts. Furthermore, the reader may not be the person who will act to solve the problem or fulfill the request. If a memo includes two subjects, the reader may need to pass it along to two people. If you have two messages, write two brief memos.

Of course, more than one person may need to read your memo. Then, your heading will read like the following:

> TO: Phil and Nancy
>
> or
>
> TO: All Supervisors

Send Phil and Nancy or all supervisors copies of the memo.

Practice 9-6: Sending and Answering Memos

1. Write a memo to your boss requesting permission to leave work two hours early one day next week. Include all the facts your boss will need to make a decision.

2. Answer another student's memo. Give him or her permission to leave early.

3. Answer a second memo with a no. Give a good reason for your refusal and a positive alternative.

4. Read the letter shown in Figure 9-17 on page 310. Write a memo from Mr. Bridges to Keith to find out how the phone call to Pat Kendall went.

INFOBIT

There are no misunderstandings; there are only failures to communicate.

SENEGALESE PROVERB

TECHNOBIT

After you click the "send" icon, Internet e-mail messages are broken up into small packets, each taking the quickest route; the last packet sent might be the first to arrive. Transmission Control Protocol/Internet Protocol (TCP/IP) software on the receiver's end collects and reassembles the packets into the original message. All this happens in a matter of seconds.

INTEROFFICE MEMO

To: All Staff

From: Penny   Date: April 12, ----

Subject: E-Mail Procedures

We finally have the bugs worked out of the new e-mail system. I apologize for the delay and thank you for your patience. I think the features of EEZ-Mail make it worth the wait. Please follow these guidelines so we can get the most out of this system:

- Check for messages at the start of your shift, before or after lunch, and at the end of your shift.
- Please avoid sending junk mail.
- Check with senders before forwarding their message to some-one else. It's just common courtesy.
- Since messages take up disk space, regularly delete files you no longer need. Be aware, though, that deleted messages still exist on the tape backup.
- Although we do not regularly read messages, you can't consider them to be private. Do not send confidential information by e-mail.

Please message me if you have any questions. My e-mail user name is *doergerp*.

Figure 9-12: *A memo to multiple readers*

Sending Electronic Mail

Electronic mail, better known as **e-mail**, is communication technology that allows people to send memos from their computers directly to computers in the same building or tens of thousands of miles away. According to the Electronic Messaging Association, by 1996, 4.7 billion e-mail messages were sent per day by 51 million users. The U.S. Postal Service reports delivering 493 million messages per day during the same year.

Electronic mail combines the efficiency and low cost of memos with the speed and conversational nature of phone calls, but without the problem of "telephone tag." You can also send and receive messages 24 hours a day, 365 days a year, and your readers can respond to your messages instantly. You can easily send one message to several people, and they can just as easily reply to, print, edit, file, and forward your message. Electronic mail is the fastest way to send short messages.

ETHICS C·O·N·N·E·C·T·I·O·N

How would you feel if you found out your mail carrier regularly opened your private mail and shared it with your neighbors? If you send e-mail at work, something similar could be happening. Courts have ruled that employers are entitled to read any e-mail that passes through the organization's computers. And if you think hitting the "delete" key deletes the file, you're wrong. Often, messages are saved, deep in the company computer, for years. People have been fired for sending company secrets or exchanging unethical or illegal information. One fired employee who sued for age discrimination got a quick settlement after his lawyer found, "I hope we can get rid of the old &$#@ soon" on deleted company e-mail.

Don't e-mail it if you don't want to see it in print, posted on a bulletin board, in a newsletter, or in front of a jury.

Most e-mail messages are brief and casual. Electronic-mail software generally provides a memo format for composing messages, with boxes to fill in the name and/or e-mail address of each recipient, a subject line, the names and e-mail addresses of any people who should receive copies of the message, and the message, as shown in Figure 9-13. Informative, specific subject lines are very important to readers who receive lots of e-mail. The subject line can let them know whether the message is important or useful enough to be dealt with—or deleted— right away.

The qualities and parts of effective messages discussed earlier in this chapter also apply to writing e-mail. Some additional guidelines follow:

* Keep paragraphs short, only a few sentences each. Otherwise, your reader might lose his or her train of thought while scrolling through long paragraphs.

* Try to keep messages to one screen— about 25 lines.

* DO NOT USE ALL CAPITAL LETTERS IN YOUR MESSAGE. DOING SO MAY SAVE YOU A FEW KEYSTROKES, BUT USING ALL CAPITAL LETTERS IS HARD TO READ.

* When responding to a message, include enough information in your message so your reader knows what it's about. If your coworker sends the message, "Where do you want to go for lunch today?" and two hours later, you reply, "I don't care," your reader

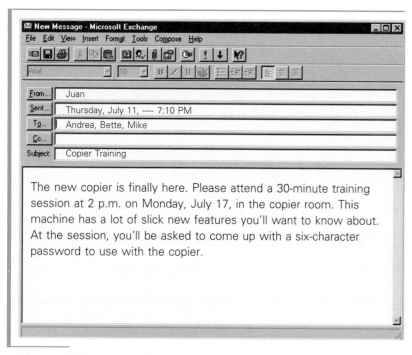

Figure 9-13: *An e-mail message*

will probably be perplexed. Instead, write, "I don't care where we go to lunch today."

* Don't send someone a message just because you can. Wasting coworkers' time with unnecessary messages is inconsiderate.

* Don't use e-mail to send bad news or criticism. Sending a "You're fired!" e-mail message would be in very bad taste.

Practice 9-7: Sending E-Mail

1. Read the letter shown in Figure 9-2 on page 285. Write an e-mail message to Toni, telling her about the compliment from Mrs. Del Gesso.

2. Read the message shown in Figure 9-13 on page 302. Send an e-mail message to Juan explaining that you cannot make it to the training session. What information will Juan need from you?

Figure 9-14: *Electronic mail replaces most paper memos in some organizations.*

Sending Business Letters

Business letters are written messages mailed to people who are outside the organization. If you read ten books on business letter writing, you will probably see ten correct—but different—ways to draft business letters. Not only that, but many organizations have their own preferences. Although this section will not attempt to show you all the variations, it will give you enough information and practice so that you can set up an effective letter.

The experts do agree upon a few requirements. Keep the following general guidelines in mind:

* Always key business letters. You may write personal notes and quick memos by hand, but key letters. Use plain 8 1/2- by 11-inch paper. Most people prefer white paper, but it can be off-white, beige, or light gray. Print the letter using a good, quality printer.

* Use **letterhead** stationery from your organization if it's available. The company name and address, and perhaps phone numbers and company logo, are preprinted on the paper. The letter shown in Figure 9-3 on page 287 was printed on letterhead stationery. Never use your employer's letterhead for letters relating to your personal business.

* Balance the letter attractively on the page. Use side margins of 1 inch or your word processor's defaults. Center the letter

> Addressee's Name
> Page X
> Date
>
> ↓2
>
> Use this heading style for all subsequent pages of letters or memorandums that exceed one page. Note that the top margin is 1 inch. The rest of the margins are the same as those used on the first page of the letter.

1" (line 7)

Figure 9-15: *Heading for the second page of a letter*

INFOBIT

"Letters are above all useful as a means of expressing the ideal self; and no other method of communication is quite so good for this purpose.... In letters we can reform without practice, beg without humiliation, snip and shape embarrassing experiences to the measure of our own desires...."

ELIZABETH HARDWICK,
U.S. AUTHOR AND CRITIC

vertically. If your equipment does not have an automatic centering feature, use a standard top margin of 2 inches (line 13) and a page ending of at least 1 inch.

* Text in the body of a letter may be left-aligned or fully justified. Ask if your employer has a preference.

* Use easy-to-read typefaces in 10- to 12-point sizes.

* Most business letters are no longer than one page. If the letter is longer, try to shorten it as you revise. If additional pages are necessary, use plain paper, not letterhead, for them. List the name of the reader, the page number, and the date in the upper, left corner. Follow with at least three lines of the body. Never place just the closing and signature block on the second page. (See Figure 9-15.)

Practice 9-8: Standard Business Letter Parts

As you read pages 304–309, complete the form on *Student Workbook* page 9-A with facts about the standard parts of business letters. Look also at the sample letter in Figure 9-16. When you are finished, you'll have a reference sheet to use next time you write a letter.

Standard Parts of Business Letters

Most business-letter styles include a heading, dateline, inside address, salutation, body, closing, and signature block. The block-style letter in Figure 9-16 on page 305 shows their placement on the page. Since many acceptable variations of the seven standard letter parts exist, learn whatever style your employer prefers. This chapter describes the most common styles. Please refer to Figure 9-16 as you read the descriptions of the standard letter parts.

The Heading

The **heading** of a letter is like the return address of an envelope. It gives the mailing address of the writer. Spell out the name of the city and words such as *Street* and *Avenue,* but use standard two-letter abbreviations for states. Separate city and state with a comma. Key the ZIP Code one space after the state. The writer's name is not part of the heading; it belongs at the end of the letter in the signature block.

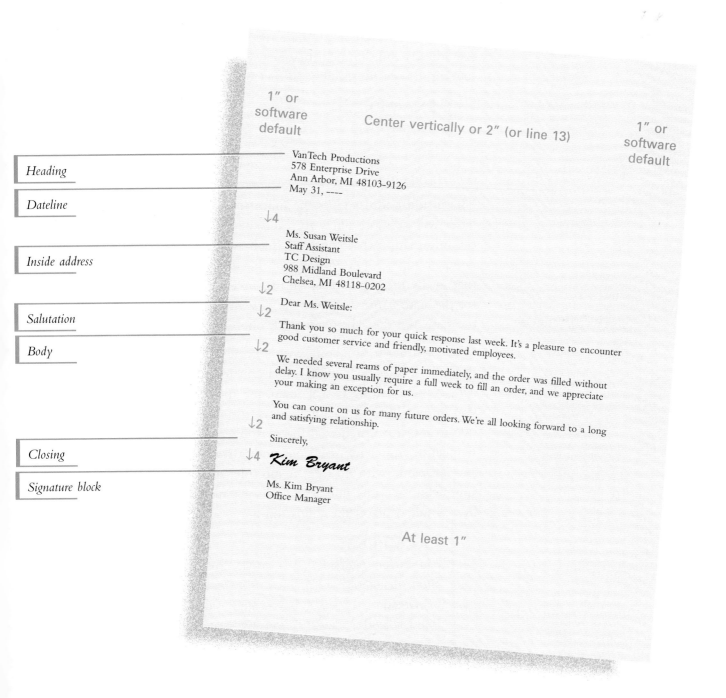

Figure 9-16: *Placement of the seven standard parts of business letters*

> ### INFOBIT
>
> "Use your good judgment in all situations.
>
> There will be no additional rules."
>
> NORDSTROM, INC.
> EMPLOYEE HANDBOOK

> **EXAMPLES:**
>
> | | |
> |---|---|
> | VanTech Productions | 578 Enterprise Drive |
> | 578 Enterprise Drive | Ann Arbor, MI 48103-9126 |
> | Ann Arbor, MI 48103-9126 | |

Do not use a heading if you are using letterhead stationery.

The Dateline

The **dateline** gives the date on which the letter was written. Do not abbreviate the month. Separate the day and the year with a comma. Key the dateline immediately below the heading. If you are using letterhead, key the dateline at the top margin.

> **EXAMPLE:**
>
> May 31, 1999

The Inside Address

The **inside address** gives the full mailing address of the reader. Your letter will be more likely to reach the right person if you include all the information that you have, such as name, title, department, and company name. The information in the inside address is the same as that in the mailing address on the envelope. Do not abbreviate except for the state name. Separate the city and state with a comma. Separate the state and the ZIP Code with one space.

When writing to someone with a professional title such as *Dr.*, use that title. For other people, use a **courtesy title** (*Miss, Ms., Mrs.,* or *Mr.*). When writing to a woman, use the courtesy title she prefers. If you do not know what she prefers, use *Ms.* If you aren't sure what title to use (for instance, if the person's name could be a man's or a woman's), and cannot find out with a reasonable effort, use the first and last name with no title. A job title, such as *Staff Assistant*, can appear on the same line as the person's name (separated from the name by a comma) or on the following line.

> **EXAMPLES:**
>
> | | |
> |---|---|
> | Ms. Susan Weitsle | Ms. Susan Weitsle, Staff Assistant |
> | Staff Assistant | TC Design |
> | TC Design | 988 Midland Boulevard |
> | 988 Midland Boulevard | Chelsea, MI 48118-0202 |
> | Chelsea, MI 48118-0202 | |

Key the inside address four lines below the dateline at the left margin. You may reduce this space to two lines for longer letters to avoid using a second page.

The Salutation

The **salutation** is sometimes called the greeting. The first name is not included, just the courtesy or professional title and the last name (if you are on a first-name basis with the person to whom you are writing, however, address that person by first name). The salutation appears two lines below the inside address.

Two different punctuation styles can be used in the salutation and closing of letters. **Open punctuation** means using no punctuation after the salutation and closing. **Mixed punctuation** means using a colon after the salutation and a comma after the closing.

The following table shows how the correct salutation depends on the information in the first line of the inside address.

SALUTATION AND INSIDE ADDRESS

Name and Title Known	Title, but Not Name, Known	Name and Title Unknown
Ms. Susan Weitsle Staff Assistant TC Design 988 Midland Boulevard Chelsea, MI 48118-0202	Attention Staff Assistant TC Design 988 Midland Boulevard Chelsea, MI 48118-0202	TC Design 988 Midland Boulevard Chelsea, MI 48118-0202
Dear Ms. Weitsle: *or* Dear Susan: (if you are on a first-name basis with her)	Ladies and Gentlemen: *or* Gentlemen and Ladies: *or* Use the simplified letter style.	Dear TC Design: *or* Ladies and Gentlemen: *or* Gentlemen and Ladies: *or* Use the simplified letter style.

The salutation is not used in the simplified block style (see Figure 9-5, page 291). Using this style when you don't know the name of your reader helps to avoid awkward salutations like "Ladies and Gentlemen."

Practice 9-9: Writing Inside Addresses

Inside addresses are written in block form. List items in this order:

NAME OF PERSON, TITLE	Mr. Charles Harper, Manager
NAME OF DEPARTMENT	Service Department
NAME OF ORGANIZATION	Good Luck Auto Parts
STREET ADDRESS	3434 Riverside Drive
CITY, STATE ZIP CODE	Durango, CO 81301-9106

(cont'd on next page)

It is also correct to key the person's job title on its own line below his or her name. Notice that a comma separates the person's name from the title if this information appears on the same line. A comma also separates the city and state, but not the state and the ZIP Code.

For each group of facts, write the inside address in block form. Use the correct postal abbreviations for the state names—two capital letters with no periods. Skip a space below each address and write a correct salutation followed by a colon.

1. The director of Jupiter Day Care Center, Georgia, Atlanta Public Schools, 30301- 2413, 413 Neptune Street, Atlanta

2. Maine, B. J. Santos, 27 Pike Street, Lobster Heaven, Augusta, 04330-1217, Chef

3. Eureka, 95501-1215, 8905 Craft Road, Paris Stables, California

4. The manager of the Customer Service Department of the Airway Heights Gas and Electric Company. This company is located at 621 Lockness Avenue in the town of Airway Heights, which is in Washington. The ZIP Code in Airway Heights is 99001-2621.

5. Arvi Saarisuu of Roettig Enterprises, located in Daisetta, a town in Texas. The company is at 877 East Karcher Road. The ZIP Code there is 77533-1126.

6. Katrina Price-Hall, the pharmacy technician who works at the pharmacy nearest your home. Don't forget the ZIP Code.

7. The personnel manager of a local business that hires people with training in your occupational field.

INFOBIT

A United States Postal Service survey indicated more than 33 percent of all mail contained incomplete or inaccurate address elements and, therefore, delivery was affected—for more than 58 billion mailpieces per year!

The Body

The **body** is the message part of the letter. It follows the guidelines for effective communication. It should answer these questions:

* What is this message about?
* What are the facts and what do they mean?
* What do we do now?

In modified block style, the first line of each paragraph may be indented five spaces, but the examples in this book have blocked paragraphs with no indentation. Single spacing is used within paragraphs; double spacing is used between paragraphs. Paragraphs are generally brief.

The Closing

The **closing** is a word or phrase used to end the message. Several acceptable business-letter closings follow, in the order of least to most formal. If you use mixed punctuation in a letter and follow the salutation with a colon, follow the closing with a comma. Capitalize only the first letter of the first word.

> **EXAMPLES:**
>
> Best wishes,   Sincerely,
>
> Cordially,   Yours truly,
>
> Sincerely yours,   Respectfully,

If you are not an experienced business-letter writer, some of these closings may sound vaguely romantic to you. They're not. Readers expect these closings. However, "Thank you" is not an acceptable closing. Your thanks belong in the body of the letter. The simplified block style, shown in Figure 9-5, does not use a closing.

The Signature Block

The **signature block** includes your keyed name below your handwritten signature. The keyed name is necessary in case the reader cannot read the signature. Sign your name in black ink. This, by the way, is a signature, not an autograph, so write legibly. Writers often sign only their first name if they know the reader well.

A woman can take this opportunity to let the reader know which courtesy title she prefers. A person whose name does not indicate gender can similarly include a courtesy title to let the reader know which title is appropriate.

INFÓBIT

"For heaven's sake sign legibly. The biggest ego trip I know is a completely illegible signature."

MALCOLM FORBES, OF FORBES MAGAZINE, ON SIGNING LETTERS

> **EXAMPLES:**
>
> Sincerely,   Yours truly,
>
> *Kim Bryant*   **Gary Eder**
>
> Ms. Kim Bryant   Gary Eder, Quality Control Manager
> Sales Representative

Practice 9-10: Correcting Letter Parts

teamwork With a partner, examine the letter in *Student Workbook* page 9-B, which contains 25 errors. Locate the errors and mark them using the proofreading marks shown on the inside, back cover of this book. In the boxes, label the letter parts. Then revise the letter. The writer intended this letter to be modified block with open punctuation.

Optional Letter Parts

Along with the seven standard letter parts, use the attention line, subject line, reference initials, enclosure line, and copy notation when you need them. The block-style letter shown in Figure 9-17 uses all five optional parts and shows their placement.

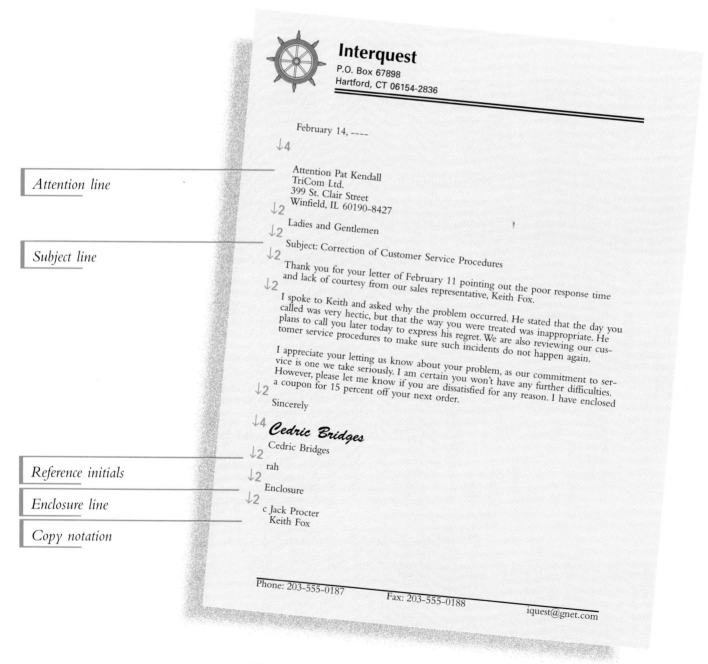

Attention line

Subject line

Reference initials

Enclosure line

Copy notation

Interquest
P.O. Box 67898
Hartford, CT 06154-2836

February 14, ----

↓4

Attention Pat Kendall
TriCom Ltd.
399 St. Clair Street
Winfield, IL 60190-8427

↓2

Ladies and Gentlemen

↓2

Subject: Correction of Customer Service Procedures

↓2

Thank you for your letter of February 11 pointing out the poor response time and lack of courtesy from our sales representative, Keith Fox.

I spoke to Keith and asked why the problem occurred. He stated that the day you called was very hectic, but that the way you were treated was inappropriate. He plans to call you later today to express his regret. We are also reviewing our customer service procedures to make sure such incidents do not happen again.

I appreciate your letting us know about your problem, as our commitment to service is one we take seriously. I am certain you won't have any further difficulties. However, please let me know if you are dissatisfied for any reason. I have enclosed a coupon for 15 percent off your next order.

↓2

Sincerely

↓4 *Cedric Bridges*

↓2 Cedric Bridges

↓2 rah

↓2 Enclosure

↓2 c Jack Procter
Keith Fox

Phone: 203-555-0187   Fax: 203-555-0188

iquest@gnet.com

Figure 9-17: *Five optional letter parts*

The Attention Line

An **attention line** allows you to send your letter officially to an organization but direct it to a specific person, position, or department. Key the word *Attention* followed by the name of a person and title, just a title, or the name of a department. Key the attention line as the first line of the inside address.

The Subject Line

The **subject line** of a letter is similar to the subject line of a memo. It tells the reader at a glance what the letter is about. Key it two lines below the salutation. In simplified letters, subject lines are keyed in all capital letters. In other letter styles, subject lines may be capitalized like titles. Including the word *Subject* is optional.

Reference Initials

The **reference initials** are the initials of the person who keyed the letter. These initials will be used only if you key letters for someone else or if someone else keys your letters for you. Reference initials are placed two lines below the keyed signature, against the left margin. They should be keyed in lowercase, not capital, letters. Reference initials can also be added to memos.

The Enclosure Line

An **enclosure** is anything in the envelope besides the letter, such as a check. Two lines below the reference initials, key the word *Enclosure* or *Enclosures*. Memos may include enclosure lines. When you have more than one enclosure, add the number of enclosures this way:

Enclosures (2)

The Copy Notation

The **copy notation** lets the reader know another person (or persons) received a copy of the letter. It goes two lines below the enclosure line. Key *c*, followed by the name or names of those receiving a copy.

Common Letter Styles

Three popular letter styles are block, modified block, and simplified block. In **block**-style letters (see Figure 9-2, page 285, and Figure 9-16, page 305) all lines begin at the left margin. In **modified block** style (see Figure 9-3, page 287) the heading (if needed), dateline, closing, and signature block are indented to the center of the page. In this style, paragraphs may be blocked at the left or indented. Letters keyed in **simplified** style (see Figure 9-5, page 291) are set up like block-style letters, but there is no salutation or closing. This style always includes a subject line in all capitals.

TECHNOBIT

The Postal Service is testing the Handwritten Address Interpretation system, which allows computer scanners to accurately read and apply bar codes to handwritten addresses on mail, allowing for automated sorting.

Unless your employer states a preference, use the style that suits you best. The block and simplified styles are easiest to key. Remember that, when keying on letterhead stationery, you do not use a heading.

Addressing Envelopes

The United States Postal Service sent a pamphlet to residential customers to explain how to address mail for faster delivery. It also gives standard abbreviations. Your teacher will give you a copy of the pamphlet.

Notice that every letter in the address is a capital letter and that all punctuation is omitted. When addresses are formatted this way, mail can be sorted automatically by the Postal Service's electronic scanners, which saves routing time. Always use the two-letter postal abbreviation for the state name. Use only the standard abbreviations for *Avenue, Street, Suite, Apartment,* and so on. Please follow U.S. Postal Service guidelines whenever you address mail.

Figures 9-18 and 9-19 show how to fold letters and insert them into two standard sizes of envelopes.

Figure 9-18: *Folding a letter for a small envelope*

Figure 9-19: *Folding a letter for a large envelope*

Practice 9-11: Addressing Mail

Use the envelope forms on *Student Workbook* page 9-C for this Practice.

1. Complete the first envelope for the letter shown in Figure 9-2 on page 285 sent from Emila Del Gesso to Roger's.

2. Complete the second envelope for a *reply* to the letter shown in Figure 9-3 on page 287. The letter would be from Paul Beauchamp to Kijiro Kimura.

3. Complete the third envelope for a letter from you to an administrator of your school district.

Practice 9-12: Writing Messages

teamwork You will need a partner for this Practice.

1. Locate the full mailing address for a local business. Write a letter in modified block style to the owner of the business—who happens to have the same name as your partner—to complain about the poor service you received from one of his or her employees yesterday. Be sure to include all three parts of an effective message. Fold the letter and address the outside as if it were an envelope. Deliver the letter to your partner.

2. Review the information in this chapter on the qualities of effective messages; then answer your partner's letter. Design letterhead for this letter and use block style. Fold the letter, address the "envelope," and deliver it.

3. Write a memo to the employee who was the subject of your partner's complaint. Make this memo as positive as you can.

WEB LINK

The Internet has sites that are like yellow pages. When you access these sites, it's easy to locate mailing addresses, Internet addresses, and phone numbers of businesses, plus maps showing how to get there.

SUMMARY

Learning to write effective notes, memos, e-mail, and letters is important for all workers. Since the written message projects an image of the writer and his or her organization, it is important to produce professional, quality correspondence. Follow these guidelines whenever you write a message:

* Specifically state the purpose.

* Communicate clearly, concisely, and courteously.

* Answer the questions What is this message about? What are the facts and what do they mean? and What do we do now?

* Use a standard style for memos and business letters.

* Address envelopes according to Postal Service guidelines.

* Carefully proofread and revise your message.

Sending a Request Letter

In this Project, you will write and send at least one business letter. Depending on your circumstances, you may choose one (or more) assignments from this list:

* Most job applications ask you to list three to five references. References are responsible people who can attest to your honesty, dependability, and positive work habits. You must, however, obtain permission from a person to list him or her as a reference. Write to someone who would give you a good reference to use next time you look for a job. Ask for permission to include his or her name on your list of references.

* When you are searching for a job, you may find it helpful to have letters of recommendation from your references to give to interviewers. Write to one of your references, asking for an open letter of recommendation. Mention what type of job you would be applying for.

* What is your dream job? How would you go about getting that job? If you have a specific career goal, write to an organization that you would like to work for in the future. What training, experience, and qualities do they expect from new employees? How can you prepare yourself for eventual employment with that organization? Call the organization to find out to whom your letter should be addressed.

* Companies sometimes donate used equipment to schools. Write to a local business in your occupational field. Briefly describe your educational program and ask if the business might be willing to donate equipment. Check with your school district to find out what the guidelines are for accepting donations.

* Write to an organization that produces goods or services related to your educational program asking for specific information about those goods or services.

1. Review information and examples. Study the Sample Project Plan and the Sample Request Letter on pages 316 and 317.

2. Complete the Project Plan on *Student Workbook* page 9-E and have your teacher check it. Consider including a self-addressed, stamped envelope to make it as easy as possible for your reader to respond.

3. Write a rough draft. Using the Rough Draft column of the Project Guide, *Student Workbook* page 9-F, check your own work with another student. Have your partner read your letter aloud to you. Ask your teacher to check the rough draft.

4. Revise your letter. Using the Final Draft column of the Project Guide, proofread your work. Make needed corrections. Print the final draft.

5. Fold your final draft and place it in a correctly addressed envelope. Do not seal the mailing envelope. Turn it in with the Project Guide.

Plan for a Request Letter

SUBJECT	Arrangements for taking certification exam
AUDIENCE	testing coordinator
PURPOSE	What actions should the audience take? give permission to take an oral exam
STYLE	☒ block ☐ modified block ☐ simplified block
HEADING	Apt. 7B 3495 Fair Acres Lane Warren, MI 48089-2327
DATELINE	12/3/--
LETTER ADDRESS	Testing Coordinator Certification Center 609 E. Main St., Suite 4-B Detroit, MI 48233-6977
SALUTA-TION	Ladies and Gentlemen:
CLOSING	Yours truly,
OTHER PARTS	reference initials

CONTENT

Background:

date of test

reason for not writing the test

Details:

have taken oral exams before

If I can't take an oral exam, what to do next?

my phone number

Action Statement:

Let me know before January.

Call if you need more information.

Polite Ending:

Thank you for your assistance.

3495 Fair Acres Lane
Apartment 7B
Warren, MI 48089-2327
December 3, ----

Attention Testing Coordinator
Certification Center
609 East Main Street
Suite 4-B
Detroit, MI 48233-6977

Ladies and Gentlemen:

I am scheduled to take my certification exam at your center on January 20, ----.
However, I am not able to write answers to the questions because I lost the use of
my hands in an accident four years ago.

Do you have a way to accommodate me? In the past, I have taken oral exams. If
you are unable to make special arrangements, what steps should I take next? Please
let me know by the end of December.

I am well-prepared and eager to take the certification exam. You may call me at
810-555-0150 if you need more information.

Thank you for any assistance that you can provide.

Yours truly,

Karen Schultz ts

Miss Karen Schultz

ts

KAREN SCHULTZ
3495 FAIR ACRES LANE APT 7B
WARREN MI 48089-2327

32¢

ATTN TESTING COORDNTR
CERTIFICATION CTR
609 E MAIN ST STE 4-B
DETROIT MI 48233-6977

Overview

Letters appear in every type of literature. In the Shakespearean play *Macbeth*, Lady Macbeth receives her husband's letter informing her of three witches' predictions for Macbeth's future. The novel *To Be Young, Gifted and Black* includes a letter addressed to the editor of the *New York Times*, expressing the disillusionments of militant blacks of the late sixties. In the following selection, the letter is written in the form of a love poem.

This poem speaks simply and directly of an arranged marriage, one that began without awareness of love or feeling. In this poem the speaker is a young Chinese woman who is writing to her husband after his five months' absence. She refers to her early marriage, her growing love for him, and her loneliness. The poet uses images from nature, such as deep moss, autumn leaves, and yellow butterflies, to suggest how long her husband has been away.

What evidence is there that the marriage has become one of mutual love and respect?

"The River-Merchant's Wife: A Letter"

Based on a poem by RIHAKU (LI T'AI PO):
(AD 700-762), one of China's greatest poets.

While my hair was still cut straight across
    my forehead
        I played about the front gate, pulling flowers.
You came by on bamboo stilts, playing horse,
You walked about my seat, playing with blue plums.
And we went on living in the village of Chokan:
Two small people, without dislike or suspicion.

I desired my dust to be mingled with yours. . . .

At fourteen I married My Lord you.
I never laughed being bashful.
Lowering my head, I looked at the wall.
Called to a thousand times, I never looked back.

At fifteen I stopped scowling,
I desired my dust to be mingled with yours
forever and forever and forever.
Why should I climb the look out?

> . . . *I will come out to meet*
>
> *you. . . .*

At sixteen you departed.
You went into far Ku-to-yen, by river of swirling eddies,
And you have been gone five months.
The monkeys make sorrowful noise overhead.

You dragged your feet when you went out.
By the gate now, the moss is grown, the different mosses,
Too deep to clear them away!
The leaves fall early this autumn, in wind.
The paired butterflies are already yellow with August

Over the grass in the West garden;
They hurt me. I grow older.
If you are coming down through the narrows of the
   river Kiang,
Please let me know beforehand,
And I will come out to meet you
           As far as Cho-fu-Sa.

—translated by Ezra Pound

Start-Up: Needless to say, the letter that this young Chinese wife writes to her husband is quite different from the letters you have been writing in this chapter. Disregard the fact that the letter is written as a poem. What other differences exist?

Connection: List the differences you find between a traditional letter and the one the Chinese woman writes. Consider letter format, standard letter parts, special letter parts, word choice, and sentence and paragraph structure.

Overview

Michel-Guillaume-Jean de Crèvecoeur (yes, this is his name) came to our country from France, his homeland, to travel and survey in the American colonies during the 1700s. He later settled on a farm near Chester, New York.

Crèvecoeur began writing his literary letters to inform Europeans of the opportunities in the New World. He idealized America as a land free of restraints and class structure. His letters, published in 1782, had a great influence on creating the image of America abroad.

from Letter III. "What Is an American"
from Letters from an American Farmer

I wish I could be acquainted with the feelings and thoughts which must agitate the heart and present themselves to the mind of an enlightened Englishman, when he first lands on this continent. . . . Here he beholds fair cities, substantial villages, extensive fields, and an immense country filled with decent houses, good roads, orchards, meadows, and bridges, where a hundred years ago all was wild, woody, and uncultivated! What a train of pleasing ideas this fair spectacle must suggest; it is a prospect which must inspire a good citizen with the most heartfelt pleasure.

The difficulty consists in the manner of viewing so extensive a scene. He is arrived on a new continent; a modern society offers itself to his contemplation, different from what he had hitherto seen. It is not composed, as in Europe, of great lords who possess everything, and a herd of people who have nothing. Here are no aristocratical families, no courts, no kings, no bishops, no ecclesiastical dominion, no invisible power giving to a few a very visible one, no great manufacturers employing thousands, no great refinements of luxury. The rich and the poor are not so far removed from each other as they are in Europe.

What then is the American, this new man? He is either a European or the descendant of a European, hence that strange mixture of blood, which you will find in no other country. I could point out to you a family whose grandfather was an Englishman, whose wife was Dutch, whose son married a

French woman, and whose present four sons have now four wives of different nations. *He* is an American who, leaving behind him all his ancient prejudices and manners, receives new ones from the new mode of life he has embraced, the new government he obeys, and the new rank he holds. He becomes an American by being received in the broad lap of our great *Alma Mater*. Here individuals of all nations are melted into a new race of men whose labors and posterity will one day cause great changes in the world.

Americans are the western pilgrims who are carrying along with them that great mass of arts, sciences, vigor, and industry which began long since in the East; they will finish the great circle. The Americans were once scattered all over Europe; here they are incorporated into one of the finest systems of population which has ever appeared, and which will hereafter become distinct by the power of the different climates they inhabit.

The American ought therefore to love this country much better than that wherein either he or his forefathers were born. Here the rewards of his industry follow with equal steps the progress of his labor; his labor is founded on the basis of nature, *self-interest;* can it want a stronger allurement? Wives and children, who before in vain demanded of him a morsel of bread, now, fat and frolicsome, gladly help their father to clear those fields whence exuberant crops are to arise to feed and to clothe them all, without any part being claimed either by a despotic prince, a rich abbot, or a mighty lord. Here religion demands but little of him—a small, voluntary salary to the minister and gratitude to God; can he refuse these? The American is a new man, who acts upon new principles; he must therefore entertain new ideas and form new opinions. From involuntary idleness, servile dependence, penury, and useless labor, he has passed to toils of a very different nature, rewarded by ample subsistence.—This is an American.

—Michel-Guillaume-Jean de Crèvecoeur

> Here individuals of all nations are melted into a new race of men whose labors and posterity will one day cause great changes in the world.

Start-Up: You have learned in this chapter that all correspondence should answer certain questions:

1. What is the message about?

2. What are the facts and what do they mean?

3. What do we do now?

Connection: Does the author answer these questions in his letter? Give examples.

Persuading

"True excellence requires a worthy dream, a good idea of how to realize it, and the courage to risk failure to achieve it."

—BILL CLINTON, 42ND PRESIDENT OF THE UNITED STATES

As you complete Chapter 10, you will

* define persuasion.

* adapt persuasive appeals to audience needs.

* identify barriers to persuading an audience.

* use the ADAM approach to persuade.

* create persuasive messages.

* distinguish among fact, opinion, and inference.

* identify and revise inappropriate persuasive language.

* revise a collection letter.

* determine why some sales letters are unsuccessful.

* plan, write, and revise an effective sales letter.

Workplace Skills in This Chapter

* Analyze persuasive messages using **resources** introduced in this chapter.

* Understand **interpersonal** preferences to create effective persuasion.

* Organize **information** into the ADAM method.

* Examine how persuasion affects communication **systems**.

* Use **technology** to create assignments.

Persuasion is everywhere. Advertising constantly bombards the public from billboards and television, from newspapers and magazines. Politicians campaign to win votes. Pizza parlors put flyers on mailboxes and coupons on doors to get people to try their products. The Marines and the Army recruit high school juniors and seniors. Teachers convince students to use safety equipment; parents urge kids to clean their rooms. All of these requests are expressed through persuasion.

Persuasion: Audience Needs

On the job, persuasion is used every day. The coworker who wants to trade days off uses persuasion. Personnel departments use pay incentives for better attendance. Your supervisor wants the best job done and uses persuasion to accomplish the purpose.

Persuasion is the conscious effort to influence attitudes or behavior. This attempt may reinforce a belief or convince a person that a point of view is right. Persuasion may also result in a direct action—or it may not succeed. But the person who persuades has pushed, and that push may cause change.

INFOBIT

The average person is bombarded with more than 1,600 advertising messages per day, according to Working Woman magazine.

Practice 10-1: Finding Everyday Persuasion

careers How does persuasion influence your life? Describe the following events when persuasion affected your life recently.

1. Describe two recent occasions when you tried to persuade someone.

2. Describe two recent occasions when someone tried to persuade you.

3. Describe two situations in your career major in which persuasion may be used.

The persuader should understand the needs of the audience. What are the unsatisfied needs? The persuasive message must satisfy the audience's needs, not the needs of the writer or of the speaker. The psychological researcher Abraham Maslow developed a sequence of needs. Maslow's sequence of needs provides a starting point in understanding and motivating an audience.

The lower-level needs must be met, or satisfied, before the higher-level needs can be met. For example, the person who is hungry and out of work must satisfy the need of hunger before he or she can search for a job. Once the person is fed, the hunger won't be the motivation; the lack of work will.

Maslow's sequence of needs (shown in Figure 10-1) is arranged in five categories:

1. Physical needs: Including food, warmth, shelter, sex, and avoidance of pain

2. Safety needs: Offering security for oneself and loved ones, having good health, and being in control of one's life

3. Love and belonging needs: Including the love of family, a sense of belonging, and concern for society

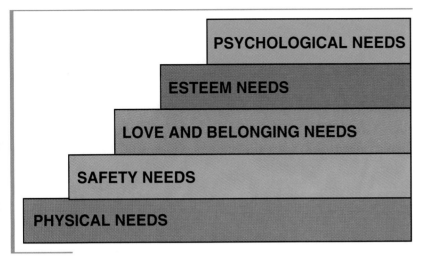

Figure 10-1: *Audience needs*

4. Esteem needs: Recognizing achievement and importance to make one feel better about oneself

5. Psychological needs (sometimes called self-actualization): Fulfilling one's potential and feeling happy about oneself; helping others

The chances of persuading an audience are greater under certain conditions. If the audience's needs are similar to the action that the persuader wants or if a person's self-esteem is low, persuasion is more likely to occur.

Practice 10-2: Identifying the Audience's Needs

careers The following persuasive arguments refer to job situations. The arguments' appeals are based on Maslow's sequence of needs. For each argument, identify the need or needs.

a. We would like you to move to our new store, along with 80 percent of our current employees. You'll still be able to socialize and eat lunch with your friends.

b. Take this new job. The employer provides wellness benefits: annual physicals, exercise equipment reimbursement, and payment for health-club membership.

c. The director took your plan to the company's branches. Now we want to reward you for a job well done by offering you a management position. Will you accept?

d. Would you speak at the annual company dinner? You've done such a tremendous job. Congratulations!

e. Working at the new job will mean I can get a reliable car, not one that breaks down when the weather is cold or wet. A new car also means that I'll get to the sitter's on time and will miss fewer days at work. I should be able to afford a dinner out once in a while. Why not change jobs?

Persuasive Appeals

After choosing the need or needs of the audience to use in the persuasive appeal, the communicator must decide the method of motivation required to get the plan or idea accepted. This motivating factor is called an **appeal**. The Greek philosopher Aristotle observed three basic types of appeals that are just as effective in persuasion today: appeals are based on the author's credibility, reason, and emotions.

Credibility: "Believe What I Say"

Persuasion is more likely to occur when the audience likes and trusts the persuader. **Credibility** is the confidence that the persuader inspires in the audience. The more trust the audience places in the communicator, the more it will rely on the communicator's judgment. The persuader's reputation, motivation, and presentation are the basis for the personal trust.

Reputation

Having knowledge of and showing familiarity with a subject will encourage a favorable reaction. When you inform your audience of your credentials, your knowledge, and your experience, you familiarize them with your reputation and inspire credibility. One way to encourage success is showing how to perform a task, demonstrate a product, or explain a procedure.

An audience is more apt to believe someone with high standards of moral conduct. A person who is perceived as dishonest will have a difficult time persuading an audience about anything. Such unethical behaviors as gross exaggeration, lying, name-calling, and misrepresenting the truth all destroy—not build—credibility.

Motivation

The person who persuades is more likely to gain credibility if he or she shows care and concern about the subject. Often we are persuaded by people whose motives we respect, even though the persuasive message may not affect our personal interest. People are more willing to accept change when they feel that the persuader serves their own personal interests.

Presentation

Many people assume that what they see is what they get. This may or may not be true. Credibility is most often built through the overall personal impression that an individual or product makes. Cheap stationery, grammar errors, and misspellings do not impress.

Figure 10-2: *Whom would you choose to cook your dinner?*

TECHNOLOGY **C·O·N·N·E·C·T·I·O·N**

A U.S. automobile manufacturer has hired Dr. Alan Hirsch, a neurologist and psychologist, to develop a smell to make car salesmen seem trustworthy to their customers, reports *Selling* magazine. The aroma would be used as a cologne or piped into a dealership. According to Dr. Hirsch's studies, smell has the greatest impact on behavior because it is associated with the part of the brain that is linked with emotion. Some examples of smells and their corresponding emotions are strawberry and buttered popcorn encouraging exercise and lavender mixed with pumpkin pie evoking feelings for the opposite sex. After all, we dress appropriately to sell products—shouldn't we smell appropriately, too?

Determining who your audience is will help you to make the best personal impression.

Reason: "Use Your Head"

Develop logic by doing the homework of **PLANNING + THINKING + RESEARCHING**. This formula will give the supportive reasoning for every "why" question that the audience is likely to ask to make a sound decision. Sound facts and statistics will support the persuasive message.

Notice how Laura applied the above formula. After discovering a defective computer sensor that regulates fuel mixture, Laura listed all the possible problems that could result if Ms. Hoover delayed her car repairs. Because Laura's argument was logical and because she was so thorough, Ms. Hoover was convinced and agreed to the additional work. By using her head, Laura successfully persuaded Ms. Hoover to approve necessary car repairs.

Emotions: "Follow the Feeling"

Persuasion works best when the writer uses language to affect emotions. The words you choose can create a persuasive effect. However, avoid words that make a person feel uncomfortable, and do not use language that leaves the audience cold. For example, the advertisement in Figure 10-3 creates little interest in the product.

So what? The company is bragging about itself. By not using any words that engage the audience's emotions, the company produced an ad with no customer appeal.

In the revised advertisement shown in Figure 10-4, the company appeals to the emotions of the consumer. The advertisement positively attempts to persuade parents who buy the product that their children will love BrocSkins. Not only that, but the children will also be eating healthy food as a bonus. By appealing to emotions, the persuader can get into the consumer's shoes. Always consider what the consumer's reactions will be.

INFOBIT

One of the most important workplace skills needed today is problem-solving ability, according to the U.S. Department of Labor.

After considerable research and expense, our company has developed a great broccoli treat—

BROCSKINS.

Figure 10-3: *"Before" ad for BrocSkins*

You won't be able to keep enough BROCSKINS in the cupboard!

BrocSkins

Our new broccoli treats have a potato-chip flavor that kids love. But parents love BROCSKINS treats for their low sodium and high vitamin C content.

Figure 10-4: *"After" ad for BrocSkins*

INFOBIT

"People can sense your emotional commitment (or lack of it) 1,000 miles away."

TOM PETERS, U.S. AUTHOR

Practice 10-3: Identifying the Appeal

For each of the following persuasive messages, identify whether the appeal is based on the author's credibility, reason, emotions, or a combination of these methods.

1. Picture calves living in darkness in a stall so tight that they can't even turn around. They are eating a milk mash until they reach the weight to become veal.

2. Two thousand cars go through this intersection every day to a four-way stop sign at Glendale and Stonegate. On Eudora Drive, 1,400 cars stop at a traffic light. Why shouldn't the busier intersection have a stoplight?

3. Our featured speaker, Bonnie Williams, is here today to speak about the needs of the Literacy Task Force. She is the chairperson of the County Commission on Literacy.

4. Would you please learn to use a computer? It takes much less time than working by hand. Plus, the computer is often more accurate in checking spelling errors than humans are.

5. When the outside temperature reaches 80 degrees, you actually use less gasoline by using your car's air conditioner than you would if you drove with your windows open. The open windows disrupt the smooth flow of air over the car, causing the car to burn more gasoline.

6. If you aren't a team player, the boss will fire you. She hates employees who won't work overtime.

7. Pesticides get into the intestines of small animals and birds through seeds. Inside their bodies, the pesticides cause bleeding and death. So avoid using pesticides.

Practice 10-4: Appealing to Needs

Using the grid on page 10-A in the *Student Workbook,* write a sales slogan for each of the following products. Identify the need or needs (according to Maslow) that your product will satisfy. Name the appeal or appeals that you used.

1. shoes
2. sports car
3. family car
4. pocket-size computer
5. day-care services
6. Doe Burgers
7. vocational education

Persuading an Audience

In addressing your audience, choose only the best for that audience. Anticipate the audience's reactions as well as its unsatisfied needs. Then adapt the argument to these reactions. For instance, in a speech describing methods of cooking over a charcoal grill, to talk about roasting meat to an audience of vegetarians is a complete waste of energy. Always consider what best appeals to the needs of your audience.

Audience Reactions

An audience's reaction to persuasion can vary. Analyzing the audience will help to predict its reaction. Is the audience favorable to the message? Does the audience have any preconceived ideas? Is the audience opposed to the persuasion? Making predictions about the audience will help form the persuasive argument. Audience reactions can vary from positive to negative.

Favorable Opinion

The audience that favors your suggestion or viewpoint is obviously the easiest to persuade. Take that favorable interest and use it to increase their commitment to your idea. For instance, a political candidate does not have to persuade voters who already support him or her.

No Opinion

Audiences that have no opinion could be uninformed; they just might not know enough about the subject to form an opinion. Provide these audiences with enough information to sway them. **Apathy**, or indifference, can also cause an audience to have no opinion. You need to create interest in the cause to get the audience's commitment to it. However, establishing that interest and getting the audience's attention may be more difficult than it sounds. Remember that if you can easily persuade the apathetic, then the opposition can easily persuade them as well.

Opposing Opinion

An audience that is against your viewpoint may range from slightly negative to very hostile. The hostile audience probably will not listen at all to your attempts to persuade it. Anything you say may have little effect, especially if the reasons you present are rooted in emotions. Also, audiences that are close-minded and see issues as either/or choices are not likely to change.

INFOBIT

"Pick battles big enough to matter, small enough to win."

JONATHAN KOZOL, U.S. AUTHOR

ETHICS C·O·N·N·E·C·T·I·O·N

You may have fallen asleep in front of the television and awakened to a smoothly produced 30-minute television commercial, often known as an infomercial. Beware of running to that telephone and ordering based on the endorsements of celebrities who are highly paid to recommend the advertised product. Often the audience sees unsubstantiated claims based on product demonstrations arranged for television with testimonials by actors who do not represent ordinary people. Is ordering the product now really saving you money? Is the free gift really free? Why can't you wait to order rather than order in the next hour? These are questions to ask yourself before ordering and while calling the local Better Business Bureau.

You can evaluate a negative audience, however. Your arguments to persuade can then be developed around unmet needs. Try not to misrepresent the opposition to earn points for the persuasion. Calling the other side "bad guys" and "idiots" harms more than persuades. Name-calling doesn't help; it only hurts. Be reasonable; persuasion that is extreme is often ignored.

Types of Conflict

Without conflict, why persuade? Everyone would just agree. There must be some sort of dissatisfaction, or an audience will not be receptive to persuasion. After discovering the need for persuasion, you need to find the type of conflict present in the majority of the audience.

Figure 10-5: *Computer fear*

Pseudo Conflict

A **pseudo**, or false, **conflict** is really not a conflict at all. All signs point to a disagreement, but no disagreement is there. Some people just feel they must choose one option or another. However, if they could see a compromise, there would be no need for a battle. For example, some people fear computers. They would rather ignore these devices or quit their jobs, rather than learn to use them to make their jobs easier. Employers who understand the pseudo conflict can ease computer fear by providing slow-paced computer classes and sympathetic instructors.

Problem/Solution Conflict

Problem/solution conflict occurs when the audience agrees with the problem but not with the suggested solution. Working to come up with alternative solutions helps. For instance, crops need to be protected from destructive insects, but many people do not want to use chemicals. Rather than have damaged vegetation, offer the use of organic pesticides.

Values Conflict

When persuasion attacks personal values (the attitudes or beliefs that a person holds), conflict may result. Such beliefs form the basis of a person's character. Be careful with **values conflict**, and proceed cautiously. Find a way, even a small way, that the audience can agree. Then slowly work on the persuasion.

Ego Conflict

Some people feel that an argument must have a winner or a loser. Instead, one can often propose a simple agreement and soften egos. Hence, both sides can win, creating a win-win situation. For example, Shanda wants to redecorate the kitchen. She feels that since she does most of the cooking, the decision is hers to make. Her husband, Brandon, feels there is no need to redo the kitchen; as the one who manages the household expenses, he feels the decision is his to make. Then Shanda proposes a compromise—that they refinish the cabinets and wallpaper the walls, thus limiting the spending. Brandon agrees, and they both settle their personal conflicts.

Managing Conflict

Conflict can be constructive if it is managed properly. Cooperation, not competition, is the key. However, you can treat conflict either positively or negatively. The ways people manage conflict vary from withdrawal and surrender to assertiveness, persuasion, and negotiation.

Withdrawal and Surrender

A person can withdraw from conflict physically or psychologically. **Physical withdrawal** is when a person *literally* moves away from the conflict situation. **Psychological withdrawal** is when a person *mentally* moves away from the conflict situation. Withdrawal may be a good or bad choice, depending on the situation.

Psychological withdrawal can also be positive or negative. Suppose Stephen and Paula have a disagreement about his keeping his room clean, and they become angry. Stephen could withdraw by daydreaming. By ignoring the conflict, he will probably only infuriate his mother more. Instead, if Stephen changes the subject tactfully, he and his mother could both calm down and resume the discussion later.

Surrender is a way of avoiding conflict—and discussion. The person who surrenders gives up the present argument, but may not necessarily give up the conflict. A person can interpret surrender as an implication that one does not care. Another explanation is that a person is a martyr if he or she surrenders: "I'll do it your way; I always do." Surrender leaves the persuader angry because the person avoids the discussion, while the person who avoids the discussion never addresses the conflict.

Assertiveness

Assertiveness is generally the most desirable way to manage conflict and to persuade, but learning to be assertive is hard. Being **assertive** is stating the position positively but firmly, using no hostility. Assertiveness requires stepping back from the issues and considering the pros and cons to find a solution.

For example, Anna wants assertively to persuade her boss, Mr. Jackson, that her new technique for wiring the circuit is more effective. First, she writes down the positive points and supports them with facts. Then Anna thinks of all the drawbacks Mr. Jackson will mention. She plans ways to disprove them. Anna's assertive approach may just sway the usually reluctant Mr. Jackson.

Persuasion

Persuasion can resolve conflict if it has a sound, logical basis. Attempting to change an attitude or behavior will work better if a person is open, not secretive. Surprising someone with a **hidden agenda**, a concealed reason for the persuasion, often ends in disaster.

Negotiation

Successful negotiation often means managing conflict through trade-off. Keeping an open mind, not being stubborn, and winning—or losing—gracefully can help with positive conflict solutions. If the negotiation is lost, discuss the reasons for failure. Improvements can be made to turn the failure into a success the next time.

A good strategy is to give the other side a little edge by first listening to what they have to say. Then, hit them with the superior argument.

INFOBIT

"Commitment may only require 5% or 10% more effort, but it makes all the difference in the world."

ART SCHWARTZ, U.S. AUTHOR

Practice 10-5: Finding and Resolving Conflict

teamwork

1. In the following situations, there is conflict. In small groups, discuss the disagreement. Then name the type of conflict, and write the reason for each disagreement.
   a. The engine is pinging in your five-year-old, low-mileage car. You just replaced the transmission and the tires, and the body is in great shape. The mechanic tells you that you

need a rebuilt engine. You feel you should sell the car, but you can't afford a new one.

b. A state agency knows that it must monitor the child-care industry closely. The Federal Health Administration agrees but wants less state inspection of activities and more federal examination of sanitary facilities. The state remains firm; it feels that child care should be state, not federally, regulated.

c. Nadro wants to hire Karen as an electronics inspector. The company has offered her a large hourly wage and flextime. In her interview, Karen asks about the company's use of radioactive materials. The company interviewer seems to avoid the question, since she feels that if Karen knew the extent to which she would be handling radioactive materials, she wouldn't take the job. Nadro wants Karen as a worker; she is experienced, with a good work record.

2. Using the guidelines for managing conflict, how could your group resolve the differences in the situations in 1a, b, and c? Brainstorm in your groups, and write down the answers.

The ADAM Method of Persuading

Motivating the audience to read or listen past the first line is a must in persuasion. If you use the ADAM approach, you will generally persuade your audience. With the ADAM method, most effective persuasion, whether visual, oral, or written, will use these four steps.

A—Attract **attention.**

D—Create **desire.**

A—**Appeal** to needs.

M—**Move** to action.

Attract Attention

Stimulate interest in the product or idea immediately—in the first line or sentence! If you do not, the audience will be lost. After deciding on the focus of your appeal, create a way to arouse and attract that interest. Some suggestions that work follow.

* Ask a question: Interest the reader by asking a question that won't take no for an answer. He or she will have to read further to get an answer.

- Startle: "In the next 12 minutes, 120 Americans will be disabled in an accident." Make a surprising statement.

- Offer something free: The free item could be a gift, a coupon, a discount, or a sale. But the audience must be required to do something to get it.

- Flatter: Flattery will appeal to the ego of the audience.

- Don't give up: Be persistent.

Anything that interrupts the message will distract the reader. Get that attention, and keep it. Combining two or more ways of attracting attention can create an even more persuasive effect.

Create Desire

Give the audience a powerful reason to act immediately while you have their attention. If you don't know your audience, research them immediately. Then go back to Maslow's needs (see pages 324 and 325), and show this audience what they're missing. Speak directly to them. For example, say, "What would you do if you had a sudden financial emergency? Would you ask for a loan? Would you dip into savings? If you think you'd have a problem, you're absolutely right."

Appeal to Needs

Now comes the pitch. Show the audience how the idea will satisfy their needs. Support every statement you make. Point out the benefits. Try appealing to the audience's needs in the following ways:

- Problem/solution: State the problem, and show them what will happen every minute that problem goes unsolved.

- Comparison of advantages: "Yes, the ROM Shop provides five times faster service than the other local computer repair shops.

- Satisfaction of requirements: "Our shop offers a full-service parts department, fully stocked with supplies, and friendly service. If you're not satisfied, we will give you a full refund."

- Testimonial: "Ruth Allan and Will Benjamin use Glo Hair Color. Come to the Nips Salon, and you, too, can have hair the color of the stars."

- Negativity: With a hostile audience, a negative approach is often needed. "The collie sheds its hair in warm weather and constantly needs grooming. Choose a Jack Russell terrier like Mollie, and you can enjoy your dog without a tedious grooming routine." When you are unsure if the audience is for or against your idea, try for less change.

INFOBIT

In a study conducted by The Ohio State University, consumers who purchased recycled greeting cards and paper products chose products with well-known brand names over others, despite the products' being the same. The brand name seems to be the assurance that, even if the product is recycled, it is quality.

Move to Action

Now it's time to get the audience to change. Hit them hard. Clinch the deal. Tell the audience the solution, and get them to do it. Make the move simple and to the point. Enclose an order form or a postcard. Invite the reader to call. Set up a meeting time. Move to action!

Practice 10-6: Anaylzing Advertising

teamwork The ADAM method is used in nearly all advertising. In this Practice, you will analyze recorded commercials to discover how the ADAM method is used.

Listen to the commercials on the CD that your teacher will play. After each commercial, answer the questions on page 10-B in your *Student Workbook*. Your teacher may have you work in small groups.

Creating a Persuasive Message

The ADAM method motivates the audience to use the product or service. When you organize the message to produce specific results, persuasion will be more effective. Together, the following persuasion-building statements help to create a persuasive message. Each persuasive action statement requires thinking about the audience and its needs and then looking in detail at each statement:

- Determine a goal.
- Give logical evidence.
- Organize the material.
- Use motivating language.
- Build credibility.
- Deliver convincingly.

Determine a Goal

The purpose or goal of the persuasion should be clear to the audience. If the audience can't figure out the goal of the persuasion, then why should it pay attention?

Give Logical Evidence

Evidence can best prove a proposition. The statements of evidence do not have to be facts, but they must support the goal. The evidence itself often has a very positive impact on the audience. Evidence that appears to be logical, yet is not a fact, may be an **inference**. An inference seems like a natural and obvious conclusion, but it is a prediction or a guess based on fact.

The following sets of examples have the same evidence. The first statement is a fact. The opinion and the inference are guesses based on that fact. The opinion is based on personal assumptions, and the inference is a presumption drawn from the fact and opinion combined.

FACT	Mom has just seen dirty dishes and half-eaten food all over the kitchen.
OPINION	Mom is angry.
INFERENCE	Mom is going to make us clean the kitchen.
FACT	Bill reads three newspapers a day.
OPINION	Bill is a brain.
INFERENCE	Bill will be the best in the class on the current events test.

Yes, Mom did see the food all over the kitchen, and Bill does read three newspapers a day. Those are facts. But the inferences may or may not come true, even though they are based on facts. Mom may be forgiving, and Bill may flunk the test. Try to avoid using inferences as facts. An audience doesn't want to be persuaded and then find out that the facts are not true. Rather than use an inference, make a statement and support it with facts.

INFOBIT

"Never show people up; they'll eventually find a way to get even."

TOM PETERS, U.S. AUTHOR

Practice 10-7: Determining Fact, Opinion, and Inference

Identify each of the following statements as fact, opinion, or inference.

1. Luke is the fastest runner in our school.

2. He can best South's runner easily.

3. It is a terrific day to go fishing.

4. The bass have been biting at the bait.

5. We'll have fish for dinner.

6. Kathy said that Springfield was 73 miles from her house.

7. We've been driving for an hour.

8. We'll be in Springfield soon.

Organize the Material

Arrange the material in a way that will produce the expected audience reaction. If the audience is familiar with the material, you will not need as much explanation. For audiences that you expect will be favorable or will have no opinion, be simple and direct, going straight to the bottom line. If you anticipate an audience to be hostile, build your argument first before stating the persuasion. Be very clear and specific.

Figure 10-6 shows a flyer for an office supply store. After there were no increases in sales, the store owner modified the flyer (Figure 10-7).

Use Motivating Language

Choose language that will persuade the audience; choose language that will motivate. For instance, Michael wrote a collection letter and ended it with, "Send your payment no later than Monday." However, Michael will be more likely to get the money for his company if he firmly states, "Send the payment by Monday."

Sometimes, plain language may not be the best choice if the words sound offensive to the audience. However, don't fall into the trap of using euphemisms. **Euphemisms** are pleasant-sounding words that substitute for unpleasant or awkward subjects. *The little girls' room* substitutes for the word *toilet*. A euphemism for *dying* is *passing away*. An *outplacement center* provides job-seeking assistance for employees who are laid off.

Our store is
outstanding in
serving your
office supply needs.

Stein's Supplies
100 Hall Drive
Waltham, MA
02254-0118

Figure 10-6: *"Before" office supply store flyer*

Our store is outstanding
in serving your
office supply needs.

>< **More locations**
>< **More salespeople**
>< **More complete catalog**
>< **More delivery trucks**
>< **and more products in stock.**

Stein's Supplies
100 Hall Drive
Waltham, MA 02254-0118

Figure 10-7: *"After" office supply store flyer*

Choose words that are to the point and not crude. Plain talk or writing is better than using a polite euphemism.

Practice 10-8: Avoiding Euphemisms

The following sentences contain euphemisms. Rewrite the sentences to be more direct and to the point.

1. Catalena bought a pre-owned car.

2. The bank charged a fee for quality for its automatic teller machine (ATM) transactions.

3. Why did you buy synthetic glass mugs instead of ceramic?

4. A domestic engineer lives and works in the same building.

5. If you don't attend your college classes, you'll expedite progress toward alternate life pursuits.

6. The employee was poorly motivated.

7. After the company began downsizing, Todd became a dislocated worker.

8. The librarian was reprimanded for weeding books.

Build Credibility

Persuasion will not take place if the audience cannot believe the persuader. Reputation, including competence and character; motive; and presentation build credibility.

Figure 10-8: *Credibility helps a sales associate persuade customers.*

Deliver Convincingly

Choosing the best method to persuade is important. By using the ADAM method effectively (see page 333), you can motivate audiences. Careful planning to structure your message presentation will increase the effectiveness of your persuasion.

You can arrange words to create a reaction in the audience. However, be careful not to use **loaded language**. These words or phrases carry strong emotional appeal, either positive or negative. The audience tends to hear the words, not the thoughts behind them.

Word choice is very important. **Inferred meaning** may cause anger in some people and no reaction in others. The careful reader or listener will sort out the message despite the emotional overtones. Nevertheless, many people will react before reading carefully.

TECHNOLOGY C·O·N·N·E·C·T·I·O·N

The Internet is emerging as a forceful marketing tool. With the Net, the small business owner can access many more customers than with traditional marketing methods. With a few hundred dollars, some writing skill, and an imagination, a Web site is relatively simple to create. However, you need to answer two questions first: (1) What can my customers gain from the Web that will help sales? (2) How do I give something free to Web users that I might otherwise charge for?

WEB LINK

Investigate the Better Business Bureau Web site for complaints concerning local and national businesses. The site also discloses unethical national advertisements and adds to the list monthly.

Practice 10-9: Eliminating Loaded Language

1. Identify the word in the series that is loaded language.

   a. child, youngster, kid, brat, toddler

   b. rookie, beginner, trainee, apprentice

   c. police officer, cop, law enforcement, security

2. Change the underlined word or phrase to eliminate loaded language, and rewrite each sentence. Be careful not to use euphemisms.

   a. The manager seemed so *egotistical,* wanting her way without discussion.

   b. The house needs an *overhaul.*

   c. Buy Garevan, the modern, *cheap* solution to the problem of trash disposal.

   d. Sir, this neighborhood is *infested with mutts.*

Practice 10-10: Writing Persuasive Messages

teamwork Choose an issue that you feel strongly about, such as a student lounge, less strict job placement policies, or animal rights. Write an "I Urge Gram" in 15 or fewer words to defend your stand. Have a partner proofread your "I Urge Gram." Then check the message to be sure it strongly supports your position.

After your teacher proofreads the "I Urge Gram," recopy it on paper your teacher provides.

INFOBIT

Small ads are like miniature bulletin boards. They should just reach out and keep you from reading the rest of the page.

Practice 10-11: Making a Business Card

careers Every second a customer looks at a business card generally translates into dollars, states Avery Pitzak of American Business Cards. Like a small-space ad, the business card has a powerful impact and reflects the business's image.

(cont'd on next page)

HEALTHY
SAVINGS!
Walk, don't ride.

**Walker's Walkers, 228 Shannon Street
Annapolis, MD 21401-1113**
(443) 555-0178

BABES! BABES! BABES!

Little Nuttin's Preschool
needs after-school volunteers.

804 Ambar
Romney, WV 26757-0804
304/555-0184

WEB LINK

A question worth investigating is whether company Web sites answer the questions in the Technology Connection on page 339.

If you or your teacher has the technology, you could build a Web page, perhaps as an Alternate Project for this chapter.

Design your own business card. This card should reflect something you are trying to sell about yourself; for example, your job search, your training skills, your speaking ability, your service learning, or even a business you are starting.

1. Decide on the focus of your business card—the element that will attract the customer and dominate the card. Keep the intended audience and the purpose of the card in mind. Will it have the intended effect? The style of your card may be professional, casual, contemporary, or elegant.

2. Choose the visual element that will make your card stand out.

EXAMPLES:

* use of white space.
* clip art.
* graphics.
* a slogan.
* the unique shape of the copy.
* creative use of fonts.

3. Include what printed information is necessary. Often included are your name (and your company's name, if appropriate).

* your address.
* your phone number.
* your e-mail address.

Collection Letters

In many situations, written persuasion is more effective than oral persuasion. Writing is permanent. For this reason, the writer should convey the message clearly, reasonably, and logically. A clear example of written persuasion is the **collection letter**.

Joseph bought a stereo from Sounders on a time payment plan. He gave the store a down payment and agreed to pay Sounders $40 a month until the stereo was paid for in full. However, Joseph lost his job at Lola's Used Cars when Lola went bankrupt. Instead of talking to Sounders, Joseph just stopped making payments on his stereo.

Sounders tried to contact Joseph through a series of messages—postcards, phone calls, and letters (see Figure 10-9 on page 343). Eventually Joseph called Sounders and worked out a new payment plan without losing his stereo. The collection letter should not offend the customer's **goodwill**, but should appeal to his or her conscience instead.

Success

Successful collections are based on the following procedures:

1. Timeliness	Within two weeks after an account is due, the creditor calls or sends the first reminder notice.	
2. Consistency	Each notice always includes the due date, the type of account and/or the account number, the amount owed, and the date the notice was sent.	
3. Regularity	After the first notice, later notices are sent every two weeks until the debtor responds.	
4. Increasing severity	Each message should be stronger than the previous message.	

A Collection Series

The collection sequence that many companies use is a three-stage series of communications. The three stages are the inquiry, the reasonable appeal, and the firm appeal.

The Inquiry

A phone call or letter goes out to gently remind the customer the account payment is due. The inquiry letter requests that the customer call, write, or stop in to explain when the customer will pay. The writer asks directly or indirectly for the overdue payment and may mention a penalty for late payment. Some companies have two steps at this level: a phone call and a letter.

The Reasonable Appeal

The company's message becomes stronger in this letter. The letter appeals to the customer's sense of fairness and refers to the customer's good credit rating. The letter explains the consequences if the customer leaves the account unpaid. Losing the merchandise, removing the service, and paying interest penalties are all possible results.

The Firm Appeal

This letter strongly urges the customer to pay the past-due account or to make contact with the company for payment arrangements by a certain date. The customer knows that the time to pay is long past. Unpleasant circumstances, such as repossession, a collection agency, or a lawsuit, could follow soon. At this point, many companies would turn the account over to a collection agency or an attorney.

Important: A company cannot legally harass a debtor or threaten physical harm. Federal, state, and local laws define what is creditor harassment.

Parts of a Collection Communication

Whether a company communicates by phone or by letter, the message should have the following three sections (see Figure 10-9):

INFOBIT

"The two words that will persuade are 'if' and 'then.' If you take this action, then you'll get this reward. Those two words will definitely help you get what you want when you're trying to persuade."

JERALD M. JELLISON, AUTHOR OF OVERCOMING RESISTANCE: A PRACTICAL GUIDE TO PRODUCING CHANGE IN THE WORKPLACE

1. Goodwill Greeting
   Open the letter or phone call with a general comment about the service or product. This remark will promote a feeling of goodwill.

2. Announcement of the Problem
   When you state the problem and the purpose of the letter, also mention the due date, as well as the type of account and/or the account number.

3. The Next Step
   Close the letter or phone call by stating what the next step is if the payment or arrangements aren't made. This statement can range from a mild warning to an ultimatum. In addition, express the hope that the customer is willing to cooperate. At any point in the letter, you may mention documents you may choose to enclose, such as an invoice or copy of a credit agreement.

Sales Letters

Selling—it's everywhere. And persuasion is the tool of sales. Selling, however, is not forcing customers to buy. Selling makes a product or service or place appealing enough that the customer is willing to spend money on it.

Selling requires more than just concentrating on what is being promoted. The goal is to create interest in the product or service right from the beginning. With a convincing, positive tone, prepare the sales pitch well. To do this, you must know your audience, product, and competition.

SOUNDERS STEREOS
1211 Queens Court
Pittsburgh, PA 15228-8840

July 8, ----

Mr. Joseph Miller
1806 Lane Street
Pittsburgh, PA 15228-8810

Dear Mr. Miller:

I hope that you are enjoying your new Sounders component stereo system. If you have any questions about the system, please contact either me or your local Sounders store.

Your long-term account requires a $40 monthly payment, due on the 20th. Sounders has not yet received your June payment.

I trust that you will contact your local Sounders store immediately to make payment arrangements. Interest penalties add to the cost of your payment daily. If you have any questions, please do not hesitate to call me at 555-0110 or contact your local Sounders store.

Sincerely yours,

Marcos Hernandez

Marcos Hernandez
Account Supervisor

PARAGRAPH 1
General comment to promote goodwill.

PARAGRAPH 2
Problem stated. Purpose of letter. Timeliness—2 weeks past due date.

PARAGRAPH 3
Next step given. Tone— firm, not harassing.

Figure 10-9: *An effective collection letter*

Practice 10-12: Revising Collection Letters

teamwork With a partner, revise the collection letter in Figure 10-10 to make it more effective. Follow the guidelines for the firm appeal letter in this chapter. You can invent details that you feel are appropriate for the letter.

Bethany Bathtubs
218 Ardwick
Bellevue, NM 87116-1806
(505) 555-0105

March 13, ----

Ms. Gladys Amora
8687 Lyon Drive
Silverdale, NM 87113-7949

Dear Ms. Amora:

Why haven't you paid your Bethany Bathtub account? You owe us $302.14. We want it now! The account is two months overdue. We've also sent you two letters. You haven't responded, and that's very frustrating. Did you forget to send your payment?

You probably have the check in the mail. Why haven't you sent the $302.14? Are you trying to cheat us? Well, Bethany Bathtubs won't stand for this. You said you liked it. We have no use for a seven-foot custom-made red bathtub, but we'll remove it from the house if you won't pay. If you do like the tub, or even if you don't, pay this bill by March 31.

Yours,

Mary Chamber

Mary Chamber
Account Supervisor

Figure 10-10: *An ineffective collection letter*

CAREER **C·O·N·N·E·C·T·I·O·N**

In the next few years, employment prospects for agriculture students are favorable, according to the *Occupational Outlook Quarterly*. More job openings will exist than students who will graduate in agriculture-related programs. However, most of the jobs won't be on the farms themselves; they will be in marketing, sales, and related science careers.

The Audience

Put yourself in the customer's head. That person may get ten sales letters a day. What will make your letter stand out? Find the emotional element to emphasize, and center everything in the letter around this emotion. Analyze the audience. What are their backgrounds? Are they a diverse or a similar group? Problems in sales come from careless analysis. Approach each audience in a personal way suitable for that audience (see Figure 10-11).

The Product

Assume that the customer needs the product and cannot function without it. Why would the customer buy it? Find out, and focus on that reason. What would be the objections to buying the product? Answer any objections by giving the customer logical reasons to buy (see Figure 10-12). Be sure to be totally familiar with the product or service. What are its strengths? Its weaknesses? Its special features? What kind of questions would the customer ask about the product or service?

The sales letter can create a solution, but first the audience must feel it has a problem or conflict. The audience must feel uncomfortable without the product. This feeling of discomfort is called **dissonance**. The greater the dissonance, the easier the sale.

The Competition

Know the competition. Emphasize the strengths of your company, rather than criticizing the competition. Give a strength for every weakness the competition has (see Figure 10-13). Show that the customer has a need for your product or service, not the competitor's.

Do you run the risk of having your house burn down?

If you have not cleaned your chimney this year, your house could easily be lost in flames.

ChimMaster — The Sweep That Cleans

837 Ashley Court, Ashland, OH 44805-1598
419/555-0113

Figure 10-11: *A chimney sweep ad*

Tireland has the best deals in town.
Good quality
Great selection
Excellent service
AND Low Prices

219 Route 40
Steamwood, IL 60103-1217
630/555-0169

Figure 10-12: *A tire ad*

High price of dining
got you down?

Come to
DIANE'S DINER

All meals $5.00

Drinks and desserts included
Can't beat our prices—or our food!!!

1015 Shannon Dale, Silver Spring, MD 20904-1015
(301) 555-0115

Open every day from 3 to 10 PM.

Figure 10-13: *A restaurant ad*

Parts of a Sales Letter

Following the ADAM approach will logically lead the audience into the letter—and into the sale. The format of a sales letter is similar to business letter format (see Figure 10-14 on page 347). Chapter 9 is your reference for a standard business letter format. The following sections discuss special parts of sales letters and some ways sales letters may differ in format from standard business letters.

The Headline

The headline is 85 percent of the power of the sales letter. That's a lot of power! When you analyze the audience, you choose the most emotional element to emphasize. Now use that element. The headline is often the salutation or greeting for the sales letter and is similar to the headline of a newspaper article. It gives the focus of the letter.

When constructing the headline, remember the ADAM method—ask a question, startle, or flatter. The headline should be a strong opener that will attract the reader's attention. You can use a single word, a phrase, a declarative sentence, or a question. Often, the headline is in a prominent font or in a contrasting color; it stands out in some way. If the headline doesn't attract the reader's attention, the reader will stop reading and throw the letter away!

In the sales letter, the headline usually appears two lines down from the address in place of the salutation (some sales letters do not have an inside address). For sales letters that include a salutation, the headline appears two lines down from the salutation and two lines from the body text. Sales letters may use unconventional salutations.

The Opening Paragraph

The opening paragraph of the sales letter is nearly as important as the headline. You may ask a question or give a free gift. Solve the audience's problem, as does the ad for Diane's Diner (see Figure 10-13). Emphasize the positive features of the product or service now, and don't mention the weaknesses. Keep that reader's attention!

The language of the sales letter should be simple and direct. Avoid using technical information for a general audience; the audience will not read the sales pitch if the language is too specialized or wordy. Repetition is the key. Restate the information over and over in different ways.

INFOBIT

"Simplicity is the ultimate sophistication."

LEONARDO DA VINCI, ITALIAN ARTIST AND INVENTOR

The Body Paragraph(s)

This paragraph (or paragraphs) solves the problem. Here you will make your claim that the product or service or place is the best the reader has ever known. Support claims with specific and truthful facts or statements that the reader will understand. Testimonials are excellent; examples support as well. Again, be as creative and unusual as possible, repeating the name of the company as many times as possible.

Letterhead

Logo

Headline

Strong opening paragraph

Eye-catching claims offering solutions

Problem solved

Tells what to do
Prompt response needed

Catchy closing

ACES
100-A Country Drive
Bartlett, OH 45123-0486

November 29, ----

Ms. Clarissa Nan
804 Robinwood Drive
Centerville, TX 75833-6916

DO YOU HAVE STRAIGHT A'S?

If you can't answer **yes** to that question, then something is **wrong**. Something needs to be changed. You can change your grades to beautiful A's—all you need is **ACES**.

ACES is your ticket to the *Honor Roll*!
ACES is your passport to high SAT and ACT scores!
ACES is the way to make your parents smile!
ACES is the *key* to the future!

ACES is a complete study system that will put YOU in charge of your grades. **ACES** costs very little, only pennies a day. The time you spend with **ACES** will more than help you *boost* your grades.

Just call 1-800-GET-ACES today to sign up for a free 30-day trial offer—or fill out the enclosed card. But hurry—the offer is limited to the first few callers only.

Today is your **ACES** day!!!

Sincerely,

Stella Zumot

Stella Zumot

President of **ACES**

Enclosure

Figure 10-14: *A sales letter*

PEOPLE **C·O·N·N·E·C·T·I·O·N**

Kathy Prasnicki's company, Sun Coast Resources, began because her high school business co-op teacher placed her as a clerk-typist at an oil distribution company. When the oil company moved out of Kathy's area of eastern Texas, she knew that she had a loyal customer base and wanted to try starting her own company. Being only 24 years old was no deterrent to her, but financing was. By working out a deal with her former company to buy on credit and sell to her customers, Kathy grew her company into a $200 million business in less than ten years. Now Kathy is the owner of one of Texas's largest petroleum wholesalers—and it all started with a high school business co-op job!

The Closing Paragraph

The closing paragraph includes an action statement. Make it easy for the customer to buy the product. Tell the reader what to do—for example, send in the enclosed postcard, send for the free gift, call for information, or fill out an order blank. You need to close the sale confidently and positively, encouraging the reader to respond *now*. The closing paragraph can either make or break the sale.

The Closing

The closing of the sales letter should be sincere and should be followed by the signature and title of the writer. Sometimes a company name is used instead of the writer's title. Sometimes a sales letter will use a sentence such as "Buy now!" instead of a typical closing.

INFOBIT

"Direct mail is what you send; junk mail is what you get."

GORDON PEERY, OFFICE SYSTEMS '97 READER

Practice 10-13: Analyzing Sales Letters

teamwork Bring in sales letters and/or promotional mailings to your teacher. In small groups, analyze at least two items by answering the following questions. You may use the grid in your *Student Workbook,* page 10-C.

1. What are the product's major and minor appeals?

2. What attracts the reader's **attention**?

3. What creates **desire**?

4. What **appeals** to the reader's needs?

5. What **moves** the reader to action?

6. What are the letter's or promotional mailing's strengths and weaknesses?

Designing Persuasive Messages

Not only the words in the persuasive message, but also the visual style can persuade the reader. Researchers have studied the influence of lettering, graphics, color, positioning for eye movement, and format.

Many readers skim sales letters. (In fact, they often call this mail junk mail.) So get the readers' attention right away so they won't junk your mail. Attract them with lettering, colors, and startling statements.

Sales letters are designed to grab the reader's attention for the sole purpose of marketing. These letters tend to use more ways of emphasizing text, such as bold, italics, capital letters, and different type sizes, than other business letters. Sales letters often use unconventional grammar, such as elliptical (condensed) expressions that represent complete sentences (*Price? No problem.*), and unconventional punctuation (*!!!*).

Lettering

Lettering can help you design an eye-catching ad very quickly and inexpensively (see Figure 10-15). Here are some tips:

* Use type that seems to shout—bold and large.

* Keep the heading short—that makes the type seem even larger.

* Avoid elaborate typefaces. They are often hard to read, especially in a small space.

Keeping your audience in mind, link the style of typeface to the emotional focus of your letter. If you are formal and professional in your tone, your lettering should be also. Mixing typefaces is fine to grab attention and for emphasis, but only mix for a reason—not to be flamboyant.

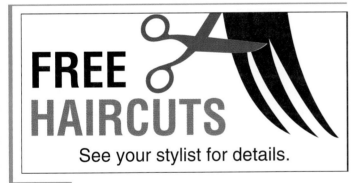

Figure 10-15: *A haircut ad*

Color and Paper Weight

Choosing the right combination of colors for paper, type, and graphics will help enhance your persuasive message. They draw the audience's attention, plus create desire and appeal to needs. What colors to use depends on who your audience is, whether you are using color copy, and what feelings you want to evoke in the reader.

For color copy, three key qualities of paper emphasize the color print's appearance: smoothness, brightness, and whiteness. The paper should be very smooth, so that the color images seem to burst off the paper. The brightness and whiteness of the paper ensure sharp color distinction. An almost blue-white shade is the best paper shade to enhance lettering.

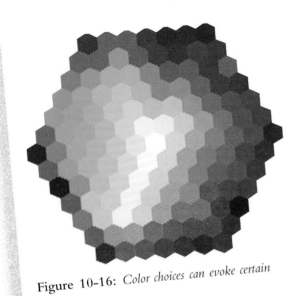

Figure 10-16: *Color choices can evoke certain feelings.*

Colored paper is fine to use, but be sure it gives the effect you want. Some combinations of paper and ink are difficult to read, such as gold lettering on orange- or melon-colored paper and black ink on red paper. Select colors for the feelings they arouse in the reader. You may want to choose color according to the following guidelines:

* Warm colors—red, orange, yellow, and pink—attract the reader.
  These colors invite the reader to read and keep reading. Red is a color most inviting for children. (Notice how cereal boxes and toy packages often use red.)

* Cool colors—blue, green, and violet—move readers away.
  Generally, avoid cool colors unless you are using them for a definite, desired effect, such as a relaxing ocean scene.

Different colors can stimulate the senses and suggest qualities such as status and self-assurance. Examples of such color uses follow.

* Taste
  Orange invites the reader to eat. Blue suggests sweetness. An orange flyer would be a good choice to promote a restaurant, and blue ink would be excellent for a candy store ad.

* Smell
  Pink, lavender, yellow, and green make readers think of smell. Green also suggests a sense of calmness, lowering stress.

* Status
  Colors of status and prestige are gold, silver, purple, and black. Navy blue commands authority. Green declares self-assurance.

Graphics

An effective graphic in a persuasive message can engage an audience more quickly than almost anything else. Graphic elements include clip art, photos, drawings, charts, and graphs. A simple way to add graphics to your message is to use type as art. Many word processing programs contain different styles of type and the means to create bullets, large capital letters, lines, boxes, screens, and reversed type. Such software usually comes with clip art and step-by-step instructions that you can use to change the shape of text.

As with any other part of a persuasive message, use graphics carefully for maximum effect. Using the same type of graphic for similar parts of a persuasive message—bulleted lists, for example—helps tie the parts

TECHNOBIT

Popular colors of the 1970s, once known as avocado and harvest gold, are now renamed sage and curry— and in vogue again. The Day-Glo colors of the post-Vietnam era meant happiness; now those colors say high-tech.

together. Placed appropriately, a single distinctive graphic can draw the reader's attention to that particular part of the message.

Positioning

For each persuasive message, choose a **focal point**, a headline, graphic, or other design element that will draw the attention of the reader. Arrange text and other graphic elements carefully on the page for attraction and interest, using white space to set off text and graphics.

The overall layout of the persuasive message should follow a geometric pattern, guiding the eye. For example, the Tireland ad in Figure 10-12, page 345, is in a T-shape. The *T* is the underlying pattern that the reader's eyes follow. The ACES letter, Figure 10-14, on page 347 is in the shape of the letter *S*. The reader's eye goes from the logo at the upper right corner to the opening lines of print on the left. It then slants to the lower right and back to the lower left.

The shape of the letter is not the only way that geometric forms can attract a reader. Letterhead, headings, underlining, and capital letters can also influence the geometric pattern. Highlighting words and adding bullets are two other eye-catching methods.

Letterhead

The sales letter should appear on letterhead stationery that includes the company name, address, and telephone number—and e-mail address, Web site, and fax number, if available. To attract the customer's attention, the letterhead should be graphically styled for the desired effect with a logo. The letterhead should end approximately 1 to 1 1/2 inches down from the top of the paper.

The text of the letterhead should set the tone of the page. The traditional way of designing letterhead is to center the company information at the top of the page. This design may be appropriate for conservative or formal audiences and messages. More innovative letterhead displays the text and logo in different ways, perhaps **asymmetrically** or **cascading** down the side or across the bottom of the page. Whatever the design, it must be distinctive and appropriate for the focus of the message.

Logos

As you learned in Chapter 2, a **logo** is a symbol or trademark that visually represents the company. If the customer becomes familiar with the logo, he or she will see the logo and automatically think of the company. Familiar logos often sell better than words. The logo should measure approximately 3/4-inch square, or five lines of text. A logo much larger will distract the customer from reading the text.

Practice 10-14: Designing a Sales Letter

The Reggae, Rock, and Rhythm letter in Figure 10-17 is not effective. The letter does not get the typical customer's interest—either to read the letter or to buy the product. Rewrite and redesign the letter, using what you have learned in this chapter.

Consider lettering, graphics, color, and positioning in redesigning this letter. Redo the letter with a logo. Use the ACES letter (see Figure 10-14) on page 347 as a convincing example.

Reggae, Rock, and Rhythm
5215 Forest Road
Buffalo, NY 14247-3548
October 13, ----

Rogers High Student Council
622 Murray Hill Road
Lincoln, NE 68537-6211

Guys and Gals—

Reggae, Rock, and Rhythm will play for your party or dance. We play any kind of music you want. Requests are our specialty.

Call us at 555-0149 today. Reasonable rates.

Book us.

Yours truly,

Matt   Ken   Brian

Matt, Ken, and Brian
Reggae, Rock, and Rhythm

Figure 10-17: *An ineffective sales letter*

QUALITY **C·O·N·N·E·C·T·I·O·N**
"Managing ahead of the headlights" means developing a long-range plan to work with change. If a change is likely to create problems, the more effective manager will plan for the problems and work solutions into the change. Then the business will run more on a long-term, rather than a day-to-day basis. Teamwork helps direct this type of planning, and employees feel as though they are part of the change too. It's often said that no one likes change except a wet baby—but not in this case.

SUMMARY

Persuasion is the attempt to influence attitudes or behavior in both positive and negative ways. Follow these guidelines in using persuasion:

* Analyze the audience's needs.

* Identify the type of appeal required to persuade the audience.

* Determine if the audience has a conflict with your persuasive message and how to resolve that conflict.

* Motivate the audience to accept your persuasive message by using the ADAM method.

* Organize the written persuasive message into an effective sales letter.

* Use design strategies to format persuasive messages for maximum impact.

Writing a Sales Letter

teamwork You are chair of the Fund-Raising Committee for your group. Your VSO (Vocational Student Organization) is starting a fund-raiser or a service learning (community service) project. To increase sales and/or volunteer participation, you and two others have decided to write a sales letter. Your goal is to persuade readers to spend money on your fund-raiser or to participate in an activity to support your service learning project.

What you choose as your fund-raiser or volunteer project determines the purpose of the letter. You may choose to have the audience

* buy a product.

* try a service, such as a car wash.

* support a cause or donate to send students to a competition.

* participate in an activity, such as a walk for pledges.

Limit the audience to one target group, defining the needs of that group. Keeping the type of fund-raiser in mind, some suggested audiences are

* parents.

* residents of the school district.

* employers.

* consumers of certain products.

* those with a particular habit or hobby.

* a group of employees.

* an age group.

In addition to writing your letter, design a letterhead, including a logo for your organization.

1. Carefully read the sales letter examples from the chapter, as well as the Sample Project Plan and the Sample Sales Letter on pages 356 and 357.

2. Choose your fund-raiser or service learning project. Then limit the audience for your letter. Check the topic with your teacher.

3. Complete the Project Plan, *Student Workbook* page 10-D.

4. Have your teacher check the Project Plan.

5. Using the information on your Project Plan, write the rough draft of the sales letter. Write quickly without stopping to consult a dictionary or to puzzle over exact wording. Just try to get your ideas down in roughly the correct form. A rough draft should be rough.

6. Design a letterhead and logo for your letter.

7. Using the Rough Draft column of the Project Guide (*Student Workbook* page 10-E), check your own work with one or more classmates. Both of you should mark the Project Guide and note any changes on the rough draft. Have your teacher check your rough draft.

8. Revise your rough draft, incorporating the changes that your classmates and your teacher suggested.

9. Using the Final Draft column of the Project Guide, proofread your work. Make needed corrections.

10. Turn in the final draft of the letter along with the Project Guide.

Plan for Writing a Sales Letter

		CONTENT
SERVICE LEARNING	Multiple Sclerosis (MS) Walk	**Attract attention.** The selfish nature of us all
AUDIENCE	Student body	
PURPOSE	**What action should the audience take?** Sign up to walk for MS	**Create desire.** Appealing to the part of the personality that needs to help others
NEED	**Physical, safety, love and belonging, esteem, psychological:** Psychological, appealing to the part of the personality that helps others	**Appeal to needs.** The Walk will raise money for the MS Society. The money will help fund MS research. Our walking for money will satisfy our need to help others.
APPEAL	**Credibility, reason, emotions:** Credibility based on motivation Emotions, secondary appeal	**Move to action.**
SOURCES	Pamphlets from the MS Society	Sign up for the Walk. Pick up MS literature.
VISUALS	**Logo, letterhead, other:** On a path of many hearts, footprints symbolize the walk with the steps of love. The path of hearts is not straight.	Start gathering pledges.

North Student Council
Bellevue, Louisiana

May 6, ----

HOW MUCH OF YOUR TIME IS SPENT HELPING OTHERS?

If you're like most of us, not much at all.

Put your money away. We don't want money—we want your legs.

The Multiple Sclerosis Walk is only two weeks away. Saturday, May 22, you can walk for MS and earn money for MS research. Your help is needed.

Sign up in the lobby. Then pick up a pledge sheet—and get pledges for every mile you walk. Friends, parents, neighbors, employers—they will all pledge. Who wouldn't want to help others? They can even earn a tax deduction! Helping others feels great. Try it. What do you have to risk—except for a Saturday morning?

Sign up today!

Margaret

Margaret Stevens
Student Council President

Overview

Thomas Paine was an American revolutionary propagandist. He wrote against tyranny and monarchy.

Paine, in the following excerpt from *The American Crisis, Number One* (the first of 16 pamphlets he started to write in December 1776), wrote these words: "These are the times that try men's souls," five months after the Declaration of Independence was signed. The morale of General George Washington's troops was at a low ebb. These words were read to Washington's troops just before they crossed the Delaware River to fight at Trenton, New Jersey.

from *The American Crisis, Number One*

These are the times that try men's souls. The summer soldier and the sunshine patriot will, in this crisis, shrink from the service of their country; but he that stands it now, deserves the love and thanks of man and woman. Tyranny, like hell, is not easily conquered; yet we have this consolation with us, that the harder the conflict, the more glorious the triumph. What we obtain too cheap, we esteem too lightly: it is dearness only that gives every thing its value. Heaven knows how to put a proper price upon its goods; and it would be strange indeed if so celestial an article as *freedom* should not be highly rated. Britain, with an army to enforce her tyranny, has declared that she has a right not only to *tax* but "to *bind* us in *all cases whatsoever*"; and if being *bound in that manner* is not slavery, then is there not such a thing as slavery upon earth. Even the expression is impious; for so unlimited a power can belong only to God.

I have as little superstition in me as any man living, but my secret opinion has ever been, and still is, that God Almighty will not give up a people to military destruction, or leave them unsupportedly to perish, who have so earnestly and so repeatedly sought to avoid the calamities of war, by every decent method which wisdom could invent. Neither have I so much of the infidel in me as to suppose that He has relinquished the government of the world, and given us up to the care of devils; and as I do not, I cannot see on what grounds the king of Britain can look up to heaven for help against us: a common murderer, a highwayman, or a housebreaker, has as good a pretense as he.

I once felt all kind of anger which a man ought to feel against the mean principles that are held by the Tories: a noted one, who kept a tavern at Amboy, was standing at his door, with as pretty a child in his hand, about eight or nine years old, as I ever saw, and after speaking his mind freely as he thought was prudent, finished with this unfatherly expression, "Well! give me peace in my day." Not a man lives on the continent but fully believes that a separation must some time or other finally take place, and a generous parent should have said, "If there must be trouble, let it be in my day, that my child may have peace"; and this single reflection, well applied, is sufficient to awaken every man to duty. Not a place upon earth might be so happy as America. Her situation is remote from all the wrangling world, and she has nothing to do but to trade with them. A man can distinguish himself between temper and principle, and I am as confident, as I am that God governs the world, that America will never be happy till she gets clear of foreign dominion. Wars, without ceasing, will break out till that period arrives, and the continent must in the end be conqueror; for though the flame of liberty may sometimes cease to shine, the coal can never expire. . . .

—Thomas Paine

Start-Up: Thomas Paine primarily uses emotional appeal to incite the American working class to fight against the British. He compares the British king to a common criminal, presents America's struggle for freedom as a holy cause, and says that America's happiness lies in being free of "foreign dominion."

Connection: Review what you know about the above situation. Then, with a partner, rewrite the above speech using the ADAM approach to persuasive speaking.

Overview

George Orwell is the pen name chosen by Eric Blair. Born in Bengal, a region of India, and schooled in England, Orwell became famous for his two novels of political satire: *Animal Farm* and *1984*.

From 1922 to 1927, Orwell served in the Indian Imperial Police in Burma, where he wrote this essay. His ability to see the plight of the underdog and to describe the difficult official relationships between the British and the Burmese explains why this essay has been ranked a classic.

"Shooting an Elephant"

In Moulmein, in lower Burma, I was hated by large numbers of people—the only time in my life that I have been important enough for this to happen to me. I was sub-divisional police officer of the town, and in an aimless, petty kind of way anti-European feeling was very bitter. No one had the guts to raise a riot, but if a European woman went through the bazaars alone somebody would probably spit betel juice over her dress. As a police officer I was an obvious target and was baited whenever it seemed safe to do so.

When a nimble Burman tripped me on the football field and the referee (another Burman) looked the other way, the crowd yelled with hideous laughter. This happened more than once. In the end the sneering yellow faces of young men that met me everywhere, the insults hooted after me when I was at a safe distance, got badly on my nerves. The young Buddhist priests were the worst of all. There were several thousands of them in the town and none of them seemed to have anything to do except stand on street corners and jeer at Europeans.

All this was perplexing and upsetting. For at that time I had already made up my mind that imperialism was an evil thing and the sooner I chucked up my job and got out of it the better. Theoretically—and secretly, of course—I was all for the Burmese and all against their oppressors, the British. As for the job I was doing, I hated it more bitterly than I can perhaps make clear. In a job like that you see the dirty work of Empire at close quarters. The wretched prisoners huddling in the stinking cages of the lock-ups, the gray cowed faces of the long-term convicts, the scarred buttocks of the men who had been flogged with bamboos—all these oppressed me with an intolerable sense of guilt. But I could get nothing into perspective. I was young and ill educated and I had had to think out my problems in the utter silence that is imposed on every Englishman in the East. I did not even know that the British Empire is dying, still less did I know that it is a great deal better than the younger empires that are going to supplant it. All I knew was that I was stuck between my hatred of the empire I served and my rage against the evil-spirited little beast who tried to make my job impossible. With one part of my mind I thought of the British Raj as an unbreakable tyranny, as something clamped down, in *saecula saeculorum*, upon the will of prostrate peoples; with another part I thought that the greatest joy in the world would be to drive a bayonet into a Buddhist priest's gut. Feelings like these are the normal by-products of imperialism; ask any Anglo-Indian official, if you catch him off duty.

One day something happened which in a roundabout way was enlightening. It was a tiny incident in itself, but it gave me a better glimpse than I had had before of the real nature of imperialism—the real motives for which despotic governments act. Early one morning the sub-inspector at a police station the other end of town rang me up on the phone and said that an elephant was ravaging the bazaar. Would I please come and do something about it? I did not know what I could do, but I wanted to see what was happening and I got onto a pony and started out. I took my rifle, an old .44 Winchester and much too small to kill an elephant, but I thought the noise might be useful in *terrorem*. Various Burmans stopped me on the way and told me about the elephant's doing. It was not, of course, a wild elephant, but a tame one which had gone "must." It had been chained up, as tame elephants always are when their attack of "must" is due, but on the previous night it had broken its chain and escaped. Its mahout, the only person who could manage it when it was in that state, had set out in pursuit, but had taken the wrong direction and was now twelve hours' journey away, and in the morning the elephant had suddenly reappeared in the town. The Burmese population had no weapons and were quite helpless against it. It had already destroyed somebody's bamboo hut, killed a cow and raided some fruit stalls and devoured the stock; also it had met the municipal rubbish van and, when the driver jumped out and took to his heels, had turned the van over and inflicted violences upon it.

The Burmese sub-inspector and some Indian constables were waiting for me in the quarter where the elephant had been seen. It was a very poor quarter, a labyrinth of squalid bamboo huts, thatched with palm-leaf, winding all over a steep hillside. I remember that it was a cloudy, stuffy morning at the beginning of the rains. We began questioning the people as to where

> *The Burmese population had no weapons and were quite helpless against it.*

the elephant had gone and, as usual, failed to get any definite information. That is invariably the case in the East; a story always sounds clear enough at a distance, but the nearer you get to the scene of the events the vaguer it becomes. Some of the people said that the elephant had gone in one direction, some said that he had gone in another, some professed not even to have heard of any elephant. I had almost made up my mind that the whole story was a pack of lies, when we heard yells a little distance away. There was a loud, scandalized cry of "Go away, child! Go away this instant!" and an old woman with a switch in her hand came round the corner of a hut, violently shooing away a crowd of naked children. Some more women followed, clicking their tongues and exclaiming; evidently there was something that the children ought not to have seen. I rounded the hut and saw a man's dead body sprawling in the mud. He was an Indian, a black Davidian coolie, almost naked, and he could not have been dead many minutes. The people said that the elephant had come suddenly upon him round the corner of the hut, caught him with its trunk, put its foot on his back and ground him into the earth. This was the rainy season and the ground was soft, and his face had scored a trench a foot deep and a couple of yards long. He was lying on his belly with arms crucified and head sharply twisted to one side. His face was coated with mud, the eyes wide open, the teeth bared and grinning with an expression of unendurable agony. (Never tell me, by the way, that the dead look peaceful. Most

(cont'd on next page)

of the corpses I have seen looked devilish.) The friction of the great beast's foot had stripped the skin from his back as neatly as one skins a rabbit. As soon as I saw the dead man I sent an orderly to a friend's house nearby to borrow an elephant rifle. I had already sent back the pony, not wanting it to go mad with fright and throw me if it smelt the elephant.

The orderly came back in a few minutes with a rifle and five cartridges, and meanwhile some Burmans had arrived and told us that the elephant was in the paddy fields below, only a few hundred yards away. As I started forward practically the whole population of the quarter flocked out of the houses and followed me. They had seen the rifle and were all shouting excitedly that I was going to shoot the elephant. They had not shown much interest in the elephant when he was ravaging their homes, but it was different now that he was going to be shot. It was a bit of fun to them, as it would be to an English crowd; besides they wanted the meat. It made me vaguely uneasy. I had no intention of shooting the elephant—I had merely sent for the rifle to defend myself if necessary— and it is always unnerving to have a crowd following you. I marched down the hill, looking and feeling a fool, with the rifle over my shoulder and an ever-growing army of people jostling at my heels. At the bottom, when you got away from the huts, there was a metalled road and beyond that a miry waste of paddy fields a thousand yards across, not yet ploughed but soggy from the first rains and dotted with coarse grass. The elephant was standing eight yards from the road; his left side toward us. He

> *They were watching me as they would watch a conjurer about to perform a trick.*

took not the slightest notice of the crowd's approach. He was tearing up bunches of grass, beating them against his knees to clean them, and stuffing them into his mouth.

I had halted on the road. As soon as I saw the elephant I knew with perfect certainty that I ought not to shoot him. It is a serious matter to shoot a working elephant—it is comparable to destroying a huge and costly piece of machinery—and obviously one ought not to do it if it can possibly be avoided. And at that distance, peacefully eating, the elephant looked no more dangerous than a cow. I thought then and I think now that his attack of "must" was already passing off; in which case he would merely wander harmlessly about until the mahout came back and caught him. Moreover, I did not in the least want to shoot him. I decided that I would watch him for a little while to make sure that he did not turn savage again, and then go home.

But at that moment I glanced round at the crowd that had followed me. It was an immense crowd, two thousand at the least and growing every minute. It blocked the road for a long distance on either side. I looked at the sea of yellow faces above the garish clothes—faces all happy and excited over this bit of fun, all certain that the elephant was going to be shot. They were watching me as they would watch a conjurer about to perform a trick. They did not like me, but with the magical rifle in my hands I was momentarily worth watching. And suddenly I realized that I should have to shoot the elephant after all. The people expected it of me and I had got to do it; I could feel their two thousand wills pressing me forward, irresistibly. And it was at this moment, as I stood there with the rifle in my hands, that I first grasped the hollowness, the futility of the white man's dominion in the East. Here was I, the white man with his gun, standing in front of the unarmed native crowd— seemingly the leading actor of the piece, but in reality I was only an absurd puppet pushed to and fro by the will of those yellow faces behind. I perceived in this moment that when the white man turns tyrant it is his own freedom that he destroys. He becomes a sort of hollow, posing dummy, the conventionalized figure of a sahib. For it is the condition of his rule that he shall spend his life in trying to impress the "natives," and so in every crisis he has got to do what the "natives" expect of him. He wears a mask, and his face grows to fit it. I had got to shoot the elephant. I had committed myself to doing it when I sent for the rifle. A sahib has got to act like a sahib; he has got to appear resolute, to know his own mind and do definite things. To come all that way, rifle in hand, with two thousand people marching at my heels, and then to trail feebly away, having done nothing— no, that was impossible. The crowd would laugh at me. And my whole life, every white man's life in the East, was one long struggle not to be laughed at.

But I did not want to shoot the elephant. I watched him beating his bunch of grass against his knees with that preoccupied grandmotherly air that elephants have. It seemed to me that it would be murder to shoot him. At that age I was not squeamish about killing animals, but I had never shot

> *. . . I had never shot an elephant and never wanted to.*

an elephant and never wanted to. (Somehow it always seems worse to kill a large animal.) Besides, there was the beast's owner to be considered. Alive, the elephant was worth at least a hundred pounds; dead, he would only be worth the value of his tusks, five pounds, possibly. But I had got to act quickly. I turned to some experienced-looking Burmans who had been there when we arrived, and asked them how the elephant had been behaving. They all said the same thing: he took no notice of you if you left him alone, but he might charge if you went too close to him.

It was perfectly clear to me what I ought to do. I ought to walk up to within, say, twenty-five yards of the elephant and test his behavior. If he charged, I could shoot; if he took no notice of me, it would be safe to leave him until the mahout came back. But also I knew that I was going to do no such thing. I was a poor shot with a rifle and the ground was soft mud into which one would sink at every step. If the elephant charged and I missed him, I should have about as much chance as a toad under a steam-roller. But even then I was not thinking particularly of my own skin, only of the watchful yellow faces behind. For at that moment, with the crowd watching me, I was not afraid in the ordinary sense, as I would have been if I had been alone. A white man mustn't be frightened in front of the "natives"; and so, in general, he isn't frightened. The sole thought in my mind was that if anything went wrong those two thousand Burmans would see me pursued, caught, trampled on, and reduced to a grinning corpse like that Indian on the hill. And if that

(cont'd on next page)

happened it was quite probable that some of them would laugh. That would never do. There was only one alternative. I shoved the cartridges into the magazine and lay down on the road to get a better aim.

The crowd grew very still, and a deep, low, happy sigh, as of people who see the theater curtain go up at last, breathed from innumerable throats. They were going to have their bit of fun after all. The rifle was a beautiful German thing with cross-hair sights. I did not then know that in shooting an elephant one would shoot to cut an imaginary bar running from ear-hole to ear-hole. I ought, therefore, as the elephant was sideways on, to have aimed straight at his earhole; actually I aimed several inches in front of this, thinking the brain would be further forward.

When I pulled the trigger I did not hear the bang or feel the kick—one never does when a shot goes home—but I heard the devilish roar of glee that went up from the crowd. In that instant, in too short a time, one would have thought, even for the bullet to get there, a mysterious, terrible change had come over the elephant. He neither stirred nor fell, but every line of his body had altered. He looked suddenly stricken, shrunken, immensely old, as though the frightful impact of the bullet had paralyzed him without knocking him down. At last, after what seemed a long time—it might have been five seconds, I dare say—he sagged flabbily to his knees. His mouth slobbered. An enormous senility seemed to have settled upon him. One could have imagined him thousands of years old. I fired again into the same spot.

He neither stirred nor fell, but every line of his body had altered.

At the second shot he did not collapse but climbed with desperate slowness to his feet and stood weakly upright with legs sagging and head dropping. I fired a third time. That was the shot that did for him. You could see the agony of it jolt his whole body and knock the last remnant of strength from his legs. But in falling he seemed for a moment to rise, for as his hind legs collapsed beneath him he seemed to tower upward like a huge rock toppling, his trunk reaching skyward like a tree. He trumpeted, for the first and only time. And then down he came, his belly toward me, with a crash that seemed to shake the ground even where I lay.

I got up. The Burmans were already racing past me across the mud. It was obvious that the elephant would never rise again, but he was not dead. He was breathing very rhythmically with long rattling gasps, his great mound of a side painfully rising and falling. His mouth was wide open—I could see far down into caverns of pale pick throat. I waited a long time for him to die, but his breathing did not weaken. Finally I fired my two remaining shots into the spot where I thought his heart must be. The thick blood welled out of him like red velvet, but still he did not die. His body did not even jerk when the shots hit him, the tortured breathing continued without a pause. He was dying very slowly and in great agony, but in some world remote from me where not even a bullet could damage him further. I felt that I had got to put an end to that dreadful noise. It seemed dreadful to see the great beast lying there, powerless to move and yet powerless to die, and not even to be able to finish him.

I sent back for my small rifle and poured shot after shot into his heart and down his throat. They seemed to make no impression. The tortured gasps continued as steadily as the ticking of a clock.

> *I had done it solely to avoid looking like a fool.*

In the end I could not stand it any longer and went away. I heard later that it took him half an hour to die. Burmans were bringing dahs and baskets even before I left, and I was told they had stripped his body almost to the bones by afternoon.

Afterward, of course, there were endless discussions about the shooting of the elephant. The owner was furious, but he was only an Indian and could do nothing. Besides, legally I had done the right thing, for a mad elephant has to be killed, like a mad dog, if its owner fails to control it. Among the Europeans opinion was divided. The older men said I was right, the younger men said it was a damn shame to shoot an elephant for killing a coolie, because an elephant was worth more than any damn Coringhee coolie. And afterward I was very glad that the coolie had been killed; it put me legally in the right and it gave me a sufficient pretext for shooting the elephant. I often wondered whether any of the others grasped that I had done it solely to avoid looking like a fool.

—George Orwell

Start-Up: Orwell allowed himself to be persuaded to shoot the elephant even though he was totally against the act. The crowd was able to pressure Orwell into taking this action because he put too much importance on how others perceived him. He did not stand up for what he believed was the right thing to do.

Connection: Cite a similar experience of being persuaded by two or more people to do something that you thought was not the right thing to do. What methods did they use to influence you?

Top 10 Reasons for Rejecting Job Applicants

10. Evasiveness (being vague or misleading)
9. Lack of confidence or overconfidence
8. Sloppy resume
7. Uninformed about the organization
6. Lack of courtesy, maturity, or tact
5. Too interested in salary or benefits
4. Lack of interest in the job
3. Poor personal appearance
2. Uncertainty about goals
1. **Inability to express oneself clearly**

Applying for a Job

"I don't like work—no man does—but I like what is in work—the chance to find yourself. Your own reality—for yourself, not for others—what no other man can ever know."

—JOSEPH CONRAD, POLISH-BORN ENGLISH NOVELIST

Workplace Skills in This Chapter

- Improve **interpersonal** skills as you practice job interviewing.

- Understand the needs of workplace **systems**.

- Gather **information** for producing resumes and cover letters.

- Manage **resources** as you plan a resume.

- Use **technology** to produce a resume and letters.

As you complete Chapter 11, you will

- list sources of job leads.

- gather data for a resume and a job application.

- identify marketable skills.

- complete a job application.

- prepare a resume, cover letter, and follow-up letter.

- participate in a mock job interview.

Y ou have been preparing for your first career position since you were small. The skills, talents, and personality traits that you bring to your first real job are not handed to you on graduation day along with your diploma; you have been developing them all through your life. On the soccer field, in the third-grade production of *The Wizard of Oz,* or in hundreds of hours of video games, you found out what you were good at and what you liked. Are you happiest when you're alone outdoors? When you're at the mall with a group of friends? When you've created something entirely original? The answers to those and many other questions form the heart of your career plan.

Finding a Career Position

Part-time jobs held during school have taught you about being dependable, working with others, taking direction, and getting through those hours when you'd rather be doing anything *but* working.

But this chapter is not about how to land that type of job. This chapter is about how to land a career position—a challenging job with opportunities for learning and advancement. A job related to your talents, interests, and occupational training. A job that pays enough to cover rent, transportation, utilities, food, and other necessities, with enough left over for having fun and for savings. A job that includes benefits, such as health insurance and paid vacations. There is a great deal of competition for these jobs, often from people who may have more training and experience than you have. The first step, though, is to locate potential employers.

INFOBIT

"Know what you love and do what you love. If you don't do what you love, you're just wasting your time."

BILLY JOEL, U.S. SINGER AND SONGWRITER

Job Leads

Most job openings are never advertised. They are filled from within the organization or by word of mouth. When you are in the market for a job, tell everyone you know what you can do and what type of job you are looking for. Work with the school counselor who handles job placement. Call organizations that hire people with your skills.

Practice 11-1: Job Leads

Do you know anyone who has the type of job you're looking for? Do you know anyone who works for an organization where you might like to work? List the names and job titles of people who might be sources of leads for career positions. Include teachers and counselors, neighbors, family members, family members of your friends, and friends of your parents, for example.

Helpful Sources of Information

Start reading the help-wanted ads in the newspaper. People often find good jobs this way. Even if the classified ads do not lead directly to a job, you can still learn a lot from reading them. For instance, the ads can answer these questions:

* What jobs are available in this area for people with my training?

* How great is the demand?

* What do these jobs pay?

* What qualities do the employers expect?

Figure 11-1 is an example of an informative help-wanted ad.

SERVICE TECHNICIANS

Reprographics company has opening for one full-time and one part-time copier repair technician. Requires copier service and electro/mechanical experience. Must be customer-oriented, reliable, self-motivated. Capable of scheduling service calls, filling out reports, maintaining a parts inventory. Full medical, tuition reimb. program. Send resume to EMH, 684 Mills Drive, Laurel, MD 20725-1426.

Figure 11-1: *Read help-wanted ads carefully and follow instructions.*

CAREER C·O·N·N·E·C·T·I·O·N

The Bureau of Labor Statistics predicts both large numbers of openings and above-average earnings for these occupations. None requires a bachelor's degree.

- Registered nurses
- Electrical and electronic technicians
- Real estate agents
- Drafters
- Police officers
- Industrial machinery mechanics
- Electricians
- Firefighters

- Postal Service mail carriers
- Sports and physical training instructors
- Sheet metal workers
- Truck drivers
- Painters and paper hangers
- Corrections officers
- Maintenance technicians
- Flight attendants
- Paralegals

Figure 11-2: *Help-wanted ads are good sources of information.*

Always follow the instructions given in the ad. For example, if the ad asks for a resume, do not call instead.

The *Occupational Outlook Handbook* is a publication of the U.S. Department of Labor that gives detailed descriptions of hundreds of jobs. Most school and public libraries have the handbook. By reading descriptions of jobs you have held and jobs you may apply for, you can find the following types of information:

- What work the job involves
- Estimated future job openings
- Necessary skills and training

- Working conditions
- Earnings
- Essential personal characteristics

Practice 11-2: Researching a Position

1. Tomorrow, begin checking the help-wanted ads in the newspaper or on the many Internet sites that post ads. Find an ad that closely matches your training and skills. But don't expect an exact match, since that rarely happens. When you find an ad that gives an address to write to, clip it or print it out and attach it to a piece of paper. You will use it later in this chapter.

2. If the book is available, find descriptions in the *Occupational Outlook Handbook* of career positions you'd like to have. Photocopy and attach them to your help-wanted ad.

Computer and Office Machine Repairers

(D.O.T. 633.261-010, -014, .281 except -026; 706.381-010 and -030; 828.261-014, .281-010, and -014)

Nature of the Work

Computer and office machine repairers install new machines, do preventive maintenance, and correct emergency problems.

Computer equipment repairers work on computers (mainframes, minis, and micros), peripheral equipment, and word processing systems, while office machine repairers work on photocopiers, cash registers, and similar equipment. They may make special cable and wiring connections when installing equipment. Repairers work closely with electricians, who install the wiring for the new system, to ensure proper layout. (A description of the work of electricians can be found elsewhere in the *Handbook*.)

Despite frequent preventive maintenance, computers and other machines do break down. To locate the cause of failures, repairers run diagnostic programs that pinpoint malfunctions. Although some of the most modern and sophisticated computers have self-diagnosing videotapes, programmed computer software, or workbooks that allow trainees to learn at their own pace.

Experienced technicians attend training sessions and read manuals to keep up with design changes and revised service procedures. Many technicians also take advanced training in a particular system or type of repair.

Good eyesight and color vision are . . . needed to inspect and work on small, delicate parts and good hearing to detect malfunctions revealed by sound. Because field repairers usually handle jobs alone, they must be able to work without close supervision. For those who have frequent contact with customers, a pleasant personality, neat appearance, and good communications skills are important. Repairers must also be trustworthy because they may be exposed to money and other valuables in places like banks and securities offices, and some employers require that they be bonded. A security clearance may be required for technicians who repair equipment or service machines in areas where people are engaged in activities related to national security.

Figure 11-3: *Excerpts from the Occupational Outlook Handbook description of computer and office machine repairers*

Preparing a Resume

INFOBIT

According to the Bureau of Labor, in any economy, 1 person in 12 is in the process of voluntarily changing careers.

Take a look at a brochure advertising any product, the Boss 450 Car Stereo System, for instance. The brochure lists the features of the system, gives data about its performance, and lets you know where to find one. The brochure is eye-catching, well-organized, and easy to read. The most important information jumps out at you. The purpose of the brochure, of course, is to interest you in buying the system. Chances are you won't call in an order based on the brochure, but you might visit a store where they sell the system so you can listen to it for yourself and get more information in person.

Your **resume** is like a sales brochure, but the product is *you*. Of course, your resume will not be colorful or flashy like the brochure. But it will be attractive and it will include essentially the same kinds of information. It summarizes the job hunter's features and performance data—education, skills, training, and experience. No one is hired based only on the information in a resume. But many employers do make decisions about whom to call for an interview based on reviewing resumes.

A decent resume cannot be prepared in a day, so it's a good idea to have one ready at all times. As is true for any other important communication, preparing a resume takes planning, organizing, writing, editing, revising, and more revising. If an employer has a large stack of resumes sitting on a desk, he or she is looking for ways to reduce this load of paperwork. Since interviews are time-consuming and the employer will only schedule a few of them, one error on your resume may be enough to cause an employer to discard it. You may lose your chance at getting a job interview.

Gathering Information

The entire job-seeking process requires a lot of information. Finding that information can take some time. For instance, exact dates, names, and addresses for the jobs that you have held are required. You also have to take a good look at yourself and identify your own strengths and skills. Unless you know what you can offer employers, how will they know?

When you are looking for a job, you must match your experience, skills, training, and personal qualities to the type of job that you want. You will need to point out to employers that you have what it takes to be a valuable employee.

Ask your instructor for a list of skills that are covered in your educational program curriculum. Talk to people who have or have had the type of job you're looking for. You must be able to show an employer what you know and what you can do. This can make the difference between being considered for a job or being rejected.

Look for ways your education and experience have prepared you for the career position you want. Honestly examine your own skills and personal characteristics.

INFOBIT

Today, a considerable amount of work gets done in teams. Find opportunities to show employers that you have accomplished things in cooperation with other people.

INFOBIT

Do let employers know if you are proficient in a second language. It's a definite plus!

Practice 11-3: Preparation for Writing a Resume

Complete the Personal Inventory form on *Student Workbook* pages 11-A through 11-D. The information that you will write on this form will be useful, not only as you plan your resume but also as you write letters, complete applications, and prepare for interviews. Take your time filling it out. You will need to look up addresses and phone numbers, check the spelling of names, and request permission from references to list their names.

Do not treat this as just another classroom exercise. You will use the information from this form to prepare a resume that will be sent to potential employers. Taking the time now to be thorough and exact will make the job of writing a resume much easier. An example of a completed Personal Inventory form is shown in Figure 11-4.

PERSONAL INFORMATION

FIRST NAME Marcus		MIDDLE NAME OR INITIAL H.	LAST NAME Davis	

STREET ADDRESS 87 Ross Ave.	CITY Laurel	STATE MD	ZIP CODE 20726-2732	NO. OF YEARS 16

PREVIOUS ADDRESS NA	CITY	STATE	ZIP CODE	NO. OF YEARS

PHONE # 301-555-0172	DATE OF BIRTH 5-3-81	MARITAL STATUS SINGLE	SOCIAL SECURITY # 202-44-8763	DRIVER'S LICENSE # PW68742

IN AN EMERGENCY, NOTIFY: NAME Diane Davis		PHONE # 555-0102	HOW MANY DAYS DID YOU MISS AT SCHOOL OR WORK DURING THE PAST 12 MONTHS? 0	

HEALTH: ☑ EXCELLENT ☐ GOOD ☐ POOR (IF POOR, EXPLAIN):

HAVE YOU EVER BEEN CONVICTED OF A FELONY? ☑ NO ☐ YES IF YES, EXPLAIN:

REFERENCES

NAME	JOB TITLE	ADDRESS	PHONE #	# OF YEARS
Mary Jones	manager	Shop 'n' Save 1007 Laurel Blvd. 20723-1130	555-0132	5 mo.
Tom Hunter	head of maintenance	Laurel Public Schools 805 Pine Rd. 20724-5423	555-0107 x 201	4
Lessa Haas	sales rep	EMH 684 Mills Dr. 20725-1426	555-0141	5
Steve Watkins	head football coach	Laurel High School 801 Pine Rd. 20724-5423	555-0107	4
Arlene Cooper	EMS teacher	Laurel Career Center 803 Pine Rd. 20724-5423	555-0107 x 114	2

Figure 11-4: *A sample personal inventory form*

I AM: PERSONAL QUALITIES — Check as many as apply to you.

☑ accurate
☐ alert
☑ calm
☐ competitive
☐ considerate
☐ creative
☑ flexible
☑ healthy
☐ imaginative
☐ loyal
☑ organized
☑ persistent
☑ quick
☑ responsible
☑ steady
☑ teachable

☑ active
☐ ambitious
☑ careful
☑ confident
☑ consistent
☑ dependable
☑ friendly
☑ helpful
☑ honest
☐ intelligent
☐ mature
☐ outgoing
☐ practical
☑ reliable
☑ self-motivated
☑ strong
☐ thorough

☐ adaptable
☐ assertive
☑ competent
☑ conscientious
☑ cooperative
☑ energetic
☑ hardworking
☐ open-minded
☐ patient
☑ punctual
☑ resourceful
☑ self-reliant
☐ tactful
☐ thoughtful

LIST YOUR FIVE STRONGEST QUALITIES WITH EVIDENCE BELOW:

1. reliable - perfect attendance. Trusted to work on school copiers.

2. teachable - A-B grade average

3. self-motivated - work unsupervised at Shop 'n' Save

4. honest - returned 3 wallets at Shop 'n' Save

5. friendly - enjoy helping customers. Lots of friends.

I CAN: SKILLS — Check as many as apply to you.

☑ listen
☑ speak clearly
☑ follow instructions
☐ train others
☐ learn from mistakes
☑ take responsibility
☐ ask questions
☐ persuade
☑ cooperate
☐ handle complaints
☑ work safely
☑ organize information
☐ organize materials
☑ follow through
☑ solve problems
☑ calculate
☐ construct
☑ maintain
☑ install
☑ drive

☑ read
☑ write clearly
☑ give instructions
☑ learn quickly
☐ accept criticism
☑ understand
☐ ask for help
☐ sell
☑ help people
☑ work with a team
☐ organize time
☐ organize people
☐ plan ahead
☑ meet deadlines
☐ handle money
☑ assemble
☑ inspect
☑ repair
☑ operate
☐ process

LIST YOUR FIVE STRONGEST SKILLS WITH EVIDENCE BELOW:

1. work with a team - played football for 3 years

2. calculate - A-B average in math

3. solve problems - I'll work on copier problems until I solve them.

4. operate computers - have used computers for 6 years

5. organize information - accurate stock & inventory, troubleshooting reports

TWO JOBS YOU'D LIKE TO HAVE:

1. copier service tech

2. pro football player

QUALITIES & SKILLS YOU HAVE FOR EACH JOB:

1. accurate, persistent, reliable, honest, competent

2. strong, quick, good team player

Figure 11-4: *(cont'd)*

EDUCATION

MOST RECENT SCHOOL ATTENDED

NAME Laurel Career Center

DATES: FROM 8-97 **TO** present

ADDRESS 803 Pine Rd. Laurel MD 20724-5423

DEGREE/CERTIFICATE 6-99

GRADE POINT AVERAGE 3.2

CLASS RANK ?

FAVORITE CLASS EMS

LEAST FAVORITE CLASS Social Studies

MOST VALUABLE CLASS EMS

SPECIAL COURSES
Applied math
Applied science
Applied English

ACTIVITIES, HONORS, AWARDS
VICA member
First place - VICA troubleshooting
Perfect attendance

SPECIAL SKILLS LEARNED
Troubleshooting, diagnosing, repair, servicing of office machines
Reading blueprints & schematics
ID components
Radio & stereo circuits

SECOND MOST RECENT SCHOOL ATTENDED

NAME Laurel High School

DATES: FROM 1995 **TO** 1997

ADDRESS 801 Pine Rd. Laurel MD 20724-5423

DEGREE/CERTIFICATE 1999

GRADE POINT AVERAGE 2.5

CLASS RANK ?

FAVORITE CLASS math

LEAST FAVORITE CLASS English

MOST VALUABLE CLASS Computer Science

SPECIAL COURSES
general studies

ACTIVITIES, HONORS, AWARDS
football - 3 years
Spanish Club - 2 years

SPECIAL SKILLS LEARNED
word processing, database, spreadsheet, computer graphics

Figure 11-4: *(cont'd)*

EXPERIENCE

CURRENT OR MOST RECENT JOB

JOB TITLE   stock clerk

DATES OF EMPLOYMENT: FROM   10 / 98   TO   / present

NAME OF BUSINESS   Shop 'n' Save

NAME OF SUPERVISOR   Mary Jones

ADDRESS   1007 Laurel Blvd., Laurel MD 20723-1130

PHONE #   555-0132

DUTIES   unpack, check, shelve products. Mark codes. Keep records, inventory. Help customers.

SECOND MOST RECENT JOB

JOB TITLE   Groundskeeper

DATES OF EMPLOYMENT: FROM   6 / 97 & 98   TO   8 / 97 & 98
Two summers

NAME OF BUSINESS   Laurel Public Schools

NAME OF SUPERVISOR   Tom Hunter

ADDRESS   805 Pine Rd., Laurel MD 20724-5423

PHONE #   555-0107 x201

DUTIES   Plant sod, maintain athletic fields, build & repair bleachers

THIRD MOST RECENT JOB

JOB TITLE   Yard maintenance

DATES OF EMPLOYMENT: FROM   5 / 94   TO   9 / 94

NAME OF BUSINESS   27 Fair Oaks Ct., Laurel MD 20725-1428

NAME OF SUPERVISOR   Ms. Lessa Haas

ADDRESS   27 Fair Oaks Ct., Laurel MD 20725-1428

PHONE #   555-0154

DUTIES   Plant & maintain lawn & garden. Perform simple household repairs. Do errands.

OTHER RELEVANT EXPERIENCES & ACTIVITIES

Details of volunteer work, hobbies, interests, and other activities that apply to a career position

Install car stereos   Carpentry
Computers   Play guitar

Figure 11-4: *(cont'd)*

TECHNOBIT

Specialized resume-writing software prompts the user for data about education and work experience and then creates a chronological or functional resume. The software also takes care of page design and formatting.

INFOBIT

"The closest to perfection a person ever comes is when he fills out a job application form."

STANLEY J. RANDALL

Drafting the Resume

Use a computer for drafting the resume; there simply is no other way to do it. Resume-writing software and word processing programs make it easy to correct errors, move sections, and improve page design. You can even create slightly different resumes for different employers. If your address or job changes after you have completed your resume, you can easily revise it if it has been saved on a disk. A resume is never finished; it is a work in progress. Once you have a good, basic resume prepared, you can modify it for years without having to start over.

Your resume will be as unique as your fingerprint. The resumes in Figures 11-5 and 11-6 will give you some ideas, but you'll need to adapt those ideas to fit your situation. Make sure that your resume says what you want it to say about you. Take advantage of this opportunity to tell the reader what you know and what you can do. It is not enough to list where and when you worked or attended school. Provide information that will tell the reader how dependable, hardworking, and trainable you are. What skills do you already have that this employer is looking for? If you don't tell the reader, who will?

Even though your resume will be unique, it will probably include the following sections:

Name, Address, and Phone Number

This information always appears at the top of the resume. Use your full name (you may use a middle initial) and your full mailing address. Write out words like *Street* and *Avenue*. Include the area code with your phone number, and make sure someone will answer at that number during business hours. If you have an answering machine, make sure your greeting is brief and businesslike. Consider including your e-mail address if you have one.

Job Objective

The **job objective** is a brief statement of your employment goal. If you are applying for a specific opening, make that job your objective. You can change your objective slightly for different jobs. Don't try to get by with something general like, "A rewarding position with opportunities for growth and advancement." That just says you have no objective. Besides, who actually *wants* a dead-end job with no rewards?

Education

Since school has been your main job so far, your education is probably the most important section of your resume. Give the name of your school, graduation date, and the name of any special course of study that would interest employers. List special job-related skills and relevant honors and awards. Include school activities, especially those in which you took leadership or demonstrated your value as a team player. If you are proud of your grade point average, include it as well.

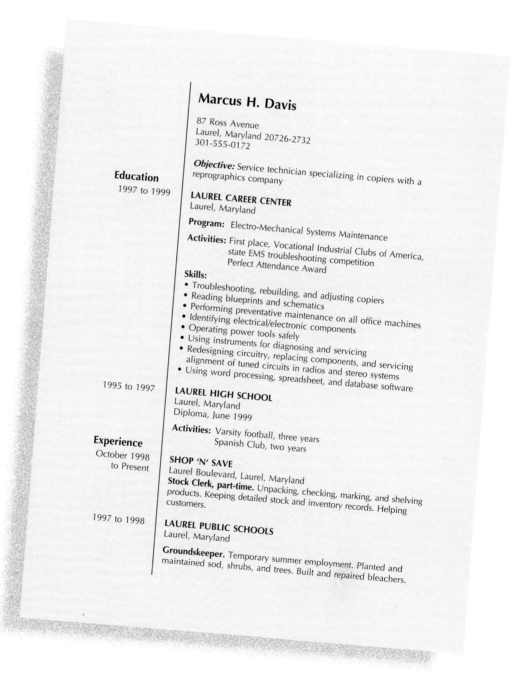

Marcus H. Davis

87 Ross Avenue
Laurel, Maryland 20726-2732
301-555-0172

Objective: Service technician specializing in copiers with a reprographics company

Education
1997 to 1999

LAUREL CAREER CENTER
Laurel, Maryland

Program: Electro-Mechanical Systems Maintenance

Activities: First place, Vocational Industrial Clubs of America, state EMS troubleshooting competition
Perfect Attendance Award

Skills:
• Troubleshooting, rebuilding, and adjusting copiers
• Reading blueprints and schematics
• Performing preventative maintenance on all office machines
• Identifying electrical/electronic components
• Operating power tools safely
• Using instruments for diagnosing and servicing
• Redesigning circuitry, replacing components, and servicing alignment of tuned circuits in radios and stereo systems
• Using word processing, spreadsheet, and database software

1995 to 1997

LAUREL HIGH SCHOOL
Laurel, Maryland
Diploma, June 1999

Activities: Varsity football, three years
Spanish Club, two years

Experience
October 1998
to Present

SHOP 'N' SAVE
Laurel Boulevard, Laurel, Maryland
Stock Clerk, part-time. Unpacking, checking, marking, and shelving products. Keeping detailed stock and inventory records. Helping customers.

1997 to 1998

LAUREL PUBLIC SCHOOLS
Laurel, Maryland

Groundskeeper. Temporary summer employment. Planted and maintained sod, shrubs, and trees. Built and repaired bleachers.

Figure 11-5: *A sample chronological resume*

INFOBIT

True story! From a resume: "I am a rabid typist."

Experience

Give the names of the organizations you worked for, when you worked there, and your job title. Briefly describe job duties. List jobs in **reverse chronological order**—with your present job first. Write about your current job in the present tense; describe the others in past tense. If you have no paid work experience, consider describing volunteer work or other valuable, relevant experiences.

Anne T. Freese
112 North Barrington Road
Salt Lake City, UT 84116-0504
801/555-0109

Job Target

A position as an administrative assistant in a business office

Office Skills

- Experience with MS Word
- Experience with WordPerfect
- Knowledge of office procedures
- Strong interpersonal skills
- Knowledge of accounting ledgers
- Experience with Excel spreadsheets
- Experience with Lotus spreadsheets
- Keying speed of 60 wpm
- Operation of switchboard
- Excellent math skills

Administrative Activities

- Assisted with clerical duties in family-owned business
- Treasurer, Sycamore High School Business Professionals of America (BPA)
  Maintained account ledger, created annual budget, balanced budget
- Co-chairperson, BPA candy sale
  Directed sales staff, planned advertising campaign, sold candy

Education

Sycamore High School, Salt Lake City, Utah
Swim team, two years
Assistant editor of school newspaper, three years

Experience

Freese's Flowers, Layton, Utah
Salesclerk and clerical assistant, part-time

Mr. and Mrs. Homer Sampson, Spring, Utah
Baby-sitter for three children, part-time

Figure 11-6: *A sample functional resume*

CULTURE C·O·N·N·E·C·T·I·O·N
Training employees is taken seriously in Japan. New employees spend up to six months in intensive training programs, which are usually held outside of the job in special training centers. On April 1, most companies observe *nyusha-shiki,* a ceremony for receiving newly hired employees into a company.

Practice 11-4: Parallel Lists

One key to designing an effective resume is consistency. For example, format all your headings and dates the same way throughout. You must also be consistent in the wording of items in lists—that is, they must be **parallel**. The following list of restaurant management duties is from the resume of a person who had worked for several years in the family business. Revise the list so all items have the same grammatical structure. Use concise phrases, not complete sentences.

* Prepared payroll for staff of 10

* Cash registers—opening and closing

* decorating and cleaning of the restaurant

* Have trained 15 servers

* Greeted and served customers

* stockroom organization and maintaining inventory

* Menu planning

* I made sure the food deliveries were of acceptable quality and that they were accurate.

* I checked to make sure the food preparation areas were orderly and clean.

* Supervise the preparation, arrangement, and serving of food

Organizational Plans

The two most common organizational plans for resumes are chronological and functional. The **chronological resume** (see Figure 11-5) lists background information in chronological (time) sequence, starting with the most recent experience first and working backward. This is the most common form and the one that most employers expect to see.

In the **functional resume** (see Figure 11-6), work experience and abilities are listed by skill areas. Resumes in this style are more difficult to put together and tend to be longer. The functional resume is most often used by people with a great deal of experience.

Resume Guidelines

When preparing a resume, follow these guidelines:

* Tell the truth. Nothing is more important than accuracy.

* Limit the resume to one page.

* Give only positive information. Do not include personal information about health or family or a photo. Do not give salary requirements or reasons for leaving other jobs. Only include hobbies and interests that relate to your ability to do the job for which you are applying. Your readers are not interested in you personally; they are interested in how you can benefit their organizations.

* Avoid using technical jargon or acronyms on printed resumes. If the reader doesn't understand them, they're just wasting space.

* Don't use the word *I* in the resume. It's not necessary because the resume is obviously about you.

* Decide whether your education or work experience will be more valuable to the reader. Put the most valuable section first.

* Use short sentences or lists to describe skills or responsibilities, with parallel structure. Begin sentences in printed resumes describing work experience with **active verbs,** like the ones listed here.

PAST-TENSE ACTIVE VERBS

achieved	handled	performed	served
analyzed	helped	planned	scheduled
arranged	improved	prepared	sold
assembled	installed	presented	solved
assisted	learned	processed	sorted
built	maintained	produced	studied
coordinated	managed	provided	trained
demonstrated	operated	recorded	won
designed	organized	repaired	worked
developed	participated	selected	wrote

* Use **key words,** nouns and noun phrases, rather than active verbs for resumes that will be sent electronically (over the Internet) or **scanned.** Some companies use special software that searches the resume for key words that match the requirements for particular positions. For example, an electrician might include the following key-word section:

TECHNOLOGY **C·O·N·N·E·C·T·I·O·N**

Nowadays, if you send your resume to a medium-size or large company, you can lay odds that the first person to read it won't be a person at all, but a computer. At some companies, resume-scanning software reads resumes and stores key words in databases. The software then uses key words to match resumes with positions. That means the resumes must be computer-friendly. This is also true if you post your resume on the Internet. If you know your resume will be scanned, follow these guidelines:

- Use nouns to emphasize specific talents rather than action verbs.
- Use industry buzzwords.
- Do not use fancy fonts, type smaller than 12 points, italics, underlining, lines and borders, bullets, or multiple columns. Begin all text at the left margin.
- Send originals printed on white paper.
- Do not fold or staple.
- Triple-check spelling.
- Include your e-mail address, but not your address and phone number, on a resume sent via the Internet.

WEB LINK

Search the Internet for the most up-to-date information on creating an electronic version of your resume.

THE FAR SIDE By GARY LARSON

Primitive resumes

THE FAR SIDE ©1992 FARWORKS, INC. Used by permission of UNIVERSAL PRESS SYNDICATE. All rights reserved.

KEY-WORD SUMMARY: Commercial wiring. Use of hand and hydraulic benders. Experience with EMT and rigid conduit. Fire alarm experience. Blueprint reading and layout. Two years' experience. Good problem-solving skills.

* There's no such thing as a cute, hip, or flashy resume. Don't even consider using adorable clip art, clever bullets, or snazzy borders. Resumes should have a businesslike, dignified appearance.

* Use a plain, readable typeface, such as Times, Palatino, or Arial.

* Use white space, headings, bold print, and bullets to make the resume attractive and easy to read.

* Balance the resume between margins.

* Do not include "References available upon request" on your resume. The employer assumes you have references. List them on a separate page so that, if an interviewer asks for this list, you have it ready. The best references are school personnel and former supervisors who can say good things about your skills and work habits. Don't ask your peers or relatives to be your references.

* Use every proofreading trick you know. Ask several people to proofread for you. Keep at it until the resume is perfect.

INFOBIT

True story! From a resume: "College, August 1880–May 1984."

* Stand several feet away from your resume to check its overall appearance.

* Use good-quality paper in a conservative color—white or off-white—and a good-quality ink-jet or laser printer. Send originals if you can, but if you must send photocopies, make sure they are clear and clean.

How would you feel as an employer if you received a resume like the one shown in Figure 11-7?

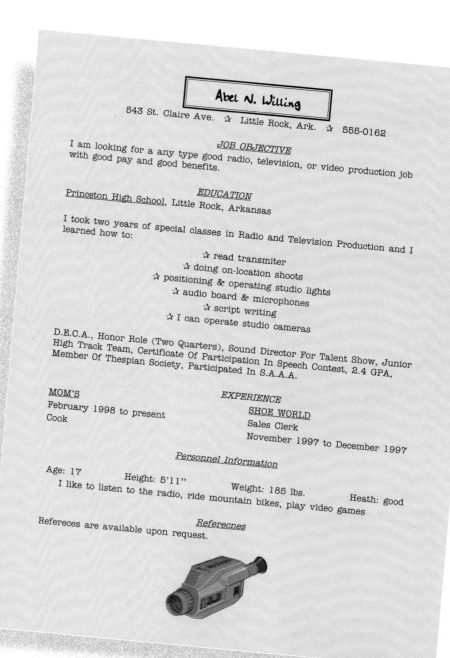

Figure 11-7: *A negative resume example*

INFOBIT

True story! From a cover letter: "Here are my qualifications for you to overlook."

Practice 11-5: Analyzing Resumes

teamwork

1. Imagine that you are an employer. After receiving the resumes shown in Figures 11-5, 11-6, and 11-7 in the mail, you immediately toss one in the trash. Why? In a group of two or three students, list ten reasons. How would you improve the other two? You'll find the three resumes on pages 377, 378, and 382.

2. What advice would you give Marc Davis for producing an electronic version of his resume, shown in Figure 11-5?

Preparing a Cover Letter

Always send **cover letters** with resumes. This is your opportunity to demonstrate your qualifications for and interest in a particular job. Figure 11-9 shows the information that is included in a cover letter, and Figure 11-10 shows the letter that Marc Davis sent with his resume. Cover letters are short and focused—no more than three or four paragraphs. And don't try to write a one-size-fits-all form letter. You may be able to recycle a few sentences, but you'll have to write a different cover letter for each job.

Convey enthusiasm in your letter. Try to include some information that will cause the reader to take notice, and to pause and think, "I'd like to know more about this person." If you know of any name to drop, such as that of a current employee of the organization, include it in your cover letter. Use a polite, professional tone.

It's more effective to address a cover letter to an individual by name. If you have the phone number, call to ask the name of the appropriate person.

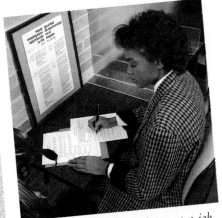

Figure 11-8: When filling out a job application, write clearly, respond to all questions, and be honest.

Completing Job Applications

If you are called for an interview, you will be asked to fill out a job application form.

It is essential to read and follow instructions on the job application. If you fail to follow instructions such as "Please print. Use blue or black ink," what will the potential employer assume about your ability to follow instructions on the job? Write clearly, respond to all questions, and be honest. Bring your resume plus a list of additional names, addresses, and dates, as well as any other information that you may need.

INFOBIT

True story! One applicant stretched out on the floor to fill out a job application. Another challenged the interviewer to arm-wrestle.

Application forms are typically designed with tiny spaces for answers. Shorten your responses and print as small as you can, but make sure your responses are legible. If you do not understand a question on the form, ask for clarification. If the question does not apply to you, write *NA* (for "not applicable") or draw a short line in the space.

Study the example of a job application in Figure 11-11.

Your Street Address
City, State ZIP Code
Date

Reader's Name
Reader's Job Title
Company Name
Street Address
City, State ZIP Code

Dear Title and Last Name:

The first paragraph explains who you are and why you are writing. If you are responding to an ad, tell where you saw it. If someone referred you, give the name and your relationship. Name the position for which you want to apply.

The next section summarizes your qualifications. Let the reader know why you want to work for this particular organization and what you can contribute to it. Don't waste space repeating the information included in your resume.

The closing provides a courteous, friendly ending. Include an action statement. For example, ask the reader for an interview or indicate when you will call to make an appointment. Include a polite ending.

Sincerely,

Your Signature

Your Name

Enclosure

Figure 11-9: *Suggested content for cover letters*

Practice 11-6: Completing a Job Application

Now it's your turn. Assume that you received an application from the organization that ran the ad that you found for Practice 11-2. Carefully complete the job application on *Student Workbook* pages 11-I and 11-J. Use information from your Personal Inventory and follow all instructions carefully. You may need to turn back to Chapter 8 to review guidelines for filling out forms.

87 Ross Avenue
Laurel, MD 20726-2732
March 3, ----

Mr. Jason Cardena
Human Resources Manager
EMH Company
684 Mills Drive
Laurel, MD 20725-1426

Dear Mr. Cardena:

I am a high school senior attending the Laurel Career Center in the Electro-Mechanical Systems Maintenance program. I would very much like to apply for the position of part-time service technician, which I read about in Sunday's *Laurel Press.*

I learned about your company during a school field trip last spring. I also recently discussed EMH with your sales representative, Ms. Lessa Haas, who encouraged me to apply. She hired me to do odd jobs for her a few years ago and has agreed to be one of my references.

My training at the Career Center has prepared me for this position, and my present job has given me experience in dealing with customers, which I enjoy. My technical skills, especially my copier repair skills, are excellent; but I plan to expand them by attending college part-time in either computer science or electrical engineering.

Because I believe my qualifications meet your needs, I would like to schedule an interview to discuss them with you. Please call me any day after 2:30. Thank you.

Sincerely,

Marcus Davis

Marcus Davis

Enclosure

Figure 11-10: *A sample cover letter*

APPLICATION FOR EMPLOYMENT

Please Print

We are an equal opportunity employer, dedicated to a policy of nondiscrimination in employment on any basis including race, color, age, sex, religion, or national origin.

PERSONAL INFORMATION

Name **Davis**　　Date **March 8, 1999**　　Social Security Number **202-44-8763**

Last **Davis**　　First **Marcus**　　Middle **H.**

Present Address　Street **87 Ross Avenue**　　City **Laurel**　　State **Maryland**　　ZIP **20726-2731**

Permanent Address　Street　　City　　State　　ZIP

Phone No. **(301) 555-0172**

ARE YOU A U.S. CITIZEN? YES ☑ NO ☐　ANY RESTRICT. ON TRAVEL YES ☐ NO ☑　IF YES, EXPLAIN

HAVE YOU EVER BEEN CONVICTED FOR OTHER THAN ☐ YES ☑ NO MINOR TRAFFIC VIOLATIONS　IF YES, WHEN?　WHERE?　REASON

EMPLOYMENT DESIRED

Position **service technician**

Are You Employed Now? **yes**　　Date You Can Start **3/15/99**

Ever Applied to This Company Before? **no**　　If So, May We Inquire of Your Present Employer? **yes**

Where?　　When?

EDUCATION

	Name and Location of School	Circle Last Year Completed	Did You Graduate?	Subjects Studied or Degree?
High School	**Laurel High School** **801 Pine Rd. Laurel MD**	1 ②3 4	☐ YES ☑ NO	**Genreal Studies Diploma 6/99**
College			☐ YES ☐ NO	
Trade, Business, or Correspondence School	**Laurel Career Center** **803 Pine Rd. Laurel MD**	1 2 3 4 ①2 3 4	☐ YES ☐ NO ☐ YES ☑ NO	**Two-Year Electro-Mechanical Systems Maintenance Program**

SPECIALIZED TECHNICAL SKILLS (e.g., Computer Programmer/Language, Equipment Operation, Special Tools or Machines Used)

Troubleshooting, maintenance, and repair of all office equipment, including copiers.

Able to use a computer and all diagnostic and servicing equipment.

Activities Other Than Religious (civic, athletic, etc.)
Exclude organizations the name or character of which indicates the race, age, sex, color, or national origin of their members.

Vocational Industrial Clubs of America

(Continued)

Figure 11-11: *A sample job application*

PHYSICAL RECORD

Do you have any disability that would substantially interfere with your ability to perform the essential duties of the job for which you have applied? If so, what can be done to accomodate your limitations

No

WORK EXPERIENCE

(List below your last four employers, starting with your present or last employer.)

Date Mo./Yr.	Name and Address of Employer	Salary	Position	Name of Supervisor	Reason for Leaving
Fr. 10/98 To Present	Shop'n'Save 1001 Laurel Blvd.	$5.75 per hour	Stock Clerk	Mary Jones	I wish to work in my trade.
Fr. Summers To 97-98	Laurel Public Schools 805 Pine Rd.	$4.00 per hour	Grounds-keeper	Tom Hunter	Temporary summer employment
Fr. 5/94 To 9/94	Ms. Lessa Haas 27 Fair Oaks Ct.	$20.00 per week	Yard Maintenance/ General Helper	——	Temporary employment
Fr. To					

May we contact your present employer?   YES ☑   NO ☐

REFERENCES

Give the names of three persons not related to you, whom you have known for at least two years.

Name and Occupation	Address	Telephone Number	Years Known
1. Ms. Lessa Haas, Sales Representative.	EMH 684 Mills Dr. Laurel, MD 20715-1426	555-0141	5
2. Ms. Arlene Cooper, EMS Instructor.	Laurel Career Center 803 Pine Rd. Laurel, MD 20714-5423	555-0107, x114	2
3. Mr. Tom Hunter, Maintenance Supervisor.	Laurel Public Schools 805 Pine Rd. Laurel, MD 20714-5423	555-0107, x201	4

I authorize investigation of all statements contained in this application. I understand that misrepresentation or omission of facts called for is cause for dismissal. Further, I understand and agree that my employment is for no definite period and may, regardless of the date of payment of my wages and salary, be terminated at any time without any previous notice.

Signature Marcus H. Davis

Date March 8, 1999

DO NOT WRITE BELOW THIS LINE.

Date

Interviewed by

Remarks

	Ability		Salary or Wages
Neatness			

	Position	Will Report	General Manager
Hired For Dept.		3.	
Approved: 1. Employment Manager	2. Dept. Head		

Figure 11-11: *(cont'd)*

Preparing for a Job Interview

Filling out the Personal Inventory form and the job application is good preparation for an interview. The employer will ask about your background, education, experience, skills, and goals.

You also need to find out about the organization to which you are applying. This shows that you are interested in working for the company. Follow these guidelines for successful interviews:

* Get plenty of rest the night before and think positively.

* Arrive clean and well groomed for the interview. Dress as you would for a day on the job, only better. Do not try to look cute, sexy, or trendy; dress conservatively and neatly. This advice also applies to hairstyle, makeup, fragrance, jewelry, and other accessories. Look like you will fit in.

* Arrive about ten minutes early. Take one or more extra copies of your resume and a pen.

* Most interviewers make their decisions within the first three minutes, so make a terrific first impression. Listen carefully to the pronunciation of the name of the person who will interview you, so you can greet him or her by name. Respond to a move to shake hands with a firm grip and a smile. Don't sit down until you're invited to do so.

* Use common courtesy and good sense. No gum or tobacco products, please.

* Watch your body language. Sit up straight and keep your hands still. Smile when appropriate, and use frequent, direct eye contact, but don't stare.

* Listen carefully to questions and answer them directly and honestly. Speak up and don't talk too fast or give one-word answers. Remember, you are trying to sell yourself.

* Most interviews last about 30 minutes. When the interviewer moves to end the interview, let him or her know you are interested in the job, say thank you, and leave.

Figure 11-12: *Be prepared to answer questions about your background, education, experience, skills, and goals.*

INFOBIT

Comedian Dennis Miller on body piercing: "A powerful, compelling visual statement that says, 'Gee, in today's competitive job market, what can I do to make myself even less employable?'"

Interview Questions

Because every interviewer has his or her own style, it is impossible to predict the exact questions you will be asked. But there are only four basic interview questions, according to Richard Nelson Bolles, author of the book *What Color Is Your Parachute: A Practical Manual for Job-Hunters and Career Changers.*

Most businesses share similar problems and want similar benefits from employees. By understanding how businesses operate, you will be in a better position to figure out ways to convince potential employers that you can make a contribution.

What You Should Know About Business

- The purpose of any business is to make a profit through creating and keeping customers.
- Any company makes a profit by offering something of value to its customers.
- To survive, companies must meet and exceed customer expectations.
- All companies require innovation to stay ahead of the competition—new products, new markets, and improvements to existing products.

Before every interview, ask yourself these questions:

- What can I do to help the organization get or keep customers?
- How can I help the organization deliver value to its customers?

INFOBIT

When Thomas Edison interviewed job applicants, he would always have them over for lunch and serve them soup. Applicants who salted the soup without tasting it were rejected. Edison was looking for people who challenged assumptions instead of acting on them.

INFOBIT

"One of the best ways to persuade others is with your ears—by listening to them."

DEAN RUSK, U.S. DEMOCRATIC POLITICIAN

Basic Questions	Examples
✴ Why did you choose this organization?	What do you know about our company?
✴ What can you offer us?	Questions about specific, job-related skills: Are you familiar with . . . Do you know how to . . . Have you received training in . . .
✴ Who are you?	How are your grades? Why did you leave your last job?
✴ Are you affordable?	How much does your current (or did your last) job pay?

Practice 11-7: Preparing Answers to Interview Questions

It's not a good idea to memorize answers to interview questions, but it is a good idea to think about them ahead of time. Write possible answers of one to three sentences to the following interview questions:

1. Tell me about yourself.

2. How did you choose your school (program, major, etc.)?

3. Where do you see yourself ten years from now?

(cont'd on next page)

INFOBIT

True story!
Questions actually
asked by
interviewers:

"Name three of
your worst qualities
and how they might
affect your job
performance."

"Give me three
reasons why I
shouldn't hire you."

"Discuss morals."

4. What do you consider to be your greatest strengths and weaknesses?

5. What have you learned from your mistakes?

6. Why do you think you would like to work for our organization?

7. How can you help our organization to be successful?

8. Do you prefer working by yourself or with others?

9. How do you handle conflicts that develop at work?

10. What kind of work do you enjoy the most? The least?

11. How much would you expect to be paid?

12. Why should I hire you?

INFOBIT

True story!
Questions actually
asked by
interviewers:

"How will your
epitaph read?"

"How would you
redesign an
elephant?"

"If you had to pick
one puppy to
euthanize out of a
litter of 12, how
would you pick?"

Inappropriate Job Interview Questions

Along with questions about your qualifications for the job, some interviewers occasionally ask questions related to applicants' personal lives. These questions have nothing to do with their ability to do the job. Most interviewers avoid these questions, since it is illegal to discriminate against applicants because of marital status, number of children, disability, age, method of transportation to work, religion, racial or ethnic group, and nationality. By law, you do not need to answer these questions (some of these questions may be asked once a person is hired, though). Of course, you can refuse to answer the question. A more effective approach, however, if you are truly interested in the job, is to give a positive "nonanswer." For example:

Question: Who will take care of your children while you are at work?

Answer: I've made arrangements so that my family life will interfere as little as possible with my work.

Question: How would you feel about working for a woman (or man)?

Answer: I have worked with both men and women while in school.

Question: Where were you born?

Answer: I'm a permanent resident of the United States and have legal permission to work here.

Practice 11-8: Responding to Inappropriate Questions

teamwork Work on this Practice with one or two partners.

How might you respond to the following interview questions? Assume you do not wish to answer directly. Instead, give a positive nonanswer.

1. Would you mind sending us a photo?

2. Do you have any disabilities?

3. What church do you attend?

4. Do you feel that your race will be a problem in performing your job?

5. How will you get to work? Do you own a car?

6. Are you planning to get married?

7. Do you have any plans to have children?

Questions from the Applicant

Most interviewers ask applicants if they have any questions. If you don't have any, the interviewer may assume you're not interested in the job. Instead of asking about pay or benefits, prepare questions such as the following:

* What would a normal workday be like?

* What are the opportunities for advancement?

* Are there opportunities for on-the-job training or further education?

* What are you looking for in an entry-level worker?

One way to prepare for the interview is by participating in practice interviews.

Practice 11-9: Interviewing for a Job

teamwork *careers* For this Practice, work with two other students. All three of you will take turns acting as applicant, interviewer, and observer. You will need your help-wanted ad, resume, completed job application form, and a pen or pencil.

Interviewer

1. Quickly read the applicant's help-wanted ad, resume, and application.

2. Shake hands with the applicant and introduce yourself. Ask the applicant to be seated.

(cont'd on next page)

INFOBIT

True story! An extremely nervous young man arrived for an interview wearing a beautiful new suit—with all the tags still attached to the sleeve.

3. Ask the applicant both general interview questions and questions about the information on the resume and application.

4. Ask follow-up questions to clarify the applicant's answers.

5. End the interview by saying, "We'll call to let you know next week."

Applicant

1. The interviewer will extend his or her hand. Shake it firmly, smile, and introduce yourself. Use the interviewer's name; for example, "I'm pleased to meet you, Ms. Woods."

2. After you have been offered a seat, sit down.

3. Watch your posture and body language.

4. Speak clearly, loudly, and slowly enough to be easily understood.

5. Answer questions directly and honestly. Do not give one-word answers, but don't ramble on too long, either.

6. Don't be afraid to pause and think before answering a question. Refer to your resume for facts when necessary.

7. Ask the interviewer at least one question.

8. The interviewer will let you know when the interview is over. Express your thanks and your interest in the job, and shake hands.

Observer

Do not participate directly in the interview. Silently watch and listen to the interview while you complete the observation form on *Student Workbook* page 11-K. Share your completed form with the applicant.

INFOBIT

True story! When asked about his hobbies, an applicant stood up and started tap dancing around the office.

INFOBIT

True story! During an interview, a young woman announced she hadn't had lunch and proceeded to eat a hamburger and French fries in the interviewer's office.

Preparing the Follow-Up Letter

Most people go through many interviews before they are hired. In rare cases, you may be hired on the spot, or you may be immediately rejected. Usually, though, the interviewer closes by saying that there are still applicants to interview and that you will receive a call by a certain date. If that day goes by and you hear nothing, you may call the interviewer a few days later.

PEOPLE C·O·N·N·E·C·T·I·O·N

Dauna Easley has owned the Learning Station, a private school for toddlers through fourth graders, for 15 years. When she lists a position in the newspaper, she only takes the first 100 calls. Here's what she said about that important initial contact:

Make no mistake about it, the phone call is an interview, so get your resume out before calling. I ask ten open-ended questions to find out if the callers would fit in with my staff and if they really want *this* job, not just *a* job. One grammatical error from callers and they are eliminated because teachers must be role models for the children. Since I only invite ten callers in for interviews, I have to find out if the parents, my *customers,* will "buy" this person. One applicant arrived with poison ivy blisters all over her face and arms. I hired her because she showed a sense of humor about the situation, and *she showed up,* both essential qualities for any employee.

INFOBIT

True story! From a follow-up letter: "Thank you for your consideration. Hope to hear from you shorty."

As soon as you get home from the interview, it's time to start writing again. The **follow-up letter** lets the employer know that you want the job and thanks the interviewer for talking to you. Send this brief, polite letter no later than two days following the interview. Even if you decide that the job for which you interviewed is not for you, or if you know that you will not receive a job offer, send a follow-up letter.

There is one more thing that you must do. Call or write to all those who helped you to get the interview. Thank them and give them the results of the interview. Chances are, you'll be interviewing again, and you may need more help.

Figure 11-13 suggests information to include in a follow-up letter. Figure 11-14 shows an example of a follow-up letter.

Being Evaluated on the Job

Finding a job can be a frustrating process. Eventually, though, efforts will pay off with an offer of a good job. The new employee must then apply all of his or her skills to that job and learn new skills and procedures.

The new employee will also have to learn what the employer expects. Most employers will make their expectations clear. If your boss does not, ask for a complete explanation of the expectations and the evaluation process.

All employees are periodically evaluated. Some organizations use an informal process; others have formal policies and procedures for evaluating employees. Whether the process is informal or formal, you may be sure that within the first few weeks or months, your supervisor will decide whether or not you fit in with the organization and whether or not you have potential for making a positive contribution. You can also expect to be evaluated periodically throughout your career.

Your Street Address
City, State ZIP Code
Date

Reader's Name
Reader's Job Title
Company Name
Street Address
City, State ZIP Code

Dear Title and Last Name:

Remind the reader when you interviewed and for what position. Express appreciation for the interviewer's time and interest.

Briefly restate your qualifications and your interest in the job. If you have any additional information that the reader may need, mention it.

Let the reader know you are looking forward to hearing from him or her again.

Sincerely,

Your Signature

Your Name

Figure 11-13: *Suggested content for follow-up letters*

Some organizations use a form similar to the one found in Figure 11-15 to rate employees. Employers make decisions about rate of pay and job classification based on the criteria listed on the form. Even in organizations where this type of form is not used, employers use similar criteria to evaluate employees.

87 Ross Avenue
Laurel, MD 20726-2732
March 10, ----

Mr. Jason Cardena
Human Resources Manager
EMH Company
684 Mills Drive
Laurel, MD 20725-1426

Dear Mr. Cardena:

Thank you for taking the time to talk with me on March 9 about the position of service technician with EMH.

I also appreciated having the opportunity of talking with Ms. Mateo. She explained the training program in detail and tested my technical skills. Ms. Mateo said that with my training and interest, I should be able to fit right in with the team and make a real contribution.

I look forward to hearing from you. Thanks again for your interest and encouragement.

Sincerely,

Marc Davis

Marc Davis

Figure 11-14: *A sample follow-up letter*

EMPLOYEE PERFORMANCE EVALUATION

Characteristics	UNSATISFACTORY (1)	SATISFACTORY (2)	EXCEPTIONAL (3)
ACCURACY	High error level.	Makes average number of mistakes.	Rarely commits errors.
ATTENDANCE	Frequently absent or late.	Satisfactory attendance level.	Rarely absent or late. Works overtime.
CONSISTENCY	Displays emotion, temper. Disrupts work.	Even temper. Manages normal job stress.	Performs well under pressure.
COOPERATION	Often uncooperative with reasonable requests.	Cooperates well with coworkers and customers.	Very cooperative. Often offers help.
COURTESY	Often rude to others.	Usually polite. Does not offend others.	Respectful of the rights and feelings of others. Polite.
CREATIVITY	Rarely or never offers suggestions.	Occasionally offers positive suggestions.	Often offers positive, innovative suggestions.
DECISION MAKING	Frequently makes unsound decisions.	Usually shows good judgment.	Shows exceptional judgment. Excellent reasoning ability.
DEPENDABILITY	Unreliable and untrustworthy.	Can be depended on to complete work.	Works with little supervision. Self-motivated.
DETERMINATION	Quits when encountering problems.	Overcomes most problems.	Shows perseverance. Reaches most goals.
HABITS AND APPEARANCE	Displays offensive habits and careless appearance.	Acceptable appearance and habits.	Properly dressed and groomed. Shows good taste in behavior.
INITIATIVE	Rarely volunteers. Does only what is demanded.	Shows initiative.	Self-starter. Accepts unpleasant jobs willingly.
LEARNING ABILITY	Slow to learn new ideas and procedures.	Understands most new ideas and procedures.	Fast, independent learner.
ORGANIZATION	Work and work area in disarray.	Usually organized and orderly.	Organized, precise, and efficient.
PRODUCTIVITY	Below-average output.	Acceptable level of output.	Very productive. Exceeds expectations.
PROFICIENCY	Lacking in job skills.	Understands the job.	Complete understanding of all job aspects.

RATING

15	20	25	30	35	40	45

UNSATISFACTORY   SATISFACTORY   EXCEPTIONAL

Figure 11-15: *An employee performance evaluation form*

No matter what evaluation system is used, the employee is usually informed about its results and is given a chance to respond. A list of tips for responding to an employee performance evaluation follows:

* Do not let compliments or positive comments make you feel uncomfortable. Accept praise with thanks.

* Ask questions to clarify any information in your evaluation that you do not understand.

* Respond in writing to any negative remarks that you believe are inaccurate. Make your response specific, factual, clear, and complete. Include documentation (proof) to support your objection.

* Ask for specific advice for improving your performance.

* Thank your supervisor for the opportunity to discuss your job performance.

SUMMARY

INFOBIT

Since communication skills are important to many employers, consider the resume, letters, and job interview as tests of how well you express yourself. Make sure you pass.

Job application materials present the qualifications of the applicant, including work experience, education, and personal information. This information may be presented as a resume, in a letter or application form, or in an interview. Whatever the format, the purpose is to persuade the audience to hire the applicant. Follow these guidelines whenever you prepare job application materials:

* Begin by collecting all relevant information about education, employment, references, skills, and personal qualities.

* Carefully draft a resume that is informative, positive, and attractive.

* Send an effective cover letter with your resume.

* Fill out application forms accurately, neatly, and completely.

* Practice interviewing skills so that you can competently participate in actual interviews.

* Write and send a follow-up letter after an interview, thanking the interviewer and expressing your interest in the job.

* Carefully proofread and revise all job application materials until they are as clear and correct as possible.

PROJECT 1 WRITING A RESUME

1. Use the Project Plan on *Student Workbook* page 11-E to plan a resume so you'll be ready next time you look for a job. Select facts for it from your Personal Inventory.

2. Use a computer for the rough draft. Experiment with fonts, spacing, and organization until the resume looks attractive and easy to read.

3. List three to five references on a separate page under the heading "References." Key your name, then block the addresses for references as you would an inside address, and center them.

4. Using the Rough Draft column of the Project Guide, *Student Workbook* page 11- F, check your rough draft with two other students. Have them record all their comments and changes on your Project Guide and rough draft. Ask them to write a constructive comment on the rough draft and sign it. Ask your teacher and an adult outside the classroom for feedback as well.

5. Revise the resume and have your teacher check it.

6. Prepare the final draft. Proofread until your resume is perfect, using the Final Draft column of the Project Guide. Turn your resume in with the Project Guide.

PROJECT 2 WRITING A COVER LETTER

1. Review information about and examples of business letters in Chapter 9.

2. Using the Project Plan, *Student Workbook* page 11-G, plan a cover letter addressed to the ad that you found for Practice 11-2. Remember that this letter will be sent with the resume, so don't repeat information from the resume.

3. Using a computer, write the rough draft. With one or more classmates, use the Rough Draft column of the Project Guide, *Student Workbook* page 11-H, to check your own work. Have them record all their comments and changes on your Project Guide and rough draft. Ask them to write a constructive comment on the rough draft and sign it. Ask your teacher to check it. Cover letters must be free of errors.

4. Revise the letter, check it using the Final Draft column of the Project Guide, and turn it in with the Project Guide.

PROJECT 3 WRITING A FOLLOW-UP LETTER

1. Assume that an interview has taken place, and you have decided you want the position for which you wrote the cover letter. Using the Project Plan on *Student Workbook* page 11-L, plan the follow-up letter. If the ad did not include a person's name, supply one for this letter, since you would have met by this time.

2. Draft the letter. Using the Rough Draft column of the Project Guide on page 11-M of the *Student Workbook,* check your own work with one or more classmates. Have them record all their comments and changes on your Project Guide and rough draft. Ask them to write a constructive comment on the rough draft and sign it. Ask your teacher to check the rough draft.

3. Revise your letter, check it using the Final Draft column of the Project Guide, and turn it in with the Project Guide.

Overview

Overnight in 1949, Arthur Miller became a famous playwright when his play *Death of a Salesman* premiered in New York. The play is a Henrik Ibsen-influenced social-problem type of drama (An excerpt from *A Doll's House* by Ibsen appears on pages 244–245). The tragedy is a story of a father, Willy Loman, a failure at the age of 63 who has imparted to his sons his own values in material success.

In the following scene near the end of the play, Biff (Willy's son) tries to explain to his brother Happy why he failed to see an employer, whom he worked for years ago, about a chance to borrow some money now and start a new business and a new life.

from *Death of a Salesman*

Happy: Did you see Oliver?

Biff: I saw him all right. Now look, I want to tell Dad a couple of things and I want you to help me.

Happy: What? Is he going to back you?

Biff: Are you crazy? You're out of your head, you know that?

Happy: Why? What happened?

Biff (breathlessly): I did a terrible thing today, Hap. It's been the strangest day I ever went through. I'm all numb, I swear.

Happy: You mean he wouldn't see you?

Biff: Well, I waited six hours for him, see? All day. Kept sending my name in. Even tried to date his secretary so she'd get me to him, but no soap.

Happy: Because you're not showin' the old confidence, Biff. He remembered you, didn't he?

Biff (stopping Happy with a gesture): Finally, about five o'clock, he comes out. Didn't remember who I was or anything. I felt like such an idiot, Hap.

Happy: Did you tell him my Florida idea?

Biff: He walked away. I saw him for one minute. I got so mad I could've torn the walls down! How . . . did I ever get the idea I was a salesman there? I even believed myself that I'd

> . . . "I realized what a ridiculous lie my whole life has been!"

been a salesman for him! And then he gave me one look and—I realized what a ridiculous lie my whole life has been! We've been talking in a dream for fifteen years. I was a shipping clerk.

Happy: What'd you do?

Biff (with great tension and wonder): Well, he left, see. And the secretary went out. I was all alone in the waiting room. I don't know what came over me, Hap. The next thing I know, I'm in his office—paneled walls, everything.

I can't explain it. I—Hap, I took his fountain pen.

Happy: Geez, did he catch you?

Biff: I ran out. I ran down all eleven flights. I ran and ran and ran.

—Arthur Miller

Start-Up: Biff had fooled himself for 15 years that he had worked for Bill Oliver as a salesman, when in actuality he had been a shipping clerk. Based on his delusion, he went to see Oliver about borrowing a substantial sum of money to start a sporting goods business. In the scene in the excerpt, Biff realizes what he actually is. He says, a few lines later, that he's got to explain to his father that "I'm not the man somebody lends that kind of money to."

Connection: Assume that Biff has applied for a job with your company. You are an assistant personnel manager who has just interviewed Biff. Your supervisor wants a written explanation for your reason(s) when you reject any applicant.

1. Based on the scene above, or on the entire play if you have seen it or read it, why is Biff *not* the kind of person you would hire if he were applying for a job? State your reasons in a grammatically correct paragraph. Be sure to support your reasons.

2. Using good judgment and tact, write a letter from the assistant personnel manager to Biff, rejecting Biff's job application.

Overview

A folktale is a story composed orally and then passed from person to person by word of mouth by illiterate or semi-literate people. Some of these stories are based on actual events. The folktale preserves a culture's ideas and customs. This Swedish folktale teaches a lesson in a humorous way.

"The Old Man and Woman Who Switched Jobs"
from *Swedish Folktales and Legends*

Once there was an old man, just like any other old man. This old man worked in the forest, chopping wood, and burning charcoal, while his old woman stayed at home spinning, cooking, and taking care of the house. In this way their days passed one after another. But the old man always complained that he had to labor and toil all day long to support both of them while the old woman merely sat at home cooking porridge, eating, and enjoying herself. Even

> . . . *he was convinced that he alone was pulling their entire load.*

though the old woman told him that there was plenty to do at home as well and that the old man would be badly fed and clothed if she did not look after the house, the old man turned a deaf ear; he was convinced that he alone was pulling their entire load.

One day, after they'd bickered longer than usual, the old woman said, "Have it your way! Tomorrow we'll switch jobs. I'll go to the forest and cut wood for the fire, and you'll stay home and do my chores."

This suited the old man just fine. "I'll take good care of the house," he said. "But how you'll fare in the woods is another story."

Early the next morning the old woman said, "Don't forget to bake the bread, churn the butter, watch the cow, and cook the greens for dinner."

These were all mere trifles, thought the old man, and soon they parted. The old woman took the old man's axe and went off to the forest while the old man began to build a fire under the oven and make the dough. When he thought it was ready, he began to bake it. But what sort of bread it was going to be was hard to say, for he forgot the yeast and put the loaves into the oven without first sweeping away the ashes.

The old man thought he'd managed the baking very well, and the thought of fresh bread awakened his appetitie.

"Fresh bread is fine," he said to himself, "but if you have some bacon to go along with it, it tastes even better."

So the next moment he went to the storehouse to fetch their last piece of bacon. But since the bacon was salty, he wanted something to drink with it. He put the bacon on the cellar steps and went downstairs.

If only I'd let mother stay at home!

Just as he was taking the plug out of the beer barrel, a dog came by and grabbed the bacon. The old man certainly didn't want to lose it, so he jumped up and ran off after the dog. But as he was running he discovered that he still had the plug in his hand, and he abandoned the bacon and ran back so that he could at least save the beer.

But it was too late. The barrel was empty and all the good beer had run out. This made him very unhappy, but he comforted himself with the thought that the old woman probably wasn't doing any better in the forest. Even if he had to do without bacon and beer, at least he still had the nice fresh-baked bread. With bread to eat, life is complete! as the saying goes.

How on earth was he going to manage it all?

But his comfort was short-lived. When he got inside the hut he found the bread burned to a crisp. Not a single bite was left for him to taste. It was a terrible state of affairs.

"This is no good at all," he moaned. "If only I'd let mother stay at home! If I'm doing this badly, how might she be doing in the forest? By now she may have chopped off both arms and legs!"

But there was no time for thinking. The sun was already high in the sky, and he had to cook greens for dinner. For greens one must have something green, the old man said to himself, and as he couldn't find anything else green, he took the old woman's homespun jacket, chopped it into little bits, and put the pieces in the pot.

He realized that he couldn't cook greens without water, but the spring was so far away. And besides, he also

(cont'd on next page)

had to churn butter! How on earth was he going to manage it all?

"If I put the churn on my back and shake it while I'm running to the spring, it'll probably turn to butter by the time I get back," he thought.

And that is what he did. But in his haste he forgot to put the lid on, and when he bent to haul up the water bucket, the cream poured over his shoulders and head and down into the spring.

Disheartened, he returned with the soupy, creamy water.

Now he had to tend to the cow, and since he couldn't be both inside and outside at the same time, how was he going to manage? On top of the house's sod roof, the grass shone a bright green in the sunshine; *there* was a juicy pasture! He tied a long rope around the cow's neck and pulled her up onto the roof, then threw the other end of the rope down the chimney.

Feeling a little happier, he went back inside the cottage and tied the tether hanging down through the chimney around his own waist so that the cow wouldn't get away from him. Then he started blowing on the fire under the pot. But while he was occupied

blowing, the cow fell off the roof and pulled him up into the chimney!

At that very moment the old woman came home with a big bundle of firewood on her back. When she saw the cow hanging alongside the cottage wall, she hurried as fast as she could and cut the rope. Then she went inside. There on the floor lay the old man, smoked, burned, and half suffocated.

> Never again was he heard to complain of his lot.

"God preserve us!" she exclaimed. "Is this how you've been managing at home?"

The poor old man couldn't utter a word; he just moaned and groaned. But it didn't take the old woman long to see how he'd managed: the bacon was gone, the beer run out, the bread burned to coal. The cream was in the spring and her jacket chopped up in the pot. The cow was hanged and the old man himself badly bruised and burned.

What happened later is not hard to guess. The old woman was allowed to care for her house in peace and quiet while the old man went off to the forest. Never again was he heard to complain of his lot.

—retold by Lone Thygesen Blecher and George Blecher

Start-Up: People are working daily all around us. Since most of us spend more hours working than doing anything else, choosing our vocation and preparing ourselves for it should be very important to us. One way to choose the right vocation is to be aware of different jobs that are available. Observe people working in your community, paying close attention to the jobs they do.

Connection: This project will take a little time to complete. Your teacher will give you instructions and a deadline.

1. Divide into groups of two or three. Each group should use a camera to take pictures of people doing their jobs in the workplace. Candid shots and pictures of men and women doing non-traditional jobs should be the goal of each group.

2. The pictures may be used to create a classroom display of the various types of work in the community.

* "Didn't the Buckeyes play better this year?"

* "Being at Snips gives me the opportunity to work with more clients than if I was employed by Trimcuts."

* "That car will run much faster than before."

* "You look healthier since you started walking every day."

Comparing and Contrasting

"There are many thousands of individuals on this planet more intelligent than I. I, however, work at it eighteen hours a day."

—ALBERT EINSTEIN, GERMAN-BORN U.S. SCIENTIST

As you complete Chapter 12, you will

* define comparing and contrasting.

* develop uses for comparison and contrast.

* discover likenesses and differences.

* organize data by constructing tables.

* prepare a comparison and contrast analysis.

* use comparison and contrast transitional signals.

Workplace Skills in This Chapter

* Manage **resources** to create analysis tools.

* Increase **interpersonal** skills by planning a presentation for a selected audience.

* Organize and analyze **information** for chapter activities.

* Utilize data for benefiting workplace **systems**.

* Use **technology** to construct a table to analyze data.

You hear remarks pointing out similarities and differences constantly in your everyday conversation. For example, Micah brags about his retuned engine compared to its formerly sluggish condition; you talk about how the spring weather is great compared to the winter's ice and snow. "There's nothing good for lunch today" compares today's lunch to yesterday's great feast.

In Chapters 5 and 6, you learned how to use analogies to show similarities. One of the best, and easiest, tools for analyzing and evaluating is comparison and contrast. This chapter will help you organize data with this tool and use it to draw conclusions and to make logical recommendations.

What Is Comparison and Contrast?

Often in making personal decisions, you will compare and contrast your options, perhaps without even realizing what you are doing. **Comparison** shows how things are alike; **contrast** shows how things are different. When comparing your athletic shoes endorsed by a basketball star to the star's actual shoes, you are talking about how both pairs of shoes are alike. When you contrast last year's grades with this year's, you emphasize the improvement, or difference, over your grades last year.

In the workplace, you often must analyze, evaluate, and/or justify your decisions to the supervisor, to coworkers, and to the customer. For example, a procedure is more efficient than one currently used; one person is better qualified for a promotion than another; or the preferred product is superior to the competitor's. You must be aware of this comparing and contrasting process in the workplace.

Figure 12-1: *Everyday comparison decisions*

Purposes for Comparison and Contrast

Comparison and contrast is used to make the unfamiliar more familiar, to analyze features, or to help make decisions. After you use comparison and contrast to analyze, you can draw conclusions and make recommendations based on that analysis.

Becoming Familiar

When you are faced with something unfamiliar, you can understand it more easily if you compare it with something familiar. Try comparing or contrasting the familiar everyday object with the new object. The similarities will make the new object a more familiar one. Here are some examples:

> * A snake sheds its skin inside out, the way you take off your sweater.
> * To begin soldering, hold the soldering iron as you hold a pen.
> * Spreadsheets and databases have similar components, but they have completely different uses.
> * The amount of carpeting needed for the floor of a room is not computed the same way as the amount of wall covering needed for the walls of a room.

Looking at the Details

People tend to look at the whole and often not at individual details or parts. Use comparison and contrast to focus the audience's attention on contrasting details in similar mechanisms. Here are some examples:

C·O·N·N·E·C·T·I·O·N
Aquaculture research specialist Kevin Fitzsimmons uses the very limited water resources of the desert to grow fish in water designated to grow crops. Fish deposit a natural fertilizer in the water; then the same water is used for growing vegetables. Thus, two crops use the same water, making the scarce resource more efficient.

* The basic difference between an omelet and scrambled eggs is the presentation.
* The horses are identical except for the colors of their manes and tails.
* Those two teachers have the same classroom rules except that one allows you to use electronic spell-checkers.
* The only way the child-care teacher can tell the twins apart is that one has blue eyes and one has green eyes.

Making Decisions

Customers all want the best buy, the best everything. Comparison and contrast will provide the tools to choose the best.

* The gas mileage is greatly improved in this car over last year's model.
* Carpenters use a circular saw on a construction site because the table saw is not portable.
* If you pay with a credit card, you are often paying 2 percent more than if you pay with cash.
* Clarissa received the gold medal in the culinary contest because her hollandaise sauce was more difficult to prepare than Rita's brown gravy.

Organizing Comparison and Contrast

Subjects are the topics of comparison and contrast. You must have at least two subjects to analyze likenesses and differences. Next, you need to have ways to analyze the subjects, called **points of comparison**. For example, if you are comparing two types of welding, the *subjects* would be MIG welding and TIG welding. Some *points of comparison* would be technique, materials, equipment, use, and so on.

Comparison and contrast discussions need to be in parallel order. In other words, the points for Subject A must be the same points—and in the same order—as the points for Subject B. If you discuss MIG welding techniques first, then you must discuss TIG welding techniques first.

The secretaries of the past are the managers of today. In the past, secretaries typed correspondence, took dictation, and answered the phones for many executives and managers. Now those same secretaries, often titled administrative assistants, are assuming the duties of downsized middle managers. Often executives receive and reply to their own voice mail, create correspondence and reports on laptops, and set up appointments. The new secretaries format and organize the correspondence, coordinate department meetings and appointments, and handle record-keeping. The majority of secretaries supervise and train others, something their predecessors never would have done. Also, in comparison, the average salary for the secretary has increased 25 percent more in the last 20 years than the average salaries of all white-collar workers, reports *Career Opportunities News*.

Practice 12-1: Discovering Similarities and Differences

Use *Student Workbook* page 12-A to complete this Practice. List similar subjects to compare from your career cluster and note the points of comparison for each subject. Then arrange the points in a logical order.

Organizing Data with a Table

When faced with large quantities of data, a reader will frequently do one of two things: either stop reading or become confused. In comparing or contrasting, a writer may use facts, numbers, and statistics to draw conclusions and to make recommendations. However, too often technical data ends up not being read at all, or at the very least, the meaning is lost. Creating a **table** to organize and to compare large quantities of data helps eliminate the confusion of wordy, fact-filled paragraphs by displaying the data visually. The table emphasizes the importance of the information and saves time for the reader.

Using a Table to Display Data

Isabel needed to make some metric conversions at her construction site. The statistical information in the reference book that her supervisor gave her only served to confuse Isabel. Try as she would, she kept getting the numbers confused in the conversion formulas. Here is an example of the information from the reference book:

> To convert feet into centimeters, multiply the feet by 30.48; to convert centimeters into feet, multiply the centimeters by 0.03281. To convert inches into centimeters, multiply the inches by 2.54; to convert meters into inches, multiply the meters by 39.37. To convert feet into meters, multiply the feet by 0.3048; to convert meters into feet, multiply the meters by 3.281.

WEB LINK

Internet searches will provide you with a wealth of information, including considerable data to include in your tables. For example, you can gather information to compare similar national or large local companies or products.

When Isabel saw the same information arranged in a table (Table 12-1), her confusion cleared, and she easily made the conversions. Table 12-1 organizes the same data as in the example paragraph, but it makes the task of converting numbers much easier. The table puts the data into categories that form the columns of the table.

TABLE I
Simplified Conversion Table
(alphabetical order)

To Convert	Into	Multiply by
centimeters	feet	0.03281
feet	centimeters	30.48
feet	meters	0.3048
inches	centimeters	2.54
meters	feet	3.281
meters	inches	39.37

Table 12-1

Using a Table to Compare and Contrast

Not only are tables excellent to organize data visually, but also they can serve another important purpose—to assist you in analyzing or evaluating data. In these situations, you can use the table setup to compare and to contrast data for the purposes of making the unfamiliar familiar, looking at details, and making decisions. Using the table allows you to draw conclusions from the data and make a recommendation.

For example, Deandra decided that she wanted to continue her education after graduating with her dental assistant certification. She and her parents are trying to determine which school she should attend to become a dental hygienist. One of the factors in their decision is the annual cost of her education at her three choices of schools. To decide which amount of money to borrow, Deandra created Table 12-2 to show typical monthly interest charges for four loan amounts over a ten-year period. Another factor in Deandra's decision-making process is the source of the loan. The Stafford Loan for students and the parent PLUS Loan are federal loans with lower interest, but State Bank is locally owned and convenient for completing paperwork and asking questions. Table 12-2 on page 412 visually displays the information to help Deandra decide both what amount to borrow and the source of the loan.

TECHNOBIT

The United States Postal Service is the chief transporter of snail mail, stamped or metered mail sent via trucks or planes. Now the post office is beginning to venture into e-mail, with a documented e-mail service that will certify that your e-mail reached its destination. With a low annual subscription, you can deliver your e-mail at one-tenth the cost of a snail-mail certified letter.

Constructing a Table

Constructing a table takes some planning, but once you do the preliminary work, the rest is relatively simple. If a computer is available, table construction becomes even easier, but again, planning is essential. Table 12-3 is an example of a well-constructed table to be used for a comparison and contrast discussion. If you decide that an audience will benefit from seeing data visually in a table, you must carefully plan, draft, and revise the data arrangement.

TABLE II
Monthly Interest for Education Loan

Loan Amount	Stafford Student Loan	PLUS Loan	State Bank Loan
$2,000	$11.67	$13.33	$16.67
4,000	23.33	26.67	33.33
5,000	29.17	33.33	41.67
7,500	43.75	50.00	62.50

Table 12-2
Source: Federal Family Education Loan Program, U.S. Department of Education

TABLE III
Average Number of Daily Messages per Worker

Major Delivery Sources	Messages Sent	Messages Received
Phone Calls/Regular, Wired Phone	23.9	31.8
Paper Messages; e.g., U.S. Mail, Notes, etc.	22.6	11.0
Voice Mail	9.5	11.2
Interoffice Mail	10.7	0
E-Mail	9.8	13.6
Fax	6.6	8.8
Pager	5.3	3.9
Phone Calls/Cell Phone	3.3	1.8
Courier Services	3.3	0
Total Number of Messages	95.0	82.1

Table 12-3
Source: Pitney Bowes, 1997

The Label and the Title

The title introduces the table to the reader and implies the table's meaning. When referring to tables in text or within a presentation, you need to number them.

* Label the table with the word *TABLE,* in capital letters and bold or normal print, centered over the data. (Tables sometimes have an informative heading instead of the word *TABLE.*)

* Give the table an informative title that will help the audience understand what is in the table, but use as few words as possible. Use title case in bold or normal print, and center it directly above the table data.

* Number tables consecutively if there is more than one table; for example, "TABLE 1," "TABLE 2," and so on.

The Layout

The layout of the table is as important as the format of a business letter. Planning is the key.

* Make a pencil sketch of the table before beginning its construction on the computer or on paper used for the final copy.

* Construct the table in such a way that it is wide enough not to crowd the data, including adequate white space and a neat appearance. The table must be easy to read. If you have access to a word processing program, use one of the automatic table formats in the program.

* Frame the table to add emphasis. Also, if necessary for easier reading, separate the columns with vertical lines. Use horizontal lines only if they will make the table easier to read.

* Label each column of data with a brief heading in bold or normal and in title case. Headings are flush left or centered in the columns. Arrange the rows logically; alphabetically or numerically, for example. Rows are arranged horizontally; columns are vertical.

* Make the units of measurement the same within all columns, including lining up the decimal points within each column. This alignment makes the table appear neat and clean. See Table 12-1 on page 411.

* Draw a short line in any blank table cells.

* Double-space between rows (tables are sometimes single-spaced).

INFOBIT

According to psychology studies reported by career development speaker Randy Dorn, readers in Western cultures (United States, European, etc.) find illustrations easier to read and friendlier in landscape orientation. Eastern cultures have positive reactions to portrait orientation.

Answering a phone call during a meeting announces to everyone present that the phone is more important than they are. During a meeting, have voice mail or someone else take your calls. Only allow an interruption if you're expecting an urgent call—and then, before the meeting starts, warn the person you are with that an interruption might occur.

The Source Line

Credit the author of the information used to construct the table by including a source line at the bottom of the table at the left margin. Avoid plagiarism when you borrow the information. Use the table illustrations in this chapter as examples.

Common knowledge requires no documentation. It consists of widely known facts that are available from many sources.

That President John F. Kennedy was assassinated in 1963 is common knowledge. The 1492 date of Columbus's discovery of America is common knowledge, even if you had to look up the date. If you base your table information on common knowledge, no source line is necessary. Chapter 7, page 222-223, will help you decide if the source should be credited or not.

INFOBIT

If you are losing a tug-of-war with a tiger, give him the rope before he gets to your arm. You can always buy a new rope.

MAX GUNTHER, U.S. MAGAZINE EDITOR AND AUTHOR

Practice 12-2: Constructing Tables

The information in the following paragraphs is very confusing. The information could be more effective if displayed visually in tables. First, read each paragraph carefully, and decide what subjects are being compared. Next, list the **points** of comparison in the first column in alphabetical order. To make the data clear, construct a table using the **details** of all the information in the paragraphs. Then add a **label,** a **title,** and the **source** of the information.

Paragraph 1

To compare his construction company with the competition, Doug Brown researched the number of building permits given by the Building Inspector's Office in Herbert County for plumbing, electrical, and construction work in 2000. According to this data, DHB Construction had 341 electrical permit applications, 555 plumbing permit applications, and 1,112 construction permit applications. Breezes Builders had 410 electrical permit applications, 689 plumbing permit applications, and 929 construction permit applications. Then there was Daring Creations with 434 electrical applications, 121 plumbing applications, and 655 construction applications. Peter Fisher received

714 electrical, 615 plumbing, and 992 construction applications. Last of all, Matthews Materials obtained 327 electrical, 615 plumbing, and 871 construction applications.

Paragraph 2

When should Haley call Adam? Even though she runs the Midwest Division of Bart Graphics, she must call after office hours and interrupt sleep schedules to save money. However, sometimes asking questions is more important than saving money. To help with her decision, she consulted the telephone directory for direct-dial, one-minute rates for long distance. On Monday from 8 a.m. to 5 p.m., the weekday full rate applies; from 5 p.m. to 11 p.m., the evening 40 percent discount rate applies; and from 11 p.m. to 8 a.m., the night and weekend 60 percent discount applies. The weekday full rate is in effect from 8 a.m. to 5 p.m. on Tuesday, the evening 40 percent discount from 5 p.m. to 11 p.m., and the night and weekend 60 percent rate from 11 p.m. to 8 a.m. Callers on Wednesday from 8 a.m. to 5 p.m. are charged the weekday full rate, from 5 p.m. to 11 p.m. the evening 40 percent discount rate, and from 11 p.m. to 8 a.m. the night and weekend 60 percent discount rate. Thursdays and Fridays are similar, with the weekday full rate in existence from 8 a.m. to 5 p.m., the evening 40 percent discount rate from 5 p.m. to 11 p.m., and the night and weekend 60 percent discount from 11 p.m. to 8 a.m.. The schedule changes from 8 a.m. Saturday to 8 a.m. Sunday, when the night and weekend 60 percent discount applies. The night and weekend 60 percent discount rate is in effect Sunday from 8 a.m. to 5 p.m. and from 11 p.m. to 8 a.m. The evening 40 percent discount rate applies from 5 p.m. to 11 p.m. Sunday.

Preparing a Comparison and Contrast Analysis

A comparison and contrast analysis helps you to examine and make decisions about two or more subjects. The discussion includes an introduction, the central section (body), conclusions, and recommendations. Whether the discussion is a written analysis or an oral presentation, each section should blend into the next.

The Introduction

This brief section sets up the comparison and contrast analysis. It prepares the reader by referring to

1. the subjects that are being compared and contrasted.

2. how the subjects are alike and/or different.

3. any necessary background information.

4. a general description of the conclusion and recommendation.

The conservation research firm Sunkeep Laboratories is changing its uniforms. A Uniform Committee was formed from its employees to choose the company that will supply the new uniforms. A subcommittee has narrowed the uniform choice to two brands— Utilitywear and StarService. Here is the first part of the subcommittee's report to the Uniform Committee:

> After researching more than eight uniform companies, the subcommittee narrowed the choices to two—the Utilitywear and the StarService uniform companies—because these companies have the type of uniforms that Sunkeep requires, and they have offices here in Minneapolis for service needs. Now the Uniform Committee must choose which uniform company to use based on the variety of sizes offered, stain resistance, durability of the uniforms, and price.

The Analysis

When you are planning a comparison and contrast analysis, consider the subjects that are being compared, the points of comparison, and the audience. These three factors will help you choose the most effective organization for the analysis. Discussing several points of one subject and then the same several points of another subject is one method of arrangement. Another method is to discuss one point for the first subject, then the same point for the other subject, the second point for the first subject, and so on. One of these two options of organization becomes the body of your comparison and contrast analysis.

Order of importance determines the order of the points. You may choose to start with the strongest point or the weakest, depending on your audience and the purpose for the analysis. Using the Sunkeep's uniform decision example, the company needs to compare the two brands using four different points: varieties of sizes, stain resistance, durability, and price. When the uniforms are compared, details and examples will then support the points of comparison. The committee feels that having uniforms to fit all employees is the most important factor in recommending a company, followed by stain resistance and durability. Price is the least important factor for Sunkeep.

QUALITY C·O·N·N·E·C·T·I·O·N
Before comparing his brand with the competition and expanding his business, Starbucks's founder, Howard Schultz, felt he needed his employees' allegiance. He hired workers who were enthusiastic and knowledgeable about his coffee. Consequently, brand loyalty overflowed from the workers to the customers, building up a devoted following for Starbucks Coffee.

The Subject-by-Subject Method

By choosing two subjects that you will compare and/or contrast, you show how the subjects are alike or different. First, you analyze one topic; then, you discuss the other topic. With subject-by-subject comparison and contrast, you select points of comparison (and/or contrast) to analyze the first subject, and then you analyze the same points in the same order for the other subject.

SUBJECTS:	POINTS OF COMPARISON:
A. Utilitywear Uniforms	1. Variety of sizes
B. StarService Uniforms	2. Stain resistance
	3. Durability
	4. Price

Here is the subject-by-subject organization:

A. Utilitywear Uniforms	B. StarService Uniforms
1. Variety of sizes	1. Variety of sizes
2. Stain resistance	2. Stain resistance
3. Durability	3. Durability
4. Price	4. Price

The Point-by-Point Method

Comparison and contrast explanations are used every day, not only with subject-by-subject analysis but also with point-by-point analysis. In point-by-point analysis, you choose three or more points to discuss for each subject. Using the previous example, one section would discuss how Utilitywear's and StarService's uniforms compare in variety of sizes offered. Then the second section would explain how the companies' uniforms compare in stain resistance; the third, in durability; and the fourth, in price.

PEOPLE C·O·N·N·E·C·T·I·O·N

Landscape architect Margarette Beckwith designed the specific garden areas of the Alois Alzheimer Center in Cincinnati, Ohio, according to the stages of the disease. The most active residents are in the gardens on their own, in an enclosed, looped unit with scattered benches and tables for strolling and visiting. The next level of patients tends to wander and become easily disoriented, so the garden for these patients is more contained. Since those in the last stages of the disease are generally wheelchair-bound, their gardens have planters raised so that patients can touch and smell the vegetation. The arrangement of the gardens keeps the patients safe inside, but offers them glimpses of the world beyond, giving them a sense of being in control.

Figure 12-2: *Courtyard Garden, Alois Alzheimer Center, Cincinnati, Ohio*

J. Hodgson, Beckwith Chapman Associates/Landscape Architects

Here is the point-by-point organization:

A. Variety of Sizes

    1. Utilitywear uniforms

    2. StarService uniforms

B. Stain Resistance

    1. Utilitywear uniforms

    2. StarService uniforms

C. Durability

    1. Utilitywear uniforms

    2. StarService uniforms

D. Price

    1. Utilitywear uniforms

    2. StarService uniforms

The Conclusions and the Recommendations

After hearing or reading all the facts and figures of the comparison and contrast analysis, you may say, "Now what?" The speaker or the writer will need to tie all the points together and draw conclusions. The conclusions will lead to recommendations—the purpose of the analysis. Tables will add to the analysis if they are used to draw conclusions based on the information analyzed and offer recommendations to make the unfamiliar familiar, examine details, or make decisions.

After inspecting all the statements, facts, figures, and tables, the speaker or writer will point out the relationships among the data in the analysis that explains the deductions in the conclusions. The following statements are examples of conclusions for the Sunkeep uniform analysis:

INFOBIT

Be a fixer, not a finger-pointer.

PRICE PRITCHETT, U.S. AUTHOR

- Utilitywear has the full size range of uniforms needed for Sunkeep's employees; StarService does not have the full range of sizes in stock.

- Since the prices for both companies' uniforms are very similar, cost should not be a consideration when choosing a uniform company.

- When tests of various weather conditions and spills of commonly used chemical agents were conducted, StarService's uniforms lasted more than 50 percent longer than Utilitywear's uniforms.

After the conclusions are stated based on the evidence, the committee must make recommendations to the company. These recommendations will endorse further action based on the evaluation of the conclusion and will solve the problem. The Sunkeep Uniform Committee made the following recommendation:

The Sunkeep Uniform Committee recommends the purchase of StarService uniforms to replace the existing uniforms of Sunkeep employees.

The speaker or writer can elaborate on the reasons for the conclusions and the recommendations, using the evidence in the analysis for support. However, these two sections, like the introduction, are much briefer than the analysis itself.

INFOBIT

"Insanity—Doing the same things over and over again and expecting different results."

ALBERT EINSTEIN, GERMAN-BORN U.S. SCIENTIST

Practice 12-3: Drawing Conclusions and Making Recommendations

teamwork Examine the following tables, and reread any introductory information given: Tables 12-2 and 12-3 on page 412; and at least one of the tables you created for Practice 12-2 on page 414. For each of the three tables, write two conclusions and one recommendation based on the information. Your teacher may have you work with a partner or in small groups.

Transitional Signals

When reading or hearing a comparison and contrast discussion without transitional signals, the audience can easily miss the points that you want stressed. Using transitions will help the audience discover the relationships between important facts. Transitional words and phrases also help to connect or blend thoughts.

CULTURE C·O·N·N·E·C·T·I·O·N

One stumbling block to communication between cultures is that many people assume that there are enough similarities to make communication simple. The belief that "people are people" emphasizes similarities and seemingly makes any differences wrong. These misinformed people believe that because humans have the common biological needs of food, shelter, and security, everyone is alike. However, the differences among cultures are often broader than the similarities, making living and working together more difficult.

Another assumption is that words in one language, when translated, have a comparative meaning in another language. Not only is this supposition often not true, but also its results can be disastrous!

INFOBIT

To command an audience: "You have to make them believe in what you're doing and take them into your world. I try to have eye contact, to see them reacting. Sometimes, when I do that, I can even hear them breathing."

OKSANA BAIUL, UKRAINIAN OLYMPIC GOLD MEDAL FIGURE SKATER

To signal a similarity, use

also	each of	likewise
and	in addition	neither
as well as	in the same way	similarly
besides	just as . . . so	too
both	like	

To signal a difference or opposition, use

although	in contrast	whereas
at the same time	nevertheless	while this may be
but	notwithstanding	true
but still	on one hand; on	yet
conversely	the other hand	
however	on the contrary	

The transitions point out the relationships within the paragraph and make the reading smoother. In addition, transitions help connect the sections of the comparison and contrast analysis, from the introduction to the recommendation.

Practice 12-4: Comparing and Contrasting with Transitions

1. Use the information in Table 12-3, and write an analysis paragraph. Use transitions from the preceding list to compare and/or contrast the types of messages sent, as reported in the table. Then underline the transitions you used before handing in your work.

2. Do the same for Practice 12-2, Paragraph 2.

ETHICS **C·O·N·N·E·C·T·I·O·N**

The Better Business Bureau (BBB) is the ethical watchdog of business. It helps consumers by acting as a clearinghouse for complaints, posting notices of scams, and actually negotiating differences with businesses. As a business owner, you can receive tips from the BBB for starting or strengthening your business. Its philosophy? "Our mission is to promote and foster the highest ethical relationship between businesses and the public. . . ."

SUMMARY

Comparing and contrasting are processes used to analyze and evaluate likenesses and differences. These tools can be used to make decisions. Follow these guidelines whenever you prepare a comparison and contrast discussion:

* Determine the points and supporting details of the subjects of comparison and contrast.

* Organize your comparison and contrast discussion with either the subject-by-subject or the point-by-point method.

* Construct a table when appropriate to illustrate the comparison and contrast conclusions and recommendations for the audience.

* Use transitions to connect the comparison and contrast discussion into one unit.

Comparing and Contrasting Products or Procedures

careers

teamwork

Your instructor, Mr. Marcos, wants your class to learn more about new procedures and products in your career cluster. Rather than duplicate many articles for you to read or for him to lecture to the class for several days, Mr. Marcos wants the class to give presentations. He suggests you begin by researching. For this presentation, you will be analyzing two or more processes or products from your career cluster. Keep your audience in mind in choosing the subjects to compare and contrast.

From sources such as Web searches, magazines, and journals, you will have numbers, statistics, and data regarding the two (or more) different procedures or products. To organize and analyze the information, you need to complete this Project effectively. Show your research results or data in a table. Then, through a presentation, draw conclusions from your analysis and make one or more recommendations based on the data.

You will need to

* research your processes or products.

* construct a table of details to support your conclusion and recommendation(s).

* present your analysis orally.

Some suggestions for subjects to compare and contrast follow:

* Closed versus accessible or opensided magnetic resonance images (MRI) procedure

* Three types of window construction

* Physical filter, activated carbon, and reverse osmosis water filtration systems

* Baking, frying, or steaming fish

* Macintosh versus Windows operating systems

* Relaxing hair versus getting a perm

* Emergency procedures for first aid

* Troubleshooting a defective piece of equipment

1. Review the examples of comparison and contrast analyses and tables in this chapter. Examine Linda Hockenberry's Sample Project Plan on page 425. Then listen to the recorded CD sample presentation based on this plan. Your teacher will show you the table that accompanies the presentation.

2. After consulting reference materials, choose what you are analyzing through comparison and contrast. List *at least six to ten points* to analyze *at least two* subjects. (Your teacher may specify exact numbers.) The items on this list are the points of comparison and contrast. Locate and record details on all points of the topics as you did for Practice 12-1.

3. Then complete the Project Plan, *Student Workbook* page 12-C.

4. Using the information from your Project Plan, construct a rough draft of your table showing the details of your analysis. If a computer is available, use it to construct the table. Include a title and the source of information, using as few words as possible.

5. Then prepare notes for your presentation. Write out the introduction and the closing completely. Briefly outline the body of the talk, including transitions to link the analysis points and details. Discuss both similarities and differences.

6. Study the Project Guide, *Student Workbook* page 12-D, for criteria for your table and for your presentation. Using the Rough Draft column of the Project Guide, check your table and your presentation notes with one or more classmates. Each of you should mark the Project Guide in all categories but the last four steps and note any changes on the rough draft. Have your teacher check your rough draft.

7. Revise your table and presentation notes, incorporating the changes that your classmate(s) and your teacher suggested. Rehearse the presentation with your table with another student, preferably a classmate who checked your table and presentation notes with the Project Guide. During the rehearsal, have the class member use the last four steps of the Rough Draft column of the Project Guide to evaluate the presentation.

8. Using the Final Draft column of the Project Guide, proofread your work. Make needed corrections.

9. Present your analysis to the class. Using the last four steps of the Final Draft column of the Project Guide, your teacher and possibly your classmates will evaluate your presentation.

10. After your presentation, turn in the final draft along with the Project Guide.

Presentation Guidelines:

1. Present your analysis and table to the class on the day assigned by your teacher.

2. Explain your analysis thoroughly by including
   * all necessary information.
   * source(s) of your information.
   * a valid conclusion and recommendation(s).

3. Do not read your presentation. Have the introduction, main points, and closing written. Use a maximum of three note cards that contain phrases only, not sentences.

Plan for Comparing and Contrasting

SUBJECTS	**(At least two)** **A.** Perch fillets cooked by baking **B.** Perch fillets cooked by frying **C.** Perch fillets cooked by steaming	
AUDIENCE	Class members and instructor **Reason(s) for choosing the subjects:** Teach about new procedures	
PURPOSE	**Conclusions:** Less healthy — frying More expertise needed, less taste — steaming **Recommendations:** Choose method best fits your lifestyle, health, expertise, taste	
FORMAT	☐ written ☒ oral ☐ other Table for visual	
SOURCES	Clark County Extension Service U.S. Department of Agriculture United Dairy Council	
METHOD	Organize by subjects Or (Organize by points)	

CONTENTS OF TABLE

Points (number may be specified by your teacher):

— yes

1.   Calories
2.   Cholesterol content
3.   Fats
4.   Proteins
5.   Sodium
6.   Added ingredients
7.   Preparation time

Analysis (details to compare and contrast):

Nutritional value

Cooking Skill

Lifestyle of cook

Overview

In the two paragraphs you are about to read from *Life on the Mississippi,* Mark Twain compares the way he saw the river as an innocent apprentice to the way he saw it as an experienced pilot.

"Two Views of the River" from *Life on the Mississippi*

Now when I had mastered the language of this water, and had come to know every trifling feature that bordered the great river as familiarly as I knew the letters of the alphabet, I had made a valuable acquisition. But I had lost something, too. I had lost something which could never be restored to me while I lived. All the grace, the beauty, the poetry, had gone out of the majestic river! I still keep in mind a certain wonderful sunset which I witnessed when steamboating was new to me. A broad expanse of the river was turned to blood; in the middle distance the red hue brightened into gold, through which a solitary log came floating black and conspicuous; in one place a long, slanting mark lay sparkling upon the water; in another the surface was broken by boiling, tumbling rings that were as many-tinted as an opal; where the ruddy flush was faintest, was a smooth spot that was covered with graceful circles and radiating lines, ever so delicately traced; the shore on our left was densely wooded, and the somber shadow that fell from this forest was broken in one place by a long, ruffled trail that shone like silver; and high above the forest wall a clean-stemmed dead tree waved a single leafy bough that glowed like a flame in the unobstructed splendor that was flowing from the sun. There were graceful curves, reflected images, woody heights, soft distances; and over the whole scene, far and near, the dissolving lights drifted steadily, enriching it every passing moment with new marvels of coloring.

I stood like one bewitched. I drank it in, in a speechless rapture. The world was new to me, and I had never seen anything like this at home. But as I have said, a day came when I began to cease from noting the glories and the charms which the moon and the sun and the twilight wrought upon the river's face; another day came when I ceased altogether to note them.

Then, if that sunset scene had been repeated, I should have looked upon it without rapture, and should have commented upon it, inwardly, after this fashion: "This sun means that we are going to have wind tomorrow; that floating log means that the river is rising, small thanks to it; that slanting mark on the water refers to a bluff reef which is going to kill somebody's steamboat one of these nights, if it keeps on stretching out like that; those tumbling 'boils' show a dissolving bar and a changing channel there; the lines and circles in the slick water over yonder are a warning that that troublesome place is shoaling up dangerously; that silver streak in the shadow of the forest is the 'break' from a new snag, and he has located himself in the very best place he could have found to fish for steamboats; that tall dead tree, with a single living branch, is not going to last long, and then how is a body ever going to get through this blind place at night without the friendly old landmark?"

—Mark Twain (pseudonym for Samuel Langhorne Clemens)

> *Then, if that sunset scene had been repeated, I should have looked upon it without rapture. . . .*

Start-Up: We all experience a change in the way we view people, places, and things as we grow older, become more knowledgeable and experienced, and set different goals in life. In this literary selection, Twain looks at the same scenes on the river from two perspectives: one when he was a young dreamer of adventure and one when he had become an experienced steamboat captain.

Connection: (1) Set a piece of paper or a word processing file in three columns (you may wish to use the table feature of your software). Make a list of the items or scenes that Twain notes in "Two Views of the River" in the first column. In the second column, list what he says about the scenes or items from the young dreamer's viewpoint. In the third column, list what he says about them from the experienced captain's viewpoint. (See the following example.)

Scene	Young Dreamer's Viewpoint	Steamboat Captain's Viewpoint
Sunset	". . . wonderful sunset . . . brightened into gold . . ."	" 'This sun means that we are going to have wind. . . .' "

(2) Imagine a situation in the workplace in which you have a beginner and an experienced employee involved in the same task. Make a similar three-columned list for that situation. Using those details, write two paragraphs: one paragraph in which you describe the procedure from the point of view of the new employee and a second paragraph in which you describe the process from the point of view of the experienced employee.

Overview

Born in Poland in 1923, Wislawa Szymborska is known as one of the best representatives, since World War II, of the ancient art of poetry in Poland.

When she started writing, her poetry dealt with political themes and the war. Her first volume of poetry, completed in 1948, was not published for four years because the government did not approve of her political views. She rewrote her volume of poetry; she tried to raise a poetic voice in tune with the revolutionary era in Poland. Her work was found wanting. Her later poems have dealt with lyrical subjects (expressing direct and usually intense personal emotions), new themes, and new poetic techniques. Undeniably, her poetry bears the stamp of originality!

"Possibilities"

I prefer movies.
I prefer cats.
I prefer oaks along the Warta River.
I prefer Dickens to Dostoyevsky.
I prefer liking people
to loving mankind.
I prefer having a needle and thread handy.
I prefer the color green.
I prefer not to assert
that reason should be blamed for everything.
I prefer exceptions.
I prefer to leave earlier.
I prefer to talk with doctors about something else.
I prefer old-fashioned, striped illustrations.
I prefer the foolishness of writing poems
to the foolishness of not writing them.

I prefer, in love, those anniversaries which are not so big,
which can be celebrated every day.
I prefer moralists
who do not promise me anything.
I prefer a crafty rather than a too credulous kindness.
I prefer the earth in civilian clothes.
I prefer the conquered to the conquering countries.
I prefer to hold doubts.
I prefer the hell of chaos to the hell of order.
I prefer tales of the Brothers Grimm to the front
    pages of newspapers.
I prefer leaves without flowers to flowers without leaves.
I prefer dogs with uncut tails.
I prefer light-colored eyes, because I have dark.
I prefer drawers.
I prefer many things which I have not specified here
to many other things also unspecified.
I prefer zeros on the loose
to those standing in line behind the number.
I prefer insects' time to stellar time.
I prefer to knock on wood.
I prefer not to ask how much longer and when.
I prefer to take into consideration even this possibility,
that life has meaning.

—Wislawa Szymborska. Translated by
    Grazyna Drabik and Austin Flynt.

Start-Up: All people have preferences. Making choices in life based on these preferences helps make us different from each other. It would be a stale, dull world if all people preferred the same things in life. The French say, "Vive la différence." Americans say, "Different strokes for different folks."

In her poem, "Possibilities," the poet briefly explains her own preferences.

Connection: Reread the poem. Write a list of your own preferences in life. Try to balance your preferences as the poet does in this example: "I prefer the foolishness of writing poems / to the foolishness of not writing them."

"My cousin Frances educated me about the press. She had been the AP White House correspondent during the Nixon and Ford administrations, and was now working for CNN. Frances would tell me stories of guys running out back doors because they're afraid of the press. From her I got the idea that the press isn't doing anything evil; the reporters are simply trying to help people know what's going on, and it doesn't do any harm to be courteous to them.

"I found out that they're really quite friendly, if you give them a chance. So I wasn't afraid of the press, and I would always answer their questions."

—Richard P. Feynman,
Nobel Prize–winning physicist,
regarding interviews with the press while serving
on the commission to investigate
the *Challenger* disaster in 1986

Interviewing for Information

"The most difficult part of an interview is gaining the trust and confidence of the interviewee."

As you complete Chapter 13, you will

* describe an informational interview.

* identify and narrow a topic.

* identify an expert for a given topic.

* plan and conduct an interview.

* present an oral report of an interview.

* edit and write the results of an informational interview.

* plan a survey involving the use of a questionnaire.

* plan and design a questionnaire.

* take a survey using a questionnaire.

* report results of a survey.

Workplace Skills in This Chapter

* Use people as **resources** in gathering information.

* Practice **interpersonal** skills as you interview.

* Use interviews and questionnaires as tools to gather, interpret, and convey **information**.

* Understand social and organizational **systems** better after working through the interview process.

* Use **technology** when designing questionnaires.

In 1968, Eliot Wigginton, a teacher, and two classes of his high school English students in the mountains of Georgia took pencils, paper, and cameras and went out to talk to people who had spent their lives in those mountains. Then they came back and put together a series of articles based on what they had seen and heard. The stories were published in a magazine and later, due to their popularity, in *The Foxfire Book,* named after the glowing foxfire plant found in that part of Georgia.

The *Foxfire* Legacy

Each year, as new students continued the *Foxfire* project, they published a regular quarterly magazine, the contents of which fed the publication of a series of books. Each book after the first one was called *Foxfire* with a number following: *Foxfire 2, Foxfire 3,* and so on. Once the name caught on, each new volume was like an old friend returning for another visit. By 1988, the tenth book was in print, and the series was selling by the thousands.

The appeal of the *Foxfire* books was twofold: the series of stories touched readers' souls by taking them into the everyday lives of people who had been in those mountains all their lives, and they told the historic details of an almost forgotten way of life. They were filled with folklore—with explanations of how quilts were made, how illnesses were cured, and details of living that had been passed on from parent to child for hundreds of years but were now almost forgotten.

Were these student authors marvelous writers who had spent years practicing their writing until, in high school, they finally perfected their craft? No. They were just normal students who had learned a big lesson from their teacher, which they then learned to pass along to others. They learned about the importance of listening to what other people had to say.

These Georgia students gathered their material, not only by sitting in the classroom and brainstorming, but by going into the mountains and interviewing people—asking them to tell the stories of their childhood, to explain how they built a wagon or made a fiddle, or what religious customs they had learned from their grandparents. And as these people talked, the students listened and took notes and took pictures and made tape recordings. Then they came back to school to piece it all together. The results were better than most teachers could ever dream that their students would produce.

Interviewing for information is nothing new—it's just that few students think of it as an approach to writing or research. In fact, most of the time, students go to the library to gather material for a term paper. They seldom think of the possibility of interviewing experts, as the *Foxfire* writers did, to get their information.

INFOBIT

"The greatest mistake you can make in life is to be continually fearing you will make one."

ELBERT HUBBARD

Using an Expert

Our world is filled with all kinds of experts. We're not talking here about the "person on the street" interviewed so often at the end of the nightly news. Such interviews do no more than reveal the collective opinion (not necessarily knowledge) of five or six people about a question like, "Which NBA team will win the tournament?"

Instead, to get good information, think about

- an in-depth interview with a trial lawyer to find out how juries are picked.

- an interview with a policewoman on the positive and negative sides of her job in a traditionally male-dominated occupation.

- an interview with the safety directors of several manufacturing firms on the types and causes of injuries in their workplaces and how often they occur.

- an interview with a man who is a registered nurse in a large hospital to find out how his patients and their families accept him in this nontraditional role.

Figure 13-1: *An expert is someone who knows how to do something well.*

In these examples, experts are practitioners in their fields, dealing with activities, skills, or concerns that we want to know more about.

Interviewing in a Workplace Situation

There may be many situations in your future work life when a personal interview will be necessary. That's why this skill is important to learn. So often students say, "That's something I'll never use." But five years later, these same students ask, "Why didn't anyone teach me how to do these things?" This chapter will teach you how to do "these things."

Let's look at several examples of interviewing on a variety of jobs. Some of them are very informal; some are very formal. An interview doesn't necessarily require three hours, a large notebook, and planned questions. But it is better to be prepared for such an interview in case you ever have to do one. Also note that one interview may be just talking and listening, while another may involve someone showing you how to do a particular task and letting you practice doing it yourself.

An interview at work might be necessary when someone needs to

* find out what witnesses observed about a major accident.

* research all phases of a sale or purchase to find out what went wrong—for example, talking to each person who signed or handled a purchase order, invoice, or shipment when tracking down a missing item.

* learn a new job from another worker in order to be able to take over in case of emergency—for example, an accounting clerk responsible for handling purchase order payments may have to learn to do payroll in case the payroll clerk has to be away from work for several days.

* get tips from a knowledgeable horse trainer on the fine points of training Arabians after working only with quarter horses for many years.

* understand how a trauma center differs from a typical emergency room when starting work in an urban trauma center after a year of working in a suburban hospital emergency room.

* discuss the design and layout of an advertisement with the owner of a small business, finding out what kind of business the person owns, what impression he or she wants to give, what audience he or she is trying to reach, and so forth.

TECHNOBIT

Motorola got its name from its first product: a car radio. The company has fulfilled the dream of its founder, Paul Galvin, who back in 1928 wanted to produce "mobile electronics." Today it manufactures cellular phones and pagers and is even involved in a satellite project.

Practice 13-1: Brainstorming Situations That Would Require an Interview

teamwork In a small group, brainstorm additional workplace situations that would require an interview. The interview may or may not include a show-and-tell of how to perform a task.

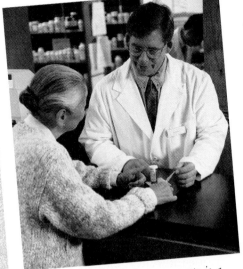

Figure 13-2: *Interviewing experts is a valuable approach to gathering information.*

The Positive Side of Interviewing an Expert

When interviewing is compared to other ways of gathering information, it is easy to see that it has certain advantages that other forms of research do not have. Here are some examples:

* Meeting an expert helps put reality into what might otherwise be an abstract topic.

* It's possible to ask clarifying questions and get answers as you go along.

* An expert can give you his or her personal insights—the kind that books rarely provide.

The Negative Side of Interviewing an Expert

On the other hand, everything about interviewing isn't always positive. It does, at times, have disadvantages. Here are some examples:

* A potential interviewee may be shy or unwilling to talk.
* It's easier to sit and read a book than to track down experts and make appointments with them, especially if you have trouble meeting strangers.
* It's impossible to go back and reread what someone says. You have to pay constant attention during an interview. (This is where recording the interview on audiocassette tape or videotape would help.)

Pinpointing Your Topic

It's going to be impossible to find the right expert to provide the information you're looking for if you're not really sure what that information is. For instance, suppose you're interested in the medical field and decide to do a report on cancer, since it is a disease that has touched nearly every family you know. Whom should you interview to get good information on cancer?

First of all, you must narrow your topic to one of the many forms of cancer that exist. Then narrow the topic further until you pinpoint a part of it that you can manage. There's no way to pick an expert until you first decide what aspect of the disease you want to know about, symptoms, treatments, and the effects of both the disease and the treatments on individuals suffering from the disease. One person is not likely to know all the details about all aspects of all types of cancer.

INFOBIT

"Designing a bridge or any other large structure is not unlike planning a trip or a vacation. The end may be clear and simple: to go from here to there. But the means may be limited only by our imaginations."

HENRY PETROSKI IN TO ENGINEER IS HUMAN: THE ROLE OF FAILURE IN SUCCESSFUL DESIGN

Practice 13-2: Narrowing and Pinpointing Your Topic

careers
teamwork

1. Look at the following example. The general topic is "Automobile Collisions," a very broad topic. Four examples of a narrowed focus on the subject of auto collisions are given. You could probably think of several others without too much difficulty. Each narrowed topic is then more finely pinpointed in the second column.

EXAMPLE:

General Topic: Automobile Collisions

Narrowed Topics:	Pinpointed Topics:
1. Two major causes of auto collisions	1-a. Speeding as a major cause of auto collisions

(cont'd on next page)

GENERAL TOPIC	NARROWED TOPIC	PINPOINTED TOPIC
All cancers	One type of cancer	One person's experience with one type of cancer

CANCER	LUNG CANCER	LIVING WITH LUNG CANCER: ONE PATIENT'S POINT OF VIEW
Includes all aspects of all types of cancers, such as lung cancer, bone cancer, brain cancer, pancreatic cancer, breast cancer, and prostate cancer, including their known causes, symptoms, treatments, side effects, survival rates, effects on family life and the workplace, etc.	Narrowed to one type of cancer. Still includes causes, symptoms, treatments, rates of cure, and effects on families and the workplace.	
Experts needed: several cancer specialists, therapists, family members, and insurance or business representatives, as well as a cancer patient	*Experts needed*: a lung cancer specialist, a therapist, family members, business representatives, and a cancer patient	*One expert needed*: a person who has lung cancer
Too broad a topic for a single interview	A bit more manageable, but still too broad for a single interview of one or two persons	Manageable for an in-depth interview with one person

Figure 13-3: *Narrowing and pinpointing a topic*

Narrowed Topics:	Pinpointed Topics:
2. Some of the most dangerous highways in our state	2-a. Highway 101: our state's most dangerous highway
3. Methods for reducing auto fatalities	3-a. The argument for seat belts as life savers
4. Some special problems repairing automobiles after a collision	4-a. Repairing a fiberglass auto body after a front-end collision

2. Page 13-A in your *Student Workbook* consists of a list of general topics. Each general topic has one narrowed topic. Work with a partner to pinpoint each of the narrowed topics as was done with the topic "Automobile Collisions." Try to relate at least one of the pinpointed topics to a career or occupational field that interests you.

Preparing for an Interview: Finding an Expert Who Knows Your Topic

After you have pinpointed your topic, you will need to find an expert who can answer your questions about it. For example, in order to learn the fine points of training a thoroughbred horse, you would have to talk to (interview) a trainer of thoroughbreds. Ask a few knowledgeable people to recommend someone who might be a good source of information for you. This person does not have to be well-educated about other matters, but he or she does have to know a great deal about the subject you are researching. For example, your father may be a great cook. He may use an old family recipe for making spaghetti sauce that always gets compliments from guests. Someone could interview him about how to make spaghetti sauce and learn a great deal. Whether or not your father has a high school diploma or even a college degree has nothing to do with how good his spaghetti sauce is.

So you have a twofold task: not only carefully pinpointing your topic, but also finding one or more persons who can provide you with enough reliable information to explore that topic adequately.

INFOBIT

A small percentage of individuals may experience epileptic seizures when exposed to certain light patterns or flashing lights. Exposure to certain patterns or backgrounds on a television screen or while playing video games may induce an epileptic seizure in these individuals.

FROM A WARNING ON A VIDEO GAME

Practice 13-3: Finding an Expert

For each of the following pinpointed topics, give a type of expert who could provide the kind of information required. Be prepared to discuss your choice with the class.

Pinpointed Topics:

1. Planting and managing a peach tree orchard
2. Computerized libraries in schools
3. Making a cheese soufflé
4. On-site experiences in the Persian Gulf during the Persian Gulf War
5. New designs in batting helmets for Little League ballplayers
6. Effects of chemical insecticides on flowering plants
7. Efficiency of seat belts as safety devices
8. Dog food as a billion-dollar industry
9. Making a fiddle
10. Head lice epidemics in child-care centers
11. Safety tips for rollerbladers
12. How an advertising campaign is put together (print, TV, or other)

Oliver Sacks is a neurologist who deals with differences in behaviors or abilities caused by anomalies in the brain. Part of his life was dramatized in the movie *Awakenings,* starring Robin Williams (Dr. Sacks) and Robert de Niro (a patient).

Dr. Sacks is interested not only in the person's affliction, but in how it manifests itself and how the person copes with it. In his book An *Anthropologist on Mars,* he describes a surgeon with Tourette's Syndrome; an autistic woman with a Ph.D. who designs more humane cattle pens based on her innate understanding of the animals; and an artist who has lost all ability to see color, but who continues to paint in leaden tones. Sacks says, "I have taken off my white coat [and] deserted, by and large, the hospitals where I have spent the last twenty-five years, to explore my subjects' lives as they live in the real world, feeling in part like a naturalist examining rare forms of life . . . but most of all like a physician, called here and there to make house calls . . . at the far borders of human experience."

Figure 13-4: *Oliver Sacks, neurologist, expert in the study of people with brain and nervous system disorders*

Setting Up the Interview

Once you have figured out the type of expert you need and get a lead or two from a reliable person such as a friend, family member, coworker, or teacher, be sure to get the expert's address and phone number. Then get your thoughts together so that you know what you want to say, and maybe jot down a few notes that you can use to introduce yourself to this person and explain why you want to interview him or her. This way you won't waste the person's time or risk being turned down because you sound unsure of what you want. Be sure to have a calendar handy so that you can set the date during your conversation.

Contacting a Potential Interviewee

Call, introduce yourself, and set up an appointment. Don't just walk in. Your expert is probably a busy person. Show courtesy by setting a meeting time that he or she selects as most convenient. This touch of courtesy will impress the expert with your professionalism and may result in greater willingness to spend time on the interview.

If the person does not have a telephone or works outdoors or for some other reason can't be reached by phone, drop by his or her place of work. Briefly explain your need to get information from an expert, and ask for a convenient time and place to meet. Some people are shy and need to be encouraged. But most would be flattered to be called an expert and would agree to talk with you.

Researching the Interviewee's Background

Do some background work on the interviewee before going to the scheduled appointment. Find out exactly what this person does and maybe what other interests the person has. Sometimes talking about other things—children, pets, sports, or mutual acquaintances, for example—gives both of you time to relax and feel more comfortable with each other.

Keeping an Open Mind

Go into the interview with an open mind. Do not allow **preconceived notions** or stereotypes to affect your opinion of this person or your behavior toward the person. If you discover that your expert is far different than you expected, have the good sense to adjust your thinking and perhaps even refocus your interview.

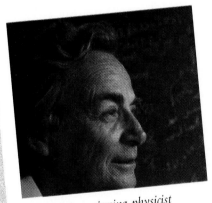

Nobel Prize winning physicist Richard Feynman

For example, let's say you've decided to interview a physicist, but that you've somewhere gotten the idea that all physicists are men, are boring, and are lost in the world of their theories. Maybe you've never met the female physicist who plays the tuba, the male physicist who leads his church choir, or his coworker who designs hang gliders and spends her weekends testing out different designs. Perhaps you haven't read *"Surely You're Joking, Mr. Feynman!": Adventures of a Curious Character,* a biography that consists largely of transcriptions of taped interviews with Feynman, so you don't know that he played the bongo drums for years, just for the fun of it, and once took second place in an international musical competition. If you had had the opportunity to learn about all these people, you might have changed your viewpoint to "What amazingly interesting and varied lives some physicists lead."

The point is, you have to suspend your judgment and make the assumption that most people lead varied and interesting lives, even when they don't realize it themselves. Your job as an interviewer is to appreciate your expert's personal uniqueness as well as learn what he or she knows about your topic.

Preparing Questions for the Interview

Write down some key questions about your topic that you want to be sure to ask. Leave a space for notes after each question. Most of the questions should be open-ended, not questions that can be answered by a simple yes or no.

Here are some questions that might be used in an interview on the topic "Cocaine Use During Pregnancy and Its Effects on the Child."

* Have you ever witnessed the births of infants to women who are addicted to cocaine?
* What differences have you observed between these infants and infants of mothers who do not consume drugs during pregnancy?
* Are there any lasting effects on the infant because of the mother's addiction, or are the effects just temporary? What are these effects? Can they be overcome? If so, how?
* What are the chances of a female cocaine addict having a normal baby?
* Is there any evidence that a father's cocaine addiction can affect the baby?

Conducting the Interview

Your interviewee will rely on you to ask appropriate questions that will provide you with the information you need. You will have to keep the interview on the topic, ask appropriate questions, get clarification on your expert's answers if you don't understand something that is said, and record your information.

Staying on the Topic During the Interview

It's easy to get caught up in the excitement of meeting an interesting or famous person and hearing stories about his or her life. However, even professionals can wander off the topic. You may need to keep bringing yourself and/or your expert back to the subject.

EXAMPLE

You are interviewing someone about emergency medical teams. You want to know what kind of training is essential to be an effective EMT (emergency medical technician).

You: "Where did you get your training?"

Member of life squad: "I started out as a volunteer with the Sycamore Branch Emergency Medical Team and took a night class twice a week. I remember one time, right after I started, when we answered a call and this kid was lying face down in a pool of blood in the kitchen. His dad was hysterical. Kept yelling at us the whole time. It was crazy."

TECHNOLOGY **C·O·N·N·E·C·T·I·O·N**

Digital cameras and scanners are excellent tools for someone who wants to publish an interview in a magazine or newspaper, at school, or elsewhere. These two tools make it possible for interviewers to take still photos of their subjects that can be incorporated into the article, using an interface program that allows them to import the photos into word processing or desktop publishing software. The digital camera uses no film, so the photographs don't have to be developed. If you do not have a digital camera, you can take a photograph with an ordinary camera and scan the picture, saving it on either the computer's hard drive or a disk. This picture can then be placed anywhere in your document as needed.

Note that your interviewee's answer, while interesting, is getting away from the point of your question. Gently get him back on topic.

> *You:* "How did you learn to deal with a situation like that? Did the night classes help prepare you for it?"

This subtle refocusing of the conversation back to the question of training will hardly be noticed by the interviewee, but it will ensure that you get the information you need. In the meantime, you will have also picked up a greater awareness of the kinds of things your expert has to endure, which adds to your understanding of your subject.

Taking Effective Notes

Don't rely on your memory to remind you of what was said during the interview. Effective notes are very important.

* *Take some phrases down* **verbatim.** Enclose them in quotes in your notes or circle them to show that they are the exact words of the speaker.

* *Read quotes or general explanations back to the interviewee to check accuracy* and to avoid recording a slip of the tongue. Remember, you are going after accurate information; you are not trying to catch the interviewee in a mistake.

* *Listen carefully and ask clarifying questions.* (Remember what you learned about the use of **clarifying questions** in Chapter 3.)

> **EXAMPLE**
>
> *Interviewee:* "I worked on the Columbus squad for a while."
>
> *You (clarifying):* "Was that in Columbus, Ohio?"
>
> *Interviewee:* "No. Columbus, Georgia. It's a college town."

Using Alternatives to Note Taking

If you're not the note-taking type, there are lots of other ways to do an interview. Be inventive about it. You might want to try an Internet interview, or you may want to tape a personal interview in case you can't keep up with note taking.

Using the Internet for On-Line Interviews

If you and your interviewee both have the necessary equipment, a face-to-face interview is possible via the Internet. If your expert agrees to the interview, you will have to arrange a time. If you do not have the capability of conducting such an interview, you can still talk to your expert via e-mail. You could also communicate through real-time correspondence if you know that a recognized expert is open for questions in a particular chat room, and you can get in on the conversation and record the answers to your questions. This last alternative could be a bit tricky due to possible interference by others on the line.

Recording Interviews

Some interviewees may allow you to record personal interviews on audiocassette tape. This procedure will allow you to listen and think during the interview rather than concentrating on getting responses down on paper. Be sure to have two new tapes (using one as a spare) and test the microphone before starting the interview, not only to be certain that it is functioning, but also in order to set it properly so that it will pick up the person's voice clearly.

If you have access to a camcorder, and if your interviewee is not uncomfortable with the idea and grants you permission, you can videotape the interview. It would be best to have someone with you who can do the videotaping while you conduct the interview. This would allow you to spend your time concentrating on the interview itself and not on whether the camera is focusing properly. Later you can review not only the words, but also the subtle body language and facial reactions of the interviewee to the questions as they were asked. You may see things that you did not notice as you were concentrating on your interviewee's words. You may note a frown, a vacant stare, an energetic walking back and forth, or other body language that can help you edit the interviewee's words with more realism and accuracy.

Record the date and time of your interview and the full name of each person you are interviewing. Write this information on the label of each tape to avoid a mix-up later and to make it easier to access information as needed.

WEB LINK

The Internet gives you access to experts all over the world. Find an individual, newsgroup, mailing list, or chat room that can answer your questions on a school or career topic or a subject of personal interest.

Carolyn, a sophomore in Cumberland, Maryland, some years ago chose as a project to learn more about the religion and education of Amish people outside Frostburg, Maryland. She got permission to visit an Amish schoolhouse and observe and talk to the students and teacher. The teacher welcomed Carolyn to the one-room schoolhouse on the scheduled day, but when she saw Carolyn's camera, she politely informed the surprised Carolyn that neither she nor the students could pose for pictures. The religious beliefs of the Amish did not allow them to pose for pictures or have their faces photographed. Carolyn also later discovered that Amish dolls were made without facial features. There were no images of human faces anywhere. Simply requesting permission to take photographs when she made her appointment would have prepared Carolyn for this event. She learned a valuable lesson about not taking for granted that everyone's values and customs are like her own.

Photo courtesy of Susan L. Kemp

It is best to start your interview by stating the full name of each person interviewed and the date of the interview just as you begin to record. It is easy to forget details or perhaps misplace notes by the time you start to work on your written version.

When the interview is ended, be sure to thank your interviewee and remember to follow up with a thank-you note within a day or two after the interview.

Editing the Interview: Making the Voice Come Through on Paper

When you begin to turn your interview into a report, let the person's voice come through as much as possible in your writing. In other words, don't try to make someone sound better or worse. What you're looking for is authenticity, the authentic response of the individual. Let the person speak for himself or herself.

Replay in your mind the way the person looked, sat, and moved. If you have videotaped the interview, watch it several times to catch aspects of the person that you may have failed to notice as you were taking notes or sorting out your thoughts. As you edit, you may want to add a word or phrase that describes something the person is doing as he or she speaks. But this should be done rarely. The most important reason for remembering the person's behavior during the interview is so that you can edit for the right tone, the right emphasis.

Depending on the effect you want, or the way the interview turns out, you will have to decide whether to put your questions and comments into the written interview or leave them out. If the interviewee began by speaking freely, providing many points of information in a smooth flow of talk without your having to ask many questions, the job is much easier. Then you can leave the questions out.

But if the person gave rather short answers to your questions, and the answers provide little or no clue to what was asked, then the questions will have to be included. For example, look at the following quote from an interview:

> "No, I don't believe that's true. He wouldn't have said something like that."

This quote tells you absolutely nothing about the subject of the interview. Was the interviewee being asked about

* how a mortician addressed the family of an accident victim?

* whether an actor criticized the writer of a television show?

* whether a teacher used vulgar language in the classroom?

* whether an employee accused his boss of neglect in a workplace accident?

The quotation is so general that it could have been the answer to any one of these questions. Therefore, it cannot be used without including the following question, which was asked in the actual interview:

> "Do you believe that the personnel director told Ms. Turner that her children would probably cause her to miss too much work?"

Once you have copied all notes and/or **transcribed** the tape, it's time to make decisions about exactly what to include in your report, what words, phrases, sentences, spacing, and punctuation are essential to the message you wish to pass on to your audience. One good rule of thumb: never omit any word or phrase, whether standard English or slang, which is essential to your interviewee's character or message.

Handling Repetition

A good rule is to omit unnecessary or repetitious words. However, you may want to keep them if they help give a clearer picture of the subject or the speaker, as is true in the following quotation:

> "Why? Why? I keep asking myself why I didn't pick up that phone. For the rest of my life I'll regret not hearing my brother's voice that one last time."

The repeated word *why* indicates the speaker's frustration with himself or herself. If communicating that frustration is important, then to remove the repeated *why* would dilute the message and give a slightly different impression of the speaker.

On the other hand, in the following quotation, the repeated phrase *you know* simply distracts from the message:

> "It was pretty scary, you know, being on duty by myself. It was, you know, like one of those Halloween movies you see, you know?"

Using Inserts

Sometimes the interviewee will use an abbreviated name, a set of initials, or some reference that would be unclear to the average reader or listener—or that is unclear even to the person conducting the interview. In this case, a clarifying question or statement would be in order. The clarification could be made in the printed report by using brackets [ ].

Brackets can help the reader understand what the speaker meant. Using brackets tells the reader that you have added something, but only to help clarify what the speaker meant, not to change the meaning or intent of the speaker.

Let's say, for example, that it is time to edit the previously quoted section of an interview with a member of an emergency medical team. The actual interview went like this:

> *Interviewee:* "I worked on the Columbus squad for a while."
>
> *You (clarifying):* "Was that in Columbus, Ohio?"
>
> *Interviewee:* "No. Columbus, Georgia. It's a college town."

A simple way to edit this exchange is to write

> "I worked on the Columbus [Georgia] squad for a while."

This approach allows you to use information from your clarifying question where it is needed and to avoid unnecessary verbiage.

Brackets can also be used to indicate movements or facial expressions, as you've seen them described in a play:

> "We had a team of ironworkers checking out that girder [he points] but they didn't find any weak spots. We even installed cameras. Nothing. We found nothing."

Using Spacing and Punctuation

Listen to the voice. If you are working from notes only, try to hear the interviewee's voice in your mind as you reread your notes. If you

INFOBIT

"I am always being asked whether a pedigree dog is easier to train than a mongrel. My answer is that all dogs can be trained if the owner is made of the right stuff. If the owner is at fault, you cannot blame or train the dog."

BARBARA WOODHOUSE IN DOG TRAINING MY WAY

have an audiocassette or videotape, listen for pauses, questions, or exclamations that might give you clues as to how to punctuate and space your sentences.

Remember that the meaning drives the editing. Strive to get on paper the meaning that the person was trying to convey by using commas, question marks, exclamation points, colons, dashes, periods, or other marks of punctuation to help convey the interviewee's intent. Also decide where to start new paragraphs.

If your interviewee gets emotionally overwrought or confused and stammers or unnecessarily repeats a word, use an ellipsis (. . .). An ellipsis shows that you have left out one or more words, but that leaving them out does not change the meaning intended by the speaker. Never omit a word, however, that will change a speaker's meaning.

Practice 13-4: Editing an Interview

Your teacher will play a CD selection for you. Listen to the voice of the man being interviewed as he tells part of his story. Then, using page 13-B in your *Student Workbook,* read along as you listen to the interview a second time. Edit the interview, using the proofreading marks listed on the inside back cover of this book to show where you need to delete a word, insert an explanation, capitalize, insert a period or other punctuation marks, and so forth.

The assignment was to interview an older worker who was fired or laid off late in his or her career. Four questions were given to the interviewee, Bill Steinemann, and then he was asked to tell his story and try to include these points as he talked. The results are a personal story in the manner of the literature selection "Nick Salerno" on page 462. The questions asked were as follows:

1. How did it feel to be fired or laid off late in life?

2. How did it affect you?

3. How did you react?

4. Did you ever get another job?

Conducting a Survey

A survey is a way to get information or opinions from a large number of people. For a survey to be effective, you have to ask all of the people exactly the same questions, or there will be no basis for comparing their answers.

For example, maybe you need to find out what 20 dentists think of TMJ (temporomandibular joint syndrome—a misalignment of the lower jaw joint). Which dentists treat it? Do any consider it a psychosomatic disorder? Do they recognize common symptoms of TMJ? Are they aware of proven methods of treatment? Do they refer TMJ patients to surgeons? Do they refer them to other professionals? Instead of having a general list of questions to keep you (the interviewer) on track, you need a very specific, carefully worded list of questions. If each person that you survey doesn't answer exactly the same questions, then you have no basis for comparing their answers.

You also have to have a means of recording responses so that the results can be tallied and compared with relative ease. One way to do this is to use a carefully prepared questionnaire.

Preparing an Appropriate Type of Questionnaire

A questionnaire makes it possible to ask a series of questions of either a select or a random group of people in order to learn how they think or feel about a particular topic. A questionnaire requires careful attention to words. Exactly what are you asking? What do you want to know?

Next, you have to think about how you are going to record all the answers (maybe ten or more) from all those people you survey. Directing people to reply in a certain way makes it possible to tally results. Of course, the way people are required to reply will vary with the type of information you are looking for. This is why you may see one or more of the following types of questions and response patterns on different questionnaires.

Type 1: Recording What People Think or Feel

On a scale of one to ten, how would you rate the Green Bay Packers? We've all heard this kind of question. When a stopwatch or game score cannot be used to judge an Olympic event, for example, judges are asked to rate the competitors on a scale of one to ten (or one to six in the case of figure skaters). Judges in such events will have guidelines to follow in arriving at their judgments, something not

"Would you say Attila is doing an excellent job, a good job, a fair job, or a poor job?"

Drawing by Chas. Addams; ©1982, The New Yorker Magazine, Inc.

INFOBIT

"I'm not so smart, it's just that I stay with problems longer."

ALBERT EINSTEIN, GERMAN-BORN U.S. SCIENTIST

always possible on a survey. But the ultimate method of replying is the same—by means of a number. Strictly speaking, the numbers used in this way cannot be added or subtracted, though people sometimes do so anyway. The numbers merely represent an opinion or judgment. One should tally how many people answered with a 7, or a 6, and so on, to report results.

To find out what people think or feel and to have an efficient way of recording their answers, many surveyors use a similar scale of five to seven numbers and ask people to rate items.

SAMPLE 1 (Rating scale)

Directions: Indicate how you rate the following media as a way of staying informed by circling the number that best reflects your response (5 = excellent, 1 = poor). If you have never used a particular medium, circle *NA*.

Medium	Excellent	Very Good	Average	Below Average	Poor	NA
Radio	5	4	3	2	1	NA
Television	5	4	3	2	1	NA
Newspapers	5	4	3	2	1	NA
The Internet	5	4	3	2	1	NA

SAMPLE 2 (Agree-Disagree scale)

Directions: Indicate your response to the following statements about products. Circle one number from 7 (strongly agree) to 1 (strongly disagree) for each product.

	Strongly Agree	Agree	No Opinion	Disagree		Strongly Disagree
Nopain is an effective painkiller.	7	6	5	4	3 2	1
Windoclear eliminates streaking.	7	6	5	4	3 2	1

SAMPLE 3 (Nonnumerical yes or no responses)

Directions: Answer each question by circling either YES or NO.

1. Do you think Nopain is an effective painkiller?   YES   NO

2. Have you ever used Windoclear?   YES   NO
   If you answered YES, does it eliminate streaks?   YES   NO

Type 2: Recording Actual Amounts

If you need to know actual amounts, you will want to set up your questionnaire so that actual amounts can be obtained and you will want to survey only knowledgeable people. The responses you get from such a questionnaire may not be exact, but they can give you a better idea than you would have gotten by estimating without asking.

SAMPLE 4 (Indicating an actual numerical range)

Directions: Check the amount that most accurately answers each question.

What percentage of your patients' insurance companies provide 100% coverage for multiple surgical procedures?

_____80% to 100%   _____60% to 79%   _____40% to 59%   _____20% to 39%   _____1% to 19%

SAMPLE 5 (Indicating exact amounts)

How many televisions are in your home? (Check answer.)

_____1   _____2   _____3   _____4 or more

Note that the arrangement of blanks and numbers can be confusing in Sample 4. People often tend to place the check mark or *X* after a number. If you wish them to place the check mark before each number, as is shown in Sample 5, be sure to use appropriate spacing so it is clear where their mark should be placed. Otherwise, your results may be inaccurate.

Be sure to set up response patterns and test them on a sample group first, so that you can correct any problems in the questionnaire format that may not have been anticipated.

Type 3: Using a Nonnumerical Checklist

In a nonnumerical checklist, actual counts are not needed. Facts or feelings may be indicated by placing a check mark next to the word(s) that answer the question.

SAMPLE 6 (Indicating objective facts)

Where did you learn about this computer? Check all the sources that apply.

_____ television commercial   _____ friend or neighbor

_____ radio commercial   _____ store display

_____ newspaper or magazine ad   _____ other

> How did you feel when you were told that your prospective employer ran a closed shop and that to work there you would have to join a labor union?
>
> _____ No reaction   _____ Angry   _____ Pleased

You may set up a questionnaire in a variety of ways. These seven examples provide you with a few to choose from. The important point to remember is that you must always consider what you want to know in order to choose an appropriate format.

Avoiding Pitfalls of Questionnaire Design

Every part of a questionnaire must be absolutely clear in its meaning—from the directions to the questions to the choices of answers. Unclear directions can result in totally unusable information. Unclear words or phrases of any kind throughout the questionnaire can cause your entire project to be worthless.

Choosing Words That Say Exactly What You Mean

The following are illustrations of some dos and don'ts in wording a questionnaire.

* Don't say *Zappo is an extraordinary roach killer.* (What does *extraordinary* mean? Interpretations may range from "extraordinarily bad" to "extraordinarily good.")

* Don't say *Zappo is a different kind of roach killer.* (Is *different* better or worse? Does *different* mean a spray, as opposed to powder or glue boards?)

Instead, say

* Zappo kills roaches effectively, or

* Zappo kills roaches better than other roach killers, or

* Zappo kills roaches without harming pets.

Avoiding Open-Ended or Essay Answers

Suppose you wanted to know whether most students like to drive American or foreign-made cars. So you asked,

"What kind of car do you like to drive?"

Think about the nightmare of tallying the responses. The respondents wouldn't know whether you were asking them to give the make, model, or style (convertible, sedan, etc.). You would have to spend hours writing down all the different answers you received. Some respondents may have said they liked two-seater sports models; others may have referred to a van or truck. Some may have said they liked Japanese- or American-made. Some may simply have said "fast" or "loud."

The responses probably wouldn't focus on any one aspect of comparing cars, because the question was so unfocused. To prevent this problem, limit the choices of the respondents. Doing so will show them the kind of answer you are looking for, as in

"What is your favorite type of radio show?" (Check one)

_____ country-western	_____ open talk	_____ bluegrass-country
_____ hip-hop	_____ New Wave	
_____ sports/sports talk	_____ jazz	_____ soft rock
_____ classical	_____ hard rock/heavy metal	_____ religious
_____ oldies		_____ other

Avoiding Loaded Statements

Statements like "I like Springbok running shoes because . . ." are a problem because they assume that the respondent does, indeed, like the product. In fact, advertisers often use such an opening line in promotional contests.

A survey, however, is not a promotional contest. It is an attempt to gather material in an unbiased way. If you assume that someone likes or dislikes anything and word your statements accordingly, the results will be biased; that is, they will be worthless as a survey.

Seeking Responses from Reliable Sources

Your respondents in a survey do not necessarily have to be experts in order to be reliable. Marketing surveys are a prime illustration of this fact. If a shoe manufacturer wants to know why people prefer a particular kind of shoe, it doesn't need a shoe expert (the company is full of shoe experts). It needs to find out which people buy shoes and why they buy them. Then it can look at their responses for ideas on what kinds of shoes to make more or fewer of in the future.

CAREER C·O·N·N·E·C·T·I·O·N

Dean Schoenewald was struck by the advice of a teacher to "Find out what you love and figure out how to make a living at it." Dean loved acting. He also had a good head for business and wanted to make money without working for somebody else. The result was Mascot Mania, whose products are familiar to millions of sports fans.

Schoenewald has worked with a generation of eye-catching, crowd-pleasing team mascots like the Philadelphia Eagle. In an interview on *CBS Morning News,* he was asked what kind of person he looks for. He said the person must first be entertaining—a ham or hot-dog personality. If you are such a person, you then have to (1) cease being yourself, (2) become the character you portray, and (3) give that character a personality. You must be able to please a crowd, because your job is to entertain thousands of sports fans in a stadium, especially when there is a lull in the action.

However, if you were to survey people about their choice of shoes in a country where only sandals or bare feet were common, you might get only puzzled looks instead of answers. The responses about shoes from those people would be unreliable.

Likewise, if you asked the fathers of 18-year-olds what their sons and daughters thought about environmental concerns, the information would not be as reliable as it would if you asked the 18-year-olds.

Constructing the Survey Questionnaire

The survey questionnaire is similar to the interview questionnaire. Both types of questionnaires

* seek information for a purpose.

* require a limited topic.

* help to direct the thoughts of the person who is responding.

The survey questionnaire, however, has to ask for specific information about the respondents before getting to the topic at hand. For example, for purposes of comparison, you may want to know

* whether the respondent is male or female.

* how old the person is.

* whether the person is married.

* how much education the person has.

* other information that might affect the responses (size of family, major in school, etc.).

This collection of facts about age, income, educational level, and other subjects for a group of people is called **demographic data.**

> **CAUTION: PROTECT ANONYMITY**
> Never ask for the names of the respondents. Protect their anonymity, so that they feel free to answer any question without fear of someone knowing how they answered.

WEB LINK

Increasingly, organizations are conducting surveys on the Internet. Take an on-line survey. How does it compare to a survey on paper? For what sorts of organizations would such a survey be useful?

Practice 13-5: Completing a Questionnaire

Fill in the questionnaire on page 13-C in your *Student Workbook*. It is also the sample Project at the end of this chapter. It is important to see how usable and appropriate a well-written and well-designed form can be before attempting one of your own. After completing the questionnaire, answer these questions.

1. Who do you think wants the information on this questionnaire?

2. Why do they want the information?

3. Why might a company that advertises in the newspaper be interested in the results of this survey?

Tallying the Survey Responses

Today, massive surveys are tallied on computers. But if you circulate only up to 50 surveys, the tallying can be done by hand.

It's easiest to work in pairs. One person reads the answer while the other marks down responses. A smaller number of responses can be tallied on a blank copy of the questionnaire itself. Larger numbers should be tallied on a separate sheet of paper. Do not write out all the questions. Write only the number and, in cases like the newspaper survey you just completed, the category.

> **EXAMPLE**
>
> 1. Yes   ~~HHH~~ ~~HHH~~ ~~HHH~~ ~~HHH~~ ~~HHH~~ ~~HHH~~ | = 31
>
>   No   ~~HHH~~ ~~HHH~~ ~~HHH~~ |||| = 19
>
>   (Tally 2 and 3 the same way.)
>
> 4. front page   ~~HHH~~ ~~HHH~~ ~~HHH~~   = 15
>
>   sports   ~~HHH~~ ~~HHH~~ ~~HHH~~ ~~HHH~~ |||| = 24
>
>   classified ads   ~~HHH~~ ~~HHH~~ | = 11

(Proceed this way for all questions. Then add up the totals for each answer.)

If you want to see how each age group answers, separate the papers into stacks by age group (all 10- to 15-year-olds in one stack, all 16- to 21-year-olds in another stack, and so forth). Then tally totals for each age group.

Reporting the Information

After tallying all of the responses on the questionnaire, the next step is to write a short report summarizing the responses. Use the following format for your report:

REPORT FORMAT

I. INTRODUCTION—STATE THE PURPOSE OF THE QUESTIONNAIRE.

II. BODY—STATE THE KINDS OF QUESTIONS ASKED.

    A. Number of Respondents
      1. Number of males
      2. Number of females
    (Note: You may want to keep the questionnaires of males and females separate and then tally all responses of males and females separately for purposes of comparison.)
    B. Ages of Respondents—Number in Each Age Category
    C. Educational Level of Respondents
    D. Income of Respondents
    E. Number of Respondents Who Receive a Newspaper in Household Each Day
    F. Number of Respondents Who Receive a Newspaper in Household at Least Once a Week
    G. Number of Respondents Who Read All or Part of a Newspaper at Least Once a Week
    H. Part of Paper Read First by Majority of Respondents
    I. Part of Newspaper Read Occasionally by Majority of Respondents
    J. How Newspaper Is Obtained by Majority

III. CONCLUSIONS

    Look at your results. What picture do you now have of your respondents? What conclusions can you draw?

Details on how to write reports containing results of your research are in Chapter 15.

SUMMARY

Interviews are an important way to gather information. In this chapter you had a chance to practice personal interviews as well as interviews of groups (commonly known as surveys). Follow these guidelines when the need or opportunity for an interview arises:

* Narrow your topic and be ready with questions that keep you focused on that topic during an interview.

* Select an expert who can shed light on your topic and arrange an interview.

* Take careful notes or, with permission, record an interview so that the full meaning of the interviewee's responses is never lost or misinterpreted.

* Represent each interviewee accurately and fairly when writing and presenting the results of an interview.

* Carefully prepare a set of questions, and ask each person the same questions when seeking information or opinions from a group using a survey.

* Tally, summarize, and report the results of your survey.

WORKS CITED

Feynman, Richard P, as told to Ralph Leighton. *"What Do YOU Care What Other People Think?": Further Adventures of a Curious Character.* New York: Norton, 1988.

Petroski, Henry. *To Engineer Is Human: The Role of Failure in Successful Design.* New York: St. Martin's, 1985.

Sacks, Oliver. *An Anthropologist on Mars: Seven Paradoxical Tales.* New York: Knopf, 1995.

Woodhouse, Barbara. *Dog Training My Way.* New York: Stein and Day, 1970.

Reporting the Results of an Interview

Before beginning this Project, study the Sample Project Plan on page 457 and the Sample Presentation, "Reporting the Results of an Interview," on page 458. Listen to the oral presentation of that interview recorded on the CD.

Then prepare a three- to five-minute oral presentation of an interview, following these steps:

1. Choose a specific (pinpointed) topic that interests you and that you think will interest others.

2. Find an expert that you can interview about this topic and who can give you interesting details about the topic. Arrange a time for an interview, and think about specific questions you can ask your expert.

3. Conduct the interview. Keep the interview reasonably short (less than an hour). Record all or part of it if possible. (Be sure to get equipment ready in advance, including extra recording tape, film, and so on.)

4. Use the Project Plan on page 13-D of the *Student Workbook* to organize your oral presentation. Choose an interesting quote or fact from the interview to use in beginning your talk. End with what you learned from the interview (a closing statement).

5. Choose a partner with whom to practice your presentation. Your partner should use the Rough Draft column of the Project Guide to evaluate your practice presentation.

6. Do another rehearsed presentation. Have your partner evaluate it using the Final Draft column of the Project Guide.

7. Give your presentation. Turn in your Project Guide.

SAMPLE PROJECT PLAN

Plan for Presentation of an Interview

SUBJECT	Man who lost job late in life—impact on his life
AUDIENCE	General audience—classmates
PURPOSE	**What actions should the audience take?** Understand what the person went through and how he felt.
FORMAT	☐ written ☒ oral ☐ other
SOURCES	a 62-year-old printing pressman who was laid off work without warning when he was 53.
VISUALS	**What visuals, if any, will make the presentation more effective?** pictures of Bill Steinemann showing him at work in the press room.
PREPARE	Get LCD projector & extension cord to use with laptop. Project pictures on screen in classroom. Set up during study hall before presentation.

CONTENT

"I thank God—I thank him every day that that kid and I got together."

Tell how Bill survived because of faith in God & in people.

Tell story from interview:
—Younger guy (friend) got fired. (Bill was in his 20s)
—Bill got him hired back.

—Later when Bill was 53—lost job when his boss sold the business.

—Guy he once re-hired offered him a job.

That was 10 years ago. Now Bill is a happy man.

(Load digital photos of Bill in pressroom into laptop computer to show class.)

Reporting the Results of an Interview

This presentation is based on an interview of a 62-year-old printing pressman. Notice that it starts with a quote from the interview you edited in Practice 13-4.

"I thank God—I thank him every day that that kid and I got together."

These are the words of a man who is very grateful and relieved to be able to support his family again. They tell you what kind of man Bill Steinemann is. He has lived by faith in God and faith in people. He has always believed that if you treat people right, they will treat you right.

When Bill was young and working in a large printing company that produced nationally known magazines and comic books, he found out through the rumor mill that a younger guy in another department had been fired. Bill knew the guy and liked him, even though he was hot-headed, which got him into trouble. This guy was only 20 years old, and his wife was pregnant. They were living on practically nothing and now he didn't even have a job. Bill put in a good word and got the guy re-hired.

The two men remained friends and their families visited one another even after each was hired by different companies a hundred miles from one another in the Midwest. Suddenly, without any warning, the owner of the company Bill worked for told him that the business had been sold. He gave Bill two weeks' notice, which meant that after two weeks and two paychecks, Bill would have no income.

Bill and his wife did not know what to do. But they couldn't stay depressed for long. They still had two teenagers at home, a girl in high school and a boy who had worked for a year and just finished a semester of college. So they were desperate to find a way to get through this disaster. Bill called his old friend and asked if he knew of any openings among the printing plants that were scattered throughout the Midwest. Within days his old friend had found him a place in his own label-making plant. The new job required Bill's family to move 100 miles, but they knew they had to do it.

When I talked to Bill, he had been working with his old friend for nearly nine years. He was proud to let me take his picture beside his new printing press, where thousands of labels are printed each day. [Project photo on screen in front of room using LCD projector.] He is proud of what he does and grateful for the power of the friendship that helped him to put his life back together.

Creating a Questionnaire

teamwork Review the Sample Project Plan for Designing a Questionnaire (on page 460) that was used in designing the questionnaire on page 13-C of your *Student Workbook*. Does the questionnaire reflect the plan? Does it do what the plan says it should do?

In this final chapter Project, use the Project Plan and Project Guide on pages 13-F and 13-G of your *Student Workbook*. Working in a group, develop a solid questionnaire of your own. Follow these steps:

1. Find a topic or an issue on which conducting a survey could provide helpful information. (Be sure that you have access to enough people who can relate to this issue.)

2. Pinpoint what you want to know about that topic.

3. Work through the Project Plan for Designing a Questionnaire (*Student Workbook* page 13-F). Decide who your audience will be (whom you need to survey) and what questions you need to ask to get the information you need.

4. Design the questionnaire for your survey based on your plan.

5. Ask a classmate to fill out and evaluate your questionnaire using the Rough Draft column of the Project Guide on page 13-G of your *Student Workbook*.

6. Revise the questionnaire if necessary based on your classmate's feedback.

7. Have another classmate fill out the questionnaire and evaluate it using the Final Draft column of the Project Guide.

8. Considering your classmate's comments, make any final adjustments to the questionnaire that are needed.

9. Conduct a survey of 25-50 people in your target audience.

10. Tally the surveys.

Save your questionnaires and tally sheets for possible interpretation and reporting in Chapters 14 and 15.

Plan for Designing a Questionnaire

SUBJECT	Find out who reads a newspaper, what parts of the newspaper they read, and where they get their paper.
AUDIENCE	Anyone over age 10.
PURPOSE	Design an effective questionnaire for this subject.
FORMAT	☒ written ☐ oral ☐ other
SOURCES	Ideas of team members in class. Brainstorm questions to put on questionnaire.
DESIGN	What layout will make the questionnaire more effective (easier to read and respond to)?

CONTENT

Need questions that will tell us
—how old the person is
—how much education the person has
—how much income the person has
—what part of the paper the person reads and how often

Write clear directions at the top of the questionnaire so people fill it out right.

Please check one reply for each piece of information requested.

Are you
male? _____
female? _____

Your age: 10-15 _____
16-21 _____
22-35 _____
36-50 _____
over 50 _____

Highest education completed
by anyone in your household:
grade school _____
some high school _____
high school graduate _____
some college _____
college graduate _____

Your family's approximate income

under $12,000 _____ $31,000 to $40,000 _____
$12,000 to $20,000 _____ $41,000 to $60,000 _____
$21,000 to $30,000 _____   over $60,000 _____

Answer the first three questions below by <u>circling the answer</u>.

1. Is there a newspaper in your household each day?   YES   NO
2. Is there a newspaper in your household at least once a week? YES   NO
3. Do you read all or part of a newspaper at least once a week? YES   NO

If you answered NO to ALL THREE questions, STOP HERE.

4. What part of the newspaper do you read first?

front page _____   editorial page _____
sports _____   puzzles/games _____
classified ads _____   comics _____
                                other _____

5. What parts of the newspaper do you read occasionally? (Check all that apply to you)

front page _____   editorial page _____
sports _____   puzzles/games _____
classified ads _____   comics _____
                                other _____

6. What best describes how you get your newspaper?

Delivered to your house _____
Buy it on the newstand _____
Read a copy you find at work _____
Pick up a used copy elsewhere _____

Overview

Studs Terkel, a writer, actor, theater manager, and television and radio show host, is an interviewer extraordinaire. Instead of interviewing celebrities, the infamous, and the heroes who make the news, he interviews the non-celebrated.

Terkel's interviews with everyday people have been published in several books, such as *Hard Times: An Oral History of the Great Depression* (1970) and *Working: People Talk About What They Do All Day and How They Feel About What They Do* (1974). In 1993 he wrote *Race: How Blacks and Whites Think and Feel About the American Obsession.*

"Nick Salerno"

He has been driving a city garbage truck for eighteen years. He is forty-one, married, has three daughters. He works a forty-hour, five-day week, with occasional overtime. He has a crew of three laborers.

I usually get up at five-fifteen. I get to the city parking lot, you check the oil, your water level, then proceed for the ward yard. I meet the men, we pick up our work sheet.

You get just like the milkman's horse, you get used to it. If you remember the milkman's horse, all he had to do was whistle and whooshhh! That's it. He knew just where to stop, didn't he? You pull up until you finish the alley. Usually thirty homes on each side. You have thirty stops in an alley. I have nineteen alleys a week. They're called units. Sometimes I can't finish 'em, that's how heavy they are, this bein' an old neighborhood. . . .

Maybe you got a problem at home. Maybe one of the children aren't feeling too good. Like my second one, she's a problem with homework. Am I doin' the right thing with her? Pressing her a little bit with math. Or you'll read the paper. You always daydream.

Some stops, there's one can, they'll throw that on, then we proceed to the next can. They signal with a buzzer or a whistle or they'll yell. The pusher blade pushes the garbage in. A good solid truckload will hold anywhere from eight thousand to twelve thousand pounds. If it's wet, it weighs more. Years ago you had people burning, a lot of people had garbage burners. You would pick up a lot of ashes. Today most of 'em have converted to gas. In place of ashes, you've got cardboard boxes, you've got wood that people aren't burning anymore.

Other people just don't care or maybe they don't know any better.

It's not like years ago, when people used everything. They're not too economy-wise today. They'll throw anything away. You'll see whole packages of meat just thrown into the garbage can without being opened. I don't know if it's spoiled from the store or not. When I first started here, I had nearly thirty alleys in this ward. Today I'm down to nineteen. And we got better trucks today. Just the way things are packaged today. Plastic. You see a lot of plastic bottles, cardboard boxes.

We try to give 'em twice-a-week service, but we can't complete the ward twice a week. Maybe I can go four alleys over. If I had an alley Monday. I might go in that alley Friday. What happens over the weekend? It just lays there.

After you dump your garbage in the hopper, the sweeper goes around to sweep it up, and the push blade pushes it in. This is where you get your sound. Does that sound bother you in the morning? (Laughs.) Sometimes it's irritating to me. If someone comes up to you to talk, and the men are working in the back, and they press the lever, you can't hear them. It's aggravating but you get used to it. We come around seven-twenty. Not too many complaints. Usually you're in the same alley the same day, once a week. The people know that you're coming and it doesn't bother them that much.

Some people will throw, will literally throw garbage out of the window—right in the alley. We have finished an alley in the morning and that same afternoon it will be like it wasn't even done. They might have a cardboard carton in the can and garbage all over the alley. People are just not takin' care of it. You get some people that takes care of their property, they'll come out and sweep around their cans. Other people just don't care or maybe they don't know any better.

Some days it's real nice. Other days, when you get off that truck you're tired, that's it! You say all you do is drive all day, but driving can be pretty tiresome—especially when the kids are out of school. They'll run through a gangway into the alley. This is what you have to watch for. Sitting in that cab, you have a lot of blind spots

(cont'd on next page)

around the truck. This is what gets you. You watch out that you don't hit any of them.

At times you get aggravated, like your truck breaks down and you get a junk as a replacement. This, believe me, you could take home with you. Otherwise, working here, if there's something on your mind, you don't hold anything in. You discuss anything with these guys. Golf, whatever. One of my laborers just bought a new home and I helped him move some of his stuff. He's helped me around my house, plumbing and painting.

We've got spotters now. It's new. (Laughs.) They're riding around in unmarked cars. They'll turn you in for stopping for coffee. I can't see that. If you have a coffee break in the alley, it's just using a little psychology. You'll get more out of them. But if you're watched continually, you're gonna lay down. There's definitely more watching today, because there was a lot of layin' down on the job. Truthfully, I'd just as soon put in my eight hours a day as easy as possible. It's hard enough comin' to work. I got a good crew, we get along together, but we have our days. . . .

> *I don't like to have my salary compared to anybody else's.*

People ask me what I do, I say, "I drive a garbage truck for the city." They call you G-man, or, "How's business, picking up?" Just the standard. . . . Or sanitary engineer. I have nothing to be ashamed of. I put in my eight hours. We make a pretty good salary. I feel I earn my money. I can go any place I want. I conduct myself as a gentleman any place I go. My wife is happy, this is the big thing. She doesn't look down at me. I think that's more important than the white-collar guy looking down at me.

They make a crack to my children at school. My kids would just love to see me do something else. I tell 'em, "Honey, this is a good job. There's nothing to be ashamed of. We're not stealin' money. You have everything you need."

I don't like to have my salary compared to anybody else's. I don't like to hear that we're makin' more than a schoolteacher. I earn my money just as well as they do. A teacher should get more money, but don't take it away from me.

—Studs Terkel

Start-Up: Studs Terkel's interview produces an in-depth look into Nick Salerno's life as a garbage truck driver. The reader learns about Salerno and his job. Imagine what sorts of questions would encourage Salerno to give us such a glimpse of himself.

Connection: What questions do you think Terkel asked Salerno to obtain the information he needed to write this interview? Write these questions individually. In groups of three, share these questions. Critique them. Make a list of the best questions.

As a class, discuss the ways that Terkel lets the interviewee's voice come through in his article.

Overview

One of America's greatest authors (and a printer and lecturer), Mark Twain has the reputation of being a great humorist. In this excerpt from his essay "How To Tell a Story," Mark Twain's responses to the interviewer are a put-on. Twain creates an absurd, comical situation.

Mark Twain, in his essay, maintains that humor in stories depends either on the manner in which the stories are told or on the story content.

from "How To Tell a Story"

I used to tell a story about a man who came to interview me once to get a sketch of my life. I consulted with a friend—a practical man—before he came, to know how I should treat him.

"Whenever you give the interviewer a fact," he said, "give him another fact that will contradict it. Then he'll go away with a jumble that he can't use at all. Be gentle, be sweet, smile like an idiot—just be natural." That's what my friend told me to do, and I did it.

The nervous, dapper young man took the chair I offered him, and said he was connected with the *Daily Thunderstorm,* and added:

"Hoping it's no harm, I've come to interview you."

"Come to what?"

"*Interview* you."

"Ah! I see. Yes—yes. Um! Yes—yes."

I was not feeling bright that morning. Indeed, my powers seemed a bit under a cloud. However, I went to the bookcase, and when I had been looking six or seven minutes, I said:

"How do you spell it?"

"Spell what?"

"Interview."

"Oh, my goodness! What do you want to spell it for?"

"I don't want just to spell it; I want to spell it to see what it means."

"In, *in,* ter, *ter, inter—*"

(cont'd on next page)

"Then you spell it with an *I*?"

"Why, certainly!"

"Oh, that is what took me so long."

"Why, my *dear* sir, what did *you* propose to spell it with?"

"Well, I—I—hardly know. I had the Unabridged, and I was looking around in the back end, among the pictures. But it's a very old edition."

"Why, my friend, they wouldn't have a *picture* of it in even the latest e— My dear sir, I beg your pardon, I mean no harm in the world, but you do not look as—as—intelligent as I had expected you would. No harm—I mean no harm at all."

"Oh, don't mention it! It has often been said, and by people who would not flatter me, that I am quite remarkable in that way. Yes—yes; they always speak of it with pleasure."

"I can easily imagine it. But about this interview. You know it is the custom, now, to interview any man who has become famous."

"Indeed, I had not heard of it before. It must be very interesting. What do you do it with?"

"Ah, well—well—well—it *ought* to be done with a club in some cases. But usually the interviewer asks questions and the interviewed answers them. It is all the rage now. Will you let me ask you certain questions to bring out the salient points of your public and private history?"

"Oh, with pleasure—with pleasure. I have a very bad memory, but I hope you will not mind that. That is to say, it is an irregular memory—very irregular. Sometimes it goes in a gallop, and then again it will be as much as a week passing a given point. This is a great grief to me."

"Oh, it is no matter, so you will try to do the best you can."

"I will. I will put my whole mind on it."

"Thanks. Are you ready to begin?"

"Ready."

Q. How old are you?

A. Nineteen, in June.

Q. Indeed. I would have taken you to be thirty-five or -six. Where were you born?

A. In Missouri.

Q. When did you begin to write?

A. In 1836.

Q. Why, how could that be, if you are only nineteen now?

A. I don't know. It does seem curious, somehow.

Q. It does, indeed. Whom do you consider the most remarkable man you ever met?

A. Aaron Burr.

Q. But you never could have met Aaron Burr, if you are only nineteen years—

A. Now, if you know more about me than I do, what do you ask me for?

Q. Well, it was only a suggestion; nothing more. How did you happen to meet Burr?

A. Well, I happened to be at his funeral one day, and he asked me to make less noise, and—

Q. But, good heavens! If you were at his funeral, he must have been dead, and if he was dead how could he care whether you made a noise or not?

A. I don't know. He was always a particular kind of man that way.

Q. Still, I don't understand it at all. You say he spoke to you, and that he was dead.

A. I didn't say he was dead.

Q. But wasn't he dead?

A. Well, some said he was, some said he wasn't.

Q. What did you think?

A. Oh, it was none of my business! It wasn't any of my funeral.

Q. Did you—However, we can never get this matter straight. Let me ask about something else. What was the date of your birth?

A. Monday, October 31, 1693.

Q. What! Impossible! That would make you a hundred and eighty years old. How do you account for that?

A. I don't account for it at all.

Q. But you said at first you were only nineteen, and now you make yourself out to be one hundred and eighty. It is an awful discrepancy.

A. Why, have you noticed that? (Shaking hands.) Many a time it has seemed to me like a discrepancy, but somehow I couldn't make up my mind. How quick you notice a thing!

Q. Thank you for the compliment, as far as it goes. Had you, or have you, any brothers or sisters?

A. Eh! I—I—I think so—yes—but I don't remember.

Q. Well, that is the most extraordinary statement I ever heard!

A. Why, what makes you think that?

Q. How could I think otherwise? Why, look here! Who is this a picture of on the wall? Isn't that a brother of yours?

A. Oh, yes, yes, yes! Now you remind me of it; that *was* a brother of mine. That's William—*Bill* we called him. Poor old Bill!

(cont'd on next page)

Q. Why? Is he dead, then?

A. Ah! Well, I suppose so. We never could tell. There was a great mystery about it.

Q. That is sad, very sad. He disappeared, then?

A. Well, yes, in a sort of general way. We buried him.

Q. *Buried* him! *Buried* him, without knowing whether he was dead or not?

A. Oh, no! Not that. He was dead enough.

Q. Well, I confess that I can't understand this. If you buried him, and you knew he was dead—

A. No! no! We only thought he was.

Q. Oh, I see! He came to life again?

A. I bet he didn't.

Q. Well, I never heard anything like this. *Somebody* was dead. *Somebody* was buried. Now, where was the mystery?

A. Ah! That's just it! That's it exactly. You see, we were twins—defunct and I—and we got mixed in the bathtub when we were only two weeks old, and one of us was drowned. But we didn't know which. Some think it was Bill. Some think it was me.

Q. Well, this *is* remarkable. What do *you* think?

A. Goodness knows! I would give whole worlds to know. This solemn, this awful mystery has cast a gloom over my whole life. But I will tell you a secret now, which I never have revealed to any creature before. One of us had a peculiar mark—a large mole on the back of his left hand; that was *me. That child was the one that was drowned!* Q. Very well, then, I don't see that there is any mystery about it, after all.

A. You don't? Well, I do. Anyway, I don't see how they could ever have been such a blundering lot as to go and bury the wrong child. But, 'sh!—don't mention it where the family can hear of it. Heaven knows they have heartbreaking troubles enough without adding this.

Q. Well, I believe I have got material enough for the present, and I am very much obliged to you for the pains you have taken. But I was a good deal interested in that account of Aaron Burr's funeral. Would you mind telling me what it was that made you think Burr was such a remarkable man?

A. Oh! It was a mere trifle! Not one man in fifty would have noticed it at all. When the sermon was over, and the procession all ready to start for the cemetery, and the body all arranged nice in the hearse, he said he wanted to take a last look at the scenery, and so he *got up and rode with the driver.*

Then the young man reverently withdrew. He was very pleasant company, and I was sorry to see him go.

—Mark Twain (pseudonym for Samuel Langhorne Clemens)

Start-Up: The interviewer should be prepared for the positive and negative sides of interviewing. On the positive side, interviews are an excellent source of primary (firsthand) information. The interviewee can provide a unique angle on a topic, something few reference books can do. On the negative side, not all interviewees give good interviews; some of them for many different reasons are reluctant to answer the interviewer's questions.

Nevertheless, the interviewer has a job to do. Twain has given his interviewer some ridiculous answers, but the young man must still write an article about Twain for his newspaper.

Connection: Assume you are the young interviewer. Write an article about Twain for your paper based on the information in the excerpt you just read.

Gold is amazing.
A mere cubic inch of it can be
    pulled into a wire 43 miles long
or beaten into a thin sheet that
    covers 1,400 square feet.
Although one of the heaviest of
    metals,
gold can be pounded so thin
    that the slightest breath
will send it floating like a cobweb
    into the air.

Using Numbers and Statistics

> "It is true that the income of the average household has been increasing. But averages often obscure the important details. After all, Shaquille O'Neal and I have an average height of six feet."
>
> —ROBERT REICH, FORMER SECRETARY OF LABOR

Workplace Skills in This Chapter

• Use numerical data as **resources** for information.

• Explain in general terms how **systems** are used to collect, process, and report data.

• Use numerical data and statistical **information** to clarify, inform, and persuade.

• Use **technology** to calculate and convey data.

• Use **interpersonal** skills in gathering and sharing numerical data.

As you complete Chapter 14, you will

* describe common uses of numbers and statistics to inform and persuade.

* identify editorializing when reading about numerical data.

* use editorializing in reporting numerical data.

* define the terms *mean, median,* and *mode.*

* construct and use tables, pie charts, bar graphs, and line graphs to illustrate numerical data.

Gold has fascinated human beings for thousands of years. It is rare and beautiful, hence expensive; but it also has great strength and **ductility**. It can be stretched and pounded into extremely fine wires and transparently thin sheets without breaking. It can hold its shape and function even when it is so thin that a **micrometer** is needed to measure it. We know that some people have spent their lifetimes working with gold. They have weighed and measured it very precisely to arrive at the measurements and observations that opened this chapter. A small part of the numerical data they have calculated can be summed up in one equation that applies uniquely to gold: 1 cubic inch = 43 miles = 1,400 square feet.

Numerical Data Fills Our Lives

Have you ever stopped to realize how many times a day we are confronted with numerical data? Numbers are so much a part of our lives that most of us pay little attention to them. But if you listen closely, you may find dozens of them in just one evening news program.

"The unemployment rate stands at 6.8 percent nationwide."

"Housing starts are down 19 percent since last April."

"Odds are one in 100 that a baby born to a woman over 40 will have Down's syndrome."

"In 1991, approximately 200,000 people in the United States were suffering from AIDS. By 1996 the number exceeded 263,000."

These comments are fairly straightforward. What we don't see is the tremendous amount of research—statistical research—behind what they say. Teams of people had to collect data from throughout the United States. The facts were then compiled, sorted, and analyzed, usually with the aid of computers. (Gathering, sorting, and analyzing numerical data is what statistics is all about.) News writers and analysts then looked through the pages and pages of information to come up with a few short, simple-sounding sentences that were slotted into the news for us to digest.

As you know from math classes, numbers can be put together in many different ways—some simple and some extremely difficult to decipher. We are going to limit ourselves in this chapter to looking at simple kinds of statistics and how they can be used not only to inform but to persuade people to think in certain ways. We will practice explaining facts in statistical terms, illustrating them with charts and graphs, and making them understandable to an audience.

Making Numerical Data Understandable

Businesses and government agencies spend a great deal of time trying to make numerical data understandable to their employees and customers, to other businesses and governments, and to the average person. We refer to the numerical data that they gather and analyze as

CAREER C·O·N·N·E·C·T·I·O·N

In 1997, according to the Cincinnati Enquirer, the average age of a tool and die maker in the United States was 56, and there were 20,000 to 30,000 openings in this trade nationwide. The shortage will be critical as current workers retire. Toolmakers build the tooling that cuts, punches, and shapes metal into the thousands of parts and products basic to our day-to-day lives. A part designed by a tool and die maker—for example, a bracket to guide the headrest on a car seat—might be purchased by an automotive supplier for about $60,000. It will then be used to produce brackets for thousands of automobiles. The precision needed to make such parts requires computerized designing followed by finely detailed workmanship on the part of the toolmaker. Although toolmakers have better-than-average salaries and have good job security, their occupation is unknown by most of the people who daily use the objects made from the parts they produce.

statistics. Statistics are used to clarify information and to help make predictions.

Some people (for example, advertisers and some political activists) use statistics in trying to convince us that we should vote, contribute, or act a certain way (*their* way). So they become expert at setting up the numbers to sway us one way or another. Sometimes the numbers are arranged somewhat deceptively. But once you understand a few basic techniques about using statistics, you're less likely to be fooled by those who use them to try to manipulate you.

Reporting Actual Numbers

When no attempt is made to influence the reader, to make predictions, or to generalize, the facts are reported just as they occur.

* Of the 65 married couples surveyed, 57 owned a dog.
* The results of the vote showed that 21 members of the senior class want to open student council meetings to all students.
* Of the 314 students in our graduating class, 11 were home-schooled until ninth grade.

These are straightforward statements of fact.

Editorializing with Numbers

Since numerical data are usually gathered for a specific purpose and not just for the pure joy of gathering information, those using it often add words and phrases that attempt to make a certain point or influence the audience in some way. Journalists call this practice **editorializing**—trying to do more than simply inform. Editorializing is used when someone is trying to sway the thinking of an audience in some way. A writer or speaker who editorializes wants the audience to make an inference about the information by picking up on certain cue words. Notice the difference when such words are added to the same three sentences that were cited above. The editorializing is underlined.

* Of the 65 married couples surveyed, <u>nearly every one of them</u> (57) owned a dog.

  (Inference the writer or speaker wanted you to make: Almost all married couples own a dog; i.e., dogs are popular with married couples.)

* The results of the vote showed that <u>only</u> 21 members of the <u>entire</u> senior class want to open student council meetings to all students.

  (Inference: The senior class is overwhelmingly against opening student council meetings to all students.)
  What might the inference be if someone instead said, "<u>A solid voting block</u> of 21 seniors want to open student council meetings to all students"? In either case, knowing the size of the senior class would put those 21 members into a clearer perspective.

* Of the 314 students in our graduating class, eleven, <u>including three honors students</u>, were home-schooled until ninth grade.

  (Inference: Having been educated at home doesn't limit a student's ability to achieve honors if he or she decides to return to school.)

Notice that the basic numerical facts have not been changed. But editorializing has subtly—and sometimes not so subtly—told readers how the writer wants them to think about those facts.

Practice 14-1: Editorializing with Numbers

teamwork Each of the following ten sentences is simply and factually stated. Working with a partner, figure out how you can rewrite each sentence, adding words or phrases that might put a different focus or slant on the facts to influence the thinking of an audience in some way (either positively or negatively). (Hint: you may want to change some of the numbers to percents or fractions to make your point stronger.)

EXAMPLE:

Statement of fact: The average income of the American car owner in 1996 was $52,000. The average income of a car owner in Europe was $102,000.

Editorialized statement: Why is it that middle-income people in the United States have to have a car, while in Europe it's those with higher incomes who spend their money on a car?

1. Two out of three married women will outlive their husbands.

2. The average man in the United States is 5 feet 10 inches tall.

3. Banks are paying 2 percent interest on money in savings accounts.

4. Daytime preschool has 20 five-year-olds enrolled, and 12 of them can recite their ABCs.

5. In a vocational student organization calculator contest, 38 percent of the students missed the second problem.

6. Last year 52 percent of high school seniors in the United States enrolled in a four-year college; 40 percent of those enrolled are expected to complete their sophomore year.

7. The U.S. Department of Labor's Bureau of Labor Statistics reported that in 1996 union members accounted for 14.9 percent of wage and salary employees. In 1995 it was 14.9 percent. In 1983 it was 20.1 percent.

8. The new computers have 4.5 gigabytes of memory on the hard drive. Our old computers had 500 megabytes.

9. Ted can enter data into the computer at the rate of 300 keystrokes per minute. The average rate is 200.

10. Twenty years ago VCRs cost approximately $2,600 and used 3/4-inch tape, which cost as much as $25 per reel. Today a VCR can cost less than $200 and videotape cassettes can be purchased for less than $3.

INFOBIT

According to Occupational Outlook Quarterly (1996), 17 percent of college graduates in the 1994 labor force were working in jobs that did not require a college education.

Rounding Numbers

Rounding is used to simplify numbers and make them more understandable to the general public.

Numbers like 527,611,432,112 are pretty unwieldy to use. Unless you are recording or researching information, you probably have no need for such an exact quantity. What is important to a general audience is to have an idea of what this number means. In a headline, it might be reported as "more than 525 billion" or "nearly 530 billion," both of which are close enough to inform people in a factual way and impress them with the quantity.

Which amount would be the rounded number for each of the following?

> **SAMPLE:**
> Round 62 to the nearest ten. (Think of counting by tens: 10, 20, 30, 40, 50, 60, 70. Is 62 closer to 60 or 70?) Remember: If your number is halfway or more than halfway between 60 and 70, the answer is 70. Is it?

1. Round 56 to the nearest 10. (Is 56 closer to 50 or 60?)

2. Round 432 to the nearest hundred. (Is 432 closer to 400 or 500?)

3. Round 9.1 to the nearest whole number. (Think: Is 9.1 closer to 9.0 or 10.0?)

Notice the way numbers are rounded in the news, in sportscasts, and in conversations. Usually some editorializing is done when the rounded number is reported.

For example, when speaking of someone with a salary of $19,850, we could say either of the following:

> He's making nearly $20,000 to start.
> He's making just under $20,000 to start.

In both cases, however, we rounded the salary to the nearest thousand when reporting it.

On certain occasions, even smaller numbers are rounded. When figuring your federal taxes, for example, rounding to the nearest dollar is acceptable. If you owe less than a dollar, you don't have to pay what you owe.

INFOBIT

"Ten men in our country could buy the whole world and ten million can't buy enough to eat."

WILL ROGERS, AMERICAN PERSONALITY AND POLITICAL COMMENTATOR (1931)

Using Ratios and Percentages

A simple way of expressing the relationship between two sets of numbers is by using a ratio. The ratio of men to women in the United States is approximately 49 to 51. For every 49 men there are 51 women.

A percentage is actually a ratio in which everything is compared to 100. (*Percent* means per hundred.) If about 49 out of every 100 persons in the United States are male, we can say that 49 percent of the U.S. population is male. With that information, we can easily figure that 51 percent of the population is female. Those numbers came from adding the millions of people in the 1990 United States census, comparing the numbers of males and females, and reducing those numbers to percents.

CULTURE **C·O·N·N·E·C·T·I·O·N**

Dogs have a unique place in the lives of Americans. Dogs are companions and the bond between human and dog is valued by many. In *The Intelligence of Dogs,* Stanley Coren takes a popular theory of human intelligence and relates it to dogs. He also ranks dogs from most to least intelligent. How did he figure out how to rank them? He sent a questionnaire to more than 400 dog obedience judges asking them to rate the 75 most popular breeds on working and obedience intelligence.

Which breeds were judged worst and best? Of the 199 judges, 121 ranked the Afghan hound one of the ten worst breeds for obedience; 99, the basenji; and 81, the chow chow. For the top ten, 190 named the border collie; 171, the shetland sheep dog; 169, the poodle; and 167, the German shepherd and golden retriever. For your dog's rank, check out pages 182 and 183 of Coren's book.

Susan Spalter Photography

Sometimes the ratios and percentages are reduced to a smaller number (like reducing fractions) and then expressed in a different way. For example:

> 25% = 25/100, or 25 out of every 100
>
> 25/100 can be reduced to 1/4 by dividing both numbers (25 and 100) by the same number: 25.
>
> $$\frac{25}{100} \div \frac{25}{25} = \frac{1}{4}$$
>
> Thus: 25 out of 100 is the same as 1 out of 4.

Generalizing from a Sample Group

Public opinion polls are good examples of the use of smaller numbers of people to represent larger groups. It is usually impossible to count everyone or everything needed to get the desired information, especially if it is needed in a short amount of time. So in news magazines and on radio and television news shows, reporting the results of a poll is a common occurrence. The agency that conducts the poll is mentioned and then a piece of information is often added that readers and listeners may not notice. The information goes something like this:

> In this opinion poll, a representative sampling of 1,000 people were asked whether they believed that women's professional sports will attract large enough crowds and sufficient media coverage within the next ten years to pay the athletes competitive salaries and to provide sports careers for large numbers of young women in the United States. (Margin of error is ± 4 percent.)

In this case, a **representative sample** of 1,000 people would have to represent a cross section of people in the United States in order to get an idea of how the American people felt. That means that men and women from all walks of life, from high, middle, and low income levels, and from a variety of ethnic and religious backgrounds would have to be surveyed. Then their responses would be generalized to the rest of the population (which means that if this group believes something, chances are that the rest of Americans do, too). This technique is acceptable and is fairly accurate if a large enough sample is used and appropriate statistical formulas are followed.

TWO PEOPLE IN A FOCUS GROUP LOVED OUR PRODUCT. SO WE'RE DOUBLING OUR PRODUCTION.

THE OPINIONS OF TWO PEOPLE ARE NOT STATISTICALLY USEFUL...

...ESPECIALLY IF YOU'RE ONE OF THE TWO PEOPLE.

I KNEW THOSE FREE SANDWICHES WERE TOO GOOD TO BE TRUE

DILBERT reprinted by permission of United Feature Syndicate, Inc.

Often, again unnoticed by the average reader or listener, the sampling error is given. The report may say, "The sampling error was plus or minus 5 percent"—a way of saying that the data aren't guaranteed to be 100 percent accurate. In fact, generalizations can never account for 100 percent of reality. To find out how all American people feel or think about anything would require asking every single one of them the same question and recording the answer. We know, of course, that that is impossible to do.

A **random sample** is different from a representative sample. How is a random sample obtained? One old-fashioned way is by lot. To get an idea of how students at a certain school with an enrollment of 850 felt about a certain issue, you could put the name of each student on a small token or card and place it in a large bin. After the bin was shaken or turned many times and all the names were thoroughly mixed, names of students could be drawn from the bin one at a time until, say, 150 students' names were on a list. This 17.6 percent of the student body could be used to predict how the rest of the students might feel about the same issue. Chances are that every grade would be represented, as would both sexes. Students from a variety of neighborhoods and family backgrounds would probably also be represented. Some would be active in sports, some would not, and so on. The point is that all students would have had an equal chance of having their names drawn.

A random sample doesn't necessarily have to equal 17.6 percent of the total group researched. The required percentage depends on a number of mathematical considerations we don't have space to detail here. The important point is that random samples are designed to give us fairly reliable data, because they provide a cross section of the society they represent.

Some researchers use the telephone directory as the basis for a kind of random sampling of a particular city. The researchers pick a name at random and then pick every 50th or 150th name after that. (The number used would depend on the number of names in the phone book and the total number needed for the sampling.) Then the researchers survey those people by telephone. This method is actually called a **systematic sample with a random start.**

With today's modern technology, computers using large databases can produce true random lists for research purposes. However, not everyone has access to such databases. And chances are that you do not. Instead, you will have to use sample groups that are available to you and describe what is true of those groups, without trying to make generalizations.

Claims Based on Questionable Generalizations

In the fictitious report on the poll of 1,000 persons cited on page 477, suppose that the following results were obtained:

* Seventy percent of adults surveyed said that women's professional sports would continue to draw crowds and to gain in popularity in the United States.

* Sixty-five percent said female athletes' salaries would increase, but would not be on a par with male athletes' salaries, in the next ten years.

* Thirty-seven percent said they would buy tickets for and attend games played by female athletes.

* Fifty-two percent agreed that women would have more opportunities to advance in sports careers in the next ten years.

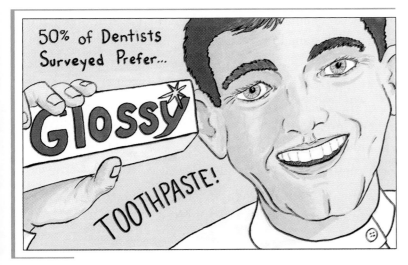

Figure 14-1: *A dentist survey*

Compare these data and the way they were obtained to the advertising claim in Figure 14-1.

In this advertisement, is any information given as to how many dentists were surveyed about their preferences? Is it possible that only four dentists were surveyed, and two of those four said they preferred Glossy toothpaste? After all, two out of four is 50 percent.

Do you think that many readers, not being as critical as you, might read such a statement and believe that 50 percent of all dentists actually prefer this toothpaste? Does the fictitious poll information you just read regarding women's professional sports and opportunities for female athletes answer these kinds of questions?

TECHNOLOGY C·O·N·N·E·C·T·I·O·N

Is agriculture a sticky business? Well, when you discover where glue comes from, you may say yes. Many common glues have for years come from plants and animals, but new high-tech methods have, in many cases, resulted in more dependability and versatility in glues.

Are old horses really sent to the glue factory? Yes. Animal bones are still part of the glues used in cartons and boxes. Other agricultural products are used to produce different kinds of glue. Tapioca is used on stamps, envelopes, and labels. Soybean glue holds plywood together. Fish glue is used in photo mounting, gummed paper, and paints. But not all glue comes from plants and animals. One of the strongest, most heat-resistant glues comes from porcelain enamel grit combined with iron oxide and stainless steel powder. It is heat-resistant to 1,500°F, which is not true of plant and animal glues. (Glover 258–263)

Identifying a Target Group

A **target group** is a subset of the population who would be most likely to provide useful information about the topic in question—so-called because they are targeted by poll-takers or surveyors as a group that has special knowledge or opinions about a subject. If you want to find out how 13-year-olds feel about being a teenager, you don't ask their parents; you ask the 13-year-olds. They are your target group for that particular subject. On the other hand, if you want to find out about the concerns parents have about their teen-aged children, parents of teens would be your target group. In the example of the survey of dentists cited previously, dentists are the target group.

Practice 14-2: Target Groups: Finding the Best Source

Students would be the target group surveyed to find out what students might believe about an issue. Dentists would be the target group surveyed to learn which dental cleaner dentists might prefer. Target groups must be carefully selected to get accurate answers to questions.

The following are eight research questions. For the first five questions, write the letter of the specific group (the target group) that would be the most reliable to survey to get the most accurate responses to each question. Starting with Question 6, there are no choices. You'll have to come up with the choice yourself. Be prepared to defend your answers.

1. How do middle-aged Republicans in Midtown, Iowa, feel about enforced retirement at the age of 65?

   Best target group:

   a. registered Republicans

   b. Republicans between the ages of 40 and 60

   c. registered voters

   d. Republican men between the ages of 35 and 50

WEB LINK

You can find limitless amounts of numerical data dealing with almost any subject on the Internet, and it's easy to find. If you're new to the Internet and want to find out about technical or liberal arts college information, for example, the easiest way to start is with search tools like Yahoo or Hotbot.

2. How many health-care workers in your town are smokers?

Best target group:

   a. tobacco companies' sales staff

   b. local hospital and medical office workers

   c. personnel in Smoke-Stoppers' Clinic

   d. doctors' spouses

3. What kind of training does the average home health-care worker in your town or city have?

Best target group:

   a. people who have hired home health-care workers

   b. human resources staff in a local technical college that has a home health-care program

   c. home health-care workers in your town

   d. representatives from agencies in your town that supply home health-care workers

4. How many workers in the local textile mill are satisfied with their jobs?

Best target group:

   a. high school students whose parents work in the textile mill

   b. supervisors of each department at the mill

   c. workers from each department at the mill

   d. union stewards at the mill

5. How do incoming ninth-grade girls in your school feel about studying math?

Best target group:

   a. math teachers at your school

   b. incoming ninth-graders

   c. your school counselors

   d. incoming ninth-grade girls

6. How do teenage fathers feel about helping to raise their children?

Best target group:

7. Do parents of 15- to 18-year-olds trust their children?

Best target group:

8. Do coaches push high school athletes in training beyond what should be physically allowed?

Best target group:

PEOPLE C·O·N·N·E·C·T·I·O·N

In 1964, when Lee Iacocca was general manager of the Ford Division of Ford Motor Company, the Mustang was introduced to the American public. It was small, sporty, strong in performance, and inexpensive, while other cars had gotten longer, wider, and more expensive every year.

After a great deal of publicity, including pictures on the covers of both *TIME* and *Newsweek,* the little car showed up in dealers' showrooms to record crowds of potential buyers. During its first year on the market, it broke all sales records for new Ford automobiles. It is now a collector's classic.

Iacocca notes in his autobiography that many people observed that the horse symbol on the front of the car was running the wrong way, because horses on a track run counterclockwise. His response: "the Mustang was a wild horse, not a domesticated race horse. And no matter which way it was running, I felt increasingly sure that it was headed in the right direction."

Ways of Looking at Groups of Numbers

When large groups of numbers are gathered, three types of simple analyses will help to reveal certain facts or trends about the group:

* Figuring the mean (the average)

* Finding the median (the midpoint)

* Looking at the mode (the most common number)

The Mean

The **mean** is simply the average, as in "The mean (average) age of the group is 25" or "The mean (average) score on the test in this class was 82 percent."

The mean test score for a given group is obtained by adding all the scores and dividing by the total number of scores. For example, here are 21 scores that students received on an American Government test:

TEST SCORES FOR AMERICAN GOVERNMENT CLASS, SECTION 402

54	82	86
66	84	88
66	84	88
72	84	94
74	84	98
74	84	100
82	86	100

Table 14-1

When the scores from all three columns in Table 14–1 are added, the total is 1,730.

Divide the total by 21:

The mean is 82.38.

$$21\overline{)1730.00}^{82.38}$$

What is the mean for each of the following groups of numbers? Round your answers to the nearest tenth.

Group X: 6, 6, 7, 9, 2, 8, 1, 5, 6

Group Y: 54, 66, 71, 73, 84, 87, 88, 91

TECHNOBIT

"... in most American households, the only people who understand how to program modern electronic devices are the children. So the V chip will presumably have to be managed by the very people it is meant to control."

CALVIN TRILLIN,
AMERICAN HUMORIST

The Median

The **median** is the midpoint. This is not the same as an average. To find the median, you simply arrange the scores in numerical order, as has been done in the list of American Government test scores in Table 14-1. Then you count down to the exact middle of the list.

List all the scores, either from low to high or from high to low. (The answer will be the same.) Then count to the halfway point in the class. That point is the median.

Identify the median in each of the following sets of numbers. The first one is identified with a circle.

1. 1, 2, ③, 4, 5

2. 0, 1, 2, 2, 5, 55, 90, 98, 98

3. 96, 88, 86, 60, 76, 74, 72

4. 121, 110, 79, 61, 42, 33, 19

You've probably noticed that every set contained an odd number of numbers. How would you figure the median if there were an even number of numbers in the set (as in the following example)?

1, 2, 2, 5, 55, 90, 98, 98

The median is between the 5 and the 55.

Add the 5 and the 55 together (5 + 55 = 60).

The median is 30 (midway between 5 and 55).

Can you identify the median in each of the following sets of numbers?

1. 16, 16, 19, 20, 21, 22, 23, 23, 24

2. 79, 77, 68, 42, 34, 22, 10, 8

3. 33, 34, 35, 38, 40, 44, 46, 51, 55, 60

4. 33, 34, 34, 38, 41, 44, 46, 51, 55, 60

The Mode

The **mode** is defined as the most common number—that is, the one that occurs most frequently. What is the most common number in this list: 1, 2, 2, 2, 3, 4, 5, 5? The answer is 2. There are more 2s than any other number. Therefore, 2 is the mode.

In the following list, there is no mode:

> 1, 2, 3, 4, 5, 6, 7, 8

Fact: Every group of numbers has a mean and a median. Not every group has a mode.

What is the mode in the following groups of numbers?

> 1. 97, 98, 99, 100, 101, 101, 101, 102, 103
>
> 2. 3, 4, 4, 5, 6, 6, 7, 7, 7, 7, 7, 7, 8, 8, 9, 10

Sometimes there is more than one mode, as in the following set of numbers:

> ③,③, 4,⑤,⑤, 6, 7

Is there a mode in the list of American Government test scores in Table 14-1?

Using Numerals When No Quantity Is Involved

Numerals can be used to indicate real quantities, as in

Count them. There are four.

Numerals can also be used in **performance ratings** and in reporting **subjective data.**

Figure 14-2: *The judges gave Mary Jo an 8.5 rating on her balance beam performance.*

Performance Ratings

Can you count the 8.5 in Mary Jo's performance rating? No, because it does not represent 8.5 things. The 8.5 that the judges gave her is not a real numerical quantity, even though we act as though it is. It is simply a judgment as to where Mary Jo ranks on a scale of 1 to 10 in her performance. We add up all the judges' ratings and divide by the number of judges to get the mean (average) number of rating points for her performance. This procedure is followed for each gymnast. The one with the highest mean score wins.

Similarly, grades of A, B, C, D, or F cannot be averaged without some number to accompany them. That is why someone developed the idea of quality points. Depending on where you go to school, an A may receive three, four, or five quality points. An A in an advanced-placement college-prep class may receive one or two extra points.

Let's say that your school is on a four-point system, and you have the following grades:

History	B
Physical Education	B
English	C
Algebra II	A
CAD Lab	A
	??? Impossible to average

With quality points, your average looks like this:

History	B = 3	
Physical Education	B = 3	
English	C = 2	
Algebra II	A = 4	
CAD Lab	A = 4	
	16	

$$\begin{array}{r} 3.2 \\ 5{\overline{\smash{\big)}\,16.0}} \\ \underline{15} \\ 10 \\ \underline{10} \\ 0 \end{array}$$

In figuring class rank, a B with a 3.2 quality-point average would outrank a 3.0. Thus, several students can have B averages, but be higher or lower than one another in class rank. Class rank could not be figured unless some numerical value were given to the letter grades. (Some schools do not have to calculate quality points since they use percentage grades. The percentages can be averaged.)

Subjective Data

Subjective data are clusters of information obtained about how people feel or think. Often, as in the case of the judges of Mary Jo's balance beam performance, those judgments are given a number.

However, judges of performances are not the only sources of subjective, nonnumerical data. In testing their clients, psychologists often use attitude scales, which involve using a number to indicate a response. A sample follows.

SAMPLE ATTITUDE SCALE

Circle the number on each scale that best describes how you feel right now.

Happy	1	2	3	4	5	6	7	Sad
Optimistic	1	2	3	4	5	6	7	Pessimistic
Wise	1	2	3	4	5	6	7	Foolish

Table 14-2

Notice that all the positive descriptive words are on the left, nearest the 1, and all the negative words are on the right, nearest the 7. If the average of all answers is 2.5, is the person feeling more positive or more negative today?

Accurate conclusions cannot be made by comparing 30 people's attitudes numerically, because attitudes are not measurable quantities. The numbers on the scale may represent something completely different to each person who participates in the survey. Special care must be taken in interpreting and using such data.

Using Tables, Charts, and Graphs

Tables, charts, and graphs are organized, attention-getting ways to present information. After surveys or other forms of research are concluded, some type of summary or report is usually made. Tables, pie charts, line graphs, and bar graphs are clear, easy-to-read ways of summarizing data.

Tables

Tables contain organized lists of information, arranged in columns and rows. For example, a student in animal science or wildlife management might find the following table of reproductive cycles of selected animals familiar:

HEAT AND GESTATION PERIODS OF SMALL MAMMALS

Mammal	Duration of Heat	Gestation Period (in days)
Ferret	Continuous, March to August	42
Guinea pig	6-11 days	67
Gerbil	4 days	24-26
Hamster	20 hours	18
Rat	13-15 hours	22
Mouse	10 hours	19

Table 14-3

All tables do not have to have three columns. The number of columns you use is dictated by the information and how it can best be arranged. Notice in Table 14-3 that each column is given a heading that describes the data in it. Selecting the right heading is important in helping the reader understand information at a glance. Tables like this may be used for handy reference when you are asking questions like, "What is the gestation period for a guinea pig?" They may also be used for comparison purposes, to answer a question like, "Do smaller animals have shorter gestation periods than larger animals?"

The most important column, or the one that is designed to be the comparison point or focal point for the reader, is put into some order—chronological, alphabetical, numerical (high to low or low to high), or some other logical arrangement. If the writer wanted to make it easier for the reader to find the animals' names, listing them in alphabetical order would be a good idea. Then, of course, the order of the information in the second and third columns would change. In Table 14-3, which column was the basis for arranging the rest of the information and thus was placed in a particular order?

Also notice that the table uses technical terms like *gestation,* since it is designed to be read by specialists, students of animal science. What changes would have to be made for a general audience?

Tables are labeled sequentially, beginning with "Table 1." If you're doing a research paper in animal science and including information on birds in Chapter 1, small mammals in Chapter 2, and reptiles in Chapter 3, the table on small mammals could be labeled "Table 2-1" (for Chapter 2, Table 1).

Practice 14-3: Putting Information into a Table

Read the following paragraph of detailed information, and decide how it can be organized into three columns. Then make a descriptive title for each column. Finally, using table construction software, if available, (as you did in Chapter 12) or the table form on *Student Workbook* page 14-A, arrange the information in a logical, readable way on the form. (A table title and setup have already been provided for you on *Student Workbook* page 14-A.)

Road construction fatalities in the Tri-State area from 1990 through 1995 often involved trucks. Causes of some of the deaths, and the places and times where they occurred, are as follows: struck by on-site truck, West Village (1990); on-site truck backed into victim, Sussex County (1991); fell off truck, Washington (1992); on-site truck backed into victim, Bluefield (1992); dump box fell from truck onto victim, Washington (1994); truck backed into victim, Mt. Storm (1994); hit by side of truck, Bills County (1995); truck ran through barricade, Jefferson County (1995).

Pie Charts

Pie charts, also known as circle graphs, got their name because they look like pies cut into slices. Pie charts always start with a circle. The circle represents 100 percent of something—the whole thing. The slices represent the parts of the whole.

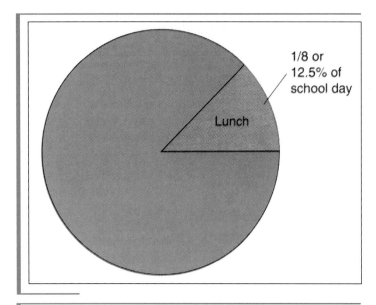

1/8 or 12.5% of school day

Lunch

Pie charts are important tools that are used to illustrate, persuade, or compare. For example, you already know what a small portion of time your lunch period is compared to the rest of the day. But when it is illustrated in a pie chart, the lunch break appears as small as it seems to you—extremely small.

The circle in Figure 14-3 represents Jason D'Amato's monthly income of $2,000. To figure out how to divide the circle, we first had to list each expense and then divide it by his total monthly income of $2,000. (See Table 14-4.) This told us what percentage of Jason's income is used for each expense. Every dollar had to be accounted for, since the pie chart had to show 100 percent of his income.

Every month, $400 is withheld from Jason's pay to cover taxes and Social Security. Jason then has to spend $500 on rent and $200 on his car payment. He usually spends about $400 a month on food, most of which he has to cook himself to save money. He is forcing himself to start saving money, so he is putting $50 a month into his savings account. He makes monthly installment payments on car and medical insurance, totaling $150 each month. The rest of his income is left for clothes, entertainment, and other expenses like household supplies and car upkeep. What percent does he have left for clothes, entertainment, and other expenses?

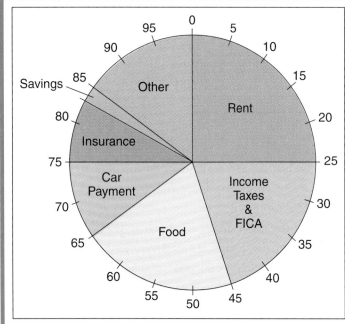

Figure 14-3: *Distribution of Jason's income*

Practice 14-4: Constructing a Pie Chart

Using page 14-B of your *Student Workbook,* complete the following:

1. Make a list of your activities for one day (24 hours). Include sleeping, eating, studying, working at a part-time job, playing basketball, or anything else you do.

2. Figure out how many hours or what part of an hour each activity takes. Some activities, like sleeping, may take eight hours. Others, like washing your car, may take only half an hour.

FIGURING JASON D'AMATO'S EXPENSES AS PERCENTAGES OF HIS INCOME

Item	Cost (Part of Income)	÷	Whole Income	=	Percentage of Income
Taxes & FICA	$400	÷	$2,000	=	20%
Rent	500	÷	2,000	=	25%
Car payment	200	÷	2,000	=	10%
Food	400	÷	2,000	=	20%
Insurance	150	÷	2,000	=	7.5%
Savings	50	÷	2,000	=	2.5%
Clothes & other expenses	300	÷	$2,000	=	15%
Total	$2,000				100%

Table 14-4

TECHNOBIT

When using a computer to make a chart or graph, you must enter information into a table before the software can translate it into a chart or graph. If you use the chart function in Microsoft Word, for example, clicking on the chart icon will cause a table to appear on the screen. Only after you enter data into the table can it be converted by Microsoft Word into the chart or graph of your choice.

3. Then figure what percent of your day each activity represents. Divide the number of hours spent on the activity by 24 (the number of hours in a day). If these numbers do not divide evenly, carry your answer to one decimal place.

EXAMPLE:

Sleeping may take 8 hours out of 24 hours.

Divide the 24 into 8.

$$24\overline{)8.000} \quad .333 = 33.3\%$$

4. Construct a pie chart showing the percentage of time you spend on each activity. Each line on the rim of the circle represents 5 percent of your day.

Line Graphs

Line graphs, like pie charts, turn numbers into drawings. The use of a line graph helps make the numbers more meaningful to the reader, because it makes a visual comparison between two kinds of change. In business a line graph often shows change in dollars earned from month to month or from year to year, so the comparison is between money and time.

QUALITY

C·O·N·N·E·C·T·I·O·N

Technology is making bloodless, non-invasive surgery more and more common. In the past, the surgery was sometimes as bad as the illness it was meant to cure. Severe trauma due to such practices as making large incisions to remove relatively small cysts and tumors required long recovery periods. Now surgery uses "keyholes rather than manholes" to reach diseased organs and remove them. In fact, in some surgeries radio waves are replacing scalpels. According to *Newsweek* writers Geoffrey Cowley and Anne Underwood, "Well-targeted radio waves can alleviate everything from joint injuries to prostate tumors without the pain or complications of traditional surgery" and require minimal recovery time besides. Now that's what we can all call 'Quality Improvement.'"

In the chart on the left, the comparison is between a child's size (in this case, weight) and time (age in years). So the graph shows gain in weight over time.

Graphs are usually plotted on graph paper if they are drawn by hand. Each vertical line that cuts through the baseline represents a number—in this case, a child's age in years: .5, 1.0, 1.5, and so on, up to 5 years. Each space between the lines, then, stands for a half year (6 months).

Each horizontal line that cuts through the vertical lines represents 5 pounds of the child's weight. Notice that a dark dot marking the child's weight at birth is placed at 0 on the horizontal line (because he or she is 0 years old) and just past the 5 on the vertical line (to indicate a weight of 6.5 pounds). The child's weight at 6 months is 12 pounds, so the dot is placed on the spot where the half-year (.5) line crosses the 12 line (between the 10- and 15-pound lines). The remainder of the dots show the amount of weight gain every 6 months until the child reaches five years of age.

Both increases and decreases can be illustrated well with a line graph. But line graphs can be misleading. Compare the two charts at the top of page 491. Which company is growing faster, based on employees on payroll? What do these two graphs tell you about the use of line graphs?

Practice 14-5: Drawing a Line Graph

Using graph paper, create a line graph to illustrate the following data: Westport Technical College had enrollments over a ten-year period as follows: 931 in 1988; 960 in 1989; 1,114 in 1990; 1,107 in 1991; 1,225 in 1992; 1,280 in 1993; 1,355 in 1994; 1,378 in 1995; 1,401 in 1996; and 1,412 in 1997.

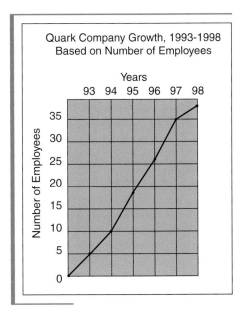

Quark Company Growth, 1993-1998
Based on Number of Employees

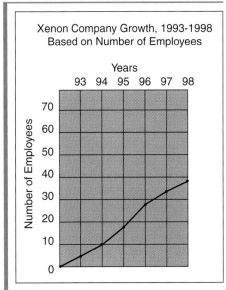

Xenon Company Growth, 1993-1998
Based on Number of Employees

Bar Graphs

Bar graphs usually compare two or more things in relation to time or space. The bars may be either vertical or horizontal. Vertical bars are used in the bar graph on page 492, which compares income per capita for four regions of the United States for 1980 and for 1993. A different-colored bar is used for each of the years for easier visual comparison.

BRAKING DISTANCES FOR FIVE SMALL, INEXPENSIVE COUPES

From 60 Mph

Make and Model	On Dry Pavement	On Wet Pavement
1996 Honda Civic	136'	152'
1996 Nissan 200SX	125'	136'
1996 Volkswagen Golf	134'	149'
1996 Pontiac Sunfire	135'	153'
1996 Dodge Neon	140'	153'

Table 14-5

Source: Consumer Reports, *May 1996*

Practice 14-6: Creating a Bar Graph

Using a computer with a software package such as Microsoft Word, create a bar graph using the information in Table 14-5. The table compares four cars, showing the distance it takes each to stop from 60 miles per hour on both dry pavement and wet pavement. If a computer is not available, use graph paper to construct your graph.

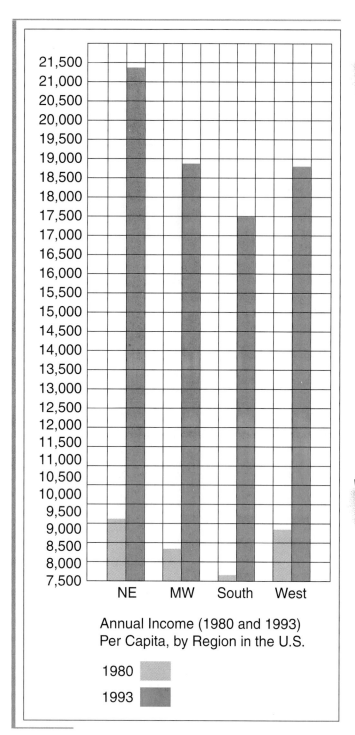

Annual Income (1980 and 1993)
Per Capita, by Region in the U.S.

1980
1993

Source: U.S. Bureau of Economic Analysis

SUMMARY

Numerical data is everywhere. It can be informative, but it can also be misleading. In gathering and reporting information, it is important to be able to use statistics and other numerical information to your advantage, especially in the following ways:

* Recognize when numbers are used accurately or inaccurately.

* Understand and use common terms like *sample group, mean,* and *median.*

* Recognize that all numbers used do not represent real numerical quantities—some are merely ratings.

* Read charts and graphs.

* Design charts and graphs to illustrate numerical information you have collected.

WORKS CITED

Cowley, Geoffrey, and Underwood, Ann. "2000, The Power of Invention." *Newsweek* Special Issue, Winter 1997-98: 77-78.

Glover, Thomas J. *Pocket Ref.* Littleton, Colorado: Sequoia Publishing, 1995.

Iacocca, Lee. *Iacocca: An Autobiography.* New York: Bantam, 1984.

————— "Midwives of Manufacturing." *The Cincinnati Enquirer,* 20 July 1997.

Illustrating Statistical Information

For this Project you will use either

* the data from your customer satisfaction questionnaire Project in Chapter 13 ("Interviewing for Information") or

* information that you research for this purpose on the Internet, in an almanac, or in other sources.

1. Fill out the Project Plan on *Student Workbook* page 14-C.

2. Illustrate the data for a general audience accurately and neatly by first putting it into a table (use table construction software, if available). If you do not have access to table construction software, use the table format on page 14-D of your *Student Workbook* to set up your information.

3. Then convert the table into (1) a pie chart, (2) a line graph, or (3) a bar graph. Use computer software if at all possible. It will give your Project a more professional look. If you do not have access to software with graphing capabilities, use either the pie chart forms on page 14-E of the *Student Workbook* or graph paper to illustrate your data. Refer to appropriate parts of this chapter for assistance on how to set up each of these illustrations, if necessary.

4. Write a short explanation telling

* how you gathered the information,

* why you illustrated it the way you did, and

* what conclusions can be drawn from the illustration.

5. Ask a classmate to check your work and use the Rough Draft column of your Project Guide (page 14-F in your *Student Workbook*) to evaluate the entire Project, including the explanation, the table, and the graph or chart.

6. After making adjustments as needed on your Project, check it again using the Final Draft column of your Project Guide.

7. Give your Project and the Project Guide to your teacher for final evaluation.

You may wish to save this Project to use as part of your report Project in Chapter 15 ("Presenting Reports").

Overview

W. H. Auden often wrote against the grain of Modernism and the technology that he feared would dehumanize us. Modernism is a series of artistic movements in the twentieth century. The movements have characteristics in common: to be new and different, to experiment with new forms, to innovate, to startle, and sometimes to shock. Modernistic literature often uses previously taboo subjects, gives attention to psychological insights, and uses imaginative symbols to evoke an emotional response in readers. The stream-of-consciousness technique of telling a story that tries to duplicate the inner workings of the characters' minds is an example of this movement in literature.

Auden wrote this poem in 1935 when he returned to England after living in Europe for a period of time. The poem is autobiographical, and the unknown citizen in the poem is Auden himself in the act of rediscovering his homeland. "The Unknown Citizen" is a satirical view of the tendency of modern society to depersonalize its citizens. Notice the use of words such as "normal," "sensible," and "necessary." The poem asks two important questions about the citizen: "Was he free? Was he happy?"

"The Unknown Citizen"

(To JS/07/M/378
This Marble Monument
Is Erected by the State)

He was found by the Bureau of Statistics to be
One against whom there was no official complaint.
And all the reports on his conduct agree
That, in the modern sense of an old-fashioned word, he was a
    saint.
For in everything he did he served the Greater Community.
Except for the War till the day he retired
He worked in a factory and never got fired,
But satisfied his employers, Fudge Motors Inc.
Yet he wasn't a scab or odd in his views,
For his Union reports that he paid his dues.
(Our report on his Union shows it was sound.)
And our Social Psychology workers found

That he was popular with his mates and liked a drink.
The Press are convinced that he bought a paper every day
And that his reactions to advertisements were normal in every way.
Policies taken out in his name prove that he was fully insured.
And his Health-card shows he was once in hospital but left it cured.
Both Producers Research and High-Grade Living declare
He was fully sensible to the advantages of the Installment Plan
And had everything necessary to the Modern Man,
A phonograph, a radio, a car and a frigidaire.
Our researchers into Public Opinion are content
That he held the proper opinions for the time of year;
When there was peace, he was for peace; when there was war,
    he went.
He was married and added five children to the population,
Which our Eugenist says was the right number for a parent of his
    generation,
And our teachers report that he never interfered with their
    education.
Was he free? Was he happy? The question is absurd:
Had anything been wrong, we should certainly have heard.

—W. H. Auden

Start-Up: The citizen in the poem is identified by all of the records available to define who he was, what he did, and how he compared to others living at the same time. The specifics of his life were a matter of public record. But what can we infer from these facts? What might we conclude about him as a person because he was for peace during peaceful times and volunteered to fight during wars? Look at the other "facts on record" and see what additional conclusions about the unknown citizen you might draw.

Connection: Today we are identified by numbers as well as facts of public record. Take five minutes and list in a column all of the numbers by which you can be identified (driver's license, social security, credit card, and so on). Your list should probably contain at least 20 numbers. Next to the numbers, write at least one conclusion that might be made about you from the numbers you've listed (e.g., a library card number might lead someone to conclude you enjoy reading). Then write a paragraph about yourself as revealed by the numbers and their implications. Write a second paragraph in which you describe yourself in ways that no numbers or facts of public record could ever reveal. Use specific examples to support your points.

Overview

From July 4, 1845, to September 6, 1847, Henry David Thoreau lived alone in a house he built for himself on the shore of Walden Pond, near his home in Concord, Massachusetts. Thoreau argued the validity of the simple life in *Walden,* a book of his essays.

In the following excerpt from his chapter on economy, Thoreau says that "The mass of men lead lives of quiet desperation" because they are in such a hurry they never stop to ask what is really necessary for their lives. He says that people need, after food, a shelter to keep themselves warm, but a shelter that requires all their energy simply to pay for it is not necessary. According to Thoreau, people should struggle to free themselves from such a condition. His experiment on Walden Pond was to free himself. In March he started building himself a house by cutting some tall white pine trees for timber. By April the house was standing, costing a grand total of 28.12\frac{1}{2}$.

from Walden

By the words, *necessary of life,* I mean whatever, of all that man obtains by his own exertions, has been from the first, or from long use has become, so important to human life that few, if any, whether from savageness, or poverty, or philosophy, ever attempt to do without it. To many creatures there is in this sense but one necessary of life, Food. To the bison of the prairie it is a few inches of palatable grass, with water to drink; unless he seeks the Shelter of the forest or the mountain's shadow. None of the brute creation requires more than Food and Shelter. The necessaries of life for man in this climate may, accurately enough, be distributed under the several heads of Food, Shelter, Clothing, and Fuel; for not till we have secured these are we prepared to entertain the true problems of life with freedom and a prospect of success. Man has invented, not only houses, but clothes and cooked food; and possibly from the accidental discovery of the warmth of fire, and the consequent use of it, at first a luxury, arose the present necessity to sit by it. We observe cats and dogs acquiring the same second nature. By proper Shelter and Clothing we legitimately retain our own internal heat; but with an excess of these, or Fuel, that is, with an external heat greater than our own internal, may not cookery properly be said to begin?. . .

As for Shelter, I will not deny that this is now a necessary of life, though there are instances of men having done without it for long periods in colder countries than this. . . .

Near the end of March, 1845, I borrowed an axe and went down to the woods by Walden Pond, nearest to where I intended to build my house, and began to cut down some tall, arrowy white pines, still in their youth, for timber. It is difficult to begin without borrowing, but perhaps it is the most generous course thus to permit your fellow-men to have an interest in your enterprise. The owner of the axe, as he released his hold on it, said that it was the apple of his eye; but I returned it sharper than I received it. . . .

I hewed the main timbers six inches square, most of the studs on two sides only, and the rafters and floor timbers on one side, leaving the rest of the bark on, so that they were just as straight and much stronger than sawed ones. Each stick was carefully mortised or tenoned by its stump, for I had borrowed other tools by this time. My days in the woods were not very long ones; yet I usually carried my dinner of bread and butter, and read the newspaper in which it was wrapped, at noon, sitting amid the green pine boughs which I had cut off, and to my bread was imparted some of their

> . . . with the help of some of my acquaintances, rather to improve so good an occasion for neighborliness than from any necessity, I set up the frame of my house.

fragrance, for my hands were covered with a thick coat of pitch. Before I had done I was more the friend than the foe of the pine tree, though I had cut down some of them, having become better acquainted with it. Sometimes a rambler in the wood was attracted by the sound of my axe, and we chatted pleasantly over the chips which I had made. . . .

By the middle of April, for I made no haste in my work, but rather made the most of it, my house was framed and ready for the raising. . . .

At length, in the beginning of May, with the help of some of my acquaintances, rather to improve so good an occasion for neighborliness than from any necessity, I set up the frame of my house. No man was ever more honored in the character of his raisers than I. They are destined, I trust, to assist at the raising of loftier structures one day. I began to occupy my house on the 4th of July, as soon as it was boarded and roofed, for the boards were carefully feather-edged and lapped, so that it was perfectly impervious to rain, but before boarding I laid the foundation of a chimney at one end, bringing two cartloads of stones up the hill from the pond in my arms. I built the chimney after my hoeing in the fall, before a fire became necessary for warmth, doing my

(cont'd on next page)

cooking the meanwhile out of doors on the ground, early in the morning: which mode I still think is in some respects more convenient and agreeable than the usual one. . . .

I have thus a tight shingled and plastered house, ten feet wide by fifteen long, and eight-feet posts, with a garret and a closet, a large window on each side, two trap-doors, one door at the end and a brick fireplace opposite. The exact cost of my house, paying the usual price for such materials as I used, but not counting the work, all of which was done by myself, was as follows; and I give the details because very few are able to tell exactly what their houses cost, and fewer still, if any, the separate cost of the various material which compose them:

Boards $8.03½
Mostly shanty boards.
Refuse shingles for roof
　and sides 4.00
Laths...1.25
Two second-hand windows
　with glass 2.43
One thousand old brick 4.00

Two casks of lime 2.40
Hair...0.31
That was high. More than I needed.
Mantle-tree iron 0.15
Nails...3.90
Hinges and screws 0.14
Latch 0.10
Chalk 0.01
Transportation 1.40
I carried a good part on my back.
　In all.................................28.12½

These are all the materials, excepting the timber, stones, and sand, which I claimed by squatter's right. I have also a small woodshed adjoining, made chiefly of the stuff which was left after building the house.

I intend to build me a house which will surpass any on the main street in Concord in grandeur and luxury, as soon as it pleases me as much and will cost me no more than my present one.

I thus found that the student who wishes for a shelter can obtain one for a lifetime at an expense not greater than the rent which he now pays annually.

—Henry David Thoreau

Start-Up: Having the ability to work effectively with numbers is important throughout your life. Number puzzles are fun to solve and help you develop your mathematics skills.

Connection: Make this activity a competitive one. Work in pairs to solve the puzzles on the following page.

Puzzle 1
If Bill Gates of Microsoft, who was reportedly worth $40 billion in 1997, spent $40 million building his home, how much should Thoreau be worth if the $28.13 he spent building his home was equally proportionate to Bill Gates's worth?

Puzzle 2
A Horse and a Pig
Thoreau bought a horse and a pig for $85. The horse cost $55 more than the pig. How much did Thoreau pay for the pig?

Puzzle 3
Thoreau's Jarring Experience
There are two jars of equal capacity. In the first jar there is one amoeba. In the second jar there are two amoebas. An amoeba can reproduce itself in three minutes. It takes the two amoebas in the second jar three hours to fill the jar to capacity. How long will it take the one amoeba in the first jar to fill that jar to capacity?

Puzzle 4
Thoreau's Zoo Story
Thoreau: How many birds and how many beasts do you have in your zoo?
Zookeeper: There are 30 heads and 100 feet.
Thoreau: I can't tell from that!
Zookeeper: Oh, yes, you can!
Can you?

"As the group [of students] hiked along a private field road on the Don Ney Farm, they noticed many frogs hopping about. . . . At one point, students accused each other of injuring the frogs because their legs were 'weird.' However, it wasn't long before they realized that this was not an injury problem—it was a developmental problem!

"Immediately, students pulled out notebooks and began collecting data about the frogs they were catching. Fully 50% of the frogs caught that day had deformities of their hind legs."

—Ryan Fisher,
10th grade,
Minnesota New Country School

Presenting Reports

> "The last thing one discovers in composing a work is what to put first."

—BLAISE PASCAL, FRENCH SCIENTIST AND PHILOSOPHER

Workplace Skills in This Chapter

- Use all available **resources** to produce a comprehensive and effective report.

- Employ **interpersonal** skills in working with others to produce a report.

- Analyze, interpret, and present **information.**

- Develop **systems** for presenting information.

- Use **technology** to find, test, record, and report information.

As you complete Chapter 15, you will

- describe four types of reports: the field report, laboratory report, progress report, and proposal (persuasive report).

- write a clear, concise conclusion.

- write an informal progress report.

- plan, write, and revise a laboratory report, a field report, or a proposal (persuasive report).

Students always seem to be writing reports—book reports, research papers, history reports, and so on. And what for? To let their teachers know that they have learned something and that they can write effectively about it.

In the world of business, industry, and science, reports are not designed to prove what you know or have learned, unless you are in training. They are simply ways of organizing information that will help a business, industry, or scientific organization to succeed in some way. They pull together information that someone needs.

Reasons for Reports in the Work World

Reports may be designed to inform, persuade, or justify a position. They convey information specific to a particular task. Reports sometimes involve original research, but they may also involve gathering information from research done by others and making it available to those who need it.

Reports can take many forms. They can be formal or informal, handwritten or laser-printed. They can be extensive and full of footnotes. They can be succinct and illustrated with original diagrams, charts, or photographs. They can be produced to be shown in full color on a computer screen using presentation software. They can be launched on the Internet. But in all cases, they contain information that someone—or a group of someones—needs.

The importance of well-researched reports can be illustrated in two real-life examples. In each case, a situation exists that demands extensive, specialized research and reporting. In the first case, the demand was met, and a large business venture succeeded. In the second, the demand was not met, and a near-disaster ensued.

Example 1: A Fried Chicken Franchise Goes to Japan

A fried chicken franchise plans to open a restaurant in Japan. However, the owners know that the average person in Japan is used to different kinds of seasonings on food than are commonly used in the southern United States, where the chicken seasoning recipe was developed. The owners also realize that there are different habits and customs in other countries. For their restaurant, they want to know what kind of external appearance, interior decorating, seating arrangement, manner of ordering food, and use of signs and symbols would be most attractive to the Japanese. So market researchers from the fried chicken company are sent to Japan to find the answers to these questions. Then, because they wish to attract customers and make money there, the owners of the business adjust the way they cook, design their restaurants, and serve their food to suit their potential Japanese customers. The fast-food restaurant is a success.

Example 2: Hillside Disaster

A civil engineer is hired by a major city in the Midwest to design a new bridge and freeway linkages for the downtown area. Unfortunately, though the engineer is familiar with the solid bedrock of his home state in the Northeast, he is unfamiliar with the shale under the surface of the midwestern city that has hired him. Worse still, he either fails to require sufficient research or ignores important parts of the research report warning him of the effects the shale may have on his project. As a result, part of his roadbed is cut through the toe of a hill, releasing loose shale, and an entire historic neighborhood is endangered as homes begin to slide down the hill with the loosened soil.

These two examples represent large-scale needs for **field research** and reporting that may take months or years to complete. In smaller businesses, information is needed and reports are made every day. These reports may range from those informal enough to be included as part of a memo, letter, or conversation to printed booklets dozens of pages in length, with elaborate and expensive photographs, graphs, and charts.

Regardless of how elaborate or how simple reports may be, they tend to fall into categories or types. In this chapter you will find four types of reports, with examples of each, that are used in a variety of job settings. Even early in your career, you may be asked to present reports like these, particularly if you are hired by a small- to medium-size business. If you become familiar with these types of reports, they'll be familiar when you encounter them at work.

In this chapter we will focus on the field report, the laboratory report, the proposal (a type of persuasive report), and the progress report.

Field Reports

Field reporting literally means reporting information found in the field. *The field* is a general term for the world outside a particular department or outside the business headquarters—perhaps a construction site, an automobile test track, a shopping mall, an oil field, a pond, or a pasture. The field is wherever you have to go to get the answers you need.

Questions That Require Field Research and Reports

In completing the survey Project in Chapter 13, you were actually doing a field study. You asked a variety of people what they thought about something and then tallied their responses. Surveying is one way of getting information, but other ways are possible. If the government wants to know how many people are in the country, it can conduct a census and count the number of people. But to find out how many sets of quadruplets were born in a certain hospital in the past ten years, a person would have to search birth records. If someone is looking for the names of his or her ancestors, genealogical records containing information on many generations of families, including birth, marriage, and death dates, can be explored.

An Example of a Student Group's Field Study That Gained National Attention

An excellent example of a field study that resulted in many other studies and reports is described in the following information published on the Internet:

THE DISCOVERY

The discovery occurred on an intended hike through the Ney Woods, which is part of a Wildlife Game Refuge near Henderson, MN. As the group hiked along a private field road on the Don Ney Farm, they noticed many frogs hopping about. As kids are prone to do, the students began catching frogs for fun. At one point, students accused each other of injuring the frogs because their legs were "weird." However, it wasn't long before they realized that this was not an injury problem—it was a developmental problem!

Immediately, students pulled out notebooks and began collecting data about the frogs they were catching. Fully 50% of the frogs caught that day had deformities of their hind legs. Many had one leg which was underdeveloped and webbed together, preventing normal function. One frog captured that day had only one hind leg, while another had two feet on one leg and a bony protrusion from the spine.

Following their return to school, students developed a list of questions to pursue. Frogs were photographed with a QuickTake camera to put on the Internet. Phone calls were made regarding types of farm chemicals used in the area. Cindy Reinitz, the teacher, made a series of phone calls which would eventually lead her to Judy Helgen, a research scientist at the Minnesota Pollution Control Agency.

The excerpt above tells about the accidental discovery of deformed frogs by students in a Nature Studies class in August of 1995 and the field research that resulted from that discovery. More than two years after the discovery of the deformed frogs, no one was yet certain as to the cause of the deformities. The Web site for this project is *www.mncs.k12.mn.us/frog/frog.html.*

Adds ninth-grader Betsy Kroon, regarding methods pursued in the study, "I have been part of the group who [h]as tested water and I

INFOBIT

The Mormons maintain the most complete genealogical records in the United States. They are accessible on CD-ROM at Mormon temples in many cities and in many public libraries. If you want to know more about your family tree, you can search these records free of charge.

WEB LINK

If you are interested in the Minnesota New School's frog project on the Internet, you might want to e-mail one of the students there for more details. Send an e-mail to the school and one of the students will answer. The school's Internet address is given on its Web site. If you have a problem, your teacher can help you find it.

Figure 15-1: *Field researchers gathering water in a Minnesota pond*

Courtesy of the Minnesota Pollution Control Agency

INFOBIT

The average home is filled with toxic substances that cause air pollution. Laboratory experiments have indicated that eight to ten spider plants in a five-room house could absorb impurities and restore clean oxygen to the house, thus providing a healthier environment for the residents.

have taken part in gathering vertebrate[s], gathering frogs and recording deformities. I have also set 'traps' in Nye Pond to catch small creatures and used large nets to gather snails, leaches, and any other animal that lives in the mucky weeds that float at the top of the water."

Betsy Kroon then raises serious questions: "I'm concerned that having these frogs in the condition they are may have a great effect on other animals in the Eco system. What happens to the animals that eat frogs? What about the animals that frogs eat? Is the insect population going to be different because they aren't at such a risk of being eaten? Are the plants around the pond [a]ffected in any way?"

Students from the frog project won first place in the sixth- to eighth-grade category in the Anheuser-Busch Theme Parks' "A Pledge and a Promise Environmental Awards." Several state and federal studies related to the Minnesota frogs are still under way and may lead to years of further field research in several states.

Practice 15-1: Identifying Methods to Use in Field Research

teamwork In the Minnesota frog project, research methods used included catching, recording data about, and photographing malformed frogs and collecting and testing samples of the pond water in which the frogs lived. What methods could be used to answer each of the following questions? Brainstorm with a partner or small group until you have at least two methods for finding the answer to each question.

1. Are there any health hazards in the new fat substitute now found in certain brands of potato chips and other snacks?

2. What types of grasses grow best along interstate highways in this state?

3. How safe are working conditions in this company's Tennessee plant?

4. What, if any, are the serious environmental hazards at this site?

5. How can ammonia levels created by pig urine in a farrowing barn be controlled in order to protect newborn pigs from toxic fumes?

6. Which of the new truck models really performs best on winding mountain roads?

QUALITY C·O·N·N·E·C·T·I·O·N

Honey has been used as a sweet and effective cure for centuries, dating back to its use in Egypt between 2600 and 2200 B.C. Honey was not only used as an effective salve to heal wounds and sores but was mixed with water to treat fevers and sore throats.

In *The Food Pharmacy,* author Jean Carper reports that Dr. P. J. Armon, a physician in South Africa, wrote an article in 1980 describing how physicians in developing countries disinfected sores and open wounds by smearing honey on them. Dr. Armon reported that honey keeps the wounds sterile and promotes healing without antibiotics.

A British surgeon in the 1970s startled fellow doctors by announcing that he put honey on wounds after certain cancer surgeries and that it helped the wounds heal faster. He and several other doctors decided to test whether the honey was actually killing bacteria, so they "put honey in test tubes with a wide range of infectious organisms. The honey killed them all."

Laboratory Reports

Although similar to field reports, laboratory reports are based on research in a highly controlled environment. The laboratory is not always like the chemistry lab at a school; instead, it could be a greenhouse or a test area within a manufacturing plant—in short, anyplace where the environment can be controlled while the subject is studied.

Laboratory reports answer questions like the following:

* Which of these two foods is best for producing healthier gerbils?
* How fast does the virus grow under these conditions?
* Can this animal be taught a language?
* What effect does water of varying acidity levels have on this paint?
* Where is the flaw in this metal alloy that causes it to crack under severe wind conditions?
* How effective is Detergent X compared to Detergent Y?
* What antibodies will kill these bacteria?

Figure 15-2: *Can this animal be taught a language?*

Both laboratory and field reports provide the results of an investigation, so they follow a similar reporting format. A common reporting format that can be used for both field reports and lab reports follows. It can be used either when testing one item or when comparing two or more items.

A Lab or Field Report Format

1. **State Your Purpose.**
   (We set out to test Item X **or** to compare Item X with Item Y.)

2. **Give Background Information.**
   (We tell why we chose Item X and/or Item Y. On what points did we test or compare them—ease of use, efficiency, comfort, cost . . .)

3. **Explain How the Investigation Was Conducted.**
   (We tell how we tested and gathered facts about the product's ease of use, durability, efficiency, cost, and so on.)

4. **Explain the Results.**
   (What qualities were found in each brand? Which item was better? In what ways? For example, if Item Y was more efficient, did it also cost less?)

5. **State Your Conclusions.**
   (What conclusions can be drawn after looking at the results of our investigation into these products?)

6. **Discuss Your Conclusions and What They Mean.**
   (We found Item X to have . . . qualities and Brand Y to have . . . qualities. **Or:** We recommend Item X because . . .)

   Adapted from Mathes and Stevenson

A Good Source for Lab and Field Reports

One popular and informative magazine that specializes in laboratory and field-test reports is *Consumer Reports*. This magazine is known for being fair and objective. Its tests and reports cover consumer products as diverse as

- cellular phones.
- household appliances.
- disposable diapers.
- electronic equipment.
- software for kids.
- power tools.
- new cars, trucks, and sports utility vehicles (SUVs).

Brands are compared and models are rated on various criteria, depending on the types of items being tested. The reports include pictures of the products, as well as comparison charts ranking the products on various points, and are written to appeal to a general adult audience.

Consumer Reports also contains informational articles that are not lab-test reports, such as a list of automobile recalls, facts about income-tax-law changes, a readers' rating of movies, and more. But every issue has several major articles devoted to lab or field-test reports designed to inform the consumer of the merit of certain products.

One reason people tend to respect what they read in this magazine may be that the Consumers Union, which publishes *Consumer Reports,* does not sell advertising space in the magazine and accepts no money from the manufacturers of products it tests.

Other magazines—such as *Motor Trend, Popular Photography,* and *Stereo Review*—are special-interest magazines that publish comparisons of automobiles, camera equipment, and stereo equipment, respectively. These magazines do contain advertising related to their readers' interests.

Practice 15-2: Analyzing a Field or Laboratory Report

1. Using a copy of a trade journal or special-interest magazine such as *Consumer Reports,* from your school library, public library, or some other source, find an article critiquing a product or comparing two or more products or services.

   Trade and professional journals are usually reliable sources of information, since they were designed to help people do their work better. A list of such journals, along with some special-interest magazines, follows.

LIST OF SELECTED TRADE AND SPECIAL INTEREST-PERIODICALS

American Artist	*Electronics Now*
American Fitness	*Flying*
American Forests	*Managing Office Technology*
American Horticulturist	*Motor Trend*
American Journal of Nursing	*National Wildlife*
American Machinist	*Nursing Homes*
American Woodworker	*Occupational Hazards*
Architectural Digest	*PC Magazine*
Aviation Week and Space Technology	*Popular Electronics*
	Popular Mechanics
Boating	*Sales and Marketing Management*
Car and Driver	*Sporting News*
Childhood Education	*Stereo Review*
Computerworld	*Television*
Consumer Reports	

Most public libraries and many high school libraries and media centers now have their periodical indexes available on CD-ROM for speedy searches. The indexes may include anywhere from 100 periodicals in small libraries to several thousand in large ones. These same indexes are available on the Internet for a fee. You begin your search by sitting down at the assigned computer and entering the subject you are trying to find, using either a key-word search or a Boolean search. In a Boolean search, you use key words but limit the search by separating the key words with *and, or,* or *not,* to indicate more precisely what you want to find (for example, enter *Chaplin and Charlie not Geraldine*). You thus avoid the hundreds of inappropriate "hits" you could get with a simple key-word search. Lists of articles containing your key words and where to find them will appear on-screen. You can then look up the articles on a separate CD-ROM or via the Internet.

2. Read the article you have selected.

3. Fill in *Student Workbook* page 15-A to find out whether the article really follows the field or lab report format. A sample analysis is provided for you below.

SUBJECT	Title of the article. "A Second Look at Minivans"	**CONCLUSIONS** **What conclusions can be drawn from this article about the better product or method? How was it better?**
AUDIENCE	General—adult	Revavan -- best fuel economy at 20 m.p.g . -- more head and leg room -- more reliable anti-lock brakes -- dual air conditioners in Deluxe model -- good support in driver's seat -- better (safer) rear door latches.
PURPOSE	What actions should the audience take after reading? Make better decision about which minivan to buy when looking at the Transtar, Aerovan, and Revavan.	
FORMAT	☒written ☐oral ☐other	
SOURCES	Magazine title and date. *Cars Galore* March 1998	
VISUALS	Visuals used to make the article effective. Photos of each van. Closeups of rear door latches & of new side doors on Aerovan.	**What do the conclusions mean for the reader?** You'll save money and be safer and more comfortable in the Revavan.
RESULTS	Which item or method was better? Renavan rated "best buy"	

Proposals (Persuasive Reports)

"Look into it."

"Let me know what you think."

"Check it out and see what we can use to get what we need for the best price."

All of the statements you just read are ways people in authority might tell you to investigate the best way to do something—and then to submit a proposal for doing it.

What, exactly, is a proposal? It is a report in which you try to persuade someone to do something based on information you have provided. A proposal is designed to be the answer to a question or problem.

A proposal might start with an idea like the following:

> * Here are some ways to tackle the attendance problem.
> * Our work area needs to be rearranged.
> * We need to advertise on the radio rather than in the newspaper.
> * We should add goat's milk and tofu to the dairy case.
> * Our department needs a new accounting software program.
> * We should replace our old delivery trucks.

Of course, there is always a *because* after these opening statements. One must state the reason for the needed change in order to make the proposal persuasive.

Then research is done to determine the best way to accomplish the needed change, by talking with knowledgeable people (interviewing), reading written materials, gathering raw data, doing Internet searches, or attending informational workshops or seminars.

And, finally, a cost must be calculated. The bottom line in business is profit, and if the proposal is not likely to help the company be more profitable, it will be rejected. Keep in mind that investing money in something like a large piece of equipment may involve a very large expense. A large expense may reap even larger profits—or it may not. Your proposal must show that it will. If you're wrong, you'll have to face the consequences. So do your homework or drop the proposal!

INFOBIT

During the 1984–85 school year, the National Collegiate Athletic Association had 91,669 female participants and 201,063 male participants. During 1995–96, there were 123,832 females and 199,556 males. This is the type of data that might be used to support a proposal for increasing the number and quality of high school programs for female athletes, as well as for increasing the number of college scholarships for female athletes. ("Gender")

A Proposal Format

A common reporting format that can be used for a proposal follows.

1. **Start with Your Conclusion.**

   State what needs to be done. (You've made up your mind. That's why you are writing this proposal.)

2. **State Your Reasons.**

   Tell why you think it should be done and how to do it. (State your most important reasons first, followed by less important reasons.) Include facts; don't just state your opinions. Find information to support your position and state where you found it.

3. **Answer Possible Objections.**

   Anticipate what your reader or listener may object to and answer those objections. For example, "I know we've never done this, but our market research shows that 40 percent of our customers want it."

4. **Restate Your Conclusion.**

   "So it is clear that . . . needs to be done."

   Adapted from Mathes and Stevenson

How to Handle a Situation Requiring a Persuasive Report

Let's say, for example, that you are in charge of maintenance in a 60-bed hospital in a medium-size town. The hospital floors have to be clean at all times, yet never slippery. Many cleaning solutions have powerful chemicals that act as disinfectants but also irritate membranes in the nasal passages. The use of these chemicals may cause additional breathing problems in patients who are already having enough trouble remaining comfortable. These and other concerns have been called to your attention by a hospital administrator who was not pleased with the previous maintenance supervisor's work at the hospital.

As a new employee, you have begun by using the supplies that were purchased before you came. In your previous job, you didn't have to deal with sick people, sterile conditions, and constant traffic, so these are new issues for you.

Figure 15-3: *Clean, safe floors are essential in a hospital.*

You go to your hospital administrator to discuss your shared concerns, knowing that solving the many facets of this floor-care problem could add to your costs. You may need a bigger budget to get the job done right. New cleaners and waxes may require special equipment. The administrator responds, "Check out the details and bring me some facts. We'll talk about them."

You know that the hospital operates on a tight budget. You are also aware that the administrator doesn't know you well enough yet to trust your judgment. What do you do?

Use the Expertise of Others

This is no time for original research, but you are going to have to put some facts and figures together for your administrator fairly quickly. Where do you get them?

First, let's look at the kinds of questions that need to be answered. You'll have to know which types of floor cleaners and waxes are available for the terrazzo and vinyl-tile floors in your hospital. Which are most effective for disinfecting and preserving the floors? Which are the safest? Which have fewer hazardous chemicals in them? How are they applied? What equipment is necessary to use them most effectively? (Buckets and mops? Electric floor scrubbers and high-speed polishers?) What is the cost of each floor cleaner and wax? What quantity will be needed to take care of the floors in your building for one year? Considering all factors (effectiveness, safety, availability of equipment to apply the products, and cost), what needs to be purchased?

Figure 15-4: *Use the expertise of others to gather information for a proposal.*

How do you get answers to these questions? Where do you look? Whom do you ask? Are letters needed or will a phone call do?

Approaching a task like this cold (without previous knowledge or preparation) can be quite a challenge.

That's why people in almost every line of work develop networks; that is, they get to know other people in their field of work, people who do the same kinds of jobs they do. They may join trade or professional organizations, many of which publish trade journals, from which they receive written information on topics pertaining to their jobs. They attend workshops on the latest products, methods, and OSHA (Occupational Safety and Health Administration) regulations.

In the case of the hospital floors, you could begin by calling the supervisors of maintenance at several other hospitals in your area or in

C·O·N·N·E·C·T·I·O·N

In the early 1990s, Garth Brooks was an ordinary country singer, mostly ignored by those in the music business. Suddenly his name was at the top of the charts, almost overnight. The reason was a change that was made in the way the record industry reported sales. When complete sales information was available, thanks to scanners and bar codes, and a data gathering system from a company named SoundScan was put into place, the true popularity of Garth Brooks was suddenly evident. And the Top 200 chart began to show which recordings were really selling, as opposed to what a number of store clerks had been reporting in questionable telephone surveys. Now, high-stakes charts are no longer based on sketchy and unreliable information; a truer picture is available through the *zap!* of a bar-code reader. Marketing practices in the music recording business can now be accurately tailored to what is actually happening in sales.

nearby towns. Have they had the same problems? What have they done about them? Can they recommend a product? Where can you buy it?

Once you get a promising lead, call the manufacturer for details about the ingredients of the products that have been recommended or about the availability of other products that might solve your problem. Most large companies today have 800 numbers, which can be dialed free of charge. Most also have an Internet Web page, which contains information about the company and its products.

Compare Products

Ask for a detailed description of each product: specifications, methods of application, and warnings related to application or use. Be sure to request the names and addresses of vendors (preferably local) from whom the product can be purchased.

Usually a vendor is happy to supply you with the names and addresses of others who use a product, so you can visit them and see for yourself how the product really works.

Compare Costs, Not Just Prices

When you have found one or two products that look promising, check with the vendor(s) for prices and shipping costs, but don't stop there. Figure the costs of using the products for one year. The new products may last longer and may not have to be stripped from the floor as often as the old ones, thus saving both time and money in the long run.

Organize Your Information

Now you are ready to put together a proposal for your administrator. Your job will be to persuade him or her to accept your recommendations, invest in special floor scrubbers (which may cost several thousands of dollars each), or do whatever else is needed.

You'll need to compare the old cleaners and waxes with several new ones and then

* recommend the purchase and use of one or more of these products.

* give several reasons for your recommendations.

* tell where you got your information.

* explain what using the new products will involve (e.g., cost, new equipment, and training of your staff in how to apply them).

* tell why you rejected other products. Restate your conviction that the hospital will benefit by using these new floor-care products. (You may be able to recommend using some of the old products in non-patient areas of the hospital, such as storage areas, business offices, or gift shops, until they are used up. This will cut down on initial expense and eliminate waste.)

* anticipate objections and concerns. Be ready to answer questions.

* restate your conclusions in your closing.

Offer More Than One Plan

Show how much the total cost would be if you gradually phased in new equipment and materials instead of buying everything new at once. Or suggest the purchase of rebuilt or reconditioned equipment, which would lower costs.

Prepare Your Thoughts in Writing

Get your thoughts together by writing down your main points. Then you can make the most convincing presentation possible. You can use these notes initially as a guide to help you speak persuasively about your conclusions; i.e., what needs to be done regarding floor care in this hospital. Then you can leave the notes for your administrator to use for future reference. (Never give away your only copy; always keep one for yourself.)

Make an Appointment to Present the Information

At the meeting, use your written information as a backup. Remember, the more knowledgeable and convincing you are, the more likely it is that your proposal will be accepted.

C·O·N·N·E·C·T·I·O·N

We're all familiar with the small shopping centers that have been built along major roads and highways and dot the American landscape. They often contain a grocery store, one or more clothing stores, a pharmacy, perhaps an electronics store, a hair styling salon, a video rental store, and two or more food stands or restaurants. The location of such a shopping center typically starts with a proposal that includes information from population surveys, studies of traffic patterns, analyses of buying habits, and other sources that would support the kinds of retail or service centers that would be frequented by people in the area. Investors who build such centers must be persuaded in advance that they will make money from them.

Practice 15-3: Writing Conclusions for a Proposal

The conclusion you reach after gathering the facts for your proposal must be worded clearly, concisely, and convincingly. A proposal may contain wonderful information but will not be persuasive if you cannot construct a strong conclusion.

Read the following weak sample conclusion and decide what's wrong with it. Be specific about what makes it sound weak. How would you change it to make it stronger?

Weak Conclusion (Sample)

(*Audience:* Office manager)

We could really use some kind of a program that's more user-friendly, like, maybe, Softwrite. This new word processing program will also work along with a spreadsheet—like you can go from one to the other— back and forth—and put stuff from your spreadsheet into what you're writing.

Improved Conclusion (Sample)

The new word processing program Softwrite is exactly what we need. It is user-friendly, and it interfaces with a spreadsheet, allowing information from the spreadsheet to be efficiently incorporated into any report.

What words or phrases helped to strengthen the improved conclusion?

This Practice contains three rambling and indistinct conclusions. After reading them carefully, write an improved version of each one. This Practice will help you learn to eliminate fuzzy thoughts, use appropriate words, and present an idea convincingly. The type of audience is specified for each conclusion.

(*cont'd on next page*)

CAREER C·O·N·N·E·C·T·I·O·N

When David Ho came to Los Angeles from Taiwan at 12, he could not speak English. His classmates thought he was dumb. But after six months of instruction in English as a second language and a lot of TV, Ho learned the language. Working intensely, he began to leave his classmates in the dust, getting straight A's in everything, including English.

Ho went to Harvard Medical School, where his training led him to the focal point of his career: how to stop HIV (the human immunodeficiency virus) from multiplying and how to eliminate it from the body.

Dr. Ho is now director of the Aaron Diamond AIDS Research Center. He hopes to eradicate AIDS (acquired immunodeficiency syndrome) by using protease inhibitors with other antiviral medications. Thanks to his research, many with HIV not only have survived, but have not developed full-blown AIDS. He was named *TIME* magazine's Man of the Year in 1996. Needless to say, no one thinks he's dumb anymore.

INFOBIT

Judge Deidra Hair is good at stating strong conclusions, often using analogies to soften them with humor. Referring to a day's work in Municipal Court, she writes, "The pace in Room A is grueling. Three hundred cases in one day is the approximate equivalent of a fourteen-hour stint in the ER, with no assisting physicians."

Weak Conclusion 1

(*Audience:* Coworkers at Designs Plus)

To improve our safety at Designs Plus, it would probably be better if we did something about all the suggestions like not plugging in electric cords across the aisle from our computers because we wouldn't want someone to trip over them. The electrical maintenance department might be able to put outlets closer to our desks if we ask them. Or we could move our desks. Maybe we could get somebody to figure out how to rearrange our area. And it would be better, I guess, to not plug three or four electric plugs into the same extension cord if we want to avoid fires.

Weak Conclusion 2

(*Audience:* Professional day-care-center workers)

We should only feed the kids in the day-care center the kind of food that doesn't have a whole lot of sugar and salt. Like fruit and stuff. Some kids get hyperactive if they get too much sugar and caffeine, like when they drink cola drinks. You have to be careful what you feed them. That's what Dr. Feingold says in his book. And it's what we've noticed ourselves with lots of kids.

Weak Conclusion 3

(*Audience:* Classmates and teacher of animal science or health occupations program)

One thing we read was that when you take small pets like dogs and cats into nursing homes, the people in there who used to not talk at all will pet the pets and talk to them. And if people have high blood pressure, just petting an animal will cause their blood pressure to go lower. We took pets into one of those places and it was true. We went there twice a week for six weeks, and the pets made a big difference.

Progress Reports

Progress reports tell what has happened so far in a project or job. Progress reports answer questions like these:

* Are plans being followed?
* Are we making a profit?
* Are we improving our products and services?
* Is the work proceeding as planned?
* How much money did we make this year?
* How many customers came back a second time this year?
* Have we been able to decrease our workdays lost due to absenteeism over the past three years?

Figure 15-5: *An on-site progress report*

Progress reports vary depending on the purpose, location, job, and degree of technology available within a company. Sometimes progress reports are written out, but often they are placed on a specially designed form. In most schools, the grade card is used as a progress report. On some jobs that require personal inspections, a checklist is used, with space for notations. (Some companies call these checklists "field reports," since they are done in the field. But they are not the same as the field reports discussed earlier in this chapter.)

A Progress Report Format

Formats for progress reports vary. One simple format follows:

1. **Summary of What's Been Done to Date**
2. **Details of Step 1**
3. **Problems Encountered So Far (If Any)**
4. **What Will Be Done Next**
5. **Recommendations**

Anyone in charge of a project that is expected to take more than a few days will gain the confidence and respect of an employer or customer by writing or calling in informal reports that indicate how the job is progressing.

A Sample Progress Report

A remodeling contractor had estimated that it would take one month for three workers to dismantle a rotting greenhouse located behind the kitchen, to remodel a second-floor bathroom, and to add a second-floor deck off the bathroom of a 130-year-old house. After one week of work, the carpenter left the handwritten note shown in Figure 15-6.

4-4-98

We're already behind schedule. The greenhouse looked rickety, but it was built to stay. It took an extra half day to remove all the #10 nails in those 2 x 4's.

We're ready for the bathroom. Hope all the brick and plaster dust isn't too bad. Leave the mop in the bucket and we'll try to clean up as we go.

PROBLEMS: It took us a full day to get the ceiling in. Old houses settle and aren't square to begin with.

The wrong color lavatory was shipped. It's going to take two weeks to get the Monroe 6 you ordered.

Meanwhile, we'll get the walls done. We won't be here till after 10:00 am Wednesday. Have to pick up lumber on the way.

Call Steve if you have concerns. He'll track me down.

—Don

Figure 15-6: *Don's report*

The note was left on a table just outside the entrance to the bathroom, since the carpenter knew that his customer would be checking to see how the work was progressing as soon as she came home from work.

Obviously, this carpenter knew that the homeowner was anxious about what was being done to her house and how unforeseen problems could add to both the cost and the inconvenience. He also knew that he would stay on good terms with his customer by keeping her fully informed and letting her know what to expect.

Although the carpenter's note is well-written, it doesn't appear at first glance to follow a progress report format. In fact, Don probably never thought of his note as more than just keeping the customer informed.

Practice 15-4: Critiquing Don's Report

Reread the steps in the progress report format reprinted in this Practice. See if Don's note contains everything in that format. What did he write in order to

1. summarize what's been done to date?

2. give details of specific tasks accomplished?

3. explain problems that have been encountered so far?

4. tell what will be done next?

5. make recommendations?

COMMUNICATING for SUCCESS

Practice 15-5: Writing a Progress Report

Report cards—with their lists of six or seven grades each report period—do not do justice to all you do as a person with your many other responsibilities, extracurricular activities, and possibly a part-time job.

Write an informal, personal progress report approximately one page in length in the form of a memo. The audience for your progress report memo can be yourself, a trusted friend, a teacher, a parent, or someone else who is interested in what you do with your life. Include the following steps:

1. A summary of what you've done this school year.

2. Details of Step 1.

3. Problems encountered so far (if any). If there have been none, say so.

4. What will be done next.

5. Recommendations you would make to yourself (e.g., "Next time I will . . .").

Other Types of Progress Reports

In addition to the basic five-step report, there are many specialized types of progress reports. A few of them are listed here.

Annual Reports to Stockholders

Publicly owned companies (those in which the public owns shares of stock in the company) publish annual reports for their shareholders. These reports may be very elaborate publications detailing profits and losses, the effects of new laws (such as those controlling air or water pollution) on their business, where their major expenditures are occurring, new product lines, and other information.

Newsletters and Magazines

Some agencies like the Union of Concerned Scientists regularly publish small magazines or newsletters outlining new projects and updating the public about their ongoing projects, such as their watchdog activities on the regulation and safety of nuclear power plants. Some departments within schools or businesses publish newsletters to keep other departments or people outside the school or business aware of the status of certain activities and projects within that department.

ETHICS C·O·N·N·E·C·T·I·O·N

The problem of inaccuracy in on-line pricing has been the subject of investigative reporting for several years. Often the discrepancies occur during a sales promotion. The sale price in the computer may be higher than the one advertised by the store. Whether the error is deliberate or simply due to an inept data entry clerk is not always clear. One thing is certain: unwary buyers could be shortchanged more frequently than they may suspect. Wise buyers will check the cash register receipt for accurate billing before they pay for their merchandise and leave the store.

The Word

February 1997   Volume 1 Issue 3

Toy Drive

The Business Technology classes got together this Christmas to help the needy families within our community.

I was very impressed with all of the support that we got from students and staff, as well as, our families and friends. This made me believe that once again we do have the spirit of giving and not just receiving. People didn't even hesitate to give money. They just did. They didn't just give once, they kept on giving.

All of the Business Technology classes and local officers were very actively involved. They raised the money, counted it, and also put barrels in the front of the school for toys. I was surprised to see the barrel filled with toys every time I walked by!

This drive only lasted for two weeks, but in those two weeks we raised over $500 and bought new toys with the money. The business classes helped wrap the toys, including the ones that were in the barrel.

With the help of Business Technology and Live Oaks, we were able to give 5 gifts to every child.

Marlene Baker, Executive Director of the H.A.N.D.S. program was very impressed with how much we raised in two weeks. Marlene wanted to make it so that every child got 2-3 gifts. With the help of Business Technology and Live Oaks, we were able to give 5 gifts to every child!
—Jillian Kautzman

From left to right: Eric Petree, Mrs. Mabel Gelter, and Rose Atwood.

Great Oaks Prepared Speech Competition

On December 17, 1996, Live Oaks held a speech competition. The speech had to be about "What Effects Technology has had on a Persons Life and Career?"

Six people competed in this Live Oaks Competition. The winners:
1st place = Eric Petree
2nd place = Rose Atwood

Eric and Rose went on to compete at the Technology Center at the Great Oaks Corporate Office. They competed against two students from each of the other three Great Oaks schools. The winners were:

1st = Eric Petree
2nd = Laura Kleiman
3rd = Christina Schneider

Congratulations to all the winners! Because of Eric's win, Live Oaks received the traveling trophy. This trophy goes to the campus who had the first place winner. The trophy stays there until the next district competition and a new winner brings the trophy home.

—Rose Atwood

Source: Live Oaks Career Development Campus, Milford, Ohio

Computerized Inventory Records

Cash registers in most large supermarkets are on-line to a central computer that keeps track of prices and inventories. This allows managers to know how much has been sold, which items need to be replaced, and the gross receipts for a given period of time—either for the whole store or for a department within the store. This record can provide management with an ongoing sales progress report.

Electronic Surveillance of Workers

In some businesses, an electronic counter or recorder provides feedback to management on how much work has been accomplished. Thus, if you are a data entry clerk, your strokes per minute and total input for the day may be recorded automatically and compared to your work on other days. In other settings, video cameras may be recording the activities of a company's employees. Workers in a variety of industries are questioning the ethics of such surveillance, claiming that it is an invasion of privacy and causes severe stress. Managers, however, argue that they can get a better idea of how to project timelines, how to spot possible illness in workers by observing their changing work patterns, and how to curtail theft—either in time or in materials. What do you think?

If you've ever gone into a grocery store outside your neighborhood, you may have noticed differences in the products sold. If a neighborhood has a large concentration of Chinese-Americans, the neighborhood super-market probably carries, in addition to the basic inventory, a stock of vegetables, spices, and other products preferred by Chinese-Americans in that community. Stores in a Mexican-American or Italian-American neighborhood would stock different items. Stores must know or research their customer base and cater to its needs.

Stores in a low-income neighborhood are less likely to have a large inventory of higher-priced specialty items. Grocery stores typically make only a small margin of profit on each item sold, so to stay in business, they must stock mainly items that large numbers of local shoppers will buy. The next time you visit a new neighborhood, head for the food mart and do a little personal research on the food there. It will give you a snapshot of the neighborhood residents.

Monthly or Annual Meetings

Sometimes progress reports are delivered in meetings as audiovisual presentations to show progress charts, pictures of new machinery, new product packaging, or other information to workers who might not otherwise be aware of these things. Such a regular update can keep all employees aware of the big picture—of what's happening throughout the company—and give them a better understanding of what's going on in the organization beyond their own departments.

Tips on Report Writing

Everything you have learned about technical communication in this course comes together in the collection of data and in the presentation of a report.

* *Audience analysis.* Audience analysis is critical. Reports may be written for customers, for company managers, or with the general public in mind. Adjust word choice and tone accordingly.

* *Clear, concise writing.* The principles of clarity and conciseness are critical. Reports are never to be padded. Less is more, provided that no necessary information is left out.

* *Tables, charts, and graphs.* Use of tables, charts, and graphs to help organize information in an attention-getting and logical way helps the reader focus on important points.

* *Layout and design.* In all technical writing, layout and design are very important. The use of headings to label and introduce each section is important, too, as is the use of white space,

CAREER C·O·N·N·E·C·T·I·O·N

In many small towns, doctors are scarce or nonexistent. In 1995, several small towns in western Kansas solved this problem by establishing a long-distance nurse practitioner training program. Training is via compressed video, at less than 2 percent of the cost of typical satellite broadcasts. Compressed video also allows specialists in another city to diagnose a serious problem. "You can hear subtle heart sounds. You can see into the ear better than you can with the naked eye," says Helen Connors, associate dean of the University of Kansas School of Nursing in Kansas City, who pushed for the program.

Qualified nurses can now take an extra two years of training, learning, for example, to suture wounds, treat joint injuries, and interpret X-rays. More nurse practitioners means more children are inoculated against diseases like whooping cough and measles. Doctors must still write prescriptions and be responsible for patients, some of whom they have never met. Despite such inconveniences, health care in western Kansas is better than ever. (Gorman)

underlining, boxes, bullets, and other devices that highlight information or help to focus the reader's attention.

* *Review for assistance.* In fact, if there is a problem with any aspect of your final report, you can get help by using the table of contents of this book and reviewing how to do it. If, for example, you are writing a persuasive report in which you are encouraging someone to buy one product rather than another, refer to Chapter 12, "Comparing and Contrasting," to review how to contrast one product with another in your report.

* *Mechanics of report writing.* Start with the topical heading. State what you are writing about. Always indicate to whom the report is addressed and by whom it was written and the date it was submitted. Sometimes a memo form is preferred. (Refer to Chapter 9 for tips on formatting a memo.)

Usually the person submitting the report signs or initials and dates the report (sometimes on each page). Follow whatever format your employer prefers.

Key all but the most informal reports. If you write or print an informal report, be sure that every letter and number is clear and legible.

In all lines of work, reports of various types play important roles. Reports may be presented orally, in writing, or both. They may require a great deal of information gathering, careful organization, and appropriate illustrations. Four types of reports that are commonly used in business and industry are

* laboratory reports, which summarize tests done on a product or process under controlled conditions.

* field reports, which require gathering information "from the field," either in the workplace or outside the workplace, in order to understand or improve upon something.

* proposals, which attempt to persuade someone to take action based on information reported and which require the use of convincing language, strong conclusions, and supporting data.

* progress reports, which show how much has been accomplished over a set period of time.

The ability to write and present a top-quality report will place you a notch above the average worker. It is the kind of skill required to be promoted to management positions, and it requires the use of all the skills you have learned in this course.

WORKS CITED

Carper, Jean. *The Food Pharmacy*. New York: Bantam, 1988.

Chua-Eoan, Howard. "The Tao of Ho." *TIME,* 6 Jan. 1997: 69–70.

"Gender Equity in Sports" [Web page] *www.arcade.uiowa.edu/proj/ge/.* (Be aware that Internet addresses are subject to change.)

Hair, Deidra. *No Shoes, No Shirt, No Trial*. Cincinnati: Symetry Publications, 1987.

Mathes, J. C., and Dwight W. Stevenson. *Designing Technical Reports.* 2d ed. New York: Macmillan, 1991.

Presenting a Report

Use the data you collected in Chapter 13, "Interviewing for Information," or Chapter 14, "Using Numbers and Statistics," or use other data that you collect. Then plan and write one of the following:

* A laboratory report (see format on pages 506–509)

* A field report (same format as laboratory report)

* A proposal (see format on pages 510–517)

1. Carefully read the Sample Project Plan and Sample Project on pages 525–527.

2. There are two Project Plans in your *Student Workbook:* one for a field or laboratory report (page 15-B) and the other for a proposal (page 15-D). Complete the one appropriate for the report you have chosen to do. There is also a Project Guide for each (pages 15-C and 15-E).

3. Locate facts that will answer the questions in your Project Plan about the topic you have chosen. Do not write complete sentences, just brief notes.

4. Using the information in your Project Plan, write a rough draft. Write quickly without worrying about getting the wording exact. Just get your ideas in roughly the correct form.

5. Use the Rough Draft column of your Project Guide (*Student Workbook* page 15-C for a field or lab report or *Student Workbook* page 15-E for a proposal), and check your own work with one or more classmates. Each of you should mark the Project Guide and note any changes on the rough draft.

6. Revise your rough draft, incorporating the changes that your classmate(s) suggested.

7. Use the Final Draft column of the Project Guide to proofread your work. Make needed corrections.

Plan for Field or Laboratory Report

SUBJECT	Report of customer satisfaction survey for Craig Bird's Lawn Care Service.
AUDIENCE	General (classmates and teachers)
PURPOSE	**What actions should the audience take?** Inform audience about how a real business survey took place, what the results were, and what the client did with the information.
FORMAT	☒ written ☐ oral ☐ other
SOURCES	**How will information be obtained? What methods will be used?** Face-to-face or phone interviews of customers. Recorded responses on questionnaire. Then tallied responses for report.
VISUALS	**What visuals, if any, will make the report more effective?** Use table to illustrate responses.
RESULTS	**What are the results of the investigation?** Most customers satisfied with service. Decided to train shrub trimmer & publicize services through flyers.

CONCLUSIONS

Hired to do customer satisfaction survey.

Total customers: 611

Number surveyed: 109

Breakdown of services used by customers who were surveyed:

1. shrub trimming -- 33
2. grass mowing -- 95
3. mulching -- 7
4. lawn weed & feed -- 61
5. aerating lawn -- 15
6. tree stakes -- 7
7. leaf-raking -- 43

Additional points on survey:

1. job clean-up
2. friendly, businesslike manner
3. billing procedures
4. pricing

Results of survey (Use notes from survey tally sheet) Highlights: 84% said lawn mowing was very good. Nearly half of shrub trim customers complained of choppy, uneven trim. Need attention to this service. 2 reported mulch piles dropped on lawn. Others rated mulching around shrubs average.

39 liked getting bill on day of service & getting questions answered. Others liked bills left inside storm door or on door knob in plastic bag. Prices rated as average.

Recommendations: Improve shrub trimming & mulching services. (Train trimmer) Keep current billing practices. Use flyers to help sell less-used services.

Field Report:
Customer Satisfaction Survey Analysis

Mr. Craig Bird and his two partners in Craig Bird's Lawn Care Service asked me to do a customer satisfaction survey of at least 100 of their 611 customers, using some questions they had put together.

They thought that if I surveyed about 25 people from each of the four neighborhoods they serve, the results would help them to see what they need to improve to keep their customers happy. They were also concerned about why they had lost 15 customers in the last six months and wanted to avoid losing more of them.

Mr. Bird gave me a list of the questions he wanted me to ask. We agreed that personal contacts either in person or by phone would be best, since very few people will fill out and mail a questionnaire. We decided that since he was into the regular spring/summer cycle with their customers here in Memphis, I would go with some of his lawn workers during our spring break and on afternoons and interview people who were at home during the day. I surveyed the others by phone in the evenings. It took a lot of hours. He let them know about the survey in advance and gave them my name so they would be expecting my call.

On the chart I put together you can see that I contacted 109 customers, a few more than Mr. Bird expected, which made him happy. From his customer records, we knew how many he mowed lawns for, trimmed shrubs for, and provided other services for. (Some of them used more than one service.) As it turned out, I did a fair job of reaching people who used all the lawn services his company provided.

The results show that most customers are satisfied with the service. The strongest satisfaction areas reported were lawn mowing and billing procedures. They liked getting their bills on the day of service and having their questions answered. The weakest areas were mulching and shrub trimming, although we didn't have as many responses in those categories. Two people said that mulch was left in their grass and on their sidewalks. Fifteen said their shrubs got a choppy trimming job and some said that the old branches weren't removed from the bushes.

We also took a hard look at how few of his customers take advantage of some of his services. Mr. Bird admits that sometimes he speaks to people who are at home when he's working in their yards, and those are the ones who hire him for a wider variety of services, like mulching in the spring and leaf raking and putting in tree stakes in the fall. I suggested that he make a flyer with a couple of garden tips on it, add a list of services and what they cost, and leave a copy of the flyer with the bill at each house as he makes his rounds. He could also leave flyers at neighboring houses. That would save mailing costs, and I could design the flyers for him on my computer. We also decided that he needs to take the time to train the person he hired to do shrub trimming so he does a better job. We think that doing these things might help the company get more business and keep it from losing more customers.

Tim Fescue
Technical Communication 213
Final Project
May 1998

SURVEY RESULTS

Craig Bird's Lawn Care Service

	Number of Customers		Responses		
Item	# Rec. Svc.	# Surveyed	Very Good	Average	Poor
1. grass mowing	517	95	80	15	0
2. shrub trimming	409	33	0	8	15
3. mulching	45	7	1	3	3
4. lawn weed & feed	387	61	31	24	6
5. aerating	76	15	13	2	0
6. tree stakes	31	7	3	4	0
7. leaf raking & removal	261	43	33	8	2
8. cleanup	611	109	27	71	11
9. friendly, businesslike	611	109	49	59	1
10. pricing	611	109	37	72	0
11. billing procedures	611	109	59	49	1

Total customers: 611. Number surveyed: 109.

Overview

The following proposal by Stephen Budiansky appeared in the magazine *U.S. News & World Report.* The topic of his memo is the U.S. government's attempt to limit immigration to the United States. He writes his proposal as one Native American to another, recommending the denial of asylum to the Pilgrims.

"1620 to 1992: Long Ago but Not So Far Away"

TO: Massasoit, Chief, Wampanoag tribe

FROM: Squanto

RE: Immigration interview report, 26 DEC 1620

One hundred so-called boat people filing claims for political asylum were interviewed. The vast majority of the claims were nonsensical. None could show a justifiable, immediate fear for their lives if they returned to Holland and/or that they had held a sensitive position in a persecuted political or religious organization. In fact, several admitted that they had only several years earlier voluntarily relocated to Holland specifically because it was an open society that would tolerate their sect ("the Separatists"). The obvious contradictions in their stories suggest that these are not bona fide political refugees but rather economic refugees, merely out to better their lives.

Their claim to permanent residency status based on special skills or professional training is likewise unsubstantiated. Most lack even the most basic job skills, as the earlier waves of boat people who were admitted to Jamestown has unfortunately demonstrated. Most of those immigrants were listed on the ship's manifest as "Gentleman," which they themselves define as "whosoever can live without manual labor." They are lazy, prone to acts of violence and unable or unwilling to become productive members of society. Established residents of the area complain of a rash of petty thefts and of outright starvation—and more than two thirds already have starved to death—they are unwilling to find gainful employment. In one well-documented incident, the immigrants chopped down their own houses for firewood. It is perhaps relevant that several prominent authorities in England have explicitly encouraged emigration to America as a way to rid their country of "idle and worthless" persons.

The conditions aboard these boats are horrendous. Interviewees report that five persons in fact died in transit. Smallpox, scurvy and typhus are rampant aboard these crowded ships, which allot a space of only 7 feet by $2\frac{1}{2}$ feet, below decks, for each passenger. More than 150 boat people died of disease on one ship that arrived in Virginia two years ago. The ships are also in poor physical condition. Interviewees reported that a second boat, the *Speedwell,* was forced to turn back twice because of leaks and eventually abandoned the voyage. Firm action now can effectively discourage other Englishmen from taking to unseaworthy vessels, which will only lead to a further unnecessary and tragic loss of life. . . .

Recommendation on applications for asylum: **DENY**.

—Stephen Budiansky

Start-Up: People write proposals in the workplace to fix a problem, meet a need, or make an improvement. Having a good idea is not enough to bring about a change. Writers must demostrate that they understand the problem or need, that they are considering the reader's position, and that they have a detailed program for putting their plans into action. A proposal must be persuasive.

In literature, proposals are written for the same reasons. Writers of literature must also plan their proposals to persuade. There is no one correct format for a proposal. However, most proposals contain certain basic parts: a conclusion (what needs to be done), the reasons (why it should be done), answers to possible objections, and a restatement of the conclusion.

Pay attention to how a proposal looks. Are headings used to help the reader determine what each paragraph contains? Are lists enumerated or bulleted? Are visuals included to help the reader understand what is being proposed? A careless presentation may result in the rejection of the proposal.

Connection: Meet in groups of four. Brainstorm for situations that exist within the school that you would like to see changed. Make a list of these situations. Also brainstorm for solutions to these situations. Each member of the group should write a proposal based on one of the situations. Use the memo format. Word-process your product and submit it to your teacher.

Overview

Does a pet have a special place in your life? On occasion, you probably have bragged about its unusually smart performances. It is just more intelligent than other pets. Right? Just how smart is your pet?

Well, two dolphin trainers asked this question about dolphins and investigated to find the answer. The following factual report pursues the answer to this question: How smart are dolphins?

"How Smart Are Dolphins?"

Malia was smart. She learned quickly, mastering many tricks after two or three lessons. She seemed to enjoy performing for audiences at Sea Life Park in Hawaii. She was so clever that her trainers, Karen Pryor and Ingrid Kang, decided to try something new.

Pryor and Kang felt that Malia's act had become too slick and polished. The dolphin knew her routines perfectly. She never made mistakes. There were no surprises. To make Malia's act more lively and interesting, Pryor and Kang decided to show their audiences how a dolphin is trained. They would teach Malia a brand-new trick at each show. When she learned the trick, she would be rewarded with a fish.

In the following days, Malia learned one new trick after another. She was rewarded only for learning something new, not for performing her old tricks. After fourteen shows, the dolphin had learned fourteen new tricks. Pryor and Kang were running out of new tricks to teach her. At one show, they couldn't come up with anything new.

Malia solved the problem herself. She began to perform new stunts she made up herself. She swam on her back with her tail in the air. She threw herself into the air backward and made an arching leap upside down. She jumped from the water and spun like a top in mid-air.

Malia had not been taught these tricks and had never performed them before. She had apparently figured out on her own that she would not be rewarded for performing old tricks. She could earn her reward only by doing something new. She seemed to realize that it didn't matter what she did, as long as she hadn't done it before.

In show after show, Malia came up with new and astonishing stunts. She performed tricks on her own that her trainers never would have imagined. The dolphin appeared to understand the abstract principle that only novelty would win a reward. She seemed to be thinking, not just learning tricks in an automatic way.

Inspired by Malia's remarkable behavior, her trainers decided to try the same thing with another dolphin, Hou. They wanted to see if Hou would also catch on to the idea that only novelty would be rewarded. This time they would keep a careful record of everything that happened.

. . . Malia and Hou had performed a feat of intelligence highly unusual in any animal.

It took a while for Hou to understand what the trainers wanted, but she did catch on. Like Malia, she began to make up and perform one new trick after another.

It seemed that Malia and Hou had performed a feat of intelligence highly unusual in any animal. Did the experiments really prove that?

Karen Pryor tried a similar experiment with pigeons. The pigeons were put through the same kind of training as the dolphins. Surprisingly, they responded in the same way.

Karen Pryor concluded that the experiments did not, after all, show how smart dolphins are. Given the same kind of training, pigeons were capable of learning the same lesson— that only new behavior would be rewarded. Apparently, the dolphins' feat did not require super-intelligence.

These experiments show how difficult it is to understand the intelligence of a creature different from ourselves. We can test an animal, but we don't always know how to interpret the results.

Dolphins live in a world of sound. Sounds tell them most of what they need to know about their underwater world. While it is not possible to see very far under water, sounds travel clearly through the water. Dolphins stay in touch with each other by sending sounds through the water. They also scan the waters around them by means of echo-location. They send out high-frequency sounds, just as bats do. The sounds bounce off objects, and the echoes bring back information about the size of the object, its shape, its texture, and its distance. By means of echo-location, a dolphin can identify a shark that is too far away to be seen.

Dolphins have much keener hearing than humans. They pick up sounds that we can't hear at all. A dolphin's acoustic nerve, which sends information to the brain, is three to four times bigger than the same nerve in humans. And a dolphin has a much larger part of its brain devoted to hearing than a human has.

Because each creature has a different kind of brain and lives in a special world of its own, it is very tricky to compare animals by means of intelligence tests. A test that is fair to one animal might not be fair to another. In general, however,

(cont'd on next page)

intelligence is closely linked to learning ability. An animal's intelligence depends, in part, on how fast it can learn, how much it can learn, and how long it can remember.

We can gain a rough idea of an animal's intelligence by looking at its brain. As a rule, smarter animals have bigger and more complex brains, but a giant brain doesn't always mean a giant intelligence.

The biggest brains on this planet belong to whales and elephants. A sperm whale has a brain that weighs about 9,000 grams, nearly 20 pounds. That's the largest brain that has ever existed on earth. An elephant's brain weighs about 6,000 grams. A bottle-nosed dolphin, a member of the whale family, has a brain of about 1,600 grams. The human brain is somewhat smaller, averaging about 1,400 grams.

Next to humans, then, dolphins have the biggest brains for their size. They also have extremely complex brains—another sign of intelligence. In some ways, the dolphin brain is even more intricate and complex than the human brain. However, it is also quite different. The human brain is longer than it is wide. A dolphin's brain is wider than it is long, and it is quite high. The part of the dolphin brain that receives and analyzes sounds appears to be much larger and more complex than in humans. There are other important differences, too. We have barely begun

Next to humans, then, dolphins have the biggest brains for their size.

to understand the workings of the human brain, and we know much less about the dolphin brain. So it's difficult to compare them. There is no question, however, that the dolphin has the brain of a highly intelligent animal.

Another way to judge the dolphin's intelligence is by its behavior. We know surprisingly little about the behavior of the dolphins in the wild. Because they live in the ocean and move rapidly over long distances, human observers have not been able to spend more than brief moments with them. It is extremely difficult to approach a group of dolphins in a boat and stay with them long enough to study their behavior. The animals are visible briefly as they surface to breathe. Then they are lost to view as they move on under the water.

We do know that dolphins travel together in groups of about twenty or more individuals. At certain times of the year, many of these groups come together to form large herds that may number thousands of dolphins.

Dolphins have been seen to cooperate with each other in a number of ways. They often work together when they hunt for food. A group of dolphins will spread out in underwater formation and advance toward a school of anchovies. They herd the anchovies up toward the ocean surface, where they close in to feed on them.

Dolphins also have been seen to aid and protect members of their group. A shark that tries to attack a dolphin may find itself surrounded by other dolphins. One by one, the dolphins charge the shark at high speed, battering it to death with their hard beaks.

If a dolphin is ill or injured and can't rise to the surface for air, other dolphins rush over and take turns lifting the injured animal to the surface, so it can breathe.

These appear to be intelligent acts. Yet many other animals cooperate in similar ways.

The best evidence for dolphins' intelligence comes from their behavior in captivity. Bottle-nosed dolphins are famous as star performers in seaquariums. They can master a wide variety of complex tricks and stunts. They catch on quickly and often learn a trick simply by watching other dolphins perform it. Trainers say that they can learn faster than any other animal.

A standard laboratory test shows just how quickly they can learn. An animal can be trained to push a lever in order to earn a reward. It takes hundreds of trials for a rhesus monkey to learn to do this. Dolphins catch on in about 20 trials.

Besides being quick learners, dolphins are talented mimics—another sign of intelligence. Sometimes they can watch an action only once and then repeat it. One dolphin watched a diver use a mechanical scraper to clean an observation window in its tank. When given the scraper, the dolphin used it just as the diver had.

With their keen hearing, dolphins also are experts at imitating sounds. Some researchers say that not only can they imitate the human voice, but they can actually learn the meaning of certain words.

Do dolphins really communicate in sophisticated ways? Scientists have conducted a number of experiments to find out.

Jarvis Bastian, a psychologist at the University of California at Davis, tried to determine if one dolphin can send specific information to another. Bastian trained two dolphins named Buzz and Doris to push underwater levers. By pushing the correct lever, they would earn their reward, a tasty fish. If they saw a flashing signal light, they had to push the lever on the left. If they saw a steady light, they had to push the lever on the right.

This is an easy lesson for dolphins. Buzz and Doris both learned it quickly.

(cont'd on next page)

Despite the years of study, researchers have never come up with convincing evidence that dolphins have a complex language. Although dolphins exchange many sounds, we have no idea what those sounds mean. As one scientist put it, "It's a bit like a man from outer space tapping into the Bell System center trying to make sense of all the beeps and switching."

One dolphin may be able to describe an underwater object to another by re-creating the sounds that bounce back from that object. Instead of "saying" a single word that stands for "sharks," for example, the dolphin would repeat the sounds that bounce back from the shark. It would create a sound-picture of the shark, which it could pass along to other dolphins, telling them how big it is, how far away it is, and possibly even what kind of shark it is.

At the moment, that is an unproven theory. The sounds exchanged by dolphins remain an unsolved mystery.

> *The dolphin's mind remains a mystery, too.*

The dolphin's mind remains a mystery, too. While everyone agrees that dolphins are smart, they don't agree on how smart they really are. Karen Pryor, who trained many dolphins at Sea Life Park, once guessed that dolphins rank in intelligence somewhere between dogs and chimpanzees. John Lilly, a devoted student of dolphins who has written many books about them, believes that they may be as intelligent as humans. "It is possible that their intelligence is comparable to ours," says Lilly, "but in a strange fashion."

Other scientists aren't too sure. According to them, we just don't have enough evidence to understand the dolphin mind or to judge the dolphin's intelligence.

—Russell Freedman

Start-Up: "How Smart Are Dolphins?" does not fit into the reporting format of either the field or the laboratory report you have studied in this chapter. However, the information in this report is ably presented. Many government and business reports are given in various formats. Often an employee is asked to write a report for which no instructions are given, making it necessary to design a format.

Connection: Researchers use two basic types of research for acquiring their information: primary and secondary research. **Primary research** is gathering firsthand information. The researcher might perform a series of experiments, conduct interviews with experts on the topic being researched, or use official records and documents. **Secondary research** is gathering and analyzing facts and ideas from published sources such as books and articles. The authors of these sources have obtained their data or information from an original source, and then they basically do what they want with it. A researcher needs to be careful with secondary research; he or she should check the sources for accuracy.

1. What type of research was used to secure information for this report: primary or secondary?

2. Analyze the literature selection by answering the following questions:

   a. What is the title of the selection?

   b. Who is the audience?

   c. What is the purpose?

   d. What is some background information?

   e. How was the investigation conducted?

   f. What were the results?

   g. What were the conclusions?

   h. Discuss the conclusions. What do they mean?

The Storeowner Who Missed Her Sale

Susan told her family that her store was going to have its biggest sale since it opened. The sale was scheduled for Tuesday, the following day. Early Tuesday morning, Susan went out to start the car but found that the car's windshield needed to be cleaned. When she entered the garage to get the windshield washer fluid, she noticed that the garage windows were open. She shut the windows, but then she stopped to clean up the water from the open windows. Susan also discovered water on the lawnmower, so she tried to start it to make sure it still worked, However, Susan found that the lawnmower needed oil. On her way to get the oil, she saw that the dog needed water. . . .

Becoming a Professional

"*We must dare to think 'unthinkable' thoughts. We must learn to explore all the options and possibilities that confront us in a complex and rapidly changing world.*"

—J. WILLIAM FULBRIGHT, U.S. SENATOR

Workplace Skills in This Chapter

- Use **resources** to set goals.

- Improve **interpersonal** skills through analysis of negotiation and team situations.

- Interpret **information** to prepare a time management plan.

- Analyze **systems** to make decisions.

- Apply **technology** to increase professional growth.

As you complete Chapter 16, you will

- analyze your use of time.

- define and set different types of goals.

- design a schedule using effective time management.

- understand leadership styles.

- analyze ineffective and effective meetings and negotiations.

- explain vocational student organizations and their importance.

- understand the purpose for joining professional organizations.

Feel overwhelmed? How can you fit everything you want to do into your week? The presentation is due for Tech Communication class, your boss needs overtime hours from you this weekend, and the local VSO competition date is fast approaching. Why is everyone asking so much from you?

Becoming a professional doesn't mean that you have to become a doctor, an attorney, or even a teacher—unless you want to become one. Becoming a professional means that not only will you have the knowledge to go out and get a job in your field, but also that you present an image. That polished image reflects the way you will conduct your professional life.

Time: A Personal Definition

Time is frustrating. You cannot touch time. Try and try again, but you cannot save or renew time. Time travels at various speeds. The clock seems to go much more slowly on Friday afternoon than it does on Saturday night. The last few pages of the assignment often take much longer to read than the first half of the chapter. Sometimes time does seem out of control. Nothing gets done on time. Deadlines are always approaching. You overslept, and you can't find the left shoe that matches the green outfit you want to wear today.

However, you can handle time. Remember, you're in charge. Effective **time management** is getting done *what* you want to do *when* you want to do it. It is also finding what you want to find when you're looking for something. Controlling time has nothing to do with being neat or perfect. Taking command of your surroundings puts you in charge of your time; then you get more out of the time you have. However, before you try to manage your time more effectively, you need to discover what you're doing with it now.

Practice 16-1: Monitoring Time

Use *Student Workbook* page 16-A to discover how you are using your time for a few days of your life. To do this monitoring, you will record your time in 30-minute periods, from 7 a.m. to 11 p.m., for the number of days your teacher tells you.

In the left column for each day, write your general activities. Driving, watching television, taking care of children, exercising, working, sleeping, and going to school are all examples of some general ways that you may spend your time.

Every two or three hours, record what you've done by darkening the boxes on the chart. Each small section represents 30 minutes.

After you have recorded the time period, total the darkened blocks for each category. Divide the total by two to find the number of hours spent on each activity. In the Comments box, record what you discovered about the totals. Save your form for use in Practice 16-2.

Wasting Time

Everyone wastes time at some point in the day. The most efficient business executive does not use every minute wisely. Throwing away minutes does add up. Catch the time wasters and save time. Descriptions of four ways to waste time follow.

CAREER C·O·N·N·E·C·T·I·O·N

For 55 percent of U.S. workers, the average part of the lunch hour actually spent eating lunch is down to just 36 minutes, according to *Career Opportunity News*. The remaining 24 minutes is used for a variety of activities, including the following:

- Socializing (53%)
- Running errands (44%)
- Catching up on work (38%)
- Reading (37%)
- Making personal phone calls (28%)

- Shopping (27%)
- Exercising (14%)
- Medical appointments (9%)
- Monitoring child care (6%)
- Interviewing for other jobs (1%)

INFOBIT

"There is nothing so useless as doing efficiently that which should not be done at all."

PETER DRUCKER, U.S. AUTHORITY ON CORPORATE MANAGEMENT

The Unproductive Task

Sometimes concentration does not come easily. As a result, other activities often take the place of what should be done. Studying for a test, for instance, is not a favorite activity. So talking on the phone, making popcorn, and brushing the dog take the place of studying. Most of us spend too much time on activities that are not urgent or not important or both.

The Wrong Task

Guests are coming to the house in one hour, and you have the house nearly straightened. All you have to do is to clean the bathroom. Choosing to straighten the desk over cleaning the bathroom may seem like a good choice. However, the bathroom is the problem; the desk is not the solution. Zeroing in on what is needed, rather than what is your preference, is necessary.

The Right Task Done the Wrong Way

Laura's assignment is to frame a window for carpentry class. Unless she attempts the project without measurements, she cannot finish the framing. All the required tasks must be done to attain the goal of finishing on schedule. However, if the details of preparing for the framing take most of the assigned time, then Laura is not planning her time wisely. Preparation, such as drawing, gathering supplies, and adjusting equipment, becomes more important than the project itself.

Too Much Detail

Not every woodworking project is a fine piece of furniture. Not every assignment is a term paper. Not every piece has to be perfect. Sometimes perfection is not necessary.

To test whether you need perfection, ask the question, "Is it a computer?" A computer must have everything perfectly

QUALITY **C·O·N·N·E·C·T·I·O·N**

Here are some ways to use time wisely.

In five minutes, I can

- make an appointment.
- stretch my back, neck, and leg muscles.

In 10 minutes, I can

- proofread a short report.
- order concert tickets.

In 30 minutes (or less), I can

- skim an article, marking sections for later study.
- organize my desktop.

working in order for it to process correctly. However, a less accurate piece of equipment, such as a toaster, can have a wire loose or be full of crumbs and still work. A rough draft does not have to be perfectly formatted; it can be handwritten on notebook paper with even a few cross-outs. On the other hand, you must correct and key the final draft perfectly.

Practice 16-2: Discovering Time Wasters

teamwork With a partner, brainstorm as many time wasters as you can write down in five minutes. You may use your time monitoring form from Practice 16-1 for ideas. Now choose two time wasters and list them. Then, on a separate sheet of paper, answer the following three questions about each time waster you listed.

1. Why is the time waster so tempting to use?

   Time Waster A:

   Time Waster B:

2. What is the benefit of using the time waster?

   Time Waster A:

   Time Waster B:

3. What is the problem with using the time waster?

   Time Waster A:

   Time Waster B:

INFOBIT

The Procrastinators' Club of America was founded in 1956. The members celebrate National Procrastination Month in March—the month before April 15 (of course!).

Procrastination

Tim is a procrastinator. He has every intention of doing what he says he will, but Tim does not follow through. He does very little of what he says he will do. In fact, he regrets saying yes ten minutes after he

INFOBIT

"It's better to have loafed and lost than never to have loafed at all."

JAMES THURBER,
U.S. AUTHOR

says it. Tim is also a charming man. He wants everyone to like him, so he has a hard time saying no. However, he also has many reasons for not finishing jobs. His excuse is usually, "I had so much to do that I didn't know where to start—so I didn't." When caught not finishing tasks, Tim claims that he works best under pressure, so he puts things off until the last minute. However, if he is constantly reminded, Tim feels that he is under too much pressure and decides not to do anything at all. That's the time when Tim looks for a rescuer. He hopes that the job will somehow disappear or someone will take over. Usually someone does.

Procrastination: A Self Check

If you find some of yourself in Tim, you may be suffering from **procrastination,** also known as *tomorrowitis.* "I'll think about it tomorrow" is the procrastinator's theme. Procrastinators often use these excuses:

* I've got too much work to start on it now.

* When I have some free time, I'll do it immediately.

* I'll get to it tomorrow.

* I've had no chance to get to it.

* After I unwind, I'll start on it.

* No problem. I'll do these other things, and then I'll get right on it.

* That's right—I've been planning to do it.

People who procrastinate avoid difficult jobs. (Actually, procrastination often takes more energy than doing the job itself.)

Procrastination may not be a problem in all parts of your life. You may be very organized at work, but you may forget to pay the bills at home. Any job involving writing may be the last job you'll do, but when a job involves speaking, you'll be the first to volunteer. Procrastination, then, may be selective because of your own personal conflict. You need to do something, but resist doing it. Rather than finding a way to resolve the dilemma, you postpone it.

Practice 16-3: Exploring Procrastination

Fill out *Student Workbook* page 16-B. Answer the questions yes or no by placing a check mark in the correct column. Answer each question honestly. Then total your score according to the instructions provided. (Don't put off doing this Practice!)

Helping to Eliminate Procrastination

Effective **time management** ensures that time is used wisely. Procrastination becomes controlled, and forgetfulness becomes manageable. The result? More time with less work. Here are some tips to help you manage your time.

* Watch for time wasters. Use Practice 16-2 on page 540 to catch those time wasters and save time.

* Do the most difficult, boring jobs first. Get these tasks over with, and the rest of the day will seem to go much more smoothly.

* Decide what is your most productive time of day. Some people work best in the early morning; others do not get motivated to work hard until late afternoon. When do you have the most energy? Make the most of your energy during that time.

* Break a large job into chunks. When you divide it into separate parts, the big job seems smaller.

* Pay attention to your attention. When you find yourself daydreaming, try to take a ten-minute break. You'll come back refreshed, with a more positive attitude. Or make a "To Do" list and a "To Think About" list; then concentrate on them.

* Ask yourself, "Is this a computer?" Remember: perfection is not always necessary. If lower standards will be acceptable, allow yourself to use them. If you're a perfectionist, make one intentional mistake a day.

INFOBIT

Ask yourself the following question. If you answer yes, then you're probably effectively managing your time. **Would I pay myself for what I did today?**

Goal Setting

What do you want out of your life? What do you believe in? What are the major goals you want to achieve in a lifetime? Asking yourself a few questions before you begin goal setting is the first step in organizing your life. **Goals** are specific expressions of your **values**. To determine your values, and the roles you want to play in your future, you need to ask yourself what activities have had special significance for you in the past. What have you really enjoyed doing and sharing? What gave you a sense of confidence and inner peace?

In his song "Blowing in the Wind," Bob Dylan sang of Spanish as being a lovely-sounding language. Not only is Spanish lovely-sounding, but in the United States, 63 percent of business executives surveyed by *Office Systems 97* magazine chose Spanish as the first preference for an employee's second language. The Japanese language finished second, followed by Chinese, German, and French. Is learning a second language one of your goals?

Practice 16-4: From the Past to the Future

The roles you choose today are probably different than the roles you chose five years ago. Ten years from now, you'll choose different roles than today. Using your memories of the past and your imaginative dreams of the future, complete the following statements. Do not answer too quickly; take the time to consider your remarks.

1. Five years ago, my most important roles were

2. Today, my most important roles are

3. In ten years, my most important roles will be

Goals

One good way to see if your values and your roles for the future really matter to you is to fit them into your goals. You can determine truly meaningful roles and values by whether you are really willing to spend time accomplishing them. After establishing the goals, break them into activities, starting with long-range plans and ending with short-term or even daily activities.

Long-Term Goals

The major targets, or ambitions, of life are **long-term goals.** Reaching these goals takes a long time. Goals such as "I want to own my own business," "I want to master a second language," or "I want to travel to every one of the 50 states" take a long time to accomplish. Long-term goals may include your career, your economic plans, and your family plans.

Midterm Goals

What do you have to do in the next two to five years to achieve your long-term goals? **Midterm goals** are activities or projects that you must accomplish to attain a long-term goal. You can't perform a goal;

you perform an activity to reach a goal. To become the owner of a beauty shop, your midterm goal might be to attain your degree in business management, in addition to having your cosmetologist's license. If you want to travel the United States for a long-term goal, plan a midterm goal of visiting a new state every year for five years.

Short-Term Goals

Midterm goals will generate the **short-term goals.** These goals can be reached in one year or less. Start taking action now or in the very near future. Taking the necessary admission tests, completing school applications, and working out a schedule with your employer are short-term goals for the midterm goal of obtaining that college degree in business management. Completing a travel itinerary for your summer vacation to Arkansas, a state you've never seen, is a short-term goal towards the midterm goal of visiting a new state every year for five years.

Barriers

Goal setting isn't always smooth. Being unsure about speaking in public (the number one fear for adults), lack of training, procrastinating about organization, or family problems are **barriers** that could prevent you from succeeding if you let them. Planning ahead for high-risk situations helps with the temptations that may get you off track. However, blaming others or feeling sorry for yourself won't help you accomplish your goals. Staying positive helps keep you on the track and tells others you believe in yourself. Department store owner R. H. Macy had seven businesses fail before his store in New York became a success. Babe Ruth struck out 1,330 times, but he also hit 714 home runs! So perseverance will reward you if you don't quit trying to achieve your goals. Remember, the only way to avoid failing is never to try.

INFOBIT

"Failure is only the opportunity to begin again more intelligently."

HENRY FORD, U.S. INVENTOR AND MANUFACTURER

Practice 16-5: Past Persistence

Think of obstacles you've overcome in the past. You probably have more tough times you've conquered than you think. Completing that complicated project, coming back from an injury, and mastering the fine art of cooking—these are examples of overcoming barriers to achieve success. List at least three barriers that you have successfully defeated. Beside each barrier, describe the way you conquered it.

EXAMPLE:

Barrier	Way I Overcame It
Memorizing algebraic formulas	Invented rhymes that start with the first letters or numbers of the formula's parts

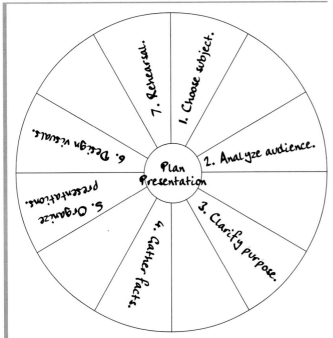

Figure 16-1: *Using the Wheel to plan a presentation*

Goal-Setting Methods

Goal setting is not just a paper-and-pencil activity, but a way of visualizing a goal and the activities you need to perform to achieve it. Each person needs to find his or her best method of putting goals on paper. Here are three practical ways of planning a presentation:

The Wheel

At the center of the wheel (sometimes known as webbing or a spidergram) is the goal. Each spoke represents an activity needed to reach the goal. You can write the activities in the order you need to do them or add timelines on the spokes. Figure 16-1 demonstrates the Wheel method.

The Fishbone

On the backbone or at the head of the fish, write the goal. On the bones of the fish, write the activities needed to reach the goal. Using the bones, you can divide activities into each action required. Figure 16-2 shows a Fishbone diagram.

Lists

Numbered lists in a column are the way many people set goals. Listing is not as visual as the Wheel or the Fishbone, which shows that all the activities support the goal. You can list tasks in order of importance or in a timeline. Figure 16-3 shows a list used to plan a presentation.

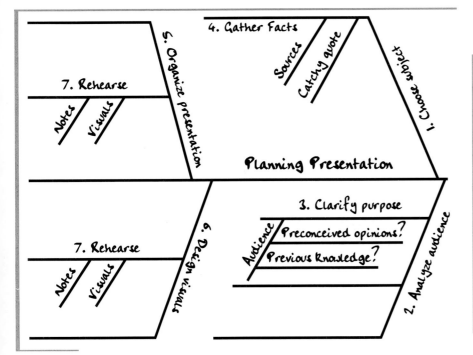

Figure 16-2: *Using the Fishbone to plan a presentation*

PLANNING A PRESENTATION

1. Choose a subject.
2. Analyze your audience.
3. Clarify your purpose.
4. Gather facts.
5. Organize the presentation.
6. Design your visuals.
7. Rehearse your presentation.

Figure 16-3: *Using a list to plan a presentation*

TECHNOLOGY C·O·N·N·E·C·T·I·O·N

With the amount of information that is available increasing daily, bookstores are flooded with publications on memory strategies. One of the easiest strategies is **mnemonics**, a technique in which you use devices such as rhymes or formulas to help in remembering. Here are several mnemonic devices:

- To remember how to spell *friend:*

  A *fri**end*** to the **end**.

- To remember how to adjust your clocks for daylight savings or standard time:

  Spring ahead; fall back.

- To remember which way to turn a bolt to tighten or remove it:

  Right is tight, left is loose.

Practice 16-6: Setting Goals

1. During the next five minutes, write down any long-term goals that come to mind. Use *Student Workbook* page 16-C if you prefer to use a Wheel or a Fishbone, adding lines to either if needed. Long-term goals may involve education, career, personal relationships, travel, possessions, savings, and other areas. When the time is up, select the three long-term goals that are the most important to you today.

2. Now select one long-term goal from the list you created above. For five minutes, write down midterm goals that will help you reach the chosen long-term goal. These goals should be activities that you can do in the next two to five years. After the five minutes are up, choose the three midterm goals that are the most realistic.

3. Select one midterm goal from the list above. In the next five minutes, write down short-term goals that will help you reach that specific midterm goal. A short-term goal can be achieved in one year or less. Exact actions, such as choosing a specific school or earning a specific amount of money, are necessary for a short-term goal. After the time is up, weed out any inappropriate goals. Then select three short-term goals that you will begin working on today.

INFOBIT

Today's workers put in 138 more hours per year than they did in the 1970s.

STEPHAN RECHTSCHAFER,
U.S. AUTHORITY
ON TIME MANAGEMENT

PEOPLE **C·O·N·N·E·C·T·I·O·N**

Art Mellor had a goal and a plan. At age 27, he had been dreaming of starting his own business for years. To realize this dream, he planned to get a job at the smallest company that would hire him. That company turned out to be Cayman Systems Inc., a descendant of the giant Apple Corporation. When Art interviewed with Cayman, he told the maker of networking software and hardware that he intended to get the skills to start his own company. And they hired him!

After three years, Art Mellor gained a considerable amount of on-the-job experience. The principal rules he learned were to be quiet and listen to customers—and to learn from the company's mistakes. Even the most successful company will make mistakes; the gain is worth the pain. Art Mellor's knowledge enabled him to start Midnight Networks Inc. with his partners in 1992. His company is continually successful today as a part of Teradyne, Inc.

Priorities

The realistic goals you develop help you set your **priorities** in life. Subgoals developed from major goals can be used in scheduling tasks. The arrangement of these tasks in order of importance gives you your priorities. Use your priorities to establish your calendars and to develop your own daily system.

Calendars

Calendars overrun mailboxes and bookstores as the new year approaches. Try using more than one calendar; scheduling on calendars yearly or weekly can be done for different purposes. Develop goals and tasks on yearly calendars, showing the preparation time to achieve a short-term goal in one year's time.

Your daily calendar system should contain a To-Do List of daily priorities. The average list should have ten things that you can reasonably expect to accomplish each day. Some of these tasks may occur every day or weekly or even monthly, but you are doing them on this particular day. In this list, you set daily priorities in relationship to your long-term, midterm, and short-term goals.

A, B, and C Priorities

By breaking larger projects into chunks, you can accomplish assignments more easily. Have a backup plan for emergencies and interruptions that may arise to prevent you from finishing that presentation for tomorrow. By planning over a span of several days or an even longer period of time, you can avoid the problem of pulling an all-nighter or facing your instructor with an incomplete assignment. Review the dates and the timelines, keeping the goal and **objective** cathy   by Cathy Guisewite

CATHY © 1991, 1992 Cathy Guisewite.
Reprinted with permission of UNIVERSAL PRESS SYNDICATE. All rights reserved.

INFOBIT

The most productive time of the day for 68 percent of U.S. workers polled by The Gallup Organization is during regular working hours. Only 14 percent said they were the most productive before working hours, and 11 percent said after working hours. The remaining 3 percent? They weren't sure when they're the most productive—and hopefully they aren't working with you!

(the *why* of the goal) in mind. To be effective, the To-Do List must be written with A, B, and C priorities and include specific timelines.

A Priorities

The A items are the most important things to do during the day. These items are due or must be done immediately. To label these items, ask the question, "What will happen if I don't get this done?" If the results will be critical, then label the item an A.

B Priorities

The B items are important but are less critical than the A items. The B priorities may be postponed for a short time if necessary. They may become As if postponed several times.

C Priorities

These items do not need immediate attention. They could be done today, but if no time is left, they can wait. Often routine items are on this list. Too many Cs can become C-fever, a problem. Sometimes it's easier to make a list full of Cs than to have to cope with As. To some people As seem too difficult or pose a greater chance of failure.

Prioritizing Tasks

How do you decide where to put a job? Learn the 80/20 rule: the important work for the day is only about 20 percent of all the items you have written down. The other 80 percent is not critical for today. So focus on the 20 percent that matters.

When is the best time to organize the calendar and the To-Do List? Slow starters organize the day better in the morning in order to arrange the day in their minds. Those people who begin work energetically in the morning plan best the night before. However, no one can plan for you except you. Having the schedule planned ahead of time and following it will make more things go the way you want more often. Reduction of chaos helps you overcome an obstacle before it becomes one.

Assess the best times for privacy and people. When do you work best by yourself? When is the best time for you to interact with people? Private time is the most productive time for work, so plan creative projects and high-demand A projects during that time in your day.

Practice 16-7: Making a Time Design

Plan your activities for the next three days on the time schedule provided by your teacher. Choose activities you actually want to finish, and schedule enough time to complete them. Use a To-Do List to jot down ideas that will fit into your schedule. Mark the items of the To-Do List as A, B, or C priorities. You won't be planning every minute, but make the Time Design as detailed as possible.

In the Actual column, record how you actually spent your time. The purpose of this column is to show you how your activities differed from your original planning.

Practice 16-8: Reaching Goals

For this Practice, use the three short-term goals from Practice 16-6, page 546. Choose one of those short-term goals, and complete the following statement:

In order to move toward this goal, I will _____ in the next 48 hours.

EXAMPLE:

study for the biology test a minimum of 3 hours.

Have your teacher check your statement. After two days, share the results with the class.

TECHNOBIT

How do people organize themselves? According to time management speaker Jeff Davidson, most use To-Do Lists and adhesive notes, but 42 percent use diaries (mostly on computers) and electronic calendars. Leaving reminders on home answering machines and e-mail on home computers is common also. At the opposite technological end, 4 percent remind themselves by writing on their hands.

Teams and Decision Making

Almost any survey of employers ranks teamwork skills as among the most necessary for success in today's work environment. In school, groups are important, but as students, you may not agree with their importance. Teams provide constant feedback, a sense of loyalty, and a win-together/lose-together feeling.

INFOBIT

Never say, "It's not my job." Why? Because you may talk yourself out of that assignment— and out of your job, too.

A good manager needs to have the team decide what needs to be done. How will the team finish the task? Who will do it? The team must consider the needs of the members or employees; however, the team must also consider the customer. The customer's needs must determine the outcome. Even classwork has a customer, for a customer is the person who receives and/or uses the work of other persons. The customer may be your teacher, your employer, a group member, or even yourself. What is good for the team is good for all, from the lowest-paid worker to the president of the company.

Practice 16-9: Team Production

teamwork After breaking the class into groups, your teacher will give each group some materials to make a product. You will have ten minutes to choose and make the product using only those supplies. *Beware:* your teacher will be making changes in each group while the process is taking place.

After completing the team production, you will be asked the following questions during class discussion:

1. How did the team choose what product to make? How did production take place?

2. What roles evolved in the process? Did the person who had the idea for the product do the most work? Who provided the most encouragement?

3. What good leadership qualities were revealed?

4. What happened when one of the team members was removed?

5. What happened when one team member was present, but did not participate?

6. What happened when the working conditions worsened?

7. How could your team have improved?

8. How does this Practice relate to work? To school?

Practice 16-10: Making Choices

teamwork Your teacher will divide the class into groups.

1. Brainstorm what choices you have made so far today. Examples may include choosing what time to get out of bed, whether to come to school, what to wear, what to eat for breakfast and/or lunch, and so on. These choices are not life-threatening, just average, everyday decisions everyone must make.

2. Your teacher has prepared four small bags. Your group must decide which bag it will pick; all group members must come to a consensus on the decision. During the decision-making process, you may ask the teacher questions. Certain questions have limitations; the one question that you cannot ask is to look inside the bag. The teacher will give you a time limit; your group must make its decision by this time.

Each group should choose a recorder and a leader who will facilitate the group discussion. (See *Student Workbook* page 5-D for an explanation of some of the group roles.) The recorder will write down the positive and negative reasons for choosing each bag. Then after your group has reached a consensus, the recorder will write down the choice that the group made and hand that choice to the teacher.

Quality

The search for quality is never-ending. In the past, image was the primary emphasis for most companies, but today the business world emphasizes quality more than image for an employee and for the customer. Generally, quality can be divided into three types:

* *Routine quality.* Routine quality means the level of service that is expected, such as a menu, a satisfactory repair, and a correct order.

* *Assumed quality.* The customer expects this type of quality as well. Examples include a pleasant greeting, prompt delivery, and clean surroundings.

* *Unanticipated quality.* This type of quality adds value to a business or a product and enhances the self-esteem of the customer. Examples of this unexpected level of service would be a follow-up call checking on product satisfaction, complimentary dessert for a birthday dinner, and a thank-you note for an extra gesture of support or encouragement.

Leadership Styles

A school of fish does not swim without direction, a place to go and a place to feed. Whether or not you can see the leader of the group, each school of fish has one. Out of hundreds of fish, the leader appears because it has certain qualities. Whether on a committee, in a class discussion, in an organization, or at work, most people have been in charge, however briefly.

The most effective leaders, however, are trained. Professional associations and vocational student organizations (VSOs) offer formal training. Observing successful leaders helps one to gain the necessary skills and confidence for leadership. What leaders do in groups is called their **leadership style.** Style influences an organization, whether the organization is a club, a classroom, or the workplace.

A leader with the **authoritarian style of leadership** maintains strict control of everything that the group will do. Groups led by authoritarian leaders tend to make decisions more quickly, make fewer mistakes, and get more work done because the leader makes all the decisions and does most of the work himself or herself.

As a result, the group depends on the leader more for guidance, rather than trying to make its own decisions. The drawback of an authoritarian group is that the leader is not really part of the group. At times, the authoritarian leader is a dictator, and the group members are the commoners. This type of leader is not a true communicator. In this age of team decision making, the authoritarian leader is generally not accepted; however when a building is burning, the person who leads the group to safety uses the authoritarian leadership style.

Laissez-faire leadership works well with highly trained, very motivated groups whose members are leaders themselves. The leader does not take part in or direct group decisions. The group is actually leading itself, for the members determine its goals, its rules, and the level or amount of participation of each person. Yet, be careful in using this style, since few groups succeed without some leadership.

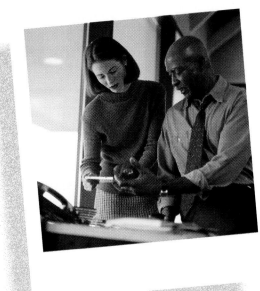

The **facilitative team leader** produces results. The group does the primary decision making, with coaching and encouragement by the leader. Although this style takes more time, group members feel a greater sense of participation in problem solving and decision making. The facilitator is open, sincere, and flexible, producing positive results. Business leaders today are giving up an authoritarian style of leadership in favor of facilitative or democratic leadership. Now the leader fosters a feeling of cooperation and esprit de corps, along with mutual respect and interdependence. The result? Increased productivity.

The team leader treats each person on the team as though he or she is the most important member. Through motivation rather than manipulation, the team leader shows the importance of each person's particular job and of him or her personally. When people know you care about them as individuals and about their team and its goals, you'll find that they will be thinking more about how to make the team successful than about their own self-importance.

An effective facilitator-leader creates a positive climate for team decision-making and problem-solving situations. The leader whose group will have the most success keeps the following observations in mind:

* Groups whose members know each other make better decisions.

* If the group is large, the members contribute less.

* If a member offers feedback, it should be stated in a positive way; then it is more readily accepted.

* If members believe their skills are weaker than others', they will be less likely to use those skills.

* A person who sits at the head of the table or in the most central position will often become the leader of the group. The foot of the table is the weakest position. A round table is a friendlier table, inviting conversation and promoting a spirit of teamwork. With a round table, the leader should be a facilitator.

* A leader's worst words are "I'll get back to you." Such a comment often makes group members feel that their concerns are worthless and that the leader has all the power. The leader has lost the group's confidence.

Practice 16-11: Evaluating Leadership Styles

careers Think about your current supervisor or the supervisor on your last job. Answer the following questions about that person's leadership style.

1. What leadership style does the supervisor use? Authoritarian? Laissez–faire? Facilitative?

2. How did you decide which style fit the supervisor?

3. Give a specific example of the supervisor's using that style.

4. What do you like or dislike about the leadership style?

5. If you were a supervisor, what leadership style would you normally use? Why?

Successful Meetings

Leadership and officer training almost always includes how to run a meeting. **Parliamentary procedure,** the rules for conducting a meeting, may seem overly formal, but many organizations use informal versions of these rules to run a meeting efficiently and fairly. Parliamentary procedure is used most often in formal meetings and competitive events.

Many meetings are more casual. Groups form to decide the theme of Career Day, to hire a new employee, to form a budget, to go over new rules, and so on. **Teleconferences** are meetings in which the participants

INFOBIT

Sixty-five percent of U.S. workers said they spend some time every day in meetings, according to Day-Timers. However, 11 percent said they spent two to seven hours a day in meetings, and more than one-third of those surveyed believed that none of the time spent in meetings is wasted. (A contradiction?)

conduct their business via a conference telephone call or videoconference to save travel. Whatever the reason for the meeting, the following basic guidelines will help to ensure its success.

1. Get the meeting started on time. If the meeting is scheduled to start at ten o'clock, then be sure to begin at ten o'clock. Otherwise, your next meeting will also start late, people will arrive late, and you will lose strength as a leader.

2. Use an **agenda.** A good agenda is practically a map of the meeting. This map is the list of items to be included in the meeting. Following the list will keep things moving. Using the agenda, you will have an objective for the meeting, an orderly plan, and an end to the meeting. Give those attending an agenda as far in advance as possible. The people attending the meeting can have roles assigned so that they can be prepared to lead parts of the meeting. This style is facilitative leadership; the group members will then feel more a part of the decision-making and problem-solving process.

3. Keep the discussion on topic. The agenda will be a guide, but often topics lead to other ideas. Then the discussion is soon off-topic. Refer to the agenda, and have the group relate the discussion to it. Shortly, the discussion will be on schedule again. Another suggestion to keep a meeting within the agenda is to appoint someone in the group to guide the discussion back on track when needed. This allows the leader to be less of a police officer and instead to concentrate on the issues. Try to schedule a time for comments at the end of the meeting, as well as a few minutes for off-topic discussion.

4. Encourage all members to participate. Think of yourself as a talk-show host. Make sure every member gets a chance to contribute. Also, try to end long-winded discussions. Asking members for agenda items before a meeting encourages participation.

5. Use questions, **paraphrases,** and summaries to keep the meeting moving. Questions enable you to point out the important points of the discussion. Paraphrasing promotes clarity; saying, "Do I understand that you meant . . . ?" invites communication. Summaries emphasize the major items. These positive techniques help keep the group on track.

6. End the meeting with a summary. The summary will finalize all decisions and discussion within the meeting. Ask for questions to make sure all members understand the results of the meeting.

To influence negotiation positively, follow these basic rules:

1. **Know what you want.** Be able to explain that goal easily. Preparation is absolutely essential. Unfortunately, it is not unusual to enter into negotiation without having done your research. For example, is your motivation more money, prestige, or career opportunities? Think it out ahead of time.

2. **Know what the other person needs.** Try to plan a solution that will meet the other person's needs—and your needs. The more you understand the other side, the more apt you are to achieve your goal.

3. **Prepare a backup plan,** an alternative solution that should meet your needs and the needs of others as well. For example, if a raise isn't possible, suggest more vacation days or flexible hours.

4. **Don't give up if your plan is rejected.** Showing your anger often stops negotiations immediately. If you regroup and offer your alternative solution, at least you are showing your determination. Getting even or getting mad is not the solution—the solution is to achieve your goal.

Conflicts and Negotiation Within Groups

Group members who know each other well will have conflict. Conflict will occur even if the group usually agrees on most subjects. Often conflict results from a change in the way things have always been. Why resist change? Well, it is easier not to change. If the group changes, it will have to see, accept, and use new ideas. If the change doesn't fit the old rules or habits, then everyone must make an adjustment.

Moving toward the future causes shifts in thinking. For example, in the early 1980s, a computer was the tool of the accountant and the data processor. If a company made a mistake, the blame was put on the computer. Today, however, computers are in many homes. Most households have computer chips in such items as microwaves, automobile dashboards, and remote control devices. Although the computer is still blamed when a mistake is made, we have learned that we can control this invention. The computer is part of us now.

There are four ways that people react to change.

1. *Do nothing.* If you ignore change, maybe it will go away.

2. *Outwardly rebel.* People who are not consulted about the change will often protest the loudest.

3. *Adapt.* Persons who adapt to change want to keep their jobs—and eventually become part of the change.

4. *Welcome the change.* These persons become motivated by the change and will eventually become the leaders.

INFOBIT

Supervisors in the United States are spending twice as much time settling employee disputes as they did in 1986, when they spent 9 percent of their time resolving personality conflicts, according to The Futurist magazine.

When group members make an effort to see one another's viewpoint, less conflict will result. Members will not always agree, but at least they will have tried shifting their thinking. The successful facilitative leader will help them.

INFOBIT

Even suggesting a seating arrangement will relieve a conflict situation. If a member is in conflict with someone, try not to have the opponents sit across from each other. Instead, seat opponents next to each other. Having the two people closer to each other makes both more vulnerable and results in less conflict.

Practice 16-12: Running a Meeting

teamwork

1. After reviewing the following questions in small groups, listen to the CD recording of a meeting that your teacher will play for you. Take notes to prepare for discussion.

    a. Do the group members have an agenda before the meeting date? Is an agenda used during the meeting?

    b. Does the meeting start on time? Explain.

    c. Who is the leader of the discussion? How can you tell?

    d. Is the meeting a decision-making situation? Why or why not?

    e. In a decision-making situation, the leader gives specific instructions to the group. What are the instructions given?

    f. Does the leader take part in the discussion? How?

    g. Is the leader in charge of the group? Is the group listening to the leader? Give some examples.

    h. How does the leader encourage all the participants to become involved?

    i. Does the leader give positive feedback to each group member? What are some of the leader's statements?

    j. Does the discussion stay on-topic? When does it stray off-topic?

    k. How does the leader keep the discussion moving? Give examples of questions, summaries, and comments used for this purpose.

    l. What is the decision made? How is the decision made?

    m. Does the leader end with a summary?

    n. How does the group display confidence in the final decision?

    o. What leadership style is displayed in this meeting? Why did you choose this style?

2. After ending the discussion on the first meeting, listen to the next selection, taking notes on the second meeting. Then discuss and answer the same questions concerning the second meeting.

Vocational Student Organizations

In a vocational program, participating in **vocational student organizations (VSOs)** is part of the curriculum. These organizations promote student involvement and education. The vocational lab, the related/applied classroom, and the VSO are all parts of the educational picture (see Figure 16-4). The classroom work cannot exist without the VSOs; the VSOs cannot exist without the classroom work.

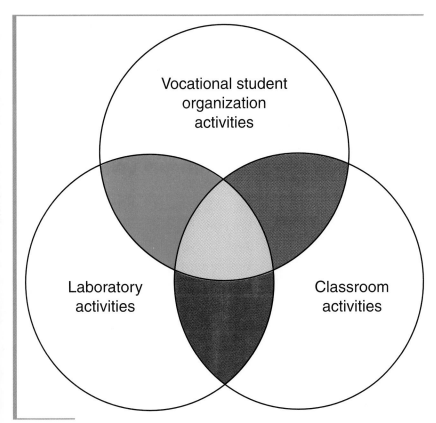

Figure 16-4: *The related parts of vocational/technical education*

Specific VSOs

Which VSO you belong to depends on your educational program. The major VSOs are described in the following sections. A VSO chapter begins at the local level, has regional or district divisions, and then branches into the state, national, and international parts of the organization. Both high schools (secondary) and postsecondary schools participate in VSOs, for VSOs are the professional organizations for students in vocational training. Many VSOs also have **alumni** organizations for graduates.

Business Professionals of America and Future Business Leaders of America (FBLA)

These two organizations are designed to meet the needs of high school and postsecondary students enrolled in vocational business and office education programs. The organizations are part of the business student's education and develop leadership, interest in American business, and competency in business occupations.

DECA

Marketing education has DECA, formerly known as the Distributive Education Clubs of America, as its member VSO. The club develops students' skills in marketing, management, and entrepreneurship. Events sponsored by DECA events stress the needs of business and industry, as well as excellence in school and work, to provide the basis for a successful career.

Figure 16-5: *Logos of major vocational student organizations*
1. Printed with permission of the National FFA Organization. 2. Used with permission of DECA. 3. By permission of Future Business Leaders of America–Phi Beta Lambda, Inc. 4. Used by permission of Future Homemakers of America, Inc. 5. Used with permission of Business Professionals of America. 6. Used by permission of Vocational Industrial Clubs of America.

FFA

The oldest vocational student organization, FFA, is the national association of students preparing for careers in the science, business, and technology of agriculture. The group's activities, honors, and awards provide incentives and practical experience. Formerly known as the Future Farmers of America, this VSO has many time-honored traditions and has excellent leadership training.

Future Homemakers of America/Home Economics-Related Occupations (FHA/HERO)

The chapters for this VSO emphasize consumer and home economics, now called family and consumer sciences. Projects focus on student concerns, including nutrition and fitness, career exploration, preparation for employment, parenting skills, family relationships, teen pregnancy, substance abuse, peer pressure, and communication among different age groups.

Health Occupations Students of America (HOSA)

Health Occupations Students of America is the organization that promotes health-care careers and education. The organization is concerned with health-care issues, leadership development, career enrichment, and environmental problems. The activities include community health projects.

Vocational Industrial Clubs of America (VICA)

The organization for trade, industrial, technical, dental assisting, cosmetology, and medical occupation students, Vocational Industrial Clubs of America, offers leadership, citizenship, and character-development programs and activities to expand student skill training related to its career clusters. This organization emphasizes respect for the dignity of work, high standards, trade ethics, workmanship, scholarship, and safety, as well as partnerships with businesses in trade and industrial careers.

VSO Responsibilities

Vocational student organizations are more than clubs that collect your dues and give you a membership card. Your VSO is the specialized organization for students that helps in your transition from school to work within your career area. The national and state VSO divisions operate along with local chapters to improve skills, strengthen interest in the vocational program, provide appropriate information for the profession, and offer guidance through advisors, training, leadership, and reading materials. Encouraging various areas of professionalism, the VSO promotes professional growth, service learning, and competition through its chapter meetings, activities, and social events.

INFOBIT

"I find the harder I work, the more luck I seem to have."

THOMAS JEFFERSON, U.S. PRESIDENT

Professional Development

Developing leadership skills is an important part of the VSO's activities. Educational programs offer training in character development, continuous quality improvement, leadership training, job seeking, self-esteem, grooming, officer training, and citizenship. Leadership opportunities vary from running for office to being an active member of a committee.

Service Learning

Helping is another facet of vocational student organizations. Chapters of VSOs have been involved in toy, clothing, food, and blood drives; Red Cross aid; and voter registration, as well as for school functions, recycling, and campus cleanup. Service learning not only helps citizens but also earns recognition for the club and the school.

Competition

Competitive events are a primary part of vocational student organizations. The desire to win is strong for most people. However, remember that the experience and education that come from competing are well worth the effort, regardless of whether you win or lose. Competitive events are classified as either skills or leadership contests.

* Skills contests use the knowledge gained in the vocational program, either first-year or advanced. One type of skills contest is the project that will have to be completed to exact specifications within a certain time period. For example, in the VICA Residential Wiring skills competition, Thomas was given a schematic diagram of a circuit using standard wiring symbols. With only the required tools and provided materials,

he had to wire a cubicle to the specifications of the in-circuit design within a $2\frac{1}{2}$-hour time period.

The other type of skills contest is a demonstration. In the FHA/HERO Focus on the Child competition, Tracey demonstrated a sound box that teaches preschoolers a game and the alphabet at the same time.

* Leadership contests are events that are not related to one specific vocational program. One of the two major types of leadership events is directly associated with leadership skills. Running a meeting using parliamentary procedure, giving a prepared or extemporaneous speech, and participating in ceremonies are examples of such an event.

The other leadership competitive event includes knowledge tests for teams or individuals. These events can be tests on subjects indirectly related to the cluster, such as math, science, or health. Other knowledge tests cover information about the club itself, current events, or general knowledge.

Preparing for competition may seem difficult, but your instructors will help you. In skills events, your lab instructor can give you the confidence to try your best and help you with the knowledge needed for competing. Other instructors, especially your academic teachers, can help by listening to your speech, by proofreading, and by coaching team practices. Just ask; they'll be glad to help.

WEB LINK

Each vocational student organization has its own national Web site. In addition, many state and local chapters have Web sites. Investigate the national site, and report the results to the class.

Practice 16-13: Investigating Leadership Activities

careers

teamwork

Each VSO has leadership training, activities that teach you the leadership qualities discussed in the previous sections of this chapter. In small groups, research your particular VSO's leadership opportunities, You may have to go to the media center, to the VSO Web site, to your chapter advisor, or to your VSO officers. After finding the answers, your group will report to the class.

Professional Organizations

Professional organizations serve their members through networking. The professional organization provides a **network,** a way of connecting with information, jobs, and other individuals in the field. Whether a formalized structure or an informal group, a network is a supplement for the usual information gained from coworkers.

Advantages of Professional Organizations

Representing the interests of members to the community, professional associations convey information through meetings or publicity. The benefits of professional organizations include the following:

Services

Organizations offer special services for their members only, such as job placement and professional consultation for problem areas. The organization may also have a **clearinghouse** for resource material; if a member needs information in a specific area, the organization can provide this service. The groups also support **lobbyists** who work to influence legislators on behalf of the organizations.

Journals, Magazines, Pamphlets, and Web Sites

With the recent publication explosion, many printed, video, and Internet materials are being produced. The **journal** provides brief evaluations of recent developments, government actions, and problems in the specific area. New products, research, and theories are introduced to readers. The beliefs and ethics of an organization are presented and discussed. Journals also provide leads to **seminars,** scholarships, courses, and jobs.

Conferences, Seminars, and Courses

During **conferences** or conventions, members of a professional organization gather to share ideas, work for legislation, and conduct business. During the meetings, problems concerning the association and plans for the future can be discussed by the membership or its representatives. Conventions meet at selected times, often every year. These meetings can be local, regional, state, or national.

The dues paid to professional organizations are an investment in the future of an occupation. Not only do the contacts and friendships offer valuable support, but also the associations may offer scholarships or job listings. Professional organizations provide opportunities for improvement in trade and professional areas.

You should join one or more professional organizations. It is your responsibility to keep up with advances in knowledge in your trade or profession. Just join with the intention of becoming president of the company. With the knowledge that you will gain, you may be in charge someday.

Mentors

Through networking in your associations, you can find and develop mentors who will support you and expand your thinking as you grow

INFOBIT

"Leadership is the ability to get other people to do what they don't want to do, and like it."

HARRY S TRUMAN, U.S. PRESIDENT

within a career and an organization. A **mentor** is similar to a coach, a person who will share his or her expertise, insights, ideas, and experiences. That person will guide you along, not help you bypass, the paths through the education and career process by offering you support. By pointing out the best pathways, the mentor teaches, shares resources and information, and helps lead you to the next step. Coaches, teachers, grandparents, and parents may be mentors, but mentors are not limited to those persons.

Figure 16-6: *A mentor can help you in your education or career.*

In choosing a mentor, find someone that you respect, someone that you feel comfortable with in asking questions and discussing decision-making situations. Then be a good listener, for your mentor will work with your inner person to offer motivation and inspiration for the journey up your career path.

Membership in a professional organization is for specialized areas of employment; the contact and membership will come after employment in the career major, generally after graduation. These organizations are often similar to vocational student organizations because both promote members' participation and continuing education within career areas. Networking uses professionalism in a less structured way, to increase participation and contacts in your career. Frequently organizations with a formalized structure, professional organizations have two basic forms: trade and professional organizations or labor unions.

Trade and Professional Associations

Any person with an interest in a specific occupation can be a member of a trade or professional association. These organizations do not require that a member have a certain occupation or place of employment, just a special interest. For instance, Women in Construction works for the interests of females in the building industry. Other examples of these types of associations are the American Welding Society and the Business Professional Women of America. The organization 9 to 5 supports the interests of workers in hourly occupations, such as secretaries and cosmetologists.

Labor Unions

Some organizations require employment in the field and possibly attaining a certain job classification before membership is offered. **Labor unions** are an example of such organizations. Members may be skilled in a certain occupation, such as carpentry or food service. The other type of union consists of workers within the same industry, such

WEB LINK

Internet searches of the Web sites of professional organizations and labor unions often provide informative articles or even on-line journals. In addition, the Web sites provide links to other sites related to the organizations' activities.

as automobile manufacturing. These workers may be constructing brake wiring systems, cleaning work areas, running machines, and supervising—all within the automotive industry.

Labor unions were created to stand behind the rights of workers. Not only do the unions help negotiate contracts between labor and management, but also they advocate workplace safety, legislative issues, and other workplace issues.

Practice 16-14: Using Professional Journals

In a library, in a classroom, at school, in the community, or on the Internet, find at least one journal pertaining to your cluster. If trade journals in your program are not available, find a related magazine in your field. Your instructor can provide appropriate titles. A list of some of these titles appears in Chapter 15 on page 508.

Write down the following information from the journal. Be as specific as possible. (Chapter 7 will provide additional help in finding the central idea of an article.) Report your information in small groups.

1. The title of the journal

2. The subject area covered by the journal

3. The date of publication

4. The number of pages in the journal

5. Does the journal include articles on the following topics? If so, identify the name of the article and the page number(s) on which it appears.

   a. New products

   b. Government action

   c. Technology

   d. Career opportunities

   e. Book reviews

6. Choose one article and identify the following information:

   a. The title of the article

   b. The author(s)

   c. The page(s)

   d. The central idea of the article

PEOPLE C·O·N·N·E·C·T·I·O·N

Carol Goldsmith gave a unique present to her mother more than ten years ago. Instead of an unneeded gift, Carol gave her mother a trip that she had longed to take and never had planned—a trip with her mother's childhood friends and their daughters. The successful journey initiated the idea for similar trips for friends. After seeing the need and doing the market research, that idea was the creative stimulus for Carol Goldsmith's company, Roots and Wings, a travel agency that plans tours for families.

SUMMARY

Your behavior is the basis of the professional image others form of you. A professional displays skills required to be successful. Follow these guidelines to be a successful professional:

* Manage your time through analyzing time wasters and procrastination.

* Set goals by determining your priorities and controlling barriers.

* Choose an effective leadership style when working in groups.

* Use strategies for conducting effective meetings and for conflict resolution.

* Become active in your vocational student organization.

* Read professional journals and join a professional organization.

WORKS CITED

Hagstrom, Jr., Robert J. *The Warren Buffett Way: Investment Strategies of the World's Greatest Investor.* New York: Wiley, 1994.

Linden, Dana Wechsler, and Dyan Machan. "The Disinheritors." *Forbes.* 19 May 1997: 152-154.

After all this work with priorities, goals, and schedules, it's time to move toward your life ambitions. This Project will help you make a commitment to carrying through with your plans. You will be writing yourself a letter that you will open in six months. The letter will contain three promises you have made to yourself in order to move toward achieving one of your long-term goals. Also included in the letter will be advice and a reward to yourself for completing the promises. Setting goals and carrying out promises are hard, so you deserve a reward for fulfillment.

1. Complete the Project Plan for this Project and have your teacher check it.

2. Complete the rough draft of the letter. Have your teacher check it.

3. Write the final draft of your letter. Have your teacher check it.

4. Place the signed letter inside a stamped, self-addressed envelope. On the back of the envelope, write, "Do not open until _____" (a date six months from now). Give the envelope to your teacher.

5. In six months, you will receive the envelope in the mail.

Overview

In the following profile of Nikki Giovanni, Lois Rosenthal describes her as "one of our age's most fearless and influential poets." Rosenthal adds that "she's earned her nickname 'priestess of black poetry.'"

Nikki Giovanni is one of America's most widely read living poets and one of the most outspoken. From the sixties, when she gained recognition as one of the prime forces in the civil rights movement, to the present, when she travels all over the world to teach and to give scores of poetry readings and lectures each year, she speaks out on whatever issues she believes are crucial. Her awards and outstanding achievements are legion.

"Nikki Giovanni"

Says Giovanni: "I use poetry as an outlet for my mind. It's my justification for living. But speaking my mind is an important part of my life as well, even when it's not a popular view. Everyone has a right to the dictates of her own heart. The one thing you cannot take away from people is their own sense of integrity. I don't want my integrity impinged upon nor will I impinge on the integrity of someone else.

". . . you can't solve a problem by shutting a person up."

"Though you cannot live your life to be intimidated by lesser people under any circumstances, I don't think you should shout people down if you disagree with them—which is what people are doing in the eighties.

"For instance, I don't agree with those who would attend a speech given by Jeanne Kirkpatrick in order to disrupt it. I think you should find out why she has the views she does and debate with her. You don't have to agree with her, but you can't solve a problem by shutting a person up. The integrity of the individual is everything."

About poets, Giovanni says:

"This is a great profession. If everybody became a poet, the world would be so much better. We would all read to each other. It would be an enhancing situation. This is not a restricted profession. There's a living out there, you just have to find it.

"People say poets can't make a living. I tell them to lower their expectations to match their income. Any young artist should stay out of debt so that, for instance, if an opportunity arises in another part of the country, she won't say, 'I can't go because I have a lease on this apartment or car payments to make.' You must be free."

Giovanni feels earning a living as a poet depends on how serious you are about it. She advises staying close to the writing profession—all facets of it. Learn to write magazine articles, book reviews. Give poetry readings to churches, restaurants, for civic organizations, any place that agrees to have them—for free if you have to. And Giovanni recommends doing every job as if it were the most important one you'll ever have. Just because it may not be the audience you dream of, don't think you can let up on the energy you put into your work.

What about all the people who want to be poets but can never hope to reach Giovanni's heights? She has a ready answer.

"Give yourself the chance to fully realize whatever your dreams are."

"Most of them won't try. They won't risk what I did. I had a son, and an apartment, and I decided I was going to try to be a poet and to do it as well as I could. If it didn't work out, I'd have still given it my best shot. Most people won't do that.

"If I have a 36-inch bust, a 24-inch waist, 38-inch hips and I lived in Stillwater, Oklahoma, and I decided to become a ballerina, I'd try. I would never say 'My chest is too big and my behind sticks out, and my measurements are all wrong for a ballerina,' I would get on my toes. Someone would have to stop me because I will not stop myself.

"Whatever I do in life, I want to do it to the absolute maximum. I want to be the best that I can be. I encourage every one of my students to do that. Give yourself the chance to fully realize whatever your dreams are."

—Lois Rosenthal

Start-Up: Nikki Giovanni's philosophy of life encourages the reading audience to take charge of their lives and live them to the maximum. She urges readers to hang on to a sense of integrity. Also, she gives advice to young poets.

What can you draw from Giovanni's remarks and that would make a good set of guidelines for becoming a professional?

Connection: First, write what you have learned from Giovanni's remarks that would make a good set of guidelines for becoming a professional. Then, write your own guidelines for becoming a professional. Share your guidelines and steps for achieving them with the rest of the class.

Overview

"In the fall of 1993, *Forbes* compiled a list of America's richest people. Several families—du Pont, Mellon, Pew, Rockefeller—and sixty-nine [other] individuals had an estimated net worth of more than $1 billion. Number one on the list was Warren Buffett, with a net worth of $8.3 billion" (Hagstrom 1). Buffett made his billions from astute stock investments and purchases of entire companies, including Berkshire Hathaway, Inc., which became the name of the holding company of which he owns controlling interest.

"In 1997, Bill Gates with his estimated $18.5 billion has become the richest man in America" (Linden and Machan 154). Gates made his billions with Microsoft computer software.

Mr. Buffett now holds the position of being the second richest man in the country.

It is interesting to note that both men feel that if their children want to be rich, they will have to work and earn money on their own. Bill Gates explains, "One thing is for sure. I won't leave a lot of money to my heirs because I don't think it would be good for them" (Linden and Machan 154).

These men are interesting to study. Here is a little information about Bill Gates and Warren Buffett.

from The Warren Buffett Way

Warren Buffett is not easy to describe. Physically he is unremarkable, with looks often described as grandfatherly. Intellectually he is considered a genius, yet his down-to-earth relationship with people is truly uncomplicated. He is simple, straightforward, forthright, and honest. He displays an engaging combination of sophisticated dry wit and cornball humor. He has a profound reverence for those things logical and a foul distaste for imbecility. He embraces the simple and avoids the complicated. . . .

Of the sixty-nine [richest] individuals, Buffett is the only one who obtained his wealth from the stock market. Berkshire Hathaway, Inc., is best understood as a holding company. In addition to . . . insurance companies, it also owns a newspaper, a candy company, a furniture store, a jewelry store, an encyclopedia publisher, a vacuum cleaner business and a company that manufactures and distributes uniforms [and a large amount of Coca Cola stock]. . . .

The story of how Buffett came to acquire these diverse businesses is interesting itself. Perhaps more to the point, the stories collectively give us a valuable insight into Buffett's way of looking at companies. It will come as little surprise that he used the same yardstick to evaluate companies for possible acquisitions as for additions to the Berkshire Hathaway stock portfolio. . . .

Reading the [Berkshire Hathaway] annual reports, one is struck by how comfortable Buffett is quoting the *Bible,* John Maynard Keynes, or Mae West. Of course the operable word is "reading." Each report is sixty to seventy pages of dense information: no pictures, no color graphics, no charts. Those who are disciplined enough to start on page one and continue uninterrupted are rewarded with a healthy dose of financial acumen, folksy humor, and unabashed honesty. Buffett is very candid in his reporting. He emphasizes both the pluses and the minuses of Berkshire's businesses. He believes that people who own stock in Berkshire Hathaway are owners of the company, and he tells them as much as he would like to be told if he were in their shoes. . . .

. . . He is always upbeat and supportive. He is genuinely excited about coming to work every day. "I have in life all I want right here," he says. "I love every day. I mean, I tap dance in here and work with nothing but people I like. There is no job in the world that is more fun than running Berkshire and I count myself lucky to be where I am."

—Robert G. Hagstrom, Jr.

William Henry Gates was born October 28, 1955, in Seattle's (Washington) Swedish Hospital. A cheerful infant, dubbed "Happy Boy" by the neighbors, he was the only son, and the second of three children. . . .

Bill was usually also the youngest in his class. . . . School authorities convinced them (classmates) that however slight Bill's physique or immature his personality, his mind was more than capable. . . .

"He knew a lot about a lot of things," Hazel Carlson [Bill's fourth-grade teacher] remembered. His IQ, which she estimated in the 160's or 170's, "was among the higher ones I've ever had. . . ."

> *On the day he was born in 1955, fewer than 500 electronic computers existed in the entire world. . . .*

Bill Gates, co-founder, chairman, chief executive officer of **Microsoft**, number one personal computer software company in the known galaxy. . . . the hyperkinetic, tousel-haired . . . computer programmer, tycoon, Harvard drop-out and multibillionaire was about to deliver the most important presentation of his presentation-filled career. (Bill's)

company . . . was about to announce the latest incarnation of **Microsoft Windows**. . . .

. . . back in 1975, Gates and his partner Paul Allen had been the very first to commercialize software for the just-born personal computer. . . . On the day he was born in 1955, fewer than 500 electronic computers existed in the entire world, their total retail value amounted to less than $200 million, and the term "software" had not yet been coined. . . .

Under the able guidance of his public relations counselor, Gates was being propelled into a curious kind of nerdy celebrityhood riddled with contradictory stories about wild womanizing on the one hand and an inability to get a date on the other, about fast cars and speeding tickets mixed with monkish workaholism. Reportedly a voracious reader, he insisted his favorite books were two novels, *The Catcher in the Rye* and *A Separate Peace,* popular largely with . . . adolescents. Described as oblivious to wealth, he was quoted boasting "I have an infinite amount of money." Bill Gates' story was never rags to riches, a Harvard friend once remarked, but riches to riches—though the initial affluence, embellished to include such fiction as a million-dollar trust fund, was now utterly insignificant. . . .

Bill Gates in his book *The Road Ahead* remarks on the Information Age: ". . . I'm optimistic about the new technology. It will enhance leisure time and enrich culture by expanding the distribution of information. . . . Technology progress will force all of society to confront tough new problems, only some of which we can foresee. . . . Societies are going to be asked to make hard choices in such areas as universal availability, investment in education, regulation, and the balance between individual privacy and community security. . . . Microsoft has been a leader in the PC era. . . . For me, a big part of the fun has always been to hire and work with smart people. I enjoy working with them. . . . They're extraordinarily talented and will contribute new visions. If Microsoft can combine these visions with listening carefully to customers, we have a chance to continue to lead the way. We can certainly keep providing better and better software to make the PC a universally empowering tool. I often say I have the best job in the world, and I mean it."

—Stephen Manes and Paul Andrews

Start-Up. Both these men have made a mark on the world through one of the ways that most of us recognize: making money. Gates and Buffett have many admirable qualities. Also, their goals are quite evident. They are similar yet different individuals.

Since just a little information is presented here, check your school media center, community library, and the Internet for more information on both of these interesting people.

Connection: Compare and contrast these two multibillionaires. Review Chapter 12 for information on comparing and contrasting, if needed.

PHOTO CREDITS

(continued from copyright page)

Chapter 1

Opener, pp. 5, 7, 8, 13, and 22: © PhotoDisc, Inc.; p. 9: © Adobe Systems Inc. All rights reserved.; p.12: © William Green Photography and Video Services, Mt. Pleasant, SC; p. 23: Donald Robinson/Corbis.

Chapter 2

Opener Photo, and pp. 49, 52: © PhotoDisc, Inc; p. 40, Photo Courtesy of Hewlett Packard; p. 48: Photo Courtesy of Xerox Corporation; p. 65: UPI/Corbis–Bettmann.

Chapter 3

Opener Photos, pp. 80, 89, 95, and 100: © PhotoDisc, Inc.; p. 77, Wally McNamee/Corbis; p. 91 Layne Kennedy/Corbis; p. 83a. MP & TV Photo Archive p. 83b. Photo by Mel Traxel/MPTV; p. 93: © Mimi Ostendorf.

Chapter 4

Opener Photo, pp. 108 (first photo), 111, 112, 131, 138: © PhotoDisc, Inc.; p. 108 (second photo) © PhotoEdit; p. 127: Reproduced by permission. Multicultural Client: Cut, Styling, and Chemical Services. By: Milady Publishing; Milady Publishing Company, a division of Delmar Publishers, Albany, New York. Copyright.

Chapter 5

Opener Photo, pp. 143, 144, 149: © PhotoDisc; p. 147: Ted Streshinsky/Corbis; p. 155: Ed Young/Corbis; p. 159: © 1998 Adobe Systems, Inc.; p. 170: Corbis-Bettmann.

Chapter 6

Opener Photo, pp. 179, 182, 184, 191, 195: © PhotoDisc; p. 188: Reproduced by permission. Multicultural Client: Cut, Styling, and Chemical Services. By: Milady Publishing; Milady Publishing Company, a division of Delmar Publishers, Albany, New York. Copyright; p. 190: Courtesy of International Business Machines Corporation. Unauthorized use not permitted. p. 194: Eric & David Hosking/Corbis; p. 204: Corel.

Chapter 7

Opener Photo, pp. 214, 215: © PhotoDisc; p. 218: © 1994 John Elk III/Stock, Boston/PNI; p. 244: Robbie Jack/Corbis.

Chapter 8

Opener Photo, pp. 248, 259, 272, 284: © PhotoDisc; p. 250: © PhotoEdit; p. 263: Eleana Rooraid/PhotoEdit.

Chapter 9

Opener Photo, pp. 297, 303, 320: © PhotoDisc, Inc. p. 280: Hulton-Deutsch Collection/Corbis; p. 288: © Alan Oddie/PhotoEdit/PNI; p. 294: Copyright 1998, Adobe Systems, Inc.

Chapter 10

Opener Photos: (top) Richard T. Nowitz/Corbis, (bottom) Bonnie Kamin/PhotoEdit; pp. 326, 338, 360: © PhotoDisc, Inc.

Chapter 11

Opener Photo: McHale Photography; pp. 369, 402: © PhotoDisc, Inc.

Chapter 12

Opener Photo, pp. 408 (soldering) and 426: © PhotoDisc, Inc.; p. 408 (computer store): Michael Newman/PhotoEdit; p. 409: Digital Research; p. 417: Photo by Digital Imaging Group, Cincinnati, OH; p. 418: Beckwith Chapman Associates.

Chapter 13

Opener Photo, pp. 432, 433, 434, 444, 462: © PhotoDisc, Inc.; p. 438: © Rosalie Winard; p. 439: Kevin Fleming/Corbis; p. 443: Susan L. Kemp; p. 467: Hulton-Deutsch Collection/Corbis.

Chapter 14

Opener Photos: (top) © PhotoDisc, Inc., (bottom): Gianni Dagli Orti/Corbis; p. 472: Copyright Adobe Systems Inc.; p. 477: Susan Spalter Photography; p. 496: Lee Snider/Corbis.

Chapter 15

Opener Photo: Matthew Borkoski/PNI; p. 503: Jennifer Lightcap; p. 505: Courtesy Minnesota Pollution Control Agency; pp. 506, 511, 530, and 533: © PhotoDisc, Inc; p. 517: © Wendt Worldwide.

Chapter 16

Opener Photo, pp. 543, 552: © PhotoDisc, Inc.; p. 538: Michael Newman/PhotoEdit; p. 539: © Coco McCoy 1994/PNI; p. 551: © Hilton Hotel Corporation; p. 554: PhotoEdit; p. 556: Bob Rowan; Progressive Image/Corbis; p. 562: James Marshall/Corbis; p. 569: Lisa Quinones/Black Star/PNI; p. 570: Judy Griesedieck/© Corbis.

(continued from copyright page)

Excerpted from "In Search of a Majority" by James Baldwin. Collected in NOBODY KNOWS MY NAME © 1960 by James Baldwin. Copyright renewed. Published by Vintage Books. Reprinted with the permission of the James Baldwin Estate.

"Pity the Poor Spiders" from ARCHY AND MEHITABEL by Don Marquis. Copyright 1927 by Doubleday, a division of Bantam, Doubleday, Dell Publishing Group, Inc. Used by permission of Doubleday, a division of Bantam, Doubleday, Dell Publishing Group, Inc.

"Charles" from THE LOTTERY by Shirley Jackson. Copyright © 1948, 1949 by Shirley Jackson, and copyright renewed © 1976, 1977 by Laurence Hyman, Barry Hyman, Mrs. Sarah Webster, and Mrs. Joanne Schnurer. Reprinted by permission of Farrar, Straus & Giroux, Inc.

"Traveller's Curse After Misdirection" by Robert Graves from THE COMPLETE POEMS OF ROBERT GRAVES edited by Beryl Graves and Dunstan Ward (3 volumes, 1995–1999), by permission of Carcanet Press Limited on behalf of the Estate of Robert Graves.

from THE JUNGLE by Upton Sinclair. Copyright 1905, 1906 by Upton Sinclair. Used by permission of Viking Penguin, a division of Penguin Books USA Inc.

"Tom Edison's Shaggy Dog," copyright 1953 by Kurt Vonnegut, Jr. from WELCOME TO THE MONKEY HOUSE by Kurt Vonnegut, Jr. Used by permission of Delacorte Press/Seymour Lawrence, a division of Bantam, Doubleday, Dell Publishing Group, Inc.

"Out, Out—" by Robert Frost. From THE POETRY OF ROBERT FROST edited by Edward Connery Lathem, Copyright 1944 by Robert Frost. Copyright 1916, © 1969 by Henry Holt and Company, Inc. Reprinted by permission of Henry Holt and Company, Inc.

"Easter" from LEAVING HOME by Garrison Keillor. Copyright © 1987 by Garrison Keillor. Used by permission of Viking Penguin, a division of Penguin Putnam Inc.

"Eyes That Do More Than See" by Isaac Asimov. Special permission granted from Weekly Reader Corporation. Copyright © 1989 by Weekly Reader Corporation. All Rights Reserved.

"The River-Merchant's Wife: A Letter" by Ezra Pound. From PERSONAE. Copyright © 1926 by Ezra Pound. Reprinted by permission of New Directions Publishing Corp.

"Shooting an Elephant" from SHOOTING AN ELEPHANT AND OTHER ESSAYS by George Orwell, copyright 1950 by Sonia Brownell Orwell and renewed 1978 by Sonia Pitt-Rivers, reprinted by permission of Harcourt Brace & Company.

from DEATH OF A SALESMAN by Arthur Miller. Copyright 1949, renewed © 1977 by Arthur Miller. Used by permission of Viking Penguin, a division of Penguin Books USA Inc.

"The Old Man and Woman Who Switched Jobs" from SWEDISH FOLKTALES AND LEGENDS by Lone Thygesen Blecher and George Blecher, editors. Copyright © 1993 by G & L Blecher Inc. Reprinted by permission of Pantheon Books, a division of Random House, Inc.

"Possibilities" by Wislawa Szymborska. Translated by Grazyna Drabik and Austin Flynt. *Quarterly Review of Literature 50th Anniversary Anthology*.

"Nick Salerno" by Studs Terkel. Reprinted by permission of Donadio & Ashworth, Inc. Copyright 1972, 1974 Studs Terkel.

"The Unknown Citizen" from COLLECTED POEMS by W. H. Auden, edited by Edward Mendelson, Faber and Faber Ltd.

"1620 to 1992: Long Ago but Not So Far Away" by Stephen Budiansky. Copyright, July 7, 1992, **U.S. News & World Report.**

"How Smart Are Dolphins?" by Russell Freedman. Reprinted with the permission of Simon & Schuster Books for Young Readers, an imprint of Simon & Schuster Children's Publishing Division from CAN BEARS PREDICT EARTHQUAKES? by Russell Freedman. Copyright © 1982 Russell Freedman.

from "Nikki Giovanni" copyright © 1989 by Lois Rosenthal. Reprinted in *On Being a Writer* copyright © 1989 by Writer's Digest Books. Used by permission of Lois Rosenthal.

from *The Warren Buffett Way* by Robert C. Hagstrom, Jr. Copyright © 1956.

from *Gates* by Stephen Manes and Paul Andrews. Copyright © 1993. Reprinted by permission of Doubleday, a division of Bantam Doubleday Dell Publishing Group, Inc.

The authors and editors have made every effort to locate the copyright owners of all selections found in this book and to make full acknowledgment for their use. Omissions brought to our attention will be corrected in subsequent editions.

CONNECTIONS INDEX

	Career Connection	Culture Connection	Ethics Connection	People Connection	Quality Connection	Technology Connection
Chapter 1	p. 6	p. 12	pp. 10, 16		p. 8	p. 18
Chapter 2	p. 56	p. 31	p. 33	pp. 44, 59	p. 45	pp. 36, 38
Chapter 3	p. 73	p. 75	p. 78	p. 77		p. 87
Chapter 4	p. 125	p. 111	p. 123	p. 130	p. 109	p. 124
Chapter 5	p. 157	p. 163	p. 146	p. 143		p. 156
Chapter 6	p. 185	p. 191		p. 181	p. 192	p. 189
Chapter 7	p. 219	p. 221	p. 223	p. 228		p. 216
Chapter 8	p. 258	p. 262	p. 251	p. 252	p. 268	p. 254
Chapter 9	p. 296		p. 302		p. 284	p. 294
Chapter 10	p. 345		p. 330	p. 348	p. 353	pp. 327, 339
Chapter 11	p. 369	p. 379		p. 393	p. 389	
Chapter 12	p. 410	p. 420	p. 421	p. 418	pp. 414, 417	p. 409
Chapter 13	p. 452	p. 443		p. 438		p. 441
Chapter 14	p. 473	p. 477		p. 482	p. 490	p. 480
Chapter 15	pp. 516, 522	pp. 512, 521	p. 520		p. 506	pp. 509, 513
Chapter 16	p. 539	p. 543		p. 547	pp. 540, 555	p. 546